ADVISORY BOARD

THE WESLEYAN EDITION OF THE
WORKS OF HENRY FIELDING

THE COVENT-GARDEN JOURNAL
AND
A PLAN OF THE UNIVERSAL REGISTER-OFFICE

BOOKS IN THE WESLEYAN EDITION OF
THE COMPLETE WORKS OF HENRY FIELDING

Amelia
Edited by Martin C. Battestin, textual introduction by Fredson Bowers

The History of Tom Jones: A Foundling
Introduction and commentary by Martin C. Battestin, text edited by
Fredson Bowers

The Jacobite's Journal and Related Writings
Edited by W. B. Coley

Joseph Andrews
Edited by Martin C. Battestin, textual introduction by Fredson Bowers

Miscellanies, Volume I
Edited by Henry Knight Miller, textual introduction by Fredson Bowers

The True Patriot and Related Writings
Edited by W. B. Coley

*An Enquiry into the Causes of the Late Increase of
Robbers, and Related Writings*
Edited by Malvin R. Zirker, textual introduction by Fredson Bowers

*The Covent-Garden Journal and
A Plan of the Universal Register-Office*
Edited by Bertrand A. Goldgar

HENRY FIELDING

The Covent-Garden Journal
and A Plan of
the Universal Register-Office

EDITED BY
BERTRAND A. GOLDGAR

Wesleyan University Press
MIDDLETOWN, CONNECTICUT

Published in the United States by Wesleyan University Press.

Published simultaneously in Great Britain by Oxford
University Press copyright © 1988 by Oxford University
Press.

All inquiries and permissions requests should be
addressed to the Publisher, Wesleyan University
Press, 110 Mt. Vernon Street, Middletown, Connecticut
06457

Library of Congress Cataloging-in-Publication Data
Fielding, Henry, 1707–1754
The Covent-Garden journal and A plan of the
universal register-office.
(The Wesleyan edition of the works of Henry Fielding)
Bibliography: p.   Includes index.
1. Goldgar, Bertrand A., 1927–   . II. Fielding,
Henry, 1707–1754. Plan of the universal
register-office. 1988.   III. Title.   IV. Series:
Fielding, Henry, 1707–1754. Works. 1983.
PR3454.C5   1988   824'.5   87–27940
ISBN 0–8195–5167–8

First American Edition

Printed in Great Britain
at the University Printing House, Oxford
by David Stanford
Printer to the University

TO LOUIS LANDA

PREFACE

THE Wesleyan Edition of *A Plan of the Universal Register-Office* and the *Covent-Garden Journal* is intended to provide reliable texts of these documents and to give the reader all the annotation and commentary necessary to understand them. The highly allusive and topical nature of the *Covent-Garden Journal* has required extensive and detailed annotation, and the General Introduction furnishes the wider historical and biographical context in which these materials were read by Fielding's original audience. After describing the background and fortunes of the Fieldings' Register Office, the Introduction explains the connection between that enterprise and the origins of the *Journal*. It then surveys the *Journal* itself—its format, its purposes, its relation to the contemporary scene, its major themes, and its reception by Fielding's contemporaries.

The Textual Introduction and the head-notes to sections of the textual apparatus at the end of the volume explain the bibliographical principles on which the text is established. In preparing that text, I have profited enormously from the generous advice of Professor Fredson Bowers about my general procedure; and, as the Textual Introduction makes clear, I have sought to follow here the guidelines he has established for the texts of previous volumes of the Wesleyan Edition. The reader should understand, however, that Professor Bowers has not examined or reviewed the results of my editorial work and is in no way responsible for any errors or flaws it may contain.

The *Plan of the Universal Register-Office* has not been reprinted since the eighteenth century. The only previous edition of the *Journal* approaching completeness is that of Gerard E. Jensen in 1915; although Jensen's edition has been useful to every student of Fielding, it includes only the leading essays, excluding the other departments of the *Journal*, and it does not seek to present a critical text. Since Jensen, of course, much has been learned about Fielding and his period on which a modern editor must base his work. In particular, the recent discovery of revisions in Fielding's hand in the Bodleian Library copy of the *Journal* and the new light which these have thrown on the text of the essays in the 1762 *Works* have made possible for the first time a text of the *Journal* incorporating authorial revisions.

Although, as with most of Fielding's journals, the authorship of a few of the numbers is in doubt, I have included all the essays in the present edition, with notes on the authorship where necessary. The texts of two of the separate departments of the *Journal*, however, are of less certain authorship and have been placed in appendices; these are the 'Covent Garden' columns commenting on cases brought before Fielding in his magistrate's court and the 'Modern History' section of excerpts from other newspapers followed by editorial comment, both reprinted here for the first time.

One of the genuine compensations for spending so many years on a project of this kind is the opportunity it affords one of working with scholars and specialists in diverse fields. It is a pleasure to record some of the many debts I have incurred in preparing this edition. I am most of all grateful to Martin C. Battestin, who first lured me into the study of Fielding and who kindly read large portions of the manuscript and offered valuable advice; both Martin and his wife Ruthe R. Battestin have been unsparing in making available to me their vast knowledge of Fielding and the eighteenth century. I am pleased also to acknowledge the very generous help of Hugh Amory, who provided benevolent advice on bibliographical problems, courteously kept me abreast of his discoveries about the Bodleian text, and gave me expert assistance on many puzzling points of annotation. Another learned friend, Thomas Lockwood, was kind enough to read and give advice on the manuscript of the General Introduction and to share with me the results of his own research on Fielding. I am similarly indebted to William B. Coley, both for his patience as Executive Editor and for the care with which he read and corrected the manuscript; and to Frederick G. Ribble for his many suggestions and corrections.

For their help with the sources, translations, and transcription of classical quotations, I wish to thank Mary Ann Rossi and my colleague Daniel J. Taylor. In the course of preparing both the annotation and the text I have benefited greatly from the learning, expertise, and helpful advice of Albert R. Braunmuller, Michael Crump, Anne Goldgar, Michael Harris, Christine Krueger, Betty Rizzo, Dennis F. Todd, Michael Treadwell, and Malvin R. Zirker.

I am grateful to Viscountess Eccles for permitting me to consult the Hyde copy of the *Covent-Garden Journal*. For their courteous assistance in the various stages of my work I wish to thank also the staffs of the British Library, the Bodleian Library, the Cambridge University Library, the University of London Library, the London Library, Yale University Library, and the Humanities Research Center of the University of Texas. My research at libraries in England would have been impossible without generous financial assistance; I am indeed grateful to Lawrence University, for numerous research grants; to the American Council of Learned Societies, for a grant-in-aid; and to the National Endowment for the Humanities, for both a summer stipend and a research fellowship.

The title-page of the *Plan of the Universal Register-Office* on page 1 is reproduced by kind permission of the Beinecke Rare Book and Manuscript Library, Yale University. The first page of the opening number of the

Covent-Garden Journal, on page 11, is reproduced by kind permission of the Harry Ransom Humanities Research Center, University of Texas at Austin.

B.A.G.

CONTENTS

ABBREVIATIONS

Baker	*A Catalogue of the Entire and Valuable Library and Books of the Late Henry Fielding, Esq; . . . sold by Auction by Samuel Baker.* [London, 1755].
CGJ	*The Covent-Garden Journal*
Cross	Wilbur L. Cross, *The History of Henry Fielding.* 3 vols., New Haven, Conn., 1918.
DA	*The Daily Advertiser.*
DNB	*Dictionary of National Biography.*
Dudden	F. Homes Dudden. *Henry Fielding, his Life, Works, and Times.* 2 vols., Oxford, 1952.
ECS	*Eighteenth-Century Studies*
GA	*The General Advertiser*
GM	*The Gentleman's Magazine.*
HLQ	*Huntington Library Quarterly.*
Jensen	*The Covent-Garden Journal By Sir Alexander Drawcansir . . . (Henry Fielding),* ed. Gerard E. Jensen. 2 vols., New Haven, Conn., 1915.
JJ	*Jacobite's Journal.*
LDA	*The London Daily Advertiser.*
LEP	*The London Evening-Post.*
LM	*The London Magazine.*
Loeb	The Loeb Classical Library.
London Stage	*The London Stage, 1660–1800.* Part 2 [1700–29], ed. Emmet L. Avery. 2 vols., Carbondale, Ill., 1960; Part 3 [1729–47], ed. Arthur H. Scouten. 2 vols., Carbondale, Ill., 1961; Part 4 [1747–76], ed. George Winchester Stone, Jr. 3 vols., Carbondale, Ill., 1962.
Miller, *Essays*	Henry Knight Miller. *Essays on Fielding's Miscellanies.* Princeton, NJ, 1961.
MLN	*Modern Language Notes.*
MLR	*Modern Language Review.*
MP	*Modern Philology.*
OE	*Old England.*
OED	*Oxford English Dictionary.*
PBSA	*Papers of the Bibliographical Society of America.*
PQ	*Philological Quarterly.*
SB	*Studies in Bibliography.*
SEL	*Studies in English Literature, 1500–1900.*
SP	*Studies in Philology.*
Tilley	Morris P. Tilley. *A Dictionary of the Proverbs in England in the Sixteenth and Seventeenth Centuries.* Ann Arbor, Michigan, 1950.

Twickenham Edn.	*The Twickenham Edition of the Poems of Alexander Pope*, ed. John Butt *et al.* 11 vols., London and New Haven, Conn., 1940–69.
Yale Walpole	*The Yale Edition of Horace Walpole's Correspondence*, ed. W. S. Lewis. 48 vols., New Haven, Conn., 1937–83.

Note: Unless otherwise indicated, the place of publication of works cited in the notes is London.

GENERAL INTRODUCTION

THE two works included in this volume date from near the end of Fielding's life, when he was burdened by the twin weights of deteriorating health and the depressing duties of a Middlesex justice of the peace. The years in question, 1751 and 1752, are also the period of his most important social tracts and of his 'darkest' novel, *Amelia*. Released, finally, from the onerous task of political writing in the narrow, partisan sense, Fielding devoted what energies he had left to the diagnosis, if not the cure, of the disorders of the body politic. Something of the range of his interests in these years is suggested by the titles of his other writings from this period: *An Enquiry into the Causes of the late Increase of Robbers* (January 1751); *Amelia* (December 1751); *Examples of the Interposition of Providence in the Detection and Punishment of Murder* (April 1752); and *A Proposal for Making an Effectual Provision for the Poor* (January 1753).

Although *A Plan of the Universal Register-Office* (February 1751) is a puff for a private business of which Fielding was part-owner and the *Covent-Garden Journal* (4 January–25 November 1752) is an essay–journal much concerned with literary satire, both works reflect the mood of social concern which dominates these other writings of his final years. Moreover, the two works are intimately connected; however much it eventually departed from its point of origin, the *Covent-Garden Journal* began as a vehicle for publicizing and advertising the Universal Register Office. Fielding's last and in many ways most significant work of journalism can, in fact, be fully understood only against the background of this curious enterprise which he and his half-brother John had operated in the Strand since February of 1750.

I. A PLAN OF THE UNIVERSAL REGISTER-OFFICE

A Plan of the Universal Register-Office, opposite Cecil-Street in the Strand, published on 21 February 1750/1, has not previously appeared in any edition of Fielding's works.[1] Its omission can be easily explained: the *Plan* is a slight piece, more an extended advertisement than a serious tract; and though Fielding's contemporaries connected him with the enterprise which the *Plan* celebrates, he was not until this century credited with the authorship of the tract itself.[2] Beginning in 1752 later editions carried a prefatory 'To the Reader' signed by Fielding's blind half-brother John,

[1] For the date of publication, see *GA*, 19 and 21 Feb. 1751.
[2] See Cross, ii. 226, iii. 321.

identifying himself there as 'One of the Proprietors', and it was John
Fielding whose name most often appeared publicly in letters to newspapers,
advertisements, and other efforts to promote the Office. Authorship of the
Plan has thus quite naturally sometimes been attributed to him. But there
can be no doubt that Henry Fielding wrote at least the theoretical framework
presented in the first half of the piece, with John perhaps responsible for the
detailed description of activities in the ten articles laid out in the second
half.[1] Such a division not only seems likely on stylistic grounds but also
corresponds to the brothers' sharing of responsibilities for the business,
since it was John who managed its day-to-day operation. In subsequent
editions of the *Plan* the theoretical introduction remained unaltered while
the catalogue of services offered expanded as the business itself expanded
and flourished.

What was the nature and background of this business? In essence the
Register Office was designed, said Fielding, 'to bring the World as it were
together into one Place' by offering the combined services of an employment
agency, a financial institution, a real estate agency, a curiosity shop, and a
travel bureau.[2] Although John Fielding in his various pronouncements
claimed originality for the scheme, there were in fact at least a half-dozen
similar enterprises in France and England during the seventeenth century.[3]
They included a 'Register for general Commerce' (1611) operated by Sir
Arthur Gorges and Sir Walter Cope; a 'Bureau d'adresse et de rencontre'
(1612) established in Paris by Theophraste Renaudot and imitated in
England by Henry Robinson (1650); Samuel Hartlib's 'Office of Addresse
for Accommodations' (1648); and similar schemes projected by Henry
Walker, T. Lawson, Adolphus Speed, Marchmont Nedham, and Oliver
Williams.[4] Interestingly enough, the avowed inspiration for some of these
projects was the same passage from a Montaigne essay (i. 34) which Fielding
quotes in his *Plan*; and like Fielding these early projectors sometimes
couched their commercial proposals in terms of general social welfare or
relief of the poor. After the Restoration these 'intelligence Offices', as they
came to be called, fell into disrepute, and until the middle of the eighteenth
century one heard little more of ambitious schemes to bring the world
together into one place. A leader in the *Daily Gazetteer* (11 November 1736)
proposed putting into practice '*Montaigne's* Office of Intelligence', and the

[1] Cross, who had not seen the 1751 edition, attributed the entire pamphlet to Henry, reserving for
John only the 'To the Reader' of the 1752 edition.   [2] *Plan*, p. 6.

[3] See M. Dorothy George, 'The Early History of Registry Offices', *Economic Journal: Economic
History Supplement*, 1 (1926–9), 570–90.

[4] Ibid., pp. 570–7; W. H. Beveridge, 'A Seventeenth-Century Labour Exchange', *Economic Journal*,
24 (1914), 371–6 and his correction on 635–6; P. S. Belasco, 'Note on the Labour Exchange Idea in
the Seventeenth Century', *Economic Journal: Economic History Supplement*, 1 (1926–9), 275–9; F. A.
Norman and L. G. Lee, 'A Further Note on Labour Exchanges in the Seventeenth Century', ibid.,
399–404.

following year a certain Vander Esch and Company advertised a Universal Register providing services much like those the Fieldings were to offer.[1] But it was only thirteen years later, when the Fieldings opened their office, that England saw a real resurgence of such enterprises. If their scheme was not really new, it was at least executed with a verve and promotional skill which produced a host of imitators and made 'Register Office' a common term in the second half of the century.

On 19 February 1749/50 the Fieldings' office opened its doors to customers for the first time, in a building opposite Cecil Street in the Strand, the third house west of Oliver's Alley. This was to remain its principal place of business until 1755, when it moved to Castle Court, across from the New Exchange Buildings.[2] The quarters were 'sufficiently decent for Business' but far from elegant, as John Fielding himself confessed, adding that the need for being in a public part of town obliged them to take a house unsuitable for entertainment.[3] Such an apology was necessary because the Register Office not only sought to attract people of fashion but also constantly stressed the fact that, unlike other such ventures, it was conducted by a 'Society of Gentlemen', whose social class would insure that customers' affairs were carried on confidentially and honestly. The identity of all these gentlemen is not known for certain; Henry owned twenty shares at the time of his death, John was obviously a substantial shareholder, and their close friend Saunders Welch, the High Constable of Holborn, was listed as a proprietor in 1755 and may have been concerned in the undertaking from the outset. It is likely that there were other partners whose names have not come to light.[4]

Although in announcing the opening of their office the partners used the somewhat opprobrious term 'the Office of Intelligence', the name was changed within a few days to Universal Register Office. Advertisements early in 1750 tended to concentrate on estates and lodgings, but by March

---

[1] *DA*, 29 Apr. 1737; I am indebted to Martin C. Battestin for these two references.

[2] On the date of opening see *GA*, 13 Feb. 1749/50; in his advertisements for the Register Office John Fielding consistently listed the year of founding as '1749', his choice of Old Style perhaps dictated by his desire to make the office appear long established. His practice misled Cross and Dudden into dating the office a year too early. On the location of the establishment, see Hugh Phillips, *Mid-Georgian London* (1964), p. 290, and the Ratebooks of the Parish of St Martins, Westminster Public Library, F5851, fos. 84, 86. The date of the move to Castle Court, about which Cross is misleading, is indicated by the imprint of the *Public Advertiser* throughout 1754 and by references in the 1755 edition of the *Plan*.

[3] *LDA*, 21 Nov. 1751.

[4] For Welch's involvement, see *Public Advertiser*, 2 Oct. 1755. Another possible partner, suggested to the editor by Dr Hugh Amory, may have been Fielding's friend Peter Taylor (1714–77), a silversmith who lived at the corner of Cecil Street and the Strand and was later an MP (1765–6, 1774–7). Fielding mentioned him in *Journal of a Voyage to Lisbon* and sent him a consignment of onions from Lisbon. See Sir Lewis Namier and John Brooke, *The History of Parliament: The House of Commons 1754–1790* (1964), iii. 517–18.

most of the functions described a year later in the *Plan* were being listed, and the note of bold expansiveness implicit in the term 'Universal' soon crept into their notices: 'As this Office takes in the Business of the whole Nation, there is nothing but what may in Time be heard of here.'[1] A broadside advertisement preserved at Yale, undated but apparently pre-dating the first edition of the *Plan*, gives a good picture of the diversity of the Register Office's services and the method of its operation. In addition to the obvious real estate transactions and employment opportunities, the office offered to arrange for private tutoring or the placing of young gentlemen in country preparatory schools; the buying and selling of china, pictures, libraries, dogs, birds, and wild beasts; the copying of books and manuscripts; the lending of money on security; the securing of dry or wet nurses and midwives; and the provision of travel information and companions. In short, 'The Interest of this Office is to bring all those together who stand in Need of each others Assistance', at the modest fee of sixpence for registration and threepence for successful enquiries.[2] One adjunct to their operation seems to have been the wide use of handbills and form letters, presumably in connection with the employment services; the ledger of the printer William Strahan includes such items printed for this office as 'Letters for a Character', 'Letters of Request', 'Letters to all Strangers', and letters beginning 'In this you have a true Copy', 'This Day applied', and so on.[3] Despite all this activity, as M. D. George points out, the scope of the Fieldings' office was not as ambitious as that of some of the seventeenth-century prototypes; it did not offer matrimonial, lost property, emigration, or detective services.[4]

During its first year of operation, before the appearance of the *Plan*, the Universal Register Office had some problem keeping the public informed of such a full range of activities. At first 'Proposals', none of which have survived, were circulated in the coffee-houses. Later in 1750 the proprietors resorted to very long and doubtless very expensive advertisements in the newspapers describing their methods and services; even so they were compelled to explain that 'as the Customs and Methods of it are too long to be inserted in an Advertisement, any Gentleman or Lady may have a full Account . . . by calling at the said Office'.[5] Shorter advertisements would refer the reader for details to the longer advertisements. Thus by the end of 1750 there was obviously a need for a plan of the office to be published and circulated. Accordingly Fielding's *Plan* appeared on 21 February 1750/1, having earlier been advertised as an account of an office 'recommended by *Henry Fielding* Esq; at the End of his Enquiry into the Causes of the late

[1] *GA*, 19 July 1750. For other advertisements, see *GA*, 13 Feb., 20, 26 Mar. 1750.
[2] 'Universal Register Office. At the Universal Register Office . . .', broadside, n.d.
[3] BL Add. MS 48803A, fos. 14–15, 23–4.
[4] George, 'The Early History of Registry Offices', pp. 581–2.
[5] *GA*, 19 July 1750; see also *GA*, 5 Sept., 11 Oct., 1 Dec. 1750.

Encrease of Street-Robberies'.[1] A threepenny pamphlet, it bore no publisher's name (though presumably printed by Strahan) and was available only at the Register Office itself.[2]

Although the earlier advertisements had spoken of the benefits which would accrue to the public from this enterprise, it remained for Fielding to provide the philosophical principles underpinning the business and to elevate it to the level of a social and economic necessity. Characteristically he opens the *Plan* with a vision of society derived in part from Aristotle's *Politics*, an optimistic vision in which a society reaches perfection by being so regulated 'that no Talent in any of its Members, which is capable of contributing to the general Good, should lie idle and unemployed, nor any of the Wants of its Members which are capable of Relief, should remain unrelieved'.[3] In the *Plan*, at least, that darker view of the evils of society, that fear of subversion of the Constitution by unruly mobs, and that denigration of the luxuries of the vulgar which had been his themes just a month earlier in the *Enquiry into the Causes of the late Increase of Robbers* are all laid aside in favor of a simpler world governed by a few unqualified mercantilist maxims: the greater the wealth of a society the greater the wants of its members, and the larger the society the more easily these wants may be supplied. No limits are set here to the desirability of growth of population and wealth, as long as all available talents find ways of being used to meet the ever-increasing needs of a prosperous society. Moreover, Fielding here simply dismisses— with an ease worthy of Mandeville himself—the protests of moralists against a society dominated by luxury: 'The Ethic Writer, indeed, will tell me, that none of these Wants arise from Nature. But let them arise from what they will, they are real, and to supply them is as essential to the Happiness of him who hath, or thinks he hath them, as it is to a Savage to supply any of these few Necessities with which a State of Nature . . . abounds.' The poor philosopher, he adds sarcastically, is considerably less happy than the rich man 'with all his Wants about him, and at the same Time, with a Capacity of supplying all these Wants'.[4]

It need hardly be said that such was not always Fielding's view.[5] In the *Enquiry*, in a somewhat similar passage, he had indeed admitted that 'as Riches are the *certain* Consequence of Trade, so is Luxury the no less *certain* Consequence of Riches'; but though certain and necessary in a flourishing

---

[1] *GA*, 19 Feb. 1751. Further advertisements for the *Plan* were placed in *GA* for 21, 23, and 25 Feb. The Fieldings may also have been prompted to publish the *Plan* at this time to avoid confusion between their office and 'the Gentlemen's Register Office', a marriage bureau in Temple Bar, which had published a *Serious Proposal* describing their function (*GA*, 23 Jan. 1751).

[2] The Strahan ledger for the Register Office begins only in 1752.

[3] *Plan*, p. 3.

[4] *Plan*, p. 4.

[5] See, for example, his attack on luxury in *True Patriot* No. 7, 17 Dec. 1745.

commercial society, luxury is there treated as an evil which must be restrained and palliated though it cannot be removed.[1] The luxury of the lower classes must be controlled and politically regulated, while that of the wealthy must be left alone (though Fielding treats it with considerable irony). No such distinctions are drawn in the *Plan*, which cheerfully accepts the luxury of an opulent society without even using that notorious term—but then the *Plan* is an extended advertisement, not a serious social tract. Fielding quickly brings the argument around to the need for a system by which members of a society can communicate their 'Wants and Talents' to each other, a need which can be met by providing 'some Place of universal Resort'. From there it is an easy step to Montaigne's famous essay and the services of the Universal Register Office.

Though the social and economic assumptions of the *Plan* exhibit none of the complexity of Fielding's thinking elsewhere on such topics, there is no reason to doubt that at heart he believed at least some of the claims of public benefits to be derived from his Register Office. Some of these benefits were related directly to his duties as a magistrate and to his writings in these years on crime and poverty. Thus at the end of his *Enquiry* a full-page notice advertising the Register Office concentrates on the problem of the 'rude Behaviour and Insolence of Servants', a problem not unlike the others addressed in that tract and solvable by the method of reliable character references the office claimed to provide. The notice ends, 'We have thought it . . . not improper to recommend this Office at the End of a Work, in which the Public Utility is sincerely intended, as it seems to deserve the Encouragement of all, who think the Public Utility worthy of their Regard.'[2] Both in the *Plan* and in newspaper advertisements or letters the Fieldings asked those who had found 'gross Faults' in servants to inform the office as a guard against their being employed by others. Still other advertisements pointed to the usefulness of the office to young people who were coming from the country to be servants or apprentices in London and who were too easily led into crime, prostitution, or poverty by being badly placed.[3] Fielding, of course, entered this business primarily to make some much-needed money; but he must have felt also that the Register Office would offer him a satisfying combination of profit and public service.

The bold claims made for the scheme soon attracted the attention of the polite world. Just a month after Fielding's *Plan* appeared, Samuel Johnson paid it the compliment of his consideration in the *Rambler*, No. 105 (19 March 1750/1):

I was lately considering, among other objects of speculation, the new attempt of an

---

[1] *An Enquiry into the Causes of the late Increase of Robbers* (1751), pp. xi–xiii, 11.

[2] *Enquiry*, p. [128].

[3] See George, 'The Early History of Registry Offices', pp. 585–7.

'universal register'. . . . My imagination soon presented to me the latitude to which this design may be extended by integrity and industry, and the advantages which may be justly hoped from a general mart of intelligence, when once its reputation shall be so established, that neither reproach nor fraud shall be feared from it; when an application to it shall not be censured as the last resource of desperation, nor its informations suspected as the fortuitous suggestions of men obliged not to appear ignorant.[1]

Johnson goes on to praise the project as worthy of the attention of both merchants and philosophers, but there is perhaps just a hint of criticism in all this, just a trace of suspicion that, however fine the idea, the men involved may prove all too fallible. That impression is not lessened by a dream described in the second half of the essay in which Justice and Truth are sent to 'register' the demands and pretensions of men, whose claims are all empty and hollow. Fielding's enterprise thus serves Johnson as an instrument of social satire from which the office itself does not entirely escape.

Others, however, must have been less skeptical, for the Register Office seemed to flourish in the next few years. One of the proprietors (probably John Fielding) declared in November 1751 that expenses had so far been great and profits small, his main reward, he added, having been the thought of distressed widows put in comfortable circumstances, orphans preserved from the streets, and country girls 'secured from dangerous Snares' by means of the Universal Register Office.[2] Perhaps he spoke sincerely, but the outward signs were those of financial success. On 6 April 1752 a new branch was opened on Bishopsgate Street next to Cornhill to serve customers in the City; and the main office in the Strand claimed to have several thousand articles registered.[3] Further branching out involved 'correspondence' with the Universal Register Office of Dublin, an independent operation begun in 1751 by 'Gentlemen and Traders' of that city and admittedly modelled directly on the Fieldings' office in London.[4] Some idea of the volume of business handled by the London Office may be gathered from the records of material printed for their use; by Strahan's account between September of 1752 and May of 1753 about 21,000 copies of the *Plan* and some 11,000 'Letters' and 'Summons' were printed; in 1754 the number of these form letters reached 16,000. Near the end of 1751 John Fielding spoke occasionally of the great crowds of people of fashion who were forced to wait

---

[1] *The Rambler*, ed. W. J. Bate and A. B. Strauss, *The Yale Edition of the Works of Samuel Johnson*, iv (1969), 194.

[2] *LDA*, 9 Nov. 1751.   [3] *CGJ* No. 27, 4 Apr. 1752.

[4] See *A Plan of the Universal Register Office Now Open'd Opposite to the Parliament-House in College-Green* (Dublin, 1751). The Dublin *Plan*, though it does not quote Montaigne or use Fielding's economic arguments, is even more hyperbolic than Fielding's in stressing the social utility of the Office in uniting mankind; the Register Office, this writer says, is the heart of the body politic and may be likened to the 'great Tree in the Vision of Nebuchadnezzar' (p. 6).

for long periods before being attended to, and though his expression of concern may have been self-serving, both the printing records and the number of competing offices which sprang up in 1751 and 1752 point to a vigorously successful undertaking.[1] Little wonder that his twenty shares of the Register Office were the only property that Fielding's will did not direct to be converted immediately into money and annuities upon his death.[2]

The later history of the Register Office is less happy. In 1761 John Fielding gave up the business, having decided, apparently, that such an enterprise could operate successfully only as a government monopoly.[3] By then the number of rival concerns had made the term 'Register Office' both commonplace and disreputable, with the old 'Intelligence Offices' now assuming the new name.[4] Their proprietors were accused of being only discarded clerks rather than gentlemen, of placing fraudulent advertisements, of cheating those who borrowed money, and, especially, of abusing the trust of those who sought to acquire places or servants.[5] By the time Joseph Reed wrote his play *The Register Office: A Farce* (1761), such establishments could be depicted as places where 'the good old Trade of Pimping is carried on with great Success and Decency', much fallen off from the laudable institution 'invented by the ingenious Author of Tom Jones'.[6]

2. THE REGISTER OFFICE AND THE BACKGROUND OF THE *COVENT-GARDEN JOURNAL*

The apparent prosperity of the Universal Register Office in 1751 and 1752 may in large part be attributed to the promotional skill of the Fieldings, who seldom let slip an opportunity to publicize its services or make extravagant claims for its usefulness to society. As one of the proprietors (presumably John Fielding) explained in a frank letter to the *London Daily Advertiser*, an intensive advertising campaign was necessary because the public was naturally suspicious of the new enterprise, the very word 'Universal' suggesting the nostrums of a quack doctor; consequently, he added, 'our

[1] BL Add. MS 48803A, fos. 14–15; *LDA*, 9 Dec. 1751.

[2] Cross, iii, 22–3.

[3] George, 'The Early History of Registry Offices', p. 589.

[4] See John Fielding's protest against this practice in *Public Advertiser*, 4 Dec. 1752. Competing offices included the Public Register Office (see below, p. xxv); the General Register-Office in Southwark, opened 20 Aug. 1752 (*LDA*, 13 Aug. 1752); and a 'New General Register Office' in Great Queen Street, Lincoln's Inn Fields (*GA*, 21 Sept. 1752).

[5] See e.g. *Spring-Garden Journal*, No. 1 (16 Nov. 1752) and 'Philanthropos', *An Appeal to the Public; Against the Growing Evil of Universal Register Offices* (1757). The latter pamphlet takes care to make an exception of the office of John Fielding, who may well have written this work himself. On the large number of such offices see the proposal for a 'literary' register office in the *Connoisseur*, No. 96 (27 Nov. 1755). See also *The Cheats of London Exposed; Or, The Tricks of the Town Laid Open* (1770?), pp. 47–8.

[6] I. i. (p. 3).

greatest Difficulty of all, was that of making the Office known and understood'.[1] Since both their advertising methods and the kinds of obstacles which they had to overcome had a direct bearing on the conception of the *Covent-Garden Journal*, to understand the background of that journal we must review the major episodes in the efforts of the Register Office to gain public attention and acceptance during 1751, between the publication of the *Plan* in February and the first number of Fielding's paper the following January.

In the spring of 1751 the Register Office, while continuing its advertisements in the *General Advertiser*, sought favorable notice in other papers as well. Fielding's friend Christopher Smart obligingly published an extended puff in the February number of his periodical the *Midwife*, celebrating the office in the Strand as fulfilling 'the Purpose of a publick Good', and in March came Johnson's rather qualified expression of approval in the *Rambler*.[2] More importantly, the proprietors began in June a series of moves to gain publicity in the *London Daily Advertiser*, in which the flamboyant Dr John Hill wrote daily leaders under the title of 'the Inspector', leaders much read by people of fashion. Two letters signed 'Z.Z.' concerning the Register Office appeared in Hill's columns, on 3 June and 21 August; both were attributed to Fielding by his nineteenth-century biographers, although neither bears the slightest trace of his style. They are, however, much in the manner of his half-brother John, and both are worth examining as examples of public relations for the Register Office.[3]

In the first of these letters 'Z.Z.' begins by eulogizing Hill (soon to be Fielding's open enemy in the 'paper war' conducted by the *Covent-Garden Journal*) and then launches into a long eyewitness account of the daily operation of the Register Office, at least the operation as the shareholders would have wished it depicted. In the series of scenes described, servants are questioned with great care about their personal background and depart 'with a better Sense of their Duty'; a clergyman is filled with surprise and joy upon learning of a vacant curacy; the proprietors are thanked by a 'curious Artist' for a recommendation to a nobleman; summer lodgings are provided for a gentleman and his wife; and a genteel young woman is rendered speechless by an 'Excess of Gratitude and tenderness' upon being placed as a maid to a lady of quality and thus saved from the misery of prostitution. Throughout these sentimentalized vignettes 'Z.Z.' harps on the fact that the Register Office is conducted by *gentlemen*, untouched, presumably, by the stigma of trade and motivated, apparently, by altruism alone.[4]

The second letter by 'Z.Z.' to the Inspector involves the controversy in the

---

[1] *LDA*, 9 Nov. 1751.   [2] *The Midwife*, 1 (1751), 225–8.
[3] On the authorship, see Cross, ii. 361, iii. 346; on Hill, see below, pp. xxxvii–xxxix.
[4] *LDA*, 3 June 1751.

summer of 1751 over the Glastonbury waters, a controversy which directly involved the Register Office and into which Fielding himself was drawn.[1] The dispute centered on the curative powers of water from a spring at the foot of Tor Hill, Glastonbury, near Fielding's birthplace. The miraculous property of this spring (derived from its legendary association with the Holy Grail) had been attested to in April by an old man named Matthew Chancellor, whose drinking of the water had been commanded by an angel in a dream; by summer the spot had become the destination of hordes of fashionable pilgrims in various stages of ill health. The commercial potential of this fad was easy to see. In June a certain Mr Brooks offered the waters for sale in London at one shilling and sixpence a quart, but in July the 'Proprietors' of the waters certified that only the Universal Register Office could sell the potion in the metropolis.[2] Claims and counter-claims, ridicule and spirited defences of the waters' efficacy, naturally abounded in the press, and the letter by 'Z.Z.' on 31 August, in response to a skeptical critique in the *General Evening Post* of 27 August, promised that a full chemical analysis would soon be published and would satisfy everyone. 'Z.Z.' himself had no doubt about the waters, for they had cured him of a stubborn, undefined ailment.[3]

No direct mention was made of the Register Office in this second letter by 'Z.Z.', but that defect was remedied by one 'T.W.' in a letter to the *London Daily Advertiser* on 7 September. Then on 8 October the *General Advertiser* carried in support of the waters a letter which, as Martin Battestin has recently demonstrated, is clearly by Henry Fielding.[4] Fielding, whose health was worsening by late summer, had visited Glastonbury in August and reportedly had received great benefit from drinking the waters there; whatever his financial interest in promoting this medicine, he appears to have been personally convinced of its power. His letter, in response to yet another unfavorable account in the press, said nothing of the Register Office, but by now the connection must have been firmly fixed in the public mind. And John Fielding, as a final reminder of his office's interest in the matter, presented another case history describing the cure in late October.[5]

---

[1] See Martin C. Battestin, 'Fielding and the Glastonbury Waters', *Yearbook of English Studies*, 10 (1980), 204–9.

[2] *GA*, 26 June 1751; *LDA*, 25 July 1751.

[3] This letter was said by *GM* 21 (1751), 416–17, to be by 'J——e F——g', but by this time both brothers were justices. It has recently been reattributed to Henry by Pat Rogers, *Henry Fielding* (1979), p. 177; but even aside from the fact that the syntax is much too tangled to have been penned by the novelist, Henry was away from London, in Glastonbury, at the time the letter appeared. Although Rogers is correct in saying Henry had a 'strong reason for celebrating' the wonders of Glastonbury, John had an equally strong reason for celebrating a product handled by the Register Office. The letter bears no resemblance to that of 8 Oct. written by Henry on the same subject.

[4] Battestin, 'Fielding and the Glastonbury Waters', reprints the letter.

[5] *LDA*, 28 Oct. 1751.

However damaging the ridicule and skepticism may have been to the sales of bottles of Glastonbury waters, the controversy had at least resulted in a spate of publicity for the Fieldings' shop in the Strand.

By October such publicity was needed more than ever, for in the middle of that month there was established in King Street, Covent Garden, the Public Register Office, the first competing agency really to pose a serious threat to the Fieldings. With a 'plan' obviously imitating that of the Universal Register Office the proprietors of this concern nonetheless claimed to be the 'original Inventors' of all such undertakings and boasted of a new method for ascertaining the true character of servants.[1] The central figure in this rival office was one Philip D'Halluin, a Belgian trained for business in London and the author of *A Compendious English Grammar, Calculated for Foreigners* (1750). The Fieldings responded to the sudden emergence of competition by attacking on several fronts. A flurry of their advertisements appeared in the *General Advertiser* (19, 23, 31 October; 9, 21, 23 November), and John Hill was somehow induced to make the rival offices the subject of his 'Inspector' essay in the *London Daily Advertiser* for 31 October. Hill's leader argues that from the very nature of the undertaking there should be but one such office, and ''tis not an undertaking for the Ignorant, or the Indigent'. And he adds, ''tis a Justice I owe not only to the proprietors of the Original Office in the Strand, but the Public also, to declare, that I know them to be Men of Fortune and Abilities'. John Fielding quickly attempted to follow this assault with a *coup de grace*. Four days later, on 4 November, he published a letter in the same paper thanking the Inspector and ridiculing the claims of the 'pretended Office' erected by 'one Dullwin, a Travelling Frenchman', who he claimed had loitered about the Universal Register Office for some months to steal its methods: 'This is . . . the only Country in Europe where a Foreigner can do an Act like this with Impunity'. To this ungenerous piece of chauvinism, D'Halluin responded two days later with his own letter to the *London Daily Advertiser*; demonstrating somewhat more dignity than John Fielding had been able to muster, he nonetheless managed to impugn the 'credit' of the proprietors of the Strand office, including 'Mr. Folding', while defending his own abilities and background. Not surprisingly, the entire affair thus turned on the integrity and social status of the various proprietors. Not content to let the matter rest, John Fielding sought in a private letter to enlist Hill's aid in another leader supporting the original office, but to no avail; Hill, for whatever reason, wrote no more essays in support of the Fieldings, and the rival office which he had attacked found no difficulty securing advertising space in the Inspector's paper.[2]

---

[1] *LDA*, 17 Oct., 29 Oct., 23 Nov., and 2 Dec. 1751.

[2] BL Stowe MS 155, fo. 124. Hill's patronage of the Universal Register Office was later a point of ridicule in *Some Remarks on the Life and Writings of Dr. J—— H——* (1752), p. 18.

In this intensified, competitive atmosphere it was particularly galling to the proprietors of the Universl Register Office that one of the major advertising outlets was closed to them. 'Z.Z.', in his first letter, had expressed his 'Surprize and Indignation . . . that the Author of, perhaps, the driest unentertaining Daily Paper, which ever did, or can exist in a sensible City, had suppressed their Advertisements, and not only absolutely refused to receive any Letter relating to the Office, but had also taken some indirect Steps to injure the Undertaking'.[1] On 9 November, just a few days after John Fielding's complaint against 'Dullwin', it was revealed in another letter to the press by 'one of the Proprietors' that the hostile paper was the *Daily Advertiser* (not to be confused with the *London Daily Advertiser*, a quite different newspaper).[2] However boring 'Z.Z.' may have found this paper, it was a vitally important medium for publicizing new enterprises, and the author of the letter of 9 November admitted that the problem of making the Universal Register Office known and understood 'would have been the least Obstacle, had the Daily Advertiser concurred with the rest of the Papers in communicating it to the Public'. What particularly annoyed this writer was that the notices of the rival office were accepted by the *Daily Advertiser* while those of the 'original' establishment were refused. In point of fact advertisements for the Public Register Office were indeed carried in that paper when it first opened, but later their notices were also rejected.[3]

The probable motive for this restrictive policy of the *Daily Advertiser* is not hard to find. A four-page daily consisting almost entirely of advertisements, it throve on the same food as the Register Office: employment opportunities, items for sale, lodgings to let, estates for sale, money to be lent, advowsons, annuities, and so on. Despite 'Z.Z.'s' hint of malice and mystery, the printer Matthew Jenour and others concerned in the *Daily Advertiser* would simply have looked on the register offices as direct competition with their own enterprise, especially since in the *Plan* Fielding had tended to disparage public advertisements as a method for executing such business as the selling of estates.

Given this climate of quarrels among rival offices and restraints on advertising, John Fielding and his partners must have seen a clear need to publish their own organ of publicity in which advertisements for the Universal Register Office could be freely displayed. Accordingly, on 31 October and 1 November their advertisements carried the announcement

[1] *LDA*, 3 June 1751.

[2] *LDA*, 9 Nov. 1751.

[3] *DA*, 17, 18 Oct. 1751. For the refusal of Public Register Office advertisements, see their notices in *GA*, 18 Apr. 1752; *LDA*, 29 Apr. 1752. A few minor advertisements for the Fielding enterprise were in fact run in the *Daily Advertiser*; e.g. an advertisement for an usher to an academy (12 Feb. 1751), for the Glastonbury waters (13 Jan. 1752), and for a 'Surgeon and Man-Midwife, who wants to settle' (7 Oct. 1752).

that at their office on 23 November would be published the *Covent-Garden Journal*, 'A Paper of Entertainment. By Several Eminent Hands.' Would-be subscribers were asked to send their names and addresses to the office in the Strand.[3]

The *Journal* did not, however, appear until 4 January 1752, and although the Register Office offered no explanation for the delay, it may be assumed that Fielding was forced to postpone its appearance while he put the finishing touches to *Amelia*, published on 18 December. But the effort to publicize the Universal Register Office suffered very little by the postponement, for Fielding worked into the fabric of *Amelia* a series of outrageous—and, given the time scheme of the novel, anachronistic—puffs for the shop in the Strand. In the first of these (and the most unfortunate from the point of view of public relations), the narrator cites Miss Mathews's maidservant as the source of his information about her, adding, 'Many other Materials of a private Nature were communicated by one of the Clerks of the Universal Register Office; who, by having a general Acquaintance with Servants, is Master of all the Secrets of every Family in the Kingdom'. After this gaffe, so clearly at odds with the proprietors' claims of confidentiality, the references are wisely limited to services performed: Mr Bennet finds a curacy and a travelling companion, Booth a new lodging, Amelia a reliable money-lender, and one of her sick children a cure in the Glastonbury waters—all through the agency of the Universal Register Office, 'a Place where all the Necessities of Life were provided for'.[2] As though these puffs were not enough, the end of the second volume displayed a full-page advertisement for the Register Office, including the caveat 'all other Offices are Counterfeits'.

When the *Covent-Garden Journal* finally appeared a few weeks later, there could be no doubt of its usefulness as a publicity medium for the Register Office in this period of commercial crisis. Not only were readers reminded of the connection by the imprint of each number, but some pains were taken in the opening issues to make the relationship explicit. Thus in No. 2 Fielding makes the Register Offfice the headquarters of his troops in his 'Journal of the Paper War', in No. 5 a long notice about the office's promotion of the manufacture of Dresden embroidery is sandwiched

---

[1] *GA*, 31 Oct. 1751; *LDA*, 1 Nov. 1751; the notice in *GA* promises publication of the *Journal* on Saturday, 6 Nov., but since 6 Nov. was not a Saturday this must be presumed a printer's error. On 21 and 23 Nov. *GA* carried a notice postponing the new periodical until a later date. Beginning on 18 and 20 Dec. advertisements for the *Journal* in *LDA* and *GA* promised its first number on 4 Jan. 1752.

[2] *Amelia* (1751), ii. 169 (Bk. v, ch. ix); iii. 51–2 (Bk. VII, ch. v); iii. 70 (Bk. VII, ch. vi); iv. 99 (Bk. x, ch. ix); iv. 156 (Bk. XI, ch. iv); iv. 187 (Bk. XI, ch. viii); iv. 296 (Bk. XII, ch. viii). These were removed in the revised edition of the novel; see *Amelia*, ed. Martin C. Battestin, Wesleyan Edn. (Oxford, 1983), pp. lix–lx and Appendix VI. For an argument that Fielding was not responsible for these deletions, see Hugh Amory, 'What Murphy Knew: His Interpolations in Fielding's *Works* (1762), and Fielding's Revision of *Amelia*', *PBSA* 77 (1983), 152–4.

between two regular departments of the paper, and a correspondent in No. 7 points to the *Journal* itself as a kind of Register Office. Moreover, in its first seven numbers the *Journal* carried no less than thirty-five notices and advertisements for its sponsoring office, whereas the proprietors placed no advertisements in the *General Advertiser* during that same period. In obvious response to this new device for gaining publicity for its rival, D'Halluin's Public Register Office in mid-January engaged Bonnell Thornton to edit a satirical counterpart; called *Have At You All: or, The Drury-Lane Journal*, Thornton's periodical did not limit its witty ridicule to Fielding alone, yet it was clearly aimed at the same market as Fielding's journal in an advertising war of the competing register offices.

By early April, however, the intensity of this rivalry had died down. Thornton's burlesque paper came to an end on 9 April, and the frequency of advertisements for the Universal Register Office in Fielding's paper slackened markedly at about the same time. Such advertising remained at a low ebb for the duration of its run. However much its conception and birth might have owed to the problems of the Universal Register Office, the *Covent-Garden Journal* had a life of its own to lead as the vehicle for the social, moral, and literary reflections of a major novelist in the last phase of his career.

3. THE *COVENT-GARDEN JOURNAL*

The *Covent-Garden Journal*, Fielding's last effort at sustained journalism, ran for 72 numbers from 4 January until 25 November 1752, appearing on Tuesdays and Saturdays until 4 July and on Saturdays only from that date until its close. Its format was like that of other essay-journals of the mid-century, with some features incorporated from Fielding's previous papers.[1] Each issue was four pages, with a typical number containing the following sections: a leader or opening essay by Fielding, sometimes varied by letters from correspondents real or imaginary; a column called 'Covent Garden', commenting upon cases which had recently come before Fielding in his capacity as a magistrate for Westminster and Middlesex; a department headed 'Modern History Abridged', consisting of news items compiled from other papers and followed by ironic or editorial comments; a section (in 17 numbers only) entitled 'Proceedings at the Court of Censorial Enquiry'; and the usual advertisements and stock reports. Amidst this material Fielding also sometimes inserted notices 'To the Public' touching on the apprehension and prosecution of criminals. After the title of each number appeared the pseudonym Fielding chose for this occasion, 'Sir Alexander Drawcansir,

---

[1] Those papers are the *Champion* (1739–41), the *True Patriot* (1745–6), and the *Jacobite's Journal* (1747–8).

Knt. Censor of Great Britain', the name being drawn from the blustering figure Drawcansir in Buckingham's *Rehearsal* and suggesting more than a touch of mock-heroism about the pose Fielding strikes here.[1]

With Drawcansir-like bravado Fielding set the price of the *Journal* at threepence, prompting a rival paper, the *Craftsman*, to remark, 'The *Covent-Garden* Hero raises his Paper a third Part above the common Price of a Journal'.[2] This higher than normal price Fielding ironically attributes to the demands of his bookseller, whose reasons, he says, include the beauty of the paper, the quantity of the matter, and the promise of classical learning to be paraded in the *Journal*'s pages.[3] If the term 'Bookseller' here is not simply a fictitious device, it would be difficult to say whom Fielding meant by it. The colophon of the first number reads, '*LONDON*: Printed, and Sold by Mrs. DODD, at the *Peacock, Temple-Bar*; and at the UNIVERSAL REGISTER OFFICE, opposite *Cecil-street*, in the *Strand*; where ADVERTISEMENTS and LETTERS to the AUTHOR are taken in.' Although there are some variations in the colophon as time goes on, Mrs Dodd's name is the only one to appear. Ann Dodd, however, was neither a copy-owning bookseller nor a printer, but only one of the more important 'mercuries' or distributors of newspapers and pamphlets. Her more famous mother (also Ann Dodd at the Peacock, without Temple-Bar) had been listed on the imprint of Fielding's *Masquerade* (1728), and the daughter's name had appeared in connection with *Shamela*, *The Crisis* (both 1741), *Ovid's Art of Love Paraphrased* (1747), and both the *True Patriot* and the *Jacobite's Journal*.[4] Her name thus signified very little with regard to the *Covent-Garden Journal* except that her shop acted as an additional distribution point along with the Universal Register Office. The actual printer of the *Journal* has not been identified.

Nor has any information come to light about the financial backing of the new periodical. As indicated earlier Fielding undertook the *Journal* in response to the demonstrated need of the Register Office for an advertising outlet, and one may assume that the partners in the Register Office were the shareholders and owners of the *Journal*—i.e., primarily if not exclusively the Fieldings themselves. On the other hand, shares of most newspapers and journals in the mid-century were owned by booksellers, who saw in such

---

[1] See George Villiers, Duke of Buckingham, *The Rehearsal* (3rd. edn., 1675), IV. i: 'I drink I huff, I strut, look big and stare; / And all this I can do, because I dare.' Cf. *Jonathan Wild*, II, viii: '. . . one of those passages in history which writers, Drawcansir-like, introduce *only because they dare.*'

[2] *Craftsman*, 7 Mar. 1752; for a similar complaint see *True Briton*, 22 Jan. 1752.

[3] *CGJ* No. 1, 4 Jan. 1752; cf. *True Patriot*, No. 1 (5 Nov. 1745), where Fielding also justifies a price of threepence instead of two by citing the claims of his bookseller.

[4] The mother, widow of a printer named Nathaniel Dodd, died in Apr. 1739, leaving the shop to her daughter Ann (born 1716). It was the mother whose name appeared on the imprint of the first edition of Pope's *Dunciad*, but the sketch of her in the Biographical Appendix to the Twickenham Edn., vol. v (1965), conflates the mother and daughter and confuses the mother with the widow of another Nathanial Dodd, whose business was once managed by Thomas Gent. I am greatly indebted to Professor J. Michael Treadwell for supplying this information on the two Ann Dodds.

papers the means of advertising their wares at cut rate; moreover, booksellers were most likely to advertise works of which they owned the copy in newspapers in which they owned shares.[1] Given these circumstances, one may well speculate that Fielding's friend and publisher Andrew Millar held shares in the *Covent-Garden Journal*, for there are throughout the run of the periodical some 159 advertisements for his books, more even than for the services of the Universal Register Office and many times more than the number of notices for the works of another well-known bookseller like Robert Dodsley, whose books are advertised only 19 times. Fielding, moreover, on several occasions devoted space in the *Journal* to puffing books published by Millar, such as the *History of the Portuguese* (No. 23, 21 March) and Charlotte Lennox's *Female Quixote* (No. 24, 24 March); and he paid personal tribute to his publisher by making him the General of his 'troops' in his mock-war on the productions of Grub Street (No. 2, 7 January). Although the commercial advantages to Millar in all this strongly suggest an arrangement that went beyond friendship, there is no documentary evidence available to support it.[2] Publicly, at least, the *Covent-Garden Journal* was simply under the proprietorship of the Universal Register Office and thus of the Fieldings themselves.

And though there were some outside contributors, Fielding himself was the author of most of the material in the *Journal*. As was customary in periodicals of the day, some 57 of the 72 numbers are signed with initials: 'C.' (19 occurrences), 'A.' (30), 'M.' (4), 'P.' (2), and 'S.' and 'J.' once each. All of these initials except 'J.' represent Fielding himself, although 'M.' usually occurs after a series of letters from readers and may signify editorial supervision rather than authorship. Of the vast majority of the remaining essays, poems, and letters—those either unsigned or signed with a pseudonym—Fielding's authorship is also not in doubt. The present edition includes all the material from the leaders and all the 'Court of Censorial Enquiry' sections, with notes on authorship only when in the editor's view Fielding's hand can be seriously questioned.[3] Outside contributors who may

[1] See Michael Harris, 'The Management of the London Newspaper Press during the Eighteenth Century', *Publishing History*, 4 (1978), 95–112, and Terry Belanger, 'Booksellers' Sales of Copyright' (Dissertation, Columbia, 1970), pp. 79 ff. For a revealing comment on the practice, see *Gray's Inn Journal*, No. 50 (29 Sept. 1753).

[2] Fielding's puff of *The Female Quixote* was reprinted as an unsigned letter in *LEP* (2 Apr. 1752), a paper unfriendly to Fielding, with no indication of source. Presumably the puff was inserted and paid for by Millar, a presumption which supports the notion that Fielding's praise of Millar's books was very conscious salesmanship.

[3] In a copy of the *Covent-Garden Journal* in the Bodleian Library (Hope Folio 11) eight essays are crossed out by hand. Since, as the Textual Introduction explains, this copy contains manuscript revisions and corrections, some of which are in Fielding's hand, and since this copy was also apparently used in the preparation of the 1762 *Works*, such markings may indicate an authoritative rejection of Fielding's authorship. In every case except one the essays are among those which on other grounds I would assign to someone other than Fielding. See below, pp. lvi–lviii, and the notes on Nos. 28, 38, 40, 41, 62, 63, 64, and 65.

be identified with at least some degree of confidence include Fielding's friend James Harris, author of *Hermes*, who unquestionably wrote the dialogue in No. 30 signed 'J.' as well as the abstract of *Hermes* in No. 21; the surgeon William Hunter, another close friend, who may have contributed articles concerning the Society of Naval Surgeons (Nos. 38 and 41); and John Fielding, who was probably the author of the letters signed 'E.R.' (Nos. 63 and 64).[1] Some scholars have also found reason to attribute pieces in the *Journal* to Christopher Smart and Arthur Murphy.[2]

Authorship of the other departments of the paper is difficult to determine, and for this reason these sections—the 'Covent Garden' columns and the 'Modern History' excerpts—have been placed in an appendix to the present edition. There can be little question that Fielding himself wrote those parts of the 'Covent Garden' columns which editorialize about issues of criminal justice; some of these, indeed, are vitally important additions to our understanding of his attitudes and mood in this period. Other comments in that section, however, and perhaps most of the simple reports on cases brought before Fielding, are the work of his law clerk, Joshua Brogden, though the Justice himself must have edited and supervised Brogden's accounts.[3]

In the same way, one cannot be certain which of the comments (other than those signed 'C.') Fielding himself appended to the news items excerpted from other papers for the 'Modern History' columns. In the second number he assures us he has assigned the task of news-collecting to a man of a 'wakeful' capacity,[4] usually identified as the Reverend William Young, the model of Parson Adams and Fielding's collaborator on an ill-fated translation of Lucian projected in *CGJ* No. 52.[5] But although Brogden's assistance is made explicit, Young's never is, and the authorship of many of the satirical comments on news items must remain a matter of conjecture. Despite a mystifying proliferation of initials and pseudonyms following these comments, Fielding himself probably was responsible for most of them.

Some of these departments or features in the *Journal* have their clear precedents in Fielding's previous journalism. The 'Court of Censorial Enquiry', which beginning with No. 5 appears here seventeen times, closely resembles both the mock-court set up in the *Champion* to expose 'whatever is wicked, hateful, absurd, or ridiculous' and the 'Court of Criticism' established in the *Jacobite's Journal* to inspect 'all Matters any wise

---

[1] See the notes on the individual numbers listed.

[2] See the notes on Nos. 50, 53, and 62. There is no evidence whatsoever that Murphy was an 'assistant' editor of the *Journal*, as some have claimed; see e.g. Matthew Grace, ed., *The Lives of Henry Fielding and Samuel Johnson together with Essays from the Gray's-Inn Journal by Arthur Murphy* (Gainesville, Fla., 1968), pp. viii–ix.

[3] See Fielding's comment in the 'Covent Garden' column for 9 Mar., below, Appendix I.

[4] 'Covent Garden' column for 6 Jan.   [5] See Dudden, p. 891; Cross, ii. 371.

concerning the Republic of Literature'.¹ Fielding had also long been irritated by the unreliability of contemporary newspapers and by their standard formulae for reporting such news items as the marriage of 'an eminent Haberdasher' to 'a young Lady posses'd of every Qualification capable of rendering the married State happy, with a genteel Fortune'.² In the *Journal* his 'Modern History, *cum notis variorum*', with its ironic or reflective commentary on such items of news, was merely a continuation of similar columns in the *True Patriot* and *Jacobite's Journal*. As the *Gentleman's Magazine* recognized in its comment on this feature of the *CGJ*, Fielding doubtless had as his model for this satiric device the similar practice of his old enemy the *Grub-street Journal* (1730–7).³

Except for some portions of the *Champion*, however, Fielding's previous journalism afforded him no model for the leading essays of the *Covent-Garden Journal*, for he here turned away almost completely from the political themes which had dominated his earlier papers. His enemies in the Opposition press pretended to find this new stance hard to believe; both *Old England* and the *Craftsman* jokingly speculated that Fielding was now trying to amuse the public simply to divert attention from the affairs of the Pelham Administration and thus serve 'as a Barrel thrown out from the Ship of Administration to some . . . Whale of the Country Interest'.⁴ But since the death of Frederick Prince of Wales in 1751 the Opposition had been in disarray, and Fielding's disclaimer of 'any Dealing in Politics' (*CGJ* No. 1) in his new periodical was seriously intended. To be sure, he manages a few compliments to Pelham in the course of the *Journal*; and he refers to recent political broils in the course of decrying the manipulation of the mob by disaffected elements and in satirizing preparations for a new Westminster election.⁵ For the most part, however, there are few partisan moments in the *Covent-Garden Journal*. Fielding's concern now is with politics in a much broader sense of the social and moral health of the body politic, with his journalistic model no longer Addison's *Freeholder* but those essays of wider range in the *Tatler* and the *Spectator*.⁶

Despite Fielding's turn away from partisan politics, his new essay-journal was strikingly rooted in the everyday life of mid-century London and unusually reflective of the most circumstantial details of the contemporary

---

¹ *Champion*, 22 Dec. 1739; *JJ* No. 6, 9 Jan. 1748.
² *DA*, 21 May 1751. For Fielding's contempt for current journalistic practices see *Champion* for 10 Apr. 1740 and *Tom Jones*, I. i.; see also Glenn W. Hatfield, *Henry Fielding and the Language of Irony* (Chicago, 1968), pp. 85–9. For a vivid sketch of the usual methods of collecting news, see *Low-Life; Or One Half of the World Knows not how the Other Half Live*, 3rd edn. (1764), pp. 85–6 (1st pub. 1752).
³ *GM* 22 (1752), 27. In *CGJ* the title of the section is changed in No. 17 (29 Feb.) to 'Modern History Abridged', and the practice of inserting comments is discontinued after No. 20 (10 Mar.).
⁴ *Craftsman*, 25 Jan. 1752; *OE*, 21 Dec. 1751, 11 and 18 Jan. 1752.
⁵ See Nos. 16, 49, and 58.
⁶ On the influence of the *Freeholder* on *JJ*, see W. B. Coley, ed., *JJ*, p. lvi.

scene. Indeed, it is instructive to compare Fielding's manner here with the generalized reflections of Johnson's *Rambler*, which was still appearing in the first few months of 1752 and which at least one reader found lacking in the concrete details of ordinary life. Writing to Mrs Elizabeth Carter about Johnson's essays, Catherine Talbot complained, 'But why then does he not write now and then on the living manners of the times?—the stage,—the follies and fashions. . . . Humour and the manners of the world are not his fort.'[1] In another letter she provides some examples of what she finds missing in the *Rambler*: 'There are many odd clubs, advertisements, societies, meetings, and devices of various kinds which this age produces; and London swarms with what would afford as amusing subjects as any in the Spectator.'[2]

Though her reaction to Fielding's journal was not recorded, Miss Talbot would surely have found it to her taste. Even the title *Covent-Garden Journal*, which Fielding had earlier used for a political satire in support of Viscount Trentham in the Westminster election of 1749,[3] suggested a world not of Johnsonian reflection but of Hogarthian bustle and busyness; the region not only housed Justice Fielding but had a reputation as the 'Grand Seraglio to the Nation', a place where 'Bawds, Whores, Thieves, Cullies, Fools and Drunkards' mixed with 'daring Pick-Pockets, fearful Passengers and frighted Constables, whose Staves are hardly of Authority sufficient to prevent their being beaten'.[4] It was on this crowded and sorry stage that Fielding held his court and Sir Alexander Drawcansir performed his duties as Censor; the 'living manners of the times' were the very stuff of the *Covent-Garden Journal*. Its 'Covent Garden' column graphically depicts the parade of felons who were appearing before Fielding, sometimes with courtroom scenes dramatized and the dialogue of witnesses or defendants reproduced, while the news columns indict contemporary journalists or editorialize about contemporary events.

Moreover, the essays themselves, even when their themes are most general, often take their rise from specific events reported in the 'Covent Garden' column or in the columns of news. Thus the murder trial of Mary Blandy, accused of parricide, leads to an essay on gallantry and seduction; a riot in Norwich provides the immediate occasion for two pieces on the mob as the 'Fourth Estate'; two essays on adultery have their origin in a reflection on a specific case reported in the 'Covent Garden' section; an allegory on methods of making capital punishment effective coincides with an account of a particular set of executions at Tyburn; a new law to suppress bawdy-

---

[1] *A Series of Letters between Mrs. Elizabeth Carter and Miss Catherine Talbot from the year 1741 to 1770* (1809), i. 371. [2] Ibid., i. 350; see also ii. 34.
[3] See M. C. with R. R. Battestin, 'Fielding, Bedford, and the Westminster Election of 1749', *ECS* 11 (1977/8), 143–85, esp. 166–74.
[4] *Covent-Garden. A Satire* (1756), p. 7; *Low-Life*, 3rd. edn. (1764), p. 19.

houses leads both Fielding and one of his correspondents to reflect on
prostitution as a social problem; Fielding's difficulty in coping with several
insane defendants brought into his court leads to a parody of the admission
regulations of St Luke's Hospital; and a subscription to help a baker whose
house was destroyed by fire occasions several general essays on the meaning
of charity.[1] The *Covent-Garden Journal* is the most generally reflective and at
the same time perhaps the most topical and allusive of Fielding's journalistic
efforts. And the interaction between the reflective essays and the specific
events which inspired them, so easy to miss when the essays are read in
isolation from the rest of the paper, is crucial to our understanding of
Fielding's purpose.

That purpose is clearly expressed by Fielding's mock-title as Drawcansir,
'Knight Censor of Great Britain'. He thus adopts here, as he had in the
Champion and *Jacobite's Journal*, the role of Censor on the Roman model, the
overseer and judge of the nation's moral health, charged with examining into
the lives and manners of its citizens.[2] As a literary vehicle for periodical
essayists, the persona of Censor derived from Isaac Bickerstaff in Steele's
Tatler,[3] but it is fair to say that for Fielding in the *Covent-Garden Journal* it is
more than a convenient device. Three years earlier he had said to the
Westminster Grand Jury, 'Grand Juries, Gentlemen, are in Reality the only
Censors of this Nation', and had reminded them that they were called 'to
this Censorial Office' by the Constitution.[4] But though he may have
recognized that juries and other officers of justice were 'in Reality' the only
Censors remaining, Fielding seems to have taken with great seriousness the
role of the writer as Censor; it was an Office, he said, which though now
degraded by mere journalists 'formerly exercised the Pens of Men of true
Learning and Genius'.[5] Again, in an important but neglected passage in one
of his letters contributed to his sister's *Familiar Letters* (1747), Fielding
partially blames the deplorable condition of the nation's morals on the fact
that 'true Wit and Genius', which ought to be charged with the responsibility
for the society's moral health, have been 'in a manner deposed, and
Imposters advanced in their Place'. 'In reality', he continues, 'what the
Ministry are to the State, the Bishops to the Church, the Chancellor and
Judges to the Law, the Generals to the Army, and the Admirals to the Fleet;
that is a great and good Writer over the Morals of his Countrymen'.[6] The
good writer's authority in morals, he goes on to explain, derives from his
superior *taste*, which he defines as 'the Knowledge of what is right and fit in

---

[1] See the notes on Nos. 20, 47, 67, 50, 45, and 39.
[2] See Plutarch, *Life of Marcus Cato*, xvi; *Champion*, 17 May 1740; and *JJ* No. 1, 5 Dec. 1747.
[3] See especially Addison's *Tatler*, No. 162, 22 Apr. 1710.
[4] *A Charge delivered to the Grand Jury* (1749), pp. 63–4.
[5] *JJ* No. 1, 5 Dec. 1747.
[6] Letter XL, *Familiar Letters between the Principal Characters in David Simple* (1747), ii. 297–8.

everything'. And because he finds an exact analogy between the taste of an age and its morals, Fielding concludes that it is unimaginable that the writer, who is capable of discerning true taste in lesser matters, should not also be able to perceive it 'in that highest and noblest Object the Human Mind'.[1]

It is the writer's true taste, then, which authorizes him to enact the role of Censor of the nation's morals. With that notion in mind we can better understand Fielding's statement of his purpose in the *Covent-Garden Journal*, as expressed in No. 5: 'However vain or romantic the Attempt may seem, I am sanguine enough to aim at serving the noble Interests of Religion, Virtue, and good Sense, by these my Lucubrations. To effect so glorious a Purpose, I know no readier a Way than by an Endeavour to restore that true and manly Taste, which hath, within these few Years, degenerated in these Kingdoms.' And precisely because he is speaking here as Censor and not as the magistrate Henry Fielding he feels able to address in the leading essays of the *Journal* those vices and corrupt diversions of 'Persons of Fashion and Fortune' which he had been careful to exclude from his *Enquiry* a year earlier. At the same time, however, Fielding is neither vain nor romantic; he knows that as writer/Censor he is without the power to act, that he is only a Drawcansir who says, like the character in the *Rehearsal*, 'all this I can do, because I dare'.[2] And so he proceeds not by serious proposals for reform but by mockery, parody, and burlesque to perform the task he had refused in the *Enquiry*, 'to satirize the Great, among whom Luxury is probably rather a moral than a political Evil'.[3]

But Fielding appears in the *Journal* not only as Censor but as Magistrate, with the columns from 'Covent Garden' vividly portraying his day-to-day administration of justice in the most sordid of settings. If, as one scholar has argued,[4] Fielding adopts the pose of Roman Censor in the Preface of his *Enquiry* and that of utilitarian magistrate in the body of the pamphlet, we have the same double role in the *Covent-Garden Journal*: the Censor of the people of fashion in the leading essays and the 'Censorial Court' is complemented by the figure of the magistrate in these other columns describing his dispensation of justice among the lower classes. Here, rather than in most of the essays, we find the Fielding of the *Enquiry* and other social pamphlets, for these sections not only report on specific cases—on occasion taking considerable delight in the speech and demeanor of the miscreants haled into court—but also sometimes provide Fielding with a

---

[1] ii. 298. Cf. *Amelia* (IX. ix), where Fielding, praising his friend Jonathan Tyers, proprietor of Spring Gardens, Vauxhall, argues that 'true Virtue is, indeed, nothing else but true Taste'.

[2] See Hugh Amory, 'Magistrate or Censor? The Problem of Authority in Fielding's Later Writings', *SEL* 12 (1972), 515.

[3] *An Enquiry into the Causes of the late Increase of Robbers* (1751), p. 4.

[4] Amory, 'Magistrate or Censor', pp. 503–18.

forum for protesting the inadequacies of the law.[1] Although, as I have indicated, Brogden appears to have been responsible for the compilation and writing of much of this material, Fielding clearly saw the column as a way of propagating a favorable image of his activities as a justice of the peace and expressing his occasional sense of frustration at various difficulties he found in the execution of his office.

For many of his readers, indeed, this section was the most interesting feature of the paper, and to some it seemed obvious that Fielding's main purpose in the *Journal* could be located in this one column. The *Gentleman's Magazine*, in reviewing the first numbers of the paper, had this comment: 'But the principal character by which he is distinguished in this his paper is that of a justice of peace; and probably his chief encouragement to this undertaking was, the opportunity which his office afforded him of amusing his readers with an account of examinations and commitments; the exploits which constables and thief-takers should atchieve by his influence and direction, and the secrets of prostitution which should be discovered by his penetration and sagacity'.[2] In the same way his enemies regarded this section of the *Journal* as outrageous self-advertisement on Fielding's part, claiming that his paper was merely a vehicle for celebrating his own industry, compassion, erudition, and impartiality in the exercise of his judicial office. Justice, suggested a particular virulent sketch in the *Craftsman* (2 May 1752), should be secret, not assume 'the Airs of a giggling, prating Wretch'; the columns in the *Journal* merely show that a 'Romance Writer' is unfit for the office of justice of the peace. Yet, despite such onslaughts, if Fielding's intention was to gain wide circulation for accurate accounts of proceedings in his court, he certainly succeeded; excerpts from the 'Covent Garden' columns regularly appeared, verbatim but without acknowledgement, amidst the news items of most of the major newspapers, even of papers otherwise hostile to the Bow Street magistrate.[4]

Both as magistrate and moralist, then, Fielding used the *Journal* as a forum for all he now wished to say, late in his career, about human nature, about the taste and manners of his age and the workings of his society. But the paper began on a note considerably less elevated. In an effort, apparently, to attract readers to his new venture, Fielding provoked a 'paper war' between himself, as representative of the 'Republic of Letters', and the united forces of Grub Street writers. This gambit, which was continued for

---

[1] See especially the 'Covent Garden' columns for 24 Feb., 4 May, 29 May, and 18 July.

[2] *GM* 22 (1752), p. 27.

[3] For similar attacks see *Drury-Lane Journal*, No. 7 (27 Feb. 1752), and *True Briton*, 4 Oct. 1752.

[4] Such papers included *GA*, *DA*, *LDA*, and *Craftsman*. One of the two copies of the *CGJ* in the British Library (Burney 447*) has manuscript additions, corrections, and deletions to the 'Covent Garden' columns which indicate that the copy was used by the editor of another newspaper in preparing excerpts for his own news columns.

three numbers and reported in a section called 'Journal of the present Paper War', turned somewhat sour, as a few of those ridiculed in the mock-war responded with personal abuse and in tones much more bitter than Fielding seems to have expected. His disparaging references, for example, to 'one Peeragrin Puckle' and 'one Rodorick Random' provoked a vicious response, usually attributed to Smollett himself, ridiculing his personal circumstances, his brother John, his political connections, and so on.[1] Since Fielding was at the same time enduring continuing attacks from his political enemies in *Old England* as well as suffering a torrent of abusive criticism of *Amelia* (with its 'noseless' heroine), it is curious that he would have opened his *Journal* with what he must have realized would be a provocative device.

Indeed, his most serious miscalculation in the first few weeks of the run of the *Journal* was to seek privately to bring the 'Inspector', John Hill, into the paper war he had initiated; the ensuing quarrel with Hill, who made his headquarters among the wits at the Bedford Coffee-House, became for contemporary readers a prime source of interest throughout the life of Fielding's periodical. Hill, it will be recalled, had been helpful to the Fieldings in publicizing the Universal Register Office, and in the previous year he had had some not uncomplimentary things to say about Fielding's work,[2] although the two men had never met before January 1752. In the second number of the *Journal* (7 January) Fielding jokingly referred to his 'Army's' plan to attack the 'Lion' Hill (in imitation of Steele) had set up in the Bedford as a receptacle for contributions; on the following day Hill, in his column in the *London Daily Advertiser*, responded only with a reference to the noselessness of Amelia and a mock news item about the attack on his lion. All of this was good-humored enough. But, by utter coincidence, on that same day, 8 January, Hill appeared in Fielding's court as a witness against a man accused of robbing him on the highway, and Fielding apparently took this chance meeting as an opportunity to suggest that the Inspector and the Censor engage in a mock-war for the amusement of the town.[3] Fielding had badly misjudged his man. On 9 January, Hill responded in print with a pompous and self-righteous disclaimer, informing the public that Fielding, whom he had never seen before, had at an accidental meeting

---

[1] *A Faithful Narrative of the Base and Inhuman Arts that were lately practiced upon the Brain of Habbakkuk Hilding, Justice, Dealer, and Chapman* (1752). On this quarrel between Fielding and Smollett, see the notes on *CGJ* No. 2.

[2] See *LDA*, 15 Mar. 1751, and G. S. Rousseau, 'Controversy or Collusion? The "Lady Vane" Tracts', *Notes and Queries*, NS 19 (1972), 377 and n. For early references by Fielding to 'one Mr. Hill', see *Champion* for 8, 15, and 29 Jan. 1739/40. For a modern, scholarly assessment of Hill see G. S. Rousseau, 'John Hill, Universal Genius Manqué: Remarks on His Life and Times, with a Checklist of His Works', in *The Renaissance Man in the Eighteenth Century* (Los Angeles, Clark Memorial Library, 1978), pp. 49–129; and *The Letters and Papers of Sir John Hill*, ed. G. S. Rousseau (New York, 1982).

[3] Hill's appearance in court on 8 Jan. is described in the 'Covent Garden' column for 10 Jan., printed originally in *CGJ* No. 3. Cross and Dudden both misdate this event by placing it in Jan. 1751.

proposed the 'insolent Deceit' of 'giving Blows that would not hurt, and sharing the Advantage of Silence'. But, says Hill, 'I hold the Public in too great Respect to trifle with it in so disingenuous a Manner', and he goes on to express his regret that the author of *Joseph Andrews* should now be 'doating' in the *Covent-Garden Journal*. The following day Hill's leader was silent on the subject of Fielding, although the second page of the paper printed 'The genuine Trial of Mary, late Cook-Maid to Sir Simon Pride, Knight, before the worshipful Mr. Justice Feeler', in large part an attack on Fielding's demeanor as a justice of the peace.[1]

In return for all this, Fielding was for once moved to invective. Speaking as 'General Alexander Drawcansir' in his 'Journal of the Paper War' (*CGJ* No. 3), he gave his version of the affair. Hill had come to his 'Tent' (i.e. court) on private business and had been told in all good humor of Drawcansir's plans to attack his lion. But Hill, the betrayer of a private treaty, has turned out to be 'absolutely the vilest Fellow that ever wore a Head'.

What had begun as a joke to improve the paper's circulation had degenerated into personal abuse, and Fielding quickly withdrew from the fray with humorous articles of a treaty of peace and with expressions of regret for the excesses of his ridicule (*CGJ* Nos. 4 and 5). But though the paper war was brought to an end, John Hill continued from time to time to figure in the various sections of the *Journal*. In early May Hill was publicly assaulted at Ranelagh by one Mountefort Brown, a young man who had thought himself slandered in the Inspector's column; in the events growing out of this incident Hill cut a bizarre and ridiculous figure, and Fielding, who had been drawn into the affair as a magistrate, satirized Hill's 'raging Vanity' in one of his leaders.[2] Again, Fielding returned to personal satire of Hill in the final two numbers of the *Journal*, this time in the course of defending Garrick's company at Drury Lane Theatre against the rival company of John Rich at Covent Garden.[3] For his part, Hill kept relatively aloof from Fielding after the end of the paper war in January, pausing only in July to laugh good-naturedly at 'Sir Alexander's declining one half of his Office' by moving to weekly publication; in August he even managed a few compliments for the author of *Tom Jones*.[4] In November, however, during the war between the theaters, Hill once more became openly abusive, calling Fielding a 'decayed Brother', the mere 'Shadow of a formidable Antagonist',

---

[1] *LDA*, 10 Jan. 1752. The main object of attack in this satire was not Fielding but Sir Samuel Prime (1701–77), King's Sergeant-at-Law. See *True Briton*, 15 Jan. 1752, and *Catalogue of Prints and Drawings in the British Museum, Division I: Political and Personal Satires*, No. 3187 (5 Mar. 1752).

[2] *CGJ* No. 60; see also the 'Covent Garden' column for 11 May 1752.

[3] See the notes on Nos. 71 and 72.

[4] *LDA*, 7 July and 10 Aug. 1752; see also *LDA* for 1 Sept. for another amiable reference to Fielding and *LDA* for 21 Sept. for one less amiable.

and pursuing his assault well after the *Covent-Garden Journal* was in its grave.[1] Moreover, throughout the run of the *Journal*, the town looked on Fielding and Hill as chief antagonists; their conflict was celebrated in epigrams, pamphlets, and newspapers, with Hill's abuse of Fielding providing a standard theme in the numerous satires on the flamboyant figure of the Inspector. In the best of these, for example, the anonymous *Some Remarks on the Life and Writings of Dr. J— H—, Inspector-General of Great Britain* (1752), a well-reasoned defense of *Amelia* is worked into the midst of a devastating mock-biography of Hill and parody of the Earl of Orrery's recent life of Swift.[2] The deterioration of the paper war into a personal quarrel may indeed have aroused more interest than Fielding's original scheme would have done.

Nevertheless, despite the attention focused on Fielding's quarrels with Smollett and Hill, such literary skirmishes were not at the heart of what he was doing in the *Covent-Garden Journal*. Nor do literary matters, strictly speaking, really dominate the paper, occupying in fact less than a third of its essays. There are, to be sure, satires in the Scriblerian manner extending the paper war against Grub Street hacks or others whose writings violate either Fielding's sense of decency or his 'Statute of Dullness'. There are essays decrying the impoverished state of literary criticism in England, defining the elusive literary terms 'Wit' and 'Humour', ridiculing the textual excesses of editors of Shakespeare, exposing the devious methods of booksellers, ironically proposing cures for the incurable vanity of authors, or sketching a mock-history of the 'Commonwealth of Literature'. And there are essays or columns of the 'Court of Censorial Enquiry' defending or celebrating particular literary works, such as Charlotte Lennox's *The Female Quixote* or the satire of Lucian or Fielding's own *Amelia*. Fielding's literary values—his admiration, for example, for the stance taken by Pope and Swift against an earlier generation of Dunces—shine through these reviews and essays, though his specific literary criticism is seldom disinterested: his assault on critics is obviously motivated by the hostile reception of *Amelia*, his essay on

---

[1] See *LDA*, 10, 16, 20, and 24 Nov., 6 and 7 Dec. 1752.

[2] *Some Remarks*, pp. 59–62. Hill attributed this satire to the antiquarian Dr John Kennedy, but Kennedy vigorously denied authorship, and it is almost certainly not his; see the 'Dedication' to *Some Observations on the Writers of the Present Age* (1752), presumably by Hill, and the 'To the Reader' prefixed to *Whipping Rods for Trifling, Scurrhill, Scriblers* (1752), by Kennedy. For other comments on Hill's relations with Fielding, see an epigram by 'C.D.' in *GA*, 18 Jan. 1752; two epigrams in the 'Covent Garden' column of 13 Jan.; *Libitina Sine Conflictu; or, A true Narrative of the untimely Death of Doctor Atall* (1752), pp. 13, 23 (attributed to Arthur Murphy by *Rules for Being a Wit* [1753], p. 15); *A Narrative of the Affair between Mr. Brown and the Inspector* (1752), pp. 23–4; *The Inspector's Rhapsody or Soliloquy on the Loss of his Wigg* (1752), p. 7; Christopher Smart, *The Hilliad* (1753), p. viii; and William Kenrick, *Fun: A Parodi-tragi-comical Satire* (1752), *passim*. Bonnell Thornton's two periodicals of 1752, *Drury-Lane Journal* and *Spring-Garden Journal*, attack both Hill and Fielding throughout. For a recent overview of the quarrel, see Betty Rizzo, 'Notes on the War between Henry Fielding and John Hill, 1752–53', *The Library*, ser. 6, 7 (1985), 338–53.

Lucian is an account of his plans for a translation, and his puffs are invariably of books published by Millar or, in the case of James Harris's *Hermes*, written by a friend. Yet, despite all these reviews and essays, and despite the fact that Fielding is more concerned with literature here than in any of his earlier journals, the overriding theme of the bulk of the material in the *Covent-Garden Journal* is not literary but moral. Fielding, of course, would not accept that disjunction; for him literary and ethical concerns were inseparable, 'base and scandalous Writings' being a prime cause of that degeneracy of taste in Britain so much at odds with 'Religion, Virtue, and good Sense' (*CGJ* No. 5). Yet as self-appointed Censor of Great Britain, free to 'satirize the Great', his main focus here is directly and explicitly moral, directed more often at bad manners than bad writing, at the immoral rather than the illiterate.

This note is struck as early as the second number, in which Fielding ironically sets out to prove 'that this is one of the most virtuous Ages, that hath ever appeared in the World' with the proof a catalogue of those social, political, and moral areas in which he felt his age to be strikingly *deficient*. And the catalogue, as it were, continues throughout the run of the paper. Fielding's assumption that the age is not virtuous but degenerate is always present as an undercurrent; it emerges as an issue directly addressed in such essays as those on 'gallantry' (No. 20), on the control and punishment of felons (No. 25), on prostitution (Nos. 50 and 57), or on adultery (Nos. 66, 67, and 68), and it lies behind the recurrent indictment in the *Journal* of fashionable vices like gaming or the taste for pornography.

The specific 'virtues' cited in *Covent-Garden Journal* No. 2 also reappear as major themes in later essays. Fielding first points to 'Liberty' as a blessing enjoyed 'in the purest Degree'. 'Doth not every Man in this Kingdom, speak, and write, and even do, whatever best pleaseth him?' As his tone here betrays, Fielding conceives of 'pure' or 'natural' liberty not as a blessing but as a threat to the operation of law and the stability of society. The confusion of 'liberty' with 'licence', especially on the part of the lower classes, was much on his mind in these years, marked as they were by his more conservative outlook on social matters. The design of his *Enquiry* (1751) had been to oppose 'those wild Notions of Liberty that are inconsistent with all Government', and he was to discourse at length on this theme in his *Voyage to Lisbon* (1754).[1] Further on in the *Journal* two essays (Nos. 47 and 49) are devoted to decrying the power of the mob, and the same concern over mistaken concepts of personal freedom underlies Fielding's ridicule of the illiterate orators of the Robin Hood debating society (Nos. 8 and 9), his sample of the political harangues to be expected at the approach of a

---

[1] *An Enquiry into the Causes of the late Increase of Robbers* (1751), p. xv; *Voyage*, 21 [16] July. See Miller, *Essays*, pp. 94–103.

Westminster election (No. 58), and even his conception of the nature of British humor (No. 55).

In the same way, the second virtue listed in *CGJ* No. 2, charity, is a prominent topic throughout the run of the paper, as it is in so much of Fielding's other writings. Along with its twin concept of 'good nature', charity in the sense of an open-hearted active benevolence arising from a natural dispensation to do good is the cornerstone of Fielding's ethics, and he takes the opportunity afforded by the *Journal* to propagate these moral principles, citing on almost each occasion the writings of his 'favourite' divine Isaac Barrow. To this end Fielding contributes letters to the *Journal* over the signature of 'Axylus', an ideally benevolent persona whose good nature is pointed up by contrast with a letter from an archetypically selfish character whom Fielding calls 'Iago'.[1] These letter-essays enable Fielding to restate and amplify ideas about morality which are essentially the same as those he had held throughout his life as a writer. Moreover, the concept of charity appears in the *Journal* by example as well as by precept; through the 'Covent Garden' column Fielding established collections for needy figures who had come to his attention in the course of his duties as a magistrate. The case of one of these, a baker whose home had been destroyed by fire, in turn prompted him to write a leader exhorting his readers to acts of charity and to invent 'letters' from contributors exhibiting contrasting reactions to a deserving case.[2]

Fielding's preoccupation in these years with the problem of the poor, a problem to which he had devoted the longest section of his *Enquiry* and which he was soon to address directly in his *Proposal for Making an Effectual Provision for the Poor* (1753), naturally figures frequently in the *Journal's* elaboration of the theme of charity. No actual proposals are advanced here, but he deals with the question ironically in a Swiftian project for restoring human sacrifice and seriously in several comments on the folly of giving money to beggars (a practice he condemned, as did most in his age). Somewhat surprisingly he also casts a skeptical eye on both the motives and the consequences of leaving benefactions to found charitable institutions or to support other acts of public charity, with the recently founded St Luke's Hospital for Lunatics serving as his example of an institution which was failing to fulfil its intended function.[3] In the *Covent-Garden Journal*, at least, Fielding was more interested in recommending private acts of charity, analyzing the moral psychology of a benevolent spirit, or attacking the moral rigorism of the 'morose' part of mankind than in celebrating the charitable institutions which flourished in the middle of the century.

[1] See *CGJ*, Nos. 16, 20, 21, and 29.
[2] See the 'Covent Garden' column for 4 May and *CGJ* Nos. 39 and 40.
[3] *CGJ* Nos. 11, 44, and 45.

Another concept long of interest to Fielding and developed further in the *Journal* is expressed by the somewhat amorphous term 'Good Breeding', which he had defined in the preface to his *Miscellanies* (1743) as 'contributing, with our utmost Power, to the Satisfaction and Happiness of all about us'.[1] As his 'Essay on Conversation' in that collection makes plain, good breeding for Fielding, as for other moralists of the day, is the social virtue of making oneself agreeable to others, a virtue which may exist naturally but which should be cultivated by good company and the right kind of education.[2] In the first of two essays in the *Journal* devoted directly to this idea (Nos. 55 and 56) Fielding calls it 'the Art of conducting yourself by certain common and general Rules', in particular by the Golden Rule; and since all men's external behavior would be essentially the same if these precepts were universally followed, the natural antithesis of good breeding is 'Humour', or singularity, produced by deliberate deviation from the common norms. Although in Fielding's view good breeding is possible in any social rank, and although he pauses on occasion to deride the lack of good breeding among the middle-class tradesmen who ape the manners of the gentry,[3] much of the satire in the *Covent-Garden Journal* is directed at violations of 'the Statute of Good Breeding' (No. 5) in the polite world, the 'Town', the closed circle of fashion with its beaus and fine ladies. Indeed, one entire essay (No. 27) ironically inverts the usual sense of class distinctions in order to deride the supposed superiority of the rich in regard to social or moral virtues, and another (No. 43) shows a worthy tradesman 'Paul Traffick' deploring his daughter's '*apparent Loss of her Good-Breeding*' through her association with 'Quality'. Violations of good breeding run through all social ranks, but Fielding's quarry in the *Journal* is that aristocratic company whose very status and education make such violations all the more reprehensible.

In a sense, then, the concept of good breeding underlies all those essays in the *Journal*, about a third of the total, satirizing the manners and taste of the glittering world of the 'People of Fashion' (No. 37). Their time-wasting diversions, their rudeness in public places, their taste for scandal and slander, their efforts to preserve exclusiveness, and their slavery to fashions in dress are all sub-themes of ill breeding which dot these pages. The 'Modern Glossary' which Fielding gives in *CGJ* No. 4 provides us with the language of the 'polite Part of Mankind', a language not otherwise to be understood by divines, moralists, or the truly learned; and since a proper education is essential to the full development of good breeding Fielding on

---

[1] *Miscellanies* (1743), ed. H. K. Miller, Wesleyan Edn. (Oxford, 1972), i. 4.
[2] On the background of the concept, see Miller, pp. 184–9; in *CGJ* Fielding refers to Bellegarde's *Reflexions upon Ridicule* (trans. 1706–7) as his chief authority on the topic.
[3] See *CGJ* Nos. 33 and 56.

several occasions lashes out at the deficiencies of the education of 'fine' gentlemen and 'fine' ladies (Nos. 42 and 56). Moreover, since its essence is the Golden Rule, there is a moral as well as social dimension to good breeding; in No. 56 Fielding tells us that the well-bred man will have no trace of ambition, covetousness, pride, anger or other passions which dominate an ill-bred man, a man of 'Humour'. And elsewhere in the *Journal* he inveighs directly against those defects of character which are also from this point of view offenses against the statute of good breeding: impudence (Nos. 48 and 53), contempt (No. 61), and ambition (No. 69).

The lack of good breeding also appears as a theme in Fielding's comments on the theater, another persistent topic in the *Journal*. In an early session of the Censorial Court (*CGJ* No. 5), wearing hats in the boxes and talking loud anywhere in the playhouse are declared to be great offences against the 'Statute of Good Breeding', and in essay after essay Fielding chastises the behavior of theater audiences, charging the obstreperous 'bucks' and self-appointed critics with a lack of humanity and judgement.[1] Most of Fielding's theatrical commentary here, however, involves his elaborate puffs of his friend David Garrick, since 1747 manager of the Theatre-Royal at Drury Lane, and his thinly disguised hostility to the rival company of John Rich at Covent Garden. Thus, at the conclusion of the paper war, Sir Alexander places Garrick's theater under his protection while relegating Rich's company to the 'Low Republic of Grub-Street'. Garrick's skill and fairness as a manager are repeatedly lauded, and leading members of his company (Clive, Bellamy, Mossop, Woodward, and Havard, for example) are singled out for praise.[2] Fielding's obvious bias did not go unrecognized, with one hostile source expressing mock-surprise that Drury Lane would accept the authority of Sir Alexander after the fiasco of Fielding's play *The Wedding Day* (1743).[3] Nevertheless, the final full essay in the *Journal* (No. 71) is a highly partisan account of the warfare between the two theaters, a warfare which had resulted in a riot nine days earlier and into which Fielding was drawn as a magistrate as well as a writer. The *Covent-Garden Journal* concludes, in fact, with a final fling at John Hill, whose conflict with Fielding had been revived because of Hill's championing of the company at Covent Garden in this dispute over theatrical taste.[4]

Although Fielding sometimes resorts to explicit moralizing in impugning the good breeding, charity, and other virtues of his age, he generally keeps

---

[1] See especially Nos. 16, 17, 26, and 27.

[2] See Nos. 3, 4, 5, 10, 15, and 28. In No. 34 Fielding appears hostile to the stage in general because of the high salaries paid to actors, but his main point is to contrast the advantages of a theatrical career with the decline of the learned professions.

[3] *The Covent-Garden Journal Extraordinary*, No. I (1752), p. 6; on *The Wedding Day*, see Fielding's comments in the Preface to the *Miscellanies* (1743).

[4] See Nos. 71 and 72.

his tone light and his manner bantering, even when engaged in learned discourses on the history of mob violence in England or the punishments of adultery among the ancients. The essays abound with passages of the deepest irony, buttressed by supporting devices like parody or 'future history' or mock-etymologies. In a number of the essays the influence of the 'immortal Swift', as Fielding calls him in No. 52, is obvious; his admiration for the Dean was not new, but some of the impetus for his praise and imitation of Swift here may perhaps be attributed to the brouhaha over Orrery's *Remarks on the Life and Writings of Swift*, recently published by Millar and widely attacked for its unfavorable portrait of that satirist.[1] Intermingled with the Swiftian irony is Fielding's characteristic display of erudite allusions and legal terminology. His interest in history and biography is especially prominent here, more so than in any of his earlier periodicals.[2] Not surprisingly, this aspect of the style of the *Journal* was mocked by Fielding's enemies, with one parody (*The Covent-Garden Journal Extraordinary*, 20 January 1752) consisting of a leader on the doctrine of Pythagoras loaded with pedantic vocabulary, Greek footnotes, and a parade of citations from ancient authorities.

But despite the irony and humor exhibited even when Fielding is developing the overriding social and moral themes of the *Journal*, his mood was not light-hearted. Readers of the *Journal*, in fact, will do well to remember that the Fielding of these years is the Fielding of *Amelia*, of the *Enquiry into the Causes of the late Increase of Robbers*, and of *Examples of the Interposition of Providence in the Detection and Punishment of Murder*. It is a period not only of his major social pamphlets but also of increased pessimism about the goodness of human nature, pessimism induced in part by 'the Sight of all those Wretches who are brought before him' at his court in Bow Street.[3] His more somber mood breaks out occasionally in the leading essays, and it also appears sometimes in the comments he appended to news items in the 'Modern History' section of the *Journal*: '*If something be not done to prevent it, Cruelty will become the Characteristic of this Nation*'; '*More Murders and horrid Barbarities have been committed within this last Twelvemonth, than*

---

[1] As examples of Swift's influence here see especially the paper war in *CGJ* Nos. 1–3, the imitation of 'A Modest Proposal' in *CGJ* No. 11, and the imagery of oratorical machines in No. 51; Fielding also directly praises Swift in Nos. 18, 52, and 60. See B. A. Goldgar, 'Swift and the Later Fielding', *The Yearbook of English Studies*, 18 (1988), 93–107. Fielding owned three copies of Orrery's *Remarks*, which was mightily puffed by John Hill (see *LDA*, 20 Nov. 1751) and greatly approved by Richardson (see his letter of 23 Feb. quoted by T. C. Duncan Eaves and Ben D. Kimbel, *Samuel Richardson: A Biography* (Oxford, 1971), pp. 579–80). For a typical attack on the *Remarks*, see *True Briton*, 8 Jan. 1752; see also Donald Berwick, *The Reputation of Jonathan Swift* (New York, 1941), p. 4.

[2] See Robert M. Wallace, 'Fielding's Knowledge of History and Biography', *SP* 44 (1947), 89–107.

[3] *CGJ* No. 16; on the change in Fielding's mood in these years, see Miller, *Essays*, pp. 84–5, 212–13.

during many preceding Years. This . . . is principally to be attributed to the Declension of Religion among the common People.[1] Such comments are not anomalous; indeed, given Fielding's poor health in his last years and his unceasing exposure to the most sordid scenes in his society, it is only surprising that a darker tone does not dominate his reflections in the *Covent-Garden Journal*.

It is difficult to determine how well these reflections were received by Fielding's contemporaries, since no circulation figures for the *Journal* are extant.[2] His enemies, of course, maintained that the *Journal* was unpopular, with its essays 'forgotten almost as soon as they are read, (if they are read at all)';[3] and it is true that what few scattered references to the periodical one can find in diaries and correspondence are generally unfavorable. Richardson claimed that with each issue of the 'Common Garden Journal' Fielding was 'contributing to his own Overthrow' and that in the paper war he was 'over-matched in his own Way, by People whom he has despised, and thought he had Vogue enough . . . to write down'.[4] Thomas Edwards, to whom Richardson made this comment, had himself expressed disappointment at the first issue of the *Journal*, warning that if Fielding 'does not improve upon his sample, his subscribers will be but indifferently off'; a few days later Edwards declared, in reference to both the *Journal* and *Amelia*, 'the Justice has spoiled the Author'. Such comments from Richardson and his circle are not surprising, but it is worth noting that one Henry Harris, writing to Fielding's friend Sir Charles Hanbury Williams, had much the same view, in mid-January dismissing the *Journal* as 'most sad trash' and by late May regarding Fielding as a writer whose force was 'quite worn out' by his success as a justice of the peace.[5] Such private reactions to the *Journal*, however, are unusually hard to come by, though the few we have suggest that at least the social range of Fielding's readers was wide—from Thomas Birch down to 'Orator' Henley.[6] Some idea of the reaction to Fielding's wit may also be gathered from a pamphlet describing an impudent hack writer's habit

---

[1] 'Modern History' sections first printed with *CGJ* Nos. 18 and 19, and the 'Modern History' section originally appearing in *CGJ* No. 6, below, Appendix I. Fielding was not the sole author of the comments on news items, but these remarks are all signed 'C.' and are by Fielding himself.

[2] Even figures on advertising duty are unavailable for 1752; see A. Aspinall, 'Statistical Accounts of the London Newspapers in the Eighteenth Century', *English Historical Review*, 63 (1948), 201–28.

[3] *Drury-Lane Journal*, No. 5.

[4] Letter of 21 Feb. 1752, as quoted by Eaves and Kimbel, pp. 301–2.

[5] Edwards, Bodl. MS 1011, pp. 309–10, 312; Harris, Hanbury Williams MS, vol. 54, p. 249; vol. 67, p. 238 (in the collection of the late W. S. Lewis, Farmington, Conn.). I am indebted to Martin Battestin for both these references.

[6] For Birch, see Hardwicke Papers, BL Add. MS 35398, letter to Philip Yorke, 4 July 1752; for evidence of Henley's reading of *CGJ*, see his notice in *DA*, 17 Apr. 1752. For a list of other possible readers, see the contributors to a collection for a poor baker, printed in the 'Covent Garden' columns for 15 May and 22 May (below, Appendix I); contributors need not have been readers, of course, but the list suggests the range of those having some contact with the *CGJ* and the Register Office.

of stealing material from the *Journal* for use in coffee-house conversation, except when 'the Relation did not take; then, my Author, said I is the J——*ce*: . . . I wonder when he will leave off writing such Nonsence—it grows worse and worse every week.'[1]

But if the scarcity of comments from individual readers suggests Fielding's enemies may have been right in calling the *Journal* a failure, the printed evidence gives a contrary impression. Fielding's reputation was clearly great enough to gain, at least at first, the attention of the town for his new venture. Although the *London Magazine* virtually ignored the *Journal*, dismissing it contemptuously at its first appearance and reprinting only two numbers, neither by Fielding,[2] the *Gentleman's Magazine* gave it its fair share of summaries and abstracts throughout the year. Moreover, other magazines also picked up material from the *Journal* and, as was their custom, reprinted it with no acknowledgment of the source, while at the same time, as I have indicated, newspapers were cheerfully plagiarizing the 'Covent Garden' column on a regular basis.[3] The most regular reprinting, however, occurred in Dublin, where on 23 January 1752 an enterprising printer named James Hoey began publishing a periodical simply called *The Covent-Garden Journal. By Sir Alexander Drawcansir . . . (Otherwise Henry Fielding, Esq.)*. Appearing at first weekly and then twice weekly, this four-page pamphlet managed to use many of Fielding's leaders and a good bit of other material from the *Journal*, all about three weeks or a month after their publication in London. As the year wore on, Hoey increasingly changed the order and numbering of Fielding's essays and added material of special interest to a Dublin audience; and after the demise of Fielding's *Journal*, Hoey simply continued his, using material from the *World* and the *Adventurer*. All this was designed primarily for the amusement of university students in Dublin and for the promotion of other books printed by Hoey, which were copiously advertised. The Dublin *Journal* had, apparently, no sanction from the Fieldings and no connection with the Dublin Universal Register Office.

As such reprints indicate, Fielding had succeeded in attracting attention to his periodical by his paper war and by his quarrel with Hill. Sir Alexander Drawcansir, in fact, became a fictional presence of some significance in the town, with a role in two plays in the spring of 1752. The first, William

---

[1] *Rules for Being a Wit* (1753), p. 6.

[2] *LM* 21 (1752), 41; the excerpts printed are from *CGJ* Nos. 28 (7 Apr.) and 38 (12 May).

[3] See above, p. xxxvi. For unacknowledged reprinting by magazines, see *Universal Magazine*, 11 (Nov. 1752), 233–5, reprinting the leader of *CGJ* No. 71; *The Repository* (1752), pp. 91–6, using excerpts from the letter of 'Benevolus' in *CGJ* No. 38; and *Ladies Magazine*, 3 (1752), 94–5 and 326–7, reprinting news items with facetious comments from *CGJ* No. 10 and the leader of *CGJ* No. 54. *True Briton*, 11 Mar. 1752, reprinted *CGJ* No. 20, but with due acknowledgments. *The Salisbury Journal*, serving an area once Fielding's home ground, also frequently reprinted essays from the *CGJ*; see Mrs Herbert Richardson, 'Wiltshire Newspapers—Past and Present, part III: The Newspapers of South Wilts', *Wiltshire Archaeological and Natural History Magazine*, 41 (1922), 58.

Kenrick's *Fun: A Parodi-tragi-comical Satire*, was printed but never performed; according to Kenrick's Preface the play was to have been performed on 13 February at Castle-Tavern, Pater-Noster Row, but was suppressed by order of the Lord Mayor and the Court of Aldermen. Kenrick gives broad hints that the suppression was instigated by Fielding himself, claiming that those who opposed it feared '*the Strength of a poor Baby* Monosyllable *might affect the Magnanimity of a Drawcansir*'.[1] Yet there is no documentary evidence linking Fielding with the affair, and it is difficult to see why he would have risked using his influence to suppress this fairly light-hearted and amusing Shakespearean parody which satirizes all parties in the battle between Drawcansir and his Grub Street enemies. To be sure, Fielding (as Justice Bobadil) is attacked for giving favored treatment in his court to prisoners of quality, and Drawcansir meets his defeat on stage at the hands of Hill; but there are complimentary passages too, such as this speech by an Iago-like Hill ('Doctor Mountain'):

> The *Covent-garden Journal*! Death and Hell!
> This, this will ruin my best labour'd Scheme.
> Two Stars keep not their Course in one same Sphere,
> Nor can one Town e'er brook the double Reign
> Of an *Inspector* and a *Censor* too.
> I hate *Drawcansir*, for on single Sheets
> He wants to do my Office; and beside
> His Works are read, while mine neglected die.[2]

Despite its unpleasant portrait of Fielding as justice of the peace, *Fun* at least is testimony to the popularity of his persona Drawcansir and of the quarrels he provoked.

The second play, *The Covent-Garden Theatre, or Pasquin Turn'd Drawcansir*, by the actor Charles Macklin, also capitalized on the popularity of the *Covent-Garden Journal*, and with no hint of adverse criticism; its plot places Pasquin in the role of 'Drawcansir and Censor of Great Britain', holding a censorial court and passing judgement on various characters of the town. Macklin, who acted in the play when it was performed as an after-piece at Covent Garden Theatre for his benefit (8 April 1752), had advertised the piece extensively in the *Journal* and other papers, but it was not a success and was not repeated.[3] Nonetheless it was excellent publicity for Fielding, whose

[1] Kenrick, *Fun* (1752), sig. A2. The printed version was advertised in *GA* as early as 17 Feb. 1752 but did not actually appear until March; Kenrick attributed the delay to his continuing efforts to have the play performed, efforts which failed because of the 'same indefatigable Opposition'.

[2] Kenrick, p. 19.

[3] The advertisements were ridiculed by George Alexander Stevens in *Distress upon Distress* (1752), pp. xiv, 21. The manuscript of *The Covent-Garden Theatre*, which was never printed, has been reproduced in Augustan Reprint Society, No. 116, ed. Jean Kern (Los Angeles, 1965). See also Esther Raushenbush, 'Charles Macklin's Lost Play about Henry Fielding', *MLN* 51 (1936), 505–14.

influence is evident throughout, from an invocation to Lucian to an indictment of gaming similar to passages in his *Enquiry*.

Macklin's slight play is something of an anomaly, however, in the friendly posture it adopts toward the *Covent-Garden Journal*. Both Fielding's previous history as a political journalist and his ridicule of other writers in the opening numbers virtually guaranteed a host of attacks on his new periodical, some motivated by literary jealousy, some by political enmity, and one, at least, by commercial rivalry. Hill's attacks in the *London Daily Advertiser* and Smollett's devastating pamphlet *Habbakkuk Hilding* clearly belong in the first category, though Smollett manages to touch on all facets of Fielding's career in the course of his satire.[1] But Hill and Smollett were not alone in pointing to the supposed defects of Fielding's style; the erudite manner of 'Covent-Garden's Word Dissector', as he was called in one poem of the day, was a frequent topic of ridicule, most notably in a full-scale parody *The Covent-Garden Journal Extraordinary*, published on 20 January by J. Sharp, whose name also appears on the imprint of *Habbukkuk Hilding*.[2] None of these attacks are very remarkable, since they are all offshoots of the paper war which Fielding himself had initiated—he must surely have expected his descent to personal satire, however light in tone, to provoke just such responses as these.

Nor could he have been too surprised to find his old political enemies in the Opposition press taking the publication of *Amelia* and the opening numbers of the *Covent-Garden Journal* as occasions to heap abuse on his head. On 21 December 1751 *Old England* began the assault, depicting Fielding as a matron in her dotage and predicting nothing of moral value from the forthcoming *Journal*: 'Here the Debauched, the Diseased, the Rotting and the Rotten, may be instructed and amused, if not cured and reformed: Here will be seen the quaint Device, the old *Badger* preaching Continence (in the *Aesopian* Stile) to the young *Wolf*.'[3] The abuse is personal, not political; there is no hint here that the writer expects the *Journal* to be a new political organ. *Old England* for 11 January, however, reverting to the usual theme of Fielding as a ministerial tool, printed a fragment of a farce in which Pelham and Lyttelton hire Fielding to carry on the *Covent-Garden Journal* as a way of deflecting the town's attention from the follies of the Administration; and the same motif is picked up in *Old England* a week later (18 January), along with a sneer at the new paper's unpopularity: 'there is not now one Coffeehouse in four which admits that Journal, new and celebrated

---

[1] See above, pp. xxxvii–xxxix.

[2] *Proceedings at the Court of Apollo* (1753), p. 7; on the parody, see above, p. xliv, and see the account by G. E. Jensen, 'The Covent-Garden Journal Extraordinary', *MLN* 34 (1919), 57–9.

[3] On this paper and its earlier attacks on Fielding, see *JJ*, ed. Coley, pp. lxxv–lxxxii, 181 n. and 214 n.

as it is'. After this *Old England* for the most part let the old badger alone, with only a final gloating letter on the occasion of the *Journal*'s demise.[1]

Fielding, of course, had disclaimed any political intention at the outset of his *Journal*, and *Old England*'s professed suspicion that the new periodical was a tale of a tub thrown out on behalf of an anxious administration was not intended to be taken seriously; Fielding's inveterate enemies on that paper were simply indulging in one more reminder of his previous service as a ministerial writer. The claim that the literary quarrels of the paper war were somehow useful to the government was laughed at even by another Opposition journal, the *Craftsman*:

There is a political Author, who supposes Sir *Alexander Drawcansir* only the Tool of a C——t, and that he is given up to the Fury of our present *Literati* to divert their Opposition from certain Persons in Power; for aught I know he may serve as a Barrel thrown out from the Ship of Administration to some other Whale of the Country Interest; but it must be a Barrel of more delicious Liquor that captivates a Quaffsman like me.[2]

The jocular tone is typical of the *Craftsman*'s reaction to Fielding's new venture, though as recently as 4 January it had been alluding to him as a venal justice and a political mercenary. By and large its jokes at the *Journal* in the opening months of the year were non-political and friendly, with an imitation of the 'Modern Glossary' of *Covent-Garden Journal* No. 4 and with occasional parodies of Fielding's mottoes and his parade of learning. The *Craftsman* writer (who a few years earlier had been Fielding's friend Thomas Cooke) seems, in fact, to enter into the spirit of the paper war ('as he *blockheaded* the *Inspector*, I suppose he intended to *hogshead* the *Quaffsman*'), almost as though he is playing the game with Fielding which Hill refused to enter.[3] In general, then, Opposition writers, however much they abused Fielding personally, found little that was politically objectionable in the *Covent-Garden Journal*. Even the Jacobite *True Briton*, which had violently assailed Fielding's *Enquiry* in 1751 and which continued to impugn his principles during 1752, made no serious complaints about the *Journal* and actually reprinted the leading essay of No. 20, with a few words of grudging admiration.[4]

But the best-known of the attacks on the *Journal* was motivated not by political bias or personal animus but by the spirit of commerce. *Have At You*

[1] *OE*, 2 Dec. 1752.

[2] *Craftsman*, 25 Jan. 1752; on the run of the *Craftsman* in 1752, see below, p. liii n. 3.

[3] See *Craftsman* of 11 and 25 Jan., 8 Feb., and 7 Mar. 1752. But the *Craftsman* of 2 May prints an extremely hostile letter; see above, p. xxxvi. Cooke was arrested in 1748 for writing the *Craftsman*, but it is unclear whether he returned to the paper after his release; see the comments by Joseph Mawbey, *GM* 62 (1792), 26–7.

[4] For the attacks, see *True Briton*, 27 Feb. 1751; 6 Mar. 1751; 26 June 1751; 29 Jan. 1752; and 27 June 1752.

All: or, The Drury-Lane Journal, a threepenny pamphlet appearing in twelve
numbers from 16 January to 9 April 1752, was published by the Public
Register Office in King Street, whose rivalry with the Universal Register
Office I have already described.[1] In the opening number the editor,
'Mrs. Roxana Termagant', traditionally said to be Bonnell Thornton,
promises to follow Fielding through all his 'turnings and windings' and tread
upon his heels once a week.[2] And follow him he does, for three months, with
a running commentary on the various sections of *Covent-Garden Journal*
intermixed with parodies of Fielding's essays and ridicule of his erudition,
legalisms, puns, and all the other turnings and windings of his style.
Fielding's court reports in the 'Covent Garden' column and his comments
on news items are also satirized, as is, of course, *Amelia*. The commercial
impulse behind the *Drury-Lane Journal* emerges in its protracted advertisements for the Public Register Office and its occasional ridicule of the
Fieldings' office in the Strand, but, like the *Covent-Garden Journal*, it masks
its function as the organ of a register office behind a display of lively and
entertaining satire. Nor is Fielding the only object of ridicule; as early as the
second number Thornton, announcing his triumph over his journalistic
counterpart, declares, 'It were tedious, as well as impertinent, to force upon
my reader continual animadversions on Sir ALEXANDER DRAWCANSIR's
blundering witticisms and fallacious reasonings'.[3] And so he slants at or
parodies Johnson, Smart, Hill, and other authors, and engages in general
literary and social satire on other aspects of his age, some of which, like the
Robin Hood Society, were also being attacked by Fielding himself; in the
fourth number, in fact, there is no reference at all to the *Covent-Garden
Journal*.

Fielding, however, remained the center of focus of the *Drury-Lane
Journal*; and with the sixth number (20 February) some of the attacks upon
him became personal and abusive, ridiculing the supposed contradiction
between his role as a magistrate and his career of 'making puns upon News-
Papers', assaulting (in a mock autobiography) his career as a political
journalist, accusing him (quite erroneously) of having edited the *Grub-street
Journal*, laughing at his exploits as manager of a puppet-show, and sneering
at his profession of moral principle: 'As I perceive my end is approaching, I
have no other refuge than to sollicit an ACT of PARLIAMENT for
monopolizing News-Papers, not for my own *Interest*, to be sure, but solely
and wholly for the *Good* of *Community*, which the *Energy of Benevolence* and

---

[1] See above, pp. xxv–xxvi.
[2] *Drury-Lane Journal* (1752), p. 6; on Thornton's authorship, see Wallace C. Brown, 'A Belated
Augustan: Bonnell Thornton, Esq.', *PQ* 34 (1955), 335–6. See also Lance Bertelsen, 'Have at You
All: Or, Bonnell Thornton's Journalism', *HLQ* 44 (1980–1), 263–8.
[3] *Drury-Lane Journal*, No. 2 (23 Jan. 1752).

the *Milk of Human Kindness* makes me always have so much at heart.'[1] It is doubtful that these abusive attacks were written by Bonnell Thornton, whose witty and telling parodies are in another key altogether; Thornton, as far as is known, had no personal enmity for Fielding and was presumably merely the paid writer engaged by D'Halluin, manager of the Public Register Office. Instead, these severe attacks upon Fielding appear to have been contributed by another hand, who has some close knowledge of Fielding's life and career; they are all signed 'X', and in the next to last issue appears the notice, 'the Person, who made use of the signiture [*sic*] X, no longer favours us with assistance'.[2] After the withdrawal of this unknown enemy, the *Drury-Lane Journal* paused for two weeks and then, on 9 April, expired.[3]

Whether Thornton's ridicule and other, less humorous attacks really harmed Fielding's enterprise cannot be determined. For whatever reason, however, the early success of the *Journal* in gaining the attention of the town in the winter and spring months of 1752 began by early summer to give way to signs of slackness. On 4 July (No. 53) Fielding announced that the paper henceforth would appear weekly, on Saturdays only instead of Tuesdays and Saturdays; it was only because of the entreaty of the whole town, he says, that Sir Alexander was not carrying through with his original intention of resigning his office altogether 'on Account of his great Age'. At the same time he announced that the price of advertisements would be raised to three shillings in order to limit their number to very few. The latter announcement smacks a bit of turning necessity into a virtue, since advertising for the preceding few weeks had already slackened considerably from the level of the opening months. At any rate, after this change of policy advertisements fell off to almost nothing except occasional notices of the Register Office or of Fielding's own projects, and beginning with No. 62 (16 September) the *Journal* even began carrying regular advertisements for Dr James's powders and one other patent medicine. This decline in the nature and number of advertisements was matched in the final months by a similar deterioration in the regular departments and features; the Censorial Court had not appeared since No. 28, the commentary on reprinted news items disappeared, and the lively 'Covent Garden' column dwindled into routine reports of cases presented and actions taken. Fortunately, however, the leaders themselves in the final twenty numbers show no signs of decay, as Fielding produces in this period some of his strongest essays, on wit and humor, on prostitution and adultery, on the pride of natural scientists, and on John Hill and the war of the theaters.

With No. 72 (25 November, 1752) Fielding brought the *Journal* to an end,

---

[1] Ibid., No. 10 (19 Mar. 1752).   [2] Ibid., No. 11 (26 Mar. 1752).

[3] The last number was numbered 'XIII', but there was apparently no twelfth number; the pagination is consecutive.

saying that he had neither inclination nor leisure to carry it on any longer and that his 'graver Friends', who had thought it below his character all along, had told him he might do more good to the public and bring more honor to himself by using his pen in other ways—social pamphlets, in other words, must replace the lighter manner of periodical journalism. No longer, he adds, except in revising his former works would he hold any 'Correspondence with the gayer Muses'. Then, as though to underline his divorce from the gayer muses, Fielding recommends to his readers the *Public Advertiser*, a new paper which was being organized as a replacement for the *General Advertiser* and which was to carry on some of the non-literary functions of the *Covent-Garden Journal*, such as public notices emanating from Fielding's court, advertisements for the Universal Register Office, and advertisements for the recovery of stolen goods. In its efforts to recover stolen goods, the new paper, according to the notice Fielding prints, was to receive the co-operation of a number of London pawnbrokers, a list of whom is given in *Covent-Garden Journal* No. 72.[1]

According to his brother John, Fielding owned shares in the *Public Advertiser*, and that there was a close working connection is obvious; advertisements for the *Advertiser* were to be taken in at the Universal Register Office and at Bow Street by Brogden, Fielding's clerk.[2] Fielding's direct involvement is also suggested by the tone of a satirical pamphlet of the day, *A Scheme for a New Public Advertiser*, bearing the imprint 'Printed for Justice *Fail-Paper*, in *Arrow-street*'.[3] It is, in fact, the *Advertiser*'s willingness to print Fielding's judicial notices that forms the focus of this little parody, which claims that the new paper will include 'a true and perfect List of all the Bawdy-Houses', 'Names of the Comedians kept by each Lady', advertisements for stolen goods inserted by criminals for the benefit of their accomplices the pawnbrokers, and the like, and which concludes with a list of subscribing bawds, whores, indorsers, thieves, bilkers, pimps, murderers, ravishers, informers, and (Drury Lane) players.[4] Subscriptions from this disreputable lot were to be accepted by Mr Justice Failpaper. There is more than a hint here of the usual charge that Fielding was a 'trading' justice, and this satire on the *Public Advertiser* is one more reminder of what kind of price he had to pay in devoting his energies fully to the half-world of criminal justice.

[1] The notice about the *Public Advertiser* which Fielding printed in *CGJ* No. 72 and which he probably wrote himself also appeared in *GA* No. 25 (27–30 Nov.) and in *LEP* (25–8 Nov.); on 1 Dec. *GA* changed its title to *Public Advertiser*.

[2] On Fielding's financial interest in the *Public Advertiser*, see John Fielding, *A Plan for preventing Robberies within Twenty Miles of London* (1755), p. 21; John here claims, rather unconvincingly, that though Henry owned shares in the paper he himself did not.

[3] In the Bodleian Library (Hope Essays fo. 43.[17]); the *Monthly Review* described this piece as ridiculing Fielding and others 'Who are said to be concerned in a daily news-paper, entitled the *public advertiser*' (8 [1753], 144). [4] *A Scheme* (n.d.), pp. 3–6.

The end of the *Covent-Garden Journal* coincided with a minor flurry of new periodicals just getting under way, some of which, such as the *Scourge* (beginning 28 November), were of ephemeral interest only but others of which, such as the *Adventurer* (7 November) and the *World* (4 January 1753), were to surpass Fielding's *Journal* in reputation. Bonnell Thornton re-emerged as the author of one of these new weekly periodicals, the *Spring-Garden Journal* (beginning 16 November), and continued his satiric parodies of Fielding. Now calling himself Priscilla Termagant, near relation to Roxana of the *Drury-Lane Journal*, Thornton, after the *Journal* had come to an end, printed yet another '*Covent-Garden Journal* Extraordinary . . . an Essay in the true Drawcansirian Stile and Sentiment', in which Fielding complains of his age and infirmities: 'I seem divested of all that Wit and Humour, all those well-grounded Sentiments of Low-life, which were a Sort of Asylum for me to fly to'.[1] This sally is followed in other numbers by Drawcansir's epitaph and a satiric last will and testament. Needless to say, Fielding's other enemies were quick to provide mock-obsequies on the occasion of the *Journal*'s demise; Hill, who currently had his hands full in a paper war with Christopher Smart, spoke of his 'Tenderness for a decayed Brother' and piously intoned 'de mortuis nil nisi bonum', while *Old England* seized the opportunity for a vicious obituary of its old political enemy, the Censor of Great Britain.[2]

Amidst this chorus of voices proclaiming Fielding's failing powers as a journalist, one new periodical essayist spoke up in his defense. In a series of essays which are now exceedingly rare and which have never been reprinted, Arthur Murphy paid repeated tribute to the author of the *Covent-Garden Journal* and even reinstituted one of that journal's departments. Murphy's comments appeared in his opening series of essays in *The Craftsman; or Gray's Inn Journal*, which began on 28 October 1752, under the pseudonym 'Joseph D'Anvers, Esq.'; and these original essays, it should be noted, bear very little resemblance to those later printed in the collected *Gray's Inn Journal* (1756).[3] Although a passing slur is made on Fielding's change of politics in an early number (11 November), Murphy in the following issue (No. 18) violently assaults Hill while praising Fielding as one 'whose Writings are likely to live'; on 9 December he began a series of Proceedings at a Court of Censorial Enquiry, in the first of which he again arraigns Hill

---

[1] *Spring-Garden Journal*, No. 3 (30 Nov. 1752), p. 60. Thornton's new venture was published by the bookseller W. Meyer, and it is interesting to note that he now ridicules the fact that both *CGJ* and his own *Drury-Lane Journal* originated in Register Offices: 'a work of Genius may more properly be introduced into the World from Mr. *Meyer*, than from Mr. *John Fielding*' (pp. 9–10).

[2] *LDA*, 6 Dec. 1752; *OE*, 2 Dec. 1752.

[3] See the important article by Simon Varey, 'The Publication of the Late *Craftsman*', *The Library*, ser. 5, 33 (1978), 230–3. As Varey points out, the originals of Murphy's opening essays exist in a possibly unique run of the *Craftsman* for 1752 held by the Archives Department, Hackney Public Library Service, to whom I am indebted for providing me access to these materials.

for his treatment of 'the immortal Author of *Jonathan Wild*, *Joseph Andrews*, and *Tom Jones*'. In a dream allegory on 30 December Murphy continues his praise, this time in regard to Fielding's plans for a translation of Lucian: 'I told *Lucian*, that the excellent Mr. *Fielding* has promised us a Translation of his Performances into the *English* Tongue, which gave the old *Grecian* great Pleasure, as he did not doubt but the Author of *Joseph Andrews* and *Tom Jones* would give the whole [t]he true Spirit of Humour.'

These comments not only give us a glimpse of Murphy's earliest views of Fielding; they also have the air already of a biography, of reflections by an admirer on a writer whose major accomplishments are over. That Murphy took seriously Fielding's farewell to the Muses in his last essay in the *Covent-Garden Journal* is indicated by the tone of a final tribute, one with which a discussion of the *Journal* may fittingly close. Writing as 'Charles Ranger' in *The Craftsman; or Gray's Inn Journal* of 30 December 1752, Murphy explains his reasons for reinstituting the Court which Fielding as Censor of Great Britain had made an important feature of the *Covent-Garden Journal*:

It having appeared strange to some Readers, that, after the Abdication of Sir *Alexander Drawcansir*, A Court of Censorial Enquiry should be continued in this Paper, we think it proper to say a few Words on that Head. This Writer saw with Regret that the admirable Mr. *Fielding* could not find Leisure to conduct his Paper any longer, and he judged that a Vehicle for Animadversions so finely imagined, as the Censorial Enquiry, ought not to cease upon his Resignation. . . . We are obliged to Mr. *Fielding*'s exquisite Humour for this Hint, and if it should not be so well carried on under the direction it is at present subject to; we hope, at least, that, while *Ulysses* is lost to the literary World, and is perhaps seeing a Variety of Men and Manners, he will permit us to try our Hand with his Bow.

TEXTUAL INTRODUCTION

THIS volume offers a critical unmodernized text of *A Plan of the Universal Register-Office* (1751) and *The Covent-Garden Journal* (1752). It follows the bibliographical aims laid down by Professor Fredson Bowers for the previous volumes of the Wesleyan Edition: 'The text is critical in that it has been established by the application of analytical criticism to the evidence of the various early documentary forms in which the materials appeared. It is unmodernized in that every effort has been made to present the text in as close a form to Fielding's own inscription and subsequent revision as the surviving documents permit, subject to normal editorial regulation'.

I. THE COPY-TEXT AND ITS TREATMENT

With the exception of a handful of revisions of the *Covent-Garden Journal* in Fielding's hand, no manuscript is known for any of the documents in the present volume, and no assignment of copyright from Fielding to the publisher is extant which would testify to the authoritative nature of the manuscripts which were sent to the press. No printing records of the *Journal* have been discovered; one may assume, however, that the *Covent-Garden Journal* was set from holograph, as was the normal practice with periodicals of the day. In the case of the *Plan of the Universal Register-Office*, the Strahan ledger, which records the printings of the editions of 1752 and subsequently, begins only in 1752 and thus contains no entry for the first edition (1751). The same printer's ornament appears in the editions of 1751 and 1752, however, and one may suppose that Strahan also printed the first edition and that it was set from holograph.

Both the *Plan* and portions of the *Journal* exist in revised editions, but the revisions differ in their authority. Of the three editions of the *Plan* appearing in Fielding's lifetime (1751, 1752, 1753), the second and third show very few variants except for the title-page and an added prefatory notice on the verso of the title-page of the third, although the text of the third has, of course, been reset. There are, on the other hand, a number of variants between the first and second editions which require further comment. The *Plan* consists of two parts: (1) a general introduction for about half the pamphlet, very clearly by Henry Fielding; and (2) a list of articles detailing the services the Register Office will provide. The list itself bears no marks of Fielding's style and is probably the work of John Fielding, who had the practical management of the office and was responsible for most of the advertising. In editions subsequent to the first (1751), almost all of the changes to the text are additions to the list of services performed, along with various notices signed by John. The introductory material ascribed to Henry remains largely unaltered, except for occasional 'updating' of information. In preparing the Wesleyan text, I have therefore used the first edition as the copy-text and accepted none of the variants from subsequent editions; the Historical Collation, similarly, is complete only for the introductory material down to the beginning of the list of articles (see Appendix VI). Another edition (octavo in fours, 12 leaves) was published in 1755, its title-page calling it the 'Eighth Edition'; this edition, appearing after Fielding's death, has no authority for an edition of Fielding's works, its revisions and additions again merely reflecting the increased business of the Register Office, and it has not been included in either the collation or the bibliographical descriptions.

The case of revisions of material in the *Covent-Garden Journal* is more complex. Until recently it was assumed that only the original numbers published in 1752 had any authority, and for the bulk of the material that claim may still be made. We now know, however, that revisions of portions of the text exist in two sources. An incomplete run of the *Journal* at the Bodleian Library (Hope Folio 11) contains a few marginal revisions and additions to the text in Fielding's own hand, as well as a few corrections in an unknown hand and occasional deletions of undetermined source (for a description and list, see Appendix VIII). These manuscript revisions and additions in Fielding's hand thus form one group of authoritative revisions of the 1752 text. Moreover, they cast an entirely new light on the text of the 26 essays from the *Covent-Garden Journal* which were selected by Arthur Murphy for inclusion in the posthumous edition of Fielding's *Works* in 1762, a text of the *Journal* previously considered of no authority. A note by Alexander Chalmers on the flyleaf of the incomplete run at the Bodleian indicates that it was once Arthur Murphy's own copy and that 'the numbers are wanting which are printed in Fielding's works; Murphy appears to have sent them to press from this collection'. In actual fact, the first and last two numbers are missing from both the Bodleian copy and from the 1762 *Works*, but otherwise Chalmers's statement is accurate: the missing numbers in Hope Folio 11 are exactly the ones reprinted in 1762 (Nos. 3, 4, 8, 9, 10, 17, 21, 23, 24, 33, 34, 35, 37, 42, 44, 47, 48, 49, 51, 53, 54, 55, 56, 59, 60, and 61). The presumption is thus very strong that these numbers in the 1762 *Works* were reprinted from the same marked copy as those surviving in the Bodleian, which for whatever reason were not selected by Murphy or by Andrew Millar for inclusion in the *Works*. As Dr Hugh Amory, who first identified Fielding's hand in Hope Folio 11, has pointed out, occasional additions to the text in the 1762 edition appear in places similar to those where Fielding added material in the Bodleian copy, i.e. at the end of paragraphs or in a footnote; and one uncorrected misprint in the 1762 addition to *CGJ* No. 48 ('De Roty' for 'De Retz') is clearly a compositorial misreading of Fielding's hand and testifies further to the authoritative nature of at least some of the substantive variants in the 1762 *Works*.[1] For these 26 numbers of the *Covent-Garden Journal*, then, the 1762 *Works* constitutes a revised edition.

Like the editors of other volumes in the Wesleyan Edition where a revised text exists, I have accepted the first edition, which lies closest to the holograph, as the most authoritative printed form of the 'accidentals' of the text, i.e. the spelling, capitalization, word-division, punctuation, use of italics, and the like. As Professor Fredson Bowers has explained in his Textual Introduction to the Wesleyan Edition of *Amelia*, 'An editor will understand that the first edition by no means represents a diplomatic reprint of the manuscript and that in many respects the accidentals are a mixture of the author's and the compositors'. But whatever the relative impurity, the first edition stands nearest to the author's own characteristics and represents the only authority in these matters that has been preserved for the texture in which his words were originally clothed'.[2] On the other hand, there is no evidence that Fielding revised the accidentals of the text in the marked copy from which the 26 issues were reprinted in the 1762 edition. The manuscript corrections and revisions of the numbers of that copy which survive in the Bodleian Library all involve the 'substantives', i.e. the words, rather than the accidentals; and, as Professor Bowers points out, authors of the time did not ordinarily tinker with the accidentals of printed copy as long as the meaning remained unaffected.[3] Moreover, the house styling of the 1762 edition was extensive, involving such changes as putting capitalized nouns into lower case, expanding contractions, increasing the use of commas, altering spelling, and removing most of the italics. Given the scope of the house styling in this posthumous edition, an editor has little chance to identify changes to accidentals that might have been Fielding's; and the evidence of both the Bodleian markings and of his general practice suggests that there were none.

In short, in the second edition of 26 numbers of the *Journal* changes to the accidentals must be rejected as unauthoritative, whereas—on the evidence of the markings in the Bodleian run—many of the changes to the substantives must be accepted as authorial. Under such circumstances the

---

[1] 'Fielding's Copy of the *Covent Garden Journal*', *Bodleian Library Record*, 11 (1983), 126–8; see also Amory's discussion of this copy in 'What Murphy Knew: His Interpolations in Fielding's *Works* (1762), and Fielding's Revision of *Amelia*', *PBSA* 77 (1983), 140–1, and in his earlier essay, 'Andrew Millar and the First Recension of Fielding's *Works* (1762)', *Trans. of the Cambridge Bibliographical Society*, 8 (1981), 66.

[2] Fredson Bowers, Textual Introduction to *Amelia*, ed. Martin C. Battestin (Oxford, 1983), pp. lxii–lxiii.

[3] Bowers, p. lxiii.

Wesleyan editor will follow Sir Walter Greg's theory of copy-text; that is, he will choose as his copy-text the document representing the most authoritative form of the accidentals, which in the absence of a manuscript will be the first edition, and into that text he will insert the substantive variants in a revised edition that he believes are the result of corrections or revisions by the author.[1] Accordingly, for the 26 numbers that were reprinted in 1762, I have sought to reproduce substantially the printer's marked copy of the original issues of 1752 in a way which would separate Fielding's additions and revisions from whatever corruption may have been involved in the resetting of the text.

The main difficulty in such a procedure, of course, is identifying the authorial revisions in the 1762 text and distinguishing them from either compositorial or editorial interventions. This problem is especially acute because (1) the number of manuscript revisions and additions in the issues remaining in the Bodleian copy is considerably less than the number of verbal changes found in the issues actually reprinted in 1762, and (2) several of the minor markings in the Bodleian run appear to be in a hand other than Fielding's (see Appendix VIII). Under these circumstances, I have sought in making my decisions to take account of Fielding's characteristic language and style, while also assuming the Bodleian markings to represent both in type and quantity the kind of authoritative changes to be expected in the 1762 edition. Given the nature of these markings, I have presumed substantive variants in 1762 to be authorial unless they can be rejected as inconsistent with Fielding's normal practice or ruled out by textual criteria as errors common in the transmission of texts. In following this conservative procedure and accepting some twenty-one substantive variants (other than corrections of obvious misprints), I may have introduced into the text an occasional non-authorial reading, but I have lessened the risk of rejecting revisions actually made by the author.

Some of the criteria which have aided me in narrowing the choices to be made may be suggested briefly.[2] Of the thirty-odd substantive or semi-substantive variants which I have rejected, many are either so minor and trivial or run so counter to Fielding's usual stylistic practice that their authority seems improbable. Thus the change of the name 'Budge' to 'Buge' (No. 8, 63.35) or the alteration of Fielding's customary usage 'cotemporary' to 'contemporary' (*passim*) manifestly fails the test of probability, whereas the revision of 'enacting' to 'promulging' (No. 23, 150.6), a more precise term

---

[1] The classic statement is Sir Walter Greg, 'The Rationale of Copy-Text', 3 (1950), 19–36; see also the summary by Bowers, p. lxiv.

[2] For full discussion of such criteria, see Bowers, pp. lxiv–lxx, commenting on Professor Battestin's treatment of these problems in the text of *Amelia*. The *Covent-Garden Journal* appeared in the same volumes of the 1762 *Works* as the revised text of *Amelia*, vol. iv of the 4° issue and vol. viii of the 8° (with *Amelia* also occupying part of vol. vii of the 8°).

in its context, is exactly the kind of change which the manuscript evidence, scanty though it is, shows Fielding interested in making. Moreover, even a minor variant must be accorded greater weight when it occurs in a number of the *Journal* in which Fielding clearly intervened. Thus the insertion of 'very' in the phrase 'a very ingenious' (No. 48, 266.23) gains in authority because it occurs in an essay to which, a few paragraphs later, Fielding made an addition of several lines (268.10–12); both of these variants in No. 48, it may be noted, also appear in places where in the Bodleian copy Fielding seems to have liked to make revisions, i.e. at the end of a column or the end of a paragraph. Familiarity with such clear cases of authorial revision aids one in distinguishing them from the overlay of editorial changes because of house styling (for example, the expansion of ' 'tis' to 'it is' throughout, or the modernization of 'thousand Pound' to 'thousand pounds') and from predictable compositorial errors: the omission of short words, confusion between similar words (e.g. 'this' and 'these', or 'farther' and 'further') or between singular and plural forms, and other compositorial variants common in the period. Finally, a number of the minor variants apparently intended as smoothing 'improvements' have been rejected as completely violating the sense or as altering Fielding's clear intention; the less obvious of these are explained in the textual notes (Appendix IX; for a full record of rejected substantive variants, see the Historical Collation, Appendix VII).

Collation of the quarto and octavo issues of the second edition has revealed only fifteen substantive variants, most of them simple errors made in the setting of the quarto and corrected to the reading of the copy by the proof-reader of the octavo issue. As Professor Bowers has explained in the Textual Introduction to *Amelia*, the quarto seems to have received little or no proof-reading before its types were rearranged and relined for the octavo issue, which was apparently proof-read with some care. Only one of these fifteen variants represents a reading in the octavo which differs from both the quarto and the first edition, and it is an obvious error ('ist it is yousefool' for 'ist it yousefool', No. 8, 61.13). The other variants show the octavo proof-reader restoring the reading of the copy in what are almost all clear cases of compositorial error in the quarto; and they have been of some aid in revealing the kinds of errors to which the compositor of the quarto was subject. Although the number of variants between quarto and octavo is much smaller proportionately in the case of the *Journal* than in *Amelia*, it may be noted that they provide further evidence for the conclusions reached by Professor Bowers about the priority of the quarto setting and the nature of the octavo proof-reading.[1]

[1] See Bowers, pp. lxv–lxx; although I have not fully collated the accidentals of the two 1762 issues against the copy-text, I have supplied a sample collation of the accidentals of 7 of the 26 numbers of the *Journal* in those issues to Professor Bowers, who has informed me that the variants between 4° and 8° are of the same nature as those in *Amelia*.

In the present text changes to the accidentals of the first editions of the *Journal* and the *Plan* have been made conservatively and for the most part have been limited to correction of obvious errors or typos. No effort has been made to achieve a consistency in spelling, punctuation, capitalization, or hyphenation that would not be characteristic of the copy-texts or of their period. In a few instances, however, I have regularized the accidentals for the convenience of the reader, especially in cases where the sense of the passage is obscured or where the original represents a departure from the normal practice of the copy-text itself. To take one example, inconsistency in the use of periods and question marks is especially striking in the *Journal*; I have generally allowed the usage of the copy-text to stand except in cases where the variation appears as an anomaly in a series of questions or series of statements.

For the most part, all such accidental as well as all substantive emendations have been listed in the textual apparatus, so that the copy-texts may be reconstructed in detail by anyone interested in doing so. The following editorial changes, however, have been made silently, in accord with the policy of previous Wesleyan volumes. (1) Errors in typography, such as turned letters, are not listed; and, in the text of the *Journal*, I have silently supplied missing or obscured letters, hyphens, or punctuation marks as long as they are clearly printed in some of the collated copies of the first edition. (2) The heading capitals and small capitals which in the first editions begin the *Plan* and each number of the *Journal*, as well as some of the separate sections within the *Journal*, have not been reproduced. (3) The original text of the *Journal* varies in its use of single and double quotation marks; I have normalized all to double, except for quotations within quotations, and omitted the running quotation marks in the left margin characteristic of the originals. Quotations are thus indicated according to modern usage, with closing quotation marks also removed silently at the end of a paragraph when the quoted material runs on into the next paragraph. The treatment of material interjected within quoted matter is very inconsistent in the original texts; I have therefore silently supplied opening and closing quotation marks to set off inserted phrases like 'he says' from the quoted matter, except when the inserted phrase is placed within parentheses in the originals. (4) When an italicized name is followed by an apostrophe and roman 's', I have kept the roman fount only if the 's' is a contraction for 'is', regularizing to italic for the possessive case. (5) Possessive apostrophes are supplied silently, or removed when they occur with pronouns. (6) Punctuation within an italicized passage is italicized, but punctuation after an italicized word followed by roman text is silently placed in roman if it is syntactically related to the roman text. (7) The treatment of the long dash used with Latin quotations has also been normalized. When the quotation is a complete sentence and would normally be followed by a period, I have placed the period before the dash. When the quotation itself is incomplete syntactically, in headings or within one of Fielding's sentences, I have used only the dash, silently omitting the period. And when a quotation which is not syntactically complete ends one of Fielding's sentences, I have put the period after the dash. (8) Similarly, when one of Fielding's complete sentences ends only with a long dash, I have silently supplied the period, placing it after the last word of the sentence and before the dash. (9) The form of address in letters to the editor has been normalized to italic fount and conventional capitalization. (10) In the mottoes and in other quotations from Latin or Greek sources, I have silently expanded titles and the names of authors; expanded the ampersand to *et* and the suffix -*q* to -*que*; removed pronunciation marks; and substituted modern lettering for Greek diphthongs. (11) Variable punctuation has been normalized to commas in the dates in the headings of the first ten numbers of the *Journal*.

In addition to the silent changes listed above, one other editorial policy requires explanation. Whenever substantive emendations are drawn from the second edition of the *Journal* (26 numbers only), the accidentals of the reading in the second edition have been silently altered so as to conform to the accidental texture of the first edition. For example, in the phrase Fielding added in his revision of *CGJ* No. 24, 'which gives a very serious, but very just Turn to this Subject' (158.13), the words 'Turn' and 'Subject', lower case in the second edition, have been given the capitalization characteristic of the first edition, since the lower-case readings in the 1762 second edition are a result of the house styling and have no authority.[1]

Finally, it should be noted that Appendix I and Appendix II both contain texts originally included in separate numbers of the *Covent-Garden Journal* but here placed in appendices because of the uncertainty of their authorship. These documents, however, have not been accorded the same bibliographical treatment. The 'Covent Garden' columns (Appendix I) have been collated and edited in the same way as the leading essays. The material in Appendix II, on the other hand, the 'Modern History' columns of excerpts from other newspapers followed by editorial comment, have not been given the same bibliographical analysis as the more important texts of the essays or the 'Covent Garden' section. Obvious printer's errors have been silently corrected, and where possible the items reprinted from other newspapers have been shortened, with omissions indicated by ellipsis.[2]

2. THE APPARATUS

For the convenience of the reader, all the textual apparatus has been placed

---

[1] See Bowers, pp. lxxiii–lxxiv. [2] See the head-notes to Appendices I and II.

in appendices (III–XI) to provide one collected body of the evidence on which the present text is based. The first three textual appendices record all emendations substantive or accidental to the text of the *Plan* (III), all substantive emendations to the *Journal* (IV), all emendations of accidentals to the *Journal* (V), and all substantive and accidental emendations of the 'Court of Censorial Enquiry' and 'Covent Garden' columns printed in Appendix I (V). These lists do not include, of course, those accidentals silently altered, as described above; and they provide only the earliest source of each accepted variant together with any readings of the editions earlier than the immediate source. For the *Journal* the only early sources of emendation are the manuscript changes in the Bodleian Library copy (indicated as 'Bodl. MS') and, for 26 numbers, the second edition of 1762, indicated as 'II' but distinguished as 'II^a' (quarto) and 'II^b' (octavo) when the two issues of the second edition vary between themselves. Accidental variants are drawn from II not because the editor believes such variants have any particular authority but because they represent the earliest printed source of an emendation considered to be necessary. All other emendations, for both the *Journal* and the *Plan*, are assigned to 'W', indicating the present edition, even if—as occurs only rarely, if at all, with the present texts—they originated with some earlier editor.

Each item in the lists begins with the page–line reference and the emended reading as printed in the present text. After the square bracket the earliest source of the emendation is indicated, and following the semicolon the entry provides the copy-text reading which has been rejected and any variant readings of editions earlier than the immediate source of emendation. (For the sigla and symbols employed, see the head-notes to Appendix IV and Appendix VIII.) For the *Journal* such variant readings are frequently missing simply because the 1762 edition reprinted only 26 of the 72 numbers and excluded all 'departments' or columns except the leading essays of the numbers selected; the immediate source for the majority of the emendations, then, especially in the list of accidentals, is 'W', with only the rejected first edition reading following the semicolon. Moreover, as explained above, when variants are drawn from II, they are silently made to conform to the accidental texture of I. Thus, for example, (No. 51, 282.21) when I have accepted the comma after 'Spelling' from II rather than the semicolon of I, I have ignored the fact that the reading is 'spelling' in II, since the point of the emendation is not the capitalization but the punctuation. The variation of the accidentals in such emendations is not recorded even when the substantive readings differ, nor, of course, when the swung dash ~ is used to indicate repeated words in emendations involving punctuation only.

The Historical Collation for the *Plan of the Universal Register-Office* (Appendix VI) uses the same system of notation and records all substantive variants from the edited text within the first three editions, those appearing in Fielding's lifetime. This list is complete, however, only for the introductory portion of the tract, since it is only this section which can be attributed to Henry Fielding (see above, p. oo).

Appendix VII provides an Historical Collation for the *Covent-Garden Journal*; it includes all substantive variants from the edited text within the first two editions, with the second edition consisting only of the 26 essays selected for the *Works* of 1762 (both quarto and octavo). The list thus records the history within the two editions of all substantive variation as well as the history of those substantive variants in the second edition rejected here as unauthoritative. The reading to the left of the bracket is that of the present edited text, whether or not it is the precise reading of the first edition or has been emended from II or W. The absence of the sigla for an edition or issue following the bracket means that its reading is the same as that of the edited text. Thus the entry for No. 53, 290.28, 'Passage] passion II^a', indicates that the reading in both the first edition and the octavo issue of the second edition is the same as that of the edited text, 'Passage'. As with the list of emendations, I have ignored accidental variation within the substantive variants to the right of the bracket.

Finally in this group of lists recording changes to the text, Appendix VIII provides an account of the copy of the *Journal* in the Bodleian Library (Hope Folio 11) and a list of all manuscript corrections, revisions, and additions to the text in that copy, regardless of handwriting, and all marginal notes that are definitely in Fielding's hand. The significance of this marked copy to an editor of the *Journal* has been noted already. The list, presented as an historical collation keyed to the present text, also distinguishes by an 'F' those markings accepted as in Fielding's hand.

The remaining sections of the apparatus include textual notes (Appendix IX), bibliographical descriptions and lists of press variants (XI), and a list of word-divisions (X) enabling the reader to reconstruct hyphenated compounds in the copy-text. Hyphenated words at the end of a line in the present text may be assumed to be the result of modern printing and absent in that form from the copy-text unless they are listed here. A second list then gives the compounds or possible compounds which are hyphenated at the end of a line in the copy-text and indicates which of those I have determined to be true hyphenated compounds on the basis of the normal practice of the copy-text. Although the hyphenation is particularly inconsistent in the printing of the *Journal* and some of my decisions about compounds are thus near-emendations, I have not recorded their treatment in the second edition.

3. COLLATION

In preparing the text of the *Covent-Garden Journal*, I collated the following
six copies of the first edition: University of London Library ([S.L.] I
[Fielding—1752] folio); British Library (Burney 447 and Burney 447*);
Cambridge University Library (CCA. 14. I); London Library (Safe-Folio);
and Bodleian Library, Oxford (Hope Folio 11). Of these, only the
Cambridge copy is complete; details of numbers missing from the other
copies are supplied in Appendix XI. Photocopies of the University of
London copy (supplemented by prints of its four missing numbers derived
from a University of Texas copy) were directly collated with the other five
listed. The press variants found in this collation (listed in Appendix XI) were
then checked against the three copies listed as 'observed' in Appendix XI,
but they were not fully collated in an effort to find new press variants.
Xeroxes of the Princeton University Library copy of the 1762 quarto issue
(3738. 1762. 11) and of the Princeton octavo issue (3728. 1762) were
collated against the 1752 copy-text edition; variants revealed in this collation
were then checked against the British Library copies of the quarto (92. g. 10)
and octavo (1493. r. 46) issues.

In preparing the text of the *Plan of the Universal Register-Office*, I collated
the following three copies of the 1751 first edition: British Library (T. 325
[2]); King's College, Cambridge (Keynes coll. E. 4. 18); and Yale University
Library (Ndn54. G6. 751f). No press variants were observed. The 1751 text
was then collated against the British Library (12230. f. 26 [7]) and University
of London (Goldsmith's Library) copies of the second edition and against
xerox of the Yale copy of the third edition (Beinecke Library, NZ 753fi).

A
P L A N

OF THE

Univerſal Regiſter-Office,

OPPOSITE

CECIL-STREET in the STRAND.

LONDON:
Printed in the Year MDCCLI.

A

PLAN

OF THE

Universal Register-Office

Man is said to be by Nature a social Animal, and this principally appears
from two Reasons; first, for that Society alone affords an Opportunity of
exerting all the human Faculties; and secondly, as it alone can provide for all
the Wants of which our Nature is susceptible.[1] In Society alone, Men can
mutually enjoy the Benefit of that vast Variety of Talents with which they are
severally endowed; the Members of the Body Corporate, like those of the
Natural Body, having their several different Uses and Qualifications, all
jointly contributing to the Good of the Whole.

If any Society ever hath been, or ever can be so regulated, that no Talent
in any of its Members, which is capable of contributing to the general Good,
should lie idle and unemployed, nor any of the Wants of its Members which
are capable of Relief, should remain unrelieved, that Society might be said to
have attained its utmost Perfection. Of this absolute Degree of Perfection,
Aristotle seems to think it capable; and if this hath never been in fact attained,
the Reason, perhaps, is neither very difficult to assign or to remove.[2]

Before I proceed to the proposed Plan, I shall lay down two Positions as
certain.

[1] See Aristotle, *Politics*, I. i. 9 (1253a 1–2). Cf. *True Patriot*, No. 8 (24 Dec. 1745): 'I have often
thought it one of the best Arguments to prove Man a Social Animal, that Nature hath severally
endow'd us with Talents so different from each other.' See also *True Patriot*, No. 25 (22 Apr. 1746)
and 'An Essay on Conversation', *Miscellanies* (1743), ed. H. K. Miller, Wesleyan Edn. (Oxford, 1972),
i. 119. The dependence of society on a diversity of human talents, the theme of Book ii (368–73) of
Plato's *Republic*, had recently been stressed by Fielding's friend James Harris in 'Concerning
Happiness, A Dialogue', *Three Treatises* (1744), pp. 148–57.

[2] See Aristotle, *Politics*, I. i. 8–11 (1252b30–1253a 20) for the passage Fielding probably has in
mind; see also *Politics*, II. i. 4–6 for the notion of 'reciprocal equality' in the exercise of talents.
Cf. Fielding's *Proposal for Making an Effectual Provision for the Poor* (1753), where he argues that 'that
Polity is the best established in which all the Members . . . are obliged to contribute a Share to the
Strength and Wealth of the Public. 2dly, That a State is capable of this degree of Perfection'
(pp. 3–4). In *CGJ* No. 15 (22 Feb. 1752) he humorously claims that a perfect distribution of talents is
possible only in the 'Theatrical State'.

First, that in Proportion to the Opulence of any Society, the Wants of its Members will be multiplied; and secondly, the more numerous its Members are, the less Likelihood will there be that any of these Wants should remain unsupplied.[1]

The former of these Positions may, perhaps, at first have the Air of a Paradox; but if we consider it in the Case of an individual Person, its Truth will immediately appear; for here we shall plainly perceive his Wants encreasing with his Riches. Insomuch that the Wants of a Man worth a single Thousand Pounds bear no Proportion to those of him who is possessed of a hundred times that Sum. The Ethic Writer, indeed, will tell me, that none of these Wants arise from Nature.[2] But let them arise from what they will, they are real, and to supply them is as essential to the Happiness of him who hath, or thinks he hath them, as it is to a Savage to supply any of those few Necessities with which a State of Nature, as some call it, abounds.[3] And yet, with Respect to the Philosopher, I shall not doubt to declare the Man with his hundred thousand Pounds in his Pocket, with all his Wants about him, and at the same Time, with a Capacity of supplying all these Wants, to be a much happier Being, than any poor *Diogenes* whatever.[4]

Now Society itself alone creates all these Wants, and at the same Time

[1] Both are mercantilist commonplaces; cf. Mandeville, *Fable of the Bees*, 'while Man advances in Knowledge, and his Manners are polish'd, we must expect to see at the same time his Desires enlarg'd, his Appetites refin'd, and his Vices increas'd' (Remark Q, 6th edn., 1732, p. 201) and his further comment that 'on the Multiplicity of those Wants depended all those mutual Services which the individual Members of a Society pay to each other, and that consequently, the greater Variety there was of Wants, the larger Number of Individuals might find their private Interest in labouring for the good of others' (Vindication of the Book, *Fable*, 6th edn., 1732, p. 465). In *Proposal for Making an Effectual Provision for the Poor* (1753) Fielding again pays tribute to the familiar mercantilist maxim that people are the riches of a nation: 'That the Strength and Riches of a Society consist in the Numbers of the People is an Assertion which hath obtained the Force of an Axiom in Politics' (p. 1). On Fielding and mercantilist thought, see Malvin R. Zirker, Jr., *Fielding's Social Pamphlets* (Berkeley and Los Angeles, 1966), pp. 101—16.

[2] Fielding refers to the countless assaults on 'luxury' by 18th-cent. moralists; see John Sekora, *Luxury: The Concept in Western Thought, Eden to Smollett* (Baltimore, 1977), chs. 2 and 3. Fielding himself had often been an 'Ethic Writer' condemning luxury as the source of the nation's ills; see his Imitation of Juvenal's Sixth Satire in *Miscellanies* (1743), Wesleyan Edn., i. 113; *True Patriot*, No. 7 (17 Dec. 1745); *Amelia*, XI. ii; *CGJ* No. 35; and *Enquiry into the Causes of the late Increase of Robbers* (1751), pp. 3–4, where luxury among the wealthy is tolerated as a moral rather than a political evil. On his shift of attitude here, see General Introduction, pp. xix–xx.

[3] Fielding would have had in mind the use of the term by both Hobbes and Locke. Cf. his reference in *Proposal for Making an Effectual Provision for the Poor* (1753) to 'what is sometimes called the State of Nature, but may more properly be called a State of Barbarism and Wildness' (pp. 4–5).

[4] Cf. the similar disparagement in the *Enquiry* (1751) of the philosopher who cries out against luxury, in contrast to the politician, who 'finds many Emoluments to compensate all the moral Evils introduced by Trade' (pp. xi–xii); on Diogenes, cf. the portrait in Fielding's 'Dialogue Between Alexander the Great and Diogenes the Cynic', *Miscellanies* (1743), in which the tub philosopher appears as the antisocial cynic whose contempt for money is exposed as hypocritical. On his unfavorable reputation in the period, see Miller, *Essays*, 402–5; cf., however, *Champion*, 26 Jan. 1740, where the idealism of Diogenes is contrasted with the worldly wisdom of Bacon. See also *JJ* No. 22 (30 Apr. 1748); *Journey from this World to the Next* (1743), I. v.

alone gives us the Methods of supplying them by the Invention of what is called Trade or Traffick.[1] And yet as Societies of Men encreased into great and populous Cities and large extended Countries, the Politician found something still wanting; and this was a Method of communicating the various Wants and Talents of the Members to each other; by which Means they might be mutually supplied. Hence the Invention of Fairs, Markets, Exchanges, and all other Publick Meetings for carrying on Traffick and Commerce between Men, in which the common and ordinary Wants of the Society are from Time to Time provided for.

All these Methods, however, are so far defective, as they fail to be Universal; for to the Perfections of a Society it is required, that none of the various Talents of the Members shall remain unknown and unemployed, nor any of their Wants unsupplied. This, as it seems, can only be attained, by providing some Place of universal Resort, where all the Members of the Society may communicate all their mutual Wants and Talents to each other. So that no Person may want what another is capable of supplying him with, provided he is able and willing to pay the Price.

In large and populous Cities, and wide extended Communities, it is most probable that every human Talent is dispersed somewhere or other among the Members; and consequently every Person who stands in Need of that Talent, might supply his Want if he knew where to find it; but to know this is the Difficulty, and this Difficulty still encreases with the Largeness of the Society. Let us illustrate this by the Case of a Shopkeeper, who deals in various Commodities: The more Goods he hath in his Warehouse, unless they are so disposed that he can easily find them, the greater is his Confusion and Inability to satisfy the Demands of his Customers.

The ingenious *Montaigne*, in his 34th Essay, hath the following Passage.

"My Father, who, for a Man that had no other Advantages, than Experience only, and his own natural Parts, was nevertheless of a very clear Judgment, has formerly told me, that he once had Thoughts of endeavouring to introduce this Practice; that there might be in every City a certain Place assigned, to which, such as stood in Need of any thing might repair, and have their Business entered by an Officer appointed for that Purpose; as for Example, one enquires[2] for a Chapman to buy my Pearl: I enquire for one that has Pearls to sell: Such a one wants Company to go to *Paris*: Such a one enquires for a Servant of such a Quality: Such a one for a Master; such a one enquires for such an Artificer, some for one Thing, some for another, every

---

[1] Cf. Josiah Tucker, 'All *Commerce* is founded upon the Wants . . . which the People of different Countries, or the different Classes of Inhabitants of the same Country, are desirous, in defect of their own single Abilities, to supply by *mutual* Intercourse', *A Brief Essay on the Advantages and Disadvantages which respectively attend France and Great Britain with Regard to Trade* (1753), p. i.

[2] Fielding's source reads 'I enquire'.

one according to what he wants. And doubtless these mutual Advertisements would be of no contemptible Advantage to the publick Correspondency and Intelligence: For there are evermore Conditions that hunt after one another, and for Want of knowing one another's Occasions, leave Men in very great Necessity."[1]

On these Principles an Office is now erected in the *Strand*, near *Southampton-street*, and opposite *Cecil-street*; the Design of which is to bring the World as it were together into one Place. Here the Buyer and the Seller, the Master and the Scholar, the Master and the Apprentice, and the Master and Servant are sure to meet: Here ingenious Persons of all Kinds will meet with those who are ready to employ them, and the Curious will be supplied with every thing which it is in the Power of Art to produce. In a Word, no useful Talent in the Society will be idle, nor will any Man long want a Seller and Purchaser of what he is desirous either to purchase or dispose of; whereas at present many a Man is Starving, while in the Possession of Talents, which would be highly serviceable to others, who could and would well reward him. Several Persons are possessed of divers Goods and Curiosities, which others are in vain enquiring after. Servants who can have the best of Characters remain out of Place, while Gentlemen are obliged in haste to accept of Persons very slightly recommended: In the same Manner the Buyer and the Seller are groping after each other in the Dark, and often, after great Expence of Time, Trouble, and Money, to no manner of Purpose. But without endeavouring to recommend a Scheme to the Public, from which they will manifestly receive so much Benefit, I shall here explain to them the Nature and Plan of that Office, under every particular Article already opened.

I. In the Register of Estates to be sold, are set down the Quantity and Quality of the Estate, *viz.* whether Freehold, Leasehold, Copyhold; whether in Manors, Lands, Houses, Rents, *&c.* the County in which it lies, the nearest City or Market Town, with the Price and every other Particular by which the Seller thinks proper to recommend it, either with or without the Parish in which it lies, and with or without the Name of the Estate, or of the Seller, at his Option. This is done at the Price of One Shilling. Now, at the Price of Three Pence only, any Gentleman who wants to buy an Estate in any County, in *Yorkshire* for Instance, naming the Nature of the Estate which he would purchase, is in a Minute informed whether there be any such Estate registered; and if not, for One Shilling more his Direction is entered in the

---

[1] Fielding quotes, with minor verbal changes, from Montaigne's *Essays in Three Books*, trans. Charles Cotton (6th edn., 1743), I. xxxiv ('Of one Defect in our Government'). Baker, item 510, lists this edition among Fielding's books.

Office, and an Account immediately sent to him the Moment any thing like what he requires is offered to be registered.

Thus the two Principals, or their immediate Agents are, at once brought together, I think I may say at no Expence at all, without the Danger and Costs of employing Jobbers, or disparaging an Estate by a public Advertisement, which though it costs from four to twenty times as much, lasts but a Day; and which, though it exposes a Man's Circumstances to all his Neighbours, escapes perhaps the Observation of the very Person for whom it was designed.[1]

II. In the Article of Lodgings, Estates, or Houses to let, we register, if it be an Estate, its Nature, Quantity, Rent, Situation, &c. If a House or Lodgings, we set it down whether furnished or unfurnished, and Number of Rooms. If in Town, the Street in which the House stands, with all its Conveniencies: If in the Country, the Town or Parish; whether any and what Garden; whether Outhouses; the Situation, Prospect, Accommodations for Travelling; with every other Particular mentioned, and the Rent if permitted. For this we require no more than Six-pence, and Three-pence from the Enquirer, as before.

The public Utility of this Article is almost too obvious to be pointed out. Many Persons will, at the Price of Six-pence, prevent the losing Weeks, Months, and sometimes a whole Season in letting their Lodgings; as on the other Hand, Gentlemen and Ladies may in a Minute's Time survey all the Houses and Lodgings which are to be let in several Streets in *London* and *Westminster*, and in a whole Parish or Town in the Country. For want of which Conveniency, they are at present obliged either to take long fruitless Walks and Rides themselves, or to trust to the Taste (too much perhaps sometimes to the Fidelity) of an Acquaintance, or a Servant; and after having contracted for a disagreeable Situation, discover to their Sorrow that they have missed the Place in which they would have been accommodated entirely to their Satisfaction.

Under the 3d Article are registered all Manner of Securities for Money, whether Real or Personal; and also the Names of those who have large or smaller Sums to dispose of; so that the Borrower and Lender are at once brought together, without Expence or Delay. And as several Persons who are willing to advance small Sums on personal Securities, on very reasonable Terms, are registered, so those who want to borrow may be assured, if they cannot be supplied here, they will fail every where else.

IV. Places and Employments to be sold, or anywise disposed of, whether Ecclesiastical, Civil, or Military; such as Chaplainships, Curacies, Patent-

---

[1] On the Fieldings' quarrel with the *DA*, see General Introduction, p. xxvi.

places, or others which the Possessor can obtain Leave to dispose of, in any Branch of the Civil Government, and Commissions of all Kinds in the Army. So that without having their Names hawked about by Jobbers, and obliged to pay great Præmiums if they succeed; their Intentions to dispose of a Place or Commission, are known only to those who are desirous to treat with them for the same; and no Expence or Reward whatever is to attend the Consummation of the Bargain.

V. Apprentices who want Masters in any Trade, and Masters who want Apprentices. Here the Trade chosen, the Age and Qualifications of the Youth, the Money to be given, and the Terms required are entered. So that for Six-pence a Master may have the choice of a hundred Apprentices, and a Parent of as many Masters for his Child.

VI. Masters and Mistresses who teach any Science or Art. If they keep a School, its Situation is registered, what they teach, what their Price, &c. If they are willing to teach Abroad; their several Recommendations; what they teach; as Languages, Music, Dancing, Fencing, &c. Their Prices, &c.

VII. Partners in Trade. The Sums ready to be advanced, and Conditions; with every Particular.

VIII. Servants of all Kinds, such as Riders, Book-keepers, and Journey-men, Stewards and Clerks; Domestic Servants, as House-Stewards, Gentlemen, Valets, Butlers, Cooks, Gardeners, Coachmen, Footmen, Grooms, Postilions, &c. Governesses, Housekeepers, Waiting-maids, Cook-maids, House-maids, Laundry-maids, dry and wet Nurses, &c. &c. Under this Head are inserted the Name, Place of Abode, Qualification, Age, married or single, whether had the Small Pox, what Place lived in last, and how long; with every Particular of their Characters, and by whom to be given. And the Public may be assured, that the utmost Care will be taken to prevent any Imposition; and that none will be registered in this Office who give the least suspicious Account of themselves, and who have lived in any disreputable Places. The great Use this Article alone will be of to the Public, is submitted to their Consideration; for the Fidelity with which it is executed, we may appeal to the Experience of Hundreds who have already been supplied at the Office; from many of whom we have received Letters of Thanks, and not from any single Person a Word of Complaint. We, however, take this Opportunity, to desire all Gentlemen and Ladies who turn away Servants for any gross Fault, to put themselves to the Expence of a Penny-post Letter to the Office, and we faithfully promise that no such Servant shall be registered there.[1]

---

[1] In promising a reliable system of character references the Fieldings were addressing one of the major problems in the employment of servants throughout the century. See e.g. *Spectator*, No. 493 (25

IX. All manner of Goods are here registered; and we desire Tradesmen would consider whether it might not be of great Use to them to send Bills of their Shops, and (particularly Mercers and Woollen-Drapers) Patterns of their Goods to the Office, where Gentlemen and Ladies may have an Opportunity of seeing them. And they may be assured, that none of the said Patterns shall be delivered from the Office, nor shewn to any others, but to such as they would willingly expose them to in their own Shops. Second Hand Goods are here likewise registered, particularly all Kinds of Vehicles, as Coaches, Landaus, Post and other Chaises. Likewise all Manner of Animals for Use or Pleasure, as Horses, Dogs, Wild Beasts, Birds, &c. And Curiosities of every Kind.

X. Lastly, Conveniencies for Travelling in all Manners by Sea or Land. Ships, whither bound, and when depart, with the Terms for Passengers. Stage Coaches; the Inns they put up; the Days and Hours they depart and arrive at, with their Prices. Bye and returned Coaches for *Bath*, and all other Places; when expected to arrive; when set out; and their Prices. Likewise all Methods of conveying Goods, either by Land or Water Carriage; Companions for Post-Chaises, &c.

This Article, surely, needs neither Explanation nor Recommendation. How advantageous on the one Hand must it be to Captains of Ships and Masters of Stage or Bye Coaches, at so trifling a Cost as Six-pence, to be certain of never missing a Passenger; as on the other Hand, how infinitely easy must it be to the Public, by the Trouble of sending to a Place, which as it is in the very Middle of the Town, cannot be far off; and at the Price of Three-pence, to know every Convenience of Travelling to the Place they are destined to!

These are the principal Articles already opened in this Office, to which, perhaps, Time and Experience may give some Additions, it being intended to make the Information as universal as possible; and we doubt not but the Public will give all due Encouragement to an Undertaking so visibly calculated for their Good; and which proposes to serve them at so cheap a Rate.

On our Side, they may be assured, that as the Proprietors of this Office are Gentlemen, and Men experienced in Business; so it will be executed with the utmost Care, Regularity, and Fidelity, and as much Secrecy always as shall be desired by the Parties themselves.

The great Utility of this Office, when its Correspondence is become

Sept. 1712), *Universal Spectator*, No. 142 (26 June 1731), *CGJ* No. 64, and *World*, No. 129 (19 June 1755); see also Dorothy Marshall, 'The Domestic Servants of the Eighteenth Century', *Economica*, 9 (1929), 15–40. Cf. the proposal, perhaps an outgrowth of the Register Office, to found a society for rewarding honest and faithful servants, who would pay a fee to register for the scheme (*A Proposal for the Amendment and Encouragement of Servants*, 1752).

universal, must be apparent to every one. Indeed, its Use consists chiefly in its Universality, and this is entirely in the Power of the Public. In this, therefore, as in every Scheme for the Common Good, if the Wise and Public-Spirited will take the Lead, they will be sure of being followed by all the rest.

The Covent-Garden Journal.

By Sir ALEXANDER DRAWCANSIR, Knt. Cenſor of GREAT BRITAIN.

SATURDAY, JANUARY 4. 1752.   Numb. I.

To be continued every TUESDAY and SATURDAY.

Credite Scriptores ——
Anglice,
By your Leave, Gentlemen.

THE World, it is certa'n, never more abounded with Authors, than at preſent; nor is there any Species more numerous than of thoſe Writers who deal forth their Lucubrations in ſmall Parcels to the Public, conſiſting partly of hiſtorical, and partly, to uſe their own Word, of *literary* Matter. So great, indeed, is their Multitude, that Homer's Simile of the Bees gives us ſcarce too vaſt an Idea of them. Some of theſe viſit the Light, daily, ſo that we may apply ſtrictly to them the

Ἀυτὶ νέον ἐρχομένων

Some of them again fly abroad only every other Day; ſome ſend forth their Works once a Week; others once a Fortnight; and others more ſparingly indulge us only at the End of every Month with their Labours.

When I ſurvey all theſe wondrous Works in my Mind, I am ſtruck with no leſs Aſtoniſhment, than was the Foreigner when he ſaw Leadenhall Market; nor can I more conceive what becomes of all this Quantity of Paper, than he could find Conſumers for ſo much Meat. The ſame Solution will, indeed, ſerve us both; for there are certainly as many B—ms in the World as there are Mouths.

Here, perhaps, I may ſeem to have advanced an Argument againſt my own Appearance, and it will poſſibly be ſaid, ſince we have ſo many, (perhaps, too many,) of theſe Writers already, what Need have we of adding a new one to the Number?

To this I ſhall firſt give the ſame Anſwer which is often made by thoſe who force themſelves into crowded Aſſemblies, when they are told the Place is too full already, " Pray, Gentlemen, make Room for me; —— I am but one. Certainly you may make Room for one more."

Secondly, I believe it is uſual in all ſuch Crowds, to find ſome few Perſons, at leaſt, who have ſufficient Decency to quit their Places and give Way to their Betters. I do not, therefore, in the leaſt queſtion, but that ſome of my cotemporary Authors will immediately, on my Appearance, have the Modeſty to retire, and leave me ſufficient Elbow Room in the World. Or, if they ſhould not, the Public will, I make no Doubt, ſo well underſtand themſelves, as to give me proper Marks of their Diſtinction, and will make Room for me by turning others out.

But, in Fact, had the great Numbers of cotemporary Writers been any Argument againſt aſſuming the Pen, the World would never have enjoyed the Works of that excellent Poet Juvenal, who tells us, that they ſwarmed in a moſt prodigious Manner in his Time; but, ſo far from declining the Poetical Function on that Account, he aſſigns this as the very Reaſon of taking it upon him.

*—— Stulta eſt Clementia, cum tot ubique
Vatibus occurras, perituræ parcere Chartæ.*

Theſe Reaſons, and this Authority, will, I believe, be ſufficient Apologies to my Readers; but it may be, perhaps, more difficult to ſatisfy my Brother Authors themſelves, to whom, I would, if poſſible, avoid giving any Kind of Umbrage. Theſe Gentlemen, I ſay it with great Concern, are ſometimes guilty of adopting Motives unworthy of the Followers of the Muſes; and, inſtead of conſulting the true Intereſt of the Republic of Letters in general, are too apt poorly and meanly to conſider their own; and, like mere Mechanics, to be envious and jealous of a Rival in their Trade.

To ſilence, therefore, effectually, all ſuch Jealouſies, and Fears, I do here declare, that it is not my Intention to encroach on the Buſineſs now carried on by my Cotemporaries, nor to deal in any of thoſe Wares which they at preſent vend to the Public.

Firſt then I diſclaim any Dealing in Politics. By Politics, here, I cannot be underſtood to mean any Diſquiſitions into thoſe Matters which reſpect the true Intereſt of this Kingdom abroad, or which relate to its domeſtic OEconomy and Government; with none of which theſe Writers have ever yet concerned themſelves. By Politics, therefore, I mean that great political Cauſe between WOODALL OUT, and TAKEALL IN, Eſqs; which hath been ſo learnedly handled in Papers, Pamphlets, and Magazines, for above thirty Years laſt paſt; and in which the Nation in general are as greatly intereſted, as they were in the late Conteſt between Thamas Kouli Kan, and the Sophy of Perſia.

Secondly, I renounce all Pretenſions to deal in perſonal Slander and Scurrility, a very extenſive article, and of which many of my Brethren have been ſo long in Poſſeſſion, that it would be in vain for me to diſpute their Title with them.

Thirdly, I do promiſe, as far as in me lies, to avoid with the utmoſt Care all Kind of Encroachment on that ſpacious Field, in which my ſaid Cotemporaries have ſuch large and undoubted Poſſeſſions; and which, from Time immemorial, hath been called the Land of DULLNESS. A late ingenious Predeceſſor of mine, in the Wantonneſs of his Heart, declared, if at any Time he appeared dull, there was a Deſign in it; on the contrary, I ſolemnly proteſt, that if I ever commit a Treſpaſs of this Kind, it will be becauſe I cannot help it. But here I muſt offer two Precautions. Firſt, that I ſhall always object to the Evidence of any of the known Proprietors of this Field, as being too much intereſted in the Cauſe to be legal Witneſſes. And, ſecondly, if my Pen ſhould, now and then, accidentally be found ſtraying in the ſaid Field, it will not thereby become a Treſpaſſer; as we Wits have, by Preſcription, a Right of Common there *per Cauſe de Vicinage*, as the Law calls it. This Right we have enjoyed from the Days of Homer, who was ſometimes found taking a ſound Nap therein.

Thus, I think, I ſhall leave theſe Gentlemen in full Poſſeſſion of all that they at preſent deal in. But there is another very good Argument to quiet their Apprehenſions; the Price of my Paper being by Half, or at leaſt, a third Part, higher than any other. To affect, therefore, any Fear of loſing their Cuſtomers by my Means, is as abſurd, as it would be in the Owners of Stalls, or Wheel-barrows, to affect any Jealouſy in Trade of THE GREAT Mr. DEARD.

The Covent-Garden Journal

By Sir ALEXANDER DRAWCANSIR, Knt. Censor of GREAT BRITAIN

SATURDAY, JANUARY 4, 1752. NUMB. I.

To be continued every TUESDAY and SATURDAY

Cedite Scriptores ——.[1]

Anglicé,

By your Leave, Gentlemen.

The World, it is certain, never more abounded with Authors, than at present;[2] nor is there any Species more numerous than of those Writers who deal forth their Lucubrations in small Parcels to the Public, consisting partly of historical, and partly, to use their own Word, of *literary* Matter. So great, indeed, is their Multitude, that Homer's Simile of the Bees gives us scarce too vast an Idea of them. Some of these visit the Light daily, so that we may apply strictly to them the

$$\text{'}Aιεὶ νέον ἐρχομενάων\text{}[3]$$

Some of them again fly abroad only every other Day; some send forth their Works once a Week; others once a Fortnight; and others more sparingly indulge us only at the End of every Month with their Labours.[4]

---

[1] Propertius, *Elegies*, II. xxxiv. 65: 'Yield ye, bards' (Loeb).

[2] Cf. the Preface to the *Tale of a Tub*, where Swift lists the varieties of this opening gambit.

[3] The simile is in *Iliad*, ii. 87 ff., describing the gathering of Greek forces: 'Even as the tribes of thronging bees go forth from some hollow rock, ever coming on afresh, and in clusters over the flowers of spring fly in throngs, . . .' (Loeb). Fielding quotes the phrase 'ever coming on afresh'.

[4] The principal daily papers were the *Daily Advertiser, London Daily Advertiser, General Advertiser,* and *London Gazetteer;* papers appearing three times a week included the *London Evening Post, Whitehall Evening Post, General Evening Post, St. James's Evening Post,* and the *Rambler* (twice weekly); appearing weekly were *Old England, Craftsman, Westminster Journal, Read's Weekly Journal, True Briton,* and Bonnell Thornton's *Drury-Lane Journal;* the *Ladies' Magazine* was published fortnightly; and the major monthly periodicals were the *Gentleman's Magazine, London Magazine, Monthly Review,* and *Universal Magazine.* For other examples, see Thornton's list of the 'flood of Magazines' that 'pour in upon us monthly', *Drury-Lane Journal,* No. 2 (23 Jan. 1752).

When I survey all these wondrous Works in my Mind, I am struck with no less Astonishment, than was the Foreigner when he saw Leadenhall Market; nor can I more conceive what becomes of all this Quantity of Paper, than he could find Consumers for so much Meat.[1] The same Solution will, indeed, serve us both; for there are certainly as many B—ms in the World as there are Mouths.

Here, perhaps, I may seem to have advanced an Argument against my own Appearance, and it will possibly be said, since we have so many, (perhaps, too many,) of these Writers already, what Need have we of adding a new one to the Number?

To this I shall first give the same Answer which is often made by those who force themselves into crowded Assemblies, when they are told the Place is too full already, "Pray, Gentlemen, make Room for me; — I am but one. Certainly you may make Room for one more."[2]

Secondly, I believe it is usual in all such Crowds, to find some few Persons, at least, who have sufficient Decency to quit their Places and give Way to their Betters. I do not, therefore, in the least question, but that some of my cotemporary Authors will immediately, on my Appearance, have the Modesty to retire, and leave me sufficient Elbow Room in the World. Or, if they should not, the Public will, I make no Doubt, so well understand themselves, as to give me proper Marks of their Distinction, and will make Room for me by turning others out.[3]

But, in Fact, had the great Numbers of cotemporary Writers been any Argument against assuming the Pen, the World would never have enjoyed the Works of that excellent Poet Juvenal, who tells us, that they swarmed in a most prodigious Manner in his Time; but, so far from declining the Poetical Function on that Account, he assigns this as the very Reason of taking it upon him.

> —— *Stulta est Clementia, cum tot ubique*
> *Vatibus occurras, perituræ parcere Chartæ.*[4]

These Reasons, and this Authority, will, I believe, be sufficient Apologies to my Readers; but it may be, perhaps, more difficult to satisfy my Brother

---

[1] Fielding alludes to the comment on Leadenhall Market by Don Pedro de Ronquillo, Spanish ambassador to the court of Charles II, who supposedly told the king 'that he believed there was more Meat sold in that Market alone in a Week than in all the Kingdom of *Spain* in a Year' (J. Macky, *A Journey through England. In Familiar Letters from a Gentleman Here, to his Friend Abroad* [1714], i. 204); Fielding owned the 5th edn. of this work (Baker, item 56). For a variant version of the story, see Defoe's *Tour* (3 vols., 1724–6), Letter VI.

[2] Cf. Swift's use of the same image in the Preface to the *Tale of a Tub*.

[3] For similar disparagement of rival newspapers, see *True Patriot*, No. 1 (5 Nov. 1745) and *JJ* No. 1 (5 Dec. 1747). It was a conventional ploy in the opening number of a new journal; cf. *Common Sense*, No. 1 (5 Feb. 1737).

[4] Juvenal, *Satires*, i. 17–18: 'It is a foolish clemency when you jostle against poets at every corner, to spare paper that will be wasted anyhow' (Loeb).

Authors themselves, to whom, I would, if possible, avoid giving any Kind of
Umbrage. These Gentlemen, I say it with great Concern, are sometimes
guilty of adopting Motives unworthy of the Followers of the Muses; and,
instead of consulting the true Interest of the Republic of Letters in general,
are too apt poorly and meanly to consider their own; and, like mere
Mechanics,[1] to be envious and jealous of a Rival in their Trade.

To silence, therefore, effectually, all such Jealousies, and Fears, I do here
declare, that it is not my Intention to encroach on the Business now carried
on by my Cotemporaries, nor to deal in any of those Wares which they at
present vend to the Public.

First then I disclaim any Dealing in Politics.[2] By Politics, here, I cannot be
understood to mean any Disquisitions into those Matters which respect the
true Interest of this Kingdom abroad, or which relate to its domestic
Œconomy and Government; with none of which these Writers have ever yet
concerned themselves. By Politics, therefore, I mean that great political
Cause between WOODALL OUT, and TAKEALL IN, Esqs; which hath been
so learnedly handled in Papers, Pamphlets, and Magazines, for above thirty
Years last past; and in which the Nation in general are as greatly interested,
as they were in the late Contest between Thamas Kouli Kan, and the
Sophy of Persia.[3]

Secondly, I renounce all Pretensions to deal in personal Slander and
Scurrility, a very extensive article, and of which many of my Brethren have
been so long in Possession, that it would be in vain for me to dispute their
Title with them.[4]

Thirdly, I do promise, as far as in me lies, to avoid with the utmost Care
all Kind of Encroachment on that spacious Field, in which my said
Cotemporaries have such large and undoubted Possessions; and which, from
Time immemorial, hath been called the Land of DULLNESS.[5] A late

---

[1] Those engaged in manual trades; low or vulgar fellows (*OED*); for a similar comment cf. *True Patriot*, No. 1 (5 Nov. 1745).

[2] In claiming that his journal is non-political, Fielding seeks to distinguish it not only from the flood of political writing which had begun thirty years earlier at the outset of the Walpole Administration but also from his own previous newspapers (*Champion, True Patriot*, and *JJ*), all of which were politically motivated. Such disclaimers were not, however, uncommon in political journals themselves; cf. *True Patriot*, No. 1 (5 Nov. 1745), *Champion*, 14 Feb. 1740, and Chesterfield's carefully non-political opening number of the Opposition journal *Common Sense* (5 Feb. 1737). Fielding's enemies were thus slow to accept his disavowal of politics in the *CGJ*; see Introduction, pp. xlviii–xlix.

[3] In 1731 Nadir Kuli, the most powerful military leader in Persia, was granted the title 'Tahmasp Kuli Khan' by the Shah (or 'Sophy') Tahmasp. After a series of intrigues and murders, Nadir Kuli was himself proclaimed Shah in 1736. Despite Fielding's remarks, interest in the affair seems to have been considerable in England, with at least five different 'Histories' of 'Kouli Kan, Sophi of Persia' published in the years 1740–2. Cf. Fielding's own reference to 'the present Persian Madman', *Champion*, 3 May 1740.

[4] Cf. *CGJ* Nos. 14 and 72, and see his Preface to the *Miscellanies* (1743).

[5] Fielding's strategy throughout this paragraph is to treat Dullness not in the mock-epic terms made familiar by Pope but in the legal language of property and trespass.

ingenious Predecessor of mine, in the Wantonness of his Heart, declared, if at any Time he appeared dull, there was a Design in it;[1] on the contrary, I solemnly protest, that if I ever commit a Trespass of this Kind, it will be because I cannot help it. But here I must offer two Precautions. First, that I shall always object to the Evidence of any of the known Proprietors of this Field, as being too much interested in the Cause to be legal Witnesses. And, secondly, if my Pen should, now and then, accidentally be found straying in the said Field, it will not thereby become a Trespasser; as we Wits have, by Prescription, a Right of Common there *per Cause de Vicinage*, as the Law calls it.[2] This Right we have enjoyed from the Days of Homer, who was sometimes found taking a sound Nap therein.[3]

Thus, I think, I shall leave these Gentlemen in full Possession of all that they at present deal in. But there is another very good Argument to quiet their Apprehensions; the Price of my Paper being by Half, or at least, a third Part, higher than any other.[4] To affect, therefore, any Fear of losing their Customers by my Means, is as absurd, as it would be in the Owners of Stalls, or Wheel-barrows, to affect any Jealousy in Trade of THE GREAT Mr. DEARD.[5]

This is a Point, indeed, infinitely below my Consideration; however, at the Desire of my Bookseller, I shall give the Public his Reasons for fixing the Price of Three-pence on this Paper, and which, he hopes, will be abundantly satisfactory.[6]

First, he insists pretty much on the extraordinary Beauty of his Paper, and Print, which alone he thinks to be worth the additional Money.

Secondly, he urges the Quantity of the Matter which this Paper will contain; being, he says, more than double the Quantity of any other, and almost twenty Times as much as is generally contained in the Daily Advertiser.[7] So that, says he,

[1] Steele, in *Tatler*, Nos. 38 (7 July 1709) and 234 (7 Oct. 1710). See *Tom Jones*, v. i., *Champion* for 22 May 1740, and *JJ* No. 31 (2 July 1748) for Fielding's other references to Steele's remark; cf. Arthur Murphy in *Gray's Inn Journal*, No. 1 (21 Oct. 1752).

[2] i.e. through lapse of time ('prescription') the Wits have a right in the lands of the Dull. 'Common because of vicinage . . . is where the tenants of two adjoining manors, the inhabitants of two adjoining townships, or the owners of two contiguous pieces of land . . . have from time immemorial "intercommoned," i.e. allowed each other's cattle to stray and pasture on each other's land.' (W. Jowitt, *Dictionary of English Law* [1959], p. 422.)

[3] Fielding alludes to Homer's 'nodding'; see Horace, *Art of Poetry*, 359.

[4] Most essay-journals were priced at twopence; cf. the *True Briton* (priced at twopence): 'The Price of our Paper will equal that of our Weekly Brethren' (2 Jan. 1751).

[5] William Deard (d. 1761), a celebrated jeweller in the Strand, often alluded to satirically by Fielding; cf. *The Temple Beau* (1730), IV. vi; *The Miser*, II. i; *Joseph Andrews*, III. vi; *Jonathan Wild*, II. iii; *Journey from This World to the Next*, I. i; *Ovid's Art of Love Paraphrased* (1747); and *Tom Jones*, XII. iv.

[6] On the argument which follows, cf. Fielding's similar claim in *True Patriot*, No. 1 (5 Nov. 1745) that the price of threepence set by the bookseller is justified because the reader will 'gain six times the Knowledge and Amusement by my Paper, compared to any other'.

[7] *DA* is no doubt singled out because it had refused the Fieldings' advertisements for the Universal Register Office; see General Introduction, p. xxvi.

	l.	*s.*	*d.*
If Ditto Contents, in Ditto Advertiser, be worth —	o	o	1½
Then Ditto Contents, in Ditto Journal, is worth —	o	2	6
Balance in Favour of the Journal,	o	2	4½

Lastly, he lays some Weight on the superior Goodness of the Matter. On this, indeed, he lays very little Stress; however, he thinks it may be reckoned at something. Modesty forces me to suppress much of what he advances on this Head. One Particular, however, I cannot forbear inserting, as there is something new and whimsical in the Thought; I shall give it in his own Words; "As you are a Man of Learning, Sir," says he, "and well travelled in the Greek and Roman Authors,[1] I shall most probably, in this Paper, import many curious Treasures of Antiquity both from Greece, and Rome. Now, as Gentlemen daily give Hundreds of Pounds for antient Busts, and Statues, they will not surely scruple to give Three-half-pence for an antient Greek or Roman Sentiment."

This is the Reasoning of my Bookseller; to imagine, indeed, that it is any Concern of mine, would be an Absurdity so great, that I shall not suspect any of my Readers to be capable of it. In an Age when all Men are so ready to serve their Country for nothing, I hope I shall not be thought an Exception.[2] For my own Part, I cannot be supposed, by an intelligent Person, to have any other View, than to correct and reform the Public; and should have taken some Pains to have prevailed with my Bookseller to distribute these Papers *gratis*, had he not assured me, that such an Example would be of great Detriment to Trade.   A.

INTRODUCTION

TO A

JOURNAL OF THE PRESENT PAPER WAR between the Forces under Sir ALEXANDER DRAWCANSIR, and the Army of GRUB-STREET.[3]

Before I had fully resolved to draw my Pen, and to take the Field in the Warfare of Writing, I duly considered not only my own Strength, but the Force of the Enemy. I am therefore well apprized of the Difficulties I have to

---

[1] Cf. Parson Adams's explanation to the Host in *Joseph Andrews*, II. xvii: 'the travelling I mean is in Books, the only way of travelling by which any Knowledge is to be acquired'.

[2] For expanded irony on this theme, see *CGJ* No. 2.

[3] Throughout his account of the paper war, Fielding's military language owes much to Swift's *Battle of the Books*; cf. also his extended analogies of the Government of the Stage in *CGJ* No. 15 and the Kingdom of Authors in *CGJ* No. 23. For the background of the paper war, see General Introduction, pp. xxxvi–xxxix.

encounter; I well know the present dreadful Condition of the great Empire of Letters; the State of Anarchy that prevails among Writers; and the great Revolution which hath lately happened in the Kingdom of Criticism; that the Constitutions of Aristotle, Horace, Longinus, and Bossu, under which the State of Criticism so long flourished, have been entirely neglected, and the Government usurped by a Set of Fellows, entirely ignorant of all those Laws.[1] The Consequence of which hath been the Dissolution of that antient Friendship and Amity which subsisted between the Author and the Critic, so much to the mutual Advantage of both People, and that the latter hath long declared War against the former. I know how cruelly this War hath been carried on, and the great Devastation which hath been made in the literary World, chiefly by means of a large Body of Irregulars, composed of Beaux, Rakes, Templars, Cits,[2] Lawyers, Mechanics, School-boys, and fine Ladies, who have been admitted to the *Jus Civitatis*,[3] by the Usurpers in the Realms of Criticism, without knowing one Word of the antient Laws, and original Constitution of that Body of which they have professed themselves to be Members. I am, farther, sensible of the Revolt which hath been of the Authors to the Critics; many of the meanest among the former, having become very considerable and principal *leaders* among the latter.

All these Circumstances put together do most certainly afford a most gloomy Prospect, and are sufficient to dismay a very enterprizing Genius; but I have often reflected with Approbation on the Advice given to Caius Piso, in Tacitus, *to appear in open Arms in Defence of a just and glorious Cause, rather than to await the Event of a tame and abject Submission.*[4] How much more noble is it in a great Author to fall with his Pen in his Hand, than quietly to sit down, and see the Press in the Possession of an Army of Scriblers, who, at present, seem to threaten the Republic of Letters with no less Devastation than that which their Ancestors the Goths, Huns, Vandals, &c. formerly poured in on the Roman Empire.

When I had taken a firm Resolution of opposing this Swarm of Vandals, I concerted my Measures in the best Manner I was able.

In the first Place I reviewed my VETERANS which were all drawn up in their Ranks before me. The Greeks led by Homer, Aristotle, Thucydides,

---

[1] Cf. *Tom Jones*, XI. i., where Fielding declares Aristotle, Horace, Longinus, and Bossu to be 'duly authorized to execute at least a judicial Authority in *Foro Literario*'. René Le Bossu (1631–80), the only modern to be included in this list of great critics, was best known for a treatise on epic poetry.

[2] 'Templars' were lawyers with chambers in the Inner or Middle Temple; 'Cits' were tradesmen or shopkeepers, in contrast to gentlemen.

[3] The rights of Roman citizenship.

[4] Fielding condenses and paraphrases the advice given to Gaius Calpurnius Piso, conspirator against Nero in AD 65; after his conspiracy was betrayed, some of his followers nonetheless urged him to take action: 'How much more honourably would he perish in the act of taking his country to his heart—of invoking help for liberty!' (Loeb.) Piso ignored the advice and killed himself when Nero's troops arrived; Tacitus, *Annals*, XV. lix.

Demosthenes, Lucian,[1] and Longinus. The Romans under the Command of Virgil, Horace, Cicero, Tacitus, Terence and Quinctilian. A most formidable Body, all in gilt Armour, and on whom I can rely with great Assurance, as I am convinced the Enemy hold not the least Correspondence with them; a Circumstance which gives me some little Suspicion of my French Forces, of which I have a considerable Body, with Moliere[2] and Bossu at their Head; but though some of the Enemy have been taken dabbling with these, I am well assured they are not likely to come to a perfect good Understanding with them.

Besides these, I have a large Body of English VETERANS, under Bacon and Locke, sent me in by Major-General A. Millar,[3] who is a faithful Ally of the Republic of Letters, and who hath himself raised this Body, all staunch Friends to the Cause.

In the next Place, I have taken sufficient Care to strengthen myself by Alliances with all the Moderns of any considerable Force; but as this hath been carried on by secret Treaties, I cannot, as yet, publish the Names of my Allies.   A.

(To be continued in our next.)

TUESDAY, JANUARY 7, 1752.   NUMB. 2.

——*Redeunt Saturnia Regna.*   Virgil.[4]

In English,

Old Sat——n himself is come to Town.

It hath been, I believe, a common Practice with Men, in all Ages, to complain of the Badness of their own Times, and as readily to commend the Goodness and Virtue of their Fore-fathers. So that it is easy to fix on several Æras in History, which have been the Subject of equal Satire and Panegyric. Succeeding Ages have sung forth the Praises of certain Periods of Time, and have recommended them as Examples to Posterity; which yet, if we believe the Historians, as well as Satyrists, who lived in those very Periods, abounded with all Kinds of Vice and Iniquity.

---

[1] The inclusion of Lucian in this array of distinguished Ancients is typical of Fielding, who regarded Lucian as 'the Father of true Humour'; see *CGJ* No. 52, below.

[2] Fielding's plays *The Mock Doctor* (1732) and *The Miser* (1733) were adaptations of Molière, and his admiration for the French playwright was expressed in *Tom Jones* (XIII. i) and again in *CGJ* No. 10.

[3] Andrew Millar (1707–68), bookseller in the Strand and Fielding's friend and publisher. Johnson called him 'the Maecenas of the age' and declared that he had 'raised the price of literature' (Boswell's *Life*, ed. G. B. Hill and L. F. Powell [Oxford, 1934], i, 287 n.–288). On Millar's possible connection with the *CGJ*, see General Introduction, pp. xxix–xxx; one of Millar's many advertisements in this number of the *CGJ* lists both *The Works of Bacon* and *The Works of Locke*.

[4] *Eclogues*, iv. 6: 'the reign of Saturn returns' (Loeb).

The present Age, notwithstanding its Improvement as well in Virtue, as in Art and Science, doth not escape from this censorious Disposition; with all the Reason which we have to set a Value on ourselves, in Preference to so many other Ages and Countries, there are still some few at this very Time, and in this very Nation, who would persuade us, that Virtue, Taste, Learning, indeed, every Thing worthy of Commendation, were never at a lower Ebb than they are at present among us.

As I am of a different Opinion from these Gentlemen, and as I am naturally inclined to catch at every Opportunity of Panegyric, I shall here endeavour to shew that we are far from deserving any such Character; and that we may be compared with many other Ages and Countries very much to our Advantage.

To say the Truth, Men often lament the Badness of their own Times, as they do the Badness of their own Circumstances, by too injudicious a Comparison. As in the latter Case, they are always lifting their Eyes to those who shine forth in the greatest Riches and Splendor; so, in the former, they have always in their Eye, two or three of those Commonwealths which have made the greatest Figure in History; whereas, if they would act in the contrary Manner, and endeavour in both Cases to make the most advantageous Comparisons, what comfortable Instances would their own Experience afford them in the one, and History in the other?

To pursue therefore this Method on the present Occasion: the first Instance I shall give is that of Sodom and Gomorah.[1] Now though the Sins of these two Cities are not very expresly set forth in Scripture, yet, from the Consequence, I think it very reasonable to conclude, that they were, at least, *somewhat worse* than we are at present.

The Moabites, according to Moses, and the Ægyptians, if we believe some Historians, may likewise afford an advantageous Comparison.[2]

The Corinthians likewise, must surely be allowed to have been worse than us, if we believe the Account given by Strabo of the rich Temple of Venus, in this City, at which above a Thousand Whores officiated as Priestesses.[3] We read likewise in other Authors, that they worshipped a Dæmon, under the Appellation of Cottys, who was the tutelar Deity of all Lewdness and Debauchery.[4] Hence, the most profligate and abandoned in such Vices, were

---

[1] Genesis 18: 20–19: 29.

[2] On the Moabites see Deuteronomy 23: 3–4 and Jeremiah 48: 29–30; for descriptions of the Egyptians of the kind Fielding has in mind, see Herodotus, II. lx, cxi, and cxxvi, or Diodorus Siculus, I. lix, lxxxviii.

[3] Strabo, *Geography*, VIII. vi. 20: 'And the temple of Aphrodite was so rich that it owned more than a thousand temple-slaves, courtesans, whom both men and women had dedicated to the goddess' (Loeb). Cf. Fielding's note on his and William Young's translation of Aristophanes' *Plutus* (1742), p. 13.

[4] Most authorities speak of Cottys as a Thracian rather than Corinthian goddess; see e.g. Strabo, *Geography*, X. iii. 16. Fielding seems to be following Suidas in associating the worship of this 'Daemon'

said Κορινθιαζειν, i.e. to *Corinthize*, or *to be as bad as a Corinthian*; which cannot, I think, be applied to us: for it is much better to have no Religion at all, as is at present our Case, than to profess such Religions as these.

To avoid Prolixity, I will mention only one more People, and these are the Romans themselves, during the Reign of Nero, of whom take the following short Account which Tacitus gives us as a Summary of the prodigious Licentiousness of those Times. "Nero," says my Author, "built a Vessel in Agrippa's Lake; in this Vessel, which was towed by others, he furnished out a Banquet. The Barges were adorned with Gold and Ivory; and the Rowers were all Pathics, placed above each other, according to their Age, or superior Skill in the Science of Debauchery. Nero had ransacked various Countries for every Kind of Flesh and Fowl, and the Ocean itself for Sea Fish: Upon one Bank of the Lake were erected Brothels, which were filled with Ladies of the first Rank; on the other Bank were exposed to View, a Number of Harlots, entirely naked. All Kinds of Lewdness were now acted over; and, as the Night came on, the neighbouring Grove, and all the Buildings near it, were illuminated, and resounded with Music. As for Nero, he defiled himself with every Kind of Lust; nor did he then seem to have left any Manner of Debauchery unpractised; and yet, a few Days afterwards, he contrived to out-do all, by being publickly married, with the utmost Solemnity, to one of his infamous Crew, a Fellow whose Name was Pythagoras. On this Occasion, the Veil in which Women are married was thrown over the Roman Emperor, and all the nuptial Ceremonies, even to the Payment of the Bride's Portion, were observed. Nor did he stop here; but all, which in a lawful Union between the Sexes, is committed to Darkness and the Night, was now acted over in the Face of the World."[1]

I have drawn this Picture at Length, as it is the most curious which, I think, History affords; and those of my Readers, at least, to whom it is new, will, I doubt not, be pleased with seeing it.

Many other Pictures of the same Kind might be drawn from the latter Ages of the Roman Empire; but I chose this from Nero's Reign, as it was a very few Years removed from the latter Days of Tiberius, in which the glorious Romans seem so entirely to have resembled our noble Selves.[2]

From what hath been said may appear the Injustice of these general and outrageous Expressions against the Wickedness of the present Age, which we often hear from the Mouths of illiterate and inconsiderate People, and with the Repetition of which I do not care to affront my polite Reader.

---

primarily with Corinth; see *Suidae Lexicon*, 3 vols. (Cambridge, 1705), s.v. κότυς. This work was in Fielding's library (Baker, item 482).

[1] Tacitus, *Annals*, xv. xxxvii; the translation, which is close, is apparently Fielding's.

[2] Fielding includes Tiberius in his list of 'anointed Tyrants' whose 'abominable Lives' ended in 'terrible Deaths', *JJ* No. 16 (19 Mar. 1748); see also *CGJ* No. 24.

And now surely it must be acknowledged, that we do not live in the worst of Times; but I will not be contented with this Concession. I will now attempt to prove, that we live in the best, in other Words, that this is one of the most virtuous Ages that hath ever appeared in the World.

And first, if Liberty be granted, as it surely must, to be the greatest of all Blessings to any People, nothing can be more manifest, than that we enjoy this in the purest Degree.[1] Doth not every Man in this Kingdom, speak, and write, and even do, whatever best pleaseth him? It is true, indeed, there are some few Exceptions, (enough only to prove a Rule) in which this natural Liberty hath been a little infringed, and I must own there are certain dead Letters,[2] (as they are very properly stiled) called Laws, by which this pure State of Liberty is somewhat abridged; but, *De non apparentibus, et non existentibus, eadem est Ratio.*[3]

Again, the greatest Virtue in the World, (according to the Tenets of a Religion some Time ago professed in this Country, and which, if my Memory fails me not, was called Christian) is Charity; the universal Extensiveness of this, I shall prove by a very strong Argument, which is by that immense Number of Beggars who frequent our Streets, and are to be found almost at every Door. This is so great a Proof of our Charity, that it would be an Affront to the Reader to endeavour to explain it. A Beggar waiting at a Man's Door doth, indeed, as effectually prove his Charity, as a Dun, or Bailiff would assure his Neighbours that he was in Debt.[4]

But there is still a higher Degree of this Virtue than what expands itself towards such Objects; and this is shewn by encouraging Merit in Arts and Sciences: This includes in it the Honour of Taste likewise; and as it very highly adorns the present Age, so doth it in a more particular Manner distinguish what we call our great Men.[5] Former Ages have, indeed, singled

---

[1] As the irony of this passage makes clear, Fielding blamed a mistaken concept of liberty for many of the social disorders and mob violence among the lower classes. See *Enquiry into the Causes of the late Increase of Robbers* (1751), p. xv; *Proposal for Making an Effectual Provision for the Poor* (1753), p. 74; *CGJ* Nos. 47, 49, 55, and 58; and his discourse on liberty in the *Journal of a Voyage to Lisbon*, 21 July [16]; see also General Introduction, p. xl.

[2] 'A writ, statute, ordinance, etc. which is or has become practically without force or inoperative, though not formally repealed or abolished' (*OED*).

[3] A familiar legal maxim, meaning 'that which does not appear will not be presumed to exist'; see Coke, 4 *Reports* 47a. Fielding quotes this also in *Tom Jones*, I. viii, and puts a garbled version in the mouth of lawyer Murphy, *Amelia*, I. x; cf. a similar maxim in *CGJ* No. 40.

[4] In actuality Fielding felt that one must discriminate carefully to find proper objects of charity, and like many in his age he was skeptical about the real needs of the beggars who infested the streets. Cf. *Spectator*, No. 232 (26 Nov. 1711). In his *Enquiry into the Cause of the late Increase of Robbers* (1751) Fielding wrote, 'Mankind are so forward to relieve the Appearance of Distress in their Fellow-creatures, that every Beggar, who can but moderately well personate Misery, is sure to find Relief and Encouragement; and this, though the Giver must have great Reason to doubt the Reality of the Distress, and when he can scarce be ignorant that his Bounty is illegal, and that he is encouraging a Nuisance' (p. 46); cf. *Journey from this World to the Next*, I. xix, and *CGJ* No. 44. For his straightforward praise of charity, see *CGJ* Nos. 29 and 39.

[5] Fielding here ironically voices a complaint which had been a stock-in-trade of the Opposition to

out one or two of the most eminent in every Art and Science, and have conferred Favours upon them as a Kind of Mark of their extraordinary Merit; but I cannot help observing there is some Cruelty in this, and that it is rather a Favour shewn to the Man than to the Art or Science itself. The nobler Method is, that which we now practise, either indiscriminately to reward all alike, at the Expence of a few Sixpences from our Pockets; or, if we make any Distinction at all, it should be, as it is, in Favour of the lowest and meanest Professors, who ought to be preferred to their Betters, as the Charity of the old English Custom preferred the younger Son to the Elder, because, as my Lord Coke observes, these were least able to provide for themselves.[1]

Another Instance of the great Virtue of this Age, is, that great Readiness which every Man shews to serve his Country, and to be employed in its most laborious Duties.

This is a Virtue beyond even the Reach of Plato's Commonwealth; as appears from the following Passage which that Philosopher puts into the Mouth of Socrates; "It seems," says he, "that if there was a City composed of good Men, the Contention among them would be, *who should not* govern, not as it is now, *who should*. Whence it is manifest, that he who is, in very Fact, a true Magistrate, is not so constituted that he may consult his own Good, but that he may provide for the Good of the Subject. Every Man therefore, being conscious of this, would rather chuse that others should labour for his Advantage, than that he should enjoy the Benefit of his own Pains."[2] In this glorious Nation, on the contrary, there is scarce a Man who scruples to plunge through thick and thin, with a View only of putting himself in the Way of serving the Public.[3]

Again, when possest of Power, with how noble and disinterested a Choice do our Great Men confer their Favours on others. That they may avoid the least Suspicion of Partiality, they commonly fill up all Vacancies with such

Walpole; cf., for example, essays in the *Champion*, 13 Dec. 1739 and 8 July 1740; see also *Amelia*, VIII. vi, where Booth reproves Colonel James for rewarding authors with no regard to merit.

[1] Sir Edward Coke, *Commentary upon Littleton*, 11th edn. (1719), II. xi. 211, quotes both Homer and Horace in support of the view that 'the younger Son (if he lack Father and Mother) because of his younger Age, may least of all his Brethren help himself'.

[2] *Republic*, I. xix (347 d).

[3] For similar irony cf. the comment Fielding puts in the mouth of a French visitor to London: 'so grateful are these people, that nobody ever doth anything for the public, but he is certain to make his fortune by it' (Letter XLI contributed to Sarah Fielding's *Familiar Letters between the Principal Characters in David Simple* [1747]). Fielding frequently expresses the ideal of public service for the common good, an ideal he associated with the Stoics; see *Jonathan Wild*, III. xiv, IV. iii, IV. vi, and IV. xi; 'An Essay on the Knowledge of the Characters of Men', *Miscellanies* (1743), ed. H. K. Miller, Wesleyan Edn. (Oxford, 1972), i. 154; and *CGJ* No. 54. In the Author's Introduction to *A Journal of a Voyage to Lisbon*, reflecting on his career as a magistrate, he says, 'I had vanity enough to rank myself with those heroes who, of old times, became voluntary sacrifices to the good of the public', although more modestly he later disclaims 'all pretence to that Spartan or Roman patriotism which loved the public so well that it was always ready to become a voluntary sacrifice to the public good'.

Persons, that it would be in the highest Degree absurd to imagine they were the Objects of any Man's particular Liking or Favour; nay, such is the Generosity of these Great Men, that it is not unusual to bestow very considerable Places on their Footmen:[1] How much more magnificent is this than that bare Manumission[2] which was thought so great a Reward by an old Roman. This is not, I must own, the Invention of these Times, but hath been so long the Practice, that it seems likely to continue *as long as we shall be a People*.

Such are, in short, the Virtues of this Age; that, to use the Words of Cicero, *Si vellem omnia percurrere Dies deficeret* —.[3] I shall therefore omit the rest; being well assured, that no Instances, equal to what I have mentioned, can be found in the Annals of any other Country upon the Face of the whole Earth.   A.

The JOURNAL of the present WAR.
Dated *January* 6, from the Head Quarters.

Nulla venenate est Litera mista Joco.[4]

Having taken all Precautions, and given all the necessary Orders, on the 4th Instant, at Break of Day, we marched into Covent-Garden, and fixed our Head Quarters at the Universal Register Office opposite unto Cecil-Street in the Strand.[5]

A little before our March, however, we sent a large Body of Forces, under the Command of General A. Millar, to take Possession of the most eminent Printing-Houses.[6] The greater Part of these were garrisoned by Detachments from the Regiment of Grub-Street, who all retired at the Approach of our Forces. A small Body, indeed, under the Command of one Peeragrin Puckle, made a slight Show of Resistance; but his Hopes were soon found to be in *Vain*; and, at the first Report of the Approach of a younger Brother of

---

[1] Cf. *Amelia*, XI. ii, in which Dr Harrison explains to a nobleman that denying a man preferment which he merits is not only 'an Act of Injustice to the Man himself, but to the Public, for whose Good principally all public Offices are, or ought to be instituted'; to the nobleman, however, all this is 'mere *Utopia*', 'the Chimerical System of *Plato's* Commonwealth with which we amused ourselves at the University'. Cf. also *Amelia*, XI. i, where Colonel James finds places for his footmen.

[2] The legal act by which slaves were released from their masters.

[3] "The day would be too short if I wished to run through them all.' The same quotation, with *velim* in place of *vellem*, appears in an essay Fielding contributed to *Common Sense* (13 May 1738), the manuscript of which has been described and printed by M. C. with R. R. Battestin, 'A Fielding Discovery, with Some Remarks on the Canon', *SB* 33 (1980), 131–43; the Battestins point out (p. 140, n. 9) that Fielding is apparently paraphrasing Cicero's *De natura deorum*, III. xxxii. 81: *Dies deficiat si velim enumerare*. Fielding uses yet another version of this quotation in *True Patriot*, No. 13 (28 Jan. 1746): *Et dies et charta deficerent si omnia vellem percurrere, multa quidem impura et impudica quae memorare nefas, recitavit.*

[4] Ovid, *Tristia*, ii. 566; the accepted text reads, *nulla venenato littera mixta ioco est*, 'Not a letter of mine is dipped in poisoned jest' (Loeb).

[5] See General Introduction, pp. xxvii–viii.   See *CGJ* No. 1, above.

General Thomas Jones, his whole Body immediately disappeared, and totally overthrew some of their own Friends, who were marching to their Assistance, under the Command of one Rodorick Random. This Rodorick, in a former Skirmish with the People called Critics, had owed some slight Success more to the Weakness of the Critics, than to any Merit of his own.[1]

At the same Time, the better to secure our Retreat in Case we should meet with any Blow at the Court End of the Town, as Success, even in the best concerted Enterprize, is always doubtful, we thought it adviseable to cause two several Bodies of our Forces to move towards the Garrisons of Tom's in Cornhill, and Dick's at Temple Bar;[2] but, to our great Pleasure, we are assured that both those Garrisons opened their Gates to our Troops at the very first Summons, and the whole Body of Critics in both unanimously declared for us; so that the secret Friends of Grub-Street have not since dared to open their Mouths.

All Things being disposed in this Manner, we marched, as I have before said, into Covent-Garden, and presently ordered a Part of our Army to file off to the Right, and to set down before the Bedford Coffee House.[3] We doubt not but we have many good Friends in the Garrison, and who are very

[1] The allusions here to Tobias Smollett's novels *Peregrine Pickle* (1751) and *Roderick Random* (1748) must be understood in the light of Smollett's quarrel with Fielding—a quarrel strictly literary, since there is no evidence the two novelists ever met. When *Peregrine Pickle* appeared in Feb. 1751, it included two sections relevant to Fielding's comments here. First, Smollett incorporated into his novel *The Memoirs of a Lady of Quality*, by the notorious Viscountess Vane (1713–88), whose amours had already been the subject of such works as John Hill's *The History of a Woman of Quality; or, The Adventures of Lady Frail* (published just before *Peregrine Pickle*; for similar efforts by Hill to capitalize on Smollett's use of the Vane memoirs, see G. S. Rousseau, 'Controversy or Collusion? The "Lady Vane" Tracts', *Notes and Queries*, NS 19 [1972], 375–7). With his pun on 'Vain' Fielding alludes to these much-talked-of memoirs. Secondly, *Peregrine Pickle* included a violent attack on Fielding's friend and patron George Lyttelton (portrayed as Sir Gosling Scrag) and a briefer but no less violent assault on Fielding himself (depicted as the poet Mr Spondy) who is advised to apply for patronage to Lyttelton so that 'when he is inclined to marry his own cook-wench, his gracious patron may condescend to give the bride away; and finally settle him in his old age, as a trading Westminster justice' (*Peregrine Pickle* [1751], iv, 123). Other than literary jealousy no motive is known for this attack, which was removed when Smollett revised the novel in 1758.

Until this number of the *CGJ* Fielding had made no response, except possibly to glance at *Peregrine Pickle* and Vane's *Memoirs* in *Amelia* (IV. i and VIII. v). Apparently in response to this paragraph in *CGJ* No. 2 there appeared on 15 Jan. 1752 *A Faithful Narrative of the Base and Inhuman Arts That were lately practised upon the Brain of Habbakkuk Hilding, Justice, Dealer, and Chapman*, a vicious attack generally attributed to Smollett, accusing Fielding, among other things, of having plagiarized the characters of Partridge in *Tom Jones* and Miss Mathews in *Amelia* from Smollett's characters Strap and Miss Williams in *Roderick Random*. For detailed treatment of the relations of the two writers, see H. S. Buck, *A Study in Smollett: Chiefly Peregrine Pickle* (New Haven, 1925), pp. 112–21, and Lewis M. Knapp, *Tobias Smollett* (Princeton, 1949), pp. 125–33.

[2] Coffee-houses. Tom's, in the City, was a rendezvous for young merchants and sometimes visited by Garrick; Dick's or Richard's, in Fleet Street, was sometimes frequented by Gray and Cowper; see B. Lillywhite, *London Coffee Houses* (1963).

[3] Celebrated as a center of wits, critics, and actors, the Bedford 'is every night crowded with men of parts' (*Connoisseur*, No. 1 [31 Jan. 1754]). See *The Memoirs of the Bedford Coffee House* (1763) and Hugh Phillips, *Mid-Georgian London* (1964), pp. 146–7. The most prominent figure to frequent the Bedford in 1752 was John Hill, with whom Fielding here begins his feud; see General Introduction, pp. xxxvii–xxxix.

desirous to admit our Forces, but, as yet, they dare not declare themselves, being kept in Awe by a strange mixed Monster, not much unlike the famous Chimera of old: for while some of our Reconnoiterers tell us that this Monster hath the Appearance of a Lion, others assure us, that his Ears are much longer than those of that generous Beast.[1] Be this as it will, as we are not yet prepared for an Attack, Yesterday, about Six in the Evening, we *blockheaded* up the said Coffee House.

On the 6th Instant, at Night, we received Intelligence at the Head Quarters, that a large and formidable Body of Critics were assembled at a certain Place in St. James's Street,[2] upon which a reconnoitring Party was presently dispatched that Way, upon whose Return we presently perceived the whole to be a false Alarm; for that the suspected Critics were very innocently engaged at certain unlawful Games, and we were well assured, that not a Man of them had looked in a Book for a Month last past. Nay, one of our Spies declared, that the current Bet of the House was Ten to One on our Side; nay, that Five hundred to Three was offered, that the Bedford Coffee House would surrender within a Week; and no Person present would take it up.   A.

(To be continued in our next.)

SATURDAY, JANUARY 11, 1752.   NUMB. 3.

Majores nusquam Rhonchi; Juvenesque, Senesque,
Et Pueri Nasum Rhinocerotis habent.

                                                                    Martial.[3]

In English,

No Town can such a Gang of Critics shew,
Ev'n Boys turn up that Nose they cannot blow.

[1] Alluding to the wooden head of a lion set up by Hill at the Bedford in Nov. 1751 as a receptacle for correspondence to 'the Inspector', under which name he wrote his daily column in *LDA*. The figure had formerly been used by Steele at Button's while Steele was writing the *Guardian*; see the description in *Guardian*, No. 114 (22 July 1713). In response to Fielding's sally here, a news item in *LDA* (8 Jan. 1752) describes how Fielding was devoured by the lion at the Bedford; see also *The March of the Lion, or the Conclusion of the War between Dunce and the Dunces* (1752), in which the 'golden Savage' departs from the Beford in search of new quarters and attacks both Hill and Fielding along the way.

[2] White's, originally a chocolate house and now a private club for aristocratic gamblers; cf. *Tom Jones*, XIII. vi.

[3] *Epigrams*, I. iii. 5–6: 'Nowhere are heard louder sneers; young men and old, even boys, have noses tilted like a rhinoceros' (Loeb); Fielding used the same lines as motto for *True Patriot*, No. 18 (4 Mar. 1746), as a portion of the motto for the *Champion*, 27 Nov. 1739, and as the epigraph for *The Intriguing Chambermaid* (1734). Like much of the rest of this leader the motto in its reference to noses is a prologue to Fielding's defense of *Amelia*; see the 'Covent Garden' Column for 11 Jan. (below, Appendix I), originally appearing in this number, and the comment about Amelia's 'noselessness' in *CGJ* No. 7.

By a Record in the Censor's Office, and now in my Custody, it appears, that at a censorial Inquisition, taken *Tricesimo qto. Eliz.*[1] by one of my illustrious Predecessors, no more than 19 Critics were enrolled in the Cities of London and Westminster; whereas at the last Inquisition taken by myself, 25°. *Geo. 2di.*[2] the Number of Persons claiming a Right to that Order, appears to amount to 276302.

This immense Encrease is, I believe, to be no otherwise accounted for, than from the very blameable Negligence of the late Censors, who have, indeed, converted their Office into a mere Sinecure, no Inquisition, as I can find, having been taken since the Censorship of Isaac Bickerstaffe, Esq; in the latter End of the Reign of Queen Anne.[3]

To the same Neglect are owing many Encroachments on all the other Orders of the Society. That of *Gentlemen* in particular, I observe to have greatly increased, and that of *Sharpers* to have decreased in the same Proportion within these few Years.

All these Irregularities it is my firm Purpose to endeavour at reforming, and to restore the high Office with which I am invested to its ancient Use and Dignity. This, however, must be attempted with Prudence and by slow Degrees: For habitual and inveterate Evils are to be cured by slow Alteratives, and not by violent Remedies. Of this the good Emperor Pertinax will be a lasting Example. "This worthy Man" (says Dion Cassius) "perished by endeavouring too hastily to reform all the Evils which infested his Country. He knew not, it seems, tho' otherwise a Man of very great Knowledge, that it is not safe, nor indeed possible, to effect a Reformation in too many Matters at once. A Rule which, if it holds true in private Life, is much more so when it is applied to those Evils that affect the Public."[4]

I thought it, therefore, not prudent, in the Hurry of my above Inquisition to make any Exceptions, but admitted all who offered to be enrolled. This is a Method which I shall not pursue hereafter, being fully resolved to enquire into the Qualifications of every Pretender.

And that all Persons may come prepared to prove their Right to the Order of Critics, I shall here set down those several Qualifications which will be insisted on before any will be admitted to that high Honour.[5] In doing this,

---

[1] The thirty-fourth year of the reign of Elizabeth, 1592; as is his custom when writing as the Censor, Fielding uses legal language throughout this essay.

[2] The twenty-fifth year of George II, i.e. 1752. With this passage cf. Swift's Preface to *A Tale of a Tub*: 'It is intended that a large Academy be erected, capable of containing nine thousand seven hundred forty and three Persons; which by modest Computation is reckoned to be pretty near the current Number of *Wits* in this Island.'

[3] Bickerstaff was Richard Steele's pseudonym in the *Tatler* (1709–11); on his role as Censor, see esp. *Tatler*, No. 144 (11 Mar. 1710) and No. 162 (22 Apr. 1710). On Fielding's adoption of the Censorial pose, see General Introduction, pp. xxxiv–xxxv.

[4] Dio Cassius, *Roman History*, LXXIV. x. 3; Publius Helvius Pertinax was Roman Emperor from 1 Jan. to 28 Mar. AD 193, when he was slain by the Praetorian guards.

[5] Cf. Fielding's condemnation of the ignorance of critics in *True Patriot*, No. 18 (4 Mar. 1746):

however, I shall strictly pursue the excellent Rule I have cited, and shall act with most perfect Moderation; for I am willing to throw open the Door as wide as I can, so that as few as possible may be rejected.

It is, I think, the Sentiment of Quinctilian, that no Man is capable of becoming a good Critic on a great Poet, but he who is himself a great Poet.[1] This would, indeed, confine the Critics on Poetry, at least, to a very small Number; and would, indeed, strike all the Antients, except only Horace and Longinus off the Roll; of the latter of whom, tho' he was no Poet, Mr. Pope finely says,

> *Thee, great Longinus, all the Nine inspire,*
> *And bless their Critic with a Poet's Fire.*[2]

But with Respect to so great a Name as that of Quinctilian, this Rule appears to me much too rigid. It seems, indeed, to be little less severe than an Injunction that no Man should criticize on Cookery but he who was himself a Cook.[3]

To require what is generally called Learning in a Critic, is altogether as absurd as to require Genius. Why should a Man in this Case, any more than in all others, be bound by any Opinions but his own? Or why should he read by Rule any more than eat by it? If I delight in a Slice of Bullock's Liver or of Oldmixon, why shall I be confined to Turtle or to Swift?[4]

The only Learning, therefore, that I insist upon, is, That my Critic BE

'The Professors of Literature, Prose-writers as well as Poets, labour under this Calamity of being try'd by Judges who never read the Laws over which they preside.' Cf. also *Champion*, 27 Nov., 4 Dec. 1739; and *Tom Jones*, XI. i.

[1] Fielding's uncertainty over the authorship of this sentiment is not surprising, for the idea was a commonplace; passages in Quintilian suggested by Jensen (ii, 154) are not close. But cf. Pope, 'Let such teach others who themselves excell, / and *censure freely* who have *written well*' (*Essay on Criticism*, ll. 15–16) and Ben Jonson, 'To judge of Poets is only the facultie of Poets; and not of all Poets, but the best' (*Timber, or Discoveries*, 1640). J. E. Spingarn points out the wide diffusion of the idea in the 17th cent. (*Critical Essays of the Seventeenth Century* [Oxford, 1908], i. 228) and gives as its ultimate source the *Rhetorica ad Herennium* (iv. 2), a treatise once erroneously attributed to Cicero and cited by Pope as the source of his lines. As Pope's Twickenham editors point out, *Tatler*, No. 239 (19 Oct. 1710) asserts, 'It is ridiculous for any man to criticize on the works of another, who has not distinguished himself by his own performances.' By Fielding's time, however, the maxim had been attacked by Dennis, Warburton, and others.

[2] *Essay on Criticism*, 675–6; Pope writes 'bold' instead of 'great'.

[3] For other examples of Fielding's fondness for cooking metaphors in literary discussion, see *CGJ* No. 28 and *Tom Jones*, I. i, with its extended image of the 'Bill of Fare to the Feast'; such language was parodied in the final number of Thornton's *Drury-Lane Journal* (9 Apr. 1752), and the *Craftsman* for 7 July 1750 wittily described Fielding as 'deeply skilled in the *Theory* of Eating'.

[4] John Oldmixon (1673–1742), Whig journalist and historian, had earned a place in Pope's *Dunciad* (ii. 283–90) by his dullness and his politics; Fielding ridicules him also in *Tom Jones* (v. i) and parodies his historical writing in *CGJ* No. 17, below. In comparing Oldmixon to ox liver and Swift to turtle, Fielding not only uses a natural contrast between two political enemies but also expresses his great admiration for Swift, a constant theme in the *CGJ*; see General Introduction, p. xliv. Turtle flesh was a great delicacy; cf. the *World*, No. 123 (8 May 1755): 'Of all the improvements in the modern kitchen, there are none that can bear a comparison with the introduction of turtle'; see also *Tom Jones*, I. i.

ABLE TO READ; and this is surely very reasonable: For I do not see how he can otherwise be called a Reader; and if I include every Reader in the Name of Critic, it is surely very just to confine every Critic within the Number of Readers.

Nor do I only require the Capacity of Reading, but the actual Exercise of that Capacity; I do here strictly forbid any Persons whatever to pass a definitive Sentence on a Book BEFORE THEY HAVE READ AT LEAST TEN PAGES IN IT, under the Penalty of being for ever rendered incapable of Admission to the Order of Critics.

Thirdly, all Critics who from and after the First Day of February next, shall condemn any Book, shall be ready to give some Reason for their Judgment: Nor shall it be sufficient for such Critic to drivel out, *I don't know not I, but all that I know is, I don't like it.* Provided, nevertheless, that any Reason how foolish or frivolous soever, shall be allowed a good and full Justification; except only the Words POOR STUFF, WRETCHED STUFF, BAD STUFF, SAD STUFF, LOW STUFF, PAULTRY STUFF. All which STUFFS I do forever banish from the Mouths of all Critics.[1]

Provided also, that the last-mentioned Clause do extend only to such Critics as openly proclaim their Censures; for it is our Intention, that all Persons shall be at Liberty to dislike privately, whatever Book they please, *without understanding, or reading one Word of it,* any Thing therein or herein contained to the contrary notwithstanding.

But as it is reasonable to extend this Power of judging for themselves, no farther in this Case of Criticism, than it is allowed to Men in some others, I do here declare, that I shall not, for the future, admit any Males to the Office of Criticism till they be of the full Age of 18, that being the Age when the Laws allow them to have a Capacity of disposing personal Chattles:[2] for, before that Time, they have only the Power of disposing of themselves in the trifling Article of Marriage. Females, perhaps, I shall admit somewhat

---

[1] Fielding may be responding here specifically to the kind of criticism *Amelia* was receiving; cf. his use of these same terms in the 'trial' of his novel in *CGJ* No. 7, below. But his general position about malicious or empty criticism had been frequently expressed earlier. Cf. the *Champion*, 27 Nov. 1739, warning that critics must be 'extremely cautious in the Use of the Words *Low, Dull, Stupid, Sad Stuff, Grub-street,* &c. which, with some few more, I wish heartily were banished out of our Language....' Precisely the same point appears in *Tom Jones*, XI. i. and *True Patriot*, No. 18 (4 Mar. 1746). Cf. the rule in Smart's the *Midwife*, 'That the Words *stuff! ridiculous! vile!* and *low!* which Sounds are the Echo of Nonsense, be made Use of by those Persons only, who are unacquainted with better language' (iii [1753], 75).

[2] Fielding has apparently slipped here, since 'full Age' in English law is 21, not 18; 'At Fourteen, which is his *Age* of Discretion, he may consent to Marriage, and chuse his Guardian; and at Twenty-one he may alien his Lands, Goods and Chattels' (Giles Jacob, *A New Law-Dictionary*, 7th edn. [1756], s.v. 'age'); see also Thomas Wood, *An Institute of the Laws of England*, 7th edn. (1745), p. 12. Though he uses the term 'full Age', Fielding may have meant only that at 18 years the male could 'make a Will for Goods and Chattels' (William Sheppard, *A Grand Abridgment of the Common and Statute Law of England* [1675], i. 131). The spelling 'Chattles' is usual with Fielding but uncommon in this period.

earlier, provided they be either witty or handsome, or have a Fortune of 5000 *l.* and upwards.[1]

Together with Childhood, I exclude all other civil Incapacities; and here I mean not only legal but real Lunatics, and Ideots. In this Number I include all Persons who, from the whole Tenour of their Conduct, appear to be incapable of discerning Good from Bad, Right from Wrong, or Wisdom from Folly, in any Instance whatever.

There are again some Persons whom I shall admit only to a partial Exercise of this Office; as, for Instance, Rakes, Beaux, Sharpers, and fine Ladies, are strictly forbidden, under Penalty of perpetual Exclusion, to presume to criticise on any Works of Religion, or Morality. All Lawyers, Physicians, Surgeons, and Apothecaries, are strictly forbidden to pass any Judgment on those Authors who attempt any Reformation in Law, or Physic. Officers of State, and wou'd-be Officers of State, (honest Men only excepted,) with all their Attendants, and Dependents, their Placemen, and wou'd-be Placemen, Pimps, Spies, Parasites, Informers, and Agents, are forbidden, under the Penalty aforesaid, to give their Opinions of any Work in which the Good of the Kingdom, in general, is designed to be advanced; but as for all Pamphlets which anywise concern the great Cause of WOODALL OUT, and TAKEALL IN, Esqs;[2] full Liberty is left to both Parties, and the one may universally cry up, and commend, and the other may universally censure and condemn, as usual. All Critics offending against this Clause, are to be deemed infamous, and their several Criticisms are hereby declared to be entirely void, and of none Effect.

No Author is to be admitted into the Order of Critics, until he hath read over, and understood, Aristotle, Horace, and Longinus, in their original Language; nor then without a Testimonial that he hath spoken well of some living Author besides himself.[3]

Lastly, all Persons are forbidden, under the Penalty *of our highest Displeasure*, to presume to criticise upon any of those Works with which WE OURSELVES shall think proper to oblige the Public;[4] and any Person who shall presume to offend in this Particular, will not only be expunged from the Roll of Critics, but will be degraded from any other Order to which he shall belong; and his Name will be forthwith entered in the Records of Grub-Street.   A.

ALEXANDER DRAWNCANSIR.

---

[1] Alluding to the extravagant claims made about brides in marriage announcements in the press, a practice Fielding ridicules in his comments in the 'Modern History' section of *CGJ*; see below, Appendix II.

[2] i.e. political pamphlets; see *CGJ* No. 1, above.

[3] For Fielding's expansion of the theme of self-praise among authors, see *CGJ* No. 60.

[4] Doubtless an allusion again to the attacks on *Amelia*, in the context of which this essay on critics must be read.

The JOURNAL *of the present* PAPER WAR.

Yesterday Morning arrived at our Head Quarters David Garrick, and James Lacy, Esqs;[1] and, after only an Hour and half's Waiting, in the Anti-chamber, they had both the Honour to be admitted into the General's Presence, and very humbly presented him with the Keys of their Theatre. The General presently returned them again into the Hands of Mr. Garrick, and was pleased to say they had never been deposited in so proper a Manner.

The General said many kind Things to Mr. Garrick, whom he declared to be, in his Belief, the best Actor the World could have ever produced. His Excellency then enquired after Mr. Woodward,[2] and spoke very highly in his Commendation. He was pleased likewise to speak much in Favour of Mrs. Clive,[3] and Mrs. Pritchard;[4] but dwelt principally on the Praises of Miss Bellamy,[5] who was, he said, not only one of the best Actresses, but one of the finest Women of her Age. "I think," said he, smiling, "if I had the same Trial of my Virtue which Scipio once had,[6] and Miss Bellamy was the Object, I should act in the same Manner; but I fear I should do it with more Reluctance."

[1] David Garrick (1717–79), the great actor, and James Lacy (d. 1774) had been patentees of Drury Lane Theatre since 1747. Garrick and Fielding had been friends from perhaps as early as 1740 (see C. B. Woods, 'The "Miss Lucy" Plays of Fielding and Garrick', *PQ* 41 [1962], 299 and n.), and Fielding's later works are dotted with compliments to him; see e.g. *JJ* No. 10 (6 Feb. 1748) and *Tom Jones*, VII. i. In *CGJ* Fielding consistently praises and supports Garrick's management of Drury Lane; see Nos. 4, 7, 9, 10, 15, 26, 28, 33, and 71.

Lacy had held the patent since 1744; under his agreement with Garrick, 'the settling or altering the business of the Stage' was to be left entirely in Garrick's hands, whereas matters of personnel and salaries were to be agreed upon by both partners. See Dougald MacMillan, *Drury Lane Calendar 1747–1776* (Oxford, 1938), p. xi.

[2] Henry Woodward (1714–77), comic actor and pantomime performer, had rejoined Drury Lane in 1748 and was to remain with Garrick for another 10 years. In Nov. 1752 he became embroiled in a quarrel with John Hill in which Fielding was involved; see *CGJ* No. 71.

[3] Catherine 'Kitty' Clive (1711–85), whom Fielding called 'in Comedy . . . certainly the best Actress the World ever produced' (*JJ* No. 9 [30 Jan. 1748]). Fielding had dedicated to Mrs Clive the printed version of his play *The Intriguing Chambermaid* (1734); for other complimentary references see *Tom Jones*, IX. i; *Miscellanies* (1743), ed. H. K. Miller, Wesleyan Edn. (Oxford, 1972), i. 93; *JJ* No. 10 (6 Feb. 1748), and *Amelia*, I. vi. See also *Joseph Andrews*, ed. Martin Battestin, Wesleyan Edn. (Oxford, 1967), p. 262 n. 5.

[4] Hannah Vaughan Pritchard (1711–68), like most of the actors and actresses mentioned here, had performed in a number of Fielding's plays and was now an important figure in Garrick's company at Drury Lane; she was best known for her role as Lady Macbeth but also performed in comic parts.

[5] George Anne Bellamy (1731?–88), tempestuous Irish actress whose ability in tragic roles and whose extravagant life off-stage made her at this point in her career one of the most popular theatrical figures. Garrick had secured her from Covent Garden at the outset of the season of 1750–1, when she opened the season playing Juliet to Garrick's Romeo, at the same time as Barry and Mrs Cibber were playing the same roles at Covent Garden, with this famous theatrical duel lasting for 12 consecutive nights. Fielding's praise for her here as a woman as well as an actress is typical of the puffs she was now receiving in the press, especially in Hill's 'Inspector' columns in *LDA*; see also *Amelia*, V. viii; Thornton's *Drury-Lane Journal*, 9 Apr. 1752; and *CGJ* No. 13.

[6] Scipio Africanus Major (235–183 BC), 'Scipio the Elder', refused the offer of a beautiful maiden after his conquest of New Carthage in Spain in 210 BC; for different versions of the story, see Plutarch, *Moralia*, 196B 1–2; Livy, xxvi. 49–50; and Aulus Gellius, *Attic Nights*, vii. 8.

Mr. Garrick and Mr. Lacy were then dismissed, both appearing to be highly satisfied with the obliging Reception which they had found; and they seemed to hug themselves greatly with the Re-possession of their Keys, without so much as the Exaction of any Tribute from them.

The General then expressed some Wonder, that Mr. Rich[1] had not yet made his Appearance; but was informed, that he was unluckily shut up in the Bedford Coffee House. Upon this, the General said with a Smile, "I have known the Time when he could have leaped out at any Window of the House; *sed* FUIT *Ilium*."[2] His Excellency then said many kind Things of Mr. Rich, and of his surprizing Genius in the Pantomime Art; and declared, that, if he would exert his Genius that Way, he would be ready to take him under his Protection; "but," added he, "though Mr. Barry and Mrs. Cibber[3] have both their Merit, I fear, in Plays, that House will never be able to contend with the other."[4]

It being reported to the General that a HILL[5] must be levelled, before the Bedford Coffee House could be taken, Orders were given accordingly; but this was afterwards found to be a Mistake, a second Express assuring us, that this HILL was only a little paultry DUNGHILL, and had long before been levelled with the Dirt. The General was then informed of a Report which had been spread by *his Lowness* the Prince of Billingsgate, in the Grub-Street Army, that his Excellency had proposed by a secret Treaty with that Prince, to carry on the War only in Appearance, against him, and so to betray the

---

[1] John Rich (1692–1761), manager of Covent Garden Theatre, pantomimist, and an old butt of Fielding's ridicule, is here associated with John Hill and the wits of the Bedford Coffee-House (see *CGJ* No. 2, above). For Fielding's attitude toward Rich's pantomimes, see *CGJ* No. 12 and notes; his point here, however, is not ridicule of pantomime but support of Garrick in the competition between the two houses.

[2] Alluding to Virgil, *Aeneid*, ii. 325: *fuimus Troes, fuit Ilium*, 'We Trojans are not, Ilium is not', an expression which became proverbial for the decline of formerly great persons or nations.

[3] Spranger Barry (1717?–77), Garrick's greatest rival as a tragic actor, had shared roles like Hamlet and Macbeth with Garrick after the latter became manager in 1747. In 1750, however, feeling constrained by the rivalry and by Garrick's management, he left Drury Lane for Rich's company at Covent Garden, where he was joined by Mrs Susannah Arne Cibber (1714–66). Mrs Cibber, the estranged wife of Colley Cibber's son Theophilus, was noted both as a singer and as an actress. Fielding compliments her in *JJ* Nos. 10 and 11 (6, 13 Feb. 1748), *Tom Jones*, IX. i, and *Amelia*, V. viii; his tone here is more restrained because he wishes to stress the superiority of Drury Lane over Covent Garden. See also *CGJ* No. 71.

[4] Fielding's confidence arises more from his hopes than from the facts of the case; the secession of Barry and Mrs Cibber meant that Covent Garden could now compete on nearly equal terms with Drury Lane in serious drama, with the first result of the new alignment being the *Romeo and Juliet* 'duel' between the two houses in Sept. 1750.

[5] John Hill (1714–75), naturalist, journalist, and miscellaneous writer; for his relations with Fielding, see General Introduction, pp. xxxvii–xxxix. For the image of levelling a hill in literary combat, cf. Swift's *Battle of the Books*, second paragraph. On Hill's career, see G. S. Rousseau, 'John Hill, Universal Genius *Manqué*: Remarks on His Life and Times, with a Checklist of his Works', in *The Renaissance Man in the Eighteenth Century: Papers read at a Clark Library Seminar* (Los Angeles, 1978), pp. 49–129; and *The Letters and Papers of Sir John Hill*, ed. G. S. Rousseau (New York, 1982).

common Cause;[1] upon which his Excellency said with a Smile, *If the Betrayer of a private Treaty could ever deserve the least Credit, yet his* Lowness *here must proclaim himself either a Liar, or a Fool. None can doubt but that he is the former, if he hath feigned this Treaty, and I think few would scruple to call him the latter, if he had rejected it.* The General then declared that the Fact stood thus: His Lowness, said he, *came to my Tent on an Affair of his own.*[2] *I treated him, though a Commander in the Enemy's Camp, with Civility, and even Kindness. I told him, with the utmost good Humour, I should attack his Lion;*[3] *and that he might, if he pleased, in the same Manner, defend him: from which, said I, no great Loss can happen to either Side.* This, the General declared, was all that past, and added, with a little more Bitterness than is usual to him, that *his Lowness* was not only among the meanest of those who ever drew a Pen, but was absolutely the vilest Fellow that ever wore a Head.[4]   A.

(To be continued.)

TUESDAY, JANUARY 14, 1752.   NUMB. 4.

———*Nanum cujusdam Atlanta vocamus:*
Æthiopem Cygnum: parvam extortamque
    puellam
Europen. Canibus pigris Scabieque vetusta
Lævibus, et siccæ lambentibus Ora lucernæ
Nomen erit Pardus, Tigris, Leo; si quid
    adhuc est
Quod fremat in Terris violentius.———

Juvenal Sat. 8.[5]

"One may observe," says Mr. Locke, "in all Languages, certain Words, that, if they be examined, will be found, in their first Original, and their appropriated Use, not to stand for any clear and distinct Ideas." Mr. Locke gives us the Instances "of Wisdom, Glory, Grace. Words which are frequent enough (says he) in every Man's Mouth; but if a great many of those who use

---

[1] Alluding to Hill's claim in his 'Inspector' column in *LDA* (9 Jan. 1752) that Fielding had proposed the two of them wage a 'Mock-fight' to amuse their readers and increase circulation of their papers.

[2] Referring to Hill's appearance in Fielding's court on 8 Jan. 1752 as a witness against one John Smith, who was accused of robbing Hill; see the 'Covent Garden column of 10 Jan., below, Appendix I, and General Introduction, p. xxxviii.   [3] See *CGJ* No. 2, above.

[4] i.e. 'powdered and pomaded hair drawn up over a cushion or stuffing, and dressed' (*OED*). Fielding may be alluding not only to Hill's lack of intelligence but also to his celebrated dandyism; the phrase is echoed sarcastically in Thornton's *Drury-Lane Journal*, Nos. 3 and 7 (30 Jan., 27 Feb. 1752). For the expression 'best He that wears a Head', see *Tom Jones*, VI. xiii, and a similar usage, ibid., VIII. ii.

[5] *Satires*, viii. 32–7: 'We call some one's dwarf an "Atlas," his blackamoor "a swan"; an ill-favoured, misshapen girl we call "Europa"; lazy hounds that are bald with chronic mange, and who lick the edges of a dry lamp, will bear the names of "Pard", "Tiger", "Lion", or of any other animal in the world that roars more fiercely' (Loeb); the accepted text reads *pravam*, not *parvam*.

them, should be asked what they mean by them, they would be at a Stand, and not know what to answer: A plain Proof, that tho' they have learned those Sounds, and have them ready at their Tongue's End; yet there are no determin'd Ideas laid up in their Minds, which are to be expressed to others by them."[1]

Besides the several Causes by him assigned of the Abuse of Words, there is one, which, tho' the great Philosopher hath omitted it, seems to have contributed not a little to the Introduction of this enormous Evil.[2] This is That Privilege which Divines and moral Writers have assumed to themselves of doing Violence to certain Words, in Favour of their own Hypotheses, and of using them in a Sense often directly contrary to that which Custom (the absolute Lord and Master, according to Horace,[3] of all the Modes of Speech) hath allotted them.

Perhaps, indeed, this Fault may be seen in somewhat a milder Light, (and I would always see the Blemishes of such Writers in the mildest.) It may not, perhaps, be so justly owing to any designed Opposition to Custom as a total Ignorance of it. An Ignorance which is almost inseparably annexed to a collegiate Life, and which any Man, indeed, may venture to own without blushing.[4]

But whatever may be the Cause of this Abuse of Words, the Consequence is certainly very bad: For whilst the Author and the World receive different Ideas from the same Words, it will be pretty difficult for them to comprehend each other's Meaning; and hence, perhaps, it is that so many Gentlemen and Ladies have contracted a general Odium to all Works of Religion or Morality; and that many others have been Readers in this Way all their Lives without understanding what they read, consequently without drawing from it any practical Use.

It would, perhaps, be an Office very worthy the Labour of a good Commentator to explain certain hard Words which frequently occur in the Works of Barrow,[5] Tillotson,[6] Clark,[7] and others of this Kind. Such are

---

[1] 'Of the Abuse of Words', *Essay Concerning Human Understanding*, III. x. 2, 3; Fielding quotes with some omissions. He owned the 1751 folio edn. of Locke's *Works* (Baker, item 456).

[2] For Fielding's concern with the corruptions of language see, among numerous instances, *Champion*, 12 and 17 Jan. 1740; Locke is cited also in this context in *Champion*, 27 Mar. 1740, in the notes to *Plutus* (1742), and in the Preface to *Tom Thumb*, 2nd. edn. (1730). On the entire subject see Glenn W. Hatfield, *Henry Fielding and the Language of Irony* (Chicago, 1968), esp. pp. 15–27 for a detailed analysis of this number of the *CGJ*. As Hatfield points out (p. 23), Fielding's telescoping of the quotation from Locke reinforces the ironic pretence that his essay is directed at unworldly divines instead of at the popular corruptions and social ills he is actually satirizing.

[3] *Art of Poetry*, 70–3: 'Many terms that have fallen out of use shall be born again, and those shall fall that are now in repute, if Usage so will it, in whose hands lies the judgement, the right and the rules of speech' (Loeb).

[4] For a full treatment of this theme, see *CGJ* No. 42.

[5] Isaac Barrow (1630–77), Master of Trinity College, Cambridge, and one of the great latitudinarian divines of the 17th cent. In No. 29 Fielding praises him as his 'favourite' divine, and his influence is obvious in the *CGJ*, where he is alluded to or quoted six times (see Nos. 24, 29, 39, 44,

Heaven, Hell, Judgment, Righteousness, Sin, &c. All which, it is reasonable to believe, are at present very little understood.

Instead, however, of undertaking this Task myself, at least, at present, I shall apply the Residue of this Paper to the Use of such Writers only. I shall here give a short Glossary of such Terms as are at present greatly in Use, and shall endeavour to fix to each those exact Ideas which are annexed to every of them in the World; for while the Learned in Colleges do, as I apprehend, consider them all in a very different Light, their Labours are not likely to do much Service to the polite Part of Mankind.

A modern Glossary.[1]

ANGEL.[2] The Name of a Woman, commonly of a very bad one.

AUTHOR. A laughing Stock. It means likewise a poor Fellow, and in general an Object of Contempt.

BEAR. A Country Gentleman; or, indeed, any Animal upon two Legs that doth not make a handsome Bow.[3]

BEAUTY. The Qualification with which Women generally go into Keeping.

BEAU. With the Article A before it, means a great Favourite of all Women.

BRUTE. A Word implying Plain-dealing and Sincerity; but more especially applied to a Philosopher.[4]

CAPTAIN.
COLONEL. } Any Stick of Wood with a Head to it, and a Piece of black Ribband upon that Head.[5]

and 69). For his place in the background of *Joseph Andrews*, see Martin Battestin, *The Moral Basis of Fielding's Art* (Middletown, Conn., 1959); see also *Tom Jones*, ed. Battestin, Wesleyan Edn. (Oxford, 1974), i. 95 n. In *Amelia* Booth is saved from infidelity by reading Barrow's sermons; see Martin Battestin, 'The Problem of *Amelia*: Hume, Barrow, and the Conversion of Captain Booth', *ELH* 41 (1974), 616 ff.

[6] John Tillotson (1630–94), Archbishop of Canterbury and important latitudinarian divine, whose stress on the doctrine of good works appealed to Fielding; see *Joseph Andrews*, I. xvi and *Champion*, 22 Jan. and 15 Mar. 1740.

[7] Samuel Clarke (1675–1729), latitudinarian divine and rationalist theologian. Fielding cites him along with Tillotson in the *Champion*, 22 Jan. 1740, as demonstrating the certainty of a future state and as providing an antidote to 'political philosophers' (Hobbes, Mandeville) who attack the notion of virtue. Clarke is again mentioned in *Amelia*, I. iii; for his influence on that novel, see A. R. Towers, 'Fielding and Dr. Samuel Clarke', *MLN* 70 (1955), 257–60. By an amusing coincidence, just three days before this leader appeared *Old England* (11 Jan. 1752) sarcastically credited Fielding with producing 'Pieces that render all the Documents of *Clark* and *Tillotson* useless'.

[1] One of the more popular items in *CGJ*, this glossary was reprinted (without acknowledgment of source) in *The New Foundling Hospital for Wit*, Part II, 2nd edn. (1768), pp. 40–4, and imitated by the *Craftsman* (8 Feb. 1752) and by Murphy in *Gray's Inn Journal*, No. 89 (29 June 1754).

[2] Described by Jensen (ii. 158) as 'a cant term for a harlot', but the present editor has been unable to confirm this reading.

[3] 'A rough, unmannerly, or uncouth person' (*OED*); Fielding's definition was cited by William Kenrick in his note to his *Pasquinade* (1753), p. 8.

[4] Cf. the dialogue between 'A Philosopher and a Fine Lady', *CGJ* No. 30.

[5] Cf. Fielding's concern with the seductive power of military officers throughout *Amelia* and in *CGJ* Nos. 20 and 68.

CREATURE. A Quality Expression of low Contempt, properly confined only to the Mouths of Ladies who are Right Honourable.[1]

CRITIC. Like *Homo*, a Name common to all human Race.

COXCOMB. A Word of Reproach, and yet, at the same Time, signifying all that is most commendable.

DAMNATION. A Term appropriated to the Theatre; though sometimes more largely applied to all Works of Invention.

DEATH. The final End of Man; as well of the *thinking Part of the Body*, as of all the other Parts.[2]

DRESS. The principal Accomplishment of Men and Women.

DULNESS. A Word applied by all Writers to the Wit and Humour of others.

EATING. A Science.

FINE. An Adjective of a very peculiar Kind, destroying, or, at least, lessening the Force of the Substantive to which it is joined: As *fine* Gentleman, *fine* Lady, *fine* House, *fine* Cloaths, *fine* Taste;—in all which *fine* is to be understood in a Sense somewhat synonymous with useless.

FOOL. A complex Idea,[3] compounded of Poverty, Honesty, Piety, and Simplicity.

GALLANTRY. Fornication and Adultery.[4]

GREAT. Applied to a Thing, signifies Bigness; when to a Man, often Littleness, or Meanness.[5]

GOOD. A Word of as many different Senses as the Greek Word Ἔχω, or as the Latin *Ago*: for which Reason it is but little used by the Polite.

HAPPINESS. Grandeur.

[1] Cf. *Champion*, 17 Nov. 1739, 'A right honourable Rogue . . . is the most contemptible, as well as Ridiculous Object in the Universe', and *Champion*, 17 Jan. 1740, where Fielding says the words 'Honourable' and 'Right Honourable' signify 'no more than if you should pronounce the . . . word *Barababatha*'. Pride in noble birth, in contrast to true virtue, is the theme of Juvenal's *Satire* viii, from which Fielding draws his motto for this leader.

[2] Cf. Fielding's assault on philosophers who deny the immortality of the soul, *Champion*, 22 Jan. 1739/40; see 'Of the Remedy of Affliction', *Miscellanies* (1743) for one of Fielding's many assertions of faith in the Christian scheme of immortality. The materialist language of this definition suggests he has Hobbes particularly in mind here.

[3] '*Ideas* thus made up of several simple ones put together, I call *Complex*' (Locke, *Essay*, II. xii. 1).

[4] For an extension of this definition, see the letter by 'Axylus' in *CGJ* No. 20. Fielding was not alone in decrying the debasement of this term by the practices of the age. Cf. *An Essay on Modern Gallantry* (1750): 'By *Gallantry*, in the modern Sense of that Word, is to be understood, a constant Application to the good Works of Adultery and Fornication; or the prevailing Art of debauching, by any Methods, the Wives and Daughters of any Men whatsoever, especially those of our dearest Friends, and most intimate Acquaintance' (p. 5).

[5] The theme of true and false greatness figures large in Fielding's work. The phrase 'The Great Man' was commonly applied to Walpole by the Opposition to his Administration in the 1730s, and the ironic use of that term is at the heart of *Jonathan Wild*. See also Fielding's discussion of greatness in the preface to his *Miscellanies* and in his poem 'Of True Greatness' (*Miscellanies* [1743]); for commentary see Miller, *Essays*, pp. 42–51.

HONOUR. Duelling.[1]

HUMOUR. Scandalous Lies, Tumbling and Dancing on the Rope.[2]

JUDGE. ⎫
JUSTICE. ⎭ An old Woman.

KNAVE. The Name of four Cards in every Pack.

KNOWLEDGE. In general, means Knowledge of the Town; as this is, indeed, the only Kind of Knowledge ever spoken of in the polite World.

LEARNING. Pedantry.

LOVE. A Word properly applied to our Delight in particular Kinds of Food; sometimes metaphorically spoken of the favourite Objects of all our *Appetites*.

MARRIAGE. A Kind of Traffic carried on between the two Sexes, in which both are constantly endeavouring to cheat each other, and both are commonly Losers in the End.[3]

MISCHIEF. Funn, Sport, or Pastime.

MODESTY. Aukwardness, Rusticity.

NO BODY. All the People in Great Britain, except about 1200.

NONSENSE. Philosophy, especially the Philosophical Writings of the Antients, and more especially of Aristotle.[4]

OPPORTUNITY. The Season of Cuckoldom.

PATRIOT. A Candidate for a Place at Court.[5]

[1] The debasement of the word 'honour' was frequently cited by those who, like Fielding, despised duelling as a violation of Christian principles. Cf. Robert South's fourth sermon on 'the mischievous Influence of Words and Names falsly applied', a sermon which perhaps influenced Fielding's glossary in a general way and which characterizes duelling as 'an outragious, ungoverned, Insolence and Revenge, frequently passing by the Name of *Sense of Honour*' (*Sermons*, 5th edn. [1722], vi, 103–4). See also Addison's *Guardian*, No. 161 (15 Sept. 1713) on true and false honor, and similar essays in the *World*, No. 49 (6 Dec. 1753) and No. 112 (20 Feb. 1755). For similar passages in Fielding, cf. *Journey from this World to the Next*, I. ii, 'the gentleman who died of honour very liberally cursed both his folly and his fencing'; *The Temple Beau* (1730), II. xii, 'You and I had strange notions of that word when we used to read the moralists at Oxford; but our honour here is as different from that as our dress. . . . it forbids us to receive injuries, but not to do them'; *Tom Jones*, VII. xiii.; and especially *Amelia*, IX. iii, where Dr Harrison tries to convince Colonel Bath that his notion of honor is false and unchristian. See also Fielding's passing condemnation of duelling in *CGJ* No. 14 and in the Modern History column of *CGJ* No. 2, below, Appendix II.

[2] See the essays on humor, *CGJ* Nos. 19 and 55.

[3] A piece of cynicism commonplace in the period, especially about marriage in fashionable circles; cf. Fielding's phrase 'legal Prostitution for Hire' to describe Mrs Western's view of marriage (*Tom Jones*, XVI. viii) and the similar attitude, expressed in all seriousness, by the correspondent signing himself 'Humphry Meanwell' in *CGJ* No. 50. Fielding himself, of course, agreed with the comment of Allworthy, 'I have always thought Love the only Foundation of Happiness in a married State' (*Tom Jones*, I. xii); see, for example, his poem 'To a Friend on the Choice of a Wife', *Miscellanies* (1743), i. 42–50.

[4] Fielding was, in fact, unusual in his period for his admiration of Aristotle. Cf. *Enquiry into the Causes of the late Increase of Robbers* (1751), p. 124; *Amelia*, III. x; and *CGJ* No. 70; see Hugh Amory, ed., 'Henry Fielding', *Sale Catalogues of Libraries of Eminent Persons*, vol. vii, *Poets and Men of Letters* (1973), pp. 134–5, and Frederick G. Ribble, 'Aristotle and the "Prudence" Theme of *Tom Jones*', *ECS* 15 (1981), 26–47.

[5] Cf. Dryden, *Absalom and Achitophel*, 'Gull'd with a patriot's name, whose modern sense / Is one

POLITICS. The Art of getting such a Place.

PROMISE. Nothing.

RELIGION. A Word of no Meaning; but which serves as a Bugbear to frighten Children with.

RICHES. The only Thing upon Earth that is really valuable, or desirable.

ROGUE. ⎱
RASCAL. ⎰   A Man of a different Party from yourself.

SERMON. A Sleeping-Dose.

SUNDAY. The best Time for playing at Cards.

SHOCKING. An Epithet which fine Ladies apply to almost every Thing. It is, indeed, an Interjection (if I may so call it) of Delicacy.

TEMPERANCE. Want of Spirit.

TASTE. The present Whim of the Town, whatever it be.[1]

TEASING. Advice; chiefly that of a Husband.

VIRTUE. ⎱
VICE. ⎰   Subjects of Discourse.

WIT. Prophaneness, Indecency, Immorality, Scurrility, Mimickry, Buffoonery. Abuse of all good Men, and especially of the Clergy.[2]

WORTH. Power. Rank. Wealth.

WISDOM. The Art of acquiring all Three.[3]

WORLD. Your own Acquaintance.[4]

                                             A.

JOURNAL *of the* WAR *concluded.*

This Morning, early, when every Man's Expectations were at the highest, of an immediate Battle between the two Armies, on a sudden we were

---

that would by law supplant his prince' (965–6). Though the irony is of general application, Fielding doubtless has partly in mind his own disillusionment with the 'Patriot' Opposition to Walpole, the leaders of which he felt had betrayed the principles of the party by their efforts to get places in the government as Walpole's fall came near; see *The Opposition: A Vision* (1741) and *Joseph Andrews*, II. vii–x. See also *True Patriot*, No. 2 (12 Nov. 1745), where Fielding distinguishes between the true and false patriot, claiming that the word 'hath of late Years been very scandalously abused by some Persons'; cf. the use of 'Woodall Out vs. Takeall In' as a designation of political controversy, *CGJ* No. 1.

[1] For Fielding's belief in a 'true and manly Taste' see *CGJ* Nos. 5 and 10; Letter XL of Sarah Fielding's *Familiar Letters between the Principal Characters in David Simple* (1747), ii. 298; and *Amelia* IX. ix; see also General Introduction, pp. xxxiv–xxxv. Cf. the *World*, No. 12 (22 Mar. 1753), quoting Locke on the abuse of language as a prelude to discussing corruptions of contemporary taste.

[2] A persistent theme in Fielding; see his essays on the 'Apology for the Clergy' in the *Champion*, 29 Mar., 5, 12, and 19 Apr. 1740; *Tom Jones*, VII. xii; and see Battestin, *The Moral Basis of Fielding's Art*, pp. 130–49.

[3] See Fielding's essay on wisdom, *CGJ* No. 69.

[4] Cf. the comment by Fielding's friend James Harris, in attacking the praise of someone for 'knowing the World': 'Why should there not be an accuracy, as well in speaking, as elsewhere? Why should our words, by our foolish hyperboles, so immensely outrun the possibility of a meaning? In praise, and dispraise, . . . all we say is little better, than a continued lie' ('Knowledge of the World, or Good Company. A Dialogue', *Upon the Rise and Progress of Criticism* [1752], p. 46).

surprized with the News of a Peace, of which the following Articles were soon after made public.

Art. 1. That there shall henceforth be a firm Peace, Amity, and Concord, between Sir Alexander Drawcansir, Knt. Lord of &c. and their Lownesses the Republic of Grub-Street.

Art. 2. That all Things shall remain in the Condition they were before the Commencement of the War; and that all Parties thereto shall sit down contented with their own Losses.

Art. 3. That Billinsgate shall be acknowledged for ever, to be a Fief of the low and unmighty Republic; and that Sir Alexander, and all the High Allies do renounce any Right, Title, or Claim, to that Fief for ever.[1]

Art. 4. Contains the Boundaries of Grub-Street, and those of Sir Alexander's Dominions, and is too long to be inserted here. The curious may consult the Treaty at large.

Art. 5. That all the Subjects of the contracting Powers shall have free Liberty to reside, and settle, if they please, in the Dominions of any of the said Powers, and shall have free Ingress, Egress, and Regress, without any Molestation, or Examination whatsoever.

Art. 6. That it shall be lawful for all the Subjects of the Low and Unmighty Republic to carry on a free and open Trade in the Dominions of Sir Alexander: Provided, however, that all Blasphemy, Profaneness, and Indecency, shall be accounted contraband Goods, and as such, be liable at all Times to be seized, and burnt; but that it shall be lawful for the Subjects of the said Republic to import their Dulness as usual; and that all the Booksellers of the said Republic, settled in the Dominions of Sir Alexander, shall have free Liberty, as usual, to vend the said Dulness, as if it was the lawful Property, and in the Name of the Subjects of the said Alexander.

Art. 7. That his Lowness the Prince of Billinsgate, and all his Liege People, shall have free Liberty to import every Kind of Scurrility, as heretofore, into the Dominions of Sir Alexander; but that the aforesaid Booksellers shall not vend the said Wares under the Name of Sir Alexander himself, or any of his Subjects.[2] And to prevent this most effectually, as well as to secure to the said Low and Unmighty Republic the sole Property of all the Productions of its said Fief, it is hereby declared, agreed, and ratified, that all Kinds of Scurrility, personal Abuse, and other the known Wares[3] of

---

[1] Literally London's fish market, but Fielding means, of course, the realm of abusive language for which 'Billingsgate' was the general term. In *JJ* Billingsgate and Grub Street are frequently coupled; see e.g. No. 1 (5 Dec. 1747), No. 20 (16 Apr. 1748), and No. 31 (2 July 1748). The Court of Criticism in *JJ* No. 11 (13 Feb. 1748) reports on proceedings between the 'Corporation of *Grub-street*, Plaintiff, and the Corporation of *Billingsgate*, Defendant' over the property of a scandalous pamphlet.

[2] Despite the light tone here, Fielding complained seriously and frequently about the common charge that he was the author of scurrilous writings; see, among many examples, the preface to *Of True Greatness* (1741); the Preface to his *Miscellanies* (1743); *Tom Jones*, XVIII. i; and *CGJ* No. 72.

[3] A legal locution; cf. the same usage in *CGJ* No. 15, 'Court of Censorial Inquiry'.

Billinsgate, shall henceforth be acknowledged to belong to, and to be the sole and undoubted Property of the Low Republic of Grub-Street aforesaid.

Art. 8. That it shall not be lawful for the said Sir Alexander, or any of his Subjects, or Allies, to publish and vend from henceforth, any more than one Paper of Entertainment and News, to be called and known by the Name of the *Covent-Garden Journal.*[1] And that all other Papers, commonly called News Papers, shall be, and remain, to the said Low Republic, as the sole and entire Property of the said Low Republic, for ever.

Art. 9. That the Theatre Royal in Drury-Lane, shall be, and remain to the said Sir Alexander for so long Time only as David Garrick and James Lacy, Esqs; the well-beloved Subjects of the said Sir Alexander, shall continue to superintend the said Theatre; and at the Expiration of the said Superintendency and Acting of the said David, the Right of the said Theatre shall again revert unto the Low Republic, to whom it had, of many Years belonged, when the said David and James first came to the Superintendency thereof.[2] That as to the Theatre in Covent-Garden, it shall still remain in the same neutral State in which it hath continued from Time immemorial.

Art. 10. That the acting Subjects of the Low Republic shall be admitted to subaltern Parts on the Stage in Drury-Lane, and to capital Parts on the other Stage, and that the writing Subjects of the said Low Republic, shall be at all Times at Liberty to puff up, and commend, their acting Brethren.

Art. 11. That Sir Alexander Drawncansir may, when he pleases, erect one Court of Criticism, and preside in the same, as he and his Predecessors, Censors of this Realm, have of Right always done.[3] And that all the Wares of the Low Republic, except the News Papers, may be tried and examined in the said Court; but that the Persons of all the Subjects of the said Republic, together with their moral, or rather immoral Characters, shall be exempted from the Jurisdiction of the said Court.

These are the most material Articles, there are some others of less Moment with which we may possibly acquaint our Readers hereafter.

On Saturday next in this Paper will be held a Court of Censorial Enquiry, of which *all Persons concerned are required to take Notice.*

---

[1] As Jensen suggests (ii. 160) Fielding may be attempting to disown the *Covent-Garden Journal Extraordinary*, but this was a parody not likely to be confused with his own work and did not appear until 20 Jan., 6 days after this comment. The remark is perhaps intended merely to distinguish in a general way his own superior product from the Grub-street level of other papers of entertainment and news.

[2] On Garrick, Lacy, and Fielding's support of Drury Lane in its rivalry with Covent Garden, see *CGJ* No. 3, above.

[3] In the *Champion*, 17 May 1740, Fielding initiated 'Proceedings at a Court of Censorial Enquiry held before Captain Hercules Vinegar, Great Champion and Censor of Great Britain'; this device he continued in *JJ*, establishing in No. 6 (9 Jan. 1748) a 'Court of Criticism', again associating such a court with his 'high Censorial Office' and with his predecessors as Censor, Addison and Steele. See General Introduction, pp. xxxiv–xxxv.

SATURDAY, JANUARY 18, 1752. NUMB. 5.

Nostrisque ductum seditionibus
Bellum resedit——. HORACE.[1]

Paraphrased.

The War, I thank Fortune, is now at an End,
Since I scarce could distinguish my Foe from my Friend.

There never was a Peace so wholesome and advantageous to any Country, but that some Persons who have found or proposed to themselves certain Emoluments from the Continuance of the War, have openly dared to censure and malign it.[2]

I do not wonder, therefore, to find that the Peace, which I have lately concluded with the Low Republic, is not received by all my Readers with universal Approbation. One of my Correspondents, in a Rage, asserts that it was base and cowardly; a second declares, that he would have made no Peace while a single Drop of his Ink had remained; and a third, with a very grave and political Air, assures me, that the Enemy was brought to such a State of Distress, and so torn with intestine Broils, there being scarce two Members of the Republic who do not heartily hate each other, that had the War continued but one Campaign, I might have obtained what Concessions I would have asked, or might have extirpated the whole Race of Grub-Street for ever.

But, notwithstanding these Opinions, all which I am well persuaded have many Supporters, I do assert, that this Peace was made by me, from very solid and substantial Reasons; and I doubt not but that after-Ages, when Party and Prejudice shall subside; when the Reason of Things, and not private Views, shall lead Mens Judgments, this Peace will be reckoned as wise a Measure as was ever concerted in the Cabinet; indeed a Master-Piece (or as the Enemy* calls it, a *Coup de Maitre*) in Politics.

Nor is the Interest, which many good People proposed to themselves in

---

* By the 14th Article of the Treaty of Covent-Garden, the Importation of French Words and Phrases in English Writings is declared to be the sole Right of Grub-Street.[3]

---

[1] *Odes*, III. iii. 29–30: 'And the war our feuds had lengthened, now has ended' (Loeb).

[2] Fielding refers to his peace treaty with Grub Street, announced in *CGJ* No. 4, but the paragraph and much of the essay which follows are highly reminiscent of his support in *JJ* of the peace policies of the Pelham wing of the Administration; see especially *JJ* No. 24 (14 May 1748) categorizing those 'who cannot be expected to concur in this general Thanksgiving' after the signing of the Preliminaries of the Treaty of Aix-la-Chapelle.

[3] One of the Articles 'of less Moment' not specified in the list given in *CGJ* No. 4. The use of French words was condemned throughout the period as a sign of foppery and affectation, though not generally associated with Grub Street writing; cf. Addison in *Spectator*, No. 165 (8 Sept. 1711) condemning the use of French phrases in newspapers; *Dunciad*, iv. 595–8; and Fielding's treatment of the fop Bellarmine in *Joseph Andrews*, II. iv.

the Continuance of the War, so great a Secret to me, as some may imagine. Sorry am I to say, that their own Diversion, and not the general good of the allied Cause, is at the Bottom of their Hearts. So powerful is the Love of Laughter in depraved Minds, that they care not what nor whom they sacrifice to its Gratification. The too general Prevalency of this Disposition hath been, in all Times, of infinite Service to Grub-Street. Had Mankind, indeed, restrained this Inclination within proper Rules, and had refused to indulge it at the Expence of common Sense and common Humanity, the Name of Grub-Street, would have long since been obliterated out of the Memory of Man.

To such Gentlemen as these I shall offer no Arguments; but to all my sober and sensible Readers, to all, in short, who know how to be *merry and wise*[1] I am convinced I shall appear to have acted very prudently in putting an End to the late War almost on any Terms.

First, it was a War in which nothing but dry Blows could be obtained on my Side; whilst the Enemy had much to hope, and as little to fear. In such a Case, notwithstanding any Superiority of Force, the wisest Measures must tend towards a Pacification.

Secondly, The unfair Methods made use of by the Enemy, are a second Reason for concluding a Peace. This may be illustrated by a familiar Instance; Mr. Sherlock[2] is, I believe, justly allowed to be superior to all Europe in the Skill of the Broad Sword; but what would this Skill avail him against a number of Blunderbusses? might he not, without any Blemish to his Courage or his Skill, retreat from such an Enemy; when these Blunderbusses were moreover loaded with ragged Bullets; and when like the poisoned Arrows of the wild Indians, they were discharged at him from lurking Holes and Places of Security?

Again, who but a Mad-man would engage with an Enemy that is invulnerable! And this, however strange it appears, was, in Reality, the Case: For several of the Enemy, as we are well assured, did in certain Skirmishes with our Forces, receive such Blows on their Heads with the sharpest Weapons, as must have proved fatal to any common Man; but to our great Surprize we found that they were not in the least hurt by these Blows, that many did not feel them, and some did even declare they were never hit.[3] In real Truth, *as Grass escapes the Scythe by being low,*[4] a Man may escape the

---

[1] Proverbial: 'Good to be merry and wise' (Tilley, G 324).

[2] Francis Sherlock, fencing-master, who in 1752 was conducting a school at Charing Cross Coffee-House and who was famed 'for his Judgment in the Broad-Sword' (*DA*, 31 Mar. 1749). Sherlock frequently accepted challenges for public combat; see *DA*, 28 Aug. 1745, 19 Dec. 1747, and 20 Apr. 1752; *GA*, 1 Apr. 1752.

[3] Cf. Pope, *Epistle to Dr. Arbuthnot*, 83–4: 'You think this cruel? take it for a rule, / No creature smarts so little as a Fool.'

[4] Source unidentified, but cf. the proverb, 'High cedars fall (are shaken) when low shrubs remain (are scarcely moved)' (Tilley, C 208).

sharpest Satire by the same means: For Ridicule may bring any Person into Contempt; but what is already the Object of our Contempt, can never be raised to be the proper Object of Ridicule.[1]

And beside these Discouragements, I had some little Reason to suspect whether I should have fair Play in the Contest. It is the Advice of Machiavel, *that when two Parties are at Variance in a City, you should side with the weakest, in order to foment and continue the War.*[2] This is a Rule in Politics, which Men are naturally enough inclined to follow; when a Superior and Inferior ingage, the World, as well as the Mob, are apt to side with the latter; and, therefore, when the comic Writer says, "There is nothing *so moving* as a great Man in Distress;"[3] I suppose he means, there is nothing so apt *to move Laughter.*

I might, however, be contented to indulge this risible Inclination in my Readers, at the Expence of having all the abusive Words in the *English* Language discharged at me, had I no other Objection; but this would too much interrupt the Design of my Paper; which, if the Public will grant me but a little of their Patience, will, I hope, appear to be much nobler than that of diverting them, by sacrificing two or three poor Writers to their Mirth. However vain or romantic the Attempt may seem, I am sanguine enough to aim at serving the noble Interests of Religion, Virtue, and good Sense, by these my Lucubrations.

To effect so glorious a Purpose, I know no readier a Way than by an Endeavour to restore that true and manly Taste, which hath, within these few Years, degenerated in these Kingdoms.[4] A Degeneracy which hath been greatly owing to those base and scandalous Writings, which the Press hath lately poured in such a Torrent upon us, that the Name of an Author is, in the Ears of all good Men, become almost an infamous Appellation. Religion, Virtue, Modesty, Decency, and the Characters of some of the best of Men, have been all violated by these Writings; insomuch, that when we consider the Impressions which young Minds are apt to conceive from Books, the very learning to read seems a dangerous Part of a Child's Education.[5]

Against Works of this Kind was the jocose War declared, and against such

---

[1] For Fielding's major statement on the proper objects of ridicule, see the Preface to *Joseph Andrews*; see also *CGJ* No. 55.

[2] *Discourses*, II. xxv; Fielding adapts, with some paraphrasing, the translation of *The Works of the Famous Nicholas Machiavel*, 3rd edn. (1720), p. 367, a volume in his library (Baker, item 447).

[3] Slightly altered from John Gay's *The Beggar's Opera* (1728), III. xv, Lucy speaking of Macheath's imminent hanging. Quoted also in *Shamela*, Letter XII.

[4] See General Introduction, pp. xxxiv–xxxv; see also *CGJ* No. 10.

[5] Cf. the 'Covent Garden' column of 13 Apr. 1752 (below, Appendix I), puffing Fielding's *Examples of the Interposition of Providence* as a book suitable for the impressionable minds of young children and citing Locke (*Essay*, II. xxxiii. 8–10) on the danger of improper connections of ideas at an early stage of education.

Attacks on calumny and scurrilous writing are a consistent theme in Fielding; for examples in the years just before the *CGJ*, see *JJ* Nos. 20, 26, 28, and 29 (16 Apr., 28 May, 11 and 18 June 1748) and *A Charge to the Grand Jury* (1749); see also *CGJ* Nos. 6, 14, and 16.

Works, Ridicule was surely no hard nor immoderate Weapon. It was not my Intention to attack the Character of any Person; and if I have been once provoked to so disagreeable an Excess,[1] no Provocation shall again hurry me so far. Vice and Folly, and not particular Men, will be the Objects of Satire in this Paper; and if any Man blushes when he reads it, he shall have the Pleasure of imputing it to his own Grace, and not to the Malignity of the Writer.

There is no Precept in the whole Christian Religion which is less a Stumbling-Block in my Way, than that which forbids us to take Vengeance on our Enemies; and I can, with great Truth, declare, that I do not at this Instant, wish Ill to any Man living. Indeed, if a Sentiment which I heard drop from the late Mr. Pope be true, *That Nature never produced a more venemous Animal than a* BAD AUTHOR,[2] I am sure that I want, at least, one Ingredient in that Character.

And as Nothing is less agreeable to my own Disposition than private Abuse, so Nothing is more foreign to the Plan of this Paper. When Hercules undertook to cleanse the Stables of Augeas, (a Work not much unlike my present Undertaking) should any little Clod of Dirt, more filthy perhaps, than all the rest, have chanced to bedawb him, how unworthy his Spirit would it have been, to have polluted his Hands, by seizing the dirty Clod, and crumbling it to Pieces. He should have known that such Accidents are incident to such an Undertaking: which, though both a useful and heroic Office, was yet none of the cleanliest; since no Man, I believe, ever removed great Quantities of Dirt from any Place, without finding some of it sticking to his Skirts.   A.

At a Court *of* Censorial Enquiry *now held this* 18th *of* January, 1752. *before the truly respectable* Sir ALEXANDER DRAWCANSIR, *Knt. Censor of* Great-Britain.

The Court was opened by the Censor, with a very learned and elegant Speech: setting forth the great Antiquity, and Usefulness of this Court, and the many Inconveniencies which had attended the Society by the long Discontinuance;[3] but as he hath been pleased to give the Public much of the Substance of this Speech in his Essay of To-day, we will not here transcribe it at large.

[1] Referring to his denunciation of John Hill in *CGJ* No. 3, above.

[2] Fielding was apparently introduced to Pope by Ralph Allen at Prior Park in the closing months of 1741; for a careful account of the meeting see Martin C. Battestin, 'Lord Hervey's Role in *Joseph Andrews*', *PQ* 42 (1963), esp. 236–9. It was during this visit to the Allens that Pope wrote *The New Dunciad*; a discussion of 'bad authors' would have been natural enough in the conversation between the two authors. At about the same time Fielding was writing *A Journey from this World to the Next*, in which Julian reports a remark made by 'some one of later days, that there are no worse men than bad authors' (I. xxiv). For Fielding's slightly ironic portrait of Pope as literary monarch, see *CGJ* No. 23.

[3] Fielding's last 'Court of Criticism' had been presented in *JJ* No. 33 (16 July 1748); see *CGJ* No. 4, above.

The Court then came to several Resolutions.

First, It was resolved, That it of Right belongs to this Court to hear, and determine, all manner of Causes, which in anywise relate to the Republic of Letters. To examine, try, recommend, or condemn, all Books, and Pamphlets, of whatever Size, or on whatever Subject.

Secondly, That it is at the Discretion of this Court to pass any of the following Sentences on such Book, or Pamphlet, as shall, after a full and fair Hearing, be judged worthy of Condemnation; that is to say, 1. To be imprisoned on the Shelf, or in the Warehouse of the Bookseller. 2. To be immediately converted into waste Paper. 3. To be burnt by the Hands of the common Hangman, or by those of some common Publisher of Scandal, which are, perhaps, much the more infamous.

Thirdly, That, after any such Judgment passed by this Court, it shall not be lawful for any Person whatever, to purchase, or read, the said Book, or Pamphlet, under the Penalty of being considered as in Contempt.

Fourthly, For the more easy carrying on our Design of examining all Books which shall, from Time to Time, be made public, it is ordered, that all Booksellers do, previous to their publishing, or vending, any Book, or Pamphlet, present unto our Clerk in Court, for our Use, one fair Copy of all such Books, and Pamphlets; and that (in Case it be a Book) the same be well bound and gilt, and do contain, in gilt Letters on the Back, the Name, or Title, of the said Book.

Fifthly, Resolved, That both the Theatres, and all other Places of Diversion and Resort, are under our Protection; and every thing which passes at any of these, is subject to our Cognizance and Jurisdiction. For which Reason, we do most earnestly and seriously recommend to all our trusty and well-beloved People to send us immediate Notice of any Misconduct or Misbehaviour that shall happen in any of the Managers of these Places of Diversion, or in any of the Performers or Spectators.[1]

Sixthly, Resolved, That all Places of general Rendezvous, tho' at a private House, shall be deemed public Places, and the Masters and Mistresses of all such Houses shall be considered in the same Light as the Managers of our public Theatres; and shall be equally subject to the Jurisdiction of this Court.

Seventhly, Whereas, by the Statute of Good-Breeding,[2] the wearing a Hat in the Boxes, at the Play-House, before or behind the Ladies, is a very great

---

[1] A constant theme in *CGJ* as in other essay-journals of the period. See *CGJ* Nos. 13, 16, 17, 26, and 27; as other instances, among many, see *Tatler*, No. 122 (19 Jan. 1710); *Spectator*, Nos. 208 (29 Oct. 1711), 235 (29 Nov. 1711), and 240 (5 Dec. 1711); and *Rambler*, No. 195 (28 Jan. 1752). For an actor's condemnation of unruly audiences, see Charles Macklin's farce *Covent-Garden Theatre; or, Pasquin turn'd Drawcansir* (1752); on the general topic of audience behavior in this period, see *London Stage*, Pt. 4, vol. i, pp. clxxxiv–cxcviii.

[2] See *CGJ* Nos. 55 and 56; and see General Introduction, pp. xlii–xliii.

Offence, that swearing or talking loud, is, likewise, under very severe Penalties forbidden by the said Statute; all our Officers in the Pit are strictly charged to see the said Law carried into vigorous Execution.

Eighthly, In the Statute of Gallantry,[1] are these Words, "Provided that for the future, a fierce Cock of the Hat be not considered as any Mark of Valour in any Person whatever, save only in Attorney's Clerks, Apprentices, Gamblers, and Bullies:" Resolved, therefore, that it shall be lawful for any honest and sober Man, at all Times to remove all such Hats from the Blocks on which they are displayed, with absolute Impunity, saving to the said Clerks, their antient Right.

Ninthly, Resolved, That laughing, grinning, whispering, and staring Modesty out of Countenance, are to be reputed Wit in any Ale-House, and at Sadler's Wells;[2] but at no other Place whatsoever.

Tenthly, Resolved, That to give an Affront or Offence at any public Place, to sober and grave Persons, to the Ladies, or to the Clergy,[3] is a very high Crime and Misdemeanor, strictly forbidden by the Laws of Decency; and whoever is convicted thereof, will be struck out of the Order of Gentlemen, at the next Inquisition to be taken of that Order.

Adjourned.

To the PUBLIC.

All Gentlemen Poets, and others, who are willing to serve and please their Country, by publishing their Elegies, Songs, Epigrams, and other short Pieces, under the Inspection of Sir ALEXANDER DRAWCANSIR, *Knt. are desired to send in their said Pieces to the* Universal Register Office, *opposite* Cecil-Street, *in the* Strand, *where they shall receive all fitting Encouragement.*　　　　A.

TUESDAY, JANUARY 21, 1752.　　NUMB. 6.

Quam multi tineas pascunt, blattasque diserti!
Et redimunt soli carmina docta coci!
Nescio quid plus est quod donat secula chartis,
Victurus genium debet habere Liber.

Martial lib.6.[4]

[1] See *CGJ* No. 4 for the meaning of this word in Fielding's 'Modern Glossary'.

[2] In Islington, a mineral water spa with a theater used primarily for pantomime, wire-walking, and the like. A middle-class resort, Sadler's Wells forms the scene of Hogarth's 'Evening' in *The Four Times of the Day* (1738); cf. a poem contrasting the 'beaux and belles' at Vauxhall with the 'happier cits' at Sadler's Wells, cited by Ronald Paulson, *Hogarth's Graphic Works* (New Haven, 1965), i. 180.

[3] Cf. *Amelia*, IX. ix., in which Amelia and Dr Harrison are affronted by young sparks at Vauxhall; and see the definition of 'wit' in the Modern Glossary, *CGJ* No. 4 above, p. 38, and n. 2.

[4] *Epigrams*, VI. lxi. 7–10: 'How many fluent writers feed moths and bookworms, and cooks alone buy their learned lays! There is something more that gives immortality to writings; a book, to live, must have a Genius' (Loeb).

How many fear the Moth's and Bookworm's Rage,
And Pastry-Cooks, sole Buyers in this Age?
What can these Murtherers of Wit controul?
To be immortal, Books must have a Soul.

There are no human Productions to which Time seems so bitter and malicious an Enemy, as to the Works of the learned: for though all the Pride and Boast of Art must sooner, or later, yield to this great Destroyer; though all the Labours of the Architect, the Statuary, and the Painter, must share the same Mortality with their Authors; yet, with these, Time acts in a gentler and milder Manner, allows them generally a reasonable Period of Existence, and brings them to an End by a gradual and imperceptible Decay: so that they may seem rather cut off by the fatal Laws of Necessity, than to be destroyed by any such Act of Violence, as this cruel Tyrant daily executes on us Writers.

It is true, indeed, there are some Exceptions to this Rule; some few Works of Learning have not only equalled, but far exceeded, all other human Labours in their Duration; but alas! how very few are these, compared to that vast Number which have been swallowed up by this great Destroyer. Many of them cut off in their very Prime; others in their early Youth; and others, again, at their very Birth; so that they can scarce be said ever to have been.[1]

And, as to the few that remain to us, is not their long Existence to be attributed to their own unconquerable Spirit, and rather to the Weakness, than to the Mercy of Time? Have not many of their Authors foreseen, and foretold, the Endeavours which would be exerted to destroy them, and have boldly asserted their just Claim to Immortality, in Defiance of all the Malice, all the Cunning, and all the Power of Time?

Indeed, when we consider the many various Engines which have been employed for this destructive Purpose, it will be Matter of Wonder, that any of the Writings of Antiquity have been able to make their Escape. This might almost lead us into a Belief, that the Writers were really possessed of that Divinity, to which some of them pretended, especially as those which seem to have had the best Pretensions to this Divinity, have been almost the only ones which have escaped into our Hands.

And here, not to mention those great Engines of Destruction which Ovid so boldly defies, such as Swords, and Fire, and the devouring Moths of

---

[1] Cf. Swift, *A Tale of a Tub*, 'Epistle Dedicatory, to His Royal Highness Prince Posterity': 'It were endless to recount the several Methods of Tyranny and Destruction, which Your *Governour* [Time] is pleased to practise upon this Occasion. His inveterate Malice is such to the Writings of our Age, that of several Thousands produced yearly from this renowned City, before the next Revolution of the Sun, there is not one to be heard of.' Fielding's essay appears to owe much to this section of Swift's *Tale*.

Antiquity,[1] how many cunning Methods hath the Malice of Time invented, of later Days, to extirpate the Works of the Learned, and to convert the Invention of Paper, and even of Printing, to the total Abolition of those very Works which they were so ingeniously calculated to perpetuate.[2]

The first of these, Decency will permit me barely to hint to the Reader. It is the Application of it to a Use for which Parchment and Vellum, the antient Repositories of Learning, would have been utterly unfit. To this cunning Invention of Time, therefore, Printing and Paper have chiefly betrayed the Learned; nor can I see, without Indignation, the Booksellers, those great Enemies of Authors, endeavouring by all their sinister Arts to propagate so destructive a Method: for what is commoner than to see Books advertised to be printed *on a superfine, delicate, soft Paper*, and again, *very proper to be had in all Families*, a plain Insinuation to what Use they are adapted, according to these Lines.

> *Lintott's for gen'ral Use are fit,*
> *For some Folks read, but all Folks* ——.[3]

By this abominable Method, the whole Works of several modern Authors have been so obliterated, that the most curious Searcher into Antiquity, hereafter, will never be able to wipe off the Injuries of Time.

And, yet, so truly do the Booksellers verify that old Observation, *dulcis odor lucri ex requalibet*,[4] that they are daily publishing several Works, manifestly calculated for this Use only; nay, I am told, that one of them is, by Means of a proper Translator, preparing the whole Works of Plato for the B—.[5]

Next to the Booksellers are the Trunk-makers, a Set of Men who have of late Years made the most intolerable Depredations on modern Learning.[6] The ingenious Hogarth hath very finely satyriz'd this, by representing

---

[1] *Metamorphoses*, xv. 871–2: 'And now my work is done, which neither the wrath of Jove, nor fire, nor sword, nor the gnawing tooth of time shall ever be able to undo' (Loeb).

[2] Cf. Swift, *A Tale of a Tub*, 'Epistle Dedicatory': 'It ill befits the Distance between *Your Highness* and Me, to send You for ocular Conviction to a *Jakes*, or an *Oven*; to the Windows of a *Bawdy-house*, or to a sordid *Lanthorn*. Books, like Men their Authors, have no more than one Way of coming into the World, but there are ten Thousand to go out of it, and return no more.'

[3] Lines 29–30 of Pope's 'Verses To be prefix'd before Bernard Lintot's New Miscellany' (1712); the original reads, 'all Folks sh—'. On the bookseller Bernard Lintot, see *CGJ* No. 19, below.

[4] An altered version of Juvenal, *Satires*, xiv. 204: *lucri bonus est odor ex re / qualibet*: 'The smell of gain is good whatever the thing from which it comes' (Loeb).

[5] 'Bum'; cf. Fielding's satire on booksellers' projects for translations of the classics, *The Author's Farce* (1730), II. vi.

[6] The routine use of waste paper for lining trunks, wrapping pies, and the like was converted into a commonplace satirical symbol for dullness and hack writing. In *JJ* No. 7 (16 Jan. 1748) Fielding's 'Court of Criticism' is approached by a 'Council who said he was employ'd by the Pastry-Cooks and the Makers of Trunks and Band-boxes' to represent their interests in the Court's efforts to prohibit bad books. Cf. Pope's promise that when he resorts to flattery his 'dirty leaves' will 'Cloath spice, line trunks, or flutt'ring in a row / Befringe the rails of Bedlam and Sohoe' (*Imit. of Horace*, Epist. II. i, 'To Augustus', 418–19). See also *CGJ* No. 24 and *Grub-street Journal*, No. 17 (30 Apr. 1730), the latter an ironic tribute to a waste-paper merchant for his 'particular Regard' to Grub Street authors.

several of the most valuable Productions of these Times on the Way to the Trunk-maker.[1] If these Persons would line a Trunk with a whole Pamphlet, they might possibly do more Good than Harm; for then, perhaps, the Works of last Year might be found in our Trunks, when they were possibly to be found no where else; but so far from this, they seem to take a Delight in dismembring Authors; and in placing their several Limbs together in the most absurd Manner. Thus while the Bottom of a Trunk contains a Piece of Poetry, the Top presents us with a Sheet of Romance, and the Sides and Ends are adorned with mangled Libels of various Kinds.

The third Species of these Depredators, are the Pastry Cooks.[2] What Indignation must it raise in a Lover of the Moderns, to see some of their best Performances stain'd with the Juice of Gooseberries, Currants, and Damascenes! But what Concern must the Author himself feel on such an Occasion; when he beholds those Writings, which were calculated to support the glorious Cause of Disaffection or Infidelity, humbled to the ignoble Purpose of supporting a Tart or a Custard! So, according to the Poet,

> *Great Alexander dead, and turn'd to Clay,*
> *May stop a Hole to keep the Wind away.*[3]

But, besides the Injuries done to Learning by this Method, there is another Mischief which these Pastry Cooks may thus propagate in the Society: For many of these wondrous Performances are calculated only for the Use and Inspection of the few, and are by no means proper Food for the Mouths of Babes and Sucklings. For Instance, that the Christian Religion is a mere Cheat and Imposition on the Public, nay, that the very Being of a God is a Matter of great Doubt and Incertainty, are Discoveries of too deep a Nature to perplex the Minds of Children with; and it is better, perhaps, till they come to a certain Age, that they should believe quite the opposite

[1] Fielding refers to the print 'Beer Street', published Feb. 1751, in which a hamper of books is directed for 'Mr. Pastem the Trunk Maker'. Among the 'valuable Productions' destined for waste paper are John Hill's *Review of the Works of the Royal Society*, George Turnbull's *Treatise upon Ancient Painting*, William Lauder's *Essay on Milton's Use and Imitation of the Moderns in his Paradise Lost* (a fraudulent effort to prove Milton a plagiarist), and volumes labeled 'Modern Tragedys Vo: 12' and 'Politicks Vol: 9999'; see Ronald Paulson, *Hogarth's Graphic Works* (New Haven, 1965), i. 209.

Fielding's admiration for his good friend William Hogarth (1697–1764) is expressed in complimentary references throughout his work; see especially the Preface to *Joseph Andrews*, the *Champion* for 10 June 1740, 'An Essay on Conversation' (*Miscellanies* [1743]), *Tom Jones* (I. xi, II. iii, and III. vi), and *CGJ* No. 52. Hogarth chose the *CGJ* (No. 24, 24 Mar. 1752) to announce plans for his work *An Analysis of Beauty* (1753).

[2] See the epigraph to this essay and note 6, above, p. 48. Cf. *Tom Jones*, IV. i, where Fielding singles out 'idle Romances which are filled with Monsters' as particularly suitable for pastry-cooks, a point repeated in the Preface to *Journal of a Voyage to Lisbon*. See, among many references to this theme, *Spectator*, No. 85 (7 June 1711); Swift, 'Epistle Dedicatory', *A Tale of a Tub*; and Pope, *Dunciad* (1743), i. 155–6.

[3] Alteration of *Hamlet*, v. i. 213–14: 'Imperious Caesar, dead and turned to clay, / Might stop a hole to keep the wind away.'

Doctrines.¹ Again, as Children are taught to obey and honour their Superiors, and to keep their Tongues from Evil-speaking, Lying, and Slandering, to what good Purposes can it tend to shew them that the very contrary is daily practised and suffered and supported in the World? Is not this to confound their Understandings, and almost sufficient to make them neglect their Learning? Lastly, there are certain Arcana Naturæ,² in disclosing which the Moderns have made great Progress; now whatever Merit there may be in such Denudations of Nature, if I may so express myself, and however exquisite a Relish they may afford to *very* adult Persons of both Sexes in their Closets, they are surely too speculative and mysterious for the Contemplation of the Young and Tender, into whose Hands Tarts and Pies are most likely to fall.³

Now as these three Subjects, namely, Infidelity, Scurrility, and Indecency, have principally exercised the Pens of the Moderns, I hope for the future, Pastry Cooks will be more cautious than they have lately been. In short, if they have no Regard to Learning, they will have some, I hope, to Morality.

The same Caution may be given to Grocers and Chandlers; both of whom are too apt to sell their Figs, Raisins, and Sugar to Children, without enough considering the poisonous Vehicle in which they are conveyed. At the waste Paper Market, the Cheapness of the Commodity is only considered; and it is easy to see with what Goods that Market is likely to abound; since tho' the Press hath lately swarmed with Libels against our Religion and Government, there is not a single Writer of any Reputation in this Kingdom, who hath attempted to draw his Pen against either.⁴

But to return to that Subject from which I seem to have a little digressed. How melancholy a Consideration must it be to a modern Author, that the Labours, I might call them the Offspring of his Brain, are liable to so many various Kinds of Destruction, that what Tibullus says of the numerous Avenues to Death may be here applied.

---

¹ Cf. *A Charge to the Grand Jury* (1749), where Fielding directs attention to the statutes against irreligious writings; see also *Amelia*, IX. x, in which a young clergyman complains that books of infidelity are propagated with impunity. Cf. the definition of 'Religion' in the Modern Glossary, *CGJ* No. 4.

² Secrets of nature.

³ On the dangers involved in allowing young children to read objectionable books, cf. *CGJ* No. 5, above, and the 'Covent Garden' column of 13 Apr., below, Appendix I.

⁴ Although the comment on anti-government libels is general, it doubtless reflects Fielding's recent activities as a pro-government writer in the *JJ* (1747–8), in *A True State of the Case of Bosavern Penlez* (1749), and in his ridicule of Opposition writers like Paul Whitehead during the bitterly fought Westminster election of 1749; see M. C. with R. R. Battestin, 'Fielding, Bedford, and the Westminster Election of 1749', *ECS* 11 (1977–8), 143–85. Ironically, in claiming that no writer of reputation opposes the government, Fielding reverses a standard motif of Opposition propaganda during the Walpole Administration (1721–42), when it was regularly claimed that 'all the wit' (including Fielding's) was united against Walpole and the Court; see Bertrand A. Goldgar, *Walpole and the Wits* (1976), pp. 8–19.

——Leti mille repente viæ.
To Death there are a thousand sudden Ways.[1]

For my own Part, I never walk into Mrs. Dodd's Shop,[2] and survey all that vast and formidable Host of Papers and Pamphlets arranged on her Shelves, but the noble Lamentation of Xerxes occurs to my Mind; who, when he reviewed his Army, on the Banks of the Hellespont, is said to have grieved, for that not one of all those Hundreds of Thousands would be living an Hundred Years from that Time.[3] In the same Manner, have I said to myself, "How dreadful a Thought is it, that of all these numerous and learned Works, none will survive to the next Year!" But, within that Time,

—— All will become,
Martyrs to Pyes, and Relics of the B—.[4]

I was led into these Reflections by an Accident which happened to me the other Day, and which all Lovers of Antiquity will esteem a very fortunate one. Having had the Curiosity to examine a written Paper, in which my Baker inclosed me two hot Rolls, I have rescued from Oblivion one of the most valuable Fragments, that I believe is now to be found in the World. I have ordered it to be fairly transcribed, and shall very soon present it to my Readers, with my best Endeavours, by a short Comment, to illustrate a Piece which appears to have remained to us from the most distant and obscure Ages.[7]   A.

We have received Letters from Tim. Buck, Dorothy Single, Sappho, P.W. *and from the Scavenger of* Covent-Garden, *all which will be inserted in our next.*

The Court *of* Censorial Enquiry *met according to Adjournment; and, after issuing forth Process to bring several Books into Court, among which was a Romance called* AMELIA, *adjourned to* Saturday *next.*

---

[1] *Elegies*, I. iii. 50. Cited also in 'Of the Remedy of Affliction', *Miscellanies* (1743).

[2] On Ann Dodd, whose shop is listed as 'at the *Peacock, Temple-Bar*' in the colophon of the *CGJ*, see General Introduction, p. xxix.

[3] Herodotus, *History*, vii. 45–6.

[4] Adapted from Dryden's *Mac Flecknoe* (1682), describing the gathering of the nations for Shadwell's coronation: 'From dusty shops neglected Authors come, / Martyrs of Pies, and Reliques of the Bum' (100–1).

[5] The 'Piece' is Fielding's satire on the Robin Hood Society; see *CGJ* Nos. 8 and 9.

SATURDAY, JANUARY 25, 1752. NUMB. 7.

Quis non invenit turba quod amaret in illa.

Ovid, de Arte Amandi.[1]

Who is there so stupid as not to find a favourite Letter in the following Collection?

To Sir ALEXANDER HUMBUG, *Censurer of* Grate Britan.

You, Sir Sawnny.[2] I must not Kritichize, must I— D—n me but I will tho in Spit of you and all your hadearents. Who the Divil are you, Mun, that you ant to be Kritichized upon.[3] But I can til you I have Kritichized upon you, and so have seferal of my Frinds; and we d—ned all your Papers tother Day in a Coffi House, and cursed Stuff they are, there, my boy, theres a Stuff your puzling Pat never thot off. I wish wee had you upon the Stage, my Dear, wed showe you a Trik worth two othat, I warrant you; but Garrak knows better than to acte such Stuff as you can write. You put me into Grub-street—You kiss—Da—n me I have 2000 l. a Year, that is, I shall have when I com from my Travels two Years hence, and shall bee of Age, but perhaps I shant travl at all but stay at home and d—n such Felows as you.

TIM BUCK.[4]

To the CENSOR

Sir,

In your Remarks on the many Encomiums made on Brides in the public News-Papers,[5] I suppose you intend to ridicule the Vanity of our Sex in publishing their own Qualifications to the World; but you will excuse me, if I have a better Opinion of the Female Part of the Species than to imagine they are ever privy to such pompous Exhibitions of themselves, and am well

---

[1] *Art of Love*, i. 175: 'Who found not in that crowd some object for his passion?' (Loeb).

[2] i.e. Sawney, a general term for a simpleton or fool; in its original sense, as a derisive name for a Scotchman, it derives from a Scottish variant of 'Sandy', short for 'Alexander' (*OED*).

[3] In the last of his rules for critics in *CGJ* No. 3 Sir Alexander forbade anyone to criticize his works.

[4] *OED* cites the definition of 'Buck' as 'a forward daring person of either sex' from *A New Canting Dictionary* (1725); by Fielding's time the term suggested wild, unruly behavior. See *Amelia*, x. ii and *CGJ* Nos. 17 and 26; for other mid-century characterizations of bucks see *Adventurer*, No. 100 (20 Oct. 1753) and *Connoisseur*, No. 28 (8 Aug. 1754). The name 'Timothy Buck' may have been suggested to Fielding by the Timothy Buck who flourished as a 'Master of the Noble Science of Defence' in the period 1710–12; see *Spectator*, No. 436 (21 July 1712).

[5] See the 'Modern History' excerpts from the newspapers of 5 January, originally included in *CGJ* No. 2 and printed below, Appendix II. Fielding frequently ridiculed the formulaic descriptions of brides as 'endowed with every Qualification requisite to render the Marriage State truly happy' and as young ladies 'of Beauty, Merit, and Fortune'; see *Tom Jones*, II. ii, *Champion*, 15 Nov. 1739, and *JJ* No. 11 (13 Feb. 1748); see also General Introduction, p. xxxii. In this letter he appears to elaborate on his pointed question after one such item in the news columns of *CGJ* No. 2, '*What are the Accomplishments necessary to render this State truly happy?*'

convinced that all these Compliments are inserted by the Bridegroom only; and they are, sometimes, I fear, the last Compliments, which he pays his Mistress.

This Matter, I own, appears to me in a very different Light from that in which it is seen by others. It raises my Indignation to read Beauty, Sense, Merit, and all Qualifications necessary to render the married State happy, at the End of every married Woman's Name, while a profound Silence is always preserved with regard to the Merits of the Husband. Good Mr. Censor, are we to understand by this that all Men are possessed of those Qualifications which can render the married State happy, or that there are really no Qualifications necessary on the Part of the Man; or lastly, that his Happiness alone, and not that of the Woman, is to be considered?

None of these I apprehend to be true; I submit, therefore, to your Judgment, whether it would not be decent for the future, either to pass over the great Endowments of the Woman, or to insert likewise those of the Man. For Instance, Yesterday A B, Esq; a Gentleman of Sense, Honour, and Good-nature, of a comely Person, and a suitable Age, was married to Miss C D, a Lady of great Beauty, &c. as usual: For every one of these Articles on the Man's Side are absolutely necessary to the Happiness of the Woman.

This, Sir, would be fair on both Sides; but as the matter now stands, may we not justly apprehend that many a Lady possessed of every Virtue and good Quality is thrown away either upon a Rake or a Fool, a Sot or a Clown, a Coxcomb or a R—scal; or, perhaps, on a Husband who possesses all these amiable Qualities together?

To conclude with a plain Truth, I sincerely believe the Qualifications necessary to married Happiness are much more common in Women than in Men, and may, therefore, better be understood, in general, to belong to our Sex than to yours. I am,

SIR,

Your humble Servant,

DOROTHY SINGLE.

Grosvenor-Street.[1]
Saturday.

To the CENSOR

Sir,

Looking lately into that Volume of the Spectators, in which is inserted the humble Petition of WHO and WHICH,[2] I could not help reflecting on many other discarded Words which might claim an equal Right of being restored

---

[1] One of the wealthiest and most fashionable areas in London; cf. *CGJ* Nos. 27 and 37.

[2] *Spectator*, No. 78 (30 May 1711), by Steele; Steele's mock-petition is an attack on bad grammar, without the moral and social satire of Fielding's imitation.

to Use, or rather of being suffered, sometimes at least, to enter into the human Mind.

The Words, I at present mean are WHY and WHEREFORE; which, if permitted to present themselves before Mankind, how many vain Pursuits would they stop in the very Beginning; and how many Scenes of Ruin and Destruction would a due Attention to them be able to prevent.

Give me Leave, therefore, to suppose these two Words, setting forth their unhappy Fate, and begging for better Quarter, in the following Complaint, addressed to you, Sir, as Censor of Great Britain. I am,

SIR,

Your humble Servant,

SOPHIA.[1]

The humble Complaint of WHY and WHEREFORE.

Sheweth,

That your Petitioners knowing of what great Use and Service we might be to all Societies, as well as to every Individual, and having a benevolent Intention of doing all the Good in our Power, are heartily grieved we so very seldom can find a Hearing.

If we present ourselves before a Fox-hunter in his Chace, he swiftly rides over us.

If we attempt to engage one Moment's Attention from the Hero marching at the Head of his Army to destroy his Fellow-Creatures, instead of listening to us, he immediately orders his Drums, and Trumpets, to strike up; in the Noise of which 'tis impossible our Voice should be distinguished.

In our Address to the Miser, the Chinking of his Gold sounds as loudly in his Ears, and as effectually prevents our being heard, as the more noisy Instruments of War made use of by the Soldier.

When the ambitious Man is sitting alone, and revolving in his Mind all his various Schemes for raising himself to the highest Pinnacle of Greatness,[2] we know that he is too much wrapped up in his own Thoughts to give Attention to any outward Sound. We therefore secretly endeavour to creep into his Breast; and though we, by this Means, gain Admittance, yet is it generally our Fate to be there smothered in a confused Croud of Images, such as Honours, Titles,—Command,—Adoration,—Fame, &c. &c. &c. But if, by Accident, this great Man falls from all his Glory, and comes into Disgrace, the large Company which before hid, and almost stifled, us, instantly vanish, and he then wonders he had not before seen us, and hearkened to our Voice.

[1] Called 'Sappho' when notice was given of these letters in *CGJ* No. 6.
[2] One of Fielding's most persistent themes; see *CGJ* No. 4 and n. 5, p. 36, above.

The Lover, whenever we apply to him, puffs us away with his Sighs; the Sot drowns our Voice with a merry Catch; nor could we ever obtain a satisfactory Answer from any Author, unless it was from some poor Wretch who was writing for a Dinner.

If we durst, Great Sir, we should put a Question to your Worship, on your attacking a Set of Wretches so much beneath your Notice as the present Race of Scribblers; but we do not expect you should do us so great an Honour, as ever to answer,

Your very good Friends,
WHY and WHEREFORE.[1]

George's Coffee House,[2] *Jan.* 14, 1752

Sir,

By a short Conversation which I had the other Day with an ingenious Friend of yours, at his Office in the Strand,[3] he told me he could supply me with every Kind of useful Person, and give me Information in every Sort of Business.—A Proposal which I own, had greatly the Air of Extravagance; but Experience soon taught me it was true: And though, as Censor, you may be highly serviceable to Society, I think your Friend is no less usefully employed than yourself, being engaged in a Design, which the more I examine, the more I approve.

For your Part, Sir Alexander, I look upon your Office, as Censor, as a *Universal Register Office* too, but of a different Kind; for while your Friend is placing every Man in the Sphere for which his Capacity and Education qualify him, you instruct the Wise, and furnish Entertainment for those of true Taste. In your Office are registered just Sentiments on every Occasion: you regulate the Minds of one Part of the World, whilst he employs the Bodies of the other. You give Information in Points of Knowledge; whilst he deals out Intelligence to Men of Business. To your Register Office, Mr. Censor, I now apply for the Meaning of a Word much used in the present Age, which, I own, conveys no distinct Idea to my Mind, nor do I believe it does to the Minds of those who make use of it. In your last Paper, in which you so ingeniously handled the Abuse of Words,[4] you have, to my great Disappointment, omitted the Word *Town*, of which I should be glad to know the Meaning. For being in an eminent Coffee House, some few Days ago, a grave Gentleman, with much Dignity of Wig and Person, who seemed

---

[1] Cf. 'The Humble Petition of Any-Body' (against Nobody) in Christopher Smart's *Midwife*, ii (1751), 157. See the reply to the petition of 'Why and Wherefore' in *CGJ* No. 32, below.

[2] Without Temple Bar, in the Strand, George's was frequented by wits of 'the town'.

[3] Fielding's half-brother John, at the Universal Register Office 'opposite Cecil-Street in the Strand'; see General Introduction, pp. xv–xxii.

[4] *CGJ* No. 4.

to be the Mouth and Oracle of the Assembly, made frequent Use of the Word *Town*, in his Harangues, which were not a little oratorical; and, speaking of some theatrical Performances he said, the *Town* would not bear it; the *Town* did not like it; the *Town* was offended; the *Town* damn'd it; the *Town* was the best Judge; the *Town* was out of Humour. In a Word, the *Town* did every Thing; the *Town* knew every Thing; and, to succeed in any Thing, a Man must please the *Town*.[1]

Now, Sir, what I want to know of you, is, who, or what, is meant by this Word *Town*; What Sort of Animal it is. And what one is to understand by it. Your Information, in this Particular, shall be gratefully acknowledged, by

Your humble Servant, and Admirer,

P.W.

P.S. *Quære*, Whether the *Town* does not signify the idle, silly, and illiterate Part of Society?

Jan. 17. 12 *o'Clock.*

Worshipful *Sir*,

Since the Publication of your Paper,[2] such an immense Quantity of Filth and Nastiness has been brought from Grub-Street and Billinsgate, and emptied in Covent-Garden, that unless your Worship, out of your great Wisdom, will contrive some Method of raising a new Tax for the Payment of the Scavenger, it will be impossible for me, had I treble the Number of Carts I have, to keep that Place tolerably decent.[3] I am, Sir,

Your humble Servant,

W. T. Master Scavenger.

---

[1] See Fielding's definition of 'the Town' in his note to *CGJ* No. 71, below; cf. his use of 'Counsellor Town' in the indictment of *Amelia* which follows in this issue, and his amusing analysis of the social groups designated by the term at various times, *True Patriot*, No. 18 (4 Mar. 1746); cf. also his reference to the 'Wit and Humour of a Set of young Gentlemen, who call themselves the Town', *Tom Jones*, xv. ii. The judgement of dramatic works by 'the Town' was a common topic of concern; see *Adventurer*, No. 26 (3 Feb. 1753), and cf. *The Address of the Town to Common Sense* (1752): 'The *Town* is a very familiar Word to every Body: if a Play is condemned, it was owing to the *Town*; if a Scene is disapproved, why the *Town* did it; . . . in short, my Name is become so very infamous, that there is not a Scene of Folly and Iniquity begun and perpetrated, but the whole is most certainly laid to my Charge' (p. 5).

[2] Referring to Fielding's description of his war with Grub Street as cleansing the Augean stables, *CGJ* No. 5, above, p. 44; see also his mock-lament for the transience of poor writing, *CGJ* No. 6. Jensen (ii. 166) finds Fielding's authorship of this letter unlikely; the present editor sees no reason to doubt it.

[3] Scavengers of the parish of St Paul Covent Garden were paid by funds from a scavenger's rate levied by the churchwardens on householders. The letter contains some irony, for by mid-century the vegetable market had made the task of keeping Covent Garden clean an acute problem for the parish administration; in 1748 the vestry had complained to the Duke of Bedford about the 'stench and filth of the Markett' (*The Parish of St. Paul Covent Garden*, vol. 36 [1970] of *A Survey of London*, gen. ed. F. H. W. Sheppard, pp. 57, 132).

P.S. Pray let Grub-Street alone, for the more you stir the more it will stink. M.

Proceedings at the Court of Censorial Enquiry, &c.

(Amelia *was set to the Bar*.)[1]

COUNSELLOR Town. May it please you, Mr. Censor, I am of Council in this Case, on the side of the Prosecution. The Book at the Bar is indicted upon the Statute of Dulness, a very antient Law, and too well known to need much expatiating upon. But it may be necessary to observe, *that that that*[2] is Dulness in one Age, is not so in another, and what says that antient Sage, and Lawgiver, Horace;

Ætatis cujusque notandi sunt tibi mores.
Every Writer is to observe the Manners of the Age.[3]

I know the Word *ætatis* is, in this Place, by some Lawyers, understood in another Sense; but what I contend for, is, that it may very well be understood in that Sense that I have here given to it: and, accordingly, the same Horace lays it down as a Rule,

Et predesse volunt, et delectare, poetæ.
Poets desire to get Money, and to please their Readers.[4]

---

[1] Fielding's last novel, published 18 Dec. 1751, was immediately attacked by the wits and critics of the town. Though exaggerated by Fielding, the bill of particulars offered by Counsellor Town includes the common charges actually made against the book: that it is dull and tedious, that Amelia is a weak and servile character, that she is described as a beauty despite her nose having been 'beat all to pieces' in an accident, and that the characters and prison scenes are 'low'. In the trial given here, however, Fielding ignores another complaint commonly made by his critics, that *Amelia* contains several glaring anachronisms. For a collection of contemporary reactions, see *Henry Fielding: The Critical Heritage*, ed. Ronald Paulson and Thomas Lockwood (1969), pp. 286–336, 345–51. Since a number of the hostile remarks appeared after the date of this issue of the *CGJ*, Fielding may have been anticipating some of the objections as well as responding to those already made; *Amelia* had, however, already been reviewed (not unfavorably) in *LM* (Dec. 1751) and the *Monthly Review* (Dec. 1751) and attacked by *OE* (21 Dec. 1751), by *The Covent-Garden Journal Extraordinary* (20 Jan. 1752), and by the first number of Bonnell Thornton's *Drury-Lane Journal* (16 Jan. 1752), which advertised a novel called *Shamelia*. For full discussion of its reception, see the Wesleyan Edn., ed. Martin Battestin (Oxford, 1983), pp. l–lvii.

[2] Counsellor Town uses the infelicitous expression complained about in the 'Petition of Who and Which' in *Spectator*, No. 78, referred to earlier in this number. Steele's passage reads: 'Nay, how often have we heard in one of the most polite and august Assemblies in the Universe, to our great Mortification, these Words, *That THAT that noble L—d urg'd*? which if one of us had had Justice done, would have sounded nobler thus, *That WHICH that noble L—d urg'd.*'

[3] *Art of Poetry*, 176: 'You must note the manners of each age' (Loeb); Horace is not referring to different ages of the world or historical periods, as Counsellor Town contends, but is urging dramatic poets to be accurate in their representations of various stages of a man's life; hence the 'gloss' on *aetatis* which follows.

[4] *Art of Poetry*, 333; the text reads, *Aut prodesse volunt aut delectare poetae*, 'Poets aim either to benefit, or to amuse' (Loeb). Counsellor Town not only distorts the text (*et . . . et* for *aut . . . aut*) but again twists Horace's meaning by interpreting *prodesse* ('to be useful') as 'to get Money': cf. Pope's *Peri Bathous*, ch. ii. where the persona Martinus Scriblerus misquotes and misinterprets this famous

For so I read the Law, and so I render it. A very good Law it is, and very wholesome to the Writers themselves.

Now the Humour, or Manners, of this Age are to laugh at every Thing, and the only Way to please them is to make them laugh; nor hath the Prisoner any Excuse, since it was so very easy to have done this in the present Case; what, indeed, more was necessary, than to have turned the Ridicule the other Way, and, in the Characters of Dr. Harrison, and Amelia herself, to have made a Jest of Religion, and the Clergy, of Virtue, and Innocence![1]

Here the Council was hastily stopt by the Censor, and desired to proceed to his Proofs.

TOWN. We shall prove then, to you, Sir, that the Book now at the Bar, is *very sad Stuff;*[2] that Amelia herself is a *low* Character, a *Fool*, and a *Milksop*; that she is very apt to faint, and apt to *drink Water*, to prevent it.[3] That she once *taps a Bottle of Wine, and drinks two Glasses.*[4] That she *shews too much Kindness for her Children*, and is too apt to *forgive the Faults of her Husband*. That she exerts *no Manner of Spirit*, unless, perhaps, in supporting Afflictions. That *her concealing the* Knowledge of her Husband's Amour, when she knew he had discontinued it, was *low and poor*.[5] That *her not abusing him*, for having lost his Money at Play, when she saw his Heart was already almost broke by it, *was contemptible Meanness*.[6] That she *dresses her Husband's Supper; dresses her Children*; and *submits* to the Thoughts of every servile Office. That she once mentions THE DEVIL, and as often swears BY HER SOUL.[7] Lastly, That she is a Beauty WITHOUT A NOSE, I say again, WITHOUT A NOSE.[8] All this we shall prove by many Witnesses.

We shall likewise prove that Dr. Harrison is a very *low, dull, unnatural*, Character, and that his arresting Booth, *only because he had all imaginable Reason to think he was a Villain*, is unpardonable.[9]

Horatian dictum in exactly the same way: 'Their true Design is *Profit* or *Gain*; in order to acquire which, 'tis necessary to procure Applause, by administring *Pleasure* to the Reader.'

[1] With Fielding's defense here, that he refused to conform to the manners of the age, cf. the comment by one of *Amelia*'s anonymous defenders that 'as the worthy Author, consulted in this Piece, his own Disposition, and true Taste, more than that of the Age; its Fate, compared with Success of those vile Pieces which disgrace the Press, will be a melancholy Caution to Writers, to apply rather to the vicious than virtuous Affections of Mankind' (*Some Remarks on the life and writings of Dr. J— H—, Inspector-General of Great Britain* [1752], pp. 60–1).

[2] See *CGJ* No. 3, above, p. 29; cf. Elizabeth Carter's comment on *Amelia* in a letter of 30 Mar. 1752: 'Methinks I long to engage you on the side of this poor unfortunate book, which I am told the fine folks are unanimous in pronouncing to be very sad stuff' (*A Series of Letters between Mrs. Elizabeth Carter and Miss Catherine Talbot* [1899], ii. 71).

[3] For Amelia's fainting, see III. ii; IV. ii. She drinks water to prevent fainting in VII. ii, vi.

[4] Ibid., XI. ix.   [5] Ibid., XII. ii.   [6] Ibid., X. vi.   [7] Ibid., VI. ii, iii.

[8] In the first edition Fielding refers to his heroine's nose having been 'beat all to Pieces' but has Booth affirm that she would still be beautiful 'without any Nose at all' (II. i). In his revision, in response to this most common point of ridicule of the work, he is careful to have the nose surgically repaired; see the 'Covent Garden' column for 11 Jan. 1752, below, Appendix I.

[9] Dr Harrison explains his conduct in *Amelia*, IX. i.

That Colonel Bath is a *foolish Character, very low, and ill-drawn.*

That the Scene of the Goal is *low and unmeaning*, and brought in by Head and Shoulders, without any Reason, or Design.[1]

That the Abbé is supposed to *wear a Sword*;[2] in short, not to descend to too many Particulars, which you will hear from the Mouths of the Witnesses, that the whole Book is a Heap of *sad Stuff, Dulness, and Nonsense*; that it contains no Wit, Humour, Knowledge of human Nature, or of the World; indeed, that the Fable, moral Characters, Manners, Sentiments, and Diction, are all alike bad and contemptible.

All these Matters, Sir, we doubt not to prove to your Satisfaction, and then we doubt not but that you will do exemplary Justice to such intolerable sad Stuff, and, will pass such a Sentence as may be a dreadful Example to all future Books, how they dare stand up in Opposition to the Humour of the Age.

A great Noise was now heard in the Court, and much female Vociferation; when the Censor was informed, that it was a married Lady, one of the Witnesses against Amelia, who was scolding at her Husband for not making her Way through the Crowd.

Mr. Town then moved, that, as there were several Persons of great Fashion, who were to be Witnesses in this Cause, Room might be made for them by the Officers, which was ordered accordingly.

C. Town. Call Lady *Dilly Dally.*—(*She appeared*) Mr. Censor, we call this young Lady to the Character of Amelia, and she will give you an Account of all the low Behaviour I have opened.—Lady *Dilly*, your Ladyship knows the Prisoner at the Bar?

L. Dilly. I cannot say I ever saw the Creature before.[3] (*At which there was a great Laugh*)

C. Town. I thought your Ladyship had said that Amelia was sad Stuff from Beginning to End.

L. Dilly. I believe I might say so.—Eh! I don't always remember what I say; but if I did say so, I was told it.—Oh! yes, now I remember very well, I did say so, and Dr. Dosewell,[4] my Physician, told me so.—The Doctor said, in a great deal of Company, that the Book, I forget the Name of it, was a sad

---

[1] The first three books of *Amelia* are set in prison; 'goal' is a common variant of 'gaol'.

[2] In the first edition (III. viii) Fielding introduces 'Mons. *L'Abbé Bagillard*', an admirer of Amelia, who later is described as drawing his sword (III. ix) in a fight with Colonel Bath; in the revision Bagillard is a layman, although, as Cross points out (ii. 352), the 18th-cent. abbé wore only semi-clerical dress which permitted a sword.

[3] See Fielding's definition of 'Creature' in the Modern Glossary, *CGJ* No. 4.

[4] In the first edition (v. ii) a 'Dr. Dosewell' is recommended to Booth, but he sends instead for the less conventional physician Thomas Thompson; Fielding is here either reacting to or anticipating criticism from the orthodox medical community for his praise in *Amelia* of Dr Thompson and other physicians whose methods were not generally accepted; see Cross, ii. 355, and *Amelia*, ed. Battestin, Wesleyan Edn., pp. xxix–xxx.

stupid Book, and that the Author had not a Bit of Wit, or Learning, or Sense, or any Thing else.

COURT. Mr. *Town*, you know this is only Hearsay, and not Evidence.—

C. TOWN. I do not contend for it. We shall call the Doctor himself by and by.—We will give your Ladyship no further Trouble.

L. DILLY.—I am heartily glad of it.—Mr. Censor, if you are the Judge, I beg, as you have brought me into this odious Place, you will see me safe out again.

Orders were then given to clear away the Crowd, which was very great, and Lady *Dilly* got safe to her Chair.

The Residue of this Trial will be in our next.

TUESDAY, JANUARY 28, 1752.   NUMB. 8.

> *Ambubaiarum Collegia, Pharmacopolæ,*
> *Mendici, Mimi, Balatrones; hoc genus omne.*

HORACE.[1]

> *A motley Mixture! in long Wigs, in Bags,*
> *In Silks, in Crapes, in Garters and in Rags.*

DUNCIAD.[2]

The following is a literal Copy of the Fragment mentioned in my Sixth Paper.[3] In what Language it was originally writ, is impossible to determine. To determine this would be, indeed, to ascertain who these Robinhoodians[4]

---

[1] *Satires*, I. ii. 1–2; 'The flute-girls' guilds, the drug-quacks, beggars, actresses, buffoons, and all that breed' (Loeb). Fielding uses the same motto for *True Patriot*, No. 4 (26 Nov. 1745); in both cases he substitutes the masculine *mimi* for the accepted reading, *mimae*. He also uses the first phrase as the motto for *JJ* No. 29 (18 June 1748).

[2] (1729), ii. 17–18; also quoted in the *Champion*, 6 Sept. 1740.   [3] On p. 51, above.

[4] Members of the Robin Hood Society, a debating club formed about 1747, which met every Monday evening at the Robin Hood in Butcher's Row to argue any questions the members chose to submit. Anyone who wished to attend and pay an entrance fee of sixpence had the right to speak for five minutes, at the end of which time the president rapped his hammer for silence. For a general account, see Robert J. Allen, *The Clubs of Augustan London* (Cambridge, Mas., 1933), pp. 129–36. In the years just preceding this essay the Society was frequently attacked for religious heterodoxy and political disaffection, precisely the grounds of Fielding's satire here. See the *Whitehall Evening Post* (29 Dec. 1750 and 31 Jan. 1751); *An Apology for the Robin-Hood Society, Wherein the Cause of Liberty and Free Enquiry is Asserted* (June, 1751), an ironic defense which in the guise of response simply expands all the earlier charges; *Genuine and Authentick Memoirs of the Stated Speakers of the Robin Hood Society* (Oct. 1751), a vicious assault on the impiety and blasphemy of the members; and Bonnell Thornton's *Drury-Lane Journal*, No. 2 (23 Jan. 1752), a comment on the Society by the *CGJ*'s chief detractor which preceded Fielding's own by just 5 days and may thus have furnished him his immediate hint. For later attacks, among many, see *Drury-Lane Journal*, No. 5 (13 Feb. 1752), Murphy's *Gray's Inn Journal*, Nos. 18 and 78 (17 Feb. 1753, 13 Apr. 1754), and *The History of the Robinhood Society* (1764), a fictitious history based on fraudulent documents. And with Fielding's pretense that the Society is a peculiar and obscure sect, cf. an advertisement for 'A Print of the Robbing-Wood Society. To which is added, An Account of the Religion, Customs, &c. of those most extraordinary People' (*DA*, 2 June

were; a Point, as we shall shew in our Comment, of the utmost Difficulty. From the apparent Difference in the Style, and Spelling of the Translation, it seems to have been *done into English* by several Hands, and probably in distant Ages. I have placed my Conjectures concerning some doubtful Words, at the Bottom of the Page, without venturing to disturb the Text.

   * *Importinent Questions cunsarning* Relidgin *and* Gubermint, *handyled by the* Robinhoodians.

March 8. 1 51.

This Evenin the Questin at the Robinhood was, whether Relidgin was of any youse to a Sosyaty; baken[†] bifor mee To'mmas Whytebred, Baker.[1]

   JAMES SKOTCHUM, Barber, spak as floweth: Sir, I ham of Upinion, that Relidgin can be of no youse to any mortal Sole; bycause as why, Relidgin is no youse to Trayd, and if Relidgin be of no youse to Trayd, how ist it yousefool to Sosyaty. Now no Body can deny but that a man maye kary on his Trayd very wel without Relidgin; nay, and beter two, for then he maye wurk won Day in a Wik mor than at present; whereof no Body can saye but that seven is mor than six: Besides, if we haf no Relidgin we shall haf no *Pairsuns*[||],[2] and that will be a grate Savin to the Sosyaty; and it is a *Maksum*[§]

* *Perhaps impertinent.*
† I think this should be read *taken*, and the Baker's being intent on his Trade, occasioned the Corruption. ||Read *Parsons.*   § Read *Maxim.*

1752). Portions of Fielding's essay are quoted in *The Robin-Hood Society: A Satire* (1756) by 'Peter Pounce' (i.e. Richard Lewis).

   Fielding's ridicule of the members as ignorant tradesmen was also a common point of satire; cf. *Genuine and Authentick Memoirs* (1751): 'This illustrious Assembly is composed of Bakers, Shoemakers, Journeymen-Barbers, *Fleet* Parsons, Psalm-singing Clerks, and Apprentice Boys, who every Monday Night make no inconsiderable Figure on the Side of Infidelity' (pp. 3–4). But a few members were slightly more illustrious; at this time Fielding's friend Charles Macklin, the actor, attended the sessions regularly, as did the actors Henry Woodward, Samuel Foote, and George Alexander Stevens, and Dr Johnson's amanuensis Robert Shiels (see the comment by Sir Joseph Mawbey, *GM* 62 [1792], 29; *Drury-Lane Journal*, No. 5 (13 Feb. 1752); and William Kenrick's *Pasquinade* [1753], pp. 19–21, which cites Fielding's satire and says Macklin was celebrated for his religious harangues at the Robin Hood).

   The religious and political questions which Fielding incorporates into his ridicule appear in other satires and were apparently typical of the group; one advertisement for a meeting posed two questions which almost seem a response to his burlesque: 'Whether the Drama is necessary to Religion? . . . Whether Novel-Writing is beneficial to Society?' (*DA*, 19 Feb. 1752). Cf. *Journal of a Voyage to Lisbon*, where Fielding concludes a mock-disquisition on why sailors behave like savages by recommending that the topic 'form a question in the Robin Hood Society' (entry of 30 June).

   [1] i.e. Caleb Jeacocke, a wealthy baker who was president of the Robin Hood Society; for serious praise of Jeacocke, see W. H. Draper, *The Morning Walk* (1751), p. 8.

   [2] Cf. *True Patriot*, No. 4 (26 Nov. 1745): 'Free-Thinkers have long regarded it as an intolerable Grievance, that a certain Body of Men called *Parsons* should, for the useless Service of Praying, Preaching, Catechising and Instructing the People, receive a certain fixed Stipend from the Public, which the Law foolishly allows them to call their own.' On Fielding's consistent support of the clergy, see *CGJ* No. 4, above, p. 38 and n. 2.

in Trayd, That a Peny sav'd is a Peny got. Whereof——The End of this Speech seems to be wanting, as doth the Beginning of the next.

——Different Opinion from the learned Gentleman who spoke first to the Question: First I deny that Trade can be carried on without Religion; for how often is the Sanction of an Oath necessary in Contracts, and how can we have Oaths without Religion? As to the gaining one Day in seven,[1] which the Gentleman seems to lay much Stress upon, I do admit it to be an Argument of great Force; but I question, as the People have been long used to Idleness on that Day, whether it would be easy to make them work upon it; and, consequently, if they had no Churches to go to, whether they would not resort to some worse Place? As to the Expence of Parsons, I cannot think it is prejudicial to the Society in general; for the Parsons are Members of this Society;[2] and whether they who do but little, or others who do nothing at all for their Livelihood, possess their Revenues, is a Matter of no manner of Concern to the Public. Indeed what the Gentleman says concerning the Dutch,[3] I shall own is highly to the Honour of those industrious People: And I question not but if Religion was to interfere with any Branch of our Trade, there is still so much good Sense left in this Nation, that we should presently sacrifice the Shadow to the Substance. But tho' some Instances should occur, in which Religion may be prejudicial, it cannot be fairly argued from thence, that Religion is therefore of no use to the Society; and 'till that can be proved, I shall not give my Vote for its Abolition. But at present—— *Hammer down.*

MR. MAC FLOURISH, Student, I shall with grate Reediness undertake that Tosk upon my Seel.—Sir, the Queestion, as I tak it, is, whether Relegion be of any use to Society? And Sir, this is a Queestion of that Degnity, that grete emportance, that when I conseder the Matter of wheech I am to speke, the Degnity of the Odience before whom I am to speke, when I refleect on the Smallness of my own Abeelities, weel may I be struck with the greetest Awe and Reveerence: For Sir, neither Demosthenes nor Eschines, nor Cecero, nor Hortensius,[4] ever handled a more emportant Queestion: And Sir, should

---

[1] Cf. Swift, *An Argument against Abolishing Christianity* (1708): 'Another Advantage proposed by the abolishing of Christianity, is, the clear Gain of one Day in Seven, which is now entirely lost, and consequently the Kingdom one Seventh less considerable in Trade, Business, and Pleasure.' Much of Fielding's strategy in satirizing the 'nominal' religion of the second speaker appears to be derived from Swift's ironic essay.

[2] i.e. 'Society in general', not the Robin Hood Society; for the same usage, cf. *CGJ* Nos. 18 and 36, below.

[3] Not given; but the Dutch, of course, were the prime example of a trading nation, and sometimes of a nation in which religion never stood in the way of economic gain. Cf. Fielding's disparaging allusion in *Tom Jones*, XIII. i, and Swift's harsh satire in *Gulliver's Travels*, III. xi; on the relation between religious toleration in Holland and the growth of its trade, see Sir William Temple, *Observations upon the United Provinces of the Netherlands* (1673), ch. 5.

[4] Aeschines (*c.*397–*c.*322 BC), Athenian orator and opponent of Demosthenes; Quintus Hortalus Hortensius (114–50 BC), eminent orator, associate and sometime opponent of Cicero.

any thing mesbecoming drop from me on this grate Occasion, tho' your Candour, your Beneevolence, might encline you to extend an unmeerited Attention, yet, Sir, these Walls, these Stones, these Boards, these very Bracks,[1] withute Ears, withute a Tongue, would tacitly express their Endeegnation. Sir, it is a Queestion, that whoever hath rede History, or deeved at all into the oxceelent Mystery of Politics, must confees, that all the grete Pheelosophers, Poets, Oraters, Historians——*Hammer down*——

MR. OCURRY, Solicitor. Upon my Shoul, I am very sorry now that the Rules of this grate Society forced the last very learned Gentleman to sit down before he told us his Opinion; but, whatever it be, I am after being of the saame. It is very true upon my Shoul, what he said, that it is a very great Question, and I do not well know fether I understand it as yet, or no: but this I think, that if Religion be a great Hurt to the Nation, I cannot for my Shoul see where the Good of it is. This I know very well, that there is a very good Religion in Ireland, and they do call it the Roman Catholic Religion, and I am of it myself, though I dont very well know what it is. There is Something about Beads and Masses, and Patty Nosters, and Ivy Marys, and I will fight for it as long as I am alive, and longer.—And upon my Shoul I will tell you a good Thing, if you are afraid of your own Religion, you may send for ours, for I know it will come; for Father Patrick Ocain did tell me, he would bring it along with him. Nay, he tould me, that he had brought it hither before he did come himself. (*at which there was a Laugh.*)

Mr. GILES SHUTTLE, Weaver.—I hope no Gentleman will treat this Thing as a Jest, whereof I thinks it to be a very great Matter of Earnest. Whereof I dont much understand your Speech-making Sort of Work, but this I thinks, that I am as a good Judge of these Sort of Matters, for I am worth a hundred Pounds, and owes no Man a Farthing. Whereof I thinks, I am as good a Man as another: for why should not any other Man have as much Sense as a Gentleman? I thinks I knows Something of Trade, that to be sure, is the main Article in every trading Nation, whereby——Here the first Paper was broke off. The Second is as follows:

Question. Whether infinite Power could make the World out of Nothing?

The Speakers to this Question were Mr. Thomas Tinderbox, the Chandler; Mr. George White, Boatswain's Mate; Mr. Edward Peacock, Victualler; Mr. Budge, the Shoemaker; Mr. Goose, the Taylor; Mr. Halt, the Maker of Pattins;[2] and one great Scholar, whose Name I do not know.

It was urged on the Behalf of infinite Power, That we have no very adequate Idea of it. That there are many Things which we see are, and yet we cannot, with any great Certainty, tell how they came to be. That so far from our Reason being able to comprehend every Thing, some wise Men

---

[1] Presumably, the speaker's rendering of 'bricks'; no sense of 'bracks' fits the context.
[2] i.e. pattens, wooden soles attached to ordinary shoes to raise the wearer out of mud or water.

have doubted, whether we do with Certainty, comprehend any Thing.[1] That whatever we may think we know, we do not know how we think. That either every Thing was made by Something, out of Nothing, or else Nothing made every Thing, either out of Something or Nothing.[2] And, lastly; that infinite Power might more reasonably be supposed to create every Thing out of Nothing, than no Power at all could be supposed to make every Thing out of any Thing.

On the contrary, it was well argued, that Nothing can be made out of Nothing, for, *ex nihil O Nothing is fit*.[3] That every Day's Experience must convince us of this: That, by infinite Power, we only meant a very great Degree of Power; but that, if the Thing to be done be not the Subject of Power, the smallest Degree will be equal to the greatest. And it was urged with great Force of Wit and Eloquence, by Mr. Goose, that the best Taylor, and the worst, were alike unable to make a Coat without Materials. That, in this Case, a Taylor with infinite Power, would be in the same Condition with a Taylor who had no Power at all. And if so small a Thing as a Coat could not be made out of Nothing, how could so large a Thing as the World be cut out of the same no Materials?[4] The Scholar gave a very good Answer to what had been offered concerning our Ignorance of infinite Power, and said, if we had no adequate Idea of it, it was a good Cause of disbelieving it; for, as Reason was to be Judge of all Things, what was not the Object of Reason, ought to be rejected by it. He admitted, that there were some Things which did exist, and that we did not as yet know, the Manner in which they came to exist; but it did not follow that such Causes were above the Reach of human Reason, because she had not yet discovered them, for, he made no Doubt, but that this Society, by Means of their free Enquiry after Truth, would, in the End, discover the Whole; and that the Manner in which a Man was

[1] i.e. Pyrrho and other Skeptics. With this debate over the limits of reason, cf. the account of Mr. Wilson's 'freethinking' Club, *Joseph Andrews*, III. iii: 'These Gentlemen were engaged in a Search after Truth, in the Pursuit of which they threw aside all the Prejudices of Education, and governed themselves only by the infallible Guide of Human Reason'. Cf. also the definition of a free-thinker, *CGJ* No. 62, below. Fielding's defense of Christianity against the rationalism of the Deists and the claims of those he called 'political philosophers' (Hobbes, Mandeville) is a constant theme throughout his works; see, among many instances, *Champion*, 5 and 22 Jan. 1740, *True Patriot*, No. 4 (26 Nov. 1745), and *Fragment of a Comment on Lord Bolingbroke's Essays* (unfinished at the time of his death).

[2] Cf. Fielding's 'An Essay on Nothing', *Miscellanies* (1743): 'Whereas in Fact, from Nothing proceeds every Thing. And this is a Truth confessed by the Philosophers of all Sects: the only Point in Controversy between them being, whether Something made the World out of Nothing, or Nothing out of Something'. One of Fielding's favorite divines calls such speculation 'a Research too great for any Mortal Enquiry'; see Robert South, *Sermons*, 5th edn. (1722), i. 44–5.

[3] A perversion of the proverbial expression, *Ex nihilo nihil fit*, which Fielding in his 'Essay on Nothing' translates by King Lear's line, 'Nothing can come of Nothing'. The idea is expressed by Epicurus but was common among all the pre-Socratics. See Diogenes Laertius, 'Epicurus', *Lives of Eminent Philosophers* (Loeb), x. 39 and n.

[4] Cf. Swift's sect of clothes philosophers, *A Tale of a Tub*, sect. II: 'They held the Universe to be a large *Suit of Cloaths*, which *invests* every Thing'.

made, would be no more a Mystery to Posterity, than it is to the present Age, how they make a Pudding. He concluded with saying, that some very wise and learned Men, who lived near 3000 Years ago, had asserted that the World had existed from all Eternity,[1] which Opinion seemed to solve all Difficulties, and was, as it appeared, highly agreeable to the Sentiments of the whole Society.

Question. Whether, in the Opinion of this Society, the Government did Right in——.[2]

Here ends this valuable Fragment, on which I shall give my Comment in my next Paper.   A.

Proceedings at the Court of Censorial Enquiry, *&c.*[3]

A Great Number of Beaus, Rakes, fine Ladies, and several formal Persons with bushy Wigs, and Canes at their Noses,[4] pushed forward, and offered themselves as Witnesses against poor Amelia, when a grave Man[5] stood up and begged to be heard; which the Court granted, and he spoke as follows.

"If you, Mr. Censor, are yourself a Parent, you will view me with Compassion when I declare I am the Father of this poor Girl the Prisoner at the Bar; nay, when I go farther, and avow, that of all my Offspring she is my favourite Child. I can truly say that I bestowed a more than ordinary Pains in her Education; in which I will venture to affirm, I followed the Rules of all those who are acknowledged to have writ best on the Subject; and if her Conduct be fairly examined, she will be found to deviate very little from the strictest Observation of all those Rules; neither Homer nor Virgil pursued them with greater Care than myself, and the candid and learned Reader will see that the latter was the noble model, which I made use of on this Occasion.

"I do not think my Child is entirely free from Faults. I know nothing human that is so; but surely she doth not deserve the Rancour[6] with which she hath been treated by the Public. However, it is not my Intention, at

---

[1] Presumably the Epicureans, although in that case the speaker is off by a thousand years. Cf. Diogenes Laertius, in summary of Epicurus: 'Moreover, the sum total of things was always such as it is now, and such it will ever remain' (*Lives of Eminent Philosophers* [Loeb], x. 39). Before Epicurus, however, Aristotle had also claimed that the world had always existed while at the same time stressing that all previous natural philosophers had believed it had a beginning in time; cf. *On the Heavens*, I. x (279b) and W. K. C. Guthrie, *History of Greek Philosophy* (1962), i. 390.

[2] Alluding to the tendency of the Robinhoodians to espouse Opposition politics.

[3] For the first scene of this trial, see *CGJ* No. 7 and notes, above.

[4] Dudden (p. 816) suggests these are physicians, angry at Fielding's praise in *Amelia* of unconventional doctors like Thomas Thompson and Robert James; see above, p. 59. Cf. *Journey from this World to the Next* (1743), I. ii.

[5] Fielding himself. But the 'grave man' as a figure of authority is common in Fielding; Bernard Shea, 'Machiavelli and Fielding's *Jonathan Wild*', *PMLA* 72 (1957), 59, traces the image to Machiavelli's *Discourses* (I. liv) and cites *Champion*, 15 Jan. 1740, *Tom Jones*, XII. vi., and *Jonathan Wild*, IV. iii.

[6] On the reception of *Amelia* see above, p. 57 n.1.

present, to make my Defence; but shall submit to a Compromise, which hath been always allowed in this Court in all Prosecutions for Dulness. I do, therefore, solemnly declare to you, Mr. Censor, that I will trouble the World no more with any Children of mine by the same Muse."

This Declaration was received with a loud Huzza, by the greater Part of the Spectators; and being allowed by the Court, was presently entered of Record. Then Amelia was delivered to her Parent, and a Scene of great Tenderness passed between them, which gave much Satisfaction to many present; some of whom, however, blamed the old Gentleman for putting an End to the Cause, and several very grave and well looking Men, who knew the whole Merits, asserted, that the Lady ought to have been honourably acquitted.

Then the Court adjourned to Saturday, Feb. 1.

SATURDAY, FEBRUARY 1, 1752.   NUMB. 9.

Dic quibus in terris et eris mihi magnus Apollo.

VIRGIL.[1]

Tell in what Clime these People did appear,
And you shall be the Laureate of next Year.

It will be a very difficult Matter to fix with any Certainty, at what Place, and amongst what People, the Robin-hood Society[2] was held, as we have not the least Light to guess from what Language the Fragment which now remains to us, was originally translated. Two Things may be averred, that this Society was held in some Country where the People were extremely free; and, secondly, that it was in a Country, where that Part of the Community which the French called *la Canaille*[3] was at the Head of Public Affairs.

From the latter of these Circumstances, it appears that these Robin-hoodians cannot be placed among the Egyptians; for Diodorus Siculus, speaking of these People, tells us, that, *Whereas in all Democracies great Injury is done to the State by the Populace interfering in the public Councils, the Egyptians very severely punished these Artificers who presumed to meddle with Matters of Government.*[*4]

---

* Diod. Sic. Fol. 68. Edit. Rhod. Hannov. πλεῖστοι δ' ἐν ταῖς δημοκρατουμέναις πόλεσιν κτλ.

[1] *Eclogues*, iii. 104: 'Tell me in what land—and you shall be my great Apollo' (Loeb); the line is part of a riddle which is appropriate to Fielding's satire of the religious questions debated by the Robin Hood Society: 'Tell me in what land . . . Heaven's space is but three ells broad' (Loeb).

[2] See *CGJ* No. 8, above.

[3] 'Rabble'; cf. Fielding's comment on a news item about a riot in Norwich, published in the news section of this number of the *CGJ* (below, Appendix II) and describing the growing power of the 'mob' in public affairs. This theme is developed at length in *CGJ* Nos. 47 and 49.

[4] *Bibliotheca historica*, I. lxxiv. 7; Fielding has adapted the passage by shortening it slightly.

Nor can I ever believe, that the Question, *Whether Religion was of any Use to the Society*, would ever have been supported amongst a People so highly devoted to Superstition, that Religion was indeed the Foundation of their civil Society.[1]

The same Objection will recur against placing this Society in Athens: For tho' Pericles, in his Speech to the Athenians, recorded in Thucydides, compliments his Countrymen with being all Politicians, *Among us*, says he, *even the Mechanics are not inferior to their fellow Citizens in Political Knowledge*.[2]† Yet in a Country where Socrates was put to Death, for attempting an Innovation in religious Matters, it is hard to believe that the Dregs of the People would have been permitted to have questioned the very first Principles of all Religion with Impunity.

And this Objection will, I apprehend, hold likewise against all other States, not only those which we call civilized, but even the Tartars, Goths, Vandals, and Picts, &c. from the Time they are recorded in History. None of these having been found without their Deities, and without a very strong Persuasion of the Truth of some Religion or other. And so far were they all from doubting whether Religion was of any Use, or as the Fragment hath it, *youse* to the Society, that they carried the Images of their Gods with them to War, and relied upon their Favours and Assistance for Success in all Affairs.

To say the Truth, the only People now upon Earth, among whose Ancestors I can suppose such an Assembly to have been held, are the Inhabitants of a certain Tract of Land in Africa, bordering on the Cape of Good Hope, commonly known unto us by the Name of the HOTTENTOTS.

I am, however, well aware that there are many Objections to this Opinion. First, that these Hottentots are supposed not to have any Knowledge of Religion at all, nor ever to have heard the Name of the Divinity;[3] whereas it appears manifestly that the Robinhoodians had some kind of Religion even established in their Country, and that the Name of G— was at least known among them.

It is unnecessary to observe, likewise, that the Members of this Society had more of the Use of Letters, and were better skilled in the Rules of

† Thucyd. lib. ii c. 40. καὶ ἑτέροις πρὸς ἔργα τετραμμένοις κτλ.

---

[1] Cf. Diodorus Siculus, I. lxxiii; Herodotus, *History*, ii. 37: 'They are beyond measure religious, more than any other nation' (Loeb).

[2] *History*, II. xl. 2.

[3] Cf. Peter Kolben, *The Present State of the Cape of Good-Hope: Or, A Particular Account of the several Nations of the Hottentots* (trans. Medley, 1731): 'It has been publish'd in several Languages, and is, I believe, at this day generally apprehended throughout *Europe*, that the *Hottentots* are so brutal a People as to be, in a Manner, incapable of Reflection: That they have no Sense of God or Religion' (i. 37); but Kolben argues that this view is exaggerated, as does William ten Rhyne, *An Account of the Cape of Good Hope and the Hottentots* in *A Collection of Voyages and Travels*, iv (1732), 779. In the popular view they were a 'Nation of Atheists' (*Spectator*, No. 389, 27 May 1712); Fielding refers to their 'blessed State of Nature' in *JJ* No. 16 (19 Mar. 1748).

Oratory than the Hottentots can be conceived to have been:[1] For as to the Speech of Mr. Mac Flourish, as well for *the Matter* as for the Eloquence of it, it might be spoken with great Applause in many of our politest Assemblies.

Upon the whole, therefore, I must confess myself intirely at a Loss in forming any probable Conjecture as to what Part of the Earth these *Robinhoodians* inhabited; not being able to trace the least Footsteps of them in any History I have ever seen.

As to the Time in which they flourished, the Fragment itself will lend us some little Assistance. It is dated 1 51; which Figures, I make no Doubt, should be all joined together, and then the only Doubt will be from what Æra this Reckoning begun.

And here, I think, there can be no Doubt, but that the Æra intended was that of the general Flood in the Time of Noah, and that the *Robinhoodians* were some Party of those People, who are said, after the Dispersion at Babel to have been scattered over the Face of the Earth.[2]

Those imperfect Notions of Religion which they appear to have entertained, admirably well agree with this Opinion: For it is very reasonable to suppose that such immediate Interpositions of Providence,[3] or to speak more adequately such Denunciations of divine Vengeance, as were exemplified in the Deluge, and the Dispersion at Babel, could scarce be so immediately eradicated as not to leave some little Impression, some small Sparks of religious Veneration in the Grand-children and Great-Grand-Children of those who had been Spectators of such dreadful Scenes; as, on the other Hand, both sacred and profane History assures us, that these Sparks were very faint, and not sufficient to kindle any true Devotion among them.

Again, as the Fragment very plainly appears to have been translated by several Hands, so may we very reasonably infer that it was translated out of as many various Languages. Another Reason to fix the Date of this Assembly soon after the abovementioned Dispersion.

Lastly, the Name of Robinhood puts the Matter beyond all Doubt or Question; this Word being, as a learned Etymologist observed to me, clearly derived from the *Tower of Babel*: for first *Robin* and *Bobin* are allowed to be the same Word; the first Syllable then is Bob, change o into a, which is only a Metathesis of one Vowel for another, and you have Bab, then supply the Termination el instead of ing (for both are only Terminations) and you have clearly the Word Babel.

---

[1] The language of the Hottentots was described as 'only an inarticulate noise' (ten Rhyne, p. 781), 'a confused *Gabble*' (*Spectator*, No. 389), and 'the Noise of irritated Turkey-cocks' (Kolben, i. 32).

[2] Genesis 11: 9.

[3] The phrase which forms the title of Fielding's collection of murder cases with moral reflections, published 13 Apr. 1752; see the 'Covent Garden' column for that date, Appendix I.

As for the H in Hood, it is known to be no Letter at all, and therefore an Etymologist may there place what Letter he pleases, and why not a T as well as any other. Then change the final d into an r, and you have Toor, which hath a better Pretence, than the known Word Tor to signify Tower.—Thus, by a few inconsiderable Changes, the Robin-Hood and Babel-Tower, appear to be one and the same Word.[1]

Two Objections have been made to the great Antiquity of this Fragment; the first is, that Ireland is mentioned in it, which as *Camden* and others would make us believe, was not peopled till many Ages after the Æra I have above mentioned:[2] But these learned Men are certainly in a Mistake; for I am well assured that several Irish Beggars, whose Ancestors were dispossessed in the Wars of the last Century, are after having now in their Possession the Title-Deeds of their said Estates from long before the Times of Noah.[3]

The other Objection is, that the Dutch are likewise mentioned in the Fragment, a People, as they are generally supposed, of a much later Rise in the World than the Period of Time which I have endeavoured to assign to this Society.

To this I answer, that tho' that Body of People, who threw off the Spanish Yoke in the Time of the Duke of Alva,[4] are extremely modern, yet are the Dutch themselves of very great Antiquity, as hath been well proved by the learned GOROPIUS BECANUS[5] from the History of Herodotus.

That Historian tells us, that one of the Assyrian Kings being desirous to

---

[1] Cf. Fielding's mock-etymology of the word 'Fashion' in *CGJ* No. 37; cf. also the devices used by the three brothers in interpreting their father's will, Swift's *A Tale of a Tub*, sect. II. For the same sort of learned joking, see the 'Etymology of Masquerades', in A. Betson, *Miscellaneous Dissertations Historical, Critical, and Moral on the Origin and Antiquity of Masquerades, Plays, Poetry, &c.* [1751].

[2] William Camden's *Britannia*, which Fielding owned in the translation by Edmund Gibson (1695; Baker, item 303), ridicules some of the ancient legends concerning the settlement of Ireland but adds, 'As I doubt not but this Island was anciently inhabited, as soon as mankind began to multiply and disperse in the World; so 'tis very plain that its first inhabitants came from Britain' (p. 966).

[3] Alluding to the extravagant claims made by Irish 'Fortune-hunters', a notorious breed in the period; cf. 'Col. *Mac-Blunder*', a member of 'the *Hibernian* Society of Fortune-Hunters', who are ordered to 'make such honourable mention of the said Colonel's high *Birth, Worth*, and other Merit, as may enable him to obtain in Marriage a beautiful young Lady, of a very considerable Fortune', in *A Trip from St. James's to the Royal Exchange* (1744), p. 19; see also *The Life and Intrigues of the late Celebrated Mrs. Mary Parrimore* (1729), p. 66, and an advertisement for a work called *The Adventures of Shelim O'Blunder . . . with a few cursory Reflections on the common Ingredients of a Teagueland Beau, or Fortune Hunter* (*DA*, 17 July 1751). Fielding makes similar allusions in *Tom Jones* (XI. vii, XV. xi) but criticizes such 'Sarcasms' in the *Champion*, 29 Mar. 1740, and in his 'Essay on Conversation' (*Miscellanies* [1743]); the latter work is cited in a defense of the Irish in the *Craftsman*, 17 Mar. 1750. In the present passage Fielding uses the phrase 'are after having' as an Irish locution; cf. the speech of Mr O'Curry, *CGJ* No. 8, above.

[4] Referring to the events of 1572–3, when the forces of the Prince of Orange and Louis of Nassau forced the recall of the Spanish governor-general, Fernando Alvarez de Toledo, Duke of Alva (1507–82).

[5] Johannes Goropius Becanus (1518–72), or Jean Van Gorp, a Belgian scholar, physician, and antiquarian who maintained that Dutch was the mother of all other languages and used bizarre etymologies to support his views.

discover who were the most ancient People, confined two Children, a Boy and a Girl, till they were at the Age of Maturity, without suffering either of them to hear one articulate Sound; having determined, I know not for what Reason, that whatever Language could claim their first Word, the People speaking that Language should be deemed the most ancient.

The Word which was first pronounced by one of them was BEKER, which in the Phænician Tongue signifies Bread: the Phænicians were therefore concluded to have been the first Planters of Mankind.[1]

Under this Mistake the World continued many Ages, till at last the learned Goropius discovered that the Word BEKER, which in the Phænician Tongue signifies *Bread*, did in the Dutch Language signify a BAKER, and that before Bread was a Baker was.[2] *Ergo, &c.*

And here I cannot help observing, that this Quotation, as it proves the Antiquity of the Dutch, so it proves the great Antiquity of *Bakers*, to whose Honour we may likewise read in Diodorus, that Isis the Wife of Osyris was immortalized among the Egyptians, for having taught them the Art of Baking.[3]

Succeeding Ages being unwilling to ascribe so great an Honour to a Woman, transferred it from her to her Husband, and called him BACCHUS, or as it is more commonly by modern Authors writ, BAKKUS, and BAKUS, which being literally *done into English* by the Change of the Latin Termination, is BAKER.[4]

Indeed it is very reasonable to imagine that before the Invention of Cookery, the Bakers were held in the highest Honours, as the People derived from their Art the greatest Dainty of which their simple Taste gave them any Idea. And the great Esteem, in which Cookery is held now, may very well account for the Preference given to Bakers in those early Ages, when these were the only Cooks.

But if none of these Reasons should be thought satisfactory, to fix, with any absolute Certainty, the exact Æra of this Assembly, the following Conclusions must be, I think, allowed by every Reader.

[1] Herodotus, *History*, ii. 2; the story is as Fielding tells it, except that the king, Psammetichus, is Egyptian, not Assyrian, and the word is 'Bekos', a Phrygian (not Phoenician) word for bread. The allusions to bread and baking throughout this portion of the essay are to ridicule Caleb Jeacocke, the baker who headed the Robin Hood Society (see above, p. 61).

[2] Goropius Becanus, *Origines Antwerpianae sive Cimmeriorum Becceselana* (Antwerp, 1569), pp. 551–2; Fielding summarizes the passage accurately, although Goropius uses the word 'Bec' in his account of the tale in Herodotus.

[3] Diodorus Siculus, *Bibliotheca historica*, I. xliii. 5, says that some attribute to Isis the discovery that bread could be made from the lotus, though he does not say she was thereby immortalized.

[4] Osiris is equated with Dionysus (Bacchus) in Herodotus, *History*, ii. 42 and Diodorus Siculus, I. xcvi. The same identification occurs in one of Fielding's favorite books, Abbé Banier's *Mythology and Fables of the Ancients Explain'd from History*, ii (1740), 438–44; Fielding cites this work, which he owned (Baker, item 219), in a similarly playful identification of Bacchus with Jacobites, *JJ* No. 6 (9 Jan. 1748).

First, that some Religion had a kind of Establishment amongst these People.

Secondly, That this Religion, whatever it was, could not have the least Sway over their Morals or Practice.

Thirdly, That this Society, in which the first Principles of Religion and Government were debated, was the chief Assembly, in this Country, and Mr. Whitebread, the Baker, the greatest Man in it.[1]

And lastly, I think it can create no Manner of Surprize in any one, that such a Nation as this hath been long since swept away from the Face of the Earth, and the very Name of such a People expunged out of the Memory of Man.   A.

Proceedings at the Court of Censorial Enquiry, &c.

Counsellor TOWN moved for an Information, in the Nature of a *Quo Warranto*[2], to be exhibited against Mr. Mossop, the Player, to shew Cause by what Authority he takes upon himself the Stile, Title, and Dignity of Macbeth, Mr. Garrick, the only true and lawful Macbeth, being at the same Time in full Life and Health.[3]

Ordered, That the said Mossop do shew Cause in this Paper on Tuesday next.

The Court was then moved by an Irish Gentleman on Behalf of a vast Number of *Practitioners* of the Law, who do not at present practise the Law at all, that they might be admitted to plead before the Censor.[4]

And it was ordered accordingly.

---

[1] See *CGJ* No. 8, above, p. 61.

[2] A writ which 'lies against any Person or Corporation that usurps any Franchise or Liberty against the King, without good Title; and is brought against the Usurpers to shew by what Right and Title they hold or claim such Franchise or Liberty' (Giles Jacob, *A New Law-Dictionary*, 7th edn. [1756], s.v. 'quo warranto'); an 'Information in the Nature of' such a writ was a device to make the process speedier (Jowitt, *Dictionary of English Law*).

[3] Henry Mossop (1729?–74?), Irish actor, had joined Garrick at Drury Lane in 1751, when he alternated with the manager in the role of Richard III. He first played Macbeth on 28 Jan. 1752 and again on the 29th. Some audience dissatisfaction on the first night is indicated by the comment recorded by Cross, the prompter: 'Mossop did Macbeth—diff—much hissing when given out again' (*London Stage*, Pt. 4, i. 288). Garrick resumed the role for the next performance, but Mossop continued to share the part with Garrick as long as he was at Drury Lane. For his 'trial', see *CGJ* No. 10.

[4] By 'Practitioners' Fielding means attorneys or solicitors (in contrast to barristers), who organized in London in 1739 as 'The Society of Gentlemen Practisers'. Fielding is, perhaps, suggesting ironically that since many of these, along with fledgling barristers doing the work of solicitors for lack of other work, cannot find business in the real courts, they might as well practise before A. Drawcansir. (The editor is indebted to Hugh Amory for that interpretation.) Cf. a passage in *A Ramble through London* (1738) describing 'people tolerably dressed, cursing themselves and everybody else', who turn out to be '*Counsellors* without Law or Clients' (p. 5); and see, on the low reputation of 'Gentlemen Practisers', Robert Robson, *The Attorney in Eighteenth-Century England* (Cambridge, 1959), pp. 13–25, 138–43. Since an Irish gentleman makes the motion, Fielding may be hitting at Irish attorneys in particular.

The Trial of B— T—,[1] on the Statute of Dulness, was then brought on, when the said B— T— pleaded to the Jurisdiction of the Court; and set forth, that, being a lawful Subject of Grub-Street, she is not liable to be tried in this Court for any such Crime as Dulness. To this Plea there was a Demurrer,[2] and a Day was given for the Argument of the same.

This is a Cause of great Importance, and the Expectations of all Men are very much raised concerning the Event.

(*Adjourned.*)

TUESDAY, FEBRUARY 4, 1752.   NUMB. 10.

> *At nostri Proavi Plautinos et numeros, et*
> *Laudavere Sales, nimium patienter utrumque,*
> *Ne dicam Stulte, mirati.*   Horace.[3]

Modernized.

> *In former Times this tasteless, silly Town*
> *Too fondly prais'd Tom D'Urfey and Tom Brown.*[4]

The present Age seems pretty well agreed in an Opinion, that the utmost Scope and End of Reading is Amusement only; and such, indeed, are now the fashionable Books, that a Reader can propose no more than mere

---

[1] Identified by a writer in *GM* 22 (1752), 54, as *The History of Miss Betsy Thoughtless*, a novel by Eliza Haywood containing a brief attack on Fielding's early plays at the Little Theatre in the Haymarket ('F———g's scandal Shop'). Although *Betsy Thoughtless* first appeared on 21 Oct. 1751, it was still much in the public eye, with a poem praising its 'moral Page' (*LDA*, 7 Dec. 1751) and a new edition advertised two weeks before Fielding wrote this passage (*DA*, 14 Jan. 1752). It has also been suggested, by Martin Battestin, that by 'B— T—' Fielding intended Bonnell Thornton, who under the pseudonym 'Roxana Termagant' was attacking him each week in *Have At You All: or, The Drury-Lane Journal*. Perhaps Fielding meant both interpretations to be possible; Thornton himself says he has been confused with 'that prolific inexhaustible authoress, who has lately oblig'd us with the history of Miss *Betsy Thoughtless*' (*Drury-Lane Journal*, No. 2 [23 Jan. 1752]). For the trial, see *CGJ* No. 15.

[2] 'A Kind of Pause or Stop, put to any Action, upon Point of Difficulty, which must be determined by the Court, before any farther Proceedings can be heard therein' (Giles Jacob, *A New Law-Dictionary*, 7th edn. [1756], s.v. 'demurrer').

[3] *Art of Poetry*, 270–2: 'Yet your forefathers, you say, praised both the measure and wit of Plautus. Too tolerant, not to say foolish, was their admiration of both' (Loeb); in the first line Fielding substitutes *nostri* for *vestri*.

[4] Tom Brown (1663–1704), miscellaneous writer, satirist, and translator, 'of facetious Memory' (Addison, *Spectator*, No. 567, 14 July 1714), and one of the most prolific and notorious of Grub Street hacks. His best known work was *Amusements, Serious and Comical* (1700); two volumes of his five-volume *Works* (1720–1) were in Partridge's library in *Tom Jones* (VIII. v). Brown was one of the translators of the *Works of Lucian* (1711), attacked by Fielding in *CGJ* No. 52.

Like Brown, Tom D'Urfey (or Durfey) (1653–1723), playwright and songwriter, had long been a butt of ridicule by the wits. Pope satirized him in *Peri Bathous* and the *Dunciad* (iii. 146). Aside from his plays, he was best known for his collection of songs, *Wit and Mirth; or Pills to Purge Melancholy* (6 vols., 1719–20). Cf. Fielding's *Author's Farce* (1730): 'this age would allow Tom Durfey a better poet than Congreve or Wycherley' (III. i), and *True Patriot*, No. 1 (5 Nov. 1745): '*Durfey*, whose Name is almost forgot'.

Entertainment, and it is sometimes very well for him if he finds even this in his Studies.

Letters, however, were surely intended for a much more noble and profitable Purpose than this. Writers are not, I presume, to be considered as mere Jack-Puddings,[1] whose Business it is only to excite Laughter: This, indeed, may sometimes be intermixed, and served up, with graver Matters, in order to titilate the Palate, and to recommend wholesome Food to the Mind; and, for this Purpose, it hath been used by many excellent Authors: *for why* (as Horace says) *should not any one promulgate Truth with a Smile on his Countenance?*[2] *Ridicule, indeed,* as he again intimates, *is commonly a stronger and better Method of attacking Vice, than the severer kind of Satire.*[3]

When Wit and Humour are introduced for such good Purposes, when the agreeable *is blended with the useful, then* is the Writer said *to have succeeded in every Point.*[4] *Pleasantry,* (as the ingenious Author of Clarissa says of a Story) *should be made only the Vehicle of Instruction;*[5] and thus Romances themselves, as well as Epic Poems, may become worthy the Perusal of the greatest of Men: But when no Moral, no Lesson, no Instruction is conveyed to the Reader, where the whole Design of the Composition is no more than to make us laugh, the Writer comes very near to the Character of a Buffoon; and his Admirers, if an old Latin Proverb[6] be true, deserve no great Compliments to be paid to their Wisdom.

After what I have here advanced, I cannot fairly, I think, be represented as an Enemy to Laughter, or to all those Kinds of Writing that are apt to

[1] A 'buffoon, clown, or merry-andrew, especially one attending on a mountebank' (*OED*, citing this essay); cf. the poem by 'John Pudding', in *JJ* No. 13 (27 Feb. 1748), and *CGJ* No. 18, below, p. 125.

[2] *Satires*, I. i. 24–5; cf. *Tom Jones*, XI. i: 'but surely a Man may speak Truth with a smiling Countenance'.

[3] Fielding paraphrases *Satires*, I. x. 14–15: *ridiculum acri / fortius et melius magnas plerumque secat res*, 'Jesting oft cuts hard knots more forcefully and effectively than gravity' (Loeb). He uses the opening phrases as the motto to *JJ* No. 1 (5 Dec. 1747).

[4] A commonplace in neo-classical criticism, derived from the twofold formula of Horace, *Aut prodesse volunt aut delectare poetae*, '*Poets aim either to benefit or to amuse*', *Art of Poetry*, 333–4. Fielding is quoting from the same passage in Horace (343): 'He has won every vote who has blended profit and pleasure, at once delighting and instructing the reader' (Loeb). Cf. 'Counsellor Town's' corruption of the dictum, *CGJ* No. 7, above, p. 57.

[5] In the Preface to the first volume of *Clarissa* (1748) Richardson gives as the opinion of his 'judicious Friends' 'That in all Works of This, and of the Dramatic Kind, STORY, or AMUSEMENT, should be considered as little more than the *Vehicle* to the more necessary INSTRUCTION' (i, p. vi). Fielding again cites this view with approval in his own Preface to *Journal of a Voyage to Lisbon* (1755). Despite his earlier ridicule of Richardson in *Shamela* and *Joseph Andrews*, Fielding admired *Clarissa*; he praised it in two numbers of *JJ* (Nos. 5 and 14, 2 Jan. and 5 Mar. 1748) and sent Richardson a private letter of enthusiastic appreciation (see E. L. McAdam, Jr., 'A New Letter from Fielding', *Yale Review*, 38 [1948], 300–10). At the same time in some passages of *Tom Jones* he seems to have invited comparisons between his own novel and *Clarissa* (see *Tom Jones*, ed. Martin Battestin, Wesleyan Edn. (Oxford, 1974), p. 793 n.). On Richardson's continuing animus toward Fielding after the publication of *Tom Jones*, see T. C. Duncan Eaves and Ben D. Kimbel, *Samuel Richardson: A Biography* (Oxford, 1971), pp. 292–306, and General Introduction, p. xlv.

[6] *Risus abundat in ore stultorum*, 'Laughter is frequent in the mouth of fools'; cf. Tilley, F 462: 'A Fool is ever laughing'.

promote it.[1] On the contrary, few Men, I believe, do more admire the Works of those great Masters who have sent their Satire (if I may use the Expression) laughing into the World. Such are that great Triumvirate, Lucian, Cervantes, and Swift.[2] These Authors I shall ever hold in the highest Degree of Esteem; not indeed for that Wit and Humour alone which they all so eminently possest, but because they all endeavoured, with the utmost Force of their Wit and Humour, to expose and extirpate those Follies and Vices which chiefly prevailed in their several Countries.

I would not be thought to confine Wit and Humour to these Writers. Shakespear, Moliere,[3] and some other Authors, have been blessed with the same Talents, and have employed them to the same Purposes. There are some, however, who tho' not void of these Talents have made so wretched a Use of them, that had the Consecration of their Labours been committed to the Hands of the Hangman, no good Man would have regretted their Loss: Nor am I afraid to mention Rabelais, and Aristophanes himself[4] in this Number. For if I may speak my Opinion freely of these two last Writers, and of their Works, their Design appears to me very plainly to have been to ridicule all Sobriety, Modesty, Decency, Virtue and Religion, out of the World. Now whoever reads over the five great Writers first mentioned in this Paragraph, must either have a very bad Head, or a very bad Heart, if he doth not become both a wiser and a better Man.

In the Exercise of the Mind, as well as in the Exercise of the Body, Diversion is a secondary Consideration, and designed only to make that agreeable, which is at the same Time useful, to such noble Purposes as Health and Wisdom. But what should we say to a Man who mounted his Chamber Hobby,[5] or fought with his own Shadow for his Amusement only?

[1] But cf. Fielding's ambivalent discourse on laughter in 'An Essay on the Knowledge of the Characters of Men', *Miscellanies* (1743), ed. H. K. Miller, Wesleyan Edn. (Oxford, 1972), i. 159–61; cf. also the opening paragraphs of *CGJ* No. 18 and the essay on false humor, *CGJ* No. 19.

[2] Cf. Fielding's list of those inspired by genius for wit and humor, *Tom Jones*, XIII. i, and the 'Comments upon Authors', *Amelia*, VIII. v; both passages pay high tribute to this 'great Triumvirate'. On Lucian, whom Fielding admired most of all, see *CGJ* No. 52 and notes, below. Cervantes, of course, Fielding had imitated in *Joseph Andrews* and earlier in *Don Quixote in England* (1734); for a slight qualification of the praise here, see his review of Charlotte Lennox, *CGJ* No. 24, below. On Swift, among many tributes, see *Champion*, 3 Jan. 1740; *Amelia*, VIII. v; and the obituary in *True Patriot*, No. 1 (5 Nov. 1745), where Fielding says, 'He possessed the Talents of a Lucian, a Rabelais, and a Cervantes, and in his Works exceeded them all'. In those passages, as here, Swift is praised for employing his wit 'to the noblest Purposes'; on Swift's noticeable influence on Fielding in the *CGJ*, see General Introduction, p. xliv.   [3] Cf. *CGJ* No. 1, above, p. 19.

[4] Fielding had praised Aristophanes in the Preface to his and William Young's translation of *Plutus* (1742) and had included both Aristophanes and Rabelais (along with Swift, Cervantes, Lucian, Molière, Shakespeare, and Marivaux) in his invocation to the Genius of Humor in *Tom Jones* (XIII. i); Swift and Rabelais are also compared, without real prejudice to the latter, in *Amelia*, VIII. v. But in his Dedication to *Don Quixote in England* (1734) Fielding condemns Aristophanes for his 'destruction' of Socrates by his misuse of the weapon of theatrical ridicule, and this point seems to have carried increased weight in the severer mood of Fielding's later years; he repeats his revised estimate of the playwright in *CGJ* No. 52.

[5] i.e. a hobby-horse, from the combining of 'chamber-horse' and 'hobby'.

How much more absurd and weak would he appear, who swallowed Poison because it was sweet.

How differently did Horace think of Study from our modern Readers.

> *Quid verum atque decens curo et rogo, et omnis in hoc sum:*
> *Condo et compono, quæ mox depromere possim.*

Truth and Decency are my whole Care and Enquiry. In this Study I am entirely occupied; these I am always laying up, and so disposing, that I can at any Time draw forth my Stores for my immediate Use.[1] The whole Epistle indeed, from which I have paraphrased this Passage, is a Comment upon it, and affords many useful Lessons of Philosophy.

When we are employed in reading a great and good Author, we ought to consider ourselves as searching after Treasures, which, if well and regularly laid up in the Mind, will be of use to us on sundry Occasions in our Lives. If a Man, for Instance, should be overloaded with Prosperity or Adversity (both of which Cases are liable to happen to us) who is there so very wise, or so very foolish, that, if he was a Master of Seneca and Plutarch, could not find great Matter of Comfort and Utility from their Doctrines?[2] I mention these rather than Plato and Aristotle, as the Works of the latter, are not, I think, yet compleatly made English; and, consequently, are less within the Reach of most of my Countrymen.[3]

But, perhaps it may be asked, Will Seneca or Plutarch make us laugh? Perhaps not; but if you are not a Fool, my worthy Friend, which I can hardly with Civility suspect, they will both, (the latter especially) please you more than if they did. For my own Part, I declare, I have not read even Lucian himself with more Delight than I have Plutarch; but surely it is astonishing, that such Scriblers as Tom Brown, Tom D'Urfy, and the Wits of our Age should find Readers, whilst the Writings of so excellent, so entertaining, and so voluminous an Author as Plutarch remain in the World, and, as I

---

[1] *Epistles*, I. i. 11–12. The epistle, addressed to Maecenas, explains why Horace has abandoned 'verses and all other toys' to pursue wisdom and virtue; the passage Fielding quotes is near the beginning, hence his remark that the remainder of the poem is a comment upon it.

[2] Cf. Fielding's praise in *Tom Jones* of the discourse on anger by Seneca, 'who hath, indeed, so well handled this Passion, that none but a very angry Man can read him without great Pleasure and Profit' (VI. ix). Despite his misgivings about some aspects of Stoic thought, Fielding's admiration for Seneca is obvious in numerous references throughout his work; see Miller, pp. 257–8. Similarly Plutarch is praised in *Tom Jones* as 'one of the best of our Brother Historians' (XVII. ii); cf. *Joseph Andrews*, I. i. Plutarch is one of the most frequently cited authors in Fielding's writings; see Robert M. Wallace, 'Fielding's Knowledge of History and Biography', *SP*44 (1947), 89–107.

[3] An 'abridg'd' edition of Plato's *Works* had been translated in 1701, not from the Greek but from the French translation by Dacier; there was no other effort to translate his writings in their entirety until 1804. Aristotle's *Works* first appeared in English in the translation by Thomas Taylor in 1812. Individual works by both philosophers were available in English in the mid-18th cent., but they represented only a small portion of the total corpus of either. On Fielding's admiration for Aristotle, see *CGJ* No. 4, above, p. 37.

apprehend, are very little known.

The Truth I am afraid is, that real Taste is a Quality with which Human Nature is very slenderly gifted. It is indeed so very rare, and so little known, that scarce two Authors have agreed in their Notions of it; and those who have endeavoured to explain it to others, seem to have succeeded only in shewing us that they knew it not themselves.[1] If I might be allowed to give my own Sentiments, I should derive it from a nice Harmony between the Imagination and the Judgment;[2] and hence perhaps it is, that so few have ever possessed this Talent in any eminent Degree. Neither of these will alone bestow it; nothing is indeed more common than to see Men of very bright Imaginations, and of very accurate Learning (which can hardly be acquired without Judgment) who are entirely devoid of Taste;[3] and Longinus, who of all Men seems most exquisitely to have possessed it, will puzzle his Reader very much if he should attempt to decide, whether Imagination or Judgment shine the brighter in that inimitable Critic.[4]

But as for the Bulk of Mankind, they are clearly void of any Degree of Taste. It is a Quality in which they advance very little beyond a State of Infancy. The first Thing a Child is fond of in a Book, is a Picture; the second is a Story; and the third a Jest. Here then is the true *Pons Asinorum*,[5] which very few Readers ever get over.

From what I have said, it may perhaps be thought to appear, that true Taste is the real Gift of Nature only; and if so, some may ask, To what

[1] For the origins and background of the concept of taste in the late 17th and early 18th cent., see J. E. Spingarn, ed., *Critical Essays of the Seventeenth Century* (Oxford, 1908), i, pp. lxxxviii–cvi, and R. W. Babcock, 'The Idea of Taste in the Eighteenth Century', *PMLA* 50 (1935), 922–6. As Fielding indicates, few critical terms were more widely debated in the first half of the century (and even more widely in the second half); some of the more notable early texts include Shaftesbury, *Soliloquy: Or, Advice to an Author* (1710); John Dennis, *A Large Account of the Taste in Poetry* (1702); Leonard Welsted, *A Dissertation Concerning the Perfection of the English Language, The State of Poetry, &c* (1724), and Francis Hutcheson, *Essay on the Nature and Conduct of the Passions and Affections* (1728). Addison, in *Spectator*, No. 409 (19 June 1712) lays out most of the issues in the critical debate, including the question which concerns Fielding here, of whether Taste is an innate faculty or one that can be learned and cultivated.

[2] Cf. Pope's efforts to harmonize 'wit' (the imaginative, inventive faculty) with 'judgment' (the restraining, controlling faculty), *Essay on Criticism*, 80–4; for the background of the problem, see the Introduction to the Twickenham Edn., pp. 212–19. On the need for both Imagination and Judgment in forming a true taste, see the concluding section of Addison's *Spectator*, No. 416 (27 June 1712). In Letter XL contributed to his sister's *Familiar Letters between the Principal Characters in David Simple* (1747), Fielding had brought taste into the realm of morality, defining it as 'no other than the Knowledge of what is right and fit in every thing' (ii. 299); cf. his comment in *Amelia*, 'true Virtue is, indeed, nothing else but true Taste' (IX. ix), and see General Introduction, pp. xxxiv–v.

[3] Cf. Addison, *Spectator*, No. 409 (19 June 1712): 'The Faculty must in some degree be born with us, and it very often happens, that those who have other Qualities in Perfection are wholly void of this'; cf. also Pope, *Essay on Criticism*, 12–13.

[4] Cf. Pope's attribution to Longinus of both judgment and 'a *Poet's Fire*', *Essay on Criticism*, 675–80; on the reputation and influence of Longinus in the period, see Samuel H. Monk, *The Sublime* (Ann Arbor, 1960), ch. 1.

[5] Bridge of asses: 'a humorous name for the fifth proposition of the first book of Euclid, from the difficulty which beginners or dull-witted persons find in getting over it' (*OED*).

Purpose have I endeavoured to show Men that they are without a Blessing, which it is impossible for them to attain?

Now, tho' it is certain that to the highest Consummation of Taste, as well as of every other Excellence, Nature must lend much Assistance; yet great is the Power of Art almost of itself, or at best with only slender Aids from Nature;[1] and to say the Truth, there are very few who have not in their Minds some small Seeds of Taste. *All Men* (says Cicero) *have a sort of tacit Sense of what is right or wrong in Arts and Sciences, even without the help of Arts.*[2] This surely it is in the Power of Art very greatly to improve. That most Men therefore proceed no farther than as I have above declared, is owing either to the want of any, or (which is perhaps yet worse) to an improper Education.

I shall, probably, therefore, in a future Paper,[3] endeavour to lay down some Rules by which all Men may acquire, at least, some Degree of Taste. In the mean while, I shall, (according to the Method observed in Innoculation)[4] recommend to my Readers, as a Preparative for their receiving my Instructions, a total Abstinence from all bad Books; I do therefore most earnestly intreat all my young Readers, that they would cautiously avoid the Perusal of any modern Book till it hath first had the Sanction of some wise and learned Man; and the same Caution I propose to all Fathers, Mothers, and Guardians.

Evil Communications corrupt good Manners, is a Quotation of St. Paul from Menander.[5] EVIL BOOKS CORRUPT AT ONCE BOTH OUR MANNERS AND OUR TASTE.   *C.*

Proceedings at the Court of Censorial Enquiry, *&c.*

Mr. Mossop[6] appeared, according to Order, and shewed Cause by his Council,

That Mr. Mossop is a young Actor of promising Abilities, and very desirous of meriting the Favour of the Public.

[1] Cf. Addison, 'But notwithstanding this Faculty must in some measure be born with us, there are several Methods for Cultivating and Improving it, and without which it will be very uncertain' (*Spectator*, No. 409, 19 June 1712).

[2] *De oratore*, III. i. 195. Cf. Pope, 'Yet if we look more closely, we shall find / Most have the *Seeds* of Judgment in their Mind' (*Essay on Criticism*, 19–20); in his note on these lines Pope cites the passage from Cicero which Fielding quotes.

[3] Never completed, as such; but cf. the essays on education, *CGJ* Nos. 42 and 56, and his affirmation that *all* his 'Lucubrations' in the *CGJ* are designed to restore true taste (*CGJ* No. 5, above).

[4] Those who were about to undergo the controversial inoculation for smallpox were commonly subjected first to a strict diet and a course of purging and vomiting to cleanse the body thoroughly; see Charles Maitland, *Mr. Maitland's Account of Inoculating the Smallpox* (1722), p. 28; and Thomas Nettleton, *An Account of the Success of Inoculating the Smallpox* (1722), p. 4.

[5] I Corinthians 15: 33; Menander, *Thais*, Fragment 2. In *Tom Jones* (v. ii) Fielding incorrectly identified the source of the proverb as Solomon; he is here correcting his error, which had been pointed out by one of his critics. The proverb is used without ascription in *Tom Jones*, XII. iii.

[6] See *CGJ* No. 9, above, p. 71.

That, in all his Attempts hitherto, he hath met with very kind Treatment, and much Encouragement from the Audience, which he presumes to derive from the extraordinary Pains that he hath taken, and from his visible Endeavours to deserve their Applause.

That he doth not presume in the Character of Macbeth to emulate the Perfections of Mr. Garrick; but that he humbly hopes he may be allowed equal to any other Actor in that Part; a Praise which, if he obtains, it will be far from raising his Vanity to any immoderate Pitch.

That Mr. Garrick hath not given up the Part of Macbeth to Mr. Mossop, nor will the former appear the more seldom in that Character, because the latter is upon the Stage.

That Mr. Garrick is not immortal, whatever his Fame may be; and that, if no Regard be had to the Succession of Actors, nor any Care taken to bring those forward into the principal Parts who shall discover the greatest theatrical Talents, the Stage will fall with himself; as was the Case when that famous Triumvirate, Booth, Wilks, and Cibber were in the Management;[1] who, by discountenancing, and keeping back any Actor of apparent Genius, left such a Set of wretched Strolers behind them, at their Departure, that our dramatic Entertainments became contemptible; and had not a Genius[2] of a surprizing Kind emerged all at once, one who was born both in a Sock, and a Buskin, the Theatre Royal was in Danger of sinking to Bartholomew-Fair.[3]

For these Reasons the Council concluded, that he hoped the Rule[4] should be discharged.

Mr. TOWN, who was on the other Side, said he had never any Intention to

---

[1] On the management of Drury Lane in the period 1713–32 by Colley Cibber (1671–1757), Robert Wilks (1665–1732), and Barton Booth (1681–1733), see *CGJ* No. 15 and n. 5 below, p. 102. Though Fielding constantly ridicules Cibber, he does not charge him elsewhere with deliberately ignoring talented young actors when manager of Drury Lane. It was, however, a common complaint, so much so that Cibber is at great pains in his *Apology* (1740) to defend himself against it: 'The most plausible Objection to our Administration, seem'd to be, that we took no Care to breed up young Actors, to succeed us; and this was imputed as the greater Fault, because it was taken for granted, that it was a Matter as easy as planting so many Cabbages: . . . Let it be our Excuse then, for that mistaken Charge against us; that since there was no Garden, or Market, where accomplish'd Actors grew, or were to be sold, we could only pick them up . . . by Chance' (pp. 323–4). See also *An Apology for the Life of Mr. T——— C———, Comedian* (1740), p. 68, a satirical work sometimes attributed to Fielding; *A Letter to a Certain Patentee* [1747], p. 23, which argues that this charge will always be made against actor-managers; and Thomas Davies, *Memoirs of the Life of David Garrick* (1780), i. 158, which accepts Cibber's excuse but praises Garrick for his encouragement of Mossop and two other young actors from Ireland.

[2] Garrick.

[3] Held every year in Smithfield, the fair was the scene of pantomimes, juggling, rope-dancing, and puppet shows as well as performances by actors from the major theatres, who set up booths there; see *London Stage*, Pt. 3, vol. i, p. xlii.

[4] An order or direction made by a court in an action, in this case 'a rule to show cause, or a rule nisi, because if no sufficient cause is shown, the rule is made absolute; otherwise it is discharged' (Jowitt, *Dictionary of English Law* [1959], s.v. 'Rule'); Mossop had been ordered to 'shew Cause' by what authority he assumed the role of Macbeth, *CGJ* No. 9.

press this Matter far against Mr. Mossop; that his Clients considered him as a promising young Man, and very likely to make in Time a great Actor; and that he had already shewn uncommon Powers in the Character of Zanga;[1] and as Mr. Garrick had declared that he did not intend to give up his great Parts, but that he had last Night appeared in that of Richard the Third, he had Instructions to give his Consent to the Discharge of the Rule.

And the Rule was discharged accordingly.

(*Adjourned.*)

SATURDAY, FEBRUARY 8, 1752.   NUMB. 11.

——*Si quid novisti rectius istis*
Candidus imperti.   HORACE.[2]

Anglicé.

If you know a better Way of providing for the Poor,
Be pleased to tell it us.

In a former Paper[3] I offered a Conjecture that the Robinhoodians must have been either the Hottentots themselves, or some such Sort of People, for which I there advanced several very plausible Reasons; the most forcible of which seems to be, *That their Religion could not have the least Sway over their Morals or Practice.* I will here add, in Support of my Opinion, that such a Religion befitted only a People who were not possessed of any Manner of Property.

On the contrary, if we look into the Doctrines and Tenets of that Institution which was accounted divine by our Ancestors, and sincerely believed at least, in this Country, we shall find it admirably calculated for the Preservation of Property; and most notably to correspond with the original Design of all Government, as we find this laid down by Thrasymachus in Plato's Dialogues de Republica. "Do you think," says Thrasymachus to Socrates, (just after he had told him that he wanted a Nurse to blow his Nose) "that those Governors of Cities, who really understand their Art, consider the People in any other Light, than as their Cattle? Do they labour Night and Day with any other View than to make their Subjects profitable to themselves?"[4]

[1] The main character in Edward Young's play, *The Revenge*; Mossop had established himself as an actor by a performance of this role at Smock Alley Theatre, Dublin (28 Nov. 1749); the play was revived at Drury Lane on 10 Oct. 1751, and Mossop continued throughout the season in this role, which Thomas Davies called 'his master-piece' (*Memoirs*, i. 162).

[2] *Epistles*, I. vi. 67–8: 'If you know something better than these precepts, pass it on, my good fellow' (Loeb); the lines come at the end of the Epistle, which has advised a 'wise indifference' to worldly riches and honors.

[3] *CGJ* No. 9, above.

[4] *Republic*, i. 343B.

Now what can more effectually establish this excellent and useful Doctrine, than that positive Assertion in the 6th Chap. of one St. Luke, 20th Verse, *Blessed are the Poor*, FOR THEIRS IS THE KINGDOM OF HEAVEN*.[1] If the Poor, or the People, (for in this Country the ΟΙ ΠΟΛΛΟΙ, and the ΟΙ ΠΤΩΧΟΙ,[2] are synonymous) could be once firmly persuaded that they had a Right to the other World, they might surely be well contented to resign all Pretensions to this. Nay, the Rich might in that Case very fairly withhold every thing in this World from them: For it would be manifestly unjust that the Poor should enjoy both. Thus the two Worlds were equally divided; and as the Rich could never be accused of making any, the least,[3] Attempt on that which was allotted to the Poor, they had surely a very good Plea to keep their own to themselves, and not to suffer the Poor to make any Encroachments on them.

And on this Principle alone that Position in our Law, that even Necessity itself is no Justification of Theft can be vindicated: For in this Instance the Roman or Civil Law, as we find in Grotius and Puffendorf,[4] differs from us. Both these Writers do indeed hold, that the Rich have much the better Title to all the good Things of this World, an Opinion which I suppose they found on the Right of Possession; but they agree, however, that a poor Wretch, absolutely to prevent Starving, may innocently take a Loaf from his opulent Neighbour, which he hath neither the Heart to give, nor the Stomach to eat.[5]

But however wise, according to the Opinion before cited from Plato, our Law may here be, I much question whether it will not want the above Sanction of Religion to support it. Could any Thing therefore be so weak in our late Governors, as to have suffered a Sett of poor Fellows,[6] who were just able to read and write, to inform their Brethren, that the Place which the

---

* *This is the Reading in Mills, and this is certainly the best.*

[1] A conflation of Luke 6: 20, 'Blessed be ye poor: for yours is the kingdom of God', and Matthew 5: 3, 'Blessed are the poor in spirit: for theirs is the kingdom of heaven.' Fielding's note refers to the edition of the New Testament by John Mill (1645–1707), published at Oxford in 1707; a later manual based in part on this edition was in his library (Amsterdam, 1735; Baker, item 37). Mill's Greek text, however, simply gives the conventional readings of the passages in both Matthew and Luke. All this has the air of deliberate confusion on Fielding's part, presumably to suit the character of his worldly persona in this essay, who throughout assumes Christianity is a dead and obscure faith (cf. the reference to 'one St. Luke' in the same passage).

[2] i.e. 'the multitude' and 'the beggars'.

[3] Cf. the same usage in *CGJ* Nos. 15, 41, and 61, below, pp. 110, 235 and 329.

[4] Hugo Grotius (1583–1645) and Samuel Pufendorf (1632–94), leading authorities on the 'laws of nature', whose works Fielding cites at length in *CGJ* No. 39.

[5] For a non-ironic discussion of the issue, see *CGJ* No. 39 where Fielding leaves no doubt that he believes necessity should be a justification of theft. The passages alluded to here are Pufendorf, *Of the Law of Nature and Nations*, II. vi. 6, and Grotius, *Of the Rights of War and Peace*, II. ii. 6. See also *Journey from this World to the Next*, I. vii, and cf. the scene of wretches imprisoned for stealing bread in *Amelia*, I. iv.

[6] i.e. the members of the Robin Hood Society, whose attack on religious orthodoxy is now ironically condemned as a disservice to the rich; see the opening paragraph of the essay.

Rich had allotted them was a mere Utopia, and an Estate, according to the usual Sense of the Phrase, in Nubibus[1] only! Could the Poor become once unanimously persuaded of this, what should hinder them from an Attempt in which the Superiority of their Numbers might give them some Hopes of Success; and when they have nothing real to risque in either World in the Trial?

This is a Matter of very serious Consideration, and, as it seems of late to have employed most of our Projectors,[2] I hope I shall be at Liberty to propose a Scheme, which I think would very effectually remove the Danger apprehended.

I have not here Time to examine all the Plans of others; one however I cannot entirely pass over in Silence, as it somewhat resembles my own, and as I know so many good People who are pleased with it; and this is the Scheme of the late Dean Swift, to force our Poor to eat their own Children, as what would not only afford Provision for our present Poor, but prevent their Encrease.[3]

But with Submission, however proper and humane this Proposal might be in Ireland, I must observe it would be extremely cruel and severe here. For there the Children of the Poor being sustained for the most Part with Milk and Potatoes, must be very delicious Food; but here, as the Children of our Poor are little better than a Composition of Gin,[4] to force their Parents to eat them, would in Reality be to force them to poison themselves. The Cruelty of which appears so monstrous at first Sight, that it need not be exaggerated.

In Truth Religion here, as in many other Instances, will best do the Business of the Politician.

As to the Restoration of the Christian Religion, tho' I must own the Expediency of it, could it be accomplished, I think it is a Matter of too much Difficulty. But perhaps another Religion may be found, which will equally answer the above Great Purpose of Government, and for which the People have not been lately inspired with any Contempt or Abhorrence; and which would have the Pleasure of Novelty to some, and of Antiquity to others to recommend it.

---

[1] In the clouds, incapable of being realized.

[2] On the renewed interest in the state of the poor and the proliferation of pamphlets on the subject in the 1750s, see Malvin R. Zirker, Jr., *Fielding's Social Pamphlets* (Berkeley and Los Angeles, 1966), pp. 9–29, 34–5; see also *CGJ* No. 36 and n. 1 below, p. 215. Fielding's serious attempt to contribute to a solution of the problem came in 1753, with his *Proposal for Making an Effectual Provision for the Poor*; see also *Enquiry into the Causes of the late Increase of Robbers* (1751), sect. IV.

[3] *A Modest Proposal* (1729), which Fielding imitates in what follows.

[4] Cf. Fielding's *Enquiry* (1751): 'What must become of the Infant who is conceived in *Gin*? with the poisonous Distillations of which it is nourished both in the Womb and at the Breast' (pp. 19–20); sect. II of the *Enquiry* is a discussion of 'Drunkenness, a second Consequence of Luxury among the Vulgar'. The evils of gin-drinking among the lower classes aroused many protests, of which the best known is Hogarth's *Gin-Lane* (1751); cf. *CGJ* No. 17, below. For an account of legislative efforts to control it, see Zirker, *Fielding's Social Pamphlets*, pp. 83–91.

Without further Preface then I shall propose the Restoration of the antient Heathen Religion; that Form of Worship I mean which was formerly practised among many Nations, nay even in this very Country, and that consisted in the Immolation of human Sacrifices.

The great Usefulness of these Sacrifices to the Purpose here contended for may partly be presumed, if we consider their true Original, of which the Learned have been hitherto so much puzzled to give an Account.

The ingenious Abbé de Boissi[1] imagines that the Heathen World derived this Practice from some incertain traditional Account of the intended Sacrifice of Isaac by his Father; a Conjecture which, while the Christian Religion flourished, might seem to have had some Weight; but at present it is unnecessary to advance any Argument to prove that a Custom could not have been derived from a Fact which is not believed to have had any Existence.

In Truth, these Sacrifices were no other than an Invention of Politicians to secure the good Things of this World to themselves, and at the same Time to make *a Legal Provision for the Poor.*

And this will more plainly appear, if we observe who were the Poor in the first Ages of the World. Now in those simple Times when Riches consisted only in Flocks and Herds, and when Kings themselves were little better than Shepherds, as the richest Men abounded only in the Necessaries of Life, so there were few or none who were left entirely destitute of them: For before the Introduction of Money, Men could not, as they do now, lock up thousands of Sheep and Oxen, and the Produce of a vast Number of Acres in a small Coffer; and consequently, every Country was found sufficient for the Maintenance of its own Inhabitants.

The Poor therefore among these People were of two Sorts only; namely adventitious Strangers, and Prisoners of War; and both these, as we learn from Diodorus Siculus, that great Penetrator into the Fogs of Antiquity, were by many Nations sacrificed to their Gods.[2]

Thus these Sacrifices were no other than an Invention of Politicians to *provide for*, or rather to remove those redundant Members in every Society, for which the better (that is the richer) Sort had no Manner of Use, and who were consequently in the Language of the Law *become chargeable.*[3] Now that the same laudable Means would produce the same desirable End is too plain to require any Proof.

---

[1] Jean-Baptiste Thiaudière de Boissy (1666–1729), whose dissertation on human sacrifice, delivered in 1710 before the Académie Royale des Inscriptions et belles Lettres, was unpublished but summarized in the Academy's official memoirs as 'Des Expiations chez les anciens Grecs & Romains'; for the point Fielding uses, see *Histoire de L'Académie Royale des Inscriptions et belles Lettres . . . avec les Mémoires de Litterature*, i (Amsterdam, 1719), 56.

[2] *Bibliotheca historica*, IV. xliv. 7–45, discussing the custom among the Tauric Chersones and in Colchis.

[3] 'Liable to be made a charge or expense (to the parish, etc.)' (*OED*).

I am however aware of one Objection, which may be made to this Scheme by some few Persons, who will not be at the Pains to give it a thorough Examination; and who, as Madam Dacier said of one of the Critics on Homer, find it more easy to cavil at an Author than to understand him.[1]

The Objection I would obviate is this; that my Scheme is rather too barbarous and inhuman.[2]

To this it might be sufficient to answer that it is for the Good of the Nation *in general*; that is to say, for the richer Part.

But in Truth it is for the Advantage of the Poor themselves; we may say indeed to these, as the Roman Soldier said to Nero, in the midst of his Distress,[3] *Usque adeone mori miserum est?* Is there such a Coward in the World, as to think Death the most miserable of all Evils? Do we not daily see Instances of Men in distressed Circumstances, that is to say, who cannot keep a Coach and Six, who fly to Death as to a Refuge? What must we think then of Wretches in a State of Hunger and Nakedness; without Bread to eat, without Clothes to cover them, without a Hut or Hovel to receive them?

When Serenus was condemned to Death by the Senate of Rome, Gallus Asinius moved to mitigate the Sentence into Banishment; and proposed to send the Convict either to the Island of Gyaros or Donusa; but Serenus despised the Alternative, as both Islands were destitute of Water; saying as Tacitus hath it, "Dandos vitæ usus cui vita concede retur." *If you grant me my Life, give me also the Necessaries of it.*[4] Without these indeed Serenus well knew that the Favour pretended to be granted to him, was a mere Insult, and in Reality an Aggravation instead of a Mitigation of his former Sentence.

In this Light, therefore, I shall be understood by my sensible Reader; and instead of that Censure of Cruelty which hath been bestowed on Dr. Swift

---

[1] Anne Lefèvre Dacier (*c.*1654–1720), celebrated critic and the wife of André Dacier, translator of Homer. Fielding seems to have admired her immensely, depicting her in one passage as sitting on Homer's lap (*Journey from this World to the Next*, I. viii); for other references, see *Tom Jones*, VII. xii; *Joseph Andrews*, III. ii; *Plutus* (1742); *Champion* for 4 Dec. 1739; *Amelia*, ed. Martin Battestin, Wesleyan Edn. (Oxford, 1983), VI. vii, VIII. v, X. i, and notes, pp. 408–9; and *CGJ* No. 67.

Fielding alludes here to Mme Dacier's famous quarrel with Antoine Houdart de la Motte (1672–1731), who, without knowing Greek, presumed in 1714 to translate the *Iliad* into rhymed French verse and to attack Homer in a critical discourse. Fielding owned Mme Dacier's reply, *Des Causes de la Corruption du Goût* (Amsterdam, 1715; Baker, item 165), which ridicules La Motte's ignorance throughout. Though she does not use the exact phrase Fielding gives here, he is apparently paraphrasing her reference to 'ces Critiques si présomptueux, qui condamnent Homere sans le connoître' (p. 31), a line she had earlier used in the life of Homer prefixed to her translation of the *Iliad* (Paris, 1711, i. 43) and now applies specifically to La Motte. On their quarrel, an aspect of the ancient–modern controversy, see Maynard Mack *et al.*, eds., Pope's translation of the *Iliad*, Twickenham Edn. of the Poems of Pope, vii (1967), pp. lxxviii–lxxix. Cf. *Champion*, 27 Nov. 1739: 'And one may apply to these Persons what *Dacier* said of a *French* Critic, who abused the last mentioned Poem. *That he found it more easy to censure him than to read him.*' On La Motte, see also *CGJ* No. 66, below, p. 348.

[2] Cf. Swift, *A Modest Proposal*: 'some scrupulous People might be apt to censure such a Practice (although indeed very unjustly) as a little bordering upon Cruelty'.

[3] Suetonius, *Nero*, xlvii; the line itself is from Virgil, *Aeneid*, xii. 646: 'Is death all so sad?' (Loeb).

[4] *Annals*, IV. xxx. 2; but it is Tiberius who makes the point, not Serenus himself.

by some very ingenious and learned Critics for his abovementioned Proposal;[1] it will be attributed to my Humane Disposition, that I have proposed to lessen the Severity of that Death which is suffered by so many Persons, who in the most miserable lingering Manner do daily perish for Want in this Metropolis. A.

Proceedings at the Court of Censorial Enquiry, &c.

The Court was moved against the following Advertisement published on Wednesday last.

(Taken from the Life by an ingenious Artist)

A Whole Length PRINT of Miss MOLLY BLANDY.

Who, with her own and her Sweetheart's Contrivance, is charged with barbarously and inhumanly poisoning her own Father; which cruel and horrid Act WAS perpetrated for his Estate.

To which are annexed,

Lines properly adapted to HER wicked Crime.
Published as a Memento to Youth of either Sex.[2]

And the Court was of Opinion, that the said Advertisement was base and infamous. That such scandalous Methods tended to prepossess the Minds of Men, and might take away that Indifference with which Jurymen ought to come to the Trial of a Prisoner. That their own Passions were too apt to biass and prejudice Men in the Trial of very flagitious Offences; for the Mind being thoroughly heated with Detestation of an inhuman Crime, is prepared to receive every slight Impression against those who are accused of it, and the Weight of the Evidence is commonly enhanced by every Circumstance which enhances the Weight of the Crime: When to this Detestation we add Prejudice against the Accused, and Prepossession of

[1] Not identified; *A Modest Proposal* was virtually ignored by the early critics of Swift, nor is there any reference to such criticism in Orrery's *Remarks* (1752) or Deane Swift's *Essay* (1755), both of which make only passing comment on this satire.

[2] This advertisement appeared in *GA*, 5 Feb. 1752; Fielding quotes it accurately, except that he has emphasized by large capitals those words ('was' and 'her') which seem most prejudicial and has omitted the name of the offending printer, B. Dickinson. Fielding's may not have been the only complaint, for on 6 Feb. *DA* carried an advertisement for the same print in language less prejudicial, referring only to 'the horrid Crime she is charged with'.

Mary Blandy was the only daughter of Francis Blandy, an attorney of Henley-on-Thames. She was courted by William Henry Cranstoun, an officer in the marines, who was in fact already married. When her father objected to Cranstoun's proposal of marriage, Mary, according to the prosecution, gave her father small doses of arsenic; he died on 14 Aug. 1751. Her father even at the point of death refused to blame Mary, who was tried and convicted at Oxford (3 Mar. 1752) and hanged on 6 Apr. 1752. Cranstoun, who was accused of inducing the poisoning, escaped but died abroad on 2 Dec. 1752. The entire affair aroused enormous comment in newspapers and pamphlets during the spring of 1752; see *CGJ* No. 20 and notes, below.

their Guilt, all Hope is removed from a Defendant nothing indeed being more difficult than to acquit those whom we have once convicted in our own Hearts. That by the Law of England all Persons were presumed innocent, 'till found guilty by their Country; but that here a Woman was adjudged guilty of the most enormous of all Crimes before Conviction. That she was here stigmatized, and hung up as an Example of the blackest Iniquity to others, at a Time when her Trial is near approaching. This, the Court said, was to hang first and try afterwards; and whereas the Council had urged, that here was no Malice, but only a Desire of getting a Penny, it was answered no more was there Malice generally in Highwaymen, Burglars, and other Rogues, who were nevertheless deservedly hanged; and that to get Money by picking Pockets was less atrocious, and by robbing on the Highway more honourable than to do it by such bad Methods as these.

The Court then passed Sentence of Infamy not only against the ingenious Artist, but against all those who indulge a vain Curiosity, by encouraging such wicked and abominable Practices.

The Argument in the Great Cause of the Censor, against B— T—, is appointed for Saturday next.[1]

On Tuesday the Court will sit on the Recommendatory Side, when all Booksellers are at Liberty to enter their Claims, and present their Books.

(*Adjourned.*)

TUESDAY, FEBRUARY 11, 1752.   NUMB. 12.

——utcunque ferent ea facta Minores.

VIRGIL.[2]

Why should we heed what after Times
Think of our Follies or our Crimes?

"Most of those Things (says the ingenious Doctor *South*) that have the mightiest and most controuling Influence upon the Affairs and Course of the World, are downright Lies. What is common Fame, which sounds from all Quarters of the World, and resounds back to them again, but generally a loud, rattling, impudent, overbearing Lye? *What are most of the Histories of the World but Lies?* Lies immortalized, and consigned over as a perpetual Abuse and Flam upon Posterity!"[3]

---

[1] See *CGJ* No. 9, above, p. 72.

[2] *Aeneid*, vi. 822: 'Unhappy he, howe'er posterity extol that deed!' (Loeb).

[3] Robert South, 'A Sermon Preached at Christ-Church, Oxon, . . . October 14, 1688', in his *Twelve Sermons Preached upon Several Occasions* (1722), i. 459. Fielding quotes with one slight omission and with the italics representing his emphasis, not South's; 'Flam' means 'deception'. This volume was in Fielding's library (Baker, item 461); South (1634–1716) was, in fact, a divine whose witty style

There is, I am afraid, too much Justice in the Charge on History in general. Juvenal hath left this Stamp of Falsehood on the Greek Histories then extant,

> ——*Quicquid Græcia mendax*
> *Audet in Historia.*[1]

And the same Character Pliny gives to the historical Writers in his own Language, "Minus profecto mirentur Græciæ Mendacia, &c. qui cogitent nostros nuper paulo minus monstrifica qædam de iisdem tradidisse." *We shall be less amazed at the monstrous Lies of the Greeks, (concerning the Gardens of the Hesperides, &c.) when we consider how little less monstrous are the Accounts of those Matters which we find in our own Tongue.*[2]

Herodian, who sets out with lamenting the little Attention to Truth, which is commonly found in these Recorders of Time, hath an Observation too pretty to be omitted. "The Writer," says he, "is more careful to embellish his Work with Propriety of Phrase, and Harmony of Stile, than with Truth: For he considers that remote Posterity will be more likely to admire the two former Excellencies, than to detect his Want of the last."[3]

I do not however conclude that the Historian whenever (in the Language of the Hounhmms) he relates *the Thing which is not,*[4] intends himself to impose a Falsehood on his Reader. We frequently meet with Lies in History; when the Writer, I am convinced, did not deserve the opprobrious Name of a Liar.

Some Writers (I confess) are hardly entitled to this candid Interpretation; such are those Historians who relate Falsehoods as of their own Knowledge, and are not only the Recorders of a Lie, but the Witnesses of it; and those again whose Works contain scarce any Thing besides Lies, such as Master Geoffry of Monmouth,[5] and some others who may be fairly said *to*

Fielding greatly admired and whose sermons he cited throughout his career, from the *Mock Doctor* (1732, sc. vi) to the *Journal of a Voyage to Lisbon* (1755, 26 [21] July). On his quotations from South, see the exchange between Allan Wendt and Arthur Sherbo, *Notes and Queries*, 202 (1957), 256–7, 378–9; for Fielding's view of South's humor, see *CGJ* No. 18, below. See also *CGJ* Nos. 57, 60, 68, and 69.

[1] *Satires*, x. 174–5: *creditur olim / velificatus Athos et quidquid Graecia mendax / audet in historia,* 'We have heard how ships once sailed through Mount Athos, and all the lying tales of Grecian history' (Loeb).

[2] *Natural History*, v. i. 4; Fielding quotes roughly, shortening the passage. Thornton ridiculed Fielding's translation as 'little less monstrous' in *Drury-Lane Journal*, No. 5 (13 Feb. 1752).

[3] Paraphrased from his *History*, i. i. 1.

[4] Swift, *Gulliver's Travels*, iv. iii: 'He replied, That I needs be mistaken, or that I *said the thing which was not.* (For they have no Word in their Language to express Lying or Falshood.)'

[5] Cf. the contempt for 'Geoffry Bechard' which Fielding includes in his parody of John Oldmixon in *CGJ* No. 17, below, pp. 120–4. Oldmixon, in fact, shared Fielding's view that Geoffrey's history was mere fable; see Pat Rogers, 'Fielding's Parody of Oldmixon', *PQ* 49 (1970), 263. Fielding's library contained Geoffrey of Monmouth's *British History* in an edition of 1718 (Baker, item 191).

immortalize Lies, and to consign them over as a perpetual Abuse and Flam upon Posterity.

But if no Latitude should be given to Historians, I am afraid not only Matthew Paris,[1] the best of our antient Annalists, but the valuable Remains of Livy, Tacitus, Suetonius, Dion Cassius, and indeed almost every History, must be condemned to the Flames. The last of these whom I have mentioned tells us, I remember, a most notable Fact, (it may indeed be called a Hummer.[2]) It is the Story of an Apparition in the Shape of Alexander the Great; who with four hundred attendant Spirits traversed great Part of Thrace to Byzantium, and then crossed the Water to Chalcedon, where after some Time they all vanished. This Story he relates as a Fact which happened in his own Time, and which was (he says) attested by many thousand of Eye-Witnesses.[3]

In Reality, there are other Apologies for the Historian, besides the Allowances which we are to make for Superstition and Credulity. Nothing is so short lived as Truth, occasioned I suppose by her extreme Indolence and Sluggishness, which are so remarkable, that she never cares to wag out of her own House, not even to visit her next Door Neighbour. Physicians may on the contrary well account for the long Life of Falsehood, by the constant Exercise which she uses: for according to Virgil,

Fama malum quo non aliud velocius ullum
Mobilitate viget, Viresque; acquirit eundo.[4]

Where Fama may very well be translated *a Lie.*

If we candidly consider therefore the Materials which the Historian is obliged to make use of, and the great Difficulty with which he can come at Truth, as a Lie is always ready to present itself to his Pen, we shall not always conclude that the Writer intended to impose a Falsehood on us, when we reject his Narrative as incredible. For my own Part, though I have not quite so much Faith at present, as I once had in the Casualties related by Sir Richard Baker, in that wonderful Chronicle which was the great Favourite of my Youth; I do yet nevertheless acquit the Writer of any Design to impose on Posterity. And tho' my Faith is now somewhat staggered in attempting to

---

[1] Monk and historian (*c.*1200–59), whose most important work, *Chronica majora*, is considered a vivid and relatively reliable record of events from 1235 to 1259; Dr Harrison attributes to Paris an anecdote in *Amelia*, IX. x, actually from Roger de Wendover's *Flowers of History*, formerly thought to be by Paris.

[2] 'A notable lie' (Partridge, *Dictionary of Slang and Unconventional English*, 6th edn. [1967], s.v. 'hummer').

[3] Dio Cassius, *History*, LXXX. xviii. 1–3, discussing events in the reign of Avitus.

[4] *Aeneid*, iv. 174–5: 'Rumour of all evils the most swift. Speed lends her strength, and she wins vigour as she goes' (Loeb). The accepted text has *qua* for *quo*. Fielding's passage on Truth is sneered at by Thornton as an example of 'the Figurative, and at the same time Familiar', *Drury-Lane Journal*, No. 5 (13 Feb. 1752).

believe *that the Devil carried away half a Church*, with many other such Miracles recorded by that great Writer, I am however well persuaded that they were firmly believed by the Writer himself.[1]

Without pursuing this Lucubration any farther, I will endeavour to illustrate what I have already said, by presenting my Reader with the Specimen of a History of the present Age, which may probably be written many hundreds of Years hence, by some future Sir Richard Baker under his favourite Title of Casualties in the Reign of George the Second.

Casualties happening in this Reign.

Towards the Beginning of this Reign there flourished in some Part of Wales, a very extraordinary Woman who brought forth at one Birth nineteen Couple of Rabbits, one of which having been eaten by the Royal Society, and by them declared to have a most delicious Relish, the Breed was afterwards propagated all over the Kingdom of England, were called Welsh Rabbets, and were a long Time in great Request.[2]

[1] See Sir Richard Baker, *A Chronicle of the Kings of England, from the time of the Romans Government unto the Death of King James*, 3rd edn. (1660), p. 178; this edition was in Fielding's library (Baker, item 297). Cf. *Joseph Andrews*, I. iii, where we are told that Baker's *Chronicle* lies open for all to read in the hall window of Sir Thomas Booby's house and where Fielding also refers to the devil carrying away half a church (only 'half the Chancell' in Baker). In his account of the reign of each monarch, Baker includes a section called 'Casualties happening in his time', and Fielding's essay from this point on parodies that feature of the *Chronicle* as a framework for satire. For another example of satiric 'future history', see *CGJ* No. 17; cf. Christopher Smart's 'Remarkable Prediction' of a History of England to be written in 1931, *The Midwife*, ii (1751), 145–9.

[2] Fielding refers to the famous case of Mary Toft (or Tofts) (d. 1763), the 'Rabbit Woman' of Godalming (Surrey), who created an enormous stir in Nov. 1726 by claiming to have been delivered of 17 rabbits. Her story was supported by Nathanael St. André, surgeon to Westminster Hospital and Anatomist to the Royal Household, but the claim was widely ridiculed in a flurry of pamphlets and poems and eventually exposed as fraudulent; Toft, who confessed the imposture, was imprisoned briefly but never brought to trial. Fielding, always ready to ridicule the Royal Society, seems to imply here that its members were taken in by the hoax, but in fact the chief figures in exposing it were Fellows of the Royal Society, the famous man-midwife Sir Richard Manningham and the equally celebrated obstetrician James Douglas (see Manningham's *An Exact Diary of what was observed during Attendance upon Mary Toft* [1726] and Douglas's *An Advertisement Occasioned by some Passages in Sir. R. Manningham's Diary* [1727]). Nor does the Royal Society figure at all in the many satires arising from the incident. For a well-known example of those satires, see Hogarth's print *Cunicularii, Or the Wise Men of Godliman in Consultation* (1726) and the detailed commentary by Dennis Todd, 'Three Characters in Hogarth's *Cunicularii*—and Some Implications', *ECS* 16 (1982), 26–46. In pointing out that 'Welsh rabbets' were for a long time in great request, Fielding may be alluding ironically to one of the great jokes of the Toft affair, that the trade in rabbits supposedly collapsed because everyone suddenly found the dish repellent; see e.g. *A Philosophical Enquiry into the wonderful Coney-Warren* (1726), p. 2, and 'Lemuel Gulliver', *The Anatomist Dissected* (1727), p. 23; I am grateful to Professor Dennis Todd for suggesting this point and providing these references.

Fielding, who had referred to the Rabbit Woman in the epilogue to the *Author's Farce* (1730), may have been reminded of the hoax at this late date by recent efforts of the eccentric divine William Whiston to defend the authenticity of the story of Toft, who he claimed fulfilled a prophecy in Esdras; Whiston propounded this thesis in lectures during Mar. 1749/50 and repeated it in his *Memoirs*, Part III (1750), pp. 109–22 (on Whiston, see below, *CGJ* No. 65). Perhaps coincidentally, the day after this issue of *CGJ* appeared, Bonnell Thornton, in his *Drury-Lane Journal*, No. 5 (13 Feb. 1752), began a parody of *Amelia* by stressing the heroine's fondness for 'a Welch rabbit'.

About the same Time a Set of infernal Spirits appeared in London, and held a nocturnal Meeting under the Name of THE HELL-FIRE CLUB.[1] One Prank of this Club is confirmed by so many Writers, that it would be ridiculous Infidelity to deny our assent to it. This was the taking up the Theatre which then stood in Lincoln's Inn Fields, and carrying it on their Shoulders, together with all the Audience, into Covent Garden, where are still some Remains of that Theatre now to be seen.[2] Here we are well assured that many Devils used frequently to appear during the Time of acting, and dance to divert the Company, 'till at last a most immense Dragon descended from above, and carried them all *up to Hell*.[3]

Several other very extraordinary Matters are reported in good Authors of this Club. Some of the Members, it is said, commenced Writers, and openly propagated Atheism, Deism, Immorality, Indecency, and all Kinds of Scurrility against the best and worthiest Men of those Times. It hath been greatly lamented by the Learned, that not the least Remains of these Works have come down to us, as this would have sufficiently silenced those

[1] In the 1720s three groups with this name sprang up in London, all apparently involving persons of quality who dedicated themselves to atheism and blasphemy; for contemporary references and an account of efforts to suppress them, see Robert J. Allen, *The Clubs of Augustan London* (Cambridge, Mass., 1933), pp. 119–24. For a later reference, cited by Allen, see the *Connoisseur*, No. 22 (27 June 1754), which claims that 'the present race of Bucks, Bloods, and Free-thinkers, are but the spawn of the Mohocks and the Hell-Fire-Club'. Cf. the club of free-thinkers joined by Mr Wilson in *Joseph Andrews*, III. iii. In the present passage, of course, Fielding deliberately merges his reference to free-thinkers with his ridicule of pantomimes.

[2] Alluding to John Rich's move in 1732 from his playhouse in Lincoln's Inn Fields, where he had enjoyed great success with his pantomimes and with the *Beggar's Opera*, to Covent Garden Theatre, which had its opening performance on 7 Dec. 1732; cf. the print 'Rich's Glory, or His Triumphant Entry into Covent Garden' (1732), questionably attributed to Hogarth. Fielding's wording reflects his usual support of Garrick's company at Drury Lane in its current rivalry with Rich's at Covent Garden; cf. also the reference from Baker's *Chronicle*, cited earlier in this essay, to the devil carrying away half a church. On Rich see *CGJ* No. 3, above, p. 32.

[3] Referring to various features of pantomime, that enormously popular form of entertainment which seemed to Fielding, as to many in his age, a chief symptom of corrupt taste. Fielding never tired of satirizing Rich, who as Harlequin and manager seemed largely responsible for its popularity; see especially *Tumble-Down Dick* (1736), a theatrical parody which Fielding published with an ironic dedication to 'Mr. John Lun'; cf. *Joseph Andrews*, I. vii; *Champion*, 22 Apr., 3 and 24 May 1740; *Tom Jones*, V. i; and *CGJ* Nos. 17 and 27. The allusions to dragons, devils, and hell touch on a characteristic element in Rich's spectacles; as Fielding says in *Tom Jones*, 'the whole Furniture of the infernal Regions hath long been appropriated by the Managers of Playhouses' (XII. xii). Cf. Pope's *Dunciad* (1743), 'All sudden, Gorgons hiss, and Dragons glare, / And ten-horn'd fiends and Giants rush to war. / Hell rises, Heav'n descends, and dance on Earth' (iii. 235–7) and his description of Cibber, 'On grinning dragons thou shalt mount the wind' (iii. 268); cf. also the dragons in Hogarth's satires on pantomime, *A Just View of the British Stage* (1724) and *Masquerades and Operas* (1724). Fielding's reference to the company being carried 'up to Hell' ridicules Rich's current success, a revival of *Harlequin Sorcerer; with the Loves of Pluto and Proserpine*, originally performed at Lincoln's Inn Fields and now performed again at Covent Garden, beginning 11 Feb. Bonnell Thornton's account of this pantomime closes with the comment, 'the scrupulous Critic must not nicely enquire into the reasons, why Harlequin is carried *upwards* into the *inferal* regions' (*Drury-Lane Journal* No. 5 [13 Feb. 1752]; Thornton's account is reprinted in *LM* 21 [1752], 81–2, and *GM* 22 [1752], 52–3). Cf. Fielding's *Tumble-Down Dick* (1736): 'Does not a Dragon descend from Hell in *Doctor Faustus*? And People go up to Hell in *Pluto and Proserpine*' (p. 12).

Objections of some Critics; who would persuade us, in Opposition to the whole Current of Historical Evidence, that all which is related of this Club is a mere Fable, and the Invention of a certain Legend Writer in the twenty-third Century.

The chief Argument which these Critics rest upon is this, that it is impossible to suppose a Nation arrived at such an enormous Degree of Corruption and Prostitution, to have existed even a few Years upon the Face of the Earth. And this, I confess, would have some Weight, was it not overthrown by that Account of the thorough Reformation, which, according to the best Chronologists, happened in the Year 1753, brought about by one General DRAWGANDSIR, who *at the Head of a vast Army*, set up his Standard in the Common Gardens,[1] and with a certain Weapon called a Ridicule, or Ridicle, or as one conjectures a Wry-Sickle, brought the People by main Force to better Manners.

But the most extraordinary Miracle of all that happened about this Time, and which indeed we should not have mentioned, had it not been so well attested by a great Number of Spectators, was this which follows. A certain Juggler placed a common Quart-Bottle on a Table, on the Stage of a public Theatre, and in the Sight of several Hundreds of People, conveyed himself into the Bottle, where he remained a decent Time; after which he again returned out of his Place of Confinement, in the same Manner as he had gone into it.[2]

And what makes this *the more remarkable*, is that this Juggler was not of the smallest Size of Men, which would indeed have added *great Credibility* to the Story; but was a well proportioned and middle-sized Man.

But strange as this Story may appear, it is extremely well attested; for it hath the Authority of a Fragment of undoubted Antiquity, in which the

---

[1] For the 'vast Army', see the 'Journal of the present Paper War', *CGJ* Nos. 1–3: 'Common Gardens' is Covent Garden; cf. Richardson's reference to the 'Common Garden Journal', cited in General Introduction, above, p. xlv.

[2] Fielding refers to the 'Bottle Conjurer' affair, the most famous hoax of the mid-century, the precise details of which are obscured by a cloud of pamphlets, advertisements, parodies, pantomimes, and satiric prints. The clearest contemporary source, 'The Bottle Bubble' in *GM* for 1749, gives these facts: Someone advertised that on the night of 16 Jan. 1749 he would place himself in a tavern quart bottle on the stage of the Haymarket Theatre, as well as play the music of every instrument on a walking cane. A great crowd assembled, waited half an hour, and became impatient; when a voice in the pit called out, 'For double prices the conjurer will go into a pint bottle,' the crowd rioted and set the theatre on fire. In the confusion the money disappeared. (*GM* 19 [1749], 42). Rumors sprang up that the hoax was the result of a wager between the Duke of Montagu and the Duke of Richmond (see *London Stage*, Pt. 4, vol. i, pp. cxcvii–cxviii; on these noblemen, see below, p. 92 nn. 1 and 2). Though the riot was a serious affair, the town seized upon the episode with delight; one notice gave as the reason for the conjurer's non-appearance 'that in all the Taverns he could not find a Bottle that held a Quart' (*DA*, 24 Jan. 1749), and the enemies of Hume's *Essay on Miracles* were said to be especially disappointed at his failure (*LM* 18 [1749], 34–5). The bibliography of the hoax is enormous, but for noteworthy examples see *A Letter to the Town concerning the Man and the Bottle* (1749), *A Modest Apology for the Man in the Bottle, by Himself* (1749), and the print 'Don Jumpedo in the Character of Harlequin Jumping down his own Throat' (1749).

Author writes *That he was himself one of the F—l—s* who were assemb——to see the Perf—rm—nce.*[1]

About this Time likewise we are assured, that a Set of Attorneys Clerks, Apprentices, Players, Fidlers, Taylors, Shoemakers, and other Mechanics, assembled themselves together to examine into the Truth of Religion.[2] They met in a Place called ROBIN'S WOOD, and were, after several Skirmishes, all dispersed by General DRAWGANDSIR.

In the Middle of the same Reign, or somewhat sooner, two blazing Stars appeared, and shone all over London for the Space of a Year or more: They were esteemed the most beautiful Stars that ever enlightened the Sky, were called *The Sisters*, and were universally admired. They at last set in two great Houses, where they long shone as bright as they had shined in the Sky before: And the Owners of those Houses were envied by all Mankind.[3]

Now in all these Instances there appears a Mixture of Truth and Falsehood, such as was probably the Case with those Accounts of the first Ages that appear in profane History, in which none of the Fables were perhaps solely the Invention of the Writer, but were originally founded on some Matter of Fact; which is however so obscured and metamorphosed in

---

* *The Original will be here imperfect.*

[1] If the 'Fragment' refers to a particular pamphlet on the Bottle Conjurer's hoax, it has not been identified; several people, however, who were accused of arranging the affair protested that they had in fact been among the fools in the audience. The most prominent of these was Fielding's old enemy Samuel Foote, the actor (see *JJ* No. 22, 30 Apr. 1748); since the hoax had occurred during a run of Foote's 'Auction of Pictures', he was charged with perpetrating it as a publicity stunt and found it necessary to defend himself from the accusation in a notice to the public (*GA*, 17 Jan. 1749). The line Fielding 'quotes' does not appear in his notice, but cf. the comment in another pamphlet by the 'Man in the Bottle' himself, 'That I was to have been in the *Bottle*, was as evident as Mr. F——'s being in the House' (*A Modest Apology* [1749], p. 7). Cf. also a notice from one John Coustos, lapidary, disclaiming any responsibility for the imposture and asserting 'there are those, who are ready to attest on oath, that he was in their company that evening, and was at the Theatre as a spectator only' (20 Jan. 1749, as repr. in 'The History of the Famous Bottle Conjurer . . . being the Advertisements that appeared in the Public Papers', in R. S. Kirby, *Wonderful and Scientific Museum*, ii [1804], 11–22).
[2] The members of the Robin Hood Society; see *CGJ* Nos. 8 and 9.
[3] Referring to the two Gunning sisters, Elizabeth (1733–90) and Maria (1732–60), who had been the center of attention in London society since mid-1751. Horace Walpole described them as 'two Irish girls of no fortune, who are declared the handsomest women alive. I think their being two, so handsome and both such perfect figures, is their chief excellence, for singly I have seen much handsomer women than either: however, they can't walk in the park, or go to Vauxhall, but such mobs follow them that they are generally driven away.' (To Horace Mann, 18 June 1751, *Yale Walpole*, xx. 260.) The 'great Houses' were those of James Hamilton, 6th Duke of Hamilton, who married Elizabeth in a clandestine ceremony on 14 Feb. 1752, and George William Coventry, 6th Earl of Coventry, whom Maria married on 5 Mar. 1752. Fielding is writing in anticipation of both marriages, but the intentions of the earl and the duke had been clear for some time; see Walpole's comment on the courtships in a letter of 27 Feb. 1752, ibid., xx. 302–3. Fielding's comment may not be without irony, for the sisters were generally thought to be as vain and silly as they were beautiful; in announcing their marriages he uses the formulaic phrases he ridicules elsewhere (see 'Covent Garden' column of *CGJ* No. 13 and news columns of No. 19; cf. the comment by 'Axylus', in *CGJ* No. 16, below, p. 116).

the Tradition, that the real Truth no more appears in the Fable, than the Seed is to be discovered in the Plant that is produced from it.

I will conclude this Paper with as Story which was communicated to me by a noble Duke lately dead,[1] and which from his Mouth I can attest to be a Fact.

A certain Nobleman taking the Air one Day, on the Downs near Salisbury, saw among the *Baras** there, one of a larger Size than the rest; This, said a Gentleman present, is I suppose the Dormitory of some Giant. The Nobleman, who was a great Lover of a Jest, took the Hint; and, when they returned home, immediately dispatched a Paragraph to be inserted in a particular News-Paper, which he knew was constantly taken in by a certain Virtuoso in that Country; in which Paragraph it was affirmed, "That the Bones of a certain Giant, supposed to have been, when alive, near ten Foot high, were lately found in a Bara near Salisbury, and were then in the Possession of a certain Clergyman, who was mentioned by Name." The Joke had its Effect with the Virtuoso, who immediately dispatched a Man and Horse for the Bones to the Clergyman, whose Patron he was; nor did it cease there, but the same silly Story was literally translated into French; and on the Authority of the News-Paper transmitted to Posterity as a real Fact, in a very voluminous Work in Folio soon after published in France.[2] A.

---

* *The Graves of those who were slain in the Wars of our Ancestors are so called in Saxon.*

---

[1] Probably Charles Lennox, 2nd Duke of Richmond (1701–50), Fielding's patron; Fielding had dedicated to Richmond *The Miser* (1733) and his poem 'Of Good-Nature' (*Miscellanies*, 1743) and had complimented him in his *Enquiry* (1751, p. 70). At the time of his death on 8 Aug. 1750 Richmond, who was a Fellow of the Royal Society, was serving as president of the Society of Antiquaries and would clearly have been interested in the story Fielding tells here. See the next note.

[2] The clergyman and the virtuoso of this story have not been identified with certainty; the nobleman, however, is very probably John Montagu, 2nd Duke of Montagu (1688?–1749), well known as 'a great Lover of a Jest'. It was Montagu who, on a wager with the Duke of Richmond, supposedly perpetrated the Bottle Conjurer hoax in 1749. For his reputation as a practical joker and for examples of his other pranks, see *The Opinions of Sarah Duchess-Dowager of Marlborough* (1787), p. 58; Francis Hardy, *Memoirs . . . of James Caulfield, Earl of Charlemont*, 2nd edn. (1812), i. 65; and *Richardsoniana* (1776), pp. 160–1. Montagu, in fact, has been suggested as the original of the 'roasting' squire in *Joseph Andrews* (see *Joseph Andrews*, ed. Martin Battestin, Wesleyan Edn. [Oxford, 1967], p. xxiv n.; I am indebted to Professor Battestin for suggesting Richmond and Montagu as the noblemen referred to in this passage). Moreover, Montagu, like Richmond, was an FRS interested in antiquarian matters; he was also from 1742 onward a patron and frequent correspondent of the famous antiquarian and clergyman Dr William Stukeley, who had much earlier investigated the barrows of Salisbury Plain and had published a work on Stonehenge in 1740. In that work Stukeley refers to Thomas Herbert, 8th Earl of Pembroke (1656–1733) as the 'patron of my studies' and describes how Pembroke in 1722–3 had opened barrows and recovered skeletons 'of a reasonable size' (Stukeley, *Stonehenge* [1740], pp. 13, 44). Pembroke, who in Pope's words collected for his seat at Wilton 'Statues, dirty Gods, and Coins' (*Moral Essays*, iv. 8), was certainly the most eminent 'virtuoso' in Wiltshire, and though hard evidence is lacking one may reasonably speculate that he is the victim of the prank Fielding describes, with Stukeley as perhaps the clergyman involved.

Proceedings at the Court of Censorial Enquiry, &c.

This Day the Court sate on the Recommendatory Side, and several Booksellers appeared, and very humbly presented their Books; which were severally ordered to be read over and examined by the Commentator General.

Complaint was made to the Court against several Print-Sellers, for exposing in the Windows of their Shops, several lewd and indecent Prints, &c.[1] And the following Letter was ordered to be read.

To the Censor of Great Britain.

"*Sir,*

The Censure you have very justly passed on the Author of the Print of Miss BLANDY,[2] is very much approved of, and 'tis hoped may have the Effect intended, to restrain such scandalous Liberties, so much of late taken. But it is hoped you will extend your Authority yet farther, and bring to Shame the Authors and Venders of those infamous Prints, exhibited in almost every Print-Shop in London, representing Lewdness in every Shape in its proper Colours. This Offence, for such I must term it, calls aloud for Redress; whether it be cognizable by the Civil Magistrate, I know not; but I am sure it properly is by you as Censor-General, and therefore have no Doubt but at your next Court you will take this Matter into Consideration, and pass such Judgment on the Offenders, as shall make them ashamed of getting a Livelihood by these scandalous Methods. There are two Prints of this Sort lately come out, which exceed all the rest, and are to be seen in Fleet-street, very finely coloured. This evidently shews the Necessity there is of stopping their Progress, else we may soon expect to see the most obscene Practices of Brothels exposed to public View, for the Edification of all young Men and Maids.

> Your Well-wisher and
> Humble Servant,
> MODESTY."

Ordered, that, as this is an Offence, contra bonos mores,[3] the Suppression of the same be recommended to the Magistrates of London, Middlesex and Westminster.

(Adjourned.)

---

[1] A common complaint; for an account of a series of prosecutions in 1745 against publishers of pornographic prints, see David Foxon, *Libertine Literature in England 1660–1745* (1965), pp. 15–18. On the general reputation of print-sellers, cf. R. Campbell, *The London Tradesman* (1747): 'Our Print Shopkeepers are mere Tradesmen: They set up any thing that offers in their Shops; if it sells, their case is answered; if not, they know not where to lay the Blame, for they are no more Judges of the intrinsic Worth of the Commodity than they are of Astronomy' (p. 136).

[2] See *CGJ* No. 11, above.   [3] 'against good morals'.

SATURDAY, FEBRUARY 15, 1752. NUMB. 13.

Βοτρυδὸν δὲ Πέτονται. HOMER.[1]

They fly in Clusters.

I shall make no other Apology for now publishing the following Letters,[2] than to some of the Writers for not publishing them sooner. For the future, however, I recommend it to my Correspondents, not too hastily to conclude that I have suppressed their Writings, because they do not immediately see them in this Paper.

Most noble Knight,
From my Toilette,
Wednes. 2 o'Clock.

The seventh Article of your Censorial Court runs thus,—*Whereas by the Statute of good Breeding, the wearing a Hat in the Boxes at the Playhouse, before or behind the Ladies, is a very great Offence; that swearing or talking loud, is likewise under very severe Penalties forbidden by the said Statute, &c.*[3]

You must know, Sir, that I am a Woman of some Rank, but unfashionable enough when I go to the Theatres to attend to the Play, and be entertained with it. I was last Week at Drury-Lane to see a Tragedy of Shakespear,[4] and was well disposed to be greatly pleased with the Performance; but most unluckily for me I was seated opposite to three Persons (Gentlemen I suppose they call themselves) whose Behaviour was so conspicuous and particular, that my Eyes were unwillingly drawn from better Objects upon them.—The Moment the Curtain was taken up, they were endeavouring to turn every Thing into Ridicule; there was not a Word or Gesture but was repeated by one of 'em, to the great Diversion of the other two;—and while every Heart but theirs in the Audience seemed to be most sensibly touched with the acting and Circumstances of the Play, they were all the while like my *Lord Froth,* upon the broad Grin.[5]——Now, Sir, tho' you have not

---

[1] *Iliad,* ii. 89, from the 'simile of the bees' cited by Fielding in *CGJ* No. 1, above.

[2] The group of letters, supposedly from contributors, is signed 'M.', an initial Fielding uses to indicate editorial supervision as well as his own authorship. Except for the 'Epitaph' most of these contributions are probably by Fielding himself, despite the uncharacteristic use of 'does' in the petition of Deborah Prateapace. Jensen (ii. 183–4) doubts Fielding's authorship not only of the epitaph but of the verses signed 'Y. Y.'; Miller (*Essays,* p. 132 n.) thinks Fielding may have written the mock-epitaph.

[3] Quoted from *CGJ* No. 5, above; on the topic of audience behavior see that essay and p. 45 n. 1.

[4] *Macbeth* was performed at Drury Lane on 8 Feb. 1752, but given the signature 'Cordelia' and the fact that the letter has supposedly been on hand for some time, the reference is probably to *King Lear,* performed on 17 Jan.

[5] Lord Froth, in Congreve's *The Double Dealer*: 'Heav'n, Sir *Paul,* you amaze me, of all things in the World. You are never pleased but when we are all upon the broad grin: all laugh and no Company; ah, then 'tis such a sight to see some teeth' (III. i).

particularly mentioned this Kind of Behaviour in the said Resolutions of your Court, I beg to know if it is not to be understood in the general Words *Misconduct* and *Misbehaviour* in your fifth Article; and whether a good Sett of Teeth, or a white Hand, may be pleaded in Excuse for grinning and gesticulating during the Representation of any well written and well acted Tragedy.——Let me likewise intreat you to tell these very fine People, that tho' Fortune has most good naturedly enabled 'em to sit in the Boxes, they have no Right to interrupt the Entertainment of sober rational Minds, or to bring their Noise, Affectation, and Ribaldry, from the Tavern to the Theatre.

I am,

Dear Knight-Errant,

Yours

CORDELIA.

P.S. If these Remarks are thought worthy of your Attention,—I shall be upon the Watch for you, and send you more.

To Sir ALEXANDER DRAWCANSIR, *&c.*

Sir,

There are certain little Registers of Wit, Humour, and Gallantry, on all the public Roads of this Kingdom, which, as they might be conducive to the Entertainment, as well as inviting to the Genius, of his Majesty's Subjects, I hope you will not think below your Notice, but favour them with your Protection. What I mean, Sir, are the Windows of the Inns, which, instead of being prophaned with Bawdry and Immorality, are certainly *meant* to be the Receptacles of Epigrams, Sonnets, and other diverting Pieces.[1] Why should not the sighing Lover, as he is travelling from the dear Object of his Wishes, vent his Complaints, and commit them to the Animadversion of others, by the Help of a Diamond-Pencil, without having the Mortification upon his Return to find his Passion laughed at? As thus, Sir, travelling lately upon that Road of this great Kingdom, which leads northward, a pretty *Sonnetist* had wrote upon a Pane of Glass, at one of the most principal Inns, as follows:

> *Give me sweet Nectar in a Kiss,*
> *That I may be replete with Bliss.*

---

[1] Cf. *Spectator*, No. 220 (12 Nov. 1711): 'I have known a Gentleman of another Turn of Humour, who . . . was a considerable Poet upon Glass. I le had a very good Epigrammatick Wit; and there was not a Parlour or Tavern Window where he visited or dined for some Years, which did not receive some Sketches or Memorials of it.' The practice was still current later in the century; cf. *The Modern Courtezan* (1751), p. 26; *Champion*, 17 May 1740, where Fielding depicts Cibber as taking his wit from verses written on windows; and *The Author's Farce* (1730), I. ii.

How pretty is this! How elegant! How it adorned the lucid Pane! 'Till there comes a Brute and writes under it

> *Give* me *sweet Nectar in a* Glass,
> *And as for kissing,—kiss my* A——.[1]

I give you this Specimen, Sir, of the wrong Use Diamond and Glass is put to; and beseech you, Sir, that at your next Censorial Court, you will be pleased to order, that the first two Lines should be stuck up as a Standard of true Window-Writing; and that the last two Lines, and all that are of the same Stamp, may be committed to the Bog-House.

I am, Sir,

Yours, &c.

PETER GRIEVOUS.

To the Worshipful Sir ALEXANDER DRAWCANSIR, *Knt. and Censor of Great Britain, the Humble Petition of Deborah Prateapace, Widow, of the Parish of St. George's Hanover-Square,*[2] *and others.*

Humbly Sheweth,

That in a Paper wrote by your Honour intitled the COVENT-GARDEN JOURNAL, and published some Weeks since,[3] your Censorship in your great Wisdom, was pleased to set forth a Prohibition, that after the 9th Day of February then next ensuing, no Females should in their Criticisms make Use of the Words sad Stuff, low Stuff, mean Stuff, vile Stuff, dirty Stuff, and so-forth: Now it does appear to a Committee of Relicts Lawfully assembled, of which I am the Chairwoman; that this Prohibition of your Worship's is Arbitrary, Illegal, and contrary to the Liberty of the Subject; for it is an antient Maxim, that the Tongue of a Female is her only Weapon of Defence, or Offence,[4] as some Millions of his Majesty's good People can testify; pray consider our Condition: Many of us from natural Weakness of Mind, many more from an illiberal Education, have very confused Ideas, and but few Words to express them: therefore it is Tyranny to forbid us the Use of those Epithets which we have acquired and perhaps with some Difficulty. Sure you cannot be so unreasonable, or indeed so foolish to attempt to condemn us to Silence! No, Sir ALEXANDER, that can never be carried into Execution, in this Land of Liberty; and as a Friend I advise you, drop that Project if you have

---

[1] For the rhyme, cf. Pope's epigram, 'Cibber! write all thy Verses upon Glasses, / The only way to save 'em from our A——s' (*Minor Poems*, Twickenham Edn., vi. 360). For other examples of such 'underwriting' on windows, see *The Merry-Thought: Or, the Glass-Window and Bog-House Miscellany*, Part I (1731), repr. Augustan Reprint Society, No. 216 (Los Angeles, 1982).

[2] A fashionable area, with socially prominent residents.

[3] *CGJ* No. 3, above.

[4] Proverbial; cf. Tilley, W 675: 'A woman's strength is in (a woman's weapon is) her tongue.'

formed it: Give us a plenary Indulgence, to talk as much silly Stuff, as we are inclined to, and all whose Names are underwritten, will as in Duty bound ever pray for your Prosperity.

> *Deborah Prateapace,*
> *Margery Tattle,*
> *Phillis Findfault,*
> *Sarah Scandal,*
> *Winifred Whisper,*
> *Theodosia Telltruth.*

P.S. If you treat us with that Humanity you have upon several Occasions expressed, you will certainly hear further from our Society; in a grateful Manner.—I do not mean a Bribe.

Mr. Censor,

Booksellers never appeared to me in the Light of Jokers, 'till the other Day calling in at a noted Shop in the Strand, I found the Authors had given one Kind of Title to their Books, and the Bookseller by an Abridgement had given another: For Instance, Mr. Chubb[1] had intitled his Book *The True Gospel,* &c. But the Bookseller on the gilded Back, called it *Chubb's Gospel*: Meaning (which indeed was the Case) that 'twas not the *Gospel* according to *Matthew, Mark,* &c. but *according to Thomas Chubb.*—But pray, Mr. Censor, let the Booksellers be put in Mind that Authors are not to be joked with by their Booksellers,

> *I am Sir,*
> *Yours, &c.*
> An AUTHOR.

BAD VERSES.

Wrote on the Back of some VERY BAD Verses, which a Gentleman made upon BELINDA's speaking some Lines from the FAIR PENITENT.[2]

> BELINDA's *Perfections strike all with Surprize,*
> *Who hear, and who see the dear Maid;*
> *The Wit, and the Fool, and the Dull and the Wise,*
> *Alike by her Charms are betray'd.*

---

[1] Thomas Chubb (1679–1747), deist, who to some extent furnished the model for Mr Square in *Tom Jones*; see the discussion by Martin Battestin, Wesleyan Edn., pp. 123–5 n. Chubb, who lived in Salisbury, was an uneducated but prolific writer of increasingly heterodox tracts. The work referred to here is *The True Gospel of Jesus Christ Asserted* (1738), published by Thomas Cox, which provoked numerous attacks.

[2] Nicholas Rowe's *The Fair Penitent* (1703), which was being performed this season at Drury Lane with Garrick and Bellamy in the leads.

So ORPHEUS *of old, as the Poets recite,*
  With his Music such Transport inspir'd,
His Strains were so moving and gave such Delight
  That Men and BRUTES *also admir'd.*

But you, fair BELINDA, *old* ORPHEUS *excel,*
  (Your Praise each that sees you rehearses)
Since the Charms of your speaking *alone can compel,*
  Ev'n DUNCES *themselves to write Verses.*

Y.Y.

Tremendous Sir,

Tho' you have not mentioned the Word EPITAPHS in your Proclamation to the Poets in one of your Papers,[1] I have ventured to send you one, made Extempore upon *a very passionate Man* and a *great Snorer.*—Do what you please with it.

EPITAPH.

The Choleric BRIN *this Grave has fill'd,*
  And rests in sweet Repose;
Each ruffl'd Passion now is still'd,
  And eke his tuneful Nose.

To our Relief Death *kindly stept,*
  And took him for our Sake;
For while in Life this Mortal slept,
  He kept Mankind awake.

To the Censor.

Sir,

It was very kind of you to mention two B——y Prints in your last Paper;[2] in which I doubt not, you had that same good Intention, that your Paper hath answered; a very large Demand having been since made for those Prints.

I shall shortly exhibit to the Public a Representation of Mars and Venus caught in Vulcan's Net, as they are described in Mr. Pope's Poem upon the Odyssey.[3] The two Figures will be *in puris*, and *finished in a high Taste.*

I am but a young Beginner, and therefore hope for the Encouragement of the Censor. If you will be so very kind to write a few Lines against my Print, and to represent it as very indecent, which I promise you it shall be, I shall

---

[1] A call for contributions in *CGJ* No. 5, above.
[2] See the letter complaining of bawdy prints, *CGJ* No. 12, above.
[3] The story is sung by the bard Demodocus at the court of Alcinous, Pope's *Odyssey* (1725), viii. 309–402.

esteem it always as a great Obligation, and will beg your Acceptance of one *for your own Use,*

I am, &c.

P.S. I intend to take the Face and Neck of Venus from your Favorite, with all that Loveliness, Modesty and Innocence in which she last Night graced the Character of Sigismunda.[1] This Boldness, I hope, she will excuse, since as Prior says,

> *'Tis Chloe's Air, and Face, and Neck and Breast,*
> *Friend Howard's Genius fancied all the rest.*[2]

M.

Proceedings at the Court of Censorial Enquiry, *&c.*

The Court of Censorial Enquiry met and adjourned to Saturday next, when the great Cause[3] so much talked of, will be certainly argued.

TUESDAY, FEBRUARY 18, 1752. NUMB. 14.

> ——*Jam sævus apertam*
> *In Rabiem verti cæpit Jocus, et per honestas*
> *Ire minax impune Domos.* HORACE.[4]

> *The Jest began to turn to open Rage,*
> *And the dull scurrilous invective Page,*
> *Fell on the greatest Worthies of the Age.*

A Good Name, says THE Dramatic Poet, *is the immediate Jewel of a Man's Soul.*[5] So high indeed is the Value which Mankind set on a good Name, that we have frequent Instances (in the Case of Duels particularly) where Men do at least run the Risque of both Life and Soul for its Preservation. This is surely going too far; but if we agree with Aristotle in his Ethics, *that not to live but to live happily* is the great Business of Man,[6] Reputation will appear of

[1] Referring to George Anne Bellamy in the role of Sigismunda in James Thomson's *Tancred and Sigismunda*, performed with Garrick at Drury Lane on 13 and 15 Feb. 1752; on Bellamy as one of Fielding's favorite actresses, see *CGJ* No. 3 and n., p. 31, above.

[2] Slightly misquoted from Prior's 'Venus Mistaken'; the first line should read, ' 'Tis Cloe's Eye, and Cheek, and Lip, and Breast'. The poem is one of three by Prior about a portrait of his mistress, Anne Durham, who had been painted by Hugh Howard (1675–1737), an Irish painter.

[3] The trial of 'B— T—'; see *CGJ* No. 9, above, p. 72.

[4] *Epistles,* II. i. 148–50: 'jest, now growing cruel, turned to open frenzy, and stalked amid the homes of honest folk, fearless in its threatening' (Loeb); Fielding quotes with some tranposing of words.

[5] Adapted from *Othello,* III. iii. 155–6; Fielding quotes the entire passage in another essay on slander, in *Champion,* 6 Mar. 1740.

[6] See *Nicomachean Ethics,* i. 4 and x. 6.

equal Value with Life itself, since our living happily so absolutely depends on our possessing this inestimable Jewel.

Hence it seems to appear, that unjustly to take away another's Reputation, is an Injury equal with that of taking away his Life; and in the only Laws which have corresponded throughout with Truth and common Sense, those Laws I mean which came from the Voice of God himself, these Injuries are both considered as Crimes of an equal Die, and as deserving an equal Punishment. The same sacred Table of Laws which forbids Murder, alike forbids us to bear false Witness against our Neighbour;[1] and whoever reads and understands the 22d Verse of the 5th Chap. of St. Matthew, will find equal Vengeance pronounced by the Divine Lawgiver of the New Testament against both these Crimes.[2]

If this be the Case, a Man may reasonably express some Wonder that in a Country whose Laws pretend to be founded on those I have just mentioned, none, or at best very small Punishments are allotted to this heinous Crime of Slander.[3] That so far from considering the taking away another's Reputation as a Crime equal to that of taking away his Life, the Laws of this Christian Country do in Reality consider the taking away a Shilling as a much more grievous Offence.[4]

Nor is it, I think, Matter of less Astonishment to see many who profess themselves Believers in the Christian Religion, very deliberately, and without the least Hesitation, plunge themselves into a Crime so positively, and under such dreadful Penalties forbidden in that holy Dispensation which they agree to have Divine Authority.

Again, that Men who pretend to Honesty and Good-Nature, nay and who appear in other Instances really to possess those amiable Qualities, should wantonly delight in doing this cruel Injury to their Fellow-Creatures, may justly seem a strange Solecism in Ethics; such a Solecism indeed that it is great Pity there should be found any Principle in human Nature which will account for it.

As the Divine Law however hath thought proper to rank this Sin with that

[1] Exodus 20: 16.

[2] Fielding is thinking not only of Matthew 5: 22 ('whosoever shall say to his brother, Raca, shall be in danger of the council: but whosoever shall say, Thou fool, shall be in danger of hell fire') but also of the preceding verse, 5: 21: 'You have heard that it was said to the men of old, "You shall not kill; and whoever kills shall be liable to judgment." '

[3] Slander was not a felony, though the party slandered could sue in an 'Action on the Case for Words' in the common law courts. Cf. *Champion*, 6 Mar. 1740: 'The laws of England are little severe against slander, unless it be against the great: for as to that action which may be brought for words, as it is founded on the supposal of a trespass, or real injury committed, so juries have so little consideration of any other injury besides what is done to the pocket; that since the statute of 21 James I. cap. 16, which limits costs, it is rarely worth any man's while to bring an action for words, unless he can prove special damages.'

[4] Stealing twelve pence or more was a felony, grand larceny, though where goods were involved juries often deliberately undervalued the property; see Fielding's *Enquiry* (1751), p. 72.

of Murder, I may be allowed to treat it in the same Light, and to consider the Degrees of Guilt in this Case, as the English Law considers those in Murder.[1]

Murder is the killing a Man, &c. with Malice propense.[2] By this we are not to understand that it is always incumbent on a Prosecutor to prove that the Murderer had a previous avowed Malice to the deceased; nor is it indeed necessary he should have had it. In every barbarous Murder, and where there is no just Provocation given, the Law very wisely implies the Malice from the Fact itself: For such a Person, say the Writers on that Subject, is supposed to bear Malice to all Mankind.[3]

In the same Manner, when we barbarously take away the Reputation of another, it is not a sufficient Excuse that we have no particular Malice to the Person whom we thus cruelly injure. Nay, the Offence becomes perhaps the more atrocious from this very Excuse: For if we have no Malice, we are the less likely to have received any Provocation; and our Cruelty is to be imputed only to that Malignity which is the rankest and most poisonous Weed that disgraces human Nature. This is that *malignant Temper* which Horace attributes to the Vulgar, when he says *he despises them*;[4] that Malignity to which Valerius Maximus *assigns* Teeth, and says, "No State of Happiness can by any Degree of Moderation escape them; a Disposition that makes Men rich in the Losses of others, fortunate from their Calamities, and Immortal from their Deaths."[5]

Nor will it mitigate the Offence that we were only in Jest, and that whatever Mischief we have done by our Slander we meant nothing more

---

[1] The parallel of murder and slander is a favorite theme with Fielding; cf. his Preface to the *Miscellanies* (1743): 'I look on the Practice of stabbing a Man's Character in the Dark, to be as base and as barbarous as that of stabbing him with a Poignard in the same Manner.' See also *Tom Jones*, XI. i, in which he finds murder by poison 'an exact Analogy' to slander, 'a more cruel Weapon than a Sword'; and *Champion* for 6 Mar. 1740, an essay which is close in thought to the present leader and which was reprinted, without attribution, in 1752 in the *Ladies Magazine*, No. 19 (25 July–8 Aug., iii. 230 ff.). For his other attacks on slander and libelling, see 'Essay on the Knowledge of the Characters of Men', *Miscellanies* (1743), *A Charge to the Grand Jury* (1749), and *CGJ* Nos. 5 and 16.

[2] i.e. malice aforethought.

[3] Cf. *JJ* No. 20 (16 Apr. 1748): 'Am I to derive all this from a natural Malevolence of Disposition, and to imply the same universal Malice in these Libellers, as the Law doth in those who kill without Provocation; who are to be presumed, says Lord *Hale*, to be *hostes humani generis*?' See Matthew Hale, *History of the Pleas of the Crown*, 2 vols. (1736), I. xxxvii. 455; cf. Giles Jacob, 'If one resolves to kill the next Man he meets, and doth kill him, it is *Murder*; here Malice is implied against all Mankind' (*A New Law-Dictionary*, 7th edn. [1756], s.v. 'Murder'); on 'previous malice' see also Edward Coke, *Third Part of the Institutes of the Laws of England*, ch. vii.

[4] See *Odes*, II. xvi. 39–40, where Horace says Fate has given him a 'fine breath of Grecian song and a scorn for the envious crowd' (*et malignum spernere vulgus*) (Loeb); cf. *Odes*, III. i. i, 'I hate the uninitiate crowd' (Loeb).

[5] *Factorum et dictorum memorabilium*, IV. vii. Ext. 2; Fielding translates with some omissions from a passage which begins, 'But there is no Prosperity so modest, that can escape the teeth of Envy' (trans. Samuel Speed, 1684). Cf. Fielding on the role of 'malice' in slander, *Champion*, 6 Mar. 1740; and his distinction between malice and envy, 'Essay on the Knowledge of the Characters of Men', *Miscellanies* (1743), i. 158–9.

than our Diversion. Many Tyrants and Slaughterers of Mankind, had there been any Power to arraign them in Foro Civili,[1] could have justly alledged this Motive for Murder; but as this will be allowed no Plea for that Crime in Foro Civili, no more will it be a Plea for Slander in Foro Conscientiæ; if there be any such Slanderer who doth not know from what Principle in his Nature this mischievous Pleasure arises, let him consult Cicero's fourth Book of his *Tusculan Questions*, where he will find *Malevolence* defined to be *that Delight which we take in the Evil that happens to others, from which we ourselves receive no Emolument.*[2]

Again in Murder, as in all other Felony, there are Principals and Accessaries. In the Case of Murder, not only he who actually kills a Man, but all who are present, and in any Manner aiding, abetting, or assisting, are Principals.[3]

In Slander, every Man who knowingly contributes to the Propagation of a Falsehood against the Character of another, is as much a Principal, as the original Deviser or Contriver; and in this Light he is regarded in the Law.

Nor will it be either a legal or conscientious Excuse for such a Publisher of Scandal to say, that he did not certainly know the Falsehood, or even that he had some Reason to believe it to be true. In Law indeed, not even Truth itself will justify a Libel or a scandalous Report;[4] but surely in no Sense whatever can the Publisher of a Falsehood to the Ruin of any Man's Reputation be deemed innocent. It would be but a poor Defence for the Murder of an honest Man, that somebody told us he was a Thief; our Ignorance of the Falsehood of the Report, would hardly extenuate the Guilt in such a Case, to pure Chance-Medley;[5] nor will the same Degree of Ignorance justify the Murder of our Neighbour's Reputation. The Injury done to him is the same, and the Guilt of the Slanderer differs very little, whether he publishes that he knows to be false, or that which he hath very little Grounds to believe to be true.

---

[1] In the civil court, in contrast to the 'court of conscience' (*in foro conscientiae*).

[2] *Tusculan Disputations*, IV. vii. 16; Fielding has extended the definition, since Cicero merely says that 'malice (taking delight in another's evil)' is a subdivision of the Stoic 'disorder' of 'pleasure' (Loeb).

[3] See Matthew Hale, *History of the Pleas of the Crown*, I. xxxiv; Jacob, *A New Law-Dictionary*, s.v. 'Murder'.

[4] i.e. in a criminal prosecution for libel, not a civil action; in the former 'it is immaterial with respect to the essence of a libel, whether the matter of it be true or false; since the provocation, and not the falsity, is the thing to be punished criminally', whereas in a civil action 'if the charge be true, the plaintiff has received no private injury, and has no ground to demand a compensation' (William Blackstone, *Commentaries on the Laws of England*, iv [1769], 150). Cf. William Hawkins, *A Treatise of the Pleas of the Crown*, i (1716): 'the greater Appearance there is of Truth in any malicious Invective, so much the more provoking it is' (p. 194).

[5] 'Accident or casualty not *purely* accidental, but of a mixed character. Chiefly in *Manslaughter by chance-medley* (for which later authors often use *chance-medley* itself): "the casual killing of a man, not altogether without the killer's fault, though without an evil intent" ' (*OED*).

Lastly as to the Death of a Man, there are Accessaries, so are there likewise in this Crime.

In Murder he who commands, counsels, or advises the killing, is an Accessary before the Fact, and his Guilt is the same with the Principal; so is the Case of Slander, and needs not to be expatiated upon; but as to Accessaries after the Fact I shall be a little more explicit.

These in a legal Sense are the Receivers, Abettors, Consenters and Encouragers of a Felon knowing him to be such; and these themselves are Felons in Law, tho' admitted to the Benefit of their Clergy.[1]

To pursue therefore the Language of the Law, we shall venture to call every Man a Slanderer, who protects, defends, assists or receives into his Company any Person who is notoriously guilty of this detestable Vice.

There is besides a particular Accessary after the Fact in Theft, and that is he who buys the stolen Goods;[2] in the same Manner may we consider the Purchase of a Libel; and this moreover falls within the former Description: For by such Means the Libeller is certainly protected and assisted. Nay we may thus become even Accessaries before the Fact, to future Libels; for by the Purchase of one Libel we encourage the Author to write another; and thus Scandal and Theft are promoted in the same Manner.

What an Encouragement indeed must it give to scandalous Writers to find that an Abuse on a private Character shall be a sufficient Recommendation of their Works; and that any Hint of this Kind in an Advertisement, shall be sure to gain them Readers. This may perhaps afford too some little Excuse for those at least who write from such absolute Necessity, as would in the Civil Law have justified a Theft;[3] but what Excuse can their Readers find, who swallow down a Potion of Dulness and Nonsense, for the Sake of the agreeable Bitter of Scurrility? Is not this as vitiated a Taste as that of a green sick Girl,[4] who devours all Kinds of the most poisonous Nastiness, for the

---

[1] Originally a way of exempting clergymen from secular jurisdiction, 'benefit of clergy' was extended by medieval common law to literate laymen; by 1550 its availability had been limited to lesser felonies and to first convictions, and the privilege continued to be limited by statute until it was abolished altogether in 1841. The 'literacy' test (reading—or reciting from memory—the so-called 'neck-verse', usually the opening of Psalm 51) was abolished for peers in 1547 and altogether in 1706. By 1769 some 160 offenses were felonies without benefit of clergy. See H. H. Baker, 'Criminal Courts and Procedure at Common Law 1550–1800', in *Crime in England 1550–1800*, ed. J. S. Cockburn (Princeton, NJ, 1977), pp. 41–2; and W. S. Holdsworth, *A History of English Law*, 3rd edn. (1923), iii. 301. On benefit of clergy and accessories, cf. Thomas Wood: 'If a Statute takes away Clergy from the Principal, It is not to be taken away from the Accessory; unless the Accessory also is particularly included. . . . So where a Statute takes away Clergy from Aiders and Abetters, yet Accessories shall have their Clergy' (*An Institute of the Laws of England*, 8th edn. [1754], p. 413). Accessories after the fact were allowed the benefit of clergy in all cases; see Blackstone, *Commentaries*, iv (1769), 39.

[2] See Fielding's discussion of this subject in *An Enquiry into the Causes of the late Increase of Robbers* (1751), sect. V.

[3] For Fielding's views on necessity as justification of theft, see *CGJ* No. 11, above, p. 80, and *CGJ* No. 39, below, pp. 226–9.

[4] i.e. one affected by greensickness, 'an anaemic disease which mostly affects young women about the age of puberty' (*OED*).

Sake of those very Savours, which a sound and healthy Appetite would nauseate?

Instead of searching into those Bogs of human Nature whence such a depraved Taste can arise, I shall recommend to all who are possessed of it, a more innocent, as well as cheap Way of gratifying it, than by contributing any longer to the Propagation of those Loads of Scurrility, which are daily sent abroad to the Dishonour of both the Press and the Nation; and this Secret I shall communicate in the following short Receipt.

Take out of Ainsworth,[1] Bailey,[2] or any other Dictionary, all the abusive scurrilous Words you can find, and apply them yourself, in your own Mind, to any grave, great or good Character you please.

P.S. Take Care none of them stick to your own Hands in the Application. Thus may we gratify Malevolence without doing any Mischief; and save both that Money and Time, which we throw away in buying and reading Scandal.

C.

SATURDAY, FEBRUARY 22, 1752.   NUMB. 15.

——populum late Regem, belloque; superbum.

VIRGIL.[3]

A Nation of Kings and Warriors.

It seems very wonderful and surprizing, that when so many learned Writers in all Ages, have discoursed on Government and its various Forms, there should still remain one Form of it unhandled, and indeed unmentioned by any of them. Plato, Aristotle, Cicero are entirely silent on the Subject; Harrington,[4] Locke, Lord Bolingbroke,[5] take no Notice of it; and even the ingenious Writer of *L'Esprit des Loix,*[6] who seems to have sifted and

---

[1] Robert Ainsworth (1660–1743), antiquarian and compiler of a Latin–English dictionary published first in 1736 as *Thesaurus Linguae Latinae Compendiarius; or, A compendious Dictionary of the Latin Tongue*; a 4th edn. was published in 1752 with improvements by Fielding's friend and associate William Young. Fielding owned a 1746 edition (Baker, item 419).

[2] Nathan or Nathaniel Bailey (d. 1742), author of *Dictionarium Britannicum: Or a Compleat Universal Etymological English Dictionary* (1721); Fielding refers to him also in *Champion*, 14 Feb. 1740 and 17 May 1740, and *Tom Jones*, VII. iii.

[3] *Aeneid*, i. 21: 'a people, kings of broad realms and proud in war' (Loeb).

[4] James Harrington (1611–77), political theorist and author of *The Commonwealth of Oceana* (1656); Fielding cites him as an anti-monarchical Republican in *JJ* No. 3 (19 Dec. 1747) and No. 7 (16 Jan. 1748); and see *Champion*, 4, 15 Nov. 1740.

[5] Henry St. John, 1st Viscount Bolingbroke (1678–1751), politician and political thinker whose major political writings included *A Dissertation upon Parties* (1735) and *The Idea of a Patriot King* (1749); Bolingbroke's free-thinking in religious matters disturbed Fielding, who was writing a *Comment on Lord Bolingbroke's Essays* at the time of his death. See also *CGJ* Nos. 46, 60, and 69; *Amelia*, I. ii.

[6] Charles-Louis de Secondat, baron de Montesquieu (1689–1755), whose *Spirit of the Laws*, written during the years 1734–48, had recently appeared in an English translation by Thomas Nugent (2 vols., 1750).

considered the several Kinds of Government with such critical Exactness, hath either thro' Negligence or Design, made not the least mention of that most extraordinary System of Politics, which I am now going to describe, with a Gravity becoming so important a Question.

Not to keep my Reader any longer in Suspence, the Government I mean is that of the Stage; a Government founded on a Set of Politics peculiar to itself, and practised by no other Nation in the known Parts of the World.[1]

No State, of which we have any Record in History, hath ever suffered a greater Variety of Revolutions, been engaged in more continued Wars, or torn to Pieces with more intestine Divisions: Yet hath it subsisted thro' an infinite Number of Ages, outlasted all the Kingdoms of the Earth, and still remains in a very prosperous and flourishing Condition. Now as the Length of its Continuance must be thought an incontestible Proof of the Excellence of its Constitution, it seems to me both an useful and amusing Speculation, to examine by what particular Maxims of Policy this extraordinary People regulate their Lives. The following slight Remarks may serve to introduce the Subject, and excite some abler Penman to discuss it more at large.

The Theatrical State can neither be called a Monarchy, an Aristocracy, or a Democracy, but seems rather a Mixture and Compound of them all. It is indeed for ever in a fluctuating Condition, inclining more or less to each of these Sorts of Government at different Times: Yet, what is very remarkable, the Revolutions happen without disordering the Constitution, and Affairs go on as usual, with very little Interruption.

Thus the Theatrical State of Drury, from which we shall chiefly derive our Example, was about an Age ago under the Jurisdiction of a Triumvirate, who called themselves Cibber, Booth and Wilks,[2] and had each of them their

[1] Cf. Fielding's comment on the 'strict resemblance between the states political and theatrical' in *The Historical Register* (1737), ii. 289 ff., and his use of the device for political satire in *Eurydice Hissed* (1737). The parallel, which governs the rest of this essay, was, of course, time-worn, but Fielding's allusions here to Colley Cibber's *Apology* (1740) would have reminded his readers of a work in which the use of the parallel was both frequent and notorious. Anti-Walpole journalists in 1740 had combated the pro-government bias of Cibber's autobiography by capitalizing on his penchant for political metaphor and perversely interpreting his book as an Apology for the Life of Sir Robert Walpole. For Fielding's contribution to this ridicule, see *Champion*, 22 Apr. 1740, where he argues that Cibber's apology is for one whose comic role 'hath been Acted on a much larger Stage than *Drury Lane*'; see also *Craftsman*, 19 July 1740. Here, however, Fielding is inverting the usual political exploitation of the theme by developing the state as a metaphor for the stage.

[2] On this triumvirate, who managed Drury Lane from 1713 until 1732, see also the Court of Enquiry in *CGJ* No. 10, above, where Fielding accuses them of suppressing talented young actors. Colley Cibber (1671–1757) was the butt of Fielding's ridicule from 1730 (in the *Author's Farce*) to 1754 (*Journal of a Voyage to Lisbon*) for his character, his politics, and his defects of language and style; for a summary account of their relations, see *Joseph Andrews*, ed. Martin Battestin, Wesleyan Edn. (Oxford, 1967), pp. 18–19 n.; see also *CGJ* Nos. 26 and 34. Barton Booth (1681–1733), noted for his leading roles in Shakespearian tragedies, is generally mentioned by Fielding with respect, but cf. the disparaging reference to Booth in 'To Celia', *Miscellanies* (1743). Robert Wilks (1665–1732), best known for his comedy roles, is satirized as 'Sparkish' in the *Author's Farce*; in the Preface to the *Miscellanies* Fielding reports that a 'slight Pique' between him and Wilks prevented his offering a play to the manager after his return from Leiden. See also *Tom Jones*, IV. i and *JJ* No. 21 (23 Apr. 1748).

distinct Provinces of Government. Booth presided over the Affairs of Tragedy, Wilks over those of Comedy, and Cibber reserved himself in a neutral State, ready to add Weight to the Scale of either of his Collegues, as the other should seem to preponderate.[1] Not long afterwards the Government changed itself into a Monarchy,[2] and is at present under the joint Power of two Consuls, both of whom are esteemed by all to be the ablest Governors, that ever ruled over that People, and the State accordingly triumphs in their Hands.[3]

These *Archons* or chief Magistrates, are usually stiled *Managers*, or, as that learned and ingenious Historian Colley Cibber spells it, *Menagers of the House*;[4] and their Business is to appoint the Members of the Commonwealth their several Stations, to instruct them in the Parts they have to act, to regulate their Salaries, to manage the public Revenues, and do many other Things too tedious here to mention. They are likewise the final Judges of all Causes and Controversies that happen within their Dominions.

The Dignity and Magnificence of these Managers may be collected from hence, that they have many Kings among the Number of their Subjects, in which they seem to resemble the Majesty of the antient Romans. Yet, like the old Romans, their Modesty is very observable, in taking upon them no higher Title than that of Managers, at the same Time that many of their Subjects arrogate to themselves the splendid Appellations of Bassas, Doges, Princes, Emperors and the like.

Another Instance of the Modesty of these Archons or Managers is, that tho' their Power seems to be absolute and unlimited, they never take any Step of Consequence without consulting their Council upon it. The Council assembles every Morning in a Chamber of State, which they call the Green-room,[5] where the vacant Places of the Government are filled up, and all Affairs relating to the Commonwealth debated.

There is a very singular Custom among these People, practised by no other Nation, of admitting Women to a Seat in the Council, and a Share in

---

[1] Fielding perhaps overstates the case; though he describes accurately their strengths as actors (cf. Cibber, *Apology*, ch. xvi), there is no evidence that their managerial duties were so divided. See *London Stage*, Pt. 2, vol. i, p. lxxxvi.

[2] With Charles Fleetwood (d. 1747) as monarch. After a series of disputes in the 1732–3 season, marked by a defection of actors led by Theophilus Cibber to the New Theatre at the Haymarket, John Highmore—who had been attempting to manage Drury Lane with the remaining actors—sold out to Fleetwood before Feb. 1734. Fleetwood remained in control for the next 10 years, with Macklin as his stage manager; see *London Stage*, Pt. 3, vol. i, pp. lxxxix–xci. For Fielding's relations with Fleetwood, see the Preface to the *Miscellanies* (1743).

[3] Garrick and James Lacy, managers since 1747; see *CGJ* No. 3, above. With Fielding's ringing praise of Garrick throughout this essay, cf. Johnson's portrait in the *Rambler* a week earlier of 'Prospero', a vain man too much affected by sudden success; according to Boswell, the portrait is of Garrick. (*Rambler*, No. 200 [15 Feb. 1752]; Boswell, *Life of Johnson*, ed. G. B. Hill and L. F. Powell [Oxford, 1934], i. 216).

[4] The spelling is used consistently by Cibber in his *Apology*.

[5] The room accommodating actors and actresses not needed on stage.

the Management of public Affairs. This is often the Cause of great Inconveniencies; for as the Ladies of this Country are extremely vain and fond of Pre-eminence, grievous Quarrels often arise among them, to the great Disturbance and Interruption of public Business. A remarkable Fray of this Kind is said to have happened two or three Years ago, which set the whole Green-room in an Uproar, and 'tis confidently reported, that one of these Ladies went so far as to call her Antagonist *a Brandy-fac'd B—ch*, even while the Council was sitting, and in the very Presence of the Managers.[1]

This is the only State perhaps in which the Talents of Men are considered, and applied to what they are most fit for, and seem directed to by Nature.[2] In other Nations it is not at all unfrequent to see a Man placed at the Head of an Army, who is entirely void of Courage and military Conduct; another created Judge, without having the least Knowledge of the Laws; a third installed Bishop or Cardinal, who is perhaps a Heathen and an Atheist: But here, in the best regulated theatrical States, if we make some few Exceptions, we shall find Men disposed and placed in such particular Offices as their Talents enable them to discharge. This especially is the Case in that famous Nation now governed by Mr. Garrick and his Coadjutor, whose Plan of Policy I would recommend as a Pattern to all his cotemporary Princes.

The theatrical State is certainly the only State under the Sun, in which Rewards are bestowed generally and universally on *Well-doers*. A certain able Politician remarks, "That altho' Rewards and Punishments are usually called the two great Hinges on which all Government turns, yet he never could observe this Maxim to be put in Practice by any Nation except that of *Lilliput*."[3] 'Tis evident from hence, that this great Statesman had either never travelled among the People I have been describing, or that he had them not in his Thoughts when he wrote the foregoing Paragraph. For it is absolutely certain, that Rewards are here generally bestowed on all who

---

[1] Referring to a quarrel between Margaret 'Peg' Woffington (c. 1714–60) and Fielding's favorite, Catherine Clive (see *CGJ* No. 3, above, p. 31), both actresses admired by Fielding but both notoriously ill-tempered. The incident occurred during a performance of *1 Henry IV* at Drury Lane in Jan. 1747, with Woffington in the minor role of Lady Percy and with the house far from crowded. In Thomas Davies's account, 'A very celebrated comic actress [Clive] triumphed in the barrenness of the pit and boxes; she threw out some expressions against the consequence [*sic*] of the Lady Percy. This produced a very cool, but cutting, answer from the other; who reminded the former of her playing, very lately, to a much thinner audience, one of her favourite parts. And now, the ladies not being able to restrain themselves within the bounds of cool conversation, a most terrible fray ensued.' (*Dramatic Miscellanies*, 2 vols. [1784], i. 231–3.) See also Davies's *Memoirs of the Life of Garrick*, 2 vols. (1780), i. 311, for comment on the bitterness of feeling between Clive and Woffington. On the epithet Fielding uses, cf. this stanza from 'The Green-Room Scuffle: Or Drury-Lane in an Uproar' (a ballad on the incident): '*Peg*, in a Taste polite, / At once began the Battle: / Says she, "you may be right; / But this is Tittle-Tattle, *Red-Fac'd* B—ch!" ' (*The Foundling Hospital for Wit*, No. 5 [1748], p. 19).

[2] For Fielding, an important attribute of a well-regulated state; cf. *A Plan of the Universal Register-Office* (1751), above, p. 3.

[3] Swift, *Gulliver's Travels*, I. vi.

discharge any Part well in the Society; and even the meanest of the People have *Benefits* assigned them in Proportion to their Merit.[1] On the contrary, Punishment, the other Hinge of Government, is very little in Use among them; and even when there is a Necessity of employing it, their most rigorous Sentences never rise higher than suspending the Salary of an Offender, or at worst, if his Crime be very atrocious, banishing him from the Community.

A great Poet, Cotemporary with the Statesman last quoted, observes in one of his Satires, that

> *The Number may be hang'd, but not be crown'd.*[2]

But this also is false with Respect to the People now under Consideration, among whom it is very common to see Crowns on the Head of the *Canaille* or Multitude. Indeed the Title of King seems to be in no great Repute among them, for except King Richard, King Lear, and one or two more, I have generally observed the regal Office to be filled by some of the meanest of the People. One of these crowned Heads, namely KING MILLS,[3] died about two Years ago, and was succeeded in Rank and Dignity by King —, the next most venerable Personage on the Stage.[4]

I could never learn with Certainty what Religion is practised in this Country. Many are of Opinion that, like the Robinhoodians,[5] they have none at all; but I think one may assert with greater Probability, that they have among them all the Religions which the World has ever produced: For I myself have seen the most opposite Rites and Ceremonies performed by them on the same Spot of Ground, and sometimes on one and the same Evening. Besides they pretend to be a Nation peculiarly favoured of Heaven, and boast that at certain Seasons the Gods descend among them; nor is this

---

[1] i.e. benefit performances, held from mid-March to the end of the season. Members of the company shared the proceeds according to their importance, with the most prominent having 'clear benefits' and the less important sharing with others. Doorkeepers, office keepers, and the like also shared in the benefits, though not stage-hands or musicians; see Dougald MacMillan, *Drury Lane Calendar, 1747–1776* (Oxford, 1938), pp. xx–xxi.

[2] Pope, *Epilogue to the Satires: Dialogue II*, 111.

[3] William Mills (d. 1750), or 'Honest Billy Mills', as Fielding called him, often played Claudius in *Hamlet* and is probably engaged in that role when Partridge sees the play in *Tom Jones*, XVI. v; see Oliver Ferguson, 'Partridge's Vile Encomium: Fielding and Honest Billy Mills', *PQ* 43 (1964), 73–8. Fielding admired his character, though not his acting, and urged attendance at his benefit performance in 1748 (*JJ* No. 21, 23 Apr. 1748); see also *Joseph Andrews*, I. viii, and *Tom Jones*, VII. i. Fielding's friendship for Mills is the subject of a jibe in an other-worldly fantasy in the *Craftsman* (4 Aug. 1751): 'A Justice of Peace . . . seem'd concern'd for fear his Friend *Billy Mills*, as he call'd him, and the *Town* should meet and quarrel in the other World; they could seldom agree, he said, in this: for whenever *Billy* offered to speak to the Town, the Town immediately threw an Apple at him.'

[4] Unidentified; but a possible candidate for the actor Fielding has in mind is Edward Berry (1706–60), who was now in his declining years and who, like Mills, played serious but secondary roles on a regular basis, including Duncan in *Macbeth* in 1750–1, previously played by Mills in 1748–9.

[5] See *CGJ* No. 8, above.

Pretence without Foundation, for I have with my own Eyes been Witness of many of these supernatural Descents. Their Patron-Deity seems to be Mercury, who is more frequent in his Visits than all the other Gods.[1]

They are a People that delight greatly in War, and carry their Passion for military Glory to the most romantic Pitch of Heroism and Extravagance. And as Heroes are ever the most susceptible of the gentle Passion of Love, so these People are of all Nations under the Sun, the most amorous, the most addicted to Love and Gallantry. *Intrigue* is of the very Essence of their Constitution, and nothing is esteemed more honourable than to contrive and carry on a Love-Plot with Success. 'Tis said moreover, that they encourage promiscuous Copulation, and that all their Wives and Daughters are in common among them; but this I take to be a groundless Calumny, maliciously invented by their Enemies, without any Appearance or the least Probability of Truth.[2]

These are some few of the Observations, which I have made in my Travels among this extraordinary People, so famous in all civilized Parts of the World. The Subject deserves to be treated more at large, and I am now preparing a Book for the Press, in which these several Matters will be more copiously explained, with many more Particulars not touched upon in this short Dissertation. In the mean Time let me recommend their Laws and Customs to the Consideration of all Statesmen, and I shall conclude with heartily wishing that all the Monarchs of Europe governed as well as Mr. Garrick.

P.

Proceedings at the Court of Censorial Enquiry, *&c.*

The Censor gave his Opinion in the Cause of B— T—,[3] against whom there was an Information on the Statute of Dulness,

That this Court hath no Jurisdiction over any of the Subjects of

---

[1] In his comment on the descent of the gods Fielding makes a sly reference to the practice of incorporating classical gods and goddesses into the 'serious' part of pantomimes; cf. *Tom Jones*, v. i, where Fielding explains, 'The *Serious* exhibited a certain Number of Heathen Gods and Heroes, who were certainly the worst and dullest Company into which an Audience was ever introduced; and . . . were actually intended so to be, in order to contrast the *Comic* Part of the Entertainment.' On the frequent appearance of Mercury, cf. *Journey from this World to the Next*, i. i, in which Mercury appears as 'a tall young gentleman in a silk waistcoat, with a wing on his left heel', etc., and Fielding's note reads, 'This is the dress in which the god appears to mortals at the theaters'. Since mercury was used as a cure for venereal disease, Fielding may also be joking here in anticipation of the allegations a few lines further about the promiscuity of the players; cf. *Spectator*, No. 275 (15 Jan. 1712).

[2] On the continuing stigma of immorality attached to professional actors and actresses in the period, see *London Stage*, Pt. 3, vol. i, p. cxxvii, and Pt. 4, vol. i, pp. xcviii, cxcix–cc.

[3] Probably *The History of Miss Betsy Thoughtless* (October, 1751), by Eliza Haywood; on this identification, see *CGJ* No. 9, above, p. 72.

Grubstreet, unless in Cases of Blasphemy, Sedition, Scurrility and Indecency.[1]

That the Corporation of Grubstreet had existed from Time, whereof the Memory of Man was not to the contrary,[2] and for all that Time had enjoyed and used the Privilege of being dull.

That tho' by the Carelessness of the Clerks, all the Records of Grubstreet were lost, so that it was scarce possible to find any of a single Year's standing, yet it well appeared by incontestable Authorities, that there had been a Grubstreet even in Greece itself, where as appears from Longinus, there were Dealers in the Turgid, the Puerile, the Vapid and other the known Wares of Grubstreet.[3]

That Grubstreet was in a flourishing State in Rome, hath been proved by many Citations from Juvenal and Horace; and even from a Line of Virgil himself, who advises the Admirers of one Grubstreet Writer, to be likewise the Admirers of another.[4]

Mr. Censor added, that all these Proofs were taken from the Writings of Men who were avowed Enemies to the Grubstreet Cause, and were consequently the most unquestionable Evidence.

Mr. Censor said, he was sorry to confess that Grubstreet had very fully made out its Title to a much greater Antiquity, than the Kingdoms of Wit and Learning. That the two last had arisen from the first, and not that from these.

That before the first Beginners of the Reformation, all was Grubstreet; and Darkness had overspread the Face of the whole Kingdom.

That tho' the Dominions of Grubstreet had been lessened since the Rise of the Kingdom of Wit and Learning, still had the low Republic continued a great and mighty Power.

That the Subjects of this Republic had never paid any, not even the least Acknowledgments to the Kingdom of Wit; but that on the contrary, the Subjects of the latter had always paid certain Tributes to Grubstreet. That Shakespear himself was obliged to this Composition; for that all his Admirers had ever accounted for certain Passages in his Works, from his having been forced to comply with the absurd Taste of his Audience, in other Words, to pay a Tribute to Grubstreet.[5]

---

[1] See the 'Treaty of Covent Garden', Article 7, *CGJ* No. 4, above.

[2] Legal terminology to indicate that 'no man then alive has heard any proof of the contrary. This is also called time of living memory, as opposed to time of legal memory, which runs from the commencement of the reign of Richard I.' (W. Jowitt, *Dictionary of English Law* [1959], s.v. 'time'.) Cf. *JJ* No. 6 (9 Jan. 1748).

[3] See *On the Sublime*, sects. iii and iv; cf. Pope's *Peri Bathous* (1728), ch. vi. On the legalism 'other the known Wares', cf. 'other the known Wares of Billinsgate', *CGJ* No. 4, above, p. 39.

[4] *Eclogues*, iii. 90: *Qui Bavium non odit, amet tua carmina, Maevi*, 'Let him who hates not Bavius love your songs, Maevius' (Loeb); Fielding uses this line as the motto of *CGJ* No. 31.

[5] A common argument in 18th-cent. criticism of Shakespeare; cf., for example, Pope, Preface to

That Ben Johnson was compelled to pay the same Acknowledgments, and very plainly writ some of his Plays, with no other View than that of offering a Tribute to the Republic;[1] and Beaumont and Fletcher often contented themselves with two Scenes of Wit, and filled the rest with Dulness from the same Motive.[2]

That Dryden is another Instance of the same Tribute exacted and complied with; witness several of his Plays; in writing which he could apparently have no other Design, than what is here alledged.[3]

I need not, said the Censor, run through all the Proofs. Even Swift himself as the late noble Writer of his Life seems to allow, suffered some Pieces to be inserted in his Works, as a Tribute to the same Republic.[4] This is an Instance equal to all the rest, if we consider either the Temper of the Man, or his known Antipathy to the Cause of Grubstreet.

The last Example I shall produce, is that of Pope, who begins the last Book of his Dunciad with an Address to Dulness.

> Yet, yet a Moment, one dim Ray of Light,
> Indulge, dread Chaos and eternal Night,
> Of Darkness visible so much be lent,
> As Half to shew, half veil the deep Intent!
> Ye Pow'rs, whose Mysteries restor'd I sing,
> To whom Time bears me on his rapid Wing;
> Suspend awhile your Force inertly strong,
> Then take at once the Poet and the Song.[5]

Works of Shakespeare (1725): 'It must be allowed that Stage-Poetry of all other, is more particularly levell'd to please the *Populace*, and its success more immediately depending upon the *Common Suffrage*. One cannot therefore wonder, if *Shakespear*, having at his first appearance no other aim in his writings than to procure a subsistence, directed his endeavours solely to hit the taste and humour that then prevailed.' Lewis Theobald similarly comments in the Preface to his edition of Shakespeare (1733) that the playwright's '*false Wit*, and descending beneath himself, may have proceeded from a Deference paid to the then *reigning Barbarism*'. See also 'An Epistle to Mr. *Southerne*, from Mr. *Fenton*', *Works of Thomas Southerne* (1721), i, sig. A2ᵛ.

[1] Cf. Dryden, 'Epilogue to the Second Part of the *Conquest of Granada*': 'They, who have best succeeded on the stage, / Have still conform'd their genius to their age. / Thus *Jonson* did mechanic humour show, / When men were dull, and conversation low.' Fielding usually mentions Jonson with great respect; see e.g. the Preface to *Plutus* (1742), where he recommends that a reader accustomed to modern comedy read a few plays by Jonson before essaying Aristophanes; see, however, his comments in *CGJ* No. 55.

[2] Cf. Thomas Cooke: '*Beaumont* and *Fletcher* were . . . Poets of irregular Genius; . . . their Works are a Garden over-run with as many Weeds, without so many Flowers, as *Shakespear*'s' (*An Ode on the Powers of Poetry* [1751], p. 5).

[3] Referring especially to Dryden's tragedies, which are satirized throughout Fielding's *Tragedy of Tragedies* (1731).

[4] John Earl of Orrery, *Remarks on the Life and Writings of Dr. Jonathan Swift* (1752): 'it seems as if the author . . . imagined the public under an absolute necessity of accepting the basest coin from the same hand, that had exhibited the purest' (p. 80); for similar passages, see pp. 128–30, 229, and 283. On the controversy surrounding Orrery's work, of which Fielding owned three copies, see General Introduction, above, p. xliv.

[5] *Dunciad* (1743), iv. 1–8.

Here the Poet confesses the great Power of Grub-street, and seems to allow explicitly that the greatest Wits write only through the Indulgence of that Republic.

Upon the whole as Mr. Cibber, that great and profound Lawyer, long since discovered that we had no Right to any Liberty before the Revolution,[1] so it appears to me that no Wits were at Liberty to write without paying a Tax to Grubstreet, 'till this was stipulated for them by the late Treaty of Covent-Garden.

On the contrary, no single Instance hath been shewn where any Author of Grub-street hath paid any Tribute to the Kingdom of Wit, but have in all Ages claimed, had, and used the full Privilege of being as dull as they please, and this Privilege is secured to them by the above Treaty.

For all which Reasons Judgment was ordered to be entered for the Defendant.

(*Adjourned.*)

TUESDAY, FEBRUARY 25, 1752.   NUMB. 16.

Homo sum; nihil humani a me alienum puto.

TERENCE.[2]

I am a Man myself; and have an Interest in the Concerns of all other Men.

An eminent Frenchman now alive, in his Letters on the English Nation, hath cast a Reflexion on us, which we by no Means deserve. *The present English*, says he, *no more resemble their Ancestors in the Days of Oliver Cromwell, than the modern Italians resemble the antient Romans.*[3]

---

[1] Referring to a passage in *An Apology for the Life of Mr. Colley Cibber* (1740): 'I will boldly say then, it is, to the Revolution only, we owe the full Possession of what, 'til then, we never had more than a perpetually contested Right to' (p. 40). This statement particularly outraged the Opposition writers who attacked Cibber's book, for they recognized it as a commonplace of Walpole's apologists in their effort to counter the Opposition's use of Whig history. See *Champion* for 6 May and 6 Sept. 1740. For other attacks on Cibber see B. A. Goldgar, *Walpole and the Wits* (Lincoln, Nebr., 1976), pp. 193–4; for the controversy over the date of the birth of liberty, see Isaac Kramnick, 'Augustan Politics and English Historiography: The Debate on the English Past', *History and Theory*, 6 (1967), 33–56.

[2] *Heauton Timorumenos* ('The Self-Tormentor'), i. 75; Fielding transposes words, writing *nihil humani* for *humani nil*. This well-known line also is cited in *Tom Jones*, XV. viii and *Amelia*, X. ix.

[3] The eminent Frenchman is Voltaire, but the passage is not in his *Letters on the English Nation* but in the 'Discourse' prefixed to his *History of Charles XII* (1731). In the original edition the line used the phrase Fielding translates, 'aux Anglais de Cromwell'; after the *Craftsman* of 15 Apr. 1732, in a review generally favorable, strongly objected to the statement, Voltaire wrote to a friend in England that the printer 'should have printed, *aux fanatiques de Cromwell*; and thus it is to be read in the errata and in the late editions'; and he adds, 'never would I utter a single word that could be shocking to a free and generous nation which I admire, which I regret, and to whom I am indebted' (*Voltaire's Correspondence*, ed. Theodore Besterman [Geneva, 1953–65], ii. 315, 316 n.). Fielding has in mind the original reading and perhaps the *Craftsman*'s objections; cf. *Champion*, 6 Dec. 1739, where he writes of the 'Scoundrels and Cowards' who adhered to Cromwell, 'such they were, that I think we of the present Age are obliged to Mr. *Voltaire*, for representing us as greatly unlike them'.

The Satire here, as the Context plainly shews, is levelled at the Bravery of our present Countrymen; the Injustice of which all those French who were present at the late Battles in Germany and Flanders have very freely and loudly acknowledged.[1] Had one of our Allies indeed been no more deficient in Bravery or Integrity at the great Action at Fontenoy, France had possibly felt the Force of English Valour on that fatal Day, with as bitter Lamentations as the Fields of Cressy or Agincourt, of Blenheim or Ramelie had ever occasioned; and our glorious General as he deserved no less, so would he have gathered no less Laurels, than the most successful of his Predecessors had been ever crowned with.[2]

In real Truth, we are by no Means degenerated in Valour from our Ancestors. The British Lion is still as formidable as ever. I am afraid I cannot say the same of every other Virtue. In that particularly which hath been said so peculiarly to belong to us, that the Word which implies it, cannot be adequately rendered into any other Language, I fear we have very sensibly begun to decline. The Virtue, and the Word which I mean, is Good-Nature;[3] a Quality, in which, tho' there is little of glaring Pomp and Ostentation, there is much of solid and intrinsic Worth; if it be not admirable, it is in the highest Degree amiable; if it doth not constitute the heroic, it adorns the human, and is essential to the Christian Character.

This Virtue, I am sorry to say, seems of late Years to have decreased among us; and the Reason of this Decrease is but too apparent.

In the worthiest human Minds, there are some small innate Seeds of Malignity, which it is greatly in our Power either to suffocate and suppress, or to forward and improve their Growth, 'till they blossom and bear their poisonous Fruit; for which execrable Purpose, there is no Manure so effectual as those of Scandal, Scurrility and Abuse.[4]

---

[1] Alluding to the battles of the War of the Austrian Succession (1740–8), in particular to the battle at Fontenoy in May 1745, in which the British army under the Duke of Cumberland, youngest son of George II, acquitted itself courageously while suffering defeat. Cf. *True Patriot*, No. 6 (10 Dec. 1745), where Fielding refers to 'a Set of starved enslaved *Frenchmen*, whose Ancestors have always fled before us, and who at *Fontenoy* run from our Forces (tho' they were but a third of their Number) til their Cannon gave them a dishonourable Victory'.

[2] The ally referred to is Holland, whose attitude toward the war was unenthusiastic and whose reluctance to enter it as a principal against France played a crucial role in the series of defeats Britain suffered in the Austrian Netherlands in 1744–6. Fielding's claim here is that Cumberland would have triumphed at Fontenoy had it not been for the withdrawal of Dutch troops.

[3] The central concept in Fielding's ethics. In 'An Essay on the Knowledge of the Characters of Men' (*Miscellanies*, 1743) he defines it as 'that benevolent and amiable Temper of Mind which disposes us to feel the Misfortunes, and enjoy the Happiness of others; and consequently pushes us on to promote the latter, and prevent the former; and that without any abstract Contemplation on the Beauty of Virtue, and without the Allurements or Terrors of Religion'. His other major discussions of the idea occur in the *Champion*, 27 Mar. 1740, and the poem 'Of Good Nature' (*Miscellanies*, 1743). For commentary on the sources of the concept and its role in Fielding's thought, see Martin Battestin, *The Moral Basis of Fielding's Art* (Middletown, Conn., 1959), pp. 55–81, and Miller, *Essays*, pp. 54–88. See also *Enquiry into the Causes of the late Increase of Robbers* (1751), pp. 106–10.

[4] For Fielding's other expressions of this favourite theme, see *CGJ* Nos. 5, 6, and 14 and notes; on

That our Conversation, our Stage, and our Press have lately abounded with all these, will, I believe, be readily admitted; nor is it difficult to trace these horrid Evils to their Source. Party[1] is indeed the Fountain whence all have flowed. This it was which first set all our malignant Humours afloat, and taught us to shun, to hate, to malign and to vilify each other.

Very mischievous is this Spirit of Party of itself, and very bad were the Consequences which it produced; but they ended not here. Bad Passions being once kindled in the Mind are not so easily extinguished. There is, indeed, so much Pleasure in their Gratification, that instead of desiring to extinguish, we are apt to apply ourselves only to procure them the Fuel, in which they delight. This is a Matter too well known, and Numbers are consequently ready to get their Livelihood by administring this Fuel to us. Thus whilst our great Men are at Peace among themselves,[2] and the Press and other Engines of Party are no longer used to spread Political Dissension, the lowest of the People lay hold on those very Engines to deal forth Food to Malignity; and all those noxious Passions which Party had raised, are fed with every Kind of Scandal and Scurrility.

Instead of pursuing this disagreeable Subject any further, I will present my Reader with a Picture of a very different Temper of Mind; and then leave it with him to oppose the amiable Character, which is here drawn at full Length, to that Sketch which I have given him above: I will only add, that it is greatly within his Power to resemble which of the two he pleases, in other Words to imitate the most benevolent and virtuous, or the most wicked and base of all Beings.[3]

---

politically motivated slander in particular, see especially *JJ* Nos. 26, 28, and 29 (28 May, 11, 18 June 1748). As Fielding himself suggests at the end of the letter from 'Axylus' in this issue, his daily contact with the 'Wretches' brought into his court made him take an increasingly pessimistic view of human nature. Yet he was by no means consistent in weighing the relative effects of the 'innate Seeds of Malignity' and of man's natural goodness. For discussion of the ambiguity of his position on this topic, see Miller, *Essays*, pp. 206–14.

[1] Cf. *True Patriot*, No. 14 (4 Feb. 1746): 'Indeed this absurd and irrational Distinction of Parties hath principally contributed to poison our Constitution'. The 'spirit of party' was generally condemned in the first half of the century, often by those who were themselves fiercely partisan; cf., among many examples, Swift, *Examiner*, No. 13 (2 Nov. 1710); Addison, *Spectator*, Nos. 125 (24 July 1711) and 507 (11 Oct. 1712). The anti-party sentiment received its most theoretical exposition in Bolingbroke's *Dissertation upon Parties* (1735) and *The Idea of a Patriot King* (written 1738–9), writings which provided an ideology for the 'Patriot' opposition to Walpole.

[2] Cf. the 'Covent Garden' column of 6 Jan. 1752, printed below, Appendix I. The unusual political tranquility of these months resulted from the death of the Prince of Wales on 20 Mar. 1751, which left the Opposition to the Pelham Administration in disarray; cf. Horace Walpole's comment in a letter of 12 Dec. 1751: 'our diversions, politics, quarrels, are buried all in our Alphonso's grave' (*Yale Walpole*, xx. 291). Although the Duke of Bedford, who had been forced out of the government in June 1751, attempted to form some sort of parliamentary Opposition, the Pelhams easily dominated both Houses of Parliament. See Archibald Foord, *His Majesty's Opposition, 1714–1830* (Oxford, 1964), pp. 279–80; see also Horace Walpole, *Memoirs of the Reign of King George the Second*, 2nd edn. (1847), i. 228, where Walpole explains the reasons for 'opposition . . . having in a manner ceased at this period'.

[3] On Fielding's attitude toward freedom of the will, see Miller, *Essays*, pp. 217–19, and Martin

Mr. Censor,

From what I have read of yours, and from what I have heard of yourself, from some Persons who know you, I have concluded that you possess in an eminent Degree, that Quality, which of all others I most esteem, I mean Good-nature. I have therefore ventured to send you the Character of one, whom tho' you may imagine an odd, you will perhaps think a Good-natured, Man.

Without further Preface I am now in the sixty-fifth Year of my Age, and a Batchelor. I have an Income of five hundred a Year, and have no near Relation in the World, nor indeed any Relation with whom I am acquainted. When I tell you I am a Batchelor at these Years, I would not have you conclude that I am an Enemy to the tender Sex. In Truth I have loved one of them much too well for my Quiet. I lost her within a few Days of our intended Marriage, and still do, and ever shall, cherish her dear Memory.

From the Day of that grievous Loss to this, I have never enjoyed but one Pleasure beyond trifling Amusements, and the common Satisfactions of our ordinary Appetites, and that is—will you believe me, Mr. Censor, the Pleasure I receive from seeing and hearing the Happiness of other People.

It is natural for the Mind of Man to hunt after those Objects in which it takes Delight, and to shun those which give it Pain; for which Reason I am a constant Frequenter of Scenes of innocent Mirth, Jollity, and Happiness, and run from the Reverse as I would from a Plague. I do not mean by this that I always shun the Unfortunate; on the contrary, whenever I can by my Company, by my Advice, or by my Purse, relieve the Solitary, the Simple, or the Distressed, I never fail of doing it; and when my Endeavours are crowned with Success, I enjoy a most exquisite Pleasure. But when I should only see and feel those Miseries which I cannot redress or alleviate, I run hastily from the Scene.

I keep my Ears shut to all tragical and scandalous Stories. The Hawkers are in fee with me,[1] never to cry any Murders, last dying Speeches, or any Kind of Scurrility, in the Court where I live; but a merry Ballad is greatly my Delight, and the Singers of them receive from me many a good Penny. In a Word, I cannot bear those Pictures which represent human Nature in a wretched, or in an odious Light; but cherish every Thing which fills my Mind with Ideas of the Wisdom, the Goodness, the Mirth, and the Happiness of Mankind.

In Seasons of public Calamity I am the most wretched of Men; for I have at such Seasons the Weight of a whole Nation on my Shoulders; but I am fully repaid in Times of Joy and Prosperity; for then I may be said (tho'

Battestin, 'The Problem of *Amelia*: Hume, Barrow, and the Conversion of Captain Booth', *ELH* 41 (1974), 629–35.

[1] i.e. 'in the pay or service of, under an obligation to' (*OED*).

not in the usual Sense of the Phrase) to ride upon the Backs of all the People.[1]

I often express great Gratitude to the Almighty, that I was born in a Country where I can reflect with constant Pleasure on the Freedom, the Wealth, and indeed every political Happiness of the People. I again exult that I live in that very Age when they enjoy all these Blessings in the purest Manner. I look up with unfeigned Gratitude to the Authors, under Heaven, of these Blessings to us. With these Views I frequent the Court, and a certain Levee in Arlington-Street,[2] with more Devotion than any of the Candidates for Preferment.

Of all my Life, I think, I never enjoyed so happy a Winter as this last, in which there hath been such perfect Unanimity among all Parties, and the sole Attention of all our great Men seems to have been the Good of the Public.

Within this last Fortnight too, I have been extremely delighted. The Happiness which within that Time hath accrued to a private Family, hath almost intoxicated me with Joy. That noble, generous, Duke![3] How worthy of the highest Blessings of Life! In my Opinion how sure of them!

I have, I must confess, had lately some little Allays to my Pleasures. I was on Tuesday last at the new Play, it being the second Night (for I never go on the first). I was not so well entertained as I expected; I do not mean with the Play (for that was very pretty) but with the Audience.[4] Surely, Mr. Censor, this is unfair and illegal; for by the Law of England a Man cannot be tried twice for the same Crime.

I have likewise heard lately some obscure Hints of a Woman, somewhere

---

[1] The usual sense would be 'to assert mastery over'; cf. *Tempest*, II. i. 110–11, *Measure for Measure*, I. ii. 147–8. Axylus, of course, means that the general happiness of the people sustains him.

[2] At the home of Henry Pelham (1695?–1754), Chancellor of the Exchequer or 'prime minister', who lived at No. 17 on the site where Walpole had once lived. Fielding was a consistent supporter of the Pelham Administration ('those great and good Men') in *JJ* (1747–8) and in his later writings, dedicating to Pelham his *Proposal for Making an Effectual Provision for the Poor* (1753).

[3] James Hamilton, 6th Duke of Hamilton, who on 14 Feb. 1752 had married Elizabeth Gunning, the younger of the two famous sisters who were the toast and talk of the town (see *CGJ* No. 12, above, p. 91). Axylus' warm-hearted praise is perhaps not to be taken at face value, for the episode contains elements which Fielding consistently satirized; the Duke is described as 'hot, debauched, extravagant, and equally damaged in his fortune and person' by Horace Walpole, who further reports that the Duke fell in love at a masquerade and that the marriage was an 'extempore' affair. It was performed by one of the assistants of the notorious Revd Alexander Keith. See *Yale Walpole*, xx. 302–3.

[4] The play, Philip Francis's *Eugenia* (adapted from *Cénie* by Françoise Paula Huguet de Grafigny) opened at Drury Lane on 17 Feb., when, according to the prompter Cross, there was 'a great Noise before ye play began, occasioned by ye Music not playing what they lik'd . . . Mr Garrick went on, order'd ye Music in, & all was quiet—went off with great Applause'. On the second night, 18 Feb., when 'Axylus' supposedly attended, Cross reports the play 'went off very dull, & great hissing &c. when over' (*London Stage*, Pt. 4, i. 293–4). Fielding may be inserting this complaint because *Eugenia* was published by Andrew Millar, who also sold tickets for Francis's benefit on 22 Feb.; the play had its last performance on 25 Feb.

or other, suspected of poisoning her Father;[1] but I always shut my Ears, as I have told you, on such Occasions. I hope it is a great Way off; and what is better, I hope she is innocent.

How can your neighbouring Justice[2] bear the Sight of all those Wretches who are brought before him; but perhaps he hath sometimes Opportunities of doing Good, which make him amends. I greatly enjoyed your Story of the Man and his Ass. It brought to my Mind the famous Story of the Lion and the Man in the Roman Historian.[3] I wish I had ever seen such an Instance as either.

> I am,
> My worthy and good Sir,
> Your honest, sincere Friend,
> And most hearty Wellwisher,
> AXYLUS.[4]
>
> C.

Proceedings at the Court of Censorial Enquiry, &c.

The following Letter[5] was ordered to be read and printed.

To the Right worthy the Censor, &c.

Sir,   *Feb.* 23. 1752.

As Censor of great Britain, Misbehaviour in public Places seems to come within your Notice,and the Authors of it ought to suffer your Rebuke; tho' I must confess I am heartily sorry, that verbal Chastisement is the only Punishment you can inflict on him, whose Behaviour the other Night at Mr. Rich's House has thus raised my Indignation. For was I to see him marching at the Tail of a Cart, from Charing-Cross to Temple-Bar, with a proper Officer at his left Hand, I cannot say it wou'd give me any Pain. But not to keep you any longer in Suspence, you must know that very lately I carried my

---

[1] Mary Blandy; see *CGJ* No. 11 (above, p. 84) and No. 20, below.

[2] i.e. Fielding himself.

[3] For the story of the Man and the Ass, see the 'Covent Garden' column for 21 Feb., below, Appendix I; the other story alluded to is the famous one of Androclus and the lion, as told by Aulus Gellius in *Attic Nights*, v. xiv.

[4] Fielding takes the name from *Iliad*, vi. 12–19, where Axylus is described as 'a man rich in substance, that was beloved of all men; for he dwelt in a home by the high-road and was wont to give entertainment to all' (Loeb); Pope, whose translation chracterizes him as 'a friend to human race', notes that Axylus is a type of 'that ancient Hospitality which we now only read of' (Twickenham Edn., viii. 323). Cf. *Journal of a Voyage to Lisbon* (22 July), and see especially *Amelia*, ix. viii, where Dr Harrison defends the figure of Axylus as embodying essentially Christian virtues, a type of 'extensive benevolence'.

[5] Probably not by Fielding; Jensen (ii. 195), Cross (ii. 377), and Dudden (p. 893) all suggest that the author is the same 'Z. Z.' who wrote two letters in 1751 to *LDA* on the Universal Register Office, i.e. probably John Fielding (see General Introduction, pp. xxiii–xxv), but the use of such double letters for anonymous contributions to the press was a common device.

Wife to see the new Entertainment[1] at Covent-Garden, which by four o'Clock one may truly say was cramm'd from Top to Bottom. During the Entertainment two Gentlemen, after having hunted in vain for Admittance, came to the Door of the Two Shilling Gallery, where several Ladies were contented to stand. One of these Gentlemen, being a Man of great Wit and Humour, and resolved to indulge his Curiosity at any Expence, turned to his Companion, and said by G— I will soon make Room, I'll clear the House in an Instant, damn me. Then, with a broad Grin upon his Face, he thrust his empty Head into the Gallery Door, and cried out Fire; which on his repeating, a Lady at the Door rebuked him in such a Manner as made him, ignorant as he was, sensible of his Folly. He looked up in her Face, damn'd her for a grave Bitch, turned upon his Heel, and went down Stairs laughing, only to conceal his Confusion. Happy was it for hundreds, that their Attention was too much fixed on their Entertainment, to suffer them to be susceptible of this false Alarm. When I consider that there might possibly be in the House that Evening several Ladies with Child, and raise in my Mind the Idea of the Confusion and the Consequence that would have attended it, had this rash, this inconsiderate, this wicked Stratagem taken place, I am shocked at the very Thought; and had not my Wife prevented me, this Coxcomb should not have gone off unpunished. I am sorry I don't know his Name, and am still more concerned to say, that his Dress bespoke him an Officer, a disbanded one I hope. In your last Paper there are great Encomiums on the good Order and Government among the Nation of Actors in Drury-Lane; I could heartily wish that there was the same Decency observed in the Behaviour of those who call themselves the Audience. Having now vented my Indignation, I leave the Criminal to your Reproof, and am with all due Respects,

SIR,

Your most obliged Humble Servant,

Z.Z.

Ordered that the Defendant do appear at the next Court, and make his Defence to the above Accusation.

---

[1] The revival of Lewis Theobald's *Harlequin Sorcerer*, which opened at Covent Garden on 11 Feb.; see *CGJ* No. 12 and note, above, p. 89. In the 'Modern History' column of *CGJ* No. 18 (5 Mar.) Fielding reprints a news item on the popularity of the pantomime; see below, Appendix II.

SATURDAY, FEBRUARY 29, 1752.   NUMB. 17.

Credite, Posteri.   HORACE.[1]

Let Posterity take my Word for it.

It is a common Expression with Historians, *That such and such Facts will hardly be believed by Posterity*; and yet these Facts are delivered by them as undoubted Truths, and very often affirmed upon their own Knowledge.

But, what is much more astonishing, many of those very Instances, which are represented as difficult Articles of Truth by future Ages, did most probably pass as common Occurrences at the Time when they happened, and might seem scarce worthy of any Notice to the Generality of People who were Eye-witnesses to the Transactions.

The Cardinal de Retz, after relating the almost incredible Distress of the then Queen of England, who was likewise the Daughter of France, and had not Credit at Paris for a Faggot to warm herself in the Month of January,[2] proceeds thus. "Nous avons horreur, en lisant les Histoires, de Lachetez moins monstreuses que celle-la, & le peu de Sentiment que je trouvais dans la plupart des Esprits sur ce fait m'a obligé de faire, je crois, plus de mille fois cette reflexion: que les Exemples du passé touchent sans comparaison plus les Hommes que ceux de leurs Siecles. Nous nous accoutumons à tout ce que nous voions; & je vous ai dit quelquefois, que je ne sais si le consulat du cheval de Caligula nous auroit autant surprit que nous nous l'imaginons." *We are shocked in reading History, at many less scandalous Instances than this; and the little Impression which I observed this made in the Generality of Men's Minds at that Time, hath caused this Reflection to recur to me a thousand Times. That the Examples of former Ages do beyond all Comparison more sensibly affect us, than those of our own Times. Custom blinds us with a Kind of Glare to those Objects before our Eyes, and I have often doubted whether we should have been as much surprised at Caligula, when he made his Horse a Consul, as we are apt to imagine we should have been.*[3]

I can with Truth declare, that I have a thousand Times reflected on the judicious Discernment of this uncommon Observation; the Justice and Excellence of which I will endeavour to illustrate to my Reader, by taking

---

[1] *Odes*, II. xix. 2; see motto to *CGJ* No. 26.

[2] The memoirs of Jean François Paul de Gondi, Cardinal de Retz (1613–79) describe his role as a leader in the Fronde and opponent of Mazarin; the queen referred to is Henrietta-Maria, queen of Charles I, though it is her daughter, Princess Henrietta, who cannot afford the fire in January.

[3] *Mémoires du Cardinal de Retz* (Amsterdam, 1719), i. 226; Fielding quotes accurately from this edition, which was in his library (Baker, item 394). Without reference to De Retz, Fielding makes the same point about the reputation of Caligula in the *Champion* for 22 Apr. 1740; for other citations of De Retz, see *CGJ* Nos. 24, 48, and 49. On the high reputation of De Retz's memoirs in Fielding's day, see Catherine Talbot's letter to Elizabeth Carter (12 Aug. 1746), *A Series of Letters* (1809), i. 161; Chesterfield also praises the passage Fielding quotes, in a letter to his son of 13 Sept. 1748.

once more a Survey of that Opinion, which Posterity may be reasonably supposed to entertain of the present Times;[1] and as I have formerly shewn that they will probably in some Instances believe much more than ourselves, so in others, it is altogether as probable, that they will believe less.

Without further Preface then let us suppose some great and profound Critic, in the fortieth Century, undertaking to comment on those Historical Materials relating to this Kingdom, with which that Age may possibly furnish him, and in what Manner may we conceive him more likely to write than in the following.

Abstract from Humphrey Newmixon's Observations on the History of Great Britain.[2]

* * * * * * * * * *

* * * * * * * *

Desunt multa.[3]

Tho' it is impossible to deliver any Thing with great Certainty of those fabulous Ages, which a little preceeded the Time, when universal Ignorance began to overspread the Face of the Earth; and more especially prevailed in this Island, till the Restoration of Learning, which first began in the 36th Century; some few Monuments of Antiquity have however triumphed over the Rage of Barbarism, which may serve us to confute the horrid Forgeries of that Legendary, Geoffry Bechard,[4] who wrote about the Year 3000.

This Geoffry writing of the Year 1751, hath the following Words. "The Inglis hat set Temps ware soe dicted to Gamein, soe that severl off the Grate Menn yous'd to mak yt thee soal Bisens off thayr Lifs; hand knot unli thee Messirs, butt also theyre Fems yous'd to spind a hole Dais, hand knits hatt thayr Cartes. Les Fems aussi bien ass Messirs cheept thayr l'Assemble forr

---

[1] For the first 'Survey' or future history, see *CGJ* No. 12, above.

[2] Although social satire on the customs and manners of his age is Fielding's main purpose in these 'Observations', he is also parodying the historiographical manner of John Oldmixon (1673–1742), whom he had earlier ridiculed in *Tom Jones* (v. i) and in *CGJ* No. 3. Pat Rogers ('Fielding's Parody of Oldmixon', *PQ* 49 [1970], 262–6) points out that Fielding's parody touches on Oldmixon's scorn for pre-Reformation England; his distaste for Laurence Echard; his habit of inserting manuscript materials; his frequent allusions to the 'Annalist' Abel Boyer; and his fanciful emendations of suspect sources.

[3] i.e. 'many lines are missing', as indicated by the rows of asterisks—both standard devices to indicate a defective manuscript.

[4] A conflation of Geoffrey of Monmouth and Laurence Echard. For Fielding's view of Geoffrey, see *CGJ* No. 12, above. Echard (1670?–1730), Archdeacon of Stow and author of a *History of England* and many other historical works, was frequently criticized by Oldmixon (see Rogers, 'Fieldings Parody', pp. 263–4). Fielding himself hits at Echard's *Roman History* in *Tom Jones* (VI. ii) and in *A Journey from this World to the Next* (I. ix). In *CGJ* No. 68, however, Fielding cites Echard's *History of England* as one of his authorities on laws against adultery in the 11th cent. See also *Joseph Andrews*, III. i.

thatt propos, hat whitch les Fems hat perdus Mundoy quelle thayres Messirs rop Koontri for get."

So far this Bishop, who was reputed to be one of the most learned Men of his Age, *quia legire & scribire potebat*,[1] says a cotemporary Author; but those who contend the most for his Learning, will be able, I am afraid, to say but little for his Honesty; since all must allow that he was either deceived himself, or hath endeavoured to deceive his Readers: For I have now by me a Record of undoubted Antiquity, by which it appears, that all Kinds of Gaming were, within a very few Years before this Period, of which this Geoffry writes, absolutely prohibited under the severest Penalties.[2] This Law might indeed be infringed by some of the lowest of the People; and there is some Reason to think it was so; for in a Speech of George the Good, delivered from the Throne in that very Year 1751,[3] a severe Execution of the Laws in this Respect is recommended to the Magistrate.

But that the great Men as the Bishop says, should fly thus in the Face, not only of those Laws which they themselves made, but of their Sovereign too, is too incredible to be imposed even on Children.

Again here is a Reflection not only on the great Men, but on the great Ladies of those Times, who are represented in a Light, which I shall not affront the present virtuous and prudent Matrons, their great Grand-daughters in the seventieth descent, by mentioning. But how inconsistent is this Character with what we find in the Writings of Sir ALEXANDER DRAWCANSIR, the only Annalist of whose Works any Part hath descended to us, who in one of his Annals or Journals, acquaints us, that there was not a

---

[1] 'Because he could read and write'. As Jensen (ii. 197) points out, by the 'cotemporary Author' Fielding perhaps means Cibber, who affirmed in his *Apology* (1740), 'As we have sometimes great Composers of Musick, who cannot sing, we have as frequently great Writers that cannot read'. This view had already been ridiculed by Fielding in the *Champion*, 29 Apr. 1740.

[2] For the most recent laws against gaming—and for Fielding's more serious views on the topic—see *CGJ* No. 66, below. As many passages in *Amelia* attest, it was a vice much on his mind in these years; see also *A Charge to the Grand Jury* (1749) and *Enquiry into the Causes of the late Increase of Robbers* (1751), sect. III, which surveys its effects on the lower classes only. For commentary, see Malvin R. Zirker, Jr., *Fielding's Social Pamphlets* (Berkeley and Los Angeles, 1966), pp. 91–5. Fielding hardly exaggerates the extent of the 'addiction'; cf. Lady Jane Coke, writing in Jan. 1750, 'Play is really grown to such an excess that it is amazing, among the women as well as men' (*Letters from Lady Jane Coke to . . . Mrs. Eyre at Derby, 1747–1758* [1899], p. 42); and Murphy, in *Gray's Inn Journal* for 10 Mar. 1753, calls gambling 'the grand Business of the Nation'. For one French visitor the English taste for an activity involving constant calculation of probabilities was easy to explain: the English 'are accustomed more to reflexion than other people' (Abbé Le Blanc, *Letters on the English and French Nations* [1745, trans. 1747], ii. 306).

[3] Referring to an address of George II to both Houses of Parliament on 14 Nov. 1751, urging 'effectual provisions to suppress these audacious crimes of robbery and violence, which are now become so frequent . . . and which have proceeded in a great measure, from that profligate spirit of irreligion, idleness, gaming, and extravagance, which has of late extended itself, in an uncommon degree, to the dishonour of the nation' (*GM* 21 [1752], 511–12).

single Lady in his Time married, who was not possessed of every Qualification to make the Marriage State happy?[1]

The same Authority is sufficient to contradict the absurd Account which this Geoffry gives in another Place of the Ladies of those Days; where he says that Women of the first Quality used to make nightly Riots in their own Houses. One Passage is so ridiculous, that I cannot omit it. The Ladies of St. James's Parish, says he, used to treat their Company with *Drums*;[2] and this was thought one of their most elegant Entertainments; some Copies, I know read *Drams*, but the former is the true Reading, nor would the latter much cure the Absurdity.

A learned Critic indeed of my Acquaintance suspects that the above Passage is corrupt, and proposes, instead of *St. James's* to read *St. Giles's*, and instead of *Drum*, to read *Dram*;[3] and then he says the above Account will agree with a Record of that Age, by which it appears, that the Women of St. Giles's Parish, were notoriously addicted to Dram-drinking at that Time. And as for the Word Lady, he urges, that it did not then, as it doth now, signify a Woman of great Rank and Distinction, but was applied promiscuously to the whole Female Sex; to support which he produces a Passage from Sir ALEXANDER DRAWNCANSIR, where the Wife of a low Mechanic is called a Lady of great Merit.[4]

Another Legend recorded by our Geoffry, is sufficient of itself to destroy his Credit. He tells us, that a HERD OF BUCKS[5] used to frequent all the public Places; nay, he says, that two or three such Animals, would sometimes venture among several thousands, of Gentlemen and Ladies, and put them all into Confusion and Disorder. This is a very scandalous Reflection on the Gentlemen of those Days; but it is at the same Time so incredible, that it needs no Refutation.

The Truth I believe is, that the Bishop was a weak and credulous Man, and very easily imposed upon; especially in those Matters with which his

---

[1] See *CGJ* No. 7 (letter from 'Dorothy Single') above, p. 52, n. 5; for examples of this formulaic description of brides, see the 'Modern History' column for 5 Jan., below, Appendix II.

[2] Defined by 'Parson Adams' in *True Patriot*, No. 13 (28 Jan. 1746) as 'large Congregations of Men and Women, who, instead of assembling together to hear something that is good; nay, or to divert themselves with Gambols, which might be allowed now and then in Holiday Times, meet for no other Purpose but that of Gaming, for a whole Guinea and much more at a Stake'; cf. another definition in *Tom Jones*, XVII. vi, and the distinction between *drum* and *rout* (a smaller group) drawn in *Amelia*, IX. vii.

[3] By suggesting these alternate readings, Fielding is satirically equating the world of fashionable assemblies in St James's with the world of the gin-drinking lower classes. Hogarth's *Gin Lane* (1751) is set in St Giles's Parish, Westminster, and in the *Enquiry into the Causes of the late Increase of Robbers* (1751, p. 91) Fielding quotes evidence from his friend Saunders Welch, High Constable of Holborn, about the number of disorderly houses in that neighborhood. St Giles is also used as a synonym for a low slum in *JJ* No. 22 (30 Apr. 1748); *Amelia*, I. iii; and *CGJ* No. 27.

[4] See the 'Modern History' column from *CGJ* No. 1 (4 Jan.), printed below, Appendix II, where news items are reprinted which use the customary phrase 'ladies of great Beauty and Merit' for the wives of 'eminent' soapboilers, builders, and coopers.

[5] On the meaning of 'buck', see *CGJ* No. 7, above, p. 52 and n. 4.

Function prevented him from being well acquainted. What he writes of their Theatrical Entertainments is beyond all Measure ridiculous. De vurst a Nite of le Play, (says he) d'Author was a put a de Stake Sur on de Theatre Stage, dare des Criticats dey palt at him, hyess him, Catadecall him; off, off him vor too dree heures. Dis be dam Playe. Des Criticats be de A perentice, Klarque, Boo, Buccuk and Gamambler.

Now I will refer it to any one whether the Historian can be conceived here to write of a civilized People, and such the Britons are allowed on all Hands to have been at that Time.

Monsieur de Belle Lettre[1] in his Melange Critique, which he published in the Year 3892, treats the whole History of this Geoffry as a Romance; and indeed what is recorded in it concerning Dogs, seems sufficiently to favour this Opinion. At this Time, says Bechard, the chief Learning among those People, was among the Dogs. Learned was then a common Epithet to several of the canine Speeches, and a great Dispute was for a long Time carried on between a French and English Individual of this Species.[2] We know not in whose Favour it was determined; but it is agreed on all Hands, that the Question was, which was the most learned of the two. The Historian adds, that several of the most eminent Writers were of the canine Kind; and were universally called sad Dogs.*[3]

The Bishop concludes his History with these Words. Monstr. incred ten tousand Pip. fiffi nit. up got zee Oostryche tap tonnobus, is pregados. dat zocurn hypor hoperad abun, idelonycus quinto pur zin inmus fi fadon addili.[4]

---

* Sad is synonimous with grave, wise: The Judges were formerly called sad Men of the Law.

---

[1] Rogers suggests ('Fielding's Parody of Oldmixon', p. 265) that Fielding may be alluding here to Oldmixon's championship of the French critic Bouhours in his *Arts of Logick and Rhetorick* (1728), a stance which had more impact on the literary world than most of Oldmixon's writings.

[2] Alluding to the current rivalry between two 'learned Dogs', the famous 'Chien savant', owned by P. Le Moine, and 'the learned English Dog', whose proprietor was one S. Dewild. The French dog was advertised widely all during 1751, the claim being that, by arranging cards in the way a printer composes, he could 'read, write, and cast Accounts', as well as answer 'many Questions out of Ovid's Metamorphosis' (*DA*, 14 Feb. 1751); he was viewed early in the year by the Prince of Wales and other members of the Royal Family (*DA*, 4 Feb. 1751). Late in 1751 and early in 1752 puffs began for Dewild's dog, who 'performs a vast Variety of surprising Actions, far beyond what the late Chien Savant . . . was ever capable of' (*DA*, 16 Jan. 1752). Cf. Thornton's ridicule of their contest in the *Drury-Lane Journal*, No. 4 (6 Feb. 1752), and Fielding's comment in the 'Modern History' column of *CGJ* No. 16, printed below, Appendix II.

[3] In this usage, employed usually 'in humorous reproof', *sad* means 'dismal looking' (*OED*); cf. Smart's *The Midwife* on sad dogs as 'the most ancient and most numerous of any in the Kingdom' (i [1751], 165).

[4] Although 'Bechard' sinks into gibberish here, the lines appear to have some reference to the pantomime *Harlequin Sorcerer*, currently in a successful run at Covent Garden. 'Monstr.' indicates the usual pantomime monsters, and 'ten tousand Pip.' may refer to the large audiences crowding into Rich's theatre for this production (see *CGJ* No. 16, above). According to Thornton's account in *Drury-Lane Journal*, No. 5 (13 Feb. 1752), the pantomime 'introduces a large Ostrich, which has a very good effect upon the audience'; Colombine's tricks with the Harlequin-Ostrich made 'the whole

Which is so ridiculous a Supposition, that I shall leave it with the Reader without any Remark.   A.

Proceedings at the Court of Censorial Enquiry, &c.

The Court of Censorial Enquiry stands adjourned to Saturday next.

TUESDAY, MARCH 3, 1752.   NUMB. 18.

> *Omnibus in terris, quæ sunt a gadibus usque,*
> *Auroram et Gangem, pauci dignoscere possunt*
> **VINA bona, atque illis multum diversa——.*
>
> JUVENAL.[1]

> *From where Cornubia's[2] hundred Boroughs end,*
> *To where the Caledonian Shores extend,*
> *How few are found with Taste to ascertain*
> *The vilest Perry,[3] and the best Champagne.*

It is from a very common but a very false Opinion, that we constantly mix the Idea of Levity with those of Wit and Humour. The gravest of Men have often possessed these Qualities in a very eminent Degree, and have exerted them on the most solemn Subjects with very eminent Success. These are to be found in many Places in the most serious Works of Plato and Aristotle, of Cicero and Seneca. Not only Swift, but South hath used them on the highest and most important of all Subjects. In the Sermons of the latter, there is perhaps more Wit, than in the Comedies of Congreve; and in his Controversy with Sherlock on the Trinity,[4] he hath not only exerted great

---

* *So I chuse to read this Passage, at least on the present Occasion.*

house ring with applause'. The thundering applause may be referred to by 'tonnobus'; and 'idelonycus' may owe something to the Latin *idolon* (spectre, image, ghost). The passage is quoted and ridiculed by Thornton in *Drury-Lane Journal*, No. 8 (5 Mar. 1752).

[1] *Satires*, x. 1–3: 'In all the lands that stretch from Gades to the Ganges and the Morn, there are but few who can distinguish true blessings from their opposites' (Loeb); Fielding, as his note indicates, substitutes *Vina* for *Vera*, so that the phrase becomes 'good wines' instead of 'true blessings'. The passage is also used as the motto to *JJ* No. 7 (16 Jan. 1748).

[2] Cornwall.

[3] A drink similar to cider but made from the fermented juice of pears; as with cider its production was particularly associated with Worcestershire.

[4] On South, see *CGJ* No. 12, above, p. 85 n. 3. Fielding refers here to the Trinitarian or 'Socinian' controversy in the last decade of the 17th cent., in which South published several anonymous attacks on the work of William Sherlock (1641?–1707), Dean of St Paul's. Sherlock had attempted to defend an orthodox position in his *Vindication of the Doctrine of the . . . Trinity* (1690); South, who despised Sherlock, responded with *Animadversions upon Dr. Sherlock's Book* (1693), demonstrating with great acerbity that Sherlock was guilty of 'tritheism', and the controversy continued until the king intervened. South's other major contribution to the dispute was *Tritheism Charged upon Dr. Sherlock's New Notion of the Trinity* (1695). Fielding quotes a satiric anecdote from the *Animadversions* in

Wit, but many Strokes of the most exquisite Drollery. Not to mention the Instance of St. Paul, whose Writings do in my Opinion contain more true Wit[1] than is to be found in the Works of the unjustly celebrated Petronius.[2]

In like Manner, and with like Error we unite the Ideas of Gravity with Dulness, as if the former was inseparably annexed to the latter. True indeed it is that Dulness appears in her own Form, and in her proper Dress, when she walks abroad in some tritical Essay[3] on a grave Subject; and many millions of Reams have in all Ages been sacrificed to her by her Votaries in this Manner; but she doth not always preserve this solemn Air. She often appears in public in Essays of Entertainment, as the Booksellers chuse to call them; and sometimes in Print, as well as on the Stage, disguises herself in a Jack-pudding[4] Coat, and condescends to divert her good Friends with sundry Feats of Dexterity and Grimace.

The late ingenious Dr. Swift, who was one of the greatest Enemies that Dulness ever had; and who hath traced her out and exposed her in all her various Disguises, likens these two different Appearances of Dulness to the different Qualities of small Beer in the Barrel, and small Beer in the Bottle.[5] The former of which is well known to be of all Things the most vapid, insipid and heavy; but the latter is altogether as airy, frothy, brisk and bouncing.

But tho' there is excellent Drollery in this Comparison, I have still another

the *Champion*, 6 May 1740, and cites it again in the *Champion*, 21 Oct. 1740. On the dispute, see W. M. T. Dodds, 'Robert South and William Sherlock: Some Unpublished Letters', *MLR* 39 (1944), 215–24; for a modern appreciation of South's wit, see James Sutherland, 'Robert South', *Review of English Literature*, 1 (1960), 5–12; for an earlier appreciation see Anthony Collins, *A Discourse concerning Ridicule and Irony in Writing* (1729). On the impact of South's witty manner on Fielding, see especially W. B. Coley, 'The Background of Fielding's Laughter', *ELH* 26 (1959), 229–52.

[1] Cf. Robert South, in contrasting light and comical preachers with St Paul, 'For *true Wit* is a severe and manly Thing. Wit in Divinity is nothing else, but Sacred Truths suitably expressed' (*Sermons*, 5th edn. [1722], iv. 47–8).

[2] Petronius Arbiter, author of the *Satyricon* and frequently identified with the *arbiter elegantiae* at the court of Nero. Fielding owned his works (Baker, item 425), but refers to him seldom. Though he was celebrated in the 18th cent., many objected to his writings and his life on moral grounds, with Fielding obviously in that number. Addison found him 'loose and dissolute' (*Spectator*, No. 349, 10 Apr. 1712); Pope praised him in the *Essay on Criticism* (667–8), but his judgement, which agreed with that of Dryden, aroused the censure of Warton, who thought Petronius a 'dissolute and effeminate writer' (see Twickenham Edn., i. 315 n.). Petronius' *Satyrical Works* were published in translation in 1708, with a life and character by Saint-Evremond.

[3] i.e. trite or commonplace. Cf. Swift's parody, *A Tritical Essay upon the Faculties of the Mind* (1711), which Fielding may be recalling here; Swift declares in his mock-dedication, 'I have been of late offended with many Writers of Essays and moral Discourses, for running into stale Topicks and threadbare Quotations, and not handling their Subject fully and closely'.

[4] See *CGJ* No. 10, above, p. 73 n. 1.

[5] Pope, *Peri Bathous* (1728), ch. iv: 'It is with the *Bathos* as with small Beer, which is indeed vapid and insipid, if left at large and let abroad; but being by our Rules confin'd, and well stopt, nothing grows so frothy, pert and bouncing.' Fielding may have attributed this Scriblerian work to Swift because it was originally published in the Swift–Pope *Miscellanies* of 1727/8 (the so-called 'last volume'); it first appeared in Pope's works in 1741. Cf. *Tom Jones*, VIII. i and IX. i, where Fielding also quotes from the work, praising but not identifying the author; see also *CGJ* No. 40. On Fielding's constant praise of Swift in *CGJ*, see General Introduction, p. lxiv.

Liquor in my Eye, which will better match this airy and brisk Kind of Dulness; at least will give the Reader a more just Idea of that very Quality which we principally intend to remark in this Paper. The Liquor I mean, is that of Perry: for as this hath been often imposed on the injudicious Palate for Champagne,[1] so hath this Kind of Dulness with no less Assurance been often vented to the Public under the Name of Wit.

As this is grown to be a very common Practice, and as the Consequence of it is very pernicious to the Society; the Understandings of Men being as capable of an Injury as their Health, and as every Taste is no more capable of distinguishing in the Case of Wit than in the Case of Champagne, I shall do, I think, no inconsiderable Service to the Public by giving them some Rules to direct their Judgment, and to arm them against this Imposition. And here I shall chiefly make use of the Words Champagne and Perry, instead of Wit and Dulness, as the two former seem the pleasanter and better sounding Words, and will equally explain my Meaning.[2]

The first Caution I shall give my Reader on this Head, is to take Care of all Shops over the Door of which is writ in great Letters the following Word, BIBLIOPOLIUM. The true Reading of which is BIBITOPERRYUM.[3] A Corruption which hath led many Men into an Error, and hath carried them into a Perry-shop by Mistake.

In the next Place, I caution all Persons to pay no Regard to the Labels with which the Perry Merchants constantly endeavour to put off the worst of their Stuff. Nothing indeed is more common than to see a Quantity of rank Perry, with a Label signifying, that it is the very best of Champagne, and approved of by all Persons of Taste. The Words *curious, eminent, learned, the 6th or seventh Edition. Done into English from the original French Vessels*, &c. written upon the Label, are all of them certain Marks of Perry.

---

[1] Cf. the landlady in *Tom Jones* (x. iii): 'I have not had a better Supper ordered this half Year . . . and so easy and good-humoured were they, that they found no Fault with my *Worcestershire* Perry, which I sold them for *Champagne*; and to be sure it is as well tasted, and as wholesome as the best *Champagne* in the Kingdom, otherwise I would scorn to give it 'em.' Perry, Fielding adds in the same chapter, 'readily answered to the Name of every Kind of Wine'. In Letter XLI contributed to his sister's *Familiar Letters between the Principal Characters in David Simple* (1747) Fielding has a French visitor comment on the practice; cf. the disdainful remark of an actual French visitor, Abbé Le Blanc: 'That which they call Champagne, is often nothing but a mixture of cyder, perry, sugar, and some other ingredients' (*Letters on the English and French Nations* [1747], ii. 37–8).

[2] Fielding draws a similar parallel, between a vintner and a bookseller, in *Champion*, 16 Sept. 1740; cf. also *True Patriot*, No. 1 (5 Nov. 1745), where he compares newspapers to 'Water-cyder', drunk only by those who 'could procure no other Liquor'. The elaborate analogy which Fielding develops here was well parodied in the *Drury-Lane Journal*, No. 7 (5 Mar. 1752), under the title of '*Covent-Garden Journal Extraordinary* No. I.'

[3] Fielding puns anagrammatically on 'toper', 'perry', and 'bib' (to drink frequently). Although 'Bibliopolium', adapted from the Greek for 'bookseller's shop', is not listed in *OED*, it was apparently in use in the way Fielding suggests; cf. Ephraim Chambers's *Cyclopaedia*: 'A like conceit has taken some London *booksellers*, to inscribe over their door, *bibliopolium*, as if people could not know a shop to be a *bookseller's* without a Latin name. Even stall-men dignify their stands with *bibliopolium*; and *Moorfields* may probably, ere long, be surrounded with *bibliopolia*' (7th edn. [1751], s.v. 'bookseller').

Nor is much more Regard to be had to the positive Assertion of the Merchant himself; for nothing is more usual in this Trade as well as with the Wine-Merchant, than to sell one Thing for another. Both of these make use indeed of the same Imposition, and as every Dealer in French Vinegar, hath the Names of the most excellent Wines always at his Tongue's End, and ready to be applied to the worst Goods in his Warehouse, so hath our Perry-Merchant constantly in his Mouth the Names of the most celebrated Authors; under one of which without any Scruple, he vends the genuine anonymous Productions of Grubstreet; the Names of Swift, Addison, Pope, Dryden, Prior, &c. have been used by the one Kind of Merchant, as of Lafeat, Latour, Bennet,[1] &c. have been by the other.

Having premised these Cautions, I come now to those Marks which may distinguish the true Champagne from Perry, even to those who are not vested with sufficient Taste to know the one from the other by their several Flavours.

The first Quality which is remarkable in Perry, is its extreme Frothiness, in which indeed it will sometimes almost wholly evaporate.

2dly, It is very apt to bounce and fly with much Noise, as it is truly little more than a Composition of Wind, and proceeded originally, according to the Observations of Butler,[2] from the Author's Incapacity of sending his Wind downwards.

An extraordinary Degree of Thinness is another manifest Sign of Perry. Let the Quantity be never so large, you can immediately see through it; nor is there every any thing to be found at the Bottom.

There are perhaps some other Differences which do not at present occur to me; but indeed the surest Way of judging is by the opposite Consequences, which never fail to attend these two Liquors.

First, as Champagne is sure to raise the Spirits, and to fill almost every Man with Mirth and Gayety; so this is as certain to depress, and render those who swallow any Quantity more heavy and dull.

If, after a large Draught, you find yourself inclined to Irreligion and

---

[1] Lafite and Latour are excellent clarets, among the three or four very best wines drunk by people of fashion in this period. 'Bennet', however, is a puzzling reference. Fielding may have intended a compliment to the wines of James and Claudius Bennet, eminent wine merchants in the Haymarket throughout the period. James Bennet had been Sir Robert Walpole's principal wine dealer in the 1730s (see J. H. Plumb, 'Sir Robert Walpole's Wine', *Wine and Food*, 71 [1951], 135–9; and *London Daily Post and General Advertiser*, 22 Nov. 1734). After James died in 1743 worth £30,000 (*GM* 13 [1743], 275), his business was apparently continued by his son Claudius (see e.g. *DA*, 22 Aug. 1754). Both James and 'Claudio' Bennet were included in a list of eligible bachelors in 1742 (*The English Register*, p. 51); but though both were obviously well-known figures, neither is known to have had any connection with Fielding. The editor is indebted to Professor Betty Rizzo for information about Claudius Bennet.

[2] *Hudibras*, Second Part, iii. 773–6: 'As wind in th' hypochondries pent / Is but a blast if downward sent, / But if it upwards chance to fly / Becomes new light and prophecy . . .'

Blasphemy, never touch a Drop more, for this is a sure Sign of the very worst of all Perry.

Again, if after sitting to it (as is the Language of Drinking)[1] an Hour or two, you find in yourself a Propensity to talking indecently, indeed to any Discourse which modest Ears should not hear; this is another manifest Indication. Nothing indeed being so very apt to corrupt the Minds of Youth,[2] to make them unfit for civil Company, and to send them to the Brothels, than this Kind of Perry. In this Instance, indeed, the metaphorical Perry, which I have been here treating of, and that genuine Liquor which comes to us from Worcestershire, seem to bear a strict Analogy to each other. And for this Reason, I suppose, it is so sacred to the Brothel, that when a Bottle of Champagne is then called for, a Bottle of Perry is sure to be brought to the Customer; that being the only Champagne which is ever admitted into these Houses, from the Tendency no doubt which it hath to propagate that Kind of Filth in which they deal.

The last odious Quality of this Kind of Perry, and which most clearly distinguishes it from that which we here call true Champaigne, is that it never fails to propagate gross Abuse and Scandal; so far indeed as to inspire Men to call Names, and to deal in all the Language of Billingsgate. So very rancorous is the Nature of Perry, that many eminent Dabblers in it have escaped the Cudgel or the Whipping Post from this Circumstance only, that they have been so absolutely intoxicated as to be unable to pronounce certain Syllables in an articulate Manner. Instead of Minister, Lord, Bishop, &c. they have only uttered such Sounds as may be imitated by pronouncing M—nst—r, L—d, B—sh—p, and so forth.[3] Thus by stripping a Name or a Title of its Vowels, they securely strip the Owner of all his Virtues and good Qualities.

Now Champagne, on the contrary, is known to inspire Men not only with the most sparkling Wit, but with the highest good Humour; and so far is it from filling the Head or Heart with Mischief and Rancour, that in France the Character which is given to the best Champagne, and that of a certain Age, is that it is *Ami d'homme*; A FRIEND TO MANKIND. An Appellation which, as it is perhaps the most glorious of all, so hath it most justly belonged to those great Men in all Ages, whom Heaven hath been pleased to distinguish with those superiour Talents which are properly said to constitute a true Genius.   A.

---

[1] Cf. *Tom Jones*: '. . . and the Squire sat in to his Cups, in which he was, by Degrees, deserted by all the Company, except the Uncle of young *Nightingale*, who loved his Bottle as well as *Western* himself. These two sat stoutly to it, during the whole Evening' (XVIII. xiii).

[2] Cf. *CGJ* No. 5, above, p. 43 and n. 5.

[3] A practice frequently satirized, and one for which Fielding coined the term 'emvowelling' (*JJ* No. 1, 5 Dec. 1747); see also *Tom Jones*, VI. ii.

SATURDAY, MARCH 7, 1752.   NUMB. 19.

Non hæc jocosæ conveniunt Lyræ.

HORACE.[1]

Such Matters are beyond a Jest.

If any Person should have the Assurance to exhibit a Set of Bristol Stones[2] to the Public as real Diamonds; or if another should call himself a China-Man, and deliver to his Customers some of the vilest Earthen-Ware, as the real Production of China or Dresden, the Consequence in both Cases is certain. The Imposition would be too gross to deceive a single Individual, and the Undertakers would immediately become the Objects of universal Ridicule and Contempt.

Again, should any Man, pretending to be a Conoisseur, go about the Town and abuse the finest Jewels in Mr. Lacan's[3] Possession as mere Counterfeits, would not such a Person presently gain the Reputation of a Madman, and be soon ashamed of shewing his ridiculous Face in public?

This, as I endeavoured to shew in my last Paper, is not the Case with the Dealers in Letters. The truest Brilliants often lie overlooked and neglected on the Booksellers' Shelves, while the most impudent Counterfeits are received, admired, and encouraged. Milton himself (I am ashamed of my Country when I say it) very narrowly escaped from the Jaws of Oblivion;[4] and, instead of shining for ever with those great Lights of Antiquity in whose Constellation he is now admitted, was like to have been bundled up with those *Ephemeran*[5] insect Authors, of whom every Day almost sees both the Birth and the Funeral.

Now may we not hence conclude, that in the Distinction of Diamonds,

---

[1] *Odes*, III. iii. 69: 'But this will not befit the sportive lyre' (Loeb); Fielding has substituted plural forms for *hoc* and *conveniet* in Horace.

[2] 'A kind of transparent rock-crystal found in the Clifton limestone near Bristol, resembling the diamond in brilliancy' (*OED*).

[3] Presumably Henry Lacam (Lacan?), whose jewelry shop was in the Strand not far from the Universal Register Office; see Hugh Phillips, *Mid-Georgian London* (1964), p. 158. See also the 'Covent Garden' column for 26 Jan. (below, Appendix I), where Fielding speaks of Lacan in connection with some stolen diamonds.

[4] Cf. *True Patriot*, No. 1 (5 Nov. 1745), on the need for authors to conform to the fashion of the times: 'by neglecting this, *Milton* himself lay long in Obscurity, and the World had nearly lost the best Poem which perhaps it hath ever seen'; cf. also *CGJ* No. 50, below, p. 274. Although modern scholars assert that Milton's fame as a poet was considerable during the last quarter of the 17th cent. (see James Thorpe, ed., *Milton Criticism: Selections from Four Centuries* [1950], p. 4), Fielding's view was common in his day, when it was sometimes said that Addison's essays on *Paradise Lost* in the *Spectator* rescued Milton from obscurity; see *An Essay on the New Species of Writing founded by Mr. Fielding* (1751), p. 6; see also Charles Gildon (?), *Les Soupirs de la Grand Britaigne* (1713), p. 69, quoted by H. J. Real and H. J. Vienken in *The Scriblerian*, 13 (1981), 129.

[5] Listed by *OED* as an obsolete form of 'ephemeral', but of course, Fielding also has in mind 'ephemera', an insect that lives for only one day.

China, and such like, from their Counterfeits, there are some certain well-known Criterions to form and direct our Judgment; and that in Matters of Invention and Learning, either there are no Rules to guide our Opinion, or that such Rules are but weakly established, and that we are in general very ignorant of them.

Hence must arise those different Notions which we so often find among Men, of the same Author and the same Work; and which Horace allegorically points at, when he says,

Tres mihi Convivæ prope dissentire videntur, &c.[1]

Thus in one Company it is very common to hear the same Book extolled to the Skies, with the Epithets of fine, excellent, inimitable, and so forth; which in another is vilified and run down, as the lowest, dullest, and saddest Stuff that ever was writ.

Of all Kinds of Writing there is none on which this Variety of Opinions is so common as in those of Humour, as perhaps there is no Word in our Language of which Men have in general so vague and indeterminate an Idea.[2] To speak very plainly, I am apt to question whether the greater Part of Mankind have any Idea at all in their Heads, when this Word drops (perhaps accidentally) from their Tongue.

I remember a Gentleman who used to have this Word very frequently in his Mouth, and bestowed it with great Liberality on most of his Acquaintance. I was sometimes inclined to wonder at his Taste, 'till I happened to be on board a Ship with him, when he rapt out a great Oath, and swore that the Ship had a great deal of Humour in it. I was now satisfied that with my Friend this Word had no Meaning at all.

What can we sometimes conceive of an Audience at a Play-House, where I have heard the dullest Chitchat between Gentlemen and Ladies called Humour, and applauded as such! On the other Side, Albumazar was but coldly received, and the little French Lawyer of Fletcher was hissed off the Stage.[3]

---

[1] *Epistles*, II. ii. 61: ''Tis, I fancy, much like three guests who disagree' (Loeb). Horace is citing the variety of tastes in his audience as one of his reasons for not writing more poems; Fielding jokingly says the line comments 'allegorically' on the variety of opinions about a particular work.

[2] For Fielding's fullest discussion of the meaning of 'humour', see *CGJ* Nos. 55 and 56 (18 and 25 July); on the shifting conceptions of the term in the first half of the century and its gradual elevation above 'wit' in the critical writing of the period, see Stuart Tave, *The Amiable Humorist* (Chicago, 1960), esp. pp. 91–139.

[3] *Albumazar* (1615) by Thomas Tomkis was one of Garrick's first revivals after becoming manager at Drury Lane; advertised as a 'celebrated Old Comedy', it was performed four times in Oct. 1747, once more in Nov., and again in Apr. 1748. It was, however, 'hissed' on 3 Oct., and Garrick was criticized in several pamphlets for reviving such a simple piece; see *London Stage*, Pt. 4, i. 10–11. *The Little French Lawyer* (c.1620), a play now assigned to Fletcher and Massinger, was acted as a farce of one act on 7 Oct. 1749, with Woodward in the title role. It was well received until the final scene, which was hissed by the crowded house. Alterations were promised, and the revised version was

And here I cannot omit a pleasant Fact to which I was myself a Witness. A certain comic Author produced a Piece on Drury-Lane Stage, called *The Highland Fair*,[1] in which he intended to display the comical Humours of the Highlanders; the Audience, who had for three Nights together sat staring at each other, scarce knowing what to make of their Entertainment, on the fourth joined in a unanimous exploding Laugh. This they had continued through an Act, when the Author, who unhappily mistook the Peels of Laughter which he heard for Applause, went up to Mr. Wilks, and, with an Air of Triumph, said——*Deel o' my Sal,*[2] *Sare, they begin to tauk the Humour at last.*

Whether the Audience or the Poet erred most on this Occasion, I shall not determine. Certain it is that it is no unusual Thing in the former, to make very gross Mistakes in this Matter, as great indeed as the late learned Bernard Lintott the Bookseller, who, having purchased the Copy of a Tragedy called Phædra and Hypolitus, lamented that the Author had not put a little more Humour in it; for that, he said, was the only Thing it wanted.[3]

In truth, there is nothing so unsettled and incertain, as our Notion of

---

performed on 10 Oct., with even less success; Cross, the prompter, reported, 'Mr. Woodward promis'd it should be done no more; notwithstanding this, they would not suffer us to end it' (*London Stage*, Pt. 4, i. 142). In this passage Fielding is, of course, defending his friends at Drury Lane, but his despair at the taste of audiences for 'the dullest Chitchat' is seriously intended. Cf. his Preface to *Plutus* (1742), where he quotes a passage of such chitchat from Cibber's *The Provok'd Husband*, adding, 'This sort of Stuff, which is, I think, called genteel Comedy . . . had some Years ago taken almost sole Possession of our Stage, and banished Shakespear, Fletcher, Johnson, &c. from it.' Coincidentally, Cibber's play was the main piece at Drury Lane on 10 Oct. 1749, when *The Little French Lawyer* was hissed off the stage.

[1] Joseph Mitchell's *The Highland Fair; or, Union of the Clans*, a 'new Scots Opera' performed at Drury Lane on 20 Mar. 1731 and on three other occasions in Mar. and Apr.; the fourth performance, to which Fielding refers, was the author's benefit. The play was not in dialect, but the music consisted of 'Select Scots Tunes', with costumes and plot appropriate to the title. Genest (*Some Account of the English Stage*, iii. 290) finds Fielding's anecdote strange, since Mitchell explains the nature of his piece in an introductory dialogue between a critic and the poet; in that dialogue, however, the poet defends the novelty of his play in terms which illustrate Fielding's point: 'Is not Novelty agreeable to the Taste of the Town? Ought not the Town to be humour'd?' By the time of this play Mitchell (1684–1738), through a series of insolent, bantering poems begging for a place from the prime minister, had become known as 'Sir Robert Walpole's Poet'; Fielding must thus have regarded this 'Planet-blasted Fool', as James Thomson called him, a proper object of ridicule. Mitchell's poem 'The Sine-Cure' is obliquely sneered at in Fielding's own poem to Walpole in 1730 (see *Miscellanies* [1743], ed. H. K. Miller, Wesleyan Edn. (Oxford, 1972), i. 58 n.), and Mitchell as late as 1735 (*A Familiar Epistle*) described Fielding as one of the crowd currying favors from Sir Robert. *The Highland Fair* was being acted at Drury Lane during the same week that Fielding's *Tragedy of Tragedies* opened at the Haymarket.

[2] i.e. 'the devil take me'; cf. *Eurydice Hissed* (1737), 87; on Wilks, see *CGJ* No. 10, above, p. 78, n. 1.

[3] *Phaedra and Hippolitus*, a tragedy by Edmund 'Rag' Smith (1672–1710), the friend of Addison and Swift, was performed four times in Apr. 1707 at the Haymarket, with a prologue by Addison and epilogue by Prior. It was based on Racine and was badly received; Addison in *Spectator*, No. 18 (21 Mar. 1711) attacked the taste of English audiences who prefer Italian operas to this 'admirable Tragedy'. The play was purchased by Barnaby Bernard Lintot (1675–1736), who published it in June 1707 and later published Smith's *Works* (1714). According to Johnson's life of Smith (*Lives of the Poets*) Lintot in purchasing the play even advanced the price from the usual 50 to 60 guineas. The source of Fielding's anecdote has not been located; on Lintot, cf. *CGJ* No. 6, above, p. 48.

Humour in general. The most common Opinion is, that whatever diverts or makes you laugh, is Humour; and in Proportion as Men are more or less risible in their Nature, they are more or less liberal in this Appellation. A merry Fellow, or a pleasant Companion as he is called (and, by the by, I have known may a dull Dog called so) never fails to obtain the Character of a Man of Humour, among his Acquaintance and Admirers. The Qualifications of these Gentlemen, are a facetious Countenance, a sagacious Leer, and somewhat of Drollery in the Voice; and their Performances are usually a merry (i.e. b——y) Catch, or a long Story, with a Sting of the same Kind in the Tail.[1]

I forbear to mention here the vast Variety of handy or practical Jests, as I have seen them touched elsewhere, all which are reputed to be Humour by the Vulgar. Such are Tweaks by the Nose, Kicks on the Backside, pulling away your Chair, snatching off your Wig, with many others.

But there is another Kind of Humour, on which I do not remember to have seen any Remarks. This is that tragical Humour which was perhaps intended by the learned Bookseller abovementioned; and which, tho' it may tend to raise Laughter in some, may however be said to have its Foundation in Tears.

As the Species of practical Humour, just before spoken of, are produced by doing little jocose Mischiefs to others, this tragical Humour consists in afflicting Men with the greatest and most serious Evils; in a Word, in ruining, destroying, and tormenting Mankind.

Histories abound with Examples of Men who have very eminently possessed this Kind of Humour. There hath scarce existed indeed a single Tyrant or Conqueror upon Earth, who, tho' otherwise perhaps extremely dull, was not a great Master this Way. Alexander the Great was much gifted with this Quality, of which we have many Instances in the Accounts of his Asiatic Expedition. His burning the City of Persepolis in particular, was a Performance of most exquisite Humour.[2]

What were the Reigns of Caligula and Claudius, of Nero and Domitian, of Commodus, Caracalla, Heliogabalus, and all those Imperial Bucks or Bloods of Rome,[3] but great tragical Farces in which one Half of Mankind was with

---

[1] Cf. 'An Essay on Conversation' and 'An Essay on the Knowledge of the Characters of Men', *Miscellanies* (1743), i. Wesleyan Edn., 148, 158–60.

[2] Alexander burned the palace of Xerxes in Persepolis in 330 BC; see Plutarch's *Lives*, 'Alexander', xxxviii, and Arrian's *Anabasis of Alexander*, III. xviii. 11, for two very different versions of the story. Plutarch and Arrian are the 'Accounts' of Alexander's expedition usually cited by Fielding, who throughout his works regards Alexander as the type of false greatness and evil 'heroism'. See especially the poem *Of True Greatness* (1741), 11, 55–66; 'A Dialogue Between Alexander the Great and Diogenes the Cynic', *Miscellanies* (1743); *Jonathan Wild*, I. i, I. iii; and, for commentary, Miller, *Essays*, pp. 398–402.

[3] Fielding gives in chronological order a catalogue of the most cruel, licentious, or ineffectual Roman emperors. The lives of Caligula (AD 12–41), Claudius (10 BC–AD 54), Nero (AD 37–68), and Domitian (AD 51–96) are described by Suetonius in the *Lives of the Twelve Caesars*. Dio Cassius, whom

much Humour put to Death and Tortures, for the Diversion of the other Half.

But of all the Performances of this Kind I have ever met with, I am most pleased with the common Story of Phalaris and Perillus.[1] The latter of these being desirous of recommending himself to the Favour of the former, who was a great Tyrant, and consequently a great Lover of the tragical Humour, acquainted his Master Phalaris that he had, with much Invention and hard Labour, contrived an Entertainment for him which would produce the highest Sport and Pastime. It was thus to be performed; the Artist had made the brazen Image of a Bull, into the Belly of which a human Creature was to be conveyed. The Bull was then to be heated 'till it was red hot, by means of which the Person inclosed within, suffering the most intolerable Torments, would bellow in such a Manner that the Sound would very near imitate, or, to speak in the present fashionable Taste, would admirably MIMIC, the Roaring of a Bull.

Phalaris highly approved of the Project; but being himself a Man of great Humour, he was willing to add somewhat of his own to the Joke. He therefore chose Perillus, the Inventor, for the Person on whom the Experiment was first to be tried, and accordingly shut him up and roasted him in his own Bull.

From this, I suppose, that pleasant Humour called ROASTING[2] was derived; for so not only the Term, but the Thing seems to intimate; this diverting Entertainment consisting in giving all the Torments possible to the Object, and may indeed be called Roasting him alive.

Hence likewise the pleasant Pastime of roasting Men's Characters may possibly take its Original. Hence all that Torrent of Humour which flows so plentifully in Libels of all Kinds, in which, Names that we ought to tremble to think of, and others which highly deserve our Reverence and Honour, are pointed out as the Marks of Ridicule and Contempt; and, to use the common Expression, ROASTED for the Entertainment of the Public.

To conclude, as Tully long ago said, that there was no Absurdity which

---

Fielding cites with some frequency in *CGJ*, would have been his probable source for details of the excesses of Commodus (AD 161–92), Caracalla (AD 188–217), and Heliogabalus (i.e. Elagabalus) (AD 204–22).

[1] Phalaris, tyrant of Acragas in Sicily (*c.*570–554 BC), whose legendary cruelty is mentioned by Pindar, *Pythian Odes*, i. 96. The story of the fate of Perillus is alluded to by Ovid in *The Art of Love*, i. 653–6, and *Ibis*, 437–9; it is recounted in full by Diodorus Siculus, ix. 18–19, and given a turn favorable to the tyrant in Lucian's *Phalaris*, i and ii. In *JJ* No. 15 (12 Mar. 1748), Fielding alludes to the fate of Perillus as an instance of being 'caught in your own Trap'.

[2] i.e. ridiculing someone in a merciless fashion. In *Joseph Andrews* (III. vii) Fielding depicts Parson Adams receiving such treatment in 'A Scene of Roasting very nicely adapted to the present Taste and Times'; and in *Champion*, 13 Mar. 1740, he devotes an entire essay to this 'Diversion', which he says 'must arise either from a great Depravity of Nature, which delights in the Miseries and Misfortunes of Mankind, or from a Pride which we take in comparing the Blemishes of others with our own Perfections'. See also *Amelia*, III. vi, for another condemnation of malicious jokes.

some of the Sophists had not maintained to be *true Philosophy*;[1] so is there no Nonsense whatever, provided it be dashed with Abuse and Scurrility; which will not pass with many for TRUE HUMOUR. C.

The Court of Censorial Enquiry is further adjourned to this Day Se'nnight.

TUESDAY, MARCH 10, 1752. NUMB. 20.

Desine molle, precor, verbis convellere pectus:
Neve mihi, quam te dicis amare, noce.
Sed sine, quam tribuit sortem Fortuna, tueri:
Nec spolium nostri turpe pudoris habe.

OVID.[2]

Cease with your Prayers, my tender Breast to move,
Nor injure her whom you profess to love:
What Fate allots me, suffer me to share,
And the base Spoils of Chastity forbear.

The good Reader will not, I believe, be displeased at seeing a second Letter from my worthy Correspondent, who signs himself AXYLUS.[3] I shall give it with only this Preface, that the Subject here treated is of the utmost Concern to the Public.

Mr. CENSOR,

In my former Letter I mentioned an imperfect Account which I had received of a late cruel Parricide,[4] which I then hoped had been committed afar off, or rather indeed, that it had not been committed at all.

This Morning, however, a Paper was sent me inclosed, called the genuine Trial of Mary Blandy, Spinster, at Oxford, for poisoning her late Father Francis Blandy, Gent. &c.[5] To whom I am indebted for this Favour, I know not; but when I had once read the Title of the Pamphlet, I was insensibly led on to read the whole: For indeed, when I was well acquainted with the Reality of the Fact, I had gone too far to recede; nor was Curiosity my only

---

[1] *De divinatione*, II. lviii. 119, though it is Stoics rather than Sophists whom Cicero there discusses; Fielding uses the same passage in *Champion*, 21 Oct. 1740, *JJ* No. 12 (20 Feb. 1748), and in the opening paragraph of 'An Essay on Conversation' (*Miscellanies*, 1743), where he translates it as 'there is no Absurdity which some Philosopher or other hath not asserted'. Cf. Swift, *Gulliver's Travels*, III. vi.

[2] *Heroides*, xvii (Helen to Paris), 111–14.

[3] For the first letter, see *CGJ* No. 16 (25 Feb.), above.

[4] Mary Blandy; for the facts of the case, see *CGJ* No. 11, above, p. 84, n. 2.

[5] *The Genuine Tryal at large of Mary Blandy, Spinster*, with the imprint bearing the names of W. Jackson and R. Walker, was published on 6 Mar. (*GA*, 6 Mar. 1752), four days before Fielding's essay; based on two accounts taken in shorthand, it reports the trial of Blandy held at Oxford Assizes on 3 Mar. 1752.

Motive for perusing the Trial; tho' this is a Passion for the Gratification of which we often suffer great Pains, as we see young People listen attentively to the Stories of Apparitions, notwithstanding all the Terrors which such Relations are seen to raise in their Minds. In Fact, I had another view. I read on in Hopes of meeting with some Circumstances that might a little alleviate the dreadful Guilt imputed to the Accused, and in some Degree lessen those Horrors which I had conceived at the first Idea of a Child's poisoning her Father.

In this Endeavour I have had some Success. I know not in what Light this miserable Wretch may appear to others; but to me there is a Circumstance of some Compassion in her Case;[1] and tho' no Man living can more abhor her Crime, yet I am not altogether without Pity for the most wretched at this Day of all human Race.

Miss Blandy (for I am now acquainted with her whole History) had the Education of a Gentlewoman. She was received as such in the Country where she lived; and her Behaviour and Conversation was so agreeable, that Ladies of great Rank and Fashion were fond and desirous of her Acquaintance. She was amiable, spritely, and extremely good humoured; and was esteemed as one of the principal Ornaments of the polite Assembly at Reading.

---

[1] *GM*, which reprinted Axylus's letter, called it 'favourable Reflections on her unhappy Case' and thereby placed Fielding, somewhat unfairly, on one side of the considerable controversy over the degree of Blandy's guilt (*GM* 22 [1752], 116–17). Her own story was presented not only at her trial but in a pamphlet published after her execution on 6 Apr. by Fielding's friend Andrew Millar, *Miss Mary Blandy's Own Account . . . Published at her dying Request* (1752); in this we are told that the doses of arsenic she administered to her father were what she believed to be 'love powders' given to her by Cranstoun to make her father more agreeable to their affair. The Millar pamphlet also praises her conduct during the trial and protests against 'the palpable Falshoods, and inhuman Calumnies' against her propagated throughout the nation (p. 56; cf. Fielding's complaint about one piece of pre-trial publicity, *CGJ* No. 11, above). Blandy persisted in her story until her death, a fact which, as Horace Walpole remarked, 'has made a kind of party in her favour; as if a woman who would not stick at a parricide, would scruple a lie!' (*Yale Walpole*, xx. 317). Fielding, however, was not fully of that party, since despite the compassion expressed here, he never raises doubts about her guilty intention; cf. the comments on this case in his *Examples of the Interposition of Providence in the Detection and Punishment of Murder* (1752), where he says only her 'infatuation' could account for her poisoning her father 'in so public and barefac'd a manner' (p. 88).

For other treatments of the case favorable to Blandy, see *Original Letters to and from Miss Blandy and C———— C————* (1752), with documents supposedly showing her innocent of any intentional crime; *Memoirs of the Life of William Henry Cranstoun* (1752); and 'A Poetical Epistle from Miss Blandy to Capt. Cranstoun', in *The Repository* (1752), pp. 37–9, in which she asks her former lover, 'with your latest Breath, / Confirm me guiltless of a Father's Death'. For accounts hostile to Blandy, see *The *** Packet Broke-Open; Or, a Letter from Miss Blandy in the Shades* (1752), a sixpenny pamphlet designed to ridicule the account published by Millar; *The Genuine Speech of the Hon. Mr. ————* (1752), giving the effective prosecution speech of Henry Bathurst, 2nd Earl Bathurst; and *Captain Cranstoun's Account* (?1753). Works which leave open the question of her guilt include *The Secret History of Miss Blandy* (1752); *The Fair Parricide* (?1752), a play attributed to a Manchester playwright, Edward Crane; and an essay in *True Briton* (15 Apr. 1752), a periodical which also reprinted the letter by 'Axylus' and which, like Fielding, views the case as one which, aside from the question of her intention, 'may excite Compassion and . . . set a Guard on our Passions'.

Such was her Demeanour in general. To her Father, she was an affectionate, dutiful, respectful Child. This many Witnesses swore at her Trial. This the Witnesses against her confessed,

'Till at the last, a cruel Spoiler came.[1]

'Till that damned Villain Cranston, as the poor Father so justly called him, returned the kindest Offices of Hospitality by *the Ruin of a poor Love-sick Girl;*[2] by bringing the Father to the Grave, and the Daughter to the Gallows.

Here then is the Cause of all that Tragedy, which hath happened in this little innocent Family; of indeed the total Destruction of a kind and tender Father; of an affectionate and dutiful Daughter. The Villain crept into the unguarded Heart of this thoughtless Girl. There he first infused those poisonous Sentiments, which were afterwards to convey Arsenic into the Veins of the best and tenderest of Fathers.

For this Fact we will leave the condemned Criminal to the Execution of that Sentence, which she hath so justly received from an earthly Judge, and to that Mercy, which, I hope, a sincere Penitence will obtain for her from that most awful, most tremendous Tribunal where she must so shortly appear.

Let us for a Moment only cast our Eyes on the Wretch, who hath caused all this, who hath hitherto escaped the Hands of Justice; perhaps to be more exquisitely punished in the State of a profligate abandoned Fugitive; sent like the first Murderer, to wander over the Earth; till he shall cry with Cain, *My Punishment is greater than I can bear.*[3]

But I will leave this Wretch likewise to the Horrors of his own Conscience, to Wandering, to Beggary, to Shame, to Contempt. This Letter is designed for the Use of the loveliest, and, I sincerely think, the best Part of the Creation, who seldom stray but when they are misled by Men; by whom they are deceived, corrupted, betrayed, and often *brought to Destruction, both of Body and Soul.*[4] In the Sequel therefore, I will treat in general of these Corrupters of the Innocence of Women; and of the extreme Baseness as well

---

[1] Otway, *The Orphan* (1680), IV. ii: 'there long she flourished, / Grew sweet to sense and lovely to the eye: / Till at the last a cruel spoiler came, / Cropt this fair rose, and rifled all its sweetness, / Then cast it like a loathsome weed away.'

[2] According to the testimony of a chambermaid, the father remarked, after forbidding his daughter to see him, '*Oh! that damn'd Villain* Cranston, *that has eat of the best and drank of the best that my House has afforded, to serve me thus, and to ruin my poor love-sick Girl!*' (*The Genuine Tryal at Large of Mary Blandy* [1752], p. 8).

[3] Genesis 4: 13. On Cranstoun's wandering in his escape, cf. *Memoirs of the Life of William Henry Cranstoun* (1752), which says he is 'now a Vagabond in the World' (p. 44); in early summer he was reported to be at Boulogne 'in a very shabby Condition' (*GA*, 3 June 1752); and on 3 Dec. 1752 he died under the name of Dunbar at Furnes in Flanders; according to some reports he cleared Mary Blandy before his death (*GM* 23 [1753], 47).

[4] Cf. Matthew 10: 28: 'but rather fear him which is able to destroy both soul and body in hell'; this passage is also quoted in the course of the discussion of the Blandy case in Fielding's *Examples of the Interposition of Providence* (1752).

as Cruelty of this Practice, how favourably soever the World may please to receive it.

This base and barbarous Man was, they say, an Officer in the Army; a Sort of People who, I know not for what Reason, live in an eternal State of real Hostility with the female Sex; and seem to think that by destroying our Enemies in War, they contract a Right to destroy our Wives and Daughters in Time of Peace.[1]

I would not be here understood to insinuate that there are many Cranstons to be found in the English Army; on the contrary, I sincerely believe it would be difficult, perhaps impossible, to pick out such another; yet certain it is, that thro' the Prevalence of Custom, the Ruin of a Woman is far from being regarded amongst our military Gentlemen, or indeed amongst others, with that Abhorrence and Detestation which it deserves. It is often made the Subject of Mirth; nay, I am deceived if, instead of being considered on the Man's Side as a Mark of Disgrace, it is not sometimes treated as a Point of Honour, viewed in the Light of a Victory, and thought to add new Lawrels to those which have been acquired in the Field.

The Reason of this, in a great Measure, is the Levity with which this Matter hath been handled by some of our fashionable Authors; who, instead of exposing so execrable a Vice in its proper odious Colours, have given it the soft Term of Gallantry;[2] have at most endeavoured to make it the Subject of Ridicule; I am afraid have even represented it in an amiable Light to their Readers.

I will endeavour therefore to strip the Monster of all its borrowed Ornaments, and to display it in its native and true Deformity;[3] such as, I

---

[1] Cf. *Memoirs of the Life of . . . Cranstoun* (1752), which generalizes about military officers 'laying waste the Territories of Beauty at home' (p. 8); see also *CGJ* No. 68, where Fielding again associates adultery specifically with officers of the army. To some extent he had depicted such officers in *Amelia*, not only in Colonel James's pursuit of the heroine but in the seduction of Miss Mathews by Hebbers, a cornet in a troop of Dragoons (*Amelia*, I. vii–viii); cf. Politic in *Rape upon Rape* (1730): 'Why should red have such charms in the eyes of a woman? The Roman senate kept their armies abroad to prevent their sharing in their lands at home: we should do the same to prevent their sharing in our wives' (V. i).

[2] Cf. the definition of Gallantry as 'Fornication and Adultery', *CGJ* No. 4; see also *Amelia*, III. ix. Addison and Steele had earlier turned their attention to the abuse of this word; see *Tatler*, 58 (23 Aug. 1709), which presents an example of 'true' gallantry in the Roman Scipio, who refused to take advantage of a virgin prisoner, and *Spectator*, No. 142 (13 Aug. 1711), attacking the 'false Notion of Gallantry in Love'. Cf. also *Guardian*, No. 123 (1 Aug. 1713), in which Addison, like Fielding here, appeals to the compassion and humanity of 'knights-errant', who appear dead to the claims of honor and virtue in their conquests of innocent young women; see also *An Essay on Modern Gallantry* (1750), *passim*. On making gallantry a subject of ridicule, cf. Dr Harrison's complaint in *Amelia*, IX. v, that adultery is treated as a 'matter of jest'; for an example see *Amelia*, X. ii; cf. *CGJ* No. 67, below.

[3] A common image in Fielding; cf. *Champion*, 24 Jan. 1740: 'if we strip virtue and vice of all their outward ornaments and appearances, and view them both naked', vice will appear a 'tawdry, painted harlot'. He uses the image more frequently in its positive sense, as the 'naked Charms' of virtue; see the Dedication to *Tom Jones*; and 'Essay on the Knowledge of the Characters of Men' and 'Essay on Conversation', both in *Miscellanies* (1743), ed. H. K. Miller, Wesleyan Edn. (Oxford, 1972), i. 143, 173–4 and note. In *Tom Jones* (Dedication) Fielding associates it with Plato, with reference to *Phaedrus*, 250d; cf. Cicero, *De officiis*, I. v. 15, *De finibus*, II. xvi. 52.

think, cannot fail of attracting all that Abhorrence and Contempt which is its Due.

I shall at present pass by all those dissuasive Arguments which Religion affords against this Practice. These are already well known; and if they are not sufficient to deter Men, the Reason is but too obvious as well as deplorable.

But tho' many of my gay Readers may be ready enough to own that they have no Faith, there are few I believe who will own they have no Honour.[1] If they have a Vanity in desiring to be thought no Christians, they will at least be ashamed of being no Gentlemen.

First then, can any thing be more dishonourable than to engage in a Combat with one who is greatly inferior in Strength; and this is surely the Case in all our Attacks on the Virtue of Women: For, without any Disparagement to the Understanding of my fair Countrywomen, their Hearts are at least weaker than ours, and it is the Heart of the Woman which is aimed at in all these Engagements.

And in what Manner are these Attacks carried on? Is not the basest Fraud and Treachery constantly used on this Occasion? Doth any Man when he first aims at this Conquest, fairly and openly assert his evil Intentions? Doth he declare War against that Chastity and Honour which he means to violate? On the contrary, doth he not approach with Smiles and Cringes, with Soothing and Flattery, with Protestations, Vows, and Oaths of the tenderest Love and the sincerest Friendship? By these Means, the innocent Heart of a poor thoughtless Girl is in a manner bribed to betray its Owner into the Arms of her Seducer.

If we consider the Matter therefore in this warlike Light, the Assailant, instead of entitling himself to any Honour by such a Conquest, deserves truly an Appellation which few military Men will affect, namely that of a treacherous Coward.

And what shall we say of this Vice, when thrown under another Allegory, and that too a very familiar one to our fine Gentlemen! What do we say of the Gamester who throws a Levant?[2] who draws another in to play for a large Stake, while he himself deposites nothing real on the other Side? Would not all Men allow such a Person to be a Cheat and a Pickpocket? And what is he who engages a Woman, where her Innocence, Honour, Interest, indeed every thing valuable of which she is possessed, are at Stake; while he himself

---

[1] Cf. *An Essay on Modern Gallantry* (1750): 'And because most of those pretty Gentlemen, with whom I have to deal in this Controversy, have Stomachs too nice to digest any Arguments drawn from Religion, I shall throw Divinity entirely out of the Question, and address myself to them in their favourite Characters, as they profess themselves *Men of Honour*, *Men of Pleasure*, and *Men of Sense*' (p. 4).

[2] A bet made with the intention of absconding if it is lost (*OED*); cf. *The Lottery* (1732), sc. iii; *Tom Jones*, VIII. xii.

plays at the Risque *only of his Damnation*, which all fine Gentlemen will allow to be nothing; or, as some Gamesters call it, MOONSHINE?

In the last Place, let me apply to the Humanity of these Gallants; and this the rather as the Latins often use the Word Humanitas for the chief Qualifications of a Gentleman.[1] Now what Man of Humanity (take the Sense of the Word from which Language you please) can bear the Reflection of having by all the Means of Baseness, Falsehood and Treachery, purchased the Affections of a young, innocent, unguarded Creature; of having made this Creature from her Affections to him, the Object of his Pleasure and Delight, and of having repaid those Affections and this Pleasure, by the utter Ruin of such a Creature! Can he bear to see her stript of her Innocence, of her Reputation, of every Thing lovely, every Thing which might have made her happy in herself, or recommended her to others; deserted and abandoned by the whole World, and exposed to Shame, Beggary, Disease, in a Word, to final Misery and Ruin! Can he see all this, and know himself to be the Cause of all this, without hanging himself? If he can, I heartily wish he was, as he well deserves to be, hanged by the Laws.[2]

I am, Sir,

Your sincere Well-wisher,

AXYLUS.

SATURDAY, MARCH 14, 1752.   NUMB. 21.

Est miserorum, ut malevolentes sint atque invideant bonis.

PLAUTUS.[3]

It is a miserable State to be malevolent and to envy good Men.

I shall publish the following Letter with the same Design, that the Spartans exposed drunken Men, to the View of their Children.[4] Examples may perhaps have more Advantage over Precepts, in teaching us to avoid what is odious, than in

---

[1] See *Champion*, 27 Mar. 1740, where Fielding cites *Humanitas* as similar to his favorite ethical concept of 'good-nature'; 'Humanity' and good nature are called the distinguishing marks of a gentleman in *Spectator*, No. 75 (26 May 1711); see also *Spectator*, Nos. 169 (13 Sept. 1711) and 230 (23 Nov. 1711). *Humanitas* is a prominent term in Cicero, who uses it both in the sense of culture or knowledge of humane studies and in the sense of sensitivity to others, 'humanity'. See, as instances of the first, *Pro archia poeta*, iii and *De oratore*, II. xxxvii. 154, III. xxiv. 94, and of the latter, *Epist. ad Atticum*, I. xvii. 4 and *Ad familiares*, III. ii. 1. Fielding's sentence brings these notions together. See the discussion by John Ferguson, *Moral Values in the Ancient World* (New York, 1959), pp. 116–17 and A. E. Douglas, *Cicero* (Oxford, 1968), p. 41.

[2] Cf. the 'Covent Garden' column for Mar. 9, originally printed with this leader, below, Appendix I.

[3] *Captivi*, III. iv. 51: 'It is characteristic of poor beggars to be ill-natured and envy the well-to-do' (Loeb).

[4] See Plutarch, *Moralia*, 239A; cf. his *Life of Lycurgus*, xxviii, and *Life of Demetrius*, i; Fielding uses this allusion also in *Champion*, 10 June 1740, calling it a 'trite story'.

impelling us to pursue what is amiable.[1] *If the Reader will peruse it with Attention,*
he will, I conceive, discover in it a very useful Moral; of which I shall give no further
Hint, than by desiring the Reader not to be offended at the Contradictions that occur
in it.

　Mr. Censor,

When I first read the Name of Axylus to a Letter in your Paper, tho' I easily
perceived the Writer to be a silly Fellow, I little guest who was the individual
Person; but in his second Performance he hath been pleased to acquaint me
who he is.[2]

This Fellow, Sir, you are to know, I have employed every Means in my
Power to persecute, ever since I was acquainted with him; not because he is a
Fool (for I have no fixed Quarrel with so numerous a Body) but because he is
in reality a good Man.

You will perhaps think this a very strange Confession; and so it would be,
if there was any Possibility of your guessing from whom it came; but I have
the Satisfaction to be assured, that tho' I am actually known both to you and
to your Friend Axylus, I shall be the last Person in the World to whom either
of you will impute the Character I shall here lay open. I well know that I pass
upon you both, and a thousand other such wise People, for one of the best
and worthiest Men alive: For, as a late Orator at the Robinhood said, *he had*
the Honour to be an Atheist;[3] so I, Sir, have the Honour to be a most profound
Hypocrite. By which Means I have universally obtained a good Character,
and perhaps a much better than what the silly Axylus hath acquired by really
deserving it: For, as Plato remarks in the second Book of his Republic, the
just Man and the unjust Man are often reciprocally mistaken by Mankind,
and do frequently pass in the World the one for the other.[4] The Reason of
which, as I take it, and as he in Plato indeed intimates, is, that the former are
for the most Part Fools, and the latter are Men of Sense.

If I could so far prevail, however, as to deprive this Axylus of all the Praise
which he receives from his Actions, and to shew him in an opprobrious Light

---

　[1] Cf. Fielding's essay on the force of 'examples of what we are to shun', *Champion*, 10 June 1740,
where Hogarth's *Rake's Progress* and *Harlot's Progress* are said to be more efficacious in the cause of
virtue than all the folios of morality ever written. Cf. the opening lines of *Joseph Andrews* (i. i), where
Fielding gives the advantage to 'amiable' examples. For other uses of this common idea, see *Spectator*,
No. 299 (12 Feb. 1712) and Pope's letter to Arbuthnot of 26 July 1734: 'Precepts only apply to our
Reason, which in most men is but weak: Examples are pictures, and strike the Senses, nay raise the
Passions, and call in those . . . to the aid of reformation' (*Correspondence of Alexander Pope*, ed. George
Sherburn [Oxford, 1956], iii. 419).

　[2] For the letters of 'Axylus', see *CGJ* Nos. 16 and 20; this letter by 'Iago' is answered in *CGJ*
No. 29.

　[3] See *CGJ* No. 8, above.

　[4] In *The Republic*, ii. 361–2, Glaucon, in order to pose the problem he wishes Socrates to solve,
depicts two extreme examples, one of a completely unjust man whom everyone mistakenly believes to
be just and the other a perfectly just man whom everyone believes to be wicked.

to the World, I might perhaps be contented, and wish him Ill no longer. And yet I am not positive that this would be the Case: For what amends can it make to a Man who sees his Mistress in his Rival's Arms, that the World in general are persuaded that he himself alone enjoys her; or could all the Flattery of his Courtiers, and all the Te-Deums of his Priests, satisfy Lewis the Fourteenth, and prevent his envying the Duke of Marlborough.[1] I am well apprized that the Reputation of Goodness is all which I aim at, and is all which a wise Man would desire, notwithstanding which, I am convinced that Praise sounds most harmonious to that Ear where it finds an Eccho from within; nay who knows the secret Comforts which a good Heart may dictate from within, even when all without are silent! I perceive Symptoms of such inward Satisfaction in Axylus, and for that Reason I envy and hate him from the Bottom of my Soul.

You will perhaps say, Why then do you not imitate him? Your Servant, Sir;[2] Shall I imitate a Fool because I see him happy in his Folly? For, Folly I am convinced it is to interest yourself in the Happiness, or in the Concerns, of others. Horace, who was a sensible Writer, and knew the World, advises every Man to roll himself up in himself, as a polished Bowl which admits of no Rubs from without;[3] and the old Greek, like a wise Rogue, exclaims; *When I am dead let the Earth be consumed by Fire. It is no Concern of mine; all my Affairs are well settled.*[4]

Here again it may be objected, why do you envy one whom you condemn as a Fool? To this, I own it is not easy to give an Answer. In Fact Nature hath moulded up with the wisest Clay of Man some very simple Ingredients. Hence we covet those Commendations which we know are seldom bestowed without a Sneer, and which are annexed to Characters that we despise. The Truth I am afraid is, that I would willingly be this very Man. That I have sometimes such a Fear, I confess to you, as I think it impossible you should ever guess from whence the Confession comes; for I would not for ten

---

[1] Cf. *A Journey from this World to the Next* (1743), I. iv, in which the narrator learns that Louis XIV has prevented tapestry depicting the victories of Marlborough from being hung among the walls of the Palace of Death. Marlborough (1650–1722) is always spoken of by Fielding in terms of high praise; see, among many examples, 'Of True Greatness' and 'Liberty', both in *Miscellanies* (1743); and *True Patriot*, No. 8 (24 Dec. 1745).

[2] 'A mode of expressing submission to another's opinion, often equivalent to "there is nothing more to be said upon the subject" ' (*OED*).

[3] *Satires*, II. vii. 86–8; see *Tom Jones*, VIII. xiii, where Fielding's note provides this translation by Philip Francis: 'Firm in himself, who on himself relies, / Polish'd and round, who runs his proper Course, / And breaks Misfortunes with superior Force.' Fielding's disapproval of this image of complete self-sufficiency is suggested by his paraphrase of the passage further in *Tom Jones* (XIV. vi), where he contrasts Jones's good nature and compassion with 'that noble Firmness of Mind, which rolls a Man, as it were, within himself, and, like a polished Bowl, enables him to run through the World without being once stopped by the Calamities which happen to others'.

[4] A quotation cited in Greek by Suetonius, *Nero*, xxxviii, and ascribed only to 'someone in a general conversation'; Dio Cassius calls it an old sentiment and says it was uttered frequently by Tiberius (*Roman History*, LVIII. xxiii).

thousand Pound, that any Man should know, I had ever such a Wish; nay I would not for an equal Sum know myself that I had it.

And from this Fear, this Suspicion (for I once more assure you, and myself, that it is no more than a Suspicion) I heartily detest this Axylus. For this Reason, I have hitherto pursued him with the most inveterate Hatred; have industriously taken every Occasion to plague him, and have let slip no Opportunity of ruining his Reputation.

I am aware I may have let drop something which may lead you into an Opinion, that I really esteem this Character, which I would endeavour to persuade you I despise; but, before I finish this Letter, I flatter myself I shall place this Fellow in so contemptible a Light, that I shall have no Reason to apprehend your drawing any such Conclusion.

First, notwithstanding all the secret Comforts which Axylus pretends to receive from the *Energies of Benevolence*,[1] as he calls them, I cannot persuade myself, that there is really any Pleasure in a good Action. I must own to you, I do not speak this absolutely on my own Knowledge, for I do not remember to have done one truly good, benevolent Action in my whole Life. Indeed I should heartily despise myself if I had any such Recollection.

And if there be no Pleasure in Goodness, I am sure there is no Profit in it. This, Axylus himself will, I doubt not, be ready to confess. No Man hath ever made or improved, tho' many have injured, and some have destroyed their Fortunes this Way.

In the last Place, as to the Motives which arise from our Vanity, and which, as that very wise Writer Dr. Mandevil[2] observes, are much the strongest Supports of what is generally called Benevolence, I think to make the Folly of doing good from such Motives very plainly appear. I am far from being an Enemy to Praise, or from expressing that Contempt for a good

[1] See the response to this letter in *CGJ* No. 29, where Fielding ('Axylus') quotes Aristotle on the pleasure to be found in '*the Energy itself of Virtue*', probably with reference to *Nicomachean Ethics*, 1099a 13–15. Cf. Fielding's praise of the 'natural Energies' of a 'tender-hearted and compassionate Disposition' in *Enquiry into the Causes of the late Increase of Robbers* (1751), pp. 106–7 (sect. VII). His emphasis on the natural energy of benevolence placed Fielding in opposition to the rigorism and rationalism of other benevolist writers; see Miller, *Essays*, pp. 68–70, and Frederick G. Ribble, 'Aristotle and the "Prudence" Theme of *Tom Jones*', *ECS* 15 (1981), 31–3, 38. Cf. also the constant use of the word 'Energies' in a similar context by Fielding's Aristotelian friend James Harris in 'Concerning Happiness, a Dialogue', *Three Treatises* (1744), pp. 176, 200, 208, 237.

[2] i.e. Bernard Mandeville (1670–1733). The theme Fielding points to here is common in Mandeville, but he probably has specifically in mind *An Essay on Charity and Charity-Schools*, added to *The Fable of the Bees* in the edition of 1723. In the opening pages of this essay, which Mandeville claimed initiated the first real outcry against his work, charity is made dependent on self-love: 'Pride and Vanity have built more Hospitals than all the Virtues together'. Although Fielding himself wavers on the question of man's 'natural goodness' and sometimes uses arguments similar to Mandeville's (see *CGJ* No. 44), he generally denounces as a group those like Mandeville and Hobbes who have 'very much alarmed the World, by shewing that there were no such things as Virtue or Goodness really existing in Human Nature, and who deduced our best Actions from Pride' (*Tom Jones*, VI. i). Cf. Booth's attack on Mandeville in *Amelia* (III. v), and see *Champion*, 11 Dec. 1739, 22 Jan. 1740.

Character which some have affected. But surely it becomes a Man to purchase every Thing as cheap as he can; now why should he be at the Pains and Expence of being good in Reality, when he may so certainly obtain all the Applause he aims at, merely, by pretending to be so.

An Instance of this I give you in myself, who, without having ever done a single good Action, have universally a good Character; and this I have acquired by *only* taking upon me the Trouble of supporting one constant Series of Hypocrisy all my Days.[1]

Axylus, on the contrary, for want of undergoing this Trouble, hath miss'd the Praises he deserves. While he carelessly doth a hundred good Actions, without being at the Pains of displaying them, they are all overlooked by the World; nay often, by my Means (for I am always watchful on such Occasions) his most disinterested Benevolence is seen in a disadvantageous Light; and his Goodness, instead of being commended, turns to his Dishonour.

An Example of this I saw the other Day when you published his last Letter, where all that is said of an unhappy Woman,[2] drawn in to be guilty of the highest Degree of Wickedness, by the most wicked and profligate of Men, I am convinced flowed immediately from that Compassion which is the constant Energy of these good Hearts. Now, Sir, even this I turned against him. I represented it as a barbarous Attempt to revile the Character of a Man before he had undergone his Trial; and, can you believe it? Such is the Nature of Man. I found some Persons who could not, or would not, see the Difference between concluding a Person guilty who is in Custody, and who is to undergo a legal Disquisition into his Crimes, and concluding one to be guilty of a Fact for which he hath fled from Justice, and who, even by the Evidence given on Oath in the solemn Trial of another, appears to all the World to be guilty.[3]

But perhaps it may be said, tho' the World in general do not commend your Actions, still you are repaid for them sufficiently, by having the Esteem, the Love, the Gratitude, of those to whom they are done. To this Purpose, I will tell you a short Story. The Fact is true, and happened to Mr. Axylus himself.

That silly, good Man had done many great Services to a private Family. Indeed the very Bread they eat was for a long Time owing to his foolish Generosity, and at length by his Advice and Assistance, this Family was

---

[1] Cf. the letter from an unnamed hypocrite in *Champion*, 11 Dec. 1739; portraits of hypocrites abound in Fielding's works, but for his general indictment of the type, see 'Essay on the Knowledge of the Characters of Men', *Miscellanies* (1743).

[2] Mary Blandy; see *CGJ* No. 20.

[3] Referring to William Henry Cranstoun; see *CGJ* No. 20. Fielding is distinguishing between the unfairness of assuming the guilt of a person who has not yet been tried (see *CGJ* No. 11, above, p. 84, for his comment on Blandy in this regard) and the reasonableness of assuming the guilt of one like Cranstoun, who fled from justice and against whom sworn testimony was given in Blandy's trial.

brought from a State of Poverty and Distress to what might be called Affluence in their Condition. I was acquainted with the whole Scene and often present at it, and indeed it was one of the pleasantest I ever saw: For while the good Man was rejoicing in his own Goodness, and feeding his foolish Vanity with fond Conceits of the grateful Returns which were made to him in the Bosoms of the Obliged, they on the other Side were continually laughing at his Folly amongst themselves, and flattering their own Ingenuity with their constant Impositions on his good Nature, and ascribing every Thing which they obtained of him, to their own superior Cunning and Power of over-reaching him.

When I had enjoyed this Scene 'till I was weary of it, I was resolved to work myself another Satisfaction out of it, by tormenting the Man I hate. I accordingly communicated the Secret to Axylus, and gave him almost Demonstration of the Truth of what I told him. He answered with a Smile, he hoped I was mistaken; but if not, he was answerable for the Means only, and not for the End; and the very same Day did a new Favour to one of the Family.

I will conclude by telling you, that it was I who sent him the Trial of Miss Blandy to vex him, and I hope you will print this Letter that he may have the Plague of guessing at me, for I am sure he will guess wrong; and perhaps may fix on one of his best Friends; which will be doing him a very great Injury, and will consequently give great Pleasure to,

SIR, yours,

IAGO.

I cannot dismiss this Letter without observing, that if there be really such a Person as this Writer describes himself, the Possession of his own bad Mind is a worse Curse to him, than he himself will ever be able to inflict on the happy Axylus.   A.[1]

TUESDAY, MARCH 17, 1752.   NUMB. 22.

*Qua tamen exarsit forma? Qua capta juta est
Hippia? Quid vidit propter quod ludia dici
Sustinuit?*

JUVENAL.[2]

---

[1] For the 'Court of Censorial Enquiry' originally appearing in this number, see below, Appendix I.
[2] *Satires*, vi. 103–5: 'And what were the youthful charms which captivated Eppia? What did she see in him to allow herself to be called a "she-Gladiator"?' (Loeb.) Cf. Fielding's translation in his 'Part of Juvenal's Sixth Satire, Modernized in Burlesque Verse', *Miscellanies* (1743): 'But say, what Youth or Beauty warm'd thee / What, *Hippia*, in thy Lover charm'd thee?' For *juta* read *juventa*.

It is not Virtue, Wisdom, Valour, Wit,
Strength, Comeliness of Shape, or amplest Merit,
That Woman's Love can win or long inherit,
But what it is, hard is to say.——

MILTON.[1]

The following Story, related by Ariosto in his Orlando Furioso,[2] is so injurious to that beautiful Part of the Creation called the fair Sex, that one is at a Loss to guess what could move the ingenious Author to give it a Place in his Works. The Manners of Womankind could never, I hope, be so degenerate, as to give any just Ground for such a Satire; or if they were so in the Days when Ariosto wrote, how may we congratulate our own Times on their Improvement in Virtue? For now, when all Women, Ladies of Quality especially, are so remarkably chaste and virtuous, so distinguished for Fidelity to their Husbands, and Constancy to the Marriage bed, the following Tale will I doubt not be treated as an unnnatural Fiction, unlikely ever to have happened, and beyond all Bounds of Probability.[3] I thought it right therefore to quote my Authority, and shall leave it to the Reader's Consideration.

There reigned once in Lombardy a King named Astolpho, famous for his Beauty, and no less so for the high Conceit which he entertained of it. His Courtiers, sensible of their Master's Weakness, flattered themselves into Favour by extolling the Charms of his Person. 'Twas the current Language to call him the handsomest of Men, the Jewel of Italy, another Adonis, and

---

[1] *Samson Agonistes*, 1010–13.

[2] *Orlando Furioso*, xxviii. As Sheridan Baker has pointed out ('Fielding's *Amelia* and the Materials of Romance', *PQ* 41 [1962], 442–3), this same story is probably alluded to in the episode in *Amelia* (III. iii) in which Booth, setting out on his journey, forgets the casket which Amelia has packed for him and which she has asked him to take special care of as a symbol of his eventual return. Fielding has considerably abbreviated Ariosto's story in his version of it here and made a few changes of detail, such as substituting a bracelet of hair and a picture for the cross covered with jewels which Jucundo's wife gives him in the original. Most of his changes, in fact, make the case against women stronger than in Ariosto's story; Fielding's 'Moorish Servant' is in the original merely a young man of humble origins, and he has omitted a defense of womankind given by an old man at the conclusion of Ariosto's tale, as well as excising the fact that the two adventurers eventually return to their wives, who never cause them more trouble.

[3] For the irony here, cf. Fielding's essays on adultery, *CGJ* Nos. 67 and 68. *GM*, in excerpting this issue of *CGJ*, has the following note on this paragraph: 'There is a remarkably conformity between the sentiments in this paragraph, and those in *Caxton*'s apology for printing the *sayings of Socrates against women*' (*GM* 22 [1752], 130). A cross-reference to a previous number of *GM* provides an anecdote about Caxton, who expressed ironic wonder that a section of Socrates' remarks against women had been omitted by Anthony Earl of Rivers in his translation of *Dyctes and Sayings of the Philosophers*, given to Caxton to revise and print. Caxton printed the material in an appendix, with an apology: 'But I apperceyue, that my sayde lord knoweth verily that such defaultes ben not had ne founded in the women born and dwelling in these partyes ne regyons of this londe. . . . for I wote wel, of whatsomeuer condition women ben in grece, the women of this contre ben right good, wyse, playsant, humble, discrete, sobre, chaste, obedient to their husbands, trewe, secret, stedfast, ever besy, and never ydle, attemperat in speaking, and vertuous in alle their werkis, *or atte leste sholde be so*' (*GM* 22 [1752], 79). *GM* is suggesting that Fielding took his hint for the first paragraph of his essay from this anecdote.

many other such extravagant Appellations, to which Astolpho lent a very willing Ear.

A Rumour came at length to Court, of a young Gentleman named Jucundo, who lived at some Distance in the Country, and was said to rival the King in Beauty. Astolpho immediately had a Desire to see him, and being impatient to satisfy his Curiosity, he dispatched one of his Favourites into the Country, to invite Jucundo to Court, making him many Overtures of his Friendship and Promises of Promotion, if he complied with his Desires.

Jucundo was at this Time enjoying the most consummate Happiness, that Love and Innocence in a rural Retreat could afford him. Blest beyond Description in the Arms of a beautiful Woman, of whom he was passionately fond, and who returned his Affection with equal Rapture, he found all his Wishes complete and satisfied, and had resolved to pass his Days in Tranquillity and Retirement. When therefore the Messenger came from Court, and informed him of Astolpho's Desires, he excused himself as long as he could from complying with them. He humbly thanked his Prince for his gracious Offers, but begged Leave to represent to him, that his Views were entirely void of Ambition, that his Felicity was already perfect in the Fruition of his lovely Spouse, with whom he lived in the greatest conjugal Endearment, and that his Wishes reached no farther. To all this the Courtier remonstrated, that the Commands of Kings were not to be dispensed with, that it would be in the highest Degree unpolite to frustrate a Monarch's Desires, and that a very short Residence at Court would soon cure him of those romantic, old-fashioned Notions, about matrimonial Happiness and the Joys of Solitude, which Men who understood the *grand Monde* had long ago exploded: At least, if he determined to waste his Life in a miserable Desart, it behoved him nevertheless to make his Appearance at Court for a Time, and when the King had seen him, he might then return, if he pleased, to his Wife in the Country, and pursue that strange Scheme of Happiness, with which he seemed to be so unaccountably delighted. Jucundo replied much to this, and dwelt largely on the Difficulty of parting at all from the dear Object of his Soul, whose Happiness he knew was so entirely wrapped up in him, that the very Thought of Absence, tho' for ever so short a Time, would be worse than Death to her. But being at length overcome by the repeated Importunities of his Guest, he was obliged to consent, and agreed to attend him to Court.

This being resolvd on, the poor trembling Husband went to break the News to his Wife, who received it, as he expected, with the utmost Amazement and Affliction. She shed a Flood of Tears, and exhausted all the tender Rhetoric of Grief to dissuade him from his Purpose. At length, when she found his Honour was too far engaged to recede, she then applied herself in the warmest Manner to press his speedy Return. A thousand

Times she insisted that his Absence should not exceed a Month, and a thousand Times he vowed the sincerest Obedience to her Will. She breded[1] for him a Bracelet of her own Hairs, and gave him her Picture, to carry with him as Memorials of Love in the tedious Hours of their Separation. In short the last Scene of Tenderness, which passed between them on the Day of his Departure, exceeded any Thing that ever was recorded in History or Romance.

Jucundo then set out on his Journey; but such had been the Hurry and Agitation of his Mind at the last Interview, that he forgot to take with him the Bracelet and the Picture. When he had travelled seven or eight Miles he became sensible of this Omission, and to repair his Fault galloped back in person, not chusing to trust a Servant with the Conveyance of them. Perhaps a secret Desire of once more bidding adieu to his dear Consort, had its Share in producing this Resolution; but, however that be, he was no sooner returned and alighted from his Horse, than he flew up stairs on the Wings of Love, and with as much Impatience as if he had already been absent from her a Twelve month. And now follows the sad Part of the Story: For no sooner had he opened his Chamber-door, than he beheld his chaste Penelope, that darling Wife, on whom he doated with such Tenderness, and who had always returned his Love with such Transport, he beheld her

> *(Let me not name it to you, you chaste Stars!*
> *And thou pale Moon, turn paler at the Sound!)*[2]

fast asleep in the Arms of a Moorish Servant, who lay stretched out and snoring on the lovely Bosom of his Mistress. Imagine the Astonishment, Horror, and Indignation, that seized on Jucundo at so strange a Sight. In the first Transport of his Rage he drew his Sword, and was going to stab them both as they lay in their Embraces; but recovering himself on the Instant, "No," cried he, "perfidious Woman, thou art not worthy of my Resentment; live and riot in thy impious Amours; to the Remorse of thy own Conscience I abandon thee for ever." And so saying he locked the Chamber-Door, remounted his Horse, and pursued his Journey to Court.

But when he arrived there, he was no longer the handsome Man which Fame had reported him. Grief had entirely destroyed his Complexion, and altered his Features; his Vivacity was totally gone, and a settled Gloom reigned for ever in his Countenance. The Court-Ladies received him with

---

[1] Obsolete form of 'braided'.

[2] The first line is *Othello*, v. ii. 2; the second line has not been identified. It is not likely to be a misquotation, for Fielding knew *Othello* well; cf. *Journey from this World to the Next* (i. viii), in which Shakespeare is asked to settle a dispute about a line from the same passage as the first line given here. The moon and the stars were frequently invoked in similar passages expressing shame; cf. Rowe's *The Fair Penitent*, i. i and iv. i, and Dryden's *Indian Emperor*, iii. ii; cf. also Cowley, *Davideis*, i. 18: 'The silver Moon with Terror paler grew'.

Indifference, and sneered to think that this should be the Narcissus of whom they had heard so much, and who was to do such Execution among their Hearts. Astolpho however shewed him great Respect, appointed him an Apartment in the Palace, honoured him with his Friendship, and perhaps behaved better to him than he would have done had he found him handsomer.

But not all the King's Civilities could cure the Uneasiness of Jucundo's Mind. His Health continually decreased, and Melancholy seemed every Hour to take deeper Possession of him, when a little Accident happened which effectually restored him to himself. As he was walking one Day in a Gallery of the Palace, pensive and meditating on his unfortunate Lot, he heard a female Voice in one of the adjoining Apartments, upbraiding a Lover for want of Affection. Curiosity led him to listen, and perceiving a Chink in the Wainscot, he peeped thro' it and saw —— the Queen herself in a very wanton Attitude, caressing the King's Dwarf, who seemed to receive her Fondness with the most stupid Indifference, and appeared to look on her with Eyes of Aversion. So strange, so wonderful a Sight, threw him immediately upon Reflection, and, upon comparing it with his own Case, he began to think it was the common Behaviour of Womankind: He persuaded himself that he suffered nothing new, and that all Husbands were in the same Condition. This immediately had a good Effect; he recovered his Spirits, regained his Complexion, and soon became the Favourite of all the Women at Court.

But as he had great Obligations to Astolpho, he thought it would be making an ill Return to see him injured in so tender a Part, and suffer him to remain in Ignorance of his Wrong. One Day therefore, when he had a fair Opportunity, he gave the King Information of all he had seen. Astolpho knew not how to believe it, and at first resented so improbable a Suspicion; but by strict watching he soon became an Eye-Witness of the Fact. What Methods he took of punishing his Queen, would be a useless Enquiry; but 'tis said he soon afterwards proposed a very whimsical Project to Jucundo, and this was to make the Tour of Italy, and debauch as many Women as they could, by Way of Revenge for what they themselves had suffered from their Wives. Without Delay they began their Adventures, and took with them a large paper Book, designing to register in it the Names of all the Women who should yield to their Embraces. The Story says that the Book was soon filled, and that the two Adventurers returned to Astolpho's Palace, crowned with innumerable Lawrels.   P.

SATURDAY, MARCH 21, 1752.   NUMB. 23.

Οὐκ ἀγαθὸν πολυκοιρανίη· εἷς κοίρανος ἔστω.
Εἷς Βασιλεὺς, ᾧ ἔδωκε Κρόνου παῖς ἀγκυλομήτεω
Σκῆπτρον τ᾽ ἠδὲ θέμιστας, ἵνα σφίσιν ἐμβασιλέυη.

HOMER.[1]

————*Here is not allow'd,*
That worst of Tyrants, an usurping Crowd.
To one sole Monarch, Jove commits the Sway;
His are the Laws, and him let all obey.

POPE.[2]

Tho' of the three Forms of Government acknowledged in the Schools,[3] all have been very warmly opposed, and as warmly defended; yet, in this Point, the different Advocates will, I believe, very readily agree, that there is not one of the three which is not greatly to be preferred to a total Anarchy; a State in which there is no Subordination, no lawful Power, and no settled Government; but where every Man is at Liberty to act in whatever Manner it pleaseth him best.[4]

As this is in Reality a most deplorable State, I have long lamented, with great Anguish of Heart, that it is at present the Case of a very large Body of People in this Kingdom. An Assertion which, as it may surprize most of my Readers, I will make Haste to explain, by declaring that I mean the Fraternity of the Quill, that Body of Men to whom the Public assign the Name of AUTHORS.

However absurd Politicians may have been pleased to represent the Imperium in Imperio,[5] it will here, I doubt not, be found on a strict Examination to be extremely necessary. The Commonwealth of Literature being indeed totally distinct from the greater Commonwealth, and no more dependant upon it than the Kingdom of England is on that of France. Of this our Legislature seems to have been at all Times sensible, as they have never attempted any Provision for the Regulation or Correction of this Body. In one Instance, it is true, there are (I should rather, I believe, say there were)

---

[1] *Iliad*, ii. 204–6; the last line is an interpolated line, not in some texts.

[2] Pope's *Iliad*, ii. 241–4, with the first line slightly altered.

[3] Aristotle divides the 'right' type of constitution into the forms of kingship, aristocracy, and 'the constitutional' or 'the polity', with the 'wrong' type having the corresponding forms of tyranny, oligarchy, and democracy; see *Politics*, III. vii. By 'the Schools' Fielding presumably means scholastic philosophers or theologians; Aristotle's division was followed by Aquinas and others.

[4] Cf. Fielding's reference in *Enquiry into the Causes of the late Increase of Robbers* (1751) to 'those wild Notions of Liberty that are inconsistent with all Government' and his comment that 'Anarchy is almost sure to end in some Kind of Tyranny' (p. xv); cf. also the remarks on anarchy and liberty in *Journal of a Voyage to Lisbon* (21 [16] July). See *CGJ* No. 2, above, p. 22, No. 58, below, p. 316; and General Introduction, p. xl.

[5] An empire within an empire.

some Laws to restrain them: For Writers, if I am not mistaken, have been formerly punished for Blasphemy against God, and Libels against the Government;[1] nay I have been told, that to slander the Reputation of private Persons, was once thought unlawful here as well as among the Romans, who, as Horace tells us, had a severe Law for this Purpose.[2]

In promulging these Laws (whatever may be the Reason of suffering them to grow obsolete) the State seems to have acted very wisely; as such Kind of Writings are really of most mischievous Consequence to the Public; but alas! there are many Abuses, many horrid Evils, daily springing up in the Commonwealth of Literature, which appear to affect only that Commonwealth, at least immediately, of which none of the political Legislators have ever taken any Notice; nor hath any Civil Court of Judicature ever pretended to any Cognizance of them. Nonsense and Dulness are no Crimes in Foro Civili:[3] No Man can be questioned for bad Verses in Westminster Hall; and amongst the many Indictments for Battery, not one can be produced for breaking poor Priscian's Head,[4] tho' it is done almost every Day.

But tho' immediately, as I have said, these Evils do not affect the greater Commonwealth; yet as they tend to the utter Ruin of the lesser, so they have a remote evil Consequence, even on the State itself; which seems by having left them unprovided for, to have remitted them, for the Sake of Convenience, to the Government of Laws, and to the Superintendence of Magistrates of this lesser Commonwealth; and never to have foreseen or suspected that dreadful State of Anarchy, which at present prevails in this lesser Empire; an Empire which hath formerly made so great a Figure in this Kingdom, and that indeed almost within our own Memories.

It may appear strange, that none of our English Historians have spoken clearly and distinctly of this lesser Empire; but this may be well accounted for, when we consider that all these Histories have been written by two Sorts of Persons; that is to say, either Politicians or Lawyers. Now the former of these have had their Imaginations so entirely filled with the Affairs of the

---

[1] Such laws, of course, still existed. In his *Charge to the Grand Jury* (1749) Fielding cites blasphemy as punishable by common law and by 1 Eliz., c. 2; calls for punishment of slanderers of private persons; and lists a series of statutes against libels of public persons and magistrates. On slander, cf. *CGJ* No. 14 and notes, above. Fielding's irony is directed at what he clearly thought was the increasing frequency of writings 'of most mischievous Consequence to the Public'; for his involvement in the prosecution of a recent and sensational case of libel, Paul Whitehead's *Case of the Hon. Alexander Murray* (1751), see M. C. with R. R. Battestin, 'Fielding, Bedford, and the Westminster Election of 1749', *ECS* 11 (1977–8), 159.

[2] *Satires*, II. i. 82–3: 'If a man write ill verses against another, there is a right of action and redress by law' (Loeb).

[3] In the civil court.

[4] To break the head of Priscian, a celebrated Roman grammarian (*c.*500–53), is to violate the rules of grammar (*OED*). Cf. *JJ* No. 24 (14 May 1748).

greater Empire, that it is no Wonder the Business of the lesser should have totally escaped their Observation. And as to the Lawyers, they are well known to have been very little acquainted with the Commonwealth of Literature, and to have always acted and written in Defiance to its Laws.

From these Reasons it is very difficult to fix, with Certainty, the exact Period when this Commonwealth first began among us. Indeed if the Originals of all the greater Empires upon Earth, and even of our own, be wrapped in such Obscurity that they elude the Enquiries of the most diligent Sifters of Antiquity, we cannot be surprized that this Fate should attend our little Empire, opposed as it hath been by the Pen of the Lawyer, overlooked by the Eye of the Historian, and never once *smelt after* by the Nose of the Antiquarian.

In the earliest Ages, the literary State seems to have been an Ecclesiastical Democracy: For the Clergy are then said to have had all the Learning among them; and the great Reverence paid at that Time to it by the Laity, appears from hence, That whoever could prove in a Court of Justice that he belonged to this State, by only reading a single Verse in the Testament, was vested with the highest Privileges, and might do almost what he pleased; even commit Murder with Impunity. And this Privilege was called the Benefit of the Clergy.[1]

This Commonwealth, however, can scarce be said to have been in any flourishing State of old Time, even among the Clergy themselves; inasmuch as we are told, that a Rector of a Parish going to Law with his Parishioners about paving the Church, quoted this Authority from St. Peter, *Paveant illi non paveam ego.* Which he construed thus: *They are to pave the Church, and not I.*[2] And this by a Judge, who was likewise an Ecclesiastic, was allowed to be very good Law.

The Nobility had clearly no antient Connection with this Commonwealth, nor would submit to be bound by any of its Laws, witness that Provision in an old Act of Parliament; "that a Nobleman shall be entitled to the Benefit of his Clergy (the Privilege abovementioned) *even tho' he cannot read.*"[3] Nay the whole Body of the Laity, tho' they gave such Honours to this Commonwealth, appear to have been very few of them under its Jurisdiction; as appears by a Law cited by Judge Rolls in his Abridgement, with the Reason which he gives for it. "The Command of the Sheriff," says this Writer, "to his Officer by Word of Mouth, and without writing is good;

[1] See *CGJ* No. 14, above, p. 103, n. 1; the reading or recitation of the 'neck-verse' was abolished by statute in 1705 (6 Anne, c. 9).

[2] It is not Peter but Jeremiah who says (Vulgate, Jeremiah 17: 18) *paveant illi, et non paveam ego,* 'Let them be dismayed, but let me not be dismayed'. The source of Fielding's anecdote has not been located.

[3] The Act referred to is 1 Edward VI, c. 12 and 13 (1547), by which peers, though illiterate, were given a privilege equivalent to that of clergy. Cf. *Champion*, 25 Dec. 1739.

for it may be, that neither the Sheriff or his Officer can write or read."[1]

But not to dwell on these obscure Times, when so very little authentic can be found concerning this Commonwealth, let us come at once to the Days of Henry the Eighth, when no less a Revolution happened in the lesser than in the greater Empire: For the literary Government became absolute together with the Political, in the Hands of one and the same Monarch; who was himself a Writer,[2] and dictated not only Law but Common-Sense too, to all his People; suffering no one to write or speak but according to his own Will and Pleasure.

After this King's Demise, the literary Commonwealth was again separated from the Political; for I do not find that his Successor on the greater Throne, succeeded him likewise in the lesser. Nor did either of the two Queens, as I can learn, pretend to any Authority in this Empire, in which the Salique Law[3] hath universally prevailed; for tho' there have been some considerable Subjects of the Female Sex in the Literary Commonwealth, I never remember to have read of a Queen.

It is not easy to say with any great Exactness what Form of Government was preserved in this Commonwealth during the Reigns of Edward VI, Queen Mary and Queen Elizabeth; for tho' there were some great Men in those Times, none of them seemed to have affected the Throne of Wit: Nay Shakespear, who flourished in the latter end of the last Reign, and who seemed so justly qualified to enjoy this Crown, never thought of challenging it.

In the Reign of James I. the literary Government was an Aristocracy, for I do not chuse to give it the evil Name of Oligarchy,[4] tho' it consisted only of four, namely, Master William Shakespear, Master Benjamin Johnson,

---

[1] Fielding refers to Henry Rolle, *Un Abridgment des plusieurs Cases et Resolutions del common Ley*, 2 vols. (1668), a work he owned (Baker, item 117). The passage he cites, however, has not been located in Rolle; it appears instead to have been loosely quoted from another work in Fielding's library (Baker, item 84), Anthony Fitzherbert's *The New Natura Brevium*, 7th edn. (1730). Commenting on the Statute of Marlbridge (52 Henry III, c. 21), Fitzherbert writes as follows: 'And the Sheriff, upon a Complaint made unto him of taking of the Cattle, may command his Bailiff by Word for to replevy them; and the same is as well as if the Sheriff had made his Warrant to his Bailiff to have replevied them; for it may be that the Sheriff nor his Bailiff cannot write, or that they may want such Things wherewith they may write a Warrant, &c.' (pp. 158–9). If quoting from memory, Fielding may have confused Rolle with Fitzherbert because the latter also wrote a *Grand Abridgment* (1565; Baker, item 141). Cf. *Champion*, 25 Dec. 1739, where Fielding, giving no source, cites the same explanation for the point of law.

[2] Although Henry had a hand in various theological works issued during his reign, Fielding undoubtedly has in mind his principal work, *Assertio septem sacramentorum* (1521), a lengthy treatise against a book by Luther, as a result of which he was granted the title 'Defender of the Faith'.

[3] 'The alleged fundamental law of the French monarchy, by which females were excluded from succession to the crown' (*OED*); for Fielding's skepticism about the possibility of women becoming literary giants and about the value of women's education, see *CGJ* No. 56 and notes, below.

[4] See Aristotle, *Politics*, III. vii, viii.

Master John Fletcher and Master Francis Beaumont.[1] This Quadrumvirate, as they introduced a new Form of Government, thought proper according to Machivael's Advice, to introduce new Names,[2] they therefore called themselves THE WITS, a Name which hath been affected since by the reigning Monarchs in this Empire.

The last of this Quadrumvirate[3] enjoyed the Government alone during his Life; after which the Troubles that shortly after ensued, involved this lesser Commonwealth in all the Confusion and Ruin of the greater, nor can any Thing be found of it with sufficient Certainty, till the WITS in the Reign of Charles the Second, after many Struggles among themselves for Superiority, at last agreed to elect JOHN DRYDEN to be their King.

This King John had a very long Reign, tho' a very unquiet one; for there were several Pretenders to the Throne of Wit in his Time, who formed very considerable Parties against him, and gave him great Uneasiness, of which his Successor hath made mention in the following Lines:

> *Pride, Folly, Malice, against Dryden rose,*
> *In various Shapes, of Parsons, Critics, Beaus.*[4]

Besides which, his Finances were in such Disorder, that it is affirmed his Treasury was more than once entirely empty.[5]

He died nevertheless in a good old Age, possessed of the Kingdom of Wit, and was succeeded by King ALEXANDER, sirnamed POPE.

This Prince enjoyed the Crown many Years, and is thought to have stretched the Prerogative much farther than his Predecessor: He is said to have been extremely jealous of the Affections of his Subjects, and to have employed various Spies, by whom if he was informed of the least Suggestion against his Title, he never failed of branding the accused Person with the Word DUNCE on his Forehead in broad Letters; after which the unhappy Culprit was obliged to lay by his Pen forever; for no Bookseller would venture to print a Word that he wrote.[6]

---

[1] See also *CGJ* No. 15, 'Court of Censorial Enquiry'.

[2] *Discourses*, I. xxvi: 'Whoever makes himself Lord of a City or State (and especially if he finds himself weak, and suspects his ability to keep it) . . . the best course he can take is to subvert all, to turn every thing topsie turvy; and make all things as new as himself. To alter the Magistracy, create new Titles, elect new persons, confer new Authorities . . .' (*The Works of the Famous Nicholas Machiavel*, 3rd edn. [1720], p. 296). Fielding owned this edition of Machiavelli (Baker, item 447).

[3] i.e. Jonson, who died in 1637, having survived Fletcher by 12 years.

[4] Pope, *Essay on Criticism*, 458–9; Fielding reverses the order of 'Folly' and 'Malice' in the first line. Cf. *Champion*, 4 Dec. 1739, where he quotes and praises the entire passage on the envy of Dryden's enemies.

[5] Cf. Johnson on Dryden: 'His complaints of poverty are so frequently repeated . . . that it is impossible not to detest the age which could impose on such a man the necessity of such solicitations, or not to despise the man who could submit to such solicitations without necessity' (*Lives of the Poets*, ed. G. B. Hill [Oxford, 1905], i. 404). Refusal to take the oaths in 1689 cost Dryden his post as poet laureate, so that his final years were particularly marked by problems over money.

[6] For Fielding's relations with Pope, see *CGJ* No. 5, above, p. 44. In his reference to Pope's 'Spies',

He did indeed put a total Restraint on the Liberty of the Press: For no Person durst read any Thing which was writ without his Licence and Approbation; and this Licence he granted only to four during his Reign, namely, to the celebrated Dr. Swift, to the ingenious Dr. Young,[1] to Dr. Arbuthnot, and to one Mr. Gay, four of his principal Courtiers and Favourites.

But without diving any deeper into his Character, we must allow that King Alexander had great Merit as a Writer, and his Title to the Kingdom of Wit was better founded at least than his Enemies have pretended.

After the Demise of King Alexander, the Literary State relapsed again into a Democracy, or rather indeed into downright Anarchy; of which, as well as of the Consequences, I shall treat in a future Paper.   A.[2]

TUESDAY, MARCH 24, 1752.   NUMB. 24.

> *Nimirum sapere est abjectis utile nugis,*
> *Et tempestivum pueris concedere ludum.*

HORACE.[3]

> *Trifling Pursuits true Wisdom casts away;*
> *And leaves to Children all their childish Play.*

The Mind of Man is compared by Montaigne to a fertile Field, which tho' it be left entirely uncultivated, still retains all its genial Powers; but instead of producing any Thing lovely or profitable, sends forth only Weeds and wild Herbs of various Kinds, which serve to no Use or Emolument whatsoever.[4]

The human Mind is indeed of too active a Nature to content itself with a State of perfect Rest or Sloth. There are few Men such arrant Stocks or

he probably has in mind Richard Savage, whom Pope's victims in the *Dunciad* generally believed to be his chief informer about their activities; see James Sutherland, ed., *The Dunciad*, Twickenham Edn., v (1965), xxv–xxvi. Fielding's comments about Pope are almost always favorable, despite some early unpublished satiric verses (see Isobel Grundy, 'New Verse by Henry Fielding', *PMLA* 87 [1972], 213–45) and two essays in the *Champion* (13 Dec. 1739, 17 May 1740) lightheartedly criticizing Pope's withdrawal from political satire after 1738. There is an amusing similarity, perhaps one not absent from Fielding's thoughts, between this portrait of Pope as literary tyrant and Pope's own lines about Addison, 'Shou'd such a man, too fond to rule alone, / Bear, like the *Turk*, no brother near the throne', etc. (*Epistle to Arbuthnot*, 197 ff.).

[1] Also called 'the ingenious Dr. Young' in *CGJ* No. 60, Edward Young (1683–1765), author of *Night Thoughts*, was in fact separated both by temperament and politics from the Scriblerian wits Pope, Swift, Gay, and Arbuthnot.

[2] For the 'Court of Censorial Enquiry' originally appearing in this number, see below, Appendix I.

[3] *Epistles*, II. ii. 141–2: 'In truth, it is profitable to cast aside toys and to learn wisdom' (Loeb).

[4] A close paraphrase of the opening passage of Montaigne's essay 'Of Idleness'; after the image of the uncultivated field, Montaigne continues, 'even so it is with Wits, which if not applied to some certain Study that may fix and restrain them, run into a thousand Extravagancies, and are eternally roving here and there in the inextricable Labyrinth of restless Imagination' (*Essays*, trans. Charles Cotton, 6th edn. [3 vols., 1743], i, 40). Fielding owned this edition of Cotton's translation of Montaigne (Baker, item 510).

Stones as to be always satisfied with Idleness, or to come up to that Description in Lucretius:

> *Mortua cui vita est prope jam vivo, atque videnti*
> *Qui somno partem majorem conterit Ævi*
> *Et vigilans stertit.*[1]

St. Paul describes these Men better when, writing to the Thessalonians, he says some of them are μηδὲν ἐργαζόμενοι ἀλλὰ περιεργαζόμενοι. *Doing no Work, but busying themselves in Impertinence.*[2] Or as the Latin Author expresses the same Sentiment; *Gratis anhelans multa agendo nihil agens. Puffing and sweating to no Purpose; employed about many Things, and doing nothing.*[3]

The Original of Diversions is certainly owing to this active Temper: For to what Purpose were they calculated, but, as the very Word in our Language implies, to cast off Idleness![4] than which, to the Generality of Mankind, there is not I believe a much heavier Burthen.

But if we look a little deeper into this Matter, we shall find that there is implanted in our Nature a great Love of Business, and an equal Abhorrence of Idleness. This discovers itself very early in Children; most of whom, as I have observed, are never better pleased than when they are employed by their Elders.

The same Disposition we may perceive in Men; in those particularly to whom Fortune hath made Business unnecessary, and whom Nature very plainly appears never to have designed for any. And yet how common is it to see these Men playing at Business, if I may use the Expression, and pleasing themselves all their Lives with the Imagination that they are not idle!

From this busy Temper may be derived almost all the Works with which great Men have obliged the World. Hence it was that the great Artifex Nero arrived at so great Skill, as he himself tells us he did, in Music; to which he applied with such unwearied Industry on the Stage, that several Persons counterfeited Death, in order to be carried out of the Theatre from hearing him: for it would have been very unsafe for the *Town* of Rome to damn his Performances.[5]

---

[1] *De rerum natura*, iii. 1046–8: 'You whose life is now all but dead though you live and see, you who waste the greater part of your time in sleep, who snore open-eyed' (Loeb); Fielding's *conterit* and *stertit* should be *conteris* and *stertis*.

[2] 2 Thessalonians 3: 11: 'For we hear that there are some which walk among you disorderly, working not at all, but are busybodies'; Fielding quotes in Greek only the second half of the line.

[3] Phaedrus, *Fabulae Aesopiae*, V. iii.

[4] Fielding refers to the literal meaning of diversion as a 'turning aside' from a proper course or direction. With this passage cf. *An Enquiry into the Causes of the late Increase of Robbers* (1751), where Fielding cites Plato and Seneca as authorities for the fact that 'a necessary Relaxation from Labour was the only End for which Diversion was invented and allowed to the People' (sect. I, p. 9).

[5] Suetonius, *Nero*, xxiii, speaks of those who, because the gates to the theatre were closed, 'feigned death and were carried out as if for burial' (Loeb); on Nero's singing, cf. Tacitus, *Annals*, XIV. xv; Juvenal, *Satires*, viii. 220; Dio Cassius, *Roman History*, LXI. xx.

If Domitian had not been of a busy as well as a cruel Temper, he would never have employed so many Hours in the ingenious Employment of Fly-spitting, which he is supposed to have brought to the highest Degree of Perfection of which that Art is capable.[1] Hence it is so many industrious Critics have spent their Lives *in all such Reading as was never read*, as Mr. Pope hath it;[2] witness the laborious, and all-read Dr. Zachary Grey,[3] who to compile those wonderful Notes to his Hudibras, must have ransacked not only all the Stalls, but all the Trunks and Bandboxes in the World.[4]

Didymus the Grammarian was another Labourer of this Kind. Seneca tells us, "that he writ 4000 Books; in some of which he enquires into the Country of Homer; in others, who was the true Mother of Æneas; whether Anacreon loved wenching or drinking most; whether Sappho was a common Prostitute;"[5] with other such Learning, with which, if you had already stuffed your Head, your Study ought to be how to get it out again.

Tiberius, wise as he was in Policy, had a great Inclination to this Kind of Knowledge. He pursued it, says Suetonius, "usque ad ineptias et derisum, &c. *to a Degree of Folly and Ridicule*: For he used to ask the Grammarians, of whose Company he was very fond, such Kind of Questions as these. Who was the Mother of Hecuba? By what Name Achilles past among the Daughters of Lycomedes? What Songs the Syrens used to sing? &c."[6]

[1] Cf. Suetonius, *Domitian*, iii: 'he used to spend hours in seclusion every day, doing nothing but catch flies and stab them with a keenly sharpened stylus. Consequently when someone once asked whether anyone was in there with Caesar, Vibius Crispus made the witty reply, "Not even a fly"' (Loeb). See Dio Cassius, *Roman History*, LXV. ix, who speaks of the practice as not worthy of the dignity of history. Cf. also Robert South in a sermon of 1699: 'some Men, having compassed the greatest and noblest Objects of their Desires, . . . have betook themselves to inferior and ignoble Exercises; so that amongst the Roman emperors, . . . we find *Nero* at his *Harp*, *Domitian* killing flies, and *Commodus* playing the Fencer; and all this only to busy themselves some way or other; Nothing being so grievous and tedious to Humane Nature as perfect Idleness' (*Sermons*, 5th edn. [1722], iv. 508).

[2] *Dunciad*, iv. 249–50: 'For thee we dim the eyes, and stuff the head / With all such reading as was never read.' The entire passage is appropriate to Fielding's theme, for the lines come from the address which Aristarchus (Richard Bentley) makes to Dullness and which demonstrates that false learning may contain more true Dullness than folly itself; Pope also includes in these lines indirect praise of Isaac Barrow, whom Fielding cites at the end of this essay as 'truly learned'.

[3] Cf. Fielding's Preface to *Journal of a Voyage to Lisbon* (1755): 'if we should carry on the analogy between the traveller and the commentator, it is impossible to keep one's eye a moment off from the laborious much-read Doctor Zachary Gray, of whose redundant notes on *Hudibras* I shall only say that it is, I am confident, the single book extant in which about five hundred authors are quoted, not one of which could be found in the collection of the late Doctor Mead'. Grey (1688–1766) published his elaborate edition of *Hudibras* in 1744; the work was in Fielding's library (Baker, item 45), and he would also have been familiar with William Warburton's scornful remark in the Preface to his *Shakespeare* (1747): 'I hardly think there ever appeared, in any *learned* Language, so execrable a heap of nonsense under the name of Commentaries, as hath been lately given us on a certain satiric Poet, of the last Age, by his Editor and Coadjutor.'

[4] i.e. not only the bookstalls but all the receptacles of waste paper; see *CGJ* No. 6.

[5] *Epistulae morales*, LXXXVIII. xxxvii; Fielding conflates a few lines at the beginning of his translation. Didymus Chalcenterus (c.63 BC–AD 10), Greek grammarian, is cited by Seneca as an example of intemperance in learning; cf. Swift, *Gulliver's Travels*, III. viii.

[6] Suetonius, *Tiberius*, lxx.

Cardinal Chigi, who was afterwards Pope Alexander the Seventh, was a Genius of this Kind. He proclaimed a public Prize for that learned Man who could find a Latin Word for the Word *Chaize*. He likewise spent seven or eight Days in searching whether Musca, a *Fly*, came from Mosco or Mosco from Musca. De Retz, from whose Memoirs I have taken this Story, says that he had formerly discovered that the Cardinal was *Homme de Minutiis*; for that the said Cardinal, in a Discourse on the Studies of his Youth, had told De Retz that he had writ two Years with the same Pen.[1]

I cannot omit the excellent Remark of my Author, tho' not to my present Purpose. "It is true," says he, "this is but a Trifle; but I have often observed, that little Things afford us truer Symptoms of the Dispositions of Men, than great ones."[2]

What but the utmost Impatience of Idleness, could prompt Men to employ great Pains and Trouble, and Expence too, in making large Collections of Butterflies, Pebbles, and such other wonderful Productions; while others from the same Impatience have been no less busy in hunting after Monsters of every Kind, as if they were at Enmity with Nature, and desirous of exposing all her Errors.[3]

The Greeks have a Word for this Industry. They call it $K\epsilon\nu o\sigma\pi o\nu\delta\acute{\iota}\alpha$; and oftner $\Pi o\lambda\nu\pi\rho\alpha\gamma\mu o\sigma\acute{\nu}\nu\eta$.[4] Neither of which Words I can translate without a Periphrasis. By both is meant a vain Curiosity and Diligence in Trifles.

I make no Doubt but that the same Industry would often make a Man of a moderate Capacity a very competent Master of some notable Science, which hath made him a Proficient in some contemptible Art or rather Knack. The dextrous Juggler might have made a complete Mechanic. The same Labour, and perhaps the same Genius, which brings a Man to a Perfection at the Game of Chess, would make a great Proficiency in the Mathematics.[5] Many

---

[1] *Mémoires du Cardinal de Retz* (Amsterdam, 1719), iii. 374–5, 416; on De Retz, see *CGJ* No. 17, above, p. 119 and n. 2. Fabio Chigi (1599–1667) was in fact already Pope at the time of the 'bagatelles' described by De Retz; the word for which he sought a Latin equivalent was *chaise roulante*, and the phrase De Retz applies to him is, despite Fielding's spelling, *homme de minuties*, 'man of trifles'. On the episode of the pen, cf. Chesterfield's letter to his son of 10 Aug. 1749, which cites De Retz in warning against a 'frivolous curiosity about trifles'.

[2] *Mémoires*, iii. 375.

[3] Fielding hits here at the Royal Society and the 'virtuosi' of the age; on his consistently satirical attitude toward such enterprises, see Miller, *Essays*, pp. 326–36. Among many examples, cf. *Tom Jones*, XIII. v; *Journey from this World to the Next*, I. vii; and *CGJ* No. 70, below. Cf. also *Tatler*, No. 236 (12 Oct. 1710), and Pope's indictment in the *Dunciad* (iv. 437–59) of those who 'See Nature in some partial shape' and have learned 'but to trifle', a section which Pope places immediately after one on the 'Pains and Penalties of Idleness'.

[4] i.e. 'zealous pursuit of frivolities' and 'curiosity, officiousness, meddlesomeness'.

[5] Cf. Addison in *Spectator*, No. 160 (3 Sept. 1711): 'It is odd to consider what great Genius's are sometimes thrown away upon Trifles'; Addison goes on to cite the instance of a proficient egg-tosser, whose 'Assiduity and Attention had they been rightly applied, might have made him a greater Mathematician than *Archimedes*'. Cf. also *Rambler*, No. 83 (1 Jan. 1751), in which Johnson takes a more favorable view of the virtuoso whose 'efforts of ingenuity have been exerted in trifles'.

a Beau might have been a Scholar, if he had consulted Books with the same Attention, with which he hath consulted a Looking-Glass; and many a Foxhunter might to his great Honour have pursued the Enemies of his Country with less Labour and with less Danger than he hath encountred in the Pursuit of Foxes.

I am almost inclined to think, that if a complete History could be compiled of the eminent Works of the Κενόσπουδοι, *the Triflers*, it would manifestly appear, that more Labour and Pains, more Time (I had almost said more Genius) have been employed in the Service of Folly, than have been employed by the greatest Men in inventing and perfecting the most erudite and consummate Works of Art or Wisdom.

I will conclude this Paper with a Passage from the excellent and truly learned Dr. Barrow, which gives a very serious, but very just Turn to this Subject.[1]

"*Aliud agere*, to be impertinently busy, doing that which conduceth to no good Purpose, is in some respect worse than to do nothing, or to forbear all Action: For it is a positive Abuse of our Faculties, and trifling with God's Gifts; 'tis a throwing away Labour and Care, things valuable in themselves; 'tis often a running out of the Way, which is worse than standing still; 'tis a debasing our Reason, and declining from our Manhood; nothing being more foolish or childish, than to be solicitous and serious about Trifles: For who are more busy and active than Children? Who are fuller of Thoughts and Designs, or more eager in Prosecution of them, than they? But all is about ridiculous Toys, the Shadows of Business, suggested to them by apish Curiosity and Imitation. Of such Industry we may understand that of the Preacher, *The Labour of the Foolish wearieth every one of them*;[2] for that a Man soon will be weary of that Labour which yieldeth no Profit or beneficial Return."   C.

Proceedings at the Court of Censorial Enquiry, *&c.*

The Censor was pleased to deliver himself as follows.

"I have perused a Book called, THE FEMALE QUIXOTE, or THE ADVENTURES OF ARABELLA;[3] and I shall give my Opinion of it with no less Sincerity than Candour.

---

[1] On Fielding's 'favorite' divine, Isaac Barrow, see *CGJ* No. 4, above, p. 34, n. 5. The passage which follows is quoted from his sermon 'Of Industry in our general Calling, as Christians' (Sermon XX, *Works*, 5th edn. [1741], iii. 171); Fielding owned this edition of Barrow's *Works* (Baker, item 452).

[2] Ecclesiastes 10: 15.

[3] *The Female Quixote* by Charlotte Lennox (1720–1804) was published on 13 Mar. 1752 by Andrew Millar, having been advertised in *CGJ* Nos. 18, 20, 22, and this current number, 24. As well as puffing another of Millar's books, the review which follows gives Fielding the opportunity to express both his admiration for and misgivings about the great masterpiece he had imitated in *Don Quixote in England* (1734) and, especially, in *Joseph Andrews* (1742). Cf. his comment in *Journal of a Voyage to Lisbon*

"This is an Imitation of the famous Romance of Cervantes called *The Life and Actions of that ingenious Gentleman Don Quixote of the Mancha*, &c. A Work originally written in Spanish, and which hath been translated into most of the Languages, and admired in most of the Countries in Europe.

"I will here very frankly declare my Opinion in what Particulars the Imitation falls short; in what it equals, and in what it excels its illustrious Original.

"In the first Place, Cervantes hath the Advantage of being the Original; and consequently is intitled to that Honour of Invention, which can never be attributed to any Copy however excellent. An Advantage which Homer will always claim, and which is perhaps the only one that he can claim, over Virgil and Milton.

"In the next Place Cervantes is to be considered as an Author who intended not only the Diversion, but the Instruction and Reformation of his Countrymen: With this Intention he levelled his Ridicule at a vicious Folly, which in his Time universally prevailed in Spain, and had almost converted a civilized People into a Nation of Cutthroats.

"In this Design he imitated the three glorious Poets I have mentioned. The first of whom placed the particular Good of Greece, the second the Honour of Rome, and the third the great Cause of Christianity before their Eyes, when they planned their several Poems. And the Success of none of them was perhaps equal to that of Cervantes.

"Here again the Spanish Romance hath the Advantage of the English.

"Thirdly, the Character of Don Quixote himself, as well as that of Sancho Pancha, are superior to those of Arabella and her Maid.

"Fourthly, some of the Incidents in the Original are more exquisitely ridiculous, than any which we find in the Copy. And these I think, are all the Particulars in which an impartial Critic can give the Preference to the Spaniard. And as to the two last, I cannot help observing, they may possibly be rather owing to that Advantage, which the Actions of Men give to the Writer beyond those of Women, than to any Superiority of Genius. Don Quixote is ridiculous in performing Feats of Absurdity himself; Arabella can

(1755) that a discourse on travelling 'in the style of Don Quixote' seems 'a task reserved for my pen alone' (27 June) and his listing of Cervantes in his triumvirate of wits, *CGJ* No. 10, above.

Mrs Lennox was much befriended by Richardson and by Johnson, the latter of whom wrote the Dedication of the *Female Quixote* and most of one of the chapters (IX. xi). Fielding owned her earlier novel *The Life of Harriot Stuart* as well as the *Female Quixote* (Baker, items 385, 562). In the 'Author's Introduction' to his *Journal of a Voyage to Lisbon* he calls her 'the inimitable and shamefully distressed author of the *Female Quixote*' and credits her with reminding him of the virtues of Bishop Berkeley's treatise on tar-water. Fielding's review here excited attention; see the *Monthly Review*, 6 (Jan.–June 1752), 262 and *LEP*, 2 Apr. 1752, which reprinted it without attribution as an unsigned letter to the editor, perhaps inserted by Millar with Fielding's consent. Johnson, in reviewing Lennox's novel in *GM*, pointed to the fact that 'Mr. Fielding, however emulous of Cervantes, and jealous of a rival' had praised her work as superior in many respects to its original, 'though he has no connection with the author' (*GM* 22 [1752], 146).

only become so, in provoking and admiring the Absurdities of others. In the former Case, the Ridicule hath all the Force of a Representation; it is in a Manner subjected to the Eyes; in the latter it is conveyed, as it were, through our Ears, and partakes of the Coldness of History or Narration.

"I come now to speak of those Parts in which the two Authors appear to me upon an Equality. So they seem to be in that Care which both have taken to preserve the Affection of their Readers for their principal Characters, in the midst of all the Follies of which they are guilty. Both Characters are accordingly represented as Persons of good Sense, and of great natural Parts, and in all Cases, except one, of a very sound Judgement, and what is much more endearing, as Persons of great Innocence, Integrity and Honour, and of the highest Benevolence. Again the Fidelity and Simplicity of Sancho Pancha, are well matched by these Qualities in Arabella's Handmaid. Tho' as I have before observed, I do not think the Character of Sancho is here equalled. It is perhaps a Masterpiece in Humour of which we never have, nor ever shall see the like.

"There are probably more Instances under this Head, which I shall leave to the discerning Reader. I will proceed in the last Place to those Particulars, in which, I think, our Countrywoman hath excelled the Spanish Writer.

"And this I am not afraid to declare, she hath done in my Opinion, in all the following Particulars.

"First, as we are to grant in both Performances, that the Head of a very sensible Person is entirely subverted by reading Romances, this Concession seems to me more easy to be granted in the Case of a young Lady than of an old Gentleman. Nor can I help observing with what perfect Judgment and Art this Subversion of Brain in Arabella is accounted for by her peculiar Circumstances, and Education. To say Truth, I make no Doubt but that most young Women of the same Vivacity, and of the same innocent good Disposition, in the same Situation, and with the same Studies, would be able to make a large Progress in the same Follies.

"Secondly, the Character of Arabella is more endearing than that of Quixote. This will undoubtedly be the Case between a beautiful young Lady and an old Fellow, where equal Virtues in both become Candidates for our Favour.

"Thirdly, the Situation of Arabella is more interesting. Our Hearts are engaged very early in good Wishes for the Success of Mr. Glanville;[1] a Character entirely well drawn, as are indeed many others; for in this Particular, the English Author hath doubtless the Preference.

"Fourthly, here is a regular Story, which, tho' possibly it is not pursued with that Epic Regularity which would give it the Name of an Action, comes

---

[1] Arabella's cousin and lover, whom she eventually marries.

much nearer to that Perfection than the loose unconnected Adventures in Don Quixote; of which you may transverse the Order as you please, without any Injury to the whole.

"Fifthly, the Incidents, or, if you please, the Adventures, are much less extravagant and incredible in the English than in the Spanish Performance. The latter, in many Instances, approaches very near to the Romances which he ridicules. Such are the Stories of Cardenio and Dorothea, Ferdinand and Lucinda, &c.[1] In the former, there is nothing except the Absurdities of the Heroine herself, which is carried beyond Common-Life; nor is there any Thing even in her Character, which the Brain a little distempered may not account for. She conceives indeed somewhat preposterously of the Ranks and Conditions of Men; that is to say, mistakes one Man for another; but never advances towards the Absurdity of imagining Windmills and Wine-Bags to be human Creatures, or Flocks of Sheep to be Armies.[2]

"I might add more on this Subject, but I will pursue it no further; having already, I apprehend, given a larger Dose to Malice, Envy, and Ignorance, than they will care to swallow; but I cannot omit observing, that tho' the Humour of Romance, which is principally ridiculed in this Work, be not at present greatly in fashion in this Kingdom, our Author hath taken such Care throughout her Work, to expose all those Vices and Follies in her Sex which are chiefly predominant in our Days, that it will afford very useful Lessons to all those young Ladies who will peruse it with proper Attention.

"Upon the whole, I do very earnestly recommend it, as a most extraordinary and most excellent Performance. It is indeed a Work of true Humour, and cannot fail of giving a rational, as well as very pleasing, Amusement to a sensible Reader, who will at once be instructed and very highly diverted. Some Faults perhaps there may be, but I shall leave the unpleasing Task of pointing them out to those who will have more Pleasure in the Office. This Caution, however, I think proper to premise, that no Persons presume to find many: For if they do, I promise them, the Critic and not the Author *will be to blame.*"

SATURDAY, MARCH 28, 1752. NUMB. 25.

——*Video meliora, proboque*
Deteriora sequor. VIRGIL.[3]

I see and approve the Road to the Right;
Yet follow the left, with all my might.

---

[1] *Don Quixote*, Pt. I, chs. 27, 36.
[2] Alluding to *Don Quixote*, Pt. I, chs. 8, 18, 35.
[3] Ovid, *Metamorphoses*, vii. 20–1; Fielding incorrectly cites Virgil. Quoted also in *Amelia*, VIII. x.

Tho' I know not well what to make of the following Letter,[1] I shall however give it to the Reader, who may perhaps see farther into it than I am able; especially as it hath had the Approbation of a Friend of mine, of whose Judgment I have the highest Opinion.

Mr. *Censor,*

As I am a great Lover of Fruit, I never go to a Friend's House in the Country without paying an immediate Visit to his Kitchin Garden. To say Truth, there is nothing in the most elegant Beauties of Chiswick, or Stow,[2] which gives me equal Delight with seeing Walls well lined with Peaches, Nectarines, Cherries, Plumbs, and such like; or Rows of fine Standards[3] bowing to the Ground with the Weight of their Burden.

From this Humour of mine, I felt a very sensible Mortification the last Summer, at a Visit which I made to a Gentleman about twenty Miles from Town, whose Garden is one of the most delicious I ever saw. Here are no Evergreens, nor Forest-Trees; no Ground wasted in Walks, Lawns, Mounts, and such like. No, Sir, in this Garden which consists of about two Acres of Land, is the choicest Collection of Fruits, that is perhaps to be found in the Spot of the same Bigness in Europe; and particularly of Cherries, a Fruit of which I am above measure fond.

Guess then, Mr. Censor, what was my Concern, when upon my walking in

---

[1] Despite the pretence, the letter is by Fielding himself. It represents in parable form his protest against what he regarded as the inadequate provisions for the executions of felons in the so-called 'Murder Act' (25 Geo. II, c. 37, 'An Act for better preventing the horrid Crime of Murder'), which had received the Royal Assent on 26 Mar. 1752, just two days before this essay appeared. In the final section of his *Enquiry into the Causes of the late Increase of Robbers* (1751), Fielding had argued that if executions are to act as a deterrent they must (1) occur 'as soon as possible after the Commission and Conviction of the Crime', while the memory of the crime is still fresh in the public's mind, and (2) 'be in some degree private', so as to become 'much more shocking and terrible to the Crowd without Doors' than is the present 'Holiday at *Tyburn*' (pp. 123–6). Although the new Act provided for speedier executions and for the dissection or hanging in chains of the murderer's body, it contained no provision for private executions. On Fielding's relation to the recent laws for preventing murders and thefts, laws which his early biographers mistakenly credited him with helping to draft, see Hugh Amory, 'Henry Fielding and the Criminal Legislation of 1751–2', *PQ* 50 (1971), 175–92. In the present essay Fielding, depicting himself as 'a jesting Kind of a Gentleman', repeats some of the ideas of the *Enquiry* while reflecting on the difficulty of improving criminal law in the face of custom and the need to satisfy a variety of political interests; for his direct editorializing on the same subject, see the important 'Covent Garden' columns of 27 Mar. (originally in this number of *CGJ*) and 18 July, printed below, Appendix I.

[2] The villa at Chiswick of Richard Boyle, 3rd Earl of Burlington and 4th Earl of Cork (1695–1753), was modelled on the designs of Palladio, which Burlington published in 1730; see Pope's *Epistle IV: To Richard Boyle, Earl of Burlington* (1731). Stowe, Buckinghamshire, the estate and gardens of Sir Richard Temple, Viscount Cobham (1675–1749), was the most famous of the 18th-cent. country estates, with elaborate gardens, temples, and monumental buildings. In *Epistle IV* Pope praises both Stowe and Chiswick for their 'Spontaneous beauties', i.e. for their blending of landscape with garden. Cf. *Tom Jones*, XI. ix.

[3] Trees or shrubs 'growing on an erect stem of full height, not dwarfed or trained on a wall or espalier' (*OED*).

this Garden, I perceived on all the Trees as well Wall Trees,[1] as Standards, the Shocks of a Devastation scarce credible. Insomuch, that from a hundred of the finest Cherry-Trees in the World, I believe it was scarce possible to fill a single Bushel with that Fruit, tho' all the Children in London might have loaded themselves with Cherry-stones, to their Heart's Content.

The Master of the Place, who was then with me, perceiving my Vexation prevented my expressing it, by saying, "You see, Sir, what a dreadful Havock the Birds have made in my Garden." "I do indeed, Sir," answered I, "and am no less surprised than vexed at the Sight." "I have endeavoured all I can to prevent it," replied he. "You must perceive that I have hung up the Carcasses of several of them in Terrorem,[2] and you see that Clacker[3] there upon the Top of the Wall, which the Wind turns round all Day long." "It is visible enough," says I, "Sir; and so are four or five Blackbirds, the wickedest of all Felons, which are playing just by it, as if they enjoyed the Noise and treated it with Derision."

"It is very true," replied my Friend, "I am apt to believe they are not frightened in the least by all this: For I think they plunder my Garden every Year more and more; but still my Gardeners go on in their old Way, they now and then indeed shoot one or two; but in Fact, I believe they love *singing Birds*,[4] and are unwilling to destroy the Breed. Some Time ago a Gentleman was here, who is as fond of Fruit as yourself, and equally lamented the Depredations of the Birds. This Gentleman," continued my Friend, "acquainted us, with the Methods which he had taken in his own Gardens with Success. First he had observed, he said, that the destroying a single Bird now and then, was only throwing away Powder and Shot, and produced no Manner of Terror among the rest.[5] He therefore had ordered the Magistrates of his Garden (so he called his Gardeners, for he is a comical Man) to be very diligent and attentive for a Month together, so as not to let a single Thief escape.[6] This he said produced the desired Effect, and the Thieves in a great Measure forsook the Place. 'Again,' said he, 'as I had

---

[1] Fruit trees planted against and trained upon a wall (*OED*).

[2] i.e. as a warning, to terrify or deter others (*OED*).

[3] A rattle worked by the wind, to scare birds away.

[4] Songsters, 'usually applied to cage-birds' (*OED*). Throughout the parable Fielding may be playing on the sense of 'Bird' as 'Gaol-Bird'; cf. the phrase 'Birds of a Feather' to mean 'Rogues of the same Gang' (*A New Canting Dictionary*, 1725).

[5] Cf. *Enquiry* (1751): 'If therefore the Terror of this Example is removed (as it certainly is by frequent Pardons) the Design of the Law is rendered totally ineffectual; The Lives of the Persons executed are thrown away, and sacrificed rather to the Vengeance than to the Good of the Public, which receives no other Advantage than by getting rid of a Thief, whose Place will immediately be supplied by another' (p. 120).

[6] Cf. the 'Author's Introduction' to *Journal of a Voyage to Lisbon* (1755), where Fielding describes how, at the invitation of the Duke of Newcastle, he undertook in the autumn of 1753 just such a concentrated effort 'to demolish the then reigning gangs', executing the plan 'with such success that this hellish society were almost utterly extirpated'.

observed, that the Clacker which I had exposed publicly, availed but little, I contrived a Piece of Mechanism which should operate by Means of Clockwork. This I conveyed into the Middle of a thick Ivy Bush, where being wound up at certain Times, it discharged a dreadful Report, which was heard all over the Garden; and spread a Terror among all the feathered Felons beyond Conception, which I am convinced was much encreased by its not being seen.' This Hint the Gentleman said, he had first taken from observing the very slight Impression which was made on the Minds of Men by the public Execution of Felons, and from imagining to himself the much greater Horrors which would be inspired by the Report of their being put to death in the Presence only of the Officers of Justice."[1]

So far, Mr. Censor, my Friend related from this unknown Gentleman, and added, that he had acquainted his Gardeners with this Advice, who seemed to give very little Attention to it. That one of them answered with a Kind of Indignation, "What, Master, do you think we are to be taught our Trade by every Fool! I have been a Gardener these forty Years, and my Father was of the same Business forty Years before; and I never saw, nor ever heard of any such Thing to be done. Besides the Gentleman is a jesting Kind of a Gentleman, and to be sure knows nothing of the Matter. A likely Business truly, that if the Birds are not frightened by seeing the Clacker before their Eyes, they would be frightened by only hearing it. But the Gentleman is only in Jest, as appears by what he says about hanging Men in a public Manner. Why are Men hanged, but in order to frighten other Folks? And how can that be, if Folks can't see them hanged. It is true this will not do always; for I remember Mr. Johnson that used to work with me, was a dear Lover of going to see a Hanging-Bout; and he was hanged himself last Year for the Highway; but that argues nothing, for so he might have been, if he had never seen the Gallows before. And then as for killing all the singing Birds——to be sure it would be Matter of great Cruelty, and I would not do it for all the Fruit in the World.[2] Six or seven now and then, there is no great Matter in killing; but I would not quite destroy the Breed neither."

[1] Cf. *Enquiry* (1751), where Fielding, characteristically calling on evidence from poets and dramatists, asserts that 'The Mind of Man is so much more capable of magnifying than his Eye, that I question whether every Object is not lessened by being looked upon'. He then proposes that felons be executed at the Old Bailey as soon as sentence is pronounced, 'in the Sight and Presence of the Judges' instead of in public (pp. 123–5).

[2] Cf. Fielding's warning in the *Enquiry* (sect. VII, pp. 107–8) against giving way to our natural benevolence and compassion, which 'very often betrays Men into Errors not only hurtful to themselves, but highly prejudicial to the Society. Hence ... notorious Robbers have lived to perpetrate future Acts of Violence, through the ill-judging Tenderness and Compassion of those who could and ought to have prosecuted them.' Cf. also Johnson's *Rambler*, No. 114 (20 Apr. 1751), which responds to Fielding's hard-headed proposals by protesting the variety of offences subject to 'sanguinary justice' and arguing for 'extirpating wickedness by lenity'; on the contrast between their attitudes, see Malvin R. Zirker, Jr., *Fielding's Social Pamphlets* (Berkeley and Los Angeles, 1966), pp. 137–8.

"Such," cries my Friend, "were the Arguments of my Gardener, which were perhaps as little satisfactory to me, as they will be to you. But what is to be done?" "To be done," answered I! "Why, will you not try the Experiment, since it appears so very reasonable? will you suffer your Garden to be spoiled, and all the Fruit carried away by these Vermin, which you plainly see your present Methods will never extirpate or terrify?" "I am afraid that must be the Case," answered my Friend, "nor will there be any Thing very extraordinary in it, if it should. How common is it in Life to suffer great Inconveniencies, as well in public as in private Affairs, by adhering with the Obstinacy of those Gardeners to Habits which have no *other Sanction* but that of Custom? How often do we continue to do certain Things for no other Reason but that ourselves and our Ancestors have been used so to do, when by pursuing a contrary Method, it is very visible we should avoid some experienced Evil, or attain some very apparent Good. But, indeed, my good Friend," said he, "they know but little of the World who conclude that Men will or can always embrace what they perceive to be good, tho' it should be ever so much within their Reach, and should cost them nothing to come at it. We do great Injury to the Masters of Families or of Kingdoms, if we conceive that they do not often approve and affect right Measures, when they are obliged to pursue the contrary. The various Humours, Tempers, and Interests which both are oblig'd to consult, if they will not be Tyrants, often divert their wisest Purposes. I will tell you a short Story which may illustrate my Meaning better than the largest Dissertation. I once knew a Gentleman, whose House consisted of two Rooms below Stairs. The one was very large and commodious, the other small and inconvenient. He was a very hospitable Person, an excellent Companion, and had frequently several Friends to dine at his House, whom he constantly entertained in his lesser Apartment, by which they were often put to much Inconvenience. His Humour surprized many of his Acquaintances, and myself among the rest, as it appeared so very singular and unreasonable. One Day upon a Hint received from me, in a very intimate Conversation, he assigned the Cause of his Conduct. 'I wonder not,' said he, 'that you express your Surprize on this Occasion; for certainly it must seem very strange, that any Man will suffer Uneasiness himself, or give it to his Friends when the Redress is so very easy. You are to know then, that the Furniture of my large Room is very rich and valuable; and you know likewise, that I have a favourite Wife, who hath two favourite Lap-Dogs that are never from her, and that, without Ceremony, perform all the Offices of Nature in her Sight. They are both extremely old, and she hath promised they shall have no Successors 'till their Deaths; therefore I am contented to lose the Benefit of the best Part of my House, rather than disoblige my Wife, or spoil my Furniture.' Here you see a whole Family suffering a Grievance for the sake of two worthless Puppies, from which I desire to draw, no other Conclusion than that I am not the only silly Fellow in the World."

From what he said, as well as from his Manner of speaking, and from the Confusion which he betray'd in his Countenance, I saw he was ashamed of his Conduct in suffering the Obstinacy of his Gardener to destroy his Fruit, and therefore immediately changed the Subject to something else. When I reflected on this Scene, I thought a Moral might be drawn from it, not unworthy the Notice of the Censor. It is therefore at your Service, and do with it as you please.

I am,

SIR, &c.

C.

TUESDAY, MARCH 31, 1752.   NUMB. 26.

> *Bacchum in remotis carmina rupibus*
> *Vidi docentem (credite, posteri)*
> *Nymphasque discentes, et aures*
> *Capripedum Satyrorum acutas.*
>
> HORACE.[1]

See the Translation at the End.

Whoever can contemplate any one of our capital dramatic Pieces, and attend to the several Excellencies which adorn it; the serious, the facetious, the pathetic, the terrible, and (what is above all) the sententious, the moral, and the rational.——Whoever (I say) can contemplate all these Beauties, and mark how wonderfully they conspire in some single Performance, will not be surprized that not above ONE SHAKESPEAR should arise in a Century, and that when he comes he comes like a Prodigy of the better Sort,[2] where Nature (according to the Phrase of a great Philosopher) may be said *to have outdone her usual Outdoings.*[3]

---

[1] *Odes*, II. xix. 1–4; Fielding's translation at the end of the essay is accurate, except for the omission of the phrase *credite, posteri*, which he translates as 'Let Posterity take my Word for it' in the motto to *CGJ* No. 17.

[2] i.e. a marvel rather than a monster.

[3] The 'great Philosopher' is the time-worn butt of Fielding's ridicule, Colley Cibber (see *CGJ* No. 15, above, p. 105 n. 2). In the preface to his *Provok'd Husband* (1728) Cibber had written of Mrs Oldfield's performance, ' 'Tis not enough to say she *Here Out-did* her usual *Out-doing*'. It was, in fact, too much to say, for the sentence soon became a stock topic of ridicule by Pope, Fielding, and other enemies of the playwright. In his *Apology* (1740) Cibber admits that this 'wild Expression' is a 'most vile Jingle', but he goes on to reflect with some glee on how useful it has been to 'flat Writers', and 'provident Wags' who 'have made themselves brisk upon this single Expression; wherever the Verb *Outdo*, could come in, the pleasant Accusative, *Outdoing*, was sure to follow it' (pp. 31–2). For Fielding's ridicule of the passage from the *Apology* and of other instances of Cibber's vile English, see *Champion*, 22, 29 Apr., 10, 17 May 1740.

Should my Readers ask me to what Purpose this Observation? I must answer, 'tis to prove what they would have owned perhaps without the Help of proving, viz. that *to write capital dramatic Pieces, is not a Gift vouchsafed by Providence to the Multitude.*

I may descend even lower. 'Tis no common Gift, no mean Accomplishment, to be able TO ACT *them* with an Accuracy suitable to their intrinsic Merit. So rare is it to find a Man endowed with the natural Eminencies of Mind and Body (for both must concur) to form a perfect Actor, that I suppose it will hardly be denied that where one is born fit to rival a *Garrick* or a *Quin*,[1] many hundreds are qualified for passable Justices, for grave Doctors in any one of the Faculties; not to say thousands for Captains, Foxhunters, Stage-Coachmen, &c.

As far then as this, I take for granted, I go on Hand in Hand with my Readers. They will readily agree with me, that with Respect to dramatic Pieces, few are formed for *Actors*, and fewer still for *Writers*; I mean for such Actors, and such Writers, as may be truly said to approach the Standard of Perfection.

But from henceforward I fear we shall dissent. Tho' few think themselves qualified for Writers or Actors, yet all think themselves qualified to be adequate HEARERS: This is a Matter in which they have seldom any Scruples.

Now for my own Part, if I might venture to oppose so formidable a Body as the Multitude, and that in a Case which immediately affects them; I think there are so very few capable of being those Hearers which they fancy themselves, that take a thousand of human Race that have none of them lost their Ears, and 'tis well if there be ten among them *who have really Ears to hear*.[2] That they have the outward and visible Organs, I freely admit; so too have other Animals.——Nay, some of them possess these natural Insignia in a much more noble and enlarged Form, than the mightiest and most august among Men can pretend to. Yet 'tis plain, this is not enough. Were we to recite Hamlet or Othello to these venerable Quadrupeds, I fear we should be sentenced to lose our Labour. In short, what I would assert is this, that Ears alone are no more sufficient to make a Hearer, than a Fiddle alone is sufficient to make a Fiddler.

What then (says one) is sufficient?——The Answer to this Question will

[1] On Garrick, see *CGJ* No. 3, above, p. 31 n. 1. James Quin (1693–1766), the leading actor before Garrick, is consistently praised by Fielding; see *CGJ* No. 62. See also 'To John Hayes, Esq.' and 'Essay on Conversation', both in *Miscellanies* (1743); *JJ* No. 10 (6 Feb. 1748); *Joseph Andrews*, III. x; *Champion*, 9 Sept. 1740; and *Journal of a Voyage to Lisbon*, 19 (14) and 22 July, where Fielding repeats some of the many anecdotes about Quin.

[2] In the repeated use of this phrase Fielding means the reader to recall the repetition in Matthew of 'He that hath ears to hear, let him hear' (11: 15; 13: 9, 43). Cf. Robert South's reference to 'the furious, whimsical, ungoverned Multitude, who have *Ears to hear*, without either *Heads or Hearts to understand*' (*Sermons*, 5th edn. [1722], vi. 44–5).

more easily explain itself; in other Words, we shall be better able to shew who are truly and properly Hearers, if we consider *who in every Audience have no Pretensions to this Character.*[1]

When Mr. Handel first exhibited his Allegro and Penseroso,[2] there were two ingenious Gentlemen who had bought a Book of the Words, and thought to divert themselves by reading it before the Performance began. *Zounds* (cried one of them) *what damn'd Stuff this is!——Damn'd Stuff indeed*, replied his Friend. *God so!* (replied the other, who then first cast his Eyes on the Title-Page) *the Words are Milton's.*

It happened some Years since, that a low Farce was to be acted for the first Time after *Ben Johnson's Alchymist.* Two Heroes in the Boxes, had come there with an Intent to amuse themselves in damning the Farce. As their Attention to the Play had been taken off by their own more sublime Conversation, together with that of the Ladies who dispense Oranges, they unluckily took the End of the Play for the Beginning of the Farce, and set to hissing with the Voice not of Serpents but of Geese. The House was amazed; nor were they less amazed themselves, not to hear their Musick kindly returned by their Brother-Heroes in the Pit. In short, the Riddle was not solved, 'till one who sat near them, informed them that the Play was not yet over, and of course the Farce not yet begun. This a little discomposed them, but they soon comforted themselves by observing *'twas but a musty Piece of old Johnson's, and so it did not much signify.*[3]

There are many more such Stories to be collected. I shall, however, not dwell on a few Individuals, but pass to a common Practice of whole Crouds together. Whoever hath attended our Theatres, and seen our best Plays acted, must have heard many an exquisite Speech of the sedater Kind, delivered most exactly by an accomplished Actor, pass off unregarded in a Kind of cold Silence; while the empty Vociferation of some wretched Performer, hath been soon after rewarded with a thundering Clap of Approbation. One would imagine in such Case, that the Audience looked on the Actor as a Kind of Rival to themselves, and that they were desirous to

---

[1] On the topic of audience behavior and for Fielding's other references to the problem, see *CGJ* No. 5, above, p. 45 n. 1.

[2] The first performance of the setting of Milton's poems by George Frederick Handel (1685–1759) was on 27 Feb. 1740, at Lincoln's Inn Fields, under the title *L'Allegro il Penserose ed il Moderato*, with *il Moderato* a third part, written by Charles Jennens. Though Handel's popularity had suffered some vicissitudes since his first arrival in England in 1710, Fielding seems to have admired his music and to have spoken of him warmly; see *Champion*, 10 June 1740; the poem 'Of True Greatness' in *Miscellanies* (1743); *True Patriot*, Nos. 1 and 14 (5 Nov. 1745, 4 Feb. 1746); *Tom Jones*, IV. ii, v; and *Amelia*, IV. ix. Cf. *CGJ* No. 62.

[3] As Robert G. Noyes points out (*Ben Jonson on the English Stage 1660–1776* [Cambridge, Mass., 1935], p. 129 n.), the farce referred to was probably *George Dandin*, an afterpiece 'never acted before' and based on Molière, which had its only performance at Drury Lane after the *Alchemist* on 25 Nov. 1747; Cross, the prompter, recorded the reaction: 'Farce damn'd: bef: ist Act over' (*London Stage*, Pt. 4, i. 17).

shew him they could be louder than he was; or rather, (to give the Thing a more benevolent Explanation) that they were ambitious to pay him in his own Way, and generously to reward him with what he seemed so to delight in.

The Conclusion is, that none of these have Ears to hear; that to be *a real Hearer*, there must be SENSE, JUDGMENT, WISDOM, DISCERNMENT, call it as you please; and that not only in *Writing*, and in *Acting*, but that in HEARING too,

> ——SAPERE *est principium et fons.*[1]

Another Circumstance which disqualifies Persons for *Hearers*, is *the Want of Attention*, or at least *the Want of proper Attention*. This Defect has no small Connection with our first Defect, *the Want of Judgment and Wisdom*, tho' sufficiently distinct to merit a separate Consideration.

I remember I was once present at a theatrical Entertainment of the graver Kind, which was very excellent. The Audience were giving it much the same Attention as is given to the reading of Depositions and Affidavits, when lo! an unfortunate Cat made her Appearance and ran across the Stage. Pit, Box, and Gallery, in an Instant sympathized; their Attention became fixed to the same admirable Point; a louder Laugh never arose among Homer's Gods;[2] nor did I ever remember the best Scenes in the Rehearsal[3] to produce half so much Delight. That there are Facts of like Kind which happen every Week at the Theatres, I appeal to the Experience of those who frequent them.

When any fine Set of Company make their Appearance in the Boxes, a Scene commonly passes away before they have taken their Places. Another Scene goes off while the Bows and Curt'seys are exchanging. Then begin the Comments upon Persons and Dresses,[4] which commonly last 'till the Play is at an End, and would last were it to begin and be acted over again, the Voice of the Actors having the same Effect upon these Talkers, as the Sound of human Voices hath upon Canary-Birds and Parrots.

There is one Species of Inattention which is something peculiar, and that is Inattention arising from the Performance itself; when a Person takes Occasion from some trivial Incident (a Phrase, a Gesture, an Accent, or the like) to enter into a heavy and prolix Dissertation; to the no small Grievance

---

[1] Horace, *Art of Poetry*, 309; the full line is *Scribendi recte sapere est et principium et fons*, 'Of good writing the source and fount is wisdom' (Loeb).

[2] See *Iliad*, i. 599, 'And laughter unquenchable arose among the blessed gods' (Loeb); cf. *Odyssey*, viii. 326, 243, and Plato's objections to the laughter of the Homeric gods, *Republic*, iii. 389A.

[3] *The Rehearsal* (1671), by George Villiers, 2nd Duke of Buckingham, and others, the burlesque of heroic plays from which Fielding took his pseudonym 'Drawcansir'.

[4] A common complaint about audience behavior; for an extreme example, cf. the account of Miss Giggle in Charles Macklin's *The Covent Garden Theatre, or Pasquin Turn'd Drawcansir* (1752): 'She frequently Sets the whole House in a Titter to the Confusion of the Actors, & the general disturbance of the Audience, by constantly exposing her Nudities to publick View' (ed. Jean Kern, Augustan Reprint Soc. No. 116 [Los Angeles, 1965], p. 37).

of his rational Neighbour, whom he compels by addressing him to feed upon Husks, while a Banquet is before him of the most exquisite Kind. A dull Digresser of this Sort is not unlike an old Woman at Church, turning to her Book for the Text as soon as the Preacher hath named it; where, if the Chapter happen to be mistaken, the Spectacles to be clouded, or the Leaf to be torn out, 'tis a Chance the Sermon is half over before she hath heard a single Syllable.

The Conclusion is like the former; that those *who cannot attend*, or at least *cannot attend properly, have not Ears to hear*, and that of course to be A REAL HEARER, there must not only be UNDERSTANDING, but just and adequate ATTENTION.

The *last* and *by far the most blameable Obstacle* to becoming a real Hearer, is *the Want of Candour and Humanity*; when the Sneer, the Grin, the Hoot, and the Horse-laugh, are kept in readiness, like Troops, to appear at a Moment's Warning, and raise ungenerous Triumphs on the most iniquitous Occasions.

There are a Race of Mortals in this Country, who go by the Name of *Bucks*.[1] On what Pretence they usurp the Name of that noble Animal, 'tis hard to say, there being both Beasts and Birds of very different Species, by whose Names they would be much more aptly characterized. Be this however as it will, *Bucks* they are called. There are also two Species of Laughter; one derived from a free and social Spirit, which thro' every Part of it is harmless and inoffensive; the other, founded on Insolence and Pride, and which is Gall and Bitterness from Beginning to End. 'Tis to this last Species of Laughter, that the Bucks are commonly prone. I have beheld a Herd of these, at the most serious Scenes of a fine Tragedy, laugh with such an insolent Loudness, that the Audience who were all Attention, have not been able to hear a Word.

And what hath been the Occasion?——A stupid Witticism of their own upon the Performance; such a Witticism, as a Merry-Andrew[2] of Reputation would have been ashamed of. These same Bucks have I seen stand the high Humour of Falstaff, with as much Insensibility, as if they had not been *Bucks*, but *Pigs of Lead*. Indeed, so great is their Dulness, so incorrigible their Insolence; so ready is their malevolent Grin to display itself on every Occasion; such Enemies are they to all that is decent, to all that is orderly, to all that is even elegant and truly polite; that if ever Knight-Errants were to arise again, I could wish they would arise, to extirpate this Race; to drive them from the Face of the Earth; to force them, after the Greek Phrase, ἐις κόρακας,[3] after the English, *to the Dogs*. That such as these are no *Hearers*, is

---

[1] See the letter from 'Tim. Buck' in *CGJ* No. 7, above, p. 52 and n. 4.

[2] Originally a mountebank's assistant; in later use, a clown (*OED*).

[3] Literally, 'to the ravens' or 'to the crows': used proverbially in the sense Fielding indicates or in the sense 'go to hell' by Aristophanes (*The Peace*, 117; *The Birds*, 28; *The Plutus*, 604).

past Dispute. They have not only no *Ears* to hear; but they have neither *Heads* to hear, nor *Hearts* to hear. Humanity and Candour are Strangers to their Breasts.

Let us mark the Audience, described by Horace, in the Motto to this Paper. *I saw* (says he) *Bacchus in the remote Rocks teaching Verses; I saw the Nymphs learning, and the Ears of the goat-footed Satyrs erect.* How different as to its Behaviour is this antique Audience from a modern one? For tho' the *British* Fair may be well said to equal the fairest Nymphs of Antiquity, and tho' our Beaus with their grotesque Visages most exactly resemble the Satyrs; yet 'tis to be feared our Ladies seldom attend (like the Nymphs) *so as to learn*; and that our Beaus seldom prick up their Ears, to listen (like the Satyrs) to any Thing, worth Attention.

The Conclusion of the whole is, *that to make a perfect Hearer there must be three Things concur; that is to say,* JUDGMENT, ATTENTION, and HUMANITY.

S.

SATURDAY, APRIL 4, 1752. NUMB. 27.

——*Pudet hæc opprobria nobis,*
Et dici potuisse, et non potuisse refelli.

OVID.[1]

'Tis true 'tis Pity, and Pity 'tis, 'tis true.[2]

Of all the Oppressions which the Rich are guilty of, there seems to be none more impudent and unjust than their Endeavour to rob the Poor of a Title, which is most clearly the Property of the latter. Not contented with all the Honorables, Worshipfuls, Reverends, and a thousand other proud Epithets which they exact of the Poor, and for which they give in Return nothing but Dirt, Scrub,[3] Mob, and such like, they have laid violent Hands on a Word, to which they have not the least Pretence or Shadow of any Title.[4]

The Word I mean is the Comparative of the Adjective Good, namely BETTER, or as it is usually expressed in the Plural Number BETTERS. An Appellative which all the Rich usurp to themselves, and most shamefully use

[1] *Metamorphoses*, i. 758–9: 'Ashamed am I that such an insult could have been uttered and yet could not be answered' (Loeb).

[2] *Hamlet*, II. ii. 97–8.

[3] 'A mean insignificant fellow' (*OED*).

[4] Fielding's tone and attitude toward the poor are very different in this paragraph from the conservative language he ordinarily uses in his serious social pamphlets; see Malvin R. Zirker, *Fielding's Social Pamphlets* (Berkeley and Los Angeles, 1966), pp. 70–1. As Zirker points out, however, Fielding's emphasis in this essay 'is not on the slighted virtues of the poor but on the unpunished follies of the rich'. On his respect for traditional notions of class distinctions, on which the irony of the essay depends, see Miller, *Essays*, pp. 96–101, 188–9.

when they speak of, or to the Poor: For do we not every Day hear such Phrases as these. *Do not be saucy to your* BETTERS. *Learn to behave yourself before your* BETTERS. *Pray know your* BETTERS, &c.

It is possible that *the Rich* have been so long in Possession of this, that they may now lay a Kind of prescriptive Claim[1] to the Property; but however that be, I doubt not but to make it appear, that if the Word Better is to be understood as the Comparative of *Good*, and is meant to convey an Idea of superior Goodness, it is with the highest Impropriety applied to the Rich, in Comparison with the Poor.

And this I the rather undertake, as the Usurpation which I would obviate, hath produced a very great Mischief in Society; for the Poor having been deceived into an Opinion (for monstrous as it is, such an Opinion hath prevailed) that the Rich are their Betters, have been taught to honour, and of Consequence to imitate the Examples of those, whom they ought to have despised;[2] while the Rich on the contrary are misled into a false Contempt of what they ought to respect, and by this Means lose all the Advantage which they might draw from contemplating *the exemplary Lives* of these their *real Betters*.

First then let us imagine to ourselves, a Person wallowing in Wealth, and lolling in his Chariot, his Mind torn with Ambition, Avarice, Envy, and every other bad Passion, and his Brain distracted with Schemes to deceive and supplant some other Man, to cheat his Neighbour or perhaps the Public, what a glorious Use might such a Person derive to himself, as he is rolled through the Outskirts of the Town by due Meditations, on the Lives of those who dwell in Stalls and Cellars! What a noble Lesson of true Christian Patience and Contentment may such a Person learn from his Betters, who enjoy the highest Cheerfulness in their poor Condition; their Minds being disturbed by no unruly Passion, nor their Heads by any racking Cares!

Where again shall we look for an Example of Temperance? In the stinking Kitchins of the Rich, or under the humble Roofs of the Poor? Where for Prudence but among those who have the fewest Desires? Where for Fortitude, but among those who have every natural Evil to struggle with?

In Modesty, I think, there will be little Difficulty in knowing where we are to find our Betters: For to this Virtue there can be nothing more diametrically opposite than Pride. Whenever therefore we observe Persons stretching up their Heads and looking with an Air of Contempt on all around them, we may be well assured there is no Modesty there. Indeed I never yet

---

[1] A claim based on uninterrupted use from time immemorial, or for a period fixed by law as given in title or right (*OED*).

[2] Cf. Fielding's *Enquiry into the Causes of the late Increase of Robbers* (1751), esp. sect. I, where he addresses the 'many political Mischiefs' produced by the lower classes' imitation of the vices of the rich.

heard it enumerated among all the bad Qualities of an Oyster-woman or a Cinder-Wench,[1] that *she had a great deal of Pride*, and consequently there is at least a Possibility that such may have a great Deal of Modesty, whereas it is absolutely impossible that those to whom much Pride belongs, should have any Tincture of its opposite Virtue.

Nor are the Pretensions of these same Betters less strongly supported in that most exalted Virtue of Justice, witness the daily Examples which they give of it in their own Persons. When a Man was punished for his Crimes the Greeks said that he *gave Justice*.[2] Now this is a Gift almost totally confined to the Poor, and it is a Gift, which they very seldom fail of making as often as there is any very pressing Occasion. Who can remember to have seen a rich Man whipt at the Cart's Tail! And how seldom (I am sorry to say it) are such exalted to the Pillory, or sentenced to Transportation! And as for the more reputable, namely the capital Punishments, how rarely do we see them executed on the Rich! Whereas their Betters, to their great Honour be it spoken, do very constantly make all these Gifts of Justice to the Society, which the other Part have it much more in their Power to serve by shewing the same Regard to this Virtue.

As for Chastity, it is a Matter which I shall handle with great Delicacy and Tenderness, as it principally concerns that lovely Part of the Creation, for whom I have the sincerest Regard. On this Head therefore, I shall only whisper, that if our Ladies of Fashion were sometimes for Variety only to take a Ride through St. Giles's, they might find *Something* in the Air there as wholesome as in that of Hanover or Grosvenor-Square.[3]

It may perhaps, be objected to what I have hitherto advanced, that I have ONLY mentioned the Cardinal Virtues,[4] which, (possibly from the popish Epithet assigned to them) are at present held in so little Repute, that no Man is conceived to be the better for possessing them, or the worse for wanting them. I will now therefore proceed to a Matter so necessary to the genteel Character; that a superior Degree of Excellence in it hath been universally allowed by all Gentlemen, in the most essential Manner, to constitute *our Betters*.

---

[1] A woman who rakes cinders from among ashes.

[2] The phrase δίκην δίδοναι (to be punished, to pay the penalty) means 'to give justice' if literally construed.

[3] On the disreputable reputation of St Giles (Westminster), see *CGJ* No. 17, above, p. 122 n. 3. Hanover Square and Grosvenor Square were two of the most aristocratic and fashionable areas of London; cf. *Tom Jones*, XIII. ii, where Fielding refers to their 'happy Mansions, where Fortune segregates from the Vulgar, those magnanimous Heroes, the Descendants of ancient *Britons*, *Saxons*, or *Danes*, whose Ancestors being born in better Days, by sundry Kinds of Merit, have entailed Riches and Honour on their Posterity.'

[4] In scholastic thought the four 'natural' cardinal virtues were justice, temperance, prudence, and fortitude; Fielding has made substitutions for the last two. Cf. the auction of cardinal virtues ('temperance and chastity and a pack of stuff that I would not give three farthings for') in *Historical Register* (1737), ii. 244 ff.

My sagacious Reader, I make no Doubt, already perceives I am going to mention Decency, the Characteristic, as it is commonly thought, of a Gentleman;[1] and perhaps it formerly was so; but at present it is so far otherwise, that, if our People of Fashion will examine the Matter fairly and without Prejudice, they cannot have the least Decency left, if they refuse to allow, that, in this Instance, the Mob are most manifestly their Betters.[2]

Who that hath observed the Behaviour of an Audience at the Playhouse, can doubt a Moment to what Part he should give the Preference in Decency! Here indeed I must be forced, however against my Inclination, to prefer the upper Ladies (I mean those who sit in the upper Regions of the House) to the lower.[3] Some, perhaps, may think the Pit an Exception to this Rule; but I am sorry to say, that I have received Information by some of my Spies, that the Example of the Boxes hath of late corrupted the Manners of their Betters in the Pit; and that several Shopkeepers Wives and Daughters have begun to interrupt the Performance, by Laughing, Tittering, Giggling, Chattering, and such like Behaviour, highly unbecoming all Persons who have any Regard to Decency: Whereas nothing of this Kind hath been imputed, as I have yet heard, to the Ladies in either Gallery, who may be truly said to be ABOVE all these Irregularities.

I readily allow, that on certain Occasions the Gentlemen at the Top of the House are rather more vociferous than those at the Bottom: But to this I shall give three Answers; First, that the Voice of Men is stronger and louder than that of Beaus. Secondly, that on these Occasions, as at the first Night of a new Play, the Entertainment is to be considered as among the Audience, all

---

[1] Fielding uses the term 'Decency' here and in what follows in the sense of propriety of behavior, conformity to the standards of good taste. Cf. *Spectator*, No. 104 (29 June 1711), where Steele connects it with 'good Breeding', identifies it with 'that Rule of Life called Decorum', and cites Cicero (*De officiis*, I. xxvii. 94) on its close relationship to Virtue. See also *Spectator*, No. 292 (4 Feb. 1712). For an example of its application to audience behavior, cf. Machine in Fielding's *Tumble-Down Dick* (1736): 'Gentlemen, I must beg you to clear the Stage intirely; for in things of this serious Nature, if we do not comply with the exactest Decency, the Audience will be very justly offended' (p. 2).

[2] Although Fielding occasionally uses the word 'Mob' in this playful way for the purpose of irony directed against those in high stations (cf. *Tom Jones*, I. ix), his serious concern about the power of the mob is clear in his writings of these years. See *CGJ* Nos. 47 and 49; see also *Journal of a Voyage to Lisbon* (1755), where the case 'between the mob and their betters' is explained in terms of a mistaken idea of liberty among the lower classes (21 [16] July).

[3] The more fashionable parts of the house were the boxes and the pit, with the pit a mixed group of wealthy tradesmen, wits, law students, and the like. Prices charged at both Drury Lane and Covent Garden were 5 shillings for a box, 3 for the pit, 2 for the first gallery, and 1 for the upper gallery; see *London Stage*, Pt. 4, vol. i, pp. xxxi, xlviii. The fact that 'Persons of Fashion' were seated below other members of the audience enables Fielding to play ironically on words like 'upper', 'lower', 'above', and 'below stairs'. See the discussion of the classes of theater-goers in *Tom Jones*, VII. i. Cf. *Joseph Andrews*, II. xiii; and see also *True Patriot*, No. 23 (8 Apr. 1746), where Fielding again plays with the taste of the different classes who occupied the different sections; jokes on courtiers not paying debts are applauded, he says, in the pit and the galleries, but the boxes are greatly amused by all references to cuckoldom. Cf. the references to 'An Alderman who in the Pit was plac'd' and 'The *Dapper 'Prentice and Attorney's Clerk*' in the upper gallery, in *The Modern Courtezan* [1751], pp. 17–18.

of whom are Actors in such Scenes. Lastly, as these Entertainments all begin below-stairs, the Concurrence of the Galleries is to be attributed to the Politeness of our Betters who sit there, and to that decent Condescension which they shew in concurring with the Manners of their Inferiors.

Nor do these, our Betters, give us Examples of Decency in their own Persons only; they take the utmost Care to preserve Decency in their Inferiors, and are a Kind of Deputies to the Censor in all public Places. Who is it that prevents the Stage being crowded with grotesque Figures, a Mixture of the Human with the Baboon Species?[1] Who (I say) but the Mob? The Gentlemen in the Boxes observe always the profoundest Tranquility on all such Occasions; but no sooner doth one of these Apparitions present its frightful Figure before the Scenes, than the Mob, *from their profound Regard to Decency*, are sure to command him OFF.

And should any Persons of Fashion in the Boxes, expose themselves to public Notice by any indecent Particularities of Behaviour; from whom would they receive immediate Correction and Admonishment, but from the Mob who are (for this Purpose perhaps) placed over them?

Was it not for this tender Care of Decency in the Mob, who knows what Spectacles the Desire of Novelty and Distinction would often exhibit in our Streets? For let Persons be guilty of the highest Enormities of this Kind, they may meet a hundred People of Fashion without receiving a single Rebuke. But the Mob never fail to express their Indignation on all Indecencies of this Kind: And it is, perhaps, the Awe of the Mob alone which prevents People of Condition, as they call themselves, from becoming more egregious Apes than they are, of all the extravagant Modes and Follies of Europe.[2]

Thus, I think, I have fully proved what I undertook to prove. I do not pretend to say, that the Mob have no Faults; perhaps they have many. I assert *no more* than this, that they are in all laudable Qualities very greatly superior to those who have hitherto, with much Injustice, pretended to look down upon them.

In this Attempt I may perhaps have given Offence to some of the inferior Sort, but I am contented with the Assurance of having espoused the Cause of Truth; and in so doing, I am well convinced *I shall please all who are* REALLY MY BETTERS. A.

[1] As Jensen suggests (ii. 211), Fielding may be referring here to the fact that nobility often sat on the stage proper, sometimes impeding the performance; but he is more likely to be alluding to the representaion of lords and ladies in the plays themselves. Cf. *Tom Jones*, XIV. i, where the narrator gives this example of the failure of English writers to describe accurately the manners of 'upper Life': 'Hence those strange Monsters in Lace and Embroidery, in Silks and Brocades, with vast Wigs and Hoops; which, under the Name of Lords and Ladies, strut the Stage, to the great Delight of Attornies and their Clerks in the Pit, and of the Citizens and their Apprentices in the Galleries; and which are no more to be found in real Life, than the Centaur, the Chimera, or any other Creature of mere Fiction.'

[2] Cf. the encounter of French visitors with the mob, in Sarah Fielding's *Familiar Letters between the Principal Characters in David Simple* (1747), Letter XLI, written by Henry Fielding.

TUESDAY, APRIL 7, 1752.

NUMB. 28.[1]

————Πένθος
Δὲ πιτνεῖ Βαρὺ
Κρεσσόνων πρὸς ἀγαθῶν.
Ζώει μὲν ἐν Ὀλυμπίοις,

PINDAR. OLYMPIAN.[2]

No more let Grief bewail the Doom of Fate;
In Heav'n he lives! How glorious the Exchange!

The following Elegy on the late Prince of Wales,[3] should have been published the Middle of last Month, had it not been unfortunately mislaid. This we hope will be a sufficient Apology to the ingenious Author;[4] our Readers, we doubt not, will thank us for giving it them at any Time.

> At Frederick's Shrine, near Thame's imperial
>   Strand,
> Their Vigils all the sacred Choir shall keep;
> Mute o'er his Urn a mournful Train shall stand,
> And ev'ry Muse, and ev'ry Virtue weep.
> To dress the Spot where rests his princely Shade,
> Fresh Garlands from the Plains each Swain shall
>   bring;
> From deep'ning Vale, and Woodland high, each
>   Maid
> Shall strip the flow'ry Bosom of the Spring.

[1] Fielding appears not to have written any of the contributions printed in this number except for the 'Proceedings at the Court of Censorial Enquiry'. In the copy of *CGJ* at the Bodleian Library (Hope Folio 11), containing manuscript corrections and revisions in Fielding's hand, the first page is struck through, marking out all of the Elegy on the Prince of Wales and the first paragraph of the letter by 'Eugenio'; see General Introduction, above, p. xxx, n. 3.

[2] *Olympian Odes*, ii. 22–5: 'but their heavy sorrow was abated by the presence of greater blessings. [Semele] . . . liveth amid the gods Olympian' (Loeb).

[3] Frederick Louis, Prince of Wales (1707–51), eldest son of George II, a figure in constant conflict with his parents, had died on 20 Mar. 1751 and was buried in Westminster Abbey. This poem, appearing a year later, is typical of the flood of elegies on the Prince which had been published in 1751. Cf. Horace Walpole's comment, 'We have been overwhelmed with lamentable Cambridge and Oxford dirges on the Prince's death' (*Yale Walpole*, xx, 260–1). Collections of this verse included *The English Poems Collected from the Oxford and Cambridge Verses on the Death of . . . Frederick* (1751), *Epicedia Oxoniensia in Obitum . . . Frederici* (Oxford, 1751), and *Academiae Cantabrigiensis luctus in obitum Frederici* (Cambridge, 1751); and there were individual elegies by William Kenrick, Richard Rolt, Christopher Smart, and others. Though Fielding indicates that the present poem is printed to mark the anniversary of the Prince's death, Thornton, in his *Drury-Lane Journal* No. 13 (9 Apr. 1752), ridiculed the 'propriety, in respect to time and circumstance' of an elegy on Frederick at this late date.

[4] Not identified; because of the Cambridge connection indicated by the signature, both Smart and William Mason have been suggested as possibly the author (Jensen, ii. 211–12; Cross, ii. 381; Dudden, p. 894), but there is no good evidence for either. See Moira Dearnley, *The Poetry of Christopher Smart* (New York, 1969), pp. 86–7, and Karina Williamson, 'Christopher Smart: Problems of Attribution Reconsidered', *The Library*, 28 (1973), 119–20.

There too the graver Patriot, good and old,
Shall come, and stoop to Earth his streaming
    Cheek;
And, as he kneels to kiss, the hallow'd Mold
Shall mourn, in "Words that weep, and Tears that
    speak"![1]
Mean Time the Clouds shall drop their wat'ry
    Head,
The South and Western Breeze shall jointly blow;
And wide, upon their spicy Pinions spread
The Sweets that issue from his Tomb below.

Ah me! the Swans that fail'd in stately Pride,
And whilom stopt by Kew's[2] lov'd Vale to sing;
How slow and sad they row along the Tide!
How droop their Necks beneath their faded
    Wing!
For now, since Fate the cruel Arrow sped,
Sad Change befalls the Scenes that charm'd
    before;
The parting Genius of the Plains is fled,
The Fauns, and Dryad Train are seen no more:
The Nereids sigh beneath their coral Cave,
Their Sea-green Wreathes in rude Disorder torn;
The Bird of Calm forsakes the troubl'd Wave,
The Groves and Springs, and all their Echoe's
    mourn.[3]

From this sad Hour to many a future Day,
As led by Love to drop a pious Tear;
The Stranger takes his solitary Way,
Thro' these blest Haunts to old Remembrance
    dear:
The village Hind that wont to tread the Place,
Long Tales of his departed Lord shall tell;
With sorrowing Steps his custom'd Walks shall
    trace,
And point the Bow'r where most he lov'd to dwell.
"Beneath this Beech, beside that hallow'd Stream,
Oft with his Lyre he hail'd the op'ning Year;

---

[1] Quoted from Abraham Cowley's 'The Prophet', l. 20, in *The Mistress* (1668).
[2] Kew, Surrey, where Frederick had an estate.
[3] Cf. Milton's *Lycidas*, 39–41; the following stanza is also presumably meant to be reminiscent of
Gray's *Elegy Written in a Country Churchyard* (1751), 97–116.

And still th'harmonious Strains, and pleasing
  Theme,
Hang musical on ev'ry Shepherd's Ear.
Oft fir'd to nobler Views, with godlike Mind,
He sought yon poplar Shade in pensive Mood;
For Britain's Weal some Patriot Plan[1] design'd,
Best, firmest, Architect of public Good."
  O! how we hail'd him in his mid Career!
How dawn'd his Morn! Meridian blaz'd how
  bright!
'Till envious Death deform'd the rising Year,
In Winter's Solstice like the sudden Night!
So thron'd in Amber Car the radiant Sun,
All glorious mounts the purple Road of Day;
Before his Steeds, *Life*, *Warmth*, and *Vigour* run,
As round he pours in Tides his golden Ray:
But see!——as down he slopes his hasty Flight,
Dark, sudden Clouds obscure his Ev'ning-Eye;
In dewy Mists he shrouds his shorten'd Light,
And sets in Tears beneath the western Sky.
  But you, ye Guardians of the sacred Shears
That wheel the adamantine Spindle round;
Long, long extend Imperial Cæsar's Years,
And spare the Thread with which his Life is
  wound.
Place to the Sire's Account the just Arrear,
Due to his Annals whose fresh Loss we mourn;
Late may we shed for George a second Tear,
Late may his Ashes fill their fated Urn.
So Peace shall spread her graceful olive Shade,
Pale Faction hang her Head and shun the Light;

---

[1] There are political overtones to this phrase, for Frederick had been the leader of the 'Patriot' Opposition to Walpole in the period 1736–42 and of a revived 'Patriot' or Opposition party in 1747. Though the author of this poem was probably unaware of the fact, Frederick had in actuality drawn up a 'glorious plan' for ruining the Pelhams and taking power; see Archibald Foord, *His Majesty's Opposition 1714–1830* (Oxford, 1964), pp. 271–9. His death was thus a severe political blow to those opposed to the Pelham Administration; see *CGJ* No. 16 and notes. Cf. Fielding's definition of 'Patriot' as '*one who opposes the Ministry*' in *True Patriot*, No. 29 (20 May 1746) and his ridicule of the Patriots in *Journey from this World to the Next*, I. vii, and in *True Patriot*, No. 2 (12 Nov. 1745). The praise of George II at the end of the poem and the predicted demise of 'Pale Faction' are perhaps intended to soften any political implications of the term 'Patriot', a theme notably absent from other elegies on the Prince's death.

Fair Freedom bid her tow'ring Spires invade
The Clouds, and rival Heav'n's unmeasur'd
    Height.
Mean Time rich Commerce wide from Pole to
    Pole,
Shall stretch her Sails, remotest Climes explore;
And, wafted back by prosp'rous Breezes, roll
The Wealth of either World to Albion's Shore..

                              CANTABRIGIENSIS.

Mr. Censor,   *Pall-Mall.*

Being detained in this Town a few Weeks, like an unwilling Captive on Business, the many fine Strokes of Humour with which you delineate the Vices of this Age in your new COVENT-GARDEN JOURNAL, soon engaged my Attention, and made me ambitious of sending you one Essay on a Subject now grown ripe for your Observation.

It is the fashionable Vice of ROUTS[1] which has so bewitched the Hearts of many of my fair Countrywomen, (for as for the Men I leave them to themselves) that my Indignation is rais'd at an Evil, which, if not soon discountenanced, will extinguish the few glimmering Sparks of ancient Virtue, even yet twinkling amongst us. But this is not all, Routs are so polite and sacred an Entertainment that no Time is judged proper for them, but the tedious Evenings of every Sabbath, at which our pious Fair observe a stricter Course of Vigils, than the best Christians I fear at their Devotions. Indeed they plead with some Shew of Modesty, that some of them are constant Attenders of divine Service on Sunday Mornings, and therefore think the Evening may be very innocently devoted to Pleasure; but doth this comport with that divine Precept,[2] which tells us, that both the Outgoings of the Evening as well as Morning should praise our great Creator. I hope it will not be an improper Parallel to compare these Devotees to Gallantry to the Religious among the old Persians, who acknowledged two Principles or Deities, as Objects of their Adorations, viz. one the Author of all Good, the other of all Evil: But one unhappy Difference appears in our Case, viz. that the evil Principle has got a vast Ascendant over the Good in our Hearts and Manners.

Lest I grow tiresome on a Subject, whose dark Shades are exposed to every common Eye, I will conclude with a short Contrast, which may set this Speculation in a clearer Light than a longer Dissertation; and here if you'll reflect on the languid Spirits and emaciated Features of those, whom the Morning Sun blushes on, as they rise from broken Dreams of guilty Scenes;

---

[1] See *CGJ* No. 17, above, p. 122 n. 2.   [2] Psalms 65: 8.

and on the contrary, if you view the beauteous Bloom of Innocence, and Spring of Health and Joy, that glows in the Bosoms of unspotted and virtuous Minds; in the former you will find all the Footsteps of the Loss of Paradise and Fall of our first Ancestors, in the latter, you will see all the Display of Providence in the Dignity of Human Nature, and all the Beauty of Religion.

I am,

With great Esteem,

Sir, yours,

EUGENIO.[1]

Mr. Censor,

Nothing is more apt to mortify human Vanity, than to find ourselves deceived in any Particular on which we have built an Opinion of possessing the Esteem of others. I have lately undergone a sensible Mortification of this Kind; for to deserve Confidence, surely argues Merit; and to hold the Secrets of another, is a Post of Honour: How greatly then was I deceived by the following Accident! A Gentleman of whom the World speaks well, came to me the other Day, and, with a most important Face, told me that an ugly Affair had happened between him and a certain Lord, whose Name he could not mention; that he was in the highest Distress, nor did he know how to act. He then informed me, that the high Opinion he had as well of my Understanding as of my Honour, had induced him to come and make his Case known to me, in order to have my Advice; telling me at the same Time, that as he must be obliged to conceal nothing from me, he begg'd for God's Sake that I would not mention it to any human Creature, for that I was the only Person to whom he either had or intended to make this Affair known. He then having received proper Assurances of Secrecy, whisper'd his important Business in my Ear; on which I frankly gave him my Opinion: He received it with Joy, returned me his hearty Thanks, and left me, tho' not without reminding me of Secresy in the strongest Terms. A few Hours afterwards I was visited by an Acquaintance, who had not sat long before he told me not only my Friend's Secret, but the very Opinion I gave him upon it; expressing at the same Time his Surprize at the Boldness of my Sentiments: He said he was enjoined Secrecy; but, as he knew I was

---

[1] Unidentified; but the same writer contributed an 'Essay on Chastity, and the Matrimonial Estate' to *LM* at the end of the year, with a head-note assuring the editor 'nothing from my Pen was ever yet transplanted in your collection before, but an Epistle on Liberty, to Ralph Allen, Esq; in your Magazine of 1746, p. 309; and a paper on Routs in that of April last, . . . which I sent to the Covent-Garden Journal'. The 'Essay' is also signed 'Eugenio' and is dated from 'Wootton, Somersetshire'; both the Somersetshire address and the poem to Allen suggest someone with a connection to Fielding. See *LM* 21 (1752), 550-1.

acquainted with the Affair, he thought it no Breach of Trust to mention it. I made him little or no Answer; for I own my Vanity was hurt to find, that, after his Commendations on my Honour, he should think as well of another Man, and make him his Confident. But in the Evening a Friend of mine clear'd up the whole Matter. I ventured to tell him the Story; but had no sooner mentioned the Gentleman's Name who had thus honoured me with his Confidence, than he burst into a Horse-Laugh, and told me that my Secret was not only a Lye, but as old as Paul's;[1] and that he dar'd to say, that this Gentleman had told it to hundreds; for, says he, he is a downright Secret-Monger, a Fellow that is everlastingly inventing Lyes, and telling them to others as important Secrets; and to show you that he is in the Confidence of the Great, he never fails to mix a Lord or Lady in his Story. By this Means he has made himself a Man of Importance with many, has gain'd several Points by this Stratagem, and is a Man who is thoroughly known as yet by few; for my own Part, I should imagine that this Character is quite extravagant: But you who have div'd into the inmost Recesses of human Nature, will best know whether it be natural; I am sure it is highly ridiculous, and an Object worthy your Pen; I have related to you the plain Fact, which, when drest by a little of your Cookery,[2] will make a palatable Dish.

> I am,
>
> *Your oblig'd,*
>
> *Humble Servant,*
>
> Z. Z.[3]

M.

Proceedings at the Court of Censorial Enquiry, &c.

Mr. CENSOR was pleased to recommend the Benefit of Mr. Havard,[4] which is to be on Saturday next at Drury-Lane, in the following Manner.

"Mr. Havard is the Successor of the first Mr. Mills[5] in most of his Parts on

---

[1] i.e. as old as St. Paul's, sometimes 'as old as Paul's steeple', proverbial expression to indicate great antiquity (Tilley, P 119).

[2] Alluding, perhaps, to Fielding's penchant for food metaphors; see *CGJ* No. 3, above, p. 28 n. 3.

[3] See *CGJ* No. 16, above, p. 117 n. 5.

[4] William Havard (?1710–78), actor and playwright, had been with Garrick at Drury Lane since the new manager's first season in 1747; he continued there for 22 seasons, until his retirement in 1769 because of illness. His competence in secondary roles was well established, though he was clearly no brilliant actor. The benefit which Fielding puffs here took place on 11 Apr., with Havard as Gonsales and Garrick as Osmyn in Congreve's *The Mourning Bride*. Havard at this time lived in Broad Court, at the upper end of Bow Street, and was thus Fielding's neighbor, but Fielding indicates in *CGJ* No. 29 that they were not personally acquainted.

[5] John Mills (d. 1736), actor at Drury Lane of considerable reputation, and father of Fielding's acquaintance, the less-accomplished William Mills (see *CGJ* No. 15).

the Stage, and he no less resembles the Character of Mr. Mills in his Life, being a sober, worthy, honest Man.

"The good Judgment of the Managers shews itself therefore in their Disposition of those Parts to Mr. Havard's Share; where all the amiable Qualities of Human Nature are to be displayed; since he who exerts these Qualities in private Life, is the most likely to represent them well on the Stage; such are Horatio, the Friar in Romeo and Juliet, &c. Mr. *Havard*, says Mr. Garrick, *always acts the Part of my Friend*; and whether on the *Stage, or off, I never desire a better.*[1]

"Characters of this Kind (as well the real as the personated) seldom strike us in a very glaring Light, or carry off any loud Applause either on the Theatre or in the World; but in both Cases, they never fail to please the good and truly judicious; and in both Cases, there must be great Merit to preserve such a Character, and to support it well throughout. I have heard it farther said of Mr. Havard, *that no Man feels an Obligation with more Warmth, while none can be less susceptible of any little Injury done to his Theatrical Abilities.* Here another Parallel may be drawn between this amiable Kind of Character in Life, and on the Stage. In both, it is often oppressed by the Forward, the Insolent, and the Worthless. I am afraid Mr. Havard hath experienced some such Treatment, in having his Benefit so long postponed,[2] since, except Mr. Garrick, I do not know that he hath any Superior in Tragedy at that House.

"However my Readers may agree with me in this, there are few, I am convinced, who will not think it a great Addition to their Entertainment on Saturday next, to reflect, that they are contributing to the Ease and to the Happiness, of a sensible, modest, and Good-natured Man; and of that Family of which he is the worthy Master."

SATURDAY, APRIL 11, 1752.   NUMB. 29.

Τοῦ ἐν πάσχειν τὸ εὖ ποιεῖν οὐ μόνον κάλλιον, ἀλλὰ καὶ ΗΔΙΟΝ.

EPICURI APUD PLUTARCH.[3]

---

[1] Garrick's good opinion lasted throughout their long association. His epitaph for Havard pays tribute to his personal qualities rather than to his acting: 'Howe'er defective in the mimic art, / In real life he justly play'd his part / The noblest character he acted well, / And heaven applauded—when the curtain fell' (*Poetical Works* [2 vols., 1785], ii. 486).

[2] The order in which benefits were held was based on rank and seniority (see *London Stage*, Pt. 4, vol. I, p. cii n.); Havard's benefit had been advertised in the *CGJ* five times up to this point, the first notice appearing in No. 21 (14 Mar.), but all notices gave 11 Apr. as the date of the benefit. By 'postponement' Fielding thus means the relatively late date in the order of precedence rather than any last-minute delay.

[3] Plutarch, 'That a Philosopher Ought to Converse Especially with Men in Power', *Moralia*, 778C; the emphasis on 'delightful' is Fielding's own.

To do Good to others is not only more laudable, but more DELIGHTFUL
than to receive it from them.

To the CENSOR.

My Dear Friend,[1]

I was extremely pleased with the Recommendation of Mr. Havard's Benefit
in your last Paper;[2] and I am the more pleased with you, as I am informed
you have no other Acquaintance with the Person espoused than with his
Character, of which I am convinced, you have given a very just Account to
the Public.

This is that Conduct, my Friend, which our favourite Dr. Barrow hath
pointed out to us, in one of his excellent Sermons. "A good Man," says he,
"stints not his Benevolence to his own Family or Relations, to his
Neighbours or Benefactors; to those of his own Sect or Opinion, or of his
Humour and Disposition: to such as serve him, or oblige him, or please him,
&c.——but extends it to mere Strangers, towards such who never did him
any good, or can ever be able to do him any."[3]

So preached that worthy Divine, who truly taught the Doctrines of him,
whose Follower he professed himself, and who truly liv'd the Life he taught.
Let us set then before us both his Precept and Example; let us, in the
Language of the Poet,

——*Leave all meaner Things*
To low Ambition and the Pride of Kings;[4]

and with that first of human Kind, the glorious Patron of Amelia,[5] make
Benevolence at once the Business and the Pleasure of our Lives.

Whatever our Talents are,[6] let us convert them to the good of Mankind.

---

[1] Fielding continues here his pose as the good-natured, benevolent 'Axylus'; see the letters in *CGJ*
Nos. 16 and 20 and the answer by 'Iago' in *CGJ* No. 21.

[2] See *CGJ* No. 28, above.

[3] Quoted with slight alterations and omissions from Barrow's Sermon XXXI, 'The Duty and
Reward of Bounty to the Poor', *Works*, 5th edn. (1741), i. 304. On Isaac Barrow, see *CGJ* No. 4,
above, p. 34 n. 5; on the significance to Fielding of this sermon, quoted here three times, see Martin
Battestin, *The Moral Basis of Fielding's Art* (Middletown, Conn., 1959), pp. 18–19, 30–1, 100, and 159
n. 1, and *Tom Jones*, ed. Battestin, Wesleyan Edn. (Oxford, 1974), i. 95 n.

[4] Pope, *Essay on Man*, i. 1–2.

[5] Ralph Allen (1693–1764), philanthropist, to whom Fielding had dedicated *Amelia*, remarking,
'The best Man is the properest Patron of such an Attempt'. Allen, whose fortune had come from
improvements in the cross-country postal system, had his estate at Prior Park, near Bath, and was
noted for his charities, especially to hospitals. He was a friend of Pope, Richardson, and other men of
letters, and had been both a benefactor and friend of Fielding since 1741. In *Tom Jones*, where he
serves as the model of Squire Allworthy, Allen is also praised as 'a munificent Patron, a warm and firm
Friend, a knowing and chearful Companion, indulgent to his Servants, hospitable to his Neighbours,
charitable to the Poor, and benevolent to all Mankind' (VIII. i). See also *Joseph Andrews*, III. i, vi.

[6] The language here and in the following paragraphs draws from the Parable of the Talents,
Matthew 25: 14–30; cf. a similar use of the parable in connection with charity in *Champion* for 5 Apr.
1740.

Charity is not confined to giving Alms. If so, perhaps it would be but little within your Reach *or mine*. But the divine Founder of our Religion never intended to restrain a Virtue so essentially necessary to a Christian, to the Rich alone. As one Man's Talent lies in his Purse, another's may lie in his Pen; a third may employ his Tongue, and a fourth his Hands for the Service of others, nay the most Impotent may perhaps fully exercise this Virtue even with their Wishes, most certainly they may with their Prayers.

With what generous Pity must a Mind of this Temper look down on a Wretch who is bursting with Pride, Malice and Envy: Whose Understanding is tinctured with his Gall, who hates every Man that is better or wiser, or happier than himself; whose whole Study it is to undermine the Fame and the Fortune of his Neighbour; a secret Enemy to others, but a more secret, and perhaps more bitter Enemy to himself?[1]

There is scarce one, even among those few (for Few, I hope, they are) that resemble this Picture, who would not view it with Scorn. We will rise therefore one Step from the odious to the insipid Character, from those who delight in doing Mischief, to those who have little or no Delight either in the Good or Harm which happeneth to others. Men of this Stamp are so taken up, in contemplating themselves, that the Virtues or Vices, the Happiness or Misery of the rest of Mankind scarce ever employ their Thoughts. This is a Character, however truly contemptible it may be, which hath not wanted its Admirers among the Antients. These Men have been called Philosophers,[2] and in the heathen Systems they might deserve that Name; but in the sublimer Schools of the Christian Dispensation, they are so far from being entitled to any Honours, that they will be called to a severe Account (those especially who have received very considerable Talents of any Kind) for converting solely to their own Use, what was entrusted only to their Care for the general Good.

I proceed now, by another Gradation, to a third Species of Men, who will boldly tell us that they act upon Christian Principles; nay, and will find their Admirers among many who profess themselves very sincere Believers in the Christian Religion.

The Men I here mean, are, of all others, the greatest Usurers. Being

---

[1] See the confession by 'Iago', *CGJ* No. 21.

[2] The Stoics; cf. the characterization of Colonel James (*Amelia*, VIII. v) as a man with a mind 'formed of those firm Materials, of which Nature formerly hammered out the Stoic, and upon which the Sorrows of no Man living could make an Impression'. Fielding's attitude toward Stoicism was, however, complex, involving at times 'benevolist' anti-Stoicism in the tradition of Steele's *Christian Hero* (1701) and at times praise of its ethical ideas; for a full discussion see Miller, *Essays*, pp. 253–64. The paragraph in this leader has thus been interpreted both as an instance of his indictment of Stoic self-sufficiency and as evidence of his willingness to unite Stoic ideals and Christianity (see Battestin, *The Moral Basis of Fielding's Art*, pp. 67–8, and Miller, *Essays*, p. 259). Cf. 'Iago's' use of an image from Horace of a man rolled up within himself, *CGJ* No. 21, above, p. 141; and cf. the praise of Cicero's ethics in *CGJ* No. 39.

possessed, either by their own Roguery or by that of their Ancestors, of a thousand times more than their Share of the good things of this World, they expect by parting with the ten thousandth Part of these Things to purchase Heaven a lumping Pennyworth.[1] Every little Act of Kindness which they do, every trifling Alms which they bestow is sure to be brought into the Account, nay to be doubly posted: For first they expect, by some paultry Obligation, to bind the Person to whom it is done, in Bonds of perpetual Slavery; nor are they thus satisfied, but Heaven is made Debtor into the Bargain. This, as the Beggars tell them, and they seem to believe, is to restore them a hundred fold whatever they give on Earth.

But surely such mercenary Goodness as this, done as it were by way of Penance, can have but little Merit.[2] Such Dabs of Alms, squeez'd out of a hard-bound Generosity, can produce no very sweet smelling Savour, in the Sense of a truly wise and benevolent Being; much less of a Being who possesses, in an infinite Degree, those Qualities.

Let us, my Friend, soar a Pitch higher. Let us leave the Merit of good Actions to others, let us enjoy the Pleasure of them. *In the Energy itself of Virtue* (says Aristotle) *there is great Pleasure;*[3] and this was the Meaning of him who first said, *That Virtue was its own Reward.*[4] A Sentiment most truly just, however it hath been ridiculed by those who understood it not. If we examine the Matter abstractedly, and with due Attention, we may extend the Observation of Aristotle to every human Passion: For in what, but in the Energies themselves, can the Pleasures of Ambition, Avarice, Pride, Hatred, and Revenge, be conceived to lie? What Rewards do these severe Taskmasters bestow on their Slaves for all their Labours, but that common

---

[1] i.e. 'plenty for one's money' (*OED*).

[2] Cf. Barrow, 'The Duty and Reward of Bounty to the Poor': 'A Christian niggard is the veriest nonsense that can be'; and Barrow goes on to indict those whose liberality comes from their hopes of doing themselves material good (*Works*, 5th edn. [1741], i. 330, 305). See also the discussion on charity in *Tom Jones*, II. v; Allworthy, in refuting Captain Blifil's Methodist arguments, agrees that there is little merit in 'barely discharging a Duty', but, like Axylus here, he goes on to argue that an active charity is not only meritorious but 'so pleasant, that if any Duty could be said to be its own Reward, or to pay us while we are discharging it, it was this'. In constructing Allworthy's discourse Fielding uses the same sermon by Barrow quoted in this leader; see the notes by Battestin, ed., *Tom Jones*, Wesleyan Edn., i. 93, 95. For another condemnation of a niggardly charity, see the *Champion* for 5 Apr. 1740.

[3] *Nicomachean Ethics*, I. viii. 10 (1099a 7): 'And further, the life of active virtue is essentially pleasant' (Loeb); Aristotle had earlier used the word *energeia* to emphasize that virtue must be active. See *CGJ* No. 21, above, p. 142 n. 1, for the significance of this notion in Fielding.

[4] A Stoic aphorism going back to Zeno (see Diogenes Laertius, *Lives of Eminent Philosophers*, vii. 89); cf. Seneca, *De vita beata*, IX. iv and Cicero, *De finibus*, ii. 73, as typical instances. Fielding himself consistently argued that morality must be based on the expectation of rewards and punishments in the afterlife; in this context, however, he is stressing the pleasure of virtuous action, the 'glorious Reward' of salvation being duly addressed near the end of the leader. Cf. the remark of Allworthy in *Tom Jones*, II. v, quoted above, n. 2; cf. the 'innate Worth' of Virtue referred to in 'Essay on Knowledge of Characters of Men' (*Miscellanies* [1743], ed. H. K. Miller, Wesleyan Edn. [Oxford, 1972], p. 174) and in the *Champion*, 4 Mar. 1739/40; see also *Champion*, 24 Jan. 1740.

Reward of all Slaves, the Labour itself? Why is not Benevolence therefore as capable at least of repaying us with herself as any other Passion? Why must this most lovely of all Mistresses be pursued, not for her native Charms,[1] but for the Fortune which she is to bring us?

"As Nature (to quote once more my beloved Author Dr. Barrow) to the Acts requisite toward Preservation of our Life, hath annexed a sensible Pleasure, forcibly enticing us to the Performance of them: So hath she made the Communication of Benefits to others, to be accompanied with a very delicious Relish upon the Mind of him that practices it; nothing indeed carrying with it a more pure and savory Delight than Beneficence. A Man may be VIRTUOUSLY VOLUPTUOUS, AND A LAUDABLE EPICURE BY DOING MUCH GOOD. *For to receive Good,* even in the Judgment of Epicurus himself (the great Patron of Pleasure) *is no wise so pleasant as to do it.*"[2]

Let us cultivate therefore, my Friend, that excellent Temper of Mind, that Passion which is the Perfection of human Nature, of which the Delight is in doing Good.[3] How mean then will appear to us the Motives of those who hope for private Acknowledgments, and public Applause, for every little Benefit which they confer on Mankind. Like base Prostitutes they must be pleased and paid too, or rather indeed must be paid because they are insensible of Pleasure. The truly good Man laments not every Disappointment of private or public Gratitude. He goeth on doing Good, and enjoys it while he doth it; an Enjoyment which neither the Envy or Malice, the Folly or Malignity of Mankind, can deprive him of. And as to that glorious Reward, the only one indeed which is worthy of a wise Man's Consideration, which will attend the good Man hereafter, nothing is more certain than that he who deserves it is sure of attaining it; and the more real Delight we take in doing Good, the more we seem to acquire of such Merit.

Morose and austere Men may, if they please, preach up Mortification and Self-Denial,[4] may insinuate that a Man cannot be good and happy at the

---

[1] See *CGJ* No. 20, above, p. 137 n. 3.

[2] 'The Duty and Reward of Bounty to the Poor', *Works*, 5th edn. (1741), i. 322; the emphasis by italics and small capitals is Fielding's own.

[3] Charity is here made synonymous with Fielding's favorite doctrine of 'Good-nature'. Cf. 'the glorious Lust of doing Good' described in his poem 'Of Good-Nature' (*Miscellanies*, 1743), and see the discussion by Miller, *Essays*, pp. 63–4; see also *CGJ* No. 16.

[4] The word *morose* figures large in Fielding's condemnation of moral rigorism, whether of the Calvinist, Methodist, or philosophical variety, which he felt to be antithetical to his ideal of open-hearted, active benevolence springing from a natural disposition to charity. Cf. his references to 'the morose Part of Mankind' in *CGJ* No. 66 and 'Moroseness' in *CGJ* No. 67. In 'An Essay on the Knowledge of the Characters of Men' (*Miscellanies*, 1743) he condemns a 'sour, morose, ill-natured, censorious Sanctity' (Wesleyan Edn., p. 168); in the *Champion* (24 Jan. 1740) he argues that virtue is not 'of that morose and rigid Nature, which some mistake her to be'; and in *A Charge to the Grand Jury* (1749) he distinguishes his point of view from that of 'a morose and over-sanctified Spirit, which excludes all Kind of Diversion' (p. 51). Cf. *Journey from this World to the Next*, I, xiv; and see Frederick G. Ribble, 'Aristotle and the "Prudence" Theme of *Tom Jones*', *ECS* 15 (1981), 31–2. Cf. also James

same Time, and may deny all Merit to all Actions which are not done in Contradiction to Nature; but I say, with Dr. Barrow, *Let us improve and advance our Nature to the utmost Perfection of which it is capable,*[1] I mean by doing all the Good we can; and surely that Nature which seems to partake of the divine Goodness in this World, is the most likely to partake of the divine Happiness in the next. To speak a solemn Truth, such Natures alone are capable of such Beatitude.

I am,

My dear Friend,

Affectionately yours,

AXYLUS.

C.

TUESDAY, APRIL 14, 1752.   NUMB. 30.

Quo teneam vultus mutantem Protea nodo?

HORACE.[2]

Say, with what Ties of Reasoning shall I bind,
The Proteus Nature of the female Mind?

A

DIALOGUE[3]

AT

TUNBRIDGE-WELLS,[4]

BETWEEN

A Philosopher and a Fine Lady:

After the Manner of PLATO.[5]

Harris's condemnation of the 'meagre, mortifying System of *Self-denial*' which suppresses 'Social and Natural Affections', *Three Treatises* (1744), pp. 208–9.

[1] A paraphrased version of the opening of the paragraph in Sermon XXXI from which Fielding has just quoted: 'The very constitution, frame and temper of our nature directeth and inclineth us thereto; whence by observing those duties, we observe our own nature, we improve it, we advance it to the best perfection it is capable of' (*Works*, 5th edn. [1741], i. 322).

[2] *Epistles*, I. i. 90: 'With what knot can I hold this face-changing Proteus?' (Loeb); Horace is explaining why he refuses to follow the ever-changing whims of popular opinion.

[3] Not by Fielding. As Austin Dobson pointed out (*Later Essays* [Oxford, 1921], pp. 56–7), the 'J' who wrote this dialogue was very likely Fielding's friend James Harris of Salisbury, author of *Hermes* (see Appendix I (i), below, for a 'Court' column on *Hermes*). Harris apparently had earlier contributed two dialogues, called 'Much Ado' and 'Fashion', to Sarah Fielding's *Familiar Letters between the Principal Characters in David Simple* (1747), ii. 277 ff., the second of which especially is strikingly similar in idea and phrasing to this dialogue. Dobson's source for Harris's authorship of the dialogues in *Familiar Letters* was a comment by Samuel Johnson reported in *Diary and Letters of Madame D'Arblay*, entry for 26 Aug. 1778 (ed. Charlotte Barrett [1904], i. 86). Better evidence, however, may be found in Harris's known works; see 'Knowledge of the World, or Good Company: A Dialogue', in Harris's *Upon the Rise and Progress of Criticism* (1752), a piece which puts his authorship of this contribution to the *CGJ* beyond serious question. Cf. also his attack on an enslavement to the

Miss.

Oh! dear Mr. *Downright*, I have the strangest Piece of News to tell you, what do you think it is?

Mr.

I cannot guess.

Miss.

Then I'll tell you. Mr. *Gainlove* follows Miss *Bird*.

Mr.

If he follows her, he may e'en catch her, and eat her into the Bargain. What's that to me?

Miss.

Incurious Creature! Nay but Miss *Bird* is no Gentlewoman: And to be sure a Gentleman should marry a Gentlewoman.

Mr.

No Gentlewoman, *Miss*?

Miss.

No. I heard Lady *Brazen*, and Mrs. *Danglecourt* both say so.

Mr.

How should they know Gentlewomen? But perhaps they heard others say so.

Miss.

You are the strangest Man! Well then, I will tell you; I know she is no Gentlewoman; for her Father——

Mr.

Her Father, *Miss*! Why we are talking of the young Lady, who appears to be *genteel* in her Person, and *gentle* in her Manners: That she is a *Woman*, at present, we will take for granted. Now, *Miss*, according to my Notion of Things, if her Person and Manners are as I have described, I think Miss *Bird* may be a Gentlewoman, Lady *Brazen* and Mrs. *Danglecourt* may be two Furies, with Minds more hideous and distorted than their Bodies and Persons.

changing modes of fashion, in the Preface to *Hermes* (1751), pp. viii–xi.

⁴ In Kent, a fashionable resort and watering-place about 35 miles from London.

⁵ So labelled, presumably, because of the Socratic questioning and the 'philosopher's' use of analogy to familiar arts and sciences. Cf. Harris's description of 'Socratic Reasoning' in his *Philological Inquiries* (1780), in which he offers as an example Hamlet's response to Rosencrantz and Guildenstern (*Works*, ed. the Earl of Malmesbury [1801], ii. 408).

Miss.

Lord! Sir, you talk always to me in a quite new Language: But I won't believe one Word you say.

Mr.

That I know better than you can tell me; for Fashion will always get the better of Sense.

Miss.

Well! I suppose you in your wise Way have something to say about Fashion too.

Mr.

'Tis the Creed of Fools, and Conveniency of wise Men.

Miss.

But I shall believe in it, Mr. *Wiseman*, for all that you can say to the contrary.

Mr.

And follow it too?

Miss.

Certainly.

Mr.

But the Fashion is always changing.

Miss.

'Tis so.

Mr.

You then likewise must be always changing: And you will be aptly called the fluttering, the changing, the inconstant——.

Miss.

A Truce, pray, with your Compliments.

Mr.

No Compliments, I'll assure you, but plain Truth.——Well then, will you answer me one Question?

Miss.

What's that?

Mr.

You have learnt to cast up an Account?[1]

Miss.

I have.

Mr.

And you can play on the Spinnet?

Miss.

True.

Mr.

When you learnt to cast up an Account, you was taught that two added to two, made four; and three times three, made nine. And I am certain you would believe it the greatest Imposition on your Understanding, should any one undertake to prove that two added to two, made twenty.

Miss.

I can't see what all this tends to.

Mr.

Have a little Patience, *Miss*; you will find it of great Service in Life.——And when you learnt to play on the Spinnet, you found the Art, as far as you ever knew it, to consist of certain unvariable Principles.

Miss.

To be sure I was not to strike what Key I pleased, but what Key was proper.

Mr.

Have Courage, *Miss*, and you will become a Philosopher.——Then what was *proper* and *true* and right, you was always taught to follow in all the Arts and Sciences, which hitherto you have learnt?

Miss.

I was.

Mr.

And in all the other Arts and Sciences of human Life, don't you imagine we may reason after the same Manner? 'Tis not as we *please*, but what is *proper*. And we should take care to be rightly pleased.

[1] i.e. to add up, or calculate. Cf. the question 'You understand Arithmetic?' addressed to 'Mr. *Prim*', a mercer, in an effort to convince him of the changeableness of fashion, in 'Fashion: A Dialogue', *Familiar Letters* (1747), ii. 290; the argument then proceeds exactly as it does here.

Miss.

It may be so, for aught I know.

Mr.

It must be so. What then, *Miss*, becomes of Fashion? How comes this the chief Motive of Action? For you have acknowledged that what was *proper* and *right* should direct Fashion; and if the contrary were allowed, the Nature of Things must be subverted.[1]

Miss.

Then you would not have me be in the Fashion? And one had as good be out of the World, as out of the Fashion.

Mr.

I never said so.

Miss.

What did you say then?

Mr.

Why, I never could make Fashion a Rule for acting; but I would have higher and steadier Principles. Surely, *Miss*, it requires no great Depth of Logic, to make some Distinction between what may be convenient, and is necessary.

Miss.

Well! I could wish you did but hear Lady *Brazen* talk of the Fashion.

Mr.

I had rather hear old *Socrates*, were he alive.[2] For my Part I have no Curiosity to be acquainted with Lady *Brazen*. Tho' I know several of her Family; there is hardly a County in *England*, where her Ladyship's Relations don't flourish.—But pray answer me, Miss.

Miss.

Well, your Question.

Mr.

When you want to buy a new Gown, what Shop do you go to?

---

[1] Cf. the conclusion, 'nothing is true, or right, or good, because 'tis the Fashion; or the Fashion because 'tis true, or right, or good', in 'Fashion: A Dialogue', *Familiar Letters*, ii. 292.

[2] Cf. Harris, 'what would old *Homer* have thought, in the days of antient simplicity?' in 'Knowledge of the World, or Good Company: A Dialogue', *Upon the Rise and Progress of Criticism*, p. 47.

Miss.

Where there is the best Goods, and the most Variety, and the fairest Tradesman.

Mr.

And if you wanted to get Sense and Knowledge, to whose *Shop* would you repair?

Miss.

Your Servant, Sir!¹ I see now what you would drive at.—But really I can't stay one Moment longer;—'tis three a Clock, and I must dress myself, for I am going to dine with Lady *Brazen*, Mrs. *Danglecourt*, Capt. *Flutter*, and two or three Persons of Quality.—And so your Servant, good Mr. Philosopher.

J.

SATURDAY, APRIL 18, 1752. NUMB. 31.

Qui Bavium non odit, amet tua Carmina, Mævi.

VIRGIL.²

He who doth not hate one bad Commentator,
let him love a worse.

Sir,

You are sensible, I believe, that there is nothing in this Age more fashionable, than to criticise on Shakespeare;³ I am indeed told, that there are not less than 200 Editions of that Author, with Commentaries, Notes, Observations, &c. now preparing for the Press; as nothing therefore is more natural than to direct one's Studies by the Humour of the Times, I have

---

¹ See *CGJ* No. 21, above, p. 141 n. 2.

² *Eclogues*, iii. 90: 'Let him who hates not Bavius love your songs, Maevius' (Loeb).

³ By this time the century had already seen editions of Shakespeare by Rowe (1709), Pope (1725), Theobald (1733), Hanmer (1744), and (based on Pope's) William Warburton (1747). It is Warburton, no doubt, whom Fielding has particularly in mind in the parody which follows as well as in his comment in *Tom Jones*, 'For, perhaps, thou may'st be as learned in Human Nature as *Shakespear* himself was, and, perhaps, thou may'st be no wiser than some of his Editors' (x. i). Warburton's imperious manner of announcing variant readings and his open contempt for previous critics of Shakespeare (including Fielding's friend John Upton) had already provoked the satire of his contemporaries; see especially Thomas Edwards's *The Canons of Criticism* (1748), in which the first rule is 'A Professed Critic has a right to declare, that his Author Wrote whatever he thinks he should have written with as much positiveness as if he had been at his elbow' (3rd edn. [1750], p. 1). Since Warburton was a close friend of Fielding's patron Ralph Allen, Fielding does not satirize him openly; Warburton was, after all, only the latest and most arrogant of the commentators on Shakespeare whom Fielding had earlier ridiculed in *Journey from this World to the Next* (1743; I. viii) and the *True Patriot*, No. 16 (18 Feb. 1746). Cf. James Harris's general attack on textual critics with a 'bold conjectural spirit', as represented by Richard Bentley's notorious edition of Milton (1732) and various unspecified editions of Shakespeare, in Harris's *Upon the Rise and Progress of Criticism* (1752), pp. 16–23.

myself employed some leisure Hours on that great Poet. I here send you a short Specimen of my Labours, being some Emendations of that most celebrated Soliloquy in Hamlet, which, as I have no Intention to publish Shakespeare myself, are very much at the Service of any of the 200 Critics abovementioned.

I am, &c.

Hamlet, Act III. Scene 2.[1]
To be, or not to be; that is the Question.

This is certainly very intelligible; but if a slight Alteration were made in the former Part of the Line, and an easy Change was admitted in the last Word, the Sense would be greatly improved. I would propose then to read thus;

To be, or not. To be! that is the BASTION.

That is the strong Hold. The Fortress. So Addison in Cato.

Here will I hold——[2]

The military Terms which follow, abundantly point out this Reading.

Whether 'tis nobler in the *Mind* to *suffer*
The *Slings* and Arrows of outragious Fortune,
Or *to take Arms against a Sea* of Troubles,
And by opposing end them.

Suffering is, I allow, a Christian Virtue; but I question whether it hath ever been ranked among the heroic Qualities. Shakespeare certainly wrote BUFFET; and this leads us to supply Man for Mind; Mind being alike applicable to both Sexes, whereas Hamlet is here displaying the most masculine Fortitude. *Slings* and *Arrows* in the succeeding Line, is an Impropriety which could not have come from our Author; the former being the Engine which discharges, and the latter the Weapon discharged. To the Sling, he would have opposed the Bow; or to Arrows, Stones. Read therefore WINGED ARROWS; that is, feathered Arrows; a Figure very usual among Poets: So in the classical Ballad of Chevy Chase;

The Grey-Goose Wing that was thereon
In his Heart's Blood was wet.[3]

---

[1] III. i, in modern texts; except for substituting 'the' for 'that' and 'those' in two places (ll. 63, 81), Fielding follows Thomas Hanmer's text in the edition listed in his library (9 vols., 1748; Baker, item 376).

[2] From Cato's soliloquy on immortality in Addison's play (1713), V. i. 15.

[3] The ballad which Addison had praised so highly in *Spectator*, Nos. 70 and 74 (21, 25 May 1711); the lines quoted are in the modernized version followed by Addison, ll. 195–6. See Percy's *Reliques*, ed. H. B. Wheatley (1886), i. 1–35, 250–64.

The next Line is undoubtedly corrupt—to take Arms against a Sea, can give no Man, I think, an Idea; whereas by a slight Alteration and Transposition all will be set right, and the undoubted Meaning of Shakespeare restored.[1]

> Or *tack* against an *Arm 'oth' Sea* of Troubles,
> And by composing end them.

By composing himself to Sleep, as he presently explains himself. What shall I do? says Hamlet. Shall I *buffet* the Storm, or shall I tack about and go to Rest?

> ——*To die*, to sleep;
> No more; and by a Sleep to say we end
> The Heart-ach, and the thousand natural Shocks
> The Flesh is Heir to; 'tis a *Consummation*
> Devoutly to be wished. *To die*, to sleep;
> To sleep, perchance to dream;——

What to die first, and to go to sleep afterwards; and not only so, but to dream too?—But tho' his Commentators were dreaming of Nonsense when they read this Passage, Shakespeare was awake when he writ it. Correct it thus;

> ——To lie to sleep.

i.e. To go to sleep, a common Expression; Hamlet himself expressly says he means *no more*; which he would hardly have said, if he had talked of Death, a Matter of the greatest and highest Nature: And is not the Context a Description of the Power of Sleep, which every one knows puts an End to the Heart-ach, the Tooth-ach, Head-ach, and indeed every Ach? So our Author in his Macbeth, speaking of this very Sleep, calls it

> Balm of hurt Minds, great Nature's *second Course*.[2]

Where, by the bye, instead of second Course, I read SICKEN'D DOSE; this being, indeed, the Dose which Nature chuses to apply to all her Shocks, and may be therefore well said *devoutly to be wished for*, which surely cannot be so generally said of Death.—But how can Sleep be called a *Consummation*?— The true Reading is certainly *Consultation*; the Cause for the Effect, a common Metonymy, *i.e.* When we are in any violent Pain, and a Set of Physicians are met in a *Consultation*, it is to be hoped the Consequence will be a sleeping Dose. Death, I own, is very devoutly to be apprehended, but seldom wished, I believe, at least by the Patient himself, at all such Seasons.

For natural *Shocks*, I would read *Shakes*; indeed I know only one Argument which can be brought in Justification of the old Reading; and this

---

[1] Cf. the tone of Warburton's emendation: 'Without question' Shakespeare wrote *assail of.*
[2] *Macbeth*, II. ii. 38.

is, that *Shock* hath the same Signification, and is rather the better Word. In such Cases, the Reader must be left to his Choice.

> For in that Sleep of Death what Dreams may come,
> When we have *shuffled* off this mortal *Coil*,
> Must give us Pause——.

Read and print thus:

> For in that Sleep, of Death what Dreams may come?
> When we have *scuffled* off this mortal *Call*,
> Must give us Pause——.

i.e. Must make us stop. *Shuffle* is a paultry Metaphor, taken from playing at Cards; whereas *Scuffle* is a noble and military Word.

> The Whips and Scorns of Time.

Undoubtedly *Whips* and *Spurs*.[1]

> When he himself might his *Quietus* make
> With a bare *Bodkin*.

With a bare *Pipkin*.[2] The Reader will be pleased to observe, that Hamlet, as we have above proved, is here debating whether it were better to go to sleep, or to keep awake; as an Argument for the affirmative, he urges that no Man in his Senses would bear *the Whips and Scorns of Time, the Oppressor's Wrong*, &c. when he himself, without being at the Expence of an Apothecary, might make his *Quietus, or sleeping Dose*, with a bare PIPKIN, the cheapest of all Vessels, and consequently within every Man's Reach.

> ——Who would Fardles bear,
> To groan and sweat under a weary Life?

Who indeed would bear any thing for such a Reward? The true Reading is

> ——Who would for th' Ales bear
> To groan, &c.

Who would bear the Miseries of Life, for the Sake of the Ales. In the Days of Shakespeare, when Diversions were not arrived at that Degree of Elegance to which they have been since brought, the Assemblies of the People for Mirth were called by the Name of an ALE.[3] This was the Drum or

---

[1] Cf. Warburton: 'We may be sure' that Shakespeare wrote 'of *th*' time' because he meant 'a corrupted age or manners'.

[2] A small earthenware pot or pan used in cooking (*OED*).

[3] The name given a festival at which much ale is drunk, with 'Whitsun-ale' such an event formerly held at Whitsuntide (*OED*).

Rout of that Age, and was the Entertainment of the better Sort, as it is at this Day of the Vulgar. Such are the *Easter-Ales* and the *Whitsun-Ales*, at present celebrated all over the West of England. The Sentiment therefore of the Poet, is this; *Who would bear the Miseries of Life, to enjoy the Pleasures of it*; which latter Word is by no forced Metaphor called THE ALES OF LIFE.

> And makes us rather bear the Ills we have,
> Than fly to others that we know not of.

This, I own, is Sense as it stands; but the Spirit of the Passage will be improved, if we read

> Than try *some others*, &c.
> ——Thus the native Hue of Resolution,
> Is sicklied o'er with the pale Cast of Thought.

Read,

> ——Thus the native Blue of Resolution,
> Is pickled o'er in a stale Cask of Salt.

This restores a most elegant Sentiment; I shall leave the Relish of it therefore with the Reader, and conclude by wishing that its Taste may never be obliterated by any future Alteration of this glorious Poet.   A.

TUESDAY, APRIL 21, 1752.   NUMB. 32.

> ——*Discordia semina Rerum.*

OVID.[1]

Hints upon different Subjects.

The two first Letters which I shall give the Public this Day, the Reader will perceive have lain by me some Time, as they relate to Matters handled in my first Papers.[2] We hope they will not on that Account prove the less acceptable. The third Letter relates to a Grievance which hath been attacked by all my Predecessors; but I think not in the Light in which it is here shewn.

---

[1] *Metamorphoses*, I. ix: 'ill-matched elements heaped in one' (Loeb). In expanded form, the passage is the motto to *JJ* No. 9 (30 Jan. 1748).

[2] In No. 4 (14 Jan.) and No. 7 (25 Jan.). The claim that the letters have 'lain by' him for some time might suggest that they are not written by Fielding, but the evidence is unclear. The third letter, signed 'Humphry Gubbin' is certainly by Fielding himself, and the second is very likely his as well; the first letter, however, signed 'Jack Blood', makes use of the forms 'does' and 'has' and is therefore despite its themes not usually attributed to Fielding. See the comments by Jensen (ii. 215–16), Cross (ii. 368), and Dudden (pp. 892 n., 893); but see also *CGJ* No. 33, below, p. 202 n. 2.

TO
ALEXANDER DRAWCANSIR, Esq;
Censor of Great Britain.

Sir,

I am a Subscriber to your Paper, and therefore take the Liberty to tell you, that there is the damn'dest Letter in that of the 25th of January,[1] I ever read; and I am so enraged at it that I can hardly keep my Temper.

I did not think, Sir, that any one Person in the World could have had the Assurance to justify, countenance, or support in Print, those two abominable Words WHY and WHEREFORE. They ought, by Act of Parliament, to be entirely prohibited; they are the Bane of every Thing that's joyous. O d–mn 'em, how many Pounds have they cost me? was it not for that cursed Word WHY, a Man might debauch Country Girls, almost for as little Money as one could buy a Turkey. Then, besides the Expence of Money, what an Expence of Lies and Oaths does this infamous Word WHY put us to? For if you attack a Farmer's handsome Maid or Daughter, she presently cries, "Why would you desire to ruin a poor innocent Girl?" And there is no getting the better of this confounded WHY, till you have given her Money enough to satisfy her for what she calls her Ruin. Then if you make your Attempt higher, amongst the Parsons or Officers Daughters, which are generally our Mark, you are presently question'd with "Why would you ruin me? Why won't you marry me? &c." Z—nds, Sir, is it not abominable, that a Man of Spirit and Fortune must be so plagued and stopp'd with this impertinent Word? For what is to be done? You must either give over the Pursuit, and lose perhaps the finest Girl in the World, or satisfy these WHYS, by Lying, Swearing, and a positive Promise of future Marriage. And is it not very hard, Sir, I say, that Gentlemen must be driven to these mean Arts, as they are call'd, (and indeed I should in any other Case call them so myself) to get a fine Girl, only by that infamous Word WHY? A Word which all your d–mn'd modest Women have ever at their Fingers Ends? whilst a good honest Whore never says WHY, but *what* will you give me? and your noble generous Women of Intrigue scorn such paltry Interrogations; and only ask you When? Where? How? D–mn me, Sir, these are the Words that fill a Man with Joy and Rapture; and yet one cannot help running after those modest Toads, altho' they cost so much Pains before one gets them, and all owing to their confounded WHYS and WHEREFORES; and after all our Pains, 'tis ten to one but we have Reason, in a very few Weeks, to grow tired of them. Many Instances I could give of the Disappointments these Words WHY and WHEREFORE have cost me in the Way of Gallantry;[2] But I must tell you, Sir,

[1] *CGJ* No. 7, the 'humble Complaint of Why and Wherefore', presented by a letter signed 'Sophia'.
[2] Cf. Fielding's definition of this word in *CGJ* No. 4 and his comments on the arts of seduction in *CGJ* No. 20.

the Mischief they do in all jolly Companies; for did not those Fellows, who are called sensible Men, sometimes come among us Bloods,[1] and confound us with their WHYS and WHEREFORES, we should be the cleverest Fellows in England; and as they are generally Parsons, or old rum Dogs who have a Privilege from Years or Profession, we cannot have the Satisfaction of giving the only proper Answer to such a Question; which is knocking them down, or sending them a Challenge; and therefore know not how to deal with them. I have told a Story myself in Company, that has set every one laughing ready to kill themselves, except one of those queer Fellows, who had no Wit nor Humour,[2] and could not find out the Joke: And by G–d, Sir, this Fellow only by asking me two or three damned WHYS, turned my Story in such a manner, and set all my heroic Exploits in such a trifling View, that the Company no longer laughed at the Story, but at the Person that told it. These Things I have seen often happen to others as well as myself, to the Bane of all Wit, Humour, Fun, and Jollity: And many a charming Scheme that has been proposed for breaking Windows, or storming a Bawdy-House, have I seen spoilt and laid aside, by a queer Fellow's happening to be of the Company, and bringing up some damn'd WHY and WHEREFORE.

There was poor Tom Gallop (who broke his Neck last Year, riding a Match he had made with Ned Raquett of five hundred Guineas, on his sweet Mare Cherry Lips) about three Years ago, as I and three or four more were going to Dinner at the —— at Newberry,[3] came riding in full Speed, and, our Dinner being just ready, honest Tom made one of the Company. Down he sat in his Chair; and "D–mn me (says he) how long do you think I have been coming, on that Horse you saw me ride, from Hyde-Park Corner." I think 'tis upwards of sixty Miles; one said seven Hours, another six, and another five: At last Tom swore, and shew'd his Watch, that it was under four Hours. But unluckily one of these WHY-ERS was in Company, who says to Tom, "I presume, Sir, you are come on some important Business, by the Speed you have made." "Not I (says Tom) D–mn me. I leave Business to those stupid Dogs who cannot enjoy Pleasure." "Then pray Sir," replied the other, "*why* did you ride so hard, to tire both yourself and Horse, when there was no Necessity for it?" Tom looked like a Fool, we all laughed, and a total Stop was put to all Tom's Wit and Humour, and he sat the whole Evening in the Dumps, nor dared to open his Lips about that or any Exploits of the same Kind, with which he intended to have entertained the Company for that Night. Thus, Sir, was the Mouth stopped of one of the jollyest Fellows

---

[1] 'Bucks' or rakes (*OED*).

[2] For Fielding's attitude toward this brand of wit and humor, see *CGJ* No. 19 (7 Mar.).

[3] i.e. Newbury, about 56 miles from London, where races were held; the major inns in Newbury at this period were the Globe and the White Hart.

in the Universe; and indeed, for fear of this d–mn'd WHY, very little Wit or Humour passed all that Evening.

Now after these Stories, and a hundred more I could tell you of my own Knowledge, will you, Sir, or any Man breathing, countenance the Petition or Complaint of WHY and WHEREFORE? Z——nds, Sir, it makes me in a Passion, and I am in a Passion, and if any Man breathing was to come into the Room, and ask me *why* I was in a Passion, d–mn me if I would not knock him down.

If you take proper Notice of this Letter, and forbid the Use of these Words in all polite and jolly Companies, you shall be always esteemed as a very honest Fellow, by

Your constant Reader, &c.
JACK BLOOD.

P.S. As to the Writer of the Letter signed Sophia, if 'tis a man I am not the only one of the Bloods that would give him his Deserts, could we but find him: And if 'tis a Woman, you may let her know that if she is young and handsome, all her WHYS and WHEREFORES shall not hinder me from doing as I please with her, d–mn me.

TO
ALEXANDER DRAWCANSIR, Esq;

Sir,

'Twas with infinite Pleasure I read your Glossary,[1] and only wish'd it greatly inlarged, in which I cannot think myself capable of giving you any Assistance; but beg, for the Sake of the Public, that you would continue to explain, according to the modern Meaning, all those Words that may daily occur to your Observation, and probably you will find still a very large Number that are at present doubtful in their Signification, or quite unintelligible.

Your giving to EATING the Title of a Science, is most humourously just in this Age, and I wish you had given us the Names of all the others, in the room of those old discarded Gentry, which are now scarce ever heard of, at least out of our two Universities.

In other Languages, that is, in the Greek and Latin, most Words are either of the masculine or feminine Gender; whereas in English, few but animated Things bear any Gender, except the Neuter: And I think these old-fashioned Things called the Sciences were all of the feminine Gender, which have led some People into a silly Argument, that Women had at least an equal Claim to them with the Men;[2] and others again have from thence

---

[1] See *CGJ* No. 4, above.

[2] On the question of the role of women in science and learning, cf. Fielding's gentle ridicule of Mrs Bennet's claims in *Amelia* (VI. vii); see also *CGJ* Nos. 23 and 56.

infer'd, that they were designed as Helpmates to the Men. But to prevent any such Disputes about the modern Sciences, suppose you was to divide them as below (i.e.)

The two first to be call'd Masculine, as being only for the Study and Practice of Men.—The two next to be call'd Feminine, as chiefly studied by the Women.—The two following to be call'd of the Common of two, as being studied and practised by both.—And to make up the Number seven,[1] the last to be called Neuter, as being studied and practised by Neither.

Masculine	{ *Fencing.* *Lying.*
Feminine	{ *Dressing.* *Fainting.*
Common of two	{ *Eating.* *Gaming.*
Neuter	*Morality.*

TO
Sir ALEXANDER DRAWCANSIR, Knt.

Sir,

I am a young Fellow of twenty-five, and the only Son of a Squire, who hath an Estate of six hundred per Ann. in the West of England. Tho' I am what you call country bred, yet I have been at Grammar-School, and have learned to dance, and will dance a Hornpipe with any Man for 20 l. *I say done first.*[2]

Now, Sir, you must know that my Father, who keeps his own Estate in his Hand, sends Oxen twice a Year to Smithfield Market, and I got'un this Bout,[3] for the vurst Time, to let me come up along wi um. And to be sure it is natural for a Newcomer, to go and zee all the Zights that he can. Accordingly, Sir, I went a few Days ago to Ranilay, to the what-dye-call it, the Jubberly Ball,[4] which, thof it cost me above a Guinea, I did not begrutch my Money, vor it was the vinest Zight I ever zeed in my Life.

---

[1] So as to form the seven sciences consisting of the *trivium* and *quadrivium*.

[2] 'Done: The word by which a wager is concluded; when a wager is offered, he that accepts it says *done*' (Johnson, *Dictionary*). Cf. *Joseph Andrews*, I. xvi.

[3] i.e. 'got him this time'.

[4] i.e. a 'Jubilee' ball held at Ranelagh Gardens, the fashionable place of entertainment constructed in Chelsea in 1742 and featuring a principal room or 'Rotunda' for concerts, promenades, and masquerades. On 26 Apr. 1749 a 'Grand Jubilee in the *Venetian* taste' was held there to celebrate the peace of Aix-la-Chapelle (see *GM* 19 [1749], 185, and Horace Walpole's account, *Yale Walpole*, xx. 46–8); from time to time thereafter 'Jubilee Balls' were held again at Ranelagh in the manner of the original event (see *GA*, 22 Apr. and 4 May 1752). 'Gubbin's' letter, with its comment on the indecency of a woman's dress at Ranelagh, voices a common complaint at the time; Fielding may, in fact, be alluding ironically to a famous episode at the second 'Venetian' Jubilee masquerade (1 May 1749), when Elizabeth Chudleigh, one of the maids of honor to the Princess of Wales, caused a sensation by appearing scantily clad as 'Iphigeneia' (see *Catalogue of Prints and Drawings in the British Museum*.

But here comes the Mischief; while I was walking about there, I spied a young Woman with——. Oh! Sir, it is impossible to tell you.——I never zeed such a Zight in all my born Days.——They were as round as a Bowl Dish, and as white as Snow itself.——Ycot! I zeed every bit o'urn, and to be zure it was a Zight enuff to make any young Man run mad.

Upon this, Sir, I went to several Volk, and asked 'um who the Lady was that was Owner of zuch Goods; but nobody could or would tell me. 'Till at last I took Courage, and, having watched my Opportunity, I opened my Mind to her, told her who I was, and asked her to ha' me; to which she answered that she was engaged. This drove me quite mad, especially as I had taken two or three Mugs that Afternoon; and I could not refrain, if I had been to be hanged, from kissing what I thought she could not shew for any other Purpose, but to dispose of.

Upon this the Lady seemed angry, and told me these Goods were already bespoke. Now, Sir, as I am told you are the only Person to be applied to for such Matters, I would be glad to know therefore whether it is a Custom here in London, for Volk to expose their Goods in the Market after they are sold or bespoke, especially such Goods as must make every Man's Mouth to water that looks at them.

> I am, Sir,
>
> Your Servant to
> command
> HUMPHRY GUBBIN[1]

Division I. Political and Personal Satires [1870–83], Nos. 3030–7). For other criticism of the immodesty of women's dress at Ranelagh and Vauxhall, see *Dress: A Satire* (1754) and William Whitehead's 'Song for Ranelagh' in Dodsley's *Collection of Poems*, iv (1755), 176. Both Ranelagh and Vauxhall were also frequently attacked in more general terms for promoting lewdness and immorality; see, for example, *DA*, 17 Apr. 1751, advertising a debate on the question by the Robin Hood Society, and *Dame Ranelagh's Remonstrance in Behalf of Herself and her Sisters* (1750), ironically defending these places against charges of immorality brought by the Middlesex Grand Jury. See also a letter in *LM* 20 (1751), 129–30, attacking Fielding's claim in his *Enquiry* that Ranelagh and Vauxhall represent acceptable places of diversion as long as their pleasures are confined to the upper classes (*Enquiry into the Causes of the late Increase of Robbers* [1751], pp. 11–12). See *Amelia*, ed. Martin Battestin, Wesleyan Edn. (Oxford, 1983), p. 247 n.

[1] A name used contemptuously to indicate a naive country bumpkin; 'Humphry Gubbin' is such a character in Steele's *The Tender Husband* (1705), and the name derives apparently from an uncouth family living near Dartmoor. Cf. Chesterfield, 'clothes . . . are as uneasy to me as they were to Humphrey Gubbin', *Letters*, ed. B. Dobrée (1932), v. 2129; and see the letters signed 'Humphry Gubbins' in *JJ* Nos. 11 and 14 (13 Feb., 5 Mar. 1748).

SATURDAY, APRIL 25, 1752.   NUMB. 33.

Odi profanum Vulgus.   HORACE. [1]

I hate profane Rascals.

Sir, [2]

In this very learned and enlightened Age, in which Authors are almost as numerous as Booksellers, I doubt not but your Correspondents furnish you with a sufficient Quantity of waste Paper. I perhaps may add to the Heap; for as Men do not always know the Motive of their own Actions, I may possibly be induced by the same Sort of Vanity as other puny Authors have been, to desire to be in Print. But I am very well satisfied with you for my Judge, and if you should not think proper to take any Notice of the Hint I have here sent you, I shall conclude that I am an impertinent Correspondent, but that you are a judicious and impartial Critic. In my own Defence, however, I must say that I am never better pleased than when I see extraordinary Abilities employed in the Support of his Honour and Religion, who has so bountifully bestowed them. 'Tis for this Reason that I wish you would take some Notice of the Character, or rather Story here sent you. In my Travels westward last Summer, I lay at an Inn in Somersetshire, remarkable for its pleasant Situation, and the obliging Behaviour of the Landlord, who, tho' a downright Rustic, had an awkward Sort of Politeness, arising from his good Nature, that was very pleasing, and, if I may be allowed the Expression, was a Sort of good Breeding undrest. As I intended to make a pretty long Journey the next Day, I rose time enough to behold that glorious Luminary the Sun set out on his Course, which by the bye is one of the finest Sights the Eye can behold; and as it is a thing seldom seen by People of Fashion, unless it be at the Theatre at Covent-Garden, [3] I could not help laying some Stress upon it here. The Kitchen in this Inn was a very pleasant Room; I therefore called for some Tea, sat me in the Window that I might enjoy the Prospect which the Country afforded, and a more beautiful one is not in the Power of Imagination to frame. This House was situated on the Top of a Hill, and for two Miles below it Meadows, enlivened with Variety of Cattle, and adorned with a greater Variety of Flowers, first caught my Sight. At the Bottom of this Vale ran a River, which seemed to promise Coolness and Refreshment to the

---

[1] *Odes*, III. i. 1: 'I hate the uninitiate crowd' (Loeb); the same motto is used for *CGJ* No. 49, with a different translation and a different application.

[2] Although this letter by 'R. S.' does not use Fielding's characteristic 'hath' and 'doth', it was included in his *Works* (1762) and seems clearly to be by Fielding himself; see Jensen, ii. 216, and Cross, ii. 372.

[3] The representation of the sun in Rich's pantomimes at Covent Garden was ridiculed by Fielding in *Tumble-Down Dick* (1736), where we find 'the Sun in a great chair in the Round-house'. At one point Phoebus remarks, 'You had better send for the sun from Covent Garden house, there's a sun that hatches an egg there, and produces a Harlequin'.

thirsty Cattle. The Eye was next presented with Fields of Corn that made a Kind of an Ascent, which was terminated by a Wood, at the Top of which appeared a verdant Hill, situate as it were in the Clouds, where the Sun was just arrived, and peeping o'er the Summit, which was at this Time covered with Dew, gilded it over with his Rays, and terminated my View in the most agreeable Manner in the World. In a Word, the elegant Simplicity of every Object round me, filled my Heart with such Gratitude, and furnished my Mind with such pleasing Meditations, as made me thank Heaven I was born. But this State of joyous Tranquillity was not of long Duration: I had scarce begun my Breakfast, when my Ears were saluted with a genteel Whistle, and the Noise of a Pair of Slippers descending the Stair-Case; and soon after I beheld a Contrast to my former Prospect, being a very beauish Gentleman, with a huge laced Hat on as big as Pistol's in the Play;[1] a Wig somewhat disheveled, and a Face which at once gave you a perfect Idea of Emptiness, Assurance, and Intemperance. His Eyes, which before were scarce open, he fixt on me with a Stare which testified Surprize, and his Coat was immediately thrown open to display a very handsome second-hand Gold laced Waistcoat. In one Hand he had a Pair of Saddle-bags, and in the other a Hanger of mighty Size, both of which, with a graceful G— d–mn you, he placed upon a Chair. Then advancing towards the Landlord, who was standing by me, he said, "By G— Landlord your Wine is damnable strong." "I don't know," replied the Landlord; "it is generally reckoned pretty good, for I have it all from London." "Pray who is your Wine-Merchant?" says the Man of Importance. "A very great Man," says the Landlord, "in his Way; perhaps you may know him, Sir, his Name is Kirby." *Ah, what honest Tom; he and I have crack'd many a Bottle of Claret together; he is one of the most considerable Merchants in the City; the Dog is hellish poor, damnable poor, for I don't suppose he is worth a Farthing more than a hundred thousand Pound; only a Plumb,*[2] *that's all; he is to be our Lord-Mayor next Year.* "I ask Pardon Sir, that is not the Man, for our Mr. Kirby's Name is not Thomas, but Richard."[3] *Ay,* says the Gentleman, *that's his Brother; they are Partners together.* "I believe," says the Landlord, "you are out Sir, for that Gentleman has no Brother." *D–mn your Nonsense, with you and your Outs,* says the Beau, *as if I should not know better than you country Puts;*[4] *I who have lived in London all my Life-time.*

---

[1] A reference to Theophilus Cibber's most famous role, as Pistol in *2 Henry IV*, a role which won him the sobriquet 'Ancient Pistol'; see *Champion*, 17 May 1740, the *Historical Register* (1737), and the mock-autobiography *An Apology for the Life of Mr. T———— C———, Comedian* (1740), sometimes attributed to Fielding, all of which ridicule Cibber in this role. The print 'Cibber, in the Character of Ancient Pistol' (1733) shows him wearing a laced cocked-hat with a huge flap and a cockade (*Catalogue of Prints and Drawings in the British Museum. Division I. Political and Personal Satires* [1870–3], No. 1933); the same print forms the frontispiece to *Theophilus Cibber to David Garrick* (1759).

[2] i.e. 'plum', £100,000.

[3] Apparently fictitious; no wine merchant by that name has been identified.

[4] Louts or bumpkins (*OED*).

"I ask a thousand Pardons," says the Landlord; "I hope no Offence, Sir." *No, no*, cries the other, *We Gentlemen know how to make Allowance for your Country-breeding.* Then stepping to the Kitchen-door, with an audible Voice he called the Ostler, and in a very graceful Accent said, *D–mn your Blood, you cock-ey'd Son of a Bitch, bring me my Boots; Did not you hear me call?* Then turning to the Landlord, said, *Faith that Mr. What-de-callum, the Exciseman, is a d–mn'd jolly Fellow.* "Yes, Sir," says the Landlord, "he is a merryish Sort of a Man." "But," says the Gentleman, *As for that Schoolmaster, he is the queerest Bitch I ever saw; he looks as if he could not say Bah to a Goose.* "I don't know, Sir," says the Landlord, "he is reckoned to be a desperate good Scollard[1] about us, and the Gentry likes him vastly, for he understands the Measurement of Land and Timber, knows how to make Dials, and such Things; and for Cyphering few can out-do'en." *Ay*, says the Gentleman, *he does look like a Cypher indeed, for he did not speak three Words all last Night.* The Ostler now produced the Boots, which the Gentleman taking in his Hand, and having placed himself in a Chair, addressed in the following Speech. *My good Friends, Mr. Boots, I tell you plainly that if you plague me so damnably as you did Yesterday Morning, by G—I'll commit you to the Flames; stap my Vitals, as my Lord Huntington says in the Play:*[2] He then looked full in my Face, and asked the Landlord if he had ever been at Drury-Lane Play-House; which he answered in the Negative. *What*, says he, *did you never hear talk of Mr. Garrick* and *King Richard?* "No Sir," says the Landlord. "By G—," says the *Gent.* "he is the cleverest Fellow in *England;*" he then spouted a Speech out of *King Richard*, which begins, Give me an Horse, &c.[3] "There," says he, "that, that is just like Mr. Garrick." Having pleased himself vastly with this Performance, he shook the Landlord by the Hand with great good Humour, and said, *by G— you seem to be an honest Fellow and good Blood, if you'll come and see me in London, I'll give you your Skin full of Wine, and treat you with a Play and a Whore every Night you stay. I'll show you how it is to live, my Boy. But here, bring me some Paper, my Girl; come lets have one of your Love-Leters to air my Boots.*[4] Upon which the Landlord presented him with a Piece of an old News-Paper, *D–n you*, says the Gent. *this is not half enough, have you never a Bible or Common-Prayer Book in the House? Half a Dozen Chapters of Genesis, with a few Prayers, make an excellent Fire in a Pair of Boots.* "Oh! Lord forgive you," says the Landlord, "sure you would not burn such Books as those." *No!* cries the Spark, *Where was you born; go into a Shop of London, and buy some*

---

[1] Supposedly an illiterate person's version of 'scholar'; see *OED*, s.v. 'scollardical'.

[2] Another detail signifying the speaker's ignorance, since 'stap my Vitals' is the favorite phrase of Lord Foppington in Vanbrugh's *The Relapse* (1696), not of a 'Lord Huntington'.

[3] *Richard III*, v. iii. 177 ff. It was one of Garrick's best known roles, and Hogarth's famous painting of Garrick (1745) shows him as Richard. He was currently sharing the lead with Mossop in *Richard III* at Drury Lane, his most recent performance being 3 Feb. 1752.

[4] To 'air' one's boots was to dry them out by a fire (*OED*).

Butter or a Quartern of Tea, and then you'll see what Use is made of these Books.[1]
"Ay," says the Landlord, "we have a Saying here *in our Country*, that 'tis as
sure as the Devil is in London,[2] and if he was not there, they could not be so
wicked as they be." Here a Country-Fellow who had been standing up in
one Corner of the Kitchen, eating of cold Bacon and Beans, and who I
observed trembled at every Oath this Spark swore, took his Dish and Pot,
and marched out of the Kitchen, fearing, as I afterwards learnt, that the
House would fall down about his Ears, for he was sure, he said, *that Man in
the Gold Laced-Hat was the Devil.* The young Spark, having now displayed all
his Wit and Humour, and exerted his Talents to the utmost, thought he had
sufficiently recommended himself to my Favour, and convinced me he was a
Gentleman. He therefore with an Air addressed himself to me, and asked
me, *which Way I was travelling?* To which I gave him no Answer. He then
exalted his Voice; but at my continuing silent, he asked the Landlord if I was
deaf? Upon which, the Landlord told him he did not believe the Gentleman
was dunch,[3] for that he talked very well just now. The Man of Wit whispered
in the Landlord's Ear, and said, "I suppose he is either a Parson or a Fool."
He then drank a Dram, observing that a Man should not cool too fast; paid
Six-pence more than his Reckoning, called for his Horse, gave the Ostler a
Shilling, and gallopped out of the Inn, thoroughly satisfied that we all agreed
with him in thinking him a clever Fellow, and a Man of great Importance.
The Landlord smiling, took up his Money, and said he was a comical
Gentleman, but that it was a thousand Pities he swore so much; if it was not
for that he was a very good Customer, and as generous as a Prince, for that
the Night before, he had treated every body in the House. I then asked him,
if he knew that comical Gentleman as he called him? "No really Sir," said
the Landlord, "tho' a Gentleman was saying last Night, that he was a Sort of
Rider, or Rideout[4] to a Linen-Draper at London." This, Mr. Censor, I have
since found to be true; for having Occasion to buy some Cloth, I went last
Week into a Linen-Draper's Shop, in which I found a young Fellow whose
decent Behaviour, and plain Dress, shewed he was a Tradesman. Upon
looking full in his Face, I thought I had seen it before, nor was it long before
I recollected where it was, and that this was the same Beau I had met with in
Somersetshire. The Difference in the same Man in London, where he was
known, and in the Country where he was a Stranger, was beyond
Expression; and was it not impertinent to make Observations to you, I could
inlarge upon this Sort of Behaviour; for I am firmly of Opinion, that there is
neither Spirit or good Sense in Oaths, or any Wit or Humour in Blasphemy.

[1] See *CGJ* No. 6, above, p. 48 n. 5.
[2] Not listed by Tilley; but cf. 'as sure as God is in Gloucestershire' (Tilley, G 174).
[3] Deaf.   [4] 'Commercial traveller' (*OED*, citing this reference).

But as vulgar Errors require an abler Pen than mine to correct them, I shall leave that Task to you, and am Sir,

Your Humble Servant,

R. S.

M.

TUESDAY, APRIL 28, 1752. NUMB. 34.

Natio Comæda est.

JUVENAL.[1]

We are a Nation of Players.

It is the Advice of Solomon, to train up a Child in the Way he shall go;[2] and this in the Opinion of Quintilian can never be undertaken too early. He indeed begins his Institution even with the very Nurse.[3]

The wise Man here, very plainly supposes a previous Determination in the Parent in what Way he intends his Child shall go: For without having fixed this with Certainty, it will be impossible for any Man to fulfil the Precept.

Now all the Ways of Life, in which, in this Country, Men walk themselves, and in which they so manifestly intend to train their Children, seem to me, to be reducible to two; viz. the Way of spending an Estate and the Way of getting one. These may indeed, in this Sense, be called the two great high Roads in this Kingdom.

As to the former, it is much the less beaten and frequented Track, as it requires a certain Viaticum[4] obvious to the Reader, which is not in the Possession of every one; in this Way therefore the eldest Sons of great Families, and Heirs of great Estates, can only be trained. The Methods of training here, are no more than twofold, both very easy and apposite; it is therefore no Wonder that they are both pursued with very little Deviation by almost every Parent. The one which is universally practised in the Country, contains very few Rules, and these extremely simple; such as Drinking, Racing, Cockfighting, Hunting, with other rural Exercises. The other, which is proper to the Town, and indeed to the higher People, is somewhat more complex. This includes Dancing, Fencing, Whoring, Gaming, Travelling, Dressing, French Connoisseurship, and perhaps two or three other less material Articles.[5]

But the great and difficult Point is that of training Youth in the other great

---

[1] *Satires*, iii. 100.　　[2] Proverbs 22: 6.　　[3] *Institutio oratoria*, I. i. 1–5.

[4] A supply of money or provisions for use on a journey (*OED*).

[5] For other examples of Fielding's irony directed at the education of children of 'the higher People' in both town and country, see *CGJ* Nos. 42 and 56; see also *JJ* No. 22 (30 Apr. 1748).

Road, namely, in the Way to get an Estate. Here, as in our Journey over vast and wide Plains, the many different Tracks are apt to beget Incertainty and Confusion, and we are often extremely puzzled which of these to chuse for ourselves, and which to recommend to our Children.

The most beaten Tracks in this Road are those of the Professions, such as the Church, the Law, the Army, &c. In some one of these, the younger Children of the Nobility and Gentry have usually been trained, often with very ill Success; arising sometimes from a partial Opinion of the Talents of the Child, and more often from flattering ourselves with Hopes of more Interest with the Great, than we have really had.[1]

To all these Professions many Things may be objected, as we shall presently see, when we compare them with a Path in Life, which I am about to recommend to my Reader, and which we shall find clear from most of the Objections that may be raised against any other.

Without further Preface, the Way of Life which I mean to recommend, is that of the Stage, in which, I shall hope for the future, to see several of our young Nobility and Gentry trained up, and particularly those of the most promising Parts.

In the first Place then, the Stage at present promises a much better Provision than any of the Professions:[2] For tho' perhaps it is true that there are in the Church, the Law, the State, the Army, &c. some few Posts which yield the Possessors greater Profit than is to be acquired on the Stage; yet these bear no Proportion to the infinite Numbers who are trained in the several Professions, and who almost literally starve. The Income of an Actor of any Rank, is from six to twelve hundred a Year;[3] whereas that of two-

[1] Fielding adopts the manner here of the numerous books of the period designed to guide young people and their parents in the choice of a career, books which typically warn their readers against the difficulty of obtaining success in one of the learned professions; see, for example, *A General Description of all Trades . . . by which Parents, Guardians, and Trustees may . . . make Choice of Trades agreeable to the Capacity, Education . . . and Fortune of the Youth under their Care* (1747); R. Campbell, *The London Tradesman, Being a Compendious View of all the Trades, Professions, Arts . . . Calculated for the Information of Parents* (1747); and Joseph Collyer, *The Parent's and Guardian's Directory* (1761).

[2] In this argument Fielding's irony is directed not so much at the stage itself as at the currently low status of the traditional professions. Cf. James Bramston's advice to English youth to quit Oxford and Cambridge for Haymarket and Covent Garden: 'Boast not your incomes now, as heretofore, / Ye book-learn'd Seats! the Theatres have more: / Ye stiff-rump'd heads of Colleges be dumb, / A singing Eunuch gets a larger Sum. / Have some of you three hundred by the Year, / Booth, Rich, and Cibber, twice three thousand clear' (*The Man of Taste* [1733], p. 18). Cf. also ch. 3 of the satire on Theophilus Cibber, *An Apology for the Life of Mr. T——— C———, Comedian* (1740), describing in parody of Colley Cibber's *Apology*, 'The Author's several Chances for the Church, the Court, and the Army', none of which prove 'so profitable as the Profession of an Actor' (p. 28). See also James Ralph, *The Case of our present Theatrical Disputes* (1743), pp. 48–61, *passim*, and Ralph's more vigorous complaint against the disproportionate incomes allotted to actors in *The Case of Authors by Profession or Trade, Stated* (1758), pp. 41–6.

[3] In these paragraphs Fielding appears to exaggerate the income of actors, except for the most famous. At Covent Garden in 1761 salaries for actors and actresses of the first rank (excluding money from benefit performances) were in the range of £272–87, whereas those in the bottom level received only £35–45 a year. The leading figures could also receive a fixed seasonal sum, instead of a salary

thirds of the Gentlemen of the Army is considerably under one hundred; the Income of nine-tenths of the Clergy is less than 50 l. a Year; and the Profits in the Law, to ninety-nine in a hundred, amount not to a single Shilling.[1]

And as for those few Posts of great Emolument, upon which we all cast our Eyes, as the Adventurers in a Lottery do on the few great Prizes, if we impartially examine our own Abilities, how few of us shall dare to aspire so high; whereas on the Stage, scarce any Abilities are required, and we see Men whom no body allows to deserve the Name of Actors, enjoying Salaries of three, four, and five hundred a Year.

Again, if we consider the great Pains and Time, the Head-achs and the Heart-achs, which lead up to the Top of either the Army or the Law,

> Qui studet optatam cursu contingere metam,
> Multa tulit, fecitque puer.[2]

This Consideration will sufficiently discourage our Attempts, especially when on the other Hand we may on the Stage leap all at once into Eminence; and if we expect no more than four or five hundred Pound for the first Year of our acting, our Demands will be thought modest.

And farther in any of the Professions, all our Abilities will be thrown away, and all our Time and Labour lost, unless we have other Ingredients to recommend us. Unless we have some powerful Friend or Relation, or some beautiful Wife or Sister, we shall never procure an Opportunity of shewing the World what we are;[3] whereas to the Stage no Interest is necessary to introduce you. The publishing the Name of a Gentleman who never acted before in the Play-bills, will fill the House as surely as if he proposed to get into a Bottle,[4] and no Manager is ashamed of putting you at first into any of his principal Parts.

based on the number of performances, or even a percentage of the box-office receipts. Mrs Clive in her most successful period was guaranteed £700 a year plus a benefit. See *The London Stage*, Pt. 4, vol. I, pp. lvii–lix.

[1] Cf. the warnings against these careers in R. Campbell's *The London Tradesman* (1747): overestimating one's 'Interest' can lead to a life as a poor clergyman, than which 'there is not a more helpless Thing in Nature' (p. 36); as for attornies, 'They are so numerous that there is not Bread enough for half of them' (p. 72)—half the young barristers, Campbell claims, would starve without independent means. The poverty of the clergy is a consistent concern for Fielding in his later period; see, for example, *Joseph Andrews*, I. xvi, II. xiv, his series on the clergy in the *Champion* (29 Mar., 5, 13, 19 Apr. 1740), and the struggles of Mr Bennet in *Amelia*, VIII. The difficulty of rising in the army is, of course, also a constant theme throughout *Amelia*; see especially IV. viii, where Fielding openly calls on the public to provide better support for soldiers.

[2] Horace, *Art of Poetry*, 412–13: 'He who in the race-course craves to reach the longed-for goal, has borne much and done much as a boy' (Loeb).

[3] Cf. the debate in *Amelia*, XI. ii, between Doctor Harrison and a nobleman on the need for 'interest' rather than 'merit' in the preferment of young army officers.

[4] See *CGJ* No. 12, above, p. 90 n. 2, on the 'Bottle Conjurer'. For a contrary view of the reception accorded new actors, see the account of Garrick's first performance, in Thomas Davies's *Life of David Garrick* (1780), i. 39.

And if we view this in the Light of Ambition, the Stage will have no less Advantage over the Professions. To personate a great Character, three Hours in the twenty-four, is a Matter of more Consequence than it is generally esteemed. The World itself is commonly called a Stage; and, in the Eye of the greatest Philosophers the Actions in both appear to be equally real, and of equal Consequence. Where then is the mighty Difference between personating a Great Man on the great Theatre, or on the less? In both Cases we often assume that Character when it doth not really belong to us, and a very indifferent Player acts it sometimes better than his Right Honourable Brother, and with ten thousand times the Applause.[1]

It was not therefore without Reason that our worthy Laureat, in the excellent Apology for his Life, gave Thanks to Providence that he did not in his Youth betake himself either to the Gown or the Sword.[2] Wise indeed as well as happy was his Choice, as many of his Cotemporaries, whose ill Stars led them to the Way of those Professions, had the Question been put to them on their Death-Bed, must have acknowledged. How many of these his Cotemporaries, who have professed the Laws or Religion of their Country; how many others who have fought its Battles, after an obscure and wretched Life of Want and Misery, have bequeathed their Families to the Stalls and the Streets?[3]

That the Reverse hath been the Fate of this Gentleman I need not mention, and am pleased to think. And yet in the Days of his acting, nothing like to the present Encouragement was given on the Stage. Mrs. Oldfield herself (as I have been informed) had not half the Theatrical-Income of our present principal Actresses.[4] To what greater Height it may rise I know not;

---

[1] On the conventional parallel between the state and the stage, see *CGJ* No. 15 and page 105 n. 1.

[2] Colley Cibber, in *An Apology for the Life of Colley Cibber* (1740): 'When I look back to that time, it almost makes me tremble to think what Miseries, in fifty Years farther in Life, such an unthinking Head was liable to! To ask, why Providence afterwards took more care of me, than I did of my self, might be making too Bold an enquiry. . . . All I can say to that Point, is, that I am thankful, and amaz'd at it!' (p. 36). Fielding's annoyance with this statement comes through clearly in his allusion to it in *Joseph Andrews*, 1. i: 'How artfully doth the former, by insinuating that he *escaped* being promoted to the highest Stations in Church and State, teach us a Contempt of worldly Grandeur'; cf. *Champion*, 6 May 1740.

[3] Cf. the reaction of the Lord Chamberlain, the Duke of Grafton, upon learning in 1743 that 'a man could gain, merely by playing, the yearly salary of 500 £. His grace observed, that a near relation of his, who was then an inferior officer in the navy, exposed his life in behalf of his king and country for less than half that sum' (Thomas Davies, *Memoirs of the Life of David Garrick* [1780], i. 68).

[4] Anne Oldfield (1683–1730), the most celebrated actress of the first quarter of the century and the star of Fielding's first play (*Love in Several Masques*, 1728), received as salary and benefit for fourteen weeks of acting in 1708–9 about £57, supplemented by gifts of £120 (*London Stage*, Pt. 2, vol. i, p. cxxii). Fielding's point about the increase in salaries between that period and the mid-century is amply borne out by other testimony; see *London Stage*, Pt. 3, vol. i, p. cxxix. According to one account Oldfield's own salary increased during her career from £150 in her first season at Drury Lane to about £500 a year some years before her death, 'a Price never before given to any one'; see *Authentick Memoirs of the Life of . . . Mrs. Ann Oldfield* 3rd edn. (1730), p. 32; for yet another estimate of her salary, again in contrast to the income of later actresses, see James Ralph, *The Case of Authors by Profession or Trade, Stated* (1758), p. 42.

but from the present flourishing Condition of the Stage, and from the proportionable Decline of the learned Professions, I think it may be prophesied, that it will be as common hereafter to say, that such a particular Estate was got by the Stage, as it was formerly to see great Houses rise by the Law.

C.

SATURDAY, MAY 2, 1752. NUMB. 35.

Ἀπόλοιτο πρῶτος αὐτὸς
Ὁ τὸν ἄργυρον φιλήσας;
Διὰ τοῦτον οὐκ ἀδελφὸς,
Διὰ τοῦτον οὐ τοκῆες,
Πόλεμοι φόνοι δι' αὐτόν.

ANACREON.[1]

See the Translation afterwards.

TO
Sir ALEXANDER DRAWCANSIR.

Bedlam, Apr. 1,
1752.

Sir,

I make no Question but before you have read half through my Letter, you will be surprized at its being dated as above;[2] and may perhaps agree with the Conclusion which I have made long ago, that this Place is set apart by the English for the Confinement of all those who have more Sense than the rest of their Countrymen.

However that be, I shall begin by telling you very bluntly, that if you really intend to bring about any Reformation in this Kingdom, you will certainly miss your End, and for this simple Reason, because you are absolutely mistaken in the Means.

Physicians affirm, that before any vicious Habits can be repaired in the natural Constitution, it is necessary to know and to remove their Cause. The same holds true in the political. Without this in both Instances we may possibly patch up and palliate, but never can effectually cure.[3]

Now, Sir, give me Leave to say, you do not appear to me to have in the least guess'd at the true Source of all our political Evils, neither do you seem to be in any Likelihood of ever acquiring even a Glimpse of any such Knowledge. It is no Wonder therefore, that instead of pursuing the true

---

[1] See *Anacreontea* (Loeb), pp. 56–7; in Fielding's own edition (Baker, item 550), *Anacreontis teii Carmina*, ed. W. Baxter (1695), pp. 84–6, the poem has the Latin title *In Amorem*.

[2] i.e. from Bedlam; cf. Swift, *Tale of a Tub*, sect. IX.

[3] Cf. Fielding's *Enquiry* (1751), where political reality forces a very different conclusion: 'To say the Truth, bad Habits in the Body Politic . . . are seldom to be wholly eradicated. Palliatives alone are to be applied' (p. 5); for Fielding's habitual use of the commonplace analogy between the body politic and the human body, see Malvin R. Zirker, *Fielding's Social Pamphlets* (Berkeley and Los Angeles, 1966), pp. 65–70.

Method of Cure, you should more than once, in the Course of your Lucubrations, have thrown out Hints which would actually tend to heighten the Disease.

Know then, Sir, that it is I alone who have penetrated to the very Bottom of all the Evil. With infinite Pains and Study I have discovered the certain Cause of all that national Corruption, Luxury, and Immorality, which have polluted our Morals; and of consequence it is I alone who am capable of prescribing the Cure.

But when I lay this sole Claim to such Discovery, I would be understood to have Respect only to the Moderns. To the Philosophers among the Antients, and to some of their Poets, I am well apprized that this invaluable Secret was well known, as I could prove by numberless Quotations.[1] It occurs indeed so very often in their Works, that I am not a little surprized how it came to escape the Observation of a Gentleman who seems to have been so conversant with those illustrious Lamps of real Knowledge and Learning.

Without further Preface then, what is the true Fountain of that Complication of political Diseases which infests this Nation, but Money? Money! which, as the Greek Poet says in my Motto, *may he perish that first invented; for this it is which destroys the Relation of Brother and of Parent, and which introduces Wars and every Kind of Bloodshed into the World.*

If this be granted, as it surely must, where is the Remedy? Is it not to remove the fatal Cause, by extirpating this poisonous Metal, this Pandora's Box out of the Nation.

But tho' the Advantages arising from this Abolition, are, in my Opinion, extremely self-evident; yet as they may possibly not strike with equal Force upon the Minds of others, since no Man hath in my Memory given the least obscure Hint of such a Project; I shall mention some few of the greatest; and, to avoid a common Place of those Authors I have above mentioned, I shall confine myself to such Instances as particularly affect this Country.

First then, it would effectually put an End to all that Corruption which every Man almost complains of, and of which every Man almost partakes; for by this Means those Contentions which have begun and continued this Corruption, and which always will continue it, will immediately subside. The Struggle will be then, not who shall serve their Country in great and difficult Posts and Employments; but who shall be excused from serving it: And the People being left to themselves, will always fix upon the most capable, who

---

[1] As Fielding suggests, the corrupting power of money is a thought too common for annotation; cf. especially, however, Juvenal, *Satires*, vi. 291–4, 297–300, lines which Fielding had quoted in his *Enquiry* (1751), p. ix, as typical of a poet's outcry against the evils of luxury. In his own early translation of Juvenal's satire (*Miscellanies*, 1743), the second passage reads, 'Money's the Source of all our Woes; / Money! whence Luxury o'erflows, / And in a Torrent, like the *Nile*, / Bears off the Virtues of this Isle.'

by the Fundamental Laws of our Constitution will be compelled to enter into their Service.[1] Thus a certain Method called Election, which is of very singular Use in a Nation of Freedom, will be again revived; otherwise it may possibly sink only to a Name.[2]

For tho' I admit it possible, that bare Ambition may incite some Persons to attempt Employments for which they are utterly unfit, yet the very Powers of Bribery would be thus taken away, or would be rendered so public, that it would *then* be easily within the Power of Law to suppress it: For no Man could distribute a Herd of Cattle, or a Flock of Sheep in private.

Secondly, this Method would effectually put a Stop to Luxury, or would reduce it to that which was the Luxury of our Ancestors, and which may more properly be called Hospitality.[3]

Thirdly, it would be of the highest Advantage to Trade, for it would prevent our dealing any longer with those Bloodsucking Nations, who take not our own Commodities in Barter for theirs. This Kind of Traffic, I might perhaps be expected to speak more favourably of, as it so plainly tends to remove the Evil of which I complain, and in Process of Time would possibly effect that excellent Purpose. But I must observe, that however advantageous the End may be, the Means are not so adviseable; nay if we suffer any Money to remain among us, I think there may be good Reasons shewed, why we should retain as much as we can. It is often indeed mischievous to do that by halves, which it would be highly useful to do effectually: For this must certainly be allowed, that while Money is permitted to be the Representative of all Things; as it is at present, none but a Nation of Idiots would constantly put it into the Hands of their Enemies.[4]

[1] See *CGJ* No. 2, above, p. 23 and n. 3.

[2] Satires on the corrupt state of elections were rife in the period and had been a commonplace motif in the Opposition to Walpole; see e.g. Fielding's plays *Don Quixote in England* (1734) and *Pasquin* (1736); the brouhaha over the Westminster election of 1749 would also be fresh in Fielding's mind (see *CGJ* No. 58).

[3] The condemnation of 'luxury' was a commonplace throughout the century, with assaults on the power of money having been particularly associated with the Opposition to Walpole and with Mandeville providing the best-known answer to the usual denunciations of luxury; see Isaac Kramnick, *Bolingbroke and His Circle* (Cambridge, Mass., 1968), pp. 73–4, and John Sekora, *Luxury: The Concept in Western Thought* (Baltimore, 1977), chs. 2 and 3. Fielding often inveighed against luxury in quite conventional terms; see, for example, *Champion*, 19 Feb. 1740; *True Patriot*, No. 7 (17 Dec. 1745); *A Charge to the Grand Jury* (1749), pp. 53–4; *Amelia*, XI. ii; and Job Vinegar's voyage to a nation whose deity is 'MNEY', *Champion*, 20 Mar. 1740. In *An Enquiry into the Causes of the late Increase of Robbers* (1751), however, he accepts, with obvious reluctance, the Mandevillian view that luxury is the price paid for a flourishing commercial society, that 'Trade and Luxury do indeed support each other' (p. xii), arguing only that the mischief caused by luxury is lessened if it can 'be confined to the Palaces of the Great' (p. 4). See Zirker, *Fielding's Social Pamphlets*, pp. 76–8.

[4] Behind this paragraph is the basic mercantilist assumption that if exports exceed imports the money in a country will increase, whereas an unfavorable balance of trade will result in a disastrous decrease in the supply of gold and silver in the country; see E. Lipson, *Economic History of England* (1934), iii. 85. Concern over an unfavorable balance of trade with France, in particular, a concern which dated from the 17th cent., was much in the air in the mid-18th cent.; see *LM* 16 (1747), 356–7; Josiah Tucker, *A Brief Essay on the Advantages and Disadvantages which respectively attend France and*

Fourthly, it would restore certain excellent Things, such as Piety, Virtue, Honour, Goodness, Learning, &c. all which are totally abolished by Money, or so counterfeited by it, that no one can tell the true from the false; the Word Rich indeed is at present considered, to signify them all; but of this enough may be found in the old Philosophers and Poets, whom I have before mentioned.

Again how desirous would the Lawyers be to put a speedy End to a Suit, or the physical People to a Disease; if once my Scheme should take Place. It may be said indeed, that they would then carry away Men's Goods and Chattles, as they do now from those who have no Money; but I answer, that this is done in Order to convert them into Money; for otherwise, they would hardly admit the ragged and lousy Bed of a poor Wretch into their Houses.

For the same Reason my Scheme would effectually put an End to all Robberies; a Matter which seems so much to puzzle the Legislature:[1] For tho' our Goods are sometimes stolen as well as our Money, yet the former are only taken in Order to convert them into the latter. It is not the Use, but the Value of a Watch, Snuff-Box or Ring, that is considered by the Robber, who always thinks with Hudibras,

> *What is the Worth of any thing,*
> *But so much Money as 'twill bring?*[2]

I shall add but one Particular more; which is, that my Scheme would most certainly provide for the Poor,[3] and that by an infallible (perhaps the only infallible) Method, by removing the Rich. Where there are no Rich, there will of Consequence be found no Poor: For Providence hath in a wonderful Manner provided in every Country, a plentiful Subsistence for all its Inhabitants; and where none abound, none can want.

Having long meditated on this excellent Scheme, so long that if you will believe some People, I have cracked my Brain, I was resolved to acquit myself, and to shew by way of Example, how fully I was convinced of the Truth of my Principles. I therefore converted an Estate of three hundred Pounds a Year into Money; of this, I put a competent Sum in my Pocket, and took my next Heir with me upon the Thames, where I began to unload my Pockets into the Water. But I had scarce discharged three Handfuls, before

Great Britain with Regard to Trade, 3rd edn. (1753), pp. ii–iii, 153–4; Sir Matthew Decker, *An Essay on the Causes of the Decline of the Foreign Trade*, 2nd edn. (1750); and Malachy Postlethwayt, *Britain's Commercial Interest Explained and Improved* (1757), ii. 307.

[1] See Fielding's *Enquiry* (1751), *passim*; for the legislative efforts in 1751 and 1752 to deal with the problem, see Hugh Amory, 'Henry Fielding and the Criminal Legislation of 1751-2', *PQ* 50 (1971), 175–92. See also *CGJ* No. 25.

[2] Hudibras, Second Part, i. 465–6; the first line should read, 'For what is *worth* in any thing'.

[3] For the pamphlet literature dealing with this problem and the background to Fielding's own *Proposal* (1753) for caring for the poor, see Zirker, *Fielding's Social Pamphlets*, pp. 9–29, 34–5; see also *CGJ* Nos. 11 and 36 and *Enquiry* (1751), sect. IV.

my Heir seized me, and with the Assistance of the Waterman, conveyed me back to Shore. I was for a Day secured in an Apartment of my own House; and thence the next Morning, by a Conspiracy among my Relations, brought hither, where I am like to remain, till the rest of Mankind return to their Senses.

I am, SIR,

Your most obedient Servant,

MISARGURUS.[1]

A.

TUESDAY, MAY 5, 1752. NUMB. 36.

NEMO *adeo ferus est ut non mitescere possit.*

HORACE.[2]

NOBODY *is such a Rascal, that I have no Hopes of reclaiming him.*

Every Body to the Censor of Great-Britain, Greeting.

Sir,

Tho' I have not *altogether* the Pleasure of any personal Acquaintance with you, I have heard of your Fame, and am, *for the most Part at least,* your Admirer. I do not however preface thus, in order to induce you to do me Justice in your Censorial Capacity: this I am convinced you would do me, tho' I was a mere Stranger, nay even tho' I was your Enemy.

To you then, Sir, as Censor of Great-Britain, I make my Complaint. My Name is EVERY BODY, and the Person against whom I complain is NO-BODY. I do not love to use harsh Appellations, but I might be almost justified, if Passion should hurry me so far, since the Injuries done me by Nobody, are such as almost defy all human Patience.

You are to know, Sir, that among other Things, I am one of great Business. Indeed every thing which belongs to the Public, is properly my Care; tho' at the same Time I have the Honour to say, that I receive no Salary from the Government. Now Sir, this officious Fellow, No-body, asserts, that whatever is my Business, is his. This Falsehood, however monstrous it may appear, he hath actually persuaded the Generality of People to believe, so that if ever I meddle in public Affairs, I am sure to be laughed at for my Pains; and as this is a great Discouragement, it cannot be wondered at, that I have long declined doing any Service to my Country, the Consequence of which is, that No-body takes upon him to regulate and

---

[1] 'Hater of money'.

[2] *Epistles,* I. i. 39: 'No one is so savage that he cannot be tamed' (Loeb).

reform all Manner of public Grievances and Nusances, and when Nothing of this Kind is done as it should be, I am sure to bear the Blame.

It is incredible what a Party this Wretch hath got on his Side. Above a Year ago a certain Gentleman published a little Book, in which, he endeavoured to set forth the national Misconduct in their Manner of *providing for the Poor.*[1] I immediately fell to Work and within a few Months produced a vast Number of Schemes for redressing this Evil, when my old Antagonist began to put in his Claim, and all his Party cried out, that No-body was equal to the Task, nay it was confidently asserted, that I myself acknowledged it, tho' I solemnly assure you, I never said any such Thing.

Numberless indeed are the Instances of this horrid Kind of Injustice done me by this Monster and his wicked Crew. Nothing being commoner, than to put Words into my Mouth, and to make me the Inventor and Reporter of the most horrid Slanders, even such as I never heard of.[2] And what is most astonishing, when the Falshood of some of these Stories have been detected, and the Friends of the injured Parties have endeavoured to bear them to the Fountain-Head, No-body hath had the Assurance openly to confess himself to be the Author.

Again, Sir, when I have attempted to do Justice to some great and good Character, and if I may be allowed the Expression, to blow the Trumpet of his Fame, there have not been wanting among the Creatures of this No-body, some who have transferred the Honour of applauding Merit from me to him, and have boldly asserted, that No-body ever gave the Person a good Word, when in Reality it was I that commended, and No-body ever spoke against him.

If I was to enumerate all the Injuries done me by this Fellow and his Family, it would tire your Patience to read the Half of them. Nothing is more common than for some young Lady of the Family to report that I was present

---

[1] Fielding refers to his own *Enquiry into the Causes of the late Increase of Robbers*, published in Jan. 1751, of which the fourth and longest section concerns 'the improper Regulation of what is called the Poor in this Kingdom, arising, I think, partly from the Abuse of some Laws, and partly from the total Neglect of others; and . . . somewhat perhaps from a Defect in the Laws themselves' (p. 31). Though he analyzes the problem and makes brief reference to his having a 'Plan' to solve it, it was not until Jan. 1753 that his own *Proposal for Making an Effectual Provision for the Poor* was published. On the 'vast Number of Schemes' produced both before and after the *Enquiry*, see Malvin R. Zirker, *Fielding's Social Pamphlets* (Berkeley and Los Angeles, 1966), pp. 34–5, 117–31; as Zirker points out, royal interest in the problem, as expressed in the king's speech opening Parliament on 17 Jan. 1751, together with the work of a Parliamentary committee, was probably responsible for the sudden increase in pamphlets on the poor. As well as full-length studies and proposals, such as Thomas Alcock's *Observations on the Defects of the Poor Laws* (Jan. 1752), William Hay's *Remarks on Laws relating to the Poor* (1735; repr. Apr. 1751), and Charles Gray's *Considerations on Several Proposals Lately Made* (1751), the monthly magazines carried contributions to the debate; see e.g. *GM* 21 (1751), 659, and a series of proposals for county workhouses in *LM* 20 (1751), 499–503, 544–52. See also *CGJ* No. 11 for an ironic 'proposal' for dealing with the poor.

[2] Cf. Fielding's comments on slander in *CGJ* Nos. 5 and 14.

at a silly Drum or Rout,[1] where I should be ashamed to shew my Face; and at last it hath come out that the young Lady meant some insignificant Beau or Coxcomb who had the Impudence to personate me, tho' he was in Reality a Branch of the No-bodies.

In the same Manner I am often abused for saying Things which I never said, and doing what I never did. I am indeed brought as an Example to justify all the Folly of the Age. I am far however from laying this on Nobody, but I can with great Truth accuse his Family, the female Nobodies in particular. If one of these makes herself ridiculous by an Oddity in her Dress, and it is mentioned to her by her Friend, she immediately cries, "Why do you blame me? *Every Body wears it.*" So if you speak or act absurdly, poor Every-Body speaks and acts in the same Manner.

Infinite Mischief hath been produced in the learned World by this Method; for, whether I deserve it or no, my Taste and Judgment will be always regarded; and many a Book hath been esteemed by the Public, for no other Reason but because it hath been confidently reported that I have read it. On the contrary, tho' I am well assured that Nobody will deny it, I do assert that many a Work hath been consigned to Oblivion, merely from an Opinion that Nobody hath read it.

To shew you my Candour, however, I do not commend this Way of thinking; nay I am ready to acknowledge that I have sometimes read over the silliest Performances, and again have no doubt but that Books of much intrinsic Worth have been read by Nobody. But indeed, Sir, wonderful are the Misrepresentations of this Kind, by malicious People; I have been often reported to have slighted what I have greatly admired, merely because some few of my Relations who are Scandals to my Family, have turned up their Nose at what they have not understood; and the Commendations which I have bestowed on such Occasions, have been falsely reported to have come from Nobody's Mouth.

Upon the whole, Mr. Censor, I hope you will take this Matter into your Serious Consideration, and do me that Justice against Nobody which your censorial Capacity gives you such full Power to execute,and not only against him but against all his Adherents. I make no Question but that you are well apprized of my real Consequence in the Society, and that all Government was instituted for my Sake, and for my Sake only. This may seem a bold Word, but it is nevertheless true, notwithstanding what some of the most worthless and impudent of the Family of the Nobodies have presumed to insinuate. Nor will you, I hope, think me vain, when I aver, that unless I set about it, and that heartily, that Reformation which can alone (I say it) prevent the speedy Ruin of this Kingdom, can never be brought about. It is by my

---

[1] See *CGJ* No. 17, above, p. 122 n. 2.

Encouragement of Religion, Virtue, Science, and Art, that they can again be
brought to hold up their drooping Heads. It is I must begin, by setting the
Example in every thing that is laudable, without expecting it from others. I
am he that must first shake off Prostitution and Corruption, and every Kind
of Infamy. I alone who must resolve to give Praise and Honour to the truly
Deserving, and treat Vice and Meanness with their just Contempt, however
distinguished and elevated by Fortune, Title, or Station.

All this however, no nor any Part of this, will I perform, while you suffer
that cursed Maxim to prevail, That Every-body's Business is Nobody's.[1]

I am, Sir,

Your real Admirer,

Well-Wisher,

And Friend,

EVERY-BODY.[2]

SATURDAY, MAY 9, 1752.   NUMB. 37.

Scilicet in Vulgus manent Exempla Regentum.

CLAUDIAN.[3]

THE CREATURES *will endeavour to ape their Betters.*

There are many Phrases that Custom renders familiar to our Ears, which,
when looked into, and closely examined, will appear extremely strange, and
of which it must greatly puzzle a very learned Etymologist to account for the
Original.

Of this Sort is the Term, PEOPLE OF FASHION.[4] An Expression of such
very common Use, and so universally understood, that it is entirely needless
to set down here what is meant by it: But how it first acquired its present
Meaning, and became a Title of Honour and Distinction, is a Point, I
apprehend, of no small Difficulty to determine.

I have on this Occasion consulted several of my Friends, who are well

---

[1] For the proverb, see Tilley, B 746; Defoe used this maxim as a title for a work in 1725.

[2] See the response by 'No-Body' in *CGJ* No. 41. Cf. the dance by 'Somebody and Nobody',
Author's Farce, III. i; for the theatrical tradition behind these figures, see the note by Charles B. Woods,
ed., *The Author's Farce* (Lincoln, 1966), p. 52.

[3] *De consulatu Stilichoris* ('On Stilicho's Consulship'), i. 168: 'Of a truth their leaders' pattern passes
to the crowd' (Loeb). The accepted text reads *manant*. Fielding's use of the motto is ironic, since its
context is Claudian's description of a people united under Stilicho despite diversities of language,
arms, and dress. In his translation Fielding also repeats terms he has played with earlier; see the
definition of 'Creatures' in *CGJ* No. 4 and the discourse on 'Betters' in *CGJ* No. 27.

[4] Cf., among many examples of ridicule of the world of fashion, *True Patriot*, No. 1 (5 Nov. 1745);
and *CGJ* Nos. 27, 30 (by Harris), and 43, the last a set of replies to this leader. See also *Joseph
Andrews*, II, xiii. The topic appears often, of course, in contemporary satire, not only in periodical
essays but in separate publications; cf. Elizabeth Thomas's *The Metamorphosis of the Town* (1730);
Fashion: An Epistolary Satire (1742); *The Importance of Dress* (1752); and *Dress: A Satire* (1754).

skilled in Etymology. One of these traces the Word Fashion through the French Language up to the Latin. He brings it from the Verb FACIO, which, among other Things, signifies TO DO. Hence he supposes *People of Fashion*, according to the old Derivation of *Lucus a non lucendo*,[1] to be spoken of those who do Nothing. But this is too general, and would include all the Beggars in the Nation.

Another carries the Original no farther than the French Word FACON, which is often used to signify *Affectation*. This likewise will extend too far, and will comprehend Attorney's Clerks, Apprentices, Milliners, Mantua-makers, and an infinite Number of the lower People.

A third will bring Fashion from $\phi\acute{\alpha}\sigma\iota\varsigma$[2]. This in the genitive Plural makes $\phi\alpha\sigma\acute{\epsilon}\omega\nu$, which in English is the very Word. According to him, by People of Fashion are meant People whose Essence consisteth in Appearances, and who, while they seem to be something, are really nothing.

But tho' I am well apprized that much may be said to support this Derivation, there is a fourth Opinion, which, to speak in the proper Language, hath yet a *more smiling* Aspect.[3] This supposes the Word Fashion to be a Corruption from Fascination,[4] and that these people were formerly believed by the Vulgar to be a Kind of Conjurers, and to possess a Species of the Black Art.

In Support of this Opinion, my Friend urges the Use which these People have always made of the Word Circle, and the Pretence to be enclosed in a certain Circle,[5] like so many Conjurers, and by such Means to keep the Vulgar at a Distance from them.

To this Purpose likewise he quotes the Phrases, a polite Circle, the Circle of one's Acquaintance, People that live within a certain Circle, and many others. From all which he infers, that in those dark and ignorant Ages, when Conjurers were held in more Estimation than they are at present, the credulous Vulgar believed these People to be of the Number,[6] and consequently called them *People of Fascination*, which hath been since corrupted into *People of Fashion*.

However whimsical this Opinion may seem, or however far fetched the

---

[1] 'A grove is so called because it excludes the light'; the phrase, originating in Quintilian's account of deriving words from their opposites (*Institutio oratoria*, I. vi. 34), implies in general a misnomer or ridiculous derivation. Cf. *Tom Jones*, VIII. iv. With the mock-etymology here, cf. *CGJ* No. 9 on the origin of the name 'Robinhood'.

[2] i.e. 'appearance', as of stars on the horizon.

[3] Given the references to the occult sciences which follow, Fielding may be punning here on the astrological term 'benign' or 'friendly' *aspect*; see E. Chambers, *Cyclopaedia*, 7th edn. (1751), s.v. 'aspect'.

[4] The casting of a spell; sorcery, enchantment (*OED*).

[5] Fielding puns on the use in magic of 'circles' containing various geometric shapes 'according to the Form of the Apparition that is desired' ([Richard Boulter], *A Compleat History of Magick, Sorcery, and Witchcraft* [1716], i. 8).

[6] i.e. 'in the select group' (*OED*).

Derivation may sound to those who have not much considered the barbarous Corruption of Language, I must observe in its Favour how difficult it is by any other Method, to account not only for that odd Phrase, People of Fashion; but likewise for that Circle within which those People have always affected to live.

Even now, when Conjurers have been long laughed out of the World, the Pretence to the Circle is nevertheless maintained, and within this Circle the People of Fascination do actually insist upon living at this Day.

It is moreover extremely pleasant to observe what wonderful Care these People take to preserve their Circle safe and inviolate, and with how jealous an Eye they guard against any Intrusion of those whom they are pleased to call the Vulgar; who are on the other Hand as vigilant to watch, and as active to improve every Opportunity of invading this Circle, and breaking into it.

Within the Memory of many now living, the Circle of the People of Fascination included the whole Parish of Covent-Garden, and great Part of St. Giles's in the Fields; but here the Enemy broke in, and the Circle was presently contracted to Leicester-Fields, and Golden-Square. Hence the People of Fashion again retreated before the Foe to Hanover-Square; whence they were once more driven to Grosvenor-Square, and even beyond it, and that with such Precipitation, that had they not been stopped by the Walls of Hyde-Park, it is more than probable they would by this Time have arrived at Kensington.[1]

In many other Instances we may remark the same Flight of these People, and the same Pursuit of their Enemies. They first contrived a certain Vehicle called a Hackney-Coach to avoid the Approach of the Foe in the open Streets. Hence they were soon routed, and obliged to take Shelter in Coaches of their own. Nor did this protect them long. The Enemy likewise in great Numbers mounted into the same *armed* Vehicles*. The People of Fascination then betook themselves to Chairs;[2] in which their exempt Privileges being again invaded, I am informed that several Ladies of Quality have bespoke a Kind of Couch somewhat like the *Lectica*[3] of the Romans; in

---

* Rather *Coat of armed*.

---

[1] Fielding gives, in the words of a modern historian, 'a spirited, if somewhat exaggerated, picture' of the actual westward migration of the gentry 'from the once fashionable *piazzas* and precincts of Covent Garden, Soho and St. Giles's into the more newly developed aristocratic quarter at "the polite end of the town," in St. James's or Picadilly' (George Rudé, *Hanoverian London 1714–1808* [1971], p. 9). On the current deplorable state of St Giles's, see *CGJ* No. 17, above, p. 122 n. 3; cf. the contrast between St Giles's and the fashionable squares, *CGJ* No. 27, above, p. 173. Cf. Addison, *Spectator*, No. 403 (12 June 1712): 'When I consider this great City in its several Quarters and Divisions, I look upon it as an Aggregate of various Nations distinguished from each other by their respective Customs, Manners, and Interests.'

[2] i.e. sedan chairs.

[3] A litter or sedan chair.

which they are next Winter to be carried through the Streets upon Men's Shoulders.

The Reader will be pleased to observe, that beside the local Circle which I have described above, there is an imaginary or figurative one, which is invaded by every Imitation of the Vulgar.

Thus those People of Fascination, or if they like it better, of Fashion, who found it convenient to remain still in Coaches, observing that several of the Enemy had lately exhibited Arms on their Vehicles, by which Means, those Ornaments became vulgar and common, immediately ordered their own Arms to be blotted out, and a Cypher substituted in their Room; perhaps cunningly contriving to represent themselves instead of their Ancestors.[1]

Numberless are the Devices made use of by the People of Fashion of both Sexes, to avoid the Pursuit of the Vulgar, and to preserve the Purity of the Circle. Sometimes the Perriwig covers the whole Beau, and he peeps forth from the midst like an Owl in an Ivy-Bush; at other Times his Ears stand up behind half a dozen Hairs, and give you the Idea of a different Animal. Sometimes a large black Bag,[2] with Wings spread as broad as a Raven's adorns his Back, at other Times, a little lank Silk appears like a dead Black-bird in his Neck. To Day he borrows the Tail of a Rat, and Tomorrow that of a Monkey; for he will transform himself into the Likeness of the vilest Animal, to avoid the Resemblance of his own Species.[3]

Nor are the Ladies less watchful of the Enemy's Motions, or less anxious to avoid them. What Hoods and Hats and Caps and Coifs have fallen a Sacrifice in this Pursuit! Within my Memory the Ladies of the Circle covered their lovely Necks with a Cloak; this being routed by the Enemy, was exchanged for the Manteel; this again was succeeded by the Pelorine, the Pelorine by the Neckatee, the Neckatee by the Capuchine;[4] which hath now stood its Ground a long Time, but not without various Changes of Colour, Shape, Ornaments, &c.

And here I must not pass by the many admirable Arts made use of by these Ladies, to deceive and dodge their Imitators; when they are hunted out in

[1] Fielding puns on 'cypher' in the sense of monogram or symbolic device and in the sense of 'mere nothing', nonentity.

[2] i.e. a bag-wig, made of black taffeta, with a bow of the same material. Cf. Fielding's lines in 'Of True Greatness' (*Miscellanies*, 1743): 'The lowest Beau that skips about a Court, / The Lady's Plaything, and the Footman's Sport; / Whose Head adorn'd with Bag or Tail of Pig, / Serves very well to bear about his Wig.'

[3] Cf. *The Modern Husband* (1732), Mr. Bellamant of his son: 'I would no more comply with a ridiculous fashion than with a vicious one; nor with that which makes a man look like a monkey, than that which makes him act like any other beast' (II. ii). For other examples of the animal-like appearance of fashionable dress, especially wigs, see Elizabeth Thomas, *The Metamorphosis of the Town*, 2nd edn. (1730), p. 22; and James Kirkpatrick, *The Sea-Piece* (1750), i. 159–62.

[4] *OED*, citing this essay, defines 'Manteel' vaguely as 'some kind of cape or mantle worn by ladies' and 'Neckatee' as 'a lady's neckerchief'; a 'pelorine' is again a type of mantle or cape, and a 'Capuchine' a cloak and hood made in imitation of the dress of Capuchin monks.

any favourite Mode, the Method is to lay it by for a Time, and then to resume it again all at once, when the Enemy least expect it. Thus Patches appear and disappear several Times in a Season. I have myself seen the Enemy in the Pit, with Faces all over spotted like the Leopard, when the Circle in the Boxes have with a conscious Triumph displayed their native Alabaster, without a simple Blemish, tho' they had a few Evenings before worn a thousand: within a Month afterwards the Leopards have appeared in the Boxes to the great Mortification of the Fair Faces in the Pit.[1]

In the same Manner the Ruff after a long Discontinuance some Time since began to revive in the Circle, and advanced downwards, till it almost met the Tucker.[2] But no sooner did the Enemy pursue, than it vanished all at once, and the Boxes became a Collection of little Hills of Snow, extremely delightful to the Eyes of every Beholder.

Of all the Articles of Distinction the Hoop hath stood the longest, and with the most obstinate Resistance. Instead of giving Way, this the more it hath been pushed, hath encreased the more; till the Enemy hath been compelled to give over the Pursuit from mere Necessity; it being found impossible to convey seven Yards of Hoop into a Hackney-Coach, or to slide with it behind a Counter.[3]

But as I have mentioned some of the Arts of the Circle, it would not be fair to be silent as to those of the Enemy, among whom a certain Citizen's Wife[4] distinguished herself very remarkably, and appeared long in the very Top of the Mode. It was at last however discovered that she used a very unfair Practice, and kept a private Correspondence with one of those Milliners who were intrusted with all the Secrets of the Circle.   A.

---

[1] With Fielding's account of the use of face patches, worn to point up a lady's complexion by contrast, cf. Addison's famous essay in *Spectator*, No. 81 (2 June 1711), in which Whig and Tory ladies at the opera indicate party loyalties by the placement of their patches; cf. also *Spectator*, No. 50 (27 Apr. 1711), where an Indian king wonders at the 'little black Spots' that are 'apt to break out' in the faces of English women. On the contrast between the audience seated in the pit and in the boxes, see *CGJ* No. 27, above, p. 174 n. 3.

[2] A piece of lace worn within or around the top of the bodice (*OED*).

[3] Hoop-petticoats had been ridiculed from early in the century, as in *Spectator*, Nos. 127 and 129 (26, 28 July 1711), and their increased size at mid-century produced further satire; see Fielding's essay in *True Patriot*, No. 15 (11 Feb. 1746) proposing a tax on these products of luxury, which, he says, 'have of late grown to so very enormous, and indeed portentous a Size, that should they increase as they have done within these last ten Years, our Houses must be soon pulled down, and built with great Gates instead of Doors to admit them'. Cf. the description of a hoop 'large enough for the Top of a Tent', in *Dress: A Satire* (1754), p. 10, and Fielding's passing allusions to the fashion in *Journey from this World to the Next*, I. i, and *Tom Jones*, XIII. iv. His comment on the 'Hackney-Coach' and the 'Counter', of course, alludes to the way of life of the 'Enemy', the shopkeeping classes.

[4] i.e. the wife of a 'Cit', a tradesman or shopkeeper.

TUESDAY, MAY 12, 1752.   NUMB. 38.

Scire Potestates Herbararum, Usumque medendi.

VIRGIL.[1]

TO

Sir ALEXANDER DRAWCANSIR, Knt.

Sir,[2]

The Desire of Health was so early implanted in Man, and so originally interwove with his very Nature, that it may be said to be the genuine Child of that all ruling Principle, Self-Preservation. We see the Impulse for continuing the Search, not only diffused through the human Race; but the Brutes, from amidst an Exuberance of vegetable Variety, can select with the nicest Skill their peculiar Physic out of the Fields and Woods.

It is said, that in some Instances, Mankind have been their Pupils, and indebted to them for Instruction; that they have not only led us to the Knowledge of some useful Discoveries and Operations, but whilst their Lords, boasting of superior Reason, have been employed in the laborious Task of distinguishing the outward Characteristic of Plants, and ranging them as Matter of Curiosity, with no little Parade, the humble Beasts have taught us better Lessons; have shewn a shorter Way to the Virtues of several Simples, by making them at once the subject of their Cure, and thereby evincing their Properties.[3]

No Doubt the still lower Classes of the Creation, Reptiles, as well as Insects, have the Power given them to exercise this medicinal Art.

That the Practice of the Brutes have suffered less Mutations than that of erring Man, is a Circumstance I shall not here enlarge upon, but could have wished, that in the Systems of the latter, their Changes had always been attended, with more substantial Views of real Foundation.

Whatever Tendency to Evil this has produced, whatever Neglect and Indignity have been offered to simple Remedies, and what Attachment we have given to a useless Farrago of Drugs, the Imputation however cannot fairly be charged upon the Profession but the Professors. The Science itself is highly worthy the Pursuit of the most rational Enquirer, though perhaps, not altogether of those great Liberalities and Distinctions, which from the remotest Antiquity have been paid it. Kings as well as Peasants have at all

---

[1] *Aeneid*, xii. 396: 'He chose rather to know the virtues of herbs and the practice of healing' (Loeb).

[2] This letter, puffing the Society of the Surgeons of the Royal Navy, is not by Fielding; in the copy of *CGJ* at the Bodleian Library (Hope Folio 11), containing corrections and revisions in Fielding's hand, the entire letter is struck through. Its author may have been Fielding's friend William Hunter, the eminent surgeon; see below, p. 224 n. 1.

[3] The idea is a commonplace; cf. Pope, *Essay on Man*, iii. 173–4: 'Learn from the birds what food the thickets yield; / Learn from the beasts the physic of the field.'

Times from Choice or Necessity become its Votaries: But this is feeble Evidence of its Use, when compared to the Sanction given it by the sacred Writings of the Son of Syrac, or the divine Authority of Apostolic Function.[1] Proofs which conspire to own its noble Origin, though it must be confessed that Nations amongst the wiser Heathens were guilty of the most extravagant Excess. We read, that amongst Physicians, Crowns and Apotheoses were the attendant Honours of their Life and Death; and Macrobius speaks of Hippocrates in such applauding Strains, as can only be applied to infallible Wisdom.

——qui tam fallere quam falli nescit.[2]

This universal Persuasion, this general Acknowledgement of the Excellency of the healing Art, (which was then and indeed till late, in all its Branches, jointly exercised) will serve to demonstrate how natural, how essential it is for every Individual, the least sollicitous for its Preservation, to apply to those restoring Remedies, which God in his infinite Munificence, has so plenteously created and ordained for the Use of Man: And that Societies employed for the Advancement of Medical Learning should at all Times be encouraged by the public Suffrage. The various Seminaries of the medical Kind, both here and abroad, must necessarily give a liberal Mind very affecting Pleasure.

Those who have already availed themselves by the Powers of such Skill, may feelingly display its Use and Importance; and those who by unskilful Treatment, or empiric Ignorance, have too unhappily suffered, will have the greater Reason to approve any Institution, calculated for avoiding Error, and promoting the Good of their Fellow-Creatures. A Good, no less than that of recovering Health, that inestimable Gem, always the most valued when the least possessed, and which no temporal Blessing can be put in Competition with; for without that Comfort, no Enjoyment can have its Relish. Our Summer's Sunshine would be Zembla's Winter,[3] and terrestial Paradise, a dreary Desert.

That Physic has yet its Perplexities and Defects, its Rocks and Shoals, is a Truth I believe the warmest Advocate for its Perfection will not venture to deny. To explore those Tracks, to make Discoveries, and point out Dangers in the Regions of that Science, is a Task, however formidable, yet meritorious in those who attempt it, and of the greatest Consequence to

[1] i.e. in one of the books of the Apocrypha, Ecclesiasticus or the Wisdom of Jesus Son of Sirach 38: 1–15, a passage in praise of physicians; on the 'Apostolic Function', see Acts 3: 1–16, 9: 34, and 14: 8–11.

[2] Macrobius, *Commentary* on Cicero's *Dream of Scipio*, I. vi. 64: 'who cannot deceive or be deceived'.

[3] i.e. Novaya Zemlya, a group of islands in the Arctic Ocean, frequently cited in this period as a place of extreme cold; cf. Pope, *Essay on Man*, ii. 224, Swift, *Battle of the Books*.

Humanity. It is with no small Satisfaction that I view the laudable Endeavours of the medical Society of Surgeons of the Royal Navy directed to this salutary End.[1] A Set of Gentlemen, from whose peculiar Situations, and from those personal Visits which its Members are constantly paying to various and distant Climates, the Public may reasonably expect Improvement, as they must be more immediately enabled to investigate Diseases, and to observe Nature and her Laws, not only in the animal Œconomy, but in her manifold Productions, under the Co-operation of contrasted Soils and Seasons, from farthest India to the utmost Boundaries of the North.

Though they are not apprized of these Reflexions, much less have I their Consent for them, I shall take the Liberty to insert here the second Article of their Plan, which, as it is but in the Hands of few, tho' intended for public View, by its being printed and advertized to be called for, I hope on that Account the Members of that Society will not be offended at this Proceeding.

"II. That as one considerable Purpose of this Undertaking is to pursue, particularly, such Branches of medical Knowledge, as fall more immediately under the Observation of the Navy-Surgeons, who may be reasonably presumed to have Advantages, for some particular Disquisitions, peculiar to their Situation; such as—an Opportunity of enquiring into the Nature of Sea Diseases, and any specific or material Difference between them and those at Land;—of observing any particular Effects of Medicines at Sea;— the common Effects of the principal Operations of Surgery on that Element; especially where any remarkable Diversity occurs from their general Events on Shore; and any different Success of the same Operations in different Climates, at Sea and Land; — the Effects of Sea-Air and Diet in general, in

---

[1] On this Society, founded in Jan. 1746/7, see George C. Peachey, *A Memoir of William and John Hunter* (Plymouth, 1924), pp. 79–90, who reprints their original articles from a broadside in the British Library (Burney 415b); for the full text of their Plan, see *LM* 22(1753), 608–9. The group met at apartments in the Little Piazza, Covent Garden (not far from Fielding's home), where they heard lectures on surgery by Samuel Sharp and, later, William Hunter, and lectures on materia medica by Andrew Didier. As the article of their Plan printed here makes clear, one of the prime objects of the Society was to promote medical knowledge by gathering contributions by Navy Surgeons for publication; only one of these publications, however, has come to light, James Kirkpatrick's *Some Reflections on the Causes and Circumstances, That may Retard or Prevent the Putrefaction of Dead Bodies . . . In a Letter to the Society of Navy Surgeons* (1751), a volume which also includes an early version (1750) of their Plan. For notices of meetings, calls for papers, and other announcements in 1751–2, not noted by Peachey, see *DA*, 27 July, 25 Oct. 1751 and 6 Apr., 24 Aug., and 9 Oct. 1752; see also *GM* 22 (1752), 188.

Fielding's willingness to print these letters in *CGJ* undoubtedly stemmed from two personal connections with the Society. First, the Society's publisher was Fielding's own publisher and friend, Andrew Millar, to whom members were directed to send their papers and at whose shop their Plan was on view (see *DA*, 6 Apr. 1752). Secondly, their lecturer in surgery, William Hunter, at whose home in Covent Garden the group may have met, was also a close friend of Fielding; see *Journal of a Voyage to Lisbon* (28 June), describing ministrations to Fielding by his friend, 'the great surgeon and anatomist of Covent Garden', attended by a young sea-surgeon 'as a student'. Given this connection, it is quite possible that Hunter was 'Benevolus', author of this letter and of that in *CGJ* No. 41.

various Diseases, and the particular Changes of the Constitution, produced by them, under the Co-operation of different Seasons and Climates;—the various Distempers endemic on their different Stations; and any remarkable Diversity in the Symptoms, and the general Event of the Disease, between Natives and Strangers; with the usual Method of treating such Disease, or its ordinary supervening Symptoms, by Practitioners of the best Note and greatest Experience, in those Countries, and the most frequent Consequence of it.—It is therefore strongly recommended to them to be carefully attentive to those very material Articles: And further to improve every Opportunity of informing themselves, of the popular Methods of treating different Distempers in those Places, where Physic is little cultivated;—of attaining the natural History of the Country;—the Weather; —the Animals;—Plants (especially all indigenous physical ones) and Fossils;— to endeavour to discover the Process and Manufacture of any Drugs in it;—and to furnish themselves with the best Collection of such Productions, as they can conveniently procure. But to prevent the Multiplicity of Volumes, without adding to the Stock of useful Knowledge, it is agreed that no other Cases or Observations in Physic or Surgery shall be published, but such as may be instructive in their own Nature, or rendered so, by judicious and extensive Reflexions deduced from them, in order to the Establishment or Confirmation of general Axioms."

Such is one Article, of seven, of which their Plan at present consists. A Plan, which as Usefulness first formed, so Propriety seemingly continues to direct. In Conformity to this, they have laid a Foundation, on which an ample Superstructure is to be raised; and as they have distinguished a good Judgment in the Assortment of some Materials for their Building, it is not to be questioned but the Society will proceed in the same Method towards its farther Completion.

In order to render it as worthy their Design as possible, I am very credibly informed that no Expence within their Sphere is spared, that can contribute to its Advancement. Anatomy and Materia Medica, the two Eyes of Physick, are encouraged and publicly professed amongst them, by Persons deservedly of the first Character in their respective Classes. So that the more ingenious Part of that Body may retain and still advance in Knowledge; and the less qualified may resort to it as to a School or Nursery, whenever Convenience and the Desire of Improvement prompt them.

Great Advantage and Lustre might be derived to the Society, from the Mention of some honorary Members and Encouragers of it. Persons whose Candour, Ingenuity, and Learning, do Honour not only to this Society, but to Humanity itself. Indeed it may suffice at once to say, that of whatever is praiseworthy and of real Estimation, those Persons are the true and rightful Patrons.

Sordid Partiality, and narrow Interestedness, may seek Shelter and Protection, but seek it too in vain; for Names in this Age, however dignified, though they may greatly cherish the tender Shoots of Desert; yet they do not, neither can they, support the Offspring of spurious Knowledge.

BENEVOLUS.[1]

SATURDAY, MAY 16, 1752.   NUMB. 39.

Liberalitate nihil est Naturæ hominis accomodatius.

CICERO de Offciis. [2]

Nothing, says the great Cicero, in my Motto, *is more agreeable to the Nature of Man than Liberality.* A Sentiment which seems to flow from that noble Philosophy[3] which taught every Man to suppress, as much as possible, all narrow and selfish Principles, and to consider himself only as a Part of a Whole; a Member of that political Body to which he belongs. In this Sence, to confer Benefits on each other, and to do mutual Good, will appear to be as agreeable to Nature, as for the right Hand to assist the left, or for any one Member of the human Body to administer to the Use and Good of another; indeed to the Emolument of the Man himself. In this Sence the Roman Philosopher speaks in another Part of his Works, where he says, *that for Man to do an Injury to Man for his own private Advantage, is to act in direct Opposition to his Nature.*[4]

If this Doctrine be admitted, the Person who is void of all Liberality, is not worthy of the Name of a Man; but is to be considered as an unnatural Monster, below the Dignity of Humanity.[5]

Again, if we view this Matter in the Light in which it is placed by the Writers on the Law of Nature, the Man who refuses to relieve the Wants of

---

[1] This letter was reprinted in *LM* 21 (1752), 201–2, and, without attribution to *CGJ*, in *The Repository* (coll. edn., 1752), pp. 81–96. For a continuation of the discussion by Benevolus, see *CGJ* No. 41.

[2] *De officiis*, I. xiv. 42; Fielding adapts the line slightly.

[3] Stoicism; cf. 'An Essay on the Knowledge of the Characters of Men', *Miscellanies* (1743), referring to the doctrine of the Stoics 'by which Men were taught to consider themselves as Fellow-Citizens of the World, and to labour jointly for the common Good, without any private Distinction of their own' (ed. H. K. Miller, Wesleyan Edn. [Oxford, 1972], p. 154).

[4] It is, in fact, another part of the same work that Fielding cites, *De officiis*, III. v. 21: 'For a man to take something from his neighbour and to profit by his neighbour's loss is more contrary to nature than is death or poverty or pain or anything else' (Loeb). In the lines following this assertion Cicero develops the analogy Fielding cites between members of the physical body and members of society. On the influence of Cicero, especially of *De officiis*, on Fielding, see *Miscellanies*, Wesleyan Edn., pp. xviii–xxvii, and Miller, *Essays*, p. 257. On the body–state analogy, see also *CGJ* No. 35, above, p. 210 and n. 3.

[5] For other condemnations of avarice, among many examples in Fielding, see *CGJ* Nos. 29, 69; cf. also his poem 'Of Good-Nature' (*Miscellanies*, 1743) and *Champion*, 27 Dec. 1739, 26 Aug. 1740. See Miller, *Essays*, 333–4.

another with his own Superfluities, is guilty of great Injustice: For according to them, no Man hath any Right or Title to withhold from his Neighbour that Bread which he himself doth not want, and which his Neighbour absolutely doth want.[1]

Mr. Lock, treating of the first Methods of acquiring Property, raises the following Objection. It will perhaps be objected, says he, that *if gathering the Acorns or other Fruits of the Earth, &c. makes a Right to them, then any one may ingross as much as he will.* "To which (says he) I answer, not so. The same Law of Nature that does by this Means give us Property, does also bound that Property too. *God has given us all Things richly*, is the Voice of Reason confirmed by Inspiration. But how far has he given it us to enjoy? As much as any one can make use of to any Advantage of Life before it spoils, so much he may by his Labour fix a Property in; whatever is beyond this is more than his Share, and it belongs to others." And again, "Nature has well set the Measure of Property, by the Extent of Mens Labour and the Conveniencies of Life: No Mans Labour could subdue or appropriate all, nor could his Enjoyment consume more than a small Part; so that it was impossible for any Man, this Way, to intrench upon the Right of another, or to acquire to himself a Property to the Prejudice of his Neighbour, who would still have Room for as good and large a Possession (after the other had taken out his) as before it was appropriated."[2]

Bishop Cumberland having shewn that the Law of Nature commands an Endeavour to promote the common Good, proceeds thus: "It is manifest that this greatest and noblest End, cannot be obtained by a bare abstaining from Evil: but it is necessary that every one contribute his Share, by a true, certain, and constant Application, as well of Things external, as of his Powers towards the gaining this Point." Upon this Account it is (says he) a natural Precept, "That if at any Time, the Nature of the chief End so requiring it, we should transfer to another some Right of ours, either by Gift at present, or by Promise or Compact afterwards to be performed; we make that Promise validly and faithfully, and not with an Intention to deceive; for it is only such a firm transferring of any Thing, or of our Services to the Use of another, as I have mentioned, which can at all conduce to the End commanded us."[3]

Grotius, to the same Purpose, reasons thus.——I will translate him literally. "Let us moreover consider, whether any Right to Mankind in

---

[1] Cf. *CGJ* No. 11, where Fielding also cites authorities on the Law of Nature on the question of necessity as a justification of theft, above, pp. 79–80 and p. 80 n. 5.

[2] *Two Treatises of Government*, II. v. 31, 36; Fielding quotes, with very slight alterations, from the volume he owned (3rd edn., 1698), pp. 188, 191 (Baker, item 239).

[3] Richard Cumberland (1631–1718), Bishop of Peterborough, *A Treatise of the Laws of Nature*, trans. John Maxwell (1727), p. 68; Fielding quotes with only minor changes from this work, which was in his library (Baker, item 101).

common, may attach in us those Things which are already become the Property of others. Some may perhaps wonder this should be made a Question, as Property may seem to have absorbed all that Right which arose from the Community of Things. But this is not so: For we must examine into the Intention of those Persons who first introduced private Property (*Dominia Singularia*) which is to be interpreted so as to depart as little as possible from natural Equity: For if written Laws are as far as possible to receive this Interpretation, much more are those unwritten *Principles* or Manners, which are not bound down by the Chains of Language."

Hence it follows. First, that in the last and greatest Necessity, "that old Law of using all Things in common, revives again, as if they had always so remained; because in all human Laws, and so in the Laws of Property, this last Necessity seems to have been excepted."[1]

Puffendorf after having shewn some Difficulties which attend this Exposition, as it may give too great a Latitude to Force or Fraud, (and which are the Reasons given by Lord Hale, why this Plea of Necessity in Case of Theft is not admitted in our Law)[2] proceeds thus. "We think therefore that this Point of Dispute will be more clearly determined by the Principles and the Method which we have laid down; that is, by saying in short, that the wealthy Person is bound to relieve him, who innocently wants, by an imperfect Obligation; to the performing of which, though regularly no Man ought to be compelled by Violence, yet the Force of extreme Necessity is so great, as to make these Things recoverable by the same Means as those which are truly and rightfully due. That is by making Complaint to the Magistrate, or when the Urgency of the Distress cannot allow Time for such an Expedient, then by seizing what is ready at hand either in a secret or an open Manner."[3]

Berbeyrac in his Notes on this Passage seems to blame his Author for calling it an imperfect Obligation. "This (APPLICATION *to the Magistrate*)" says he, "is their only Refuge who believe that the greatest Necessity cannot authorize any Man of himself to take the Goods of another, but as Thomasius observes, they tacitly acknowledge, that such a Necessity gives a Man a perfect Right to require what he wants; for only those Things which

---

[1] Fielding translates from Hugo Grotius (1583–1645), *De Jure Belli ac Pacis*, II. ii. 6 (1–2), a passage located at i. 191, of the edition Fielding owned (Amsterdam, 1720; Baker, item 68). The phrase 'unwritten *Principles* or Manners' is Fielding's translation of *mores*; and the opening lines of the second paragraph, not in quotation marks, are also translated from Grotius. On the issue of justification by necessity, see *CGJ* No. 11, which also cites Grotius and Pufendorf, and *True Patriot*, No. 5 (3 Dec. 1745), where Fielding argues that debts contracted for 'the real Necessaries' should not be pursued or punished. See also *Journey from this World to the Next*, I. vii.

[2] Sir Matthew Hale, *The History of the Pleas of the Crown* (1736), i. 54–5.

[3] Samuel Pufendorf (1632–94), *Of the Law of Nature and Nations*, trans. Basil Kennett, 4th edn. (1729), II. vi. 6, pp. 208–9. This edition was in Fielding's library (Baker, item 116).

are due by Virtue of a perfect Obligation, can be subject to the Decision of the Magistrate."[1]

Upon the whole, it seems to be agreed by all these great Men, that those who want, have by the Laws of Nature A RIGHT to a Relief from the Superfluities of those who abound; by those Laws therefore it is not left to the Option of the Rich, whether they will relieve the Poor and Distressed; but those who refuse to do it, become unjust Men, and in reality deserve to be considered as ROGUES AND ROBBERS OF THE PUBLIC.

But if Liberality or Charity be so certain a Duty by the Law of Nature, how much more clearly and expressly is it enjoined by the divine Dispensation, as well the Jewish, as the Christian!——Thus in Deuteronomy; *Thou shalt not harden thy Heart, nor shut thine Hand from thy poor Brother.* And again, *Thou shalt open thy Hand wide unto thy Brother, unto thy Poor, and to thy Needy in the Land.*[2] So the Prophet, *Relieve the Oppressed, judge the Fatherless, plead for the Widow.*——And again, *Is not this the Fast which I have chosen!*——*Is it not to deal thy Bread to the Hungry, and that thou bring the Poor that are cast out to thy House; when thou seest the Naked that thou cover him, and that thou hide not thyself from thine own Flesh?*[3]

The New Testament is so full of Precepts and Exhortations to this Duty of Charity, that it would be endless to transcribe them; nor can it be in the least necessary to a Christian Reader. *Give to every Man that asketh thee,*[4] is the Command of our Saviour; who in another Place affirms, that in the Performance of this Duty consists PERFECTION. *If thou wilt be perfect sell all thou hast and give to the Poor.*[5] "These Words," says Dr. Barrow, "do indeed sound high; nor can they signify or design less than that we should be always in Affection and Disposition of Mind, ready to part with any Thing we have for the Succour of our poor Brethren, that to the utmost of *our Ability*, (according to moral Estimation prudently rated) upon all Occasions we should really express that Disposition in our Practice; that we are exceedingly obliged to the continual Exercise of these Duties in a very eminent Degree. Duties which were enforced by the constant Example of Jesus himself; and by the Preaching and Practice of all his Disciples."[6]

Upon the whole, I hope, it appears, that a Person void of Charity, is unworthy the Appellation of a Christian; that he hath no Pretence to either

---

[1] Jean Barbeyrac (1674–1729), scholar, editor, and translator of Grotius, Pufendorf, and Cumberland; Fielding loosely adapts the language of the translation of his note on Pufendorf in the edition cited above, p. 208. Barbeyrac's note on the passage refers to Christian Thomasius (1655–1728), *Institution of Divine Jurisprudence* (1709), II. ii. 171.

[2] Deuteronomy 15: 7; 15: 11.   [3] Isaiah 1: 17; 58: 6, 7.

[4] Matthew 5: 42, 'Give to him that asketh thee'.   [5] Matthew 19: 21.

[6] Isaac Barrow, Sermon XXXI, 'The Duty and Reward of Bounty to the Poor', *Works*, 5th edn. (1741), i. 306–7; Fielding quotes with some omissions and compresses considerably the thought of the last few sentences of the original passage. On Barrow, see *CGJ* No. 4, above, p. 34 n. 5; on the significance to Fielding of this particular sermon, see *CGJ* No. 29, above, p. 183 n. 3.

Goodness or Justice, or even to the Character of Humanity; that he is in honest Truth, an Infidel, a Rogue, and a Monster, and ought to be expelled not only from the Society of Christians, but of Men.   C.

TUESDAY, MAY 19, 1752.   NUMB. 40.

——*Professus grandia turget.*

HORACE.[1]

TO THE
CENSOR of Great-Britain.

Sir,[2]

Amongst the various, and almost innumerable Objects of your censorial Jurisdiction, Authorship, or the Manner of writing Books, is not the least considerable and important Article. Now tho' passing your Judgment on such as are actually published, and claim the Censor's Consideration, be the principal Duty in that Part of your Office, yet, I presume, you will not disdain to lend your Attention for a few Minutes, even to the Embryo of a Treatise, if it is remarkable and interesting.

My old Friend Jack Penflow, is, I believe, of all Men the most deeply smitten with that Disease commonly called scribendi Cacoethes,[3] or in English the Itch of Writing; I say Writing, for I think Scribbling, as it is sometimes termed, is rather too dishonourable an Appellation for my Friend's Productions. He writes in a common Way one Third Part of his whole Time. He hath by him many Reams of Manuscripts of his own Composition and Hand-Writing; and has been more than once obliged to change his Lodgings, in order to be accommodated with a light Closet, large enough to contain himself, his Bureau, and his Papers. He is withal extremely close and shy with respect to his Productions. He never vaunts of having written on this or that Subject; and can seldom or never be prevailed upon, even by his most intimate Friends, to let them have a Reading of any of his Papers. However, as he is a very great Humorist, I one Day by a Stratagem procured the Perusal of a pretty large Bundle of Sheets, which I found to contain uncommon and curious Matter; and, as I was not tied down to Secrecy, I think myself at Freedom to give some Account thereof to your

---

[1] *Art of Poetry*, 27: 'One, promising grandeur, is bombastic' (Loeb).

[2] This letter, signed 'Misotharsus', along with another bearing the same signature in *CGJ* No. 46, has been attributed to Fielding by Jensen (ii. 224–5), Cross (ii. 375), and Dudden (p. 892 n.). It should be noted, however, that in the Bodleian Library copy (Hope Folio 11) the 'Misotharsus' letter has been struck out, whereas the letters by 'Tom Thoughtless' and 'Peter Upright', both obviously by Fielding, have been left unmarked, with a note in Fielding's handwriting which reads, 'Add these 2 Letters to ye next paper'. On these markings, see General Introduction,. p. xxx n. 3. Yet several verbal parallels suggest Fielding may be the author.

[3] Juvenal, *Satires* vii. 52, the 'disease of writing' which Juvenal calls 'incurable'.

censorial Worship, as far as I can at present. The Performance is rather a Sketch or the Adversaria[1] of a Treatise, than a regular and finished one; as I believe all his Compositions are. But the Title is written out as fair and pompous, and as nicely distinguished with different Sizes of Characters, and Lengths of Lines, as if it were prepared for the Press. It stands thus,

Peri Tharsus,

A

TREATISE

ON THE

CONFIDENT and PERT,[2]

A modern Improvement in Writing;

OR,

The Art of Swaggering in Print.

A Work useful to all Kinds and Classes of Authors at this Day, but more particularly to Polemic Divines, Paradoxical Historians, Self-taught Commentators, Hypothetical and Heretical Physicians, Daily-Essay Writers, Quack-Bill Writers, and Advertisers.

I imagine my Friend, by the Floridness of this Frontispiece, designs to exhibit a Sample of his Subject,

And be himself the great pert Thing he draws.[3]

In his introductory Discourse, he observes that a Work of this Kind is a Desideratum in Literature, and wonders it hath hitherto been unattempted: "We have," says he, "a Treatise *Peri Hypsus,* or of the Sublime, by an illustrious Ancient; and another *Peri Bathus,* or of the Profound, by a no less

---

[1] 'Miscellaneous remarks or observations' (*OED*).

[2] This mock treatise on the Pert is an imitation of Pope's *Peri Bathous, or, Of the Art of Sinking in Poetry* (1728), which contains one section on 'the Pert Stile' (ch. xii, no. 2). Pope says such a style 'does in as peculiar a manner become the low in Wit, as a Pert Air does the low in Stature'; and he cites as models Tom Brown's *London Spy* and Cibber's prologues. The ironic contrast in this *CGJ* essay between ancient and modern writing is, of course, a general Scriblerian theme, but it may reflect also Pope's special claims for the Pert: 'But the Beauty and Energy of it is never so conspicuous, as when it is employ'd in *Modernizing* and *Adapting* to the *Taste of the Times* the Works of the Antients'. Cf. James Harris's warning to modern scribblers to subdue the 'spirit of pertness' when writing of 'the sublimer wits of ages past' (*Upon the Rise and Progress of Criticism* [1752], p. 19).
  'Confidence' and forwardness were conventional hallmarks of the Pert. The Greek 'Tharsûs' in its bad sense suggests audacity or impudence, and Johnson defines *pert* as 'saucy; petulant; with bold and garrulous loquacity'. But cf. Fielding's 'Weather-Glass of Wit' in *True Patriot,* No. 22 (1 Apr. 1746), in which Pertness is placed between Gravity and Dullness; 'the witty Writer', says Fielding, 'borders upon Extravagance, but the *pert* one is but one Degree above being *dull*'.

[3] Parodying Pope's comment on Longinus, 'And *Is himself* that great *Sublime* he draws' (*Essay on Criticism,* 680).

illustrious Modern.[1] We have likewise Discourses on the Logomachies of the Learned; on the Meteors of Stile; and one which comes the nearest to our present Purpose, on the Charlataneria, or Mountebankishness of Authors. But we still want a precise and full Account of the Confident or Pert, its Nature, and Usefulness in Writing; the Rules by which it may be acquired, and according to which it may be applied, and put in Practice to the best Advantage."

He next endeavours to shew, that the Doctrine and Practice of the Pert is in a great Measure a modern Invention, or at least a modern Improvement, there being very little of that Kind to be found in the Writings of the Ancients, if we except Works of Drollery, as Comedies, where a pert Character is introduced, some few controversial Tracts, and Pleadings at the Bar. He assigns Reasons why the Ancients were such poor Proficients in this Qualification; and highly extols the Ingenuity of the Moderns, to whom the Glory was reserved of rescuing it from the narrow Confinement, within which the Ancients had pent it up, and allowing it the Liberty of ranging and expatiating in Works of every Kind, without Controul or Distinction. But his own Words will best express his Meaning. "The Ancients," saith he, "were so weak as to idolize an everlasting Fame; and seemed to have expected some real Benefit, in the Grave or beyond the Grave, from the Praises bestowed on their Works by latest Posterity; to ensure which, besides the great Care they took to make their Works correct, both as to Matter and Stile; they were sollicitous to the last Degree to shun any Thing, that might disgust their most delicate Readers in their Manner of addressing them, and so bring upon themselves the Imputation of being conceited Prigs and Coxcombs. They looked upon the Public taken collectively, as superior to any single Writer whatever, were he a General, a Statesman, or even a crowned Head. Hence proceeded that bashful Modesty, or rather sheepish Diffidence, so happily expressed in French, by the Appellation of Mauvais Honte, with which they accost the Reader in their prefatory Discourses. The Moderns, on the other Hand, proceed on more demonstrative Principles. Amongst which, the chief fundamental Maxim is this undeniable one, that as Posterity neither will, nor can, do any Thing for our Advantage, it is no Business of ours to attempt any Thing for the Advantage of Posterity.[2] They wisely regard Fame, even that bestowed by Co-temporaries, as little better than Wind, and that by Posterity, as not so good; but a mere Ens rationis,[3] a

---

[1] Referring to Longinus' *On the Sublime* and Pope's *Peri Bathous*. Fielding, if he is the author, assumed *Peri Bathous* to be Swift's; see *CGJ* No. 18, above, p. 125 and n. 5.

[2] These themes are common in Scriblerian satire of the Moderns, but cf. especially Swift's *Tale of a Tub*, 'Epistle Dedicatory to His Royal Highness Prince Posterity' and 'A Digression in the Modern Kind'.

[3] A term in scholastic philosophy for an entity of reason, a creation of the mind, something which

Non-entity, according to the School Axiom, *De non existentibus, et non apparentibus idem esto judicium*.[1] They have therefore unanimously, excepting a very few old-fashioned obstinate Dissentients, exploded the fruitless Labour of compiling lasting Works, therein imitating the prudent Tenant, who, in building upon another Man's Ground, proportions his Expences to the Duration of his Lease. Moreover, by a maturer Knowledge of the World than their Ancestors, who lived near the infant State thereof, could be possessed of, they have observed, that in mixt Companies and Conversation, the confident and pert Praters are constantly applauded by the Majority, who look upon such as pretty, clever, mettled Fellows, and interpret their Self-Sufficiency, as real Ability. Hence they conclude, that a Book calculated not to last Ages, but to produce an immediate Effect ought to approach nearly to the Air and Manner of common Discourse, and catch the many, as it were by Surprise, before the Judgment of the few can interpose. To compass which desirable End, nothing conduces so much as an artful Dash of the Pert; and that not a sparing one."

I had just wrote down the last Word from the Manuscript, when I was disagreeably surprised by my Friend's starting up at my Elbow. I imagine he suspected what I was about; for he stole in, my Parlour-Door being a-jar, before I was aware. He carried off his Papers in a great Passion, and vow'd he never would communicate any more of them. But perhaps I may hereafter find Ways and Means to pacify him, and make him better than his Word. If I succeed, you shall hear more from me on the same Subject.

I am,

Sir, yours, &c.

MISOTHARSUS.[2]

You Mr. Censor,

D—n you Sir, do you think to bully us into Charity with your *Grocer*, and the Fellow whose Name begins with Puff?[3] Very pretty faith! I am obliged to give my Money, whether I will or no! However as I think the Case, a compassionate Case, I have sent you a Guinea for the Baker;[4] but I would

---

'exists only in the imagination'; see Chambers, *Cyclopaedia*, 7th edn. (1751), s.v. 'ens'. Cf. *Some Remarks on the Life and Writings of Dr. J—— H——* (1752), p. 35.

[1] 'The same judgment is made of things which do not appear as of things which do not exist,' i.e. what is not in evidence must be presumed to be non-existent; cf. the legal maxim cited in *CGJ* No. 2, although in the present context the axiom is said to be scholastic or philosophical rather than legal.

[2] 'Hater of pertness'; for the second letter on the topic, see *CGJ* No. 46.

[3] i.e. Fielding's citations of Grotius and Pufendorf in his essay on charity, *CGJ* No. 39.

[4] In the Bodleian Library copy (Hope Folio 11) a manuscript note in Fielding's hand explains, 'An unhappy poor Man who would have been ruined by Fire had not a very large Collection been set on Foot for him in this Paper'. See the 'Covent Garden' column of 15 May 1752, printed below, Appendix I.

not have you think I do it because you have persuaded me that it is my Duty. No, Sir, I do it because it pleases me, and I do not know a Way to please myself better with the Sum I send you. As for your Arguments,——

White's,[1] Saturday,
Four o'Clock.

Yours,

TOM. THOUGHTLESS.

Worthy Mr. Censor,

I have read your excellent Paper on Charity, with very high Satisfaction. You have indeed, with great Learning, demonstrated how indispensibly we are bound to that great Duty, as Men, as just Men, and as Christians. I much applaud the Goodness of your Undertaking, and I make no Doubt but it will be attended with the Success it deserves: For which Success (as well in this Case as in all your other laudable Endeavours for the Good of the Public) I shall offer up my hearty Prayers; a Matter of much more Consequence than any trifling Mite which I could add to your Subscription.

Lombard Street,
May 16, 1752.

I am,

Worthy Sir,

Your most humble Servant,

PETER UPRIGHT.[2]

SATURDAY, MAY 23, 1752.   NUMB. 41.

Audi alteram partem.[3]

Hear the Defendant.

Sir,

I am very much surprized, to see a Gentleman of your Character interfering in a private Quarrel, as you manifestly did when you published that malicious Letter signed *Every-Body*, in your Censor of the 5th Instant.[4]

As to the Writer, I may surely, with great Truth, accuse him of Malice;

---

[1] See *CGJ* No. 2, above, p. 26 n. 2.

[2] In this character, whose address in Lombard Street puts him at the banking center of the center of the City, Fielding portrays one of those 'morose and austere Men' to whom real benevolence is uknown (see *CGJ* No. 29). In his preference of prayers to charitable actions Upright reflects the Methodist view of charity; see the 'Discourse on Charity' between Allworthy and Captain Blifil, *Tom Jones*, II. v and the notes by Martin Battestin (Wesleyan Edn. [Oxford, 1974], pp. 93–6). The spontaneous action of even a Tom Thoughtless seemed preferable to Fielding, and the two letters are intended to be read as a contrasting pair. Cf. the contrast between Lombard Street and White's in *Tom Jones*, XIII. vi.

[3] An ancient legal maxim embodying the principle that no man shall be condemned unheard; Seneca's *Medea* (195) is frequently cited as a parallel. See Herbert Broom, *Selection of Legal Maxims*, 9th edn. (1924), p. 78. Used also as the motto to the *Champion* for 18 Oct. 1740 and as one of the mottoes to *The Opposition: A Vision* (1741).

[4] *CGJ* No. 36.

since he hath attacked me without any (the least) Provocation: For I have been always too wise to enter into a Quarrel, or to maintain any Dispute with him.

But since he hath thought proper to call upon me in this public Manner, I shall be justified in the Opinion of all Mankind in defending myself, and in pointing out the many Misrepresentations and Falshoods contained in his Letter.

He sets out with asserting, *that he is a Man of great Business, and that all the Concerns of the Public belong to his Care.* This is a vulgar Error, and the Cause of many political Evils. The Truth is, that Every-Body is impertinent and officious, and is too apt to meddle with the Business of Some-Body; and if Some-Body will but undertake to do his Duty, no Man can have the Assurance to charge me with interfering: But if this Some-Body will neglect his Duty, and give it up to Every-Body, I declare honestly that I shall always think it belongs to me to perform it.

As to the particular Instance of providing for the Poor, I shall only say that if Some-Body doth not undertake it, and if Every-Body, instead of planning a thousand ineffectual Schemes of his own, doth not agree without Envy or Malice, to support Some-Body in his Undertaking, that Business will never be accomplished.[1]

As to the Invention of Slanders, which is wickedly fathered upon me, I may, I think, appeal to the Public for the Proof of my Innocence; since I believe my Character is so well known, that not a single Person, except this Writer, will charge me with having been the Author of one single Article of Scandal. I do not indeed say, that Every-Body is guilty of inventing; but sure I am, that if he did not take Delight in hearing and spreading these Slanders, but would (as he ought to do) discountenance and despise them, this great Evil would soon cease in the Community.

And as to the Accusation of abusing Men of Merit, I do most solemnly deny it; and I defy him to produce a single Instance of one great and good Man, against whom No-Body ever spoke an evil Word.

Again, he upbraids me with the false Accusations brought against him by a young Lady, of being at some Drum or Rout[2] where he would be ashamed of being seen. The Fact may be true, for any thing I know to the contrary; but why am I to answer for the Behaviour of Ladies, who are so far from being my Friends, as he falsely says, that they are all such as Every-Body knows,

---

[1] See *CGJ* No. 36, above, p. 215 n. 1. In the Bodleian Library copy (Hope Folio 11) an addition in Fielding's handwriting, only partly legible, appears after the word 'accomplished': 'by any but my self; who seem [?] alone to . . . rd [*or* nd] [*page trimmed?*] its [?] Utility'. Though his writing is unclear, Fielding's intention in the revision appears to have been to emphasize the point that 'nobody' will succeed in providing for the poor until some one plan is given general support.

[2] See *CGJ* No. 17, above, p. 122 n. 2.

and would resent being thought to be acquainted with me as the most cruel Aspersion.

As for the Injury done to Books of Merit, by a Report that I have read them; is this my Fault? I might as justly lay to his Charge the Propagation of half the Nonsense, Dulness, and Scurrility, with which the Age abounds; but I CAN truly say, I HAVE no Delight in Scandal.

If I was not afraid of tiring you, or *your Reader*, with the Controversy, I could say much more; but this shall suffice. Nor do I doubt but you will do me the Justice of printing this; since I assure you, that while you persevere in exposing the Vices and Follies of the Age; while you avoid any base Attachment to Party, any servile Flattery to the Great, and any Reflections on private Characters, you will be sure to find a professed Admirer, and zealous Friend, in

Your most humble Servant,
NO-BODY.

A.

TO
Sir *Alexander Drawcansir.*

Sir,[1]

If the Society, which Crito, in the Gazetteer on the 16th Instant, somewhat invidiously calls upon, hath not yet given Proofs to the Public of its Improvements, let it be remembered by what slow Gradations every new Institution approaches to Fame.[2]

It is a well known Fact, that the Members of the Royal Academy of Surgery at Paris, were many Years before they appeared in Print;[3] and Persons suspended their Contributions and Assistance to that Work, 'till the Society had established a Character by the Press, or some other Means. No

---

[1] This letter is not by Fielding and is struck out in the Bodleian Library copy of *CGJ* (see General Introduction, p. xxx n. 3). For the possibility that its author is William Hunter and for the background of the Society of Naval Surgeons, see *CGJ* No. 38, pp. 222–4, above, and p. 224 n. 1. In preparation for printing this second letter by 'Benevolus', Fielding in *CGJ* No. 40 expressed his own approval of the Society; see the 'Covent Garden' column of 18 May, printed below, Appendix I.

[2] No copy has been found of the *London Gazetteer* of 16 May, in which 'Crito' published his criticism of the letter in *CGJ* No. 38. From what follows it is clear that 'Crito' criticized the slow progress of the naval surgeons in producing papers of interest and questioned the need for their society when the Royal Society was already flourishing. With the argument Benevolus makes here about 'slow Gradations', cf. William Hunter, *Medical Commentaries* (1762): 'Discoveries and improvements in the arts are not commonly brought to any tolerable degree of perfection in a little time; especially when they fall to the share of men who are much employed about other things, and when they require opportunities that seldom happen' (p. 60).

[3] The Académie Royale de Chirugie was founded 18 Dec. 1731; it published *Règlement pour une Académie de Chirugie* (Paris, 1732), and offered prizes in the following years, but its *Mémoires* did not appear until 1743 despite the fact that its *Règlement* (article xxxi) called for annual publication of papers if possible. The *Mémoires* were translated and published in London by Edward Cave in 1750.

Doubt the same Cause as powerfully prevails, in this our present and domestic Instance, as it must in all others of the like Kind, where Men wait only for a Specimen to be determined in their Conduct. But it must be confessed, that this is a Circumstance somewhat to be lamented; for the Friends of Science ought to consider, that were such Sentiments general, it would be impossible to form even a Beginning. The Scotch medical Essays[1] were indeed quickly perfected, but it is not difficult to assign a Reason for such uncommon Maturity.

It was the Accumulation of Papers, in some private Hands, that first gave Birth to their Proposals; hence, principally, arose that learned Association; so that it may be said, the Papers of which they were previously in Possession, gave Rise to that Society, rather than that Society to the Papers. Hence, did an able Set of Gentlemen, oblige the World, with those valuable and curious Essays, so universally known, without that usual Suspence, which has hithero attended the Productions of most other Bodies of Literature.[2] The Insinuation that the Navy Medical Society is of modern Date can scarce affect it in the slightest Degree. The trite and antient Adage that "it is never too late to do Good" may be here applied.[3] The oldest and best Institution has had its infant State.

It is not for me, in my private Capacity, to enter into the Nature of the Committee's Business; I shall only say, that all due Care is promised, in the revising and digesting Materials for the Press, and that nothing will be published, but what has undergone a fair and impartial Scrutiny. For Candor, not invective Criticism, is one of their established Rules.

In Regard to the Royal Society; that illustrious Body entertains much higher Notions of Things, than to suppose their Province invaded. Real Science is a Stranger to all Jealousy; and its true Sons ever rejoice with Company, in the Road to Truth. They well know, that there is Matter enough undetected, to exercise any different Set of Men, to all succeeding Generations. Nature is not so easily mastered, or the Springs of her Actions so soon exposed, as not to furnish almost infinite Variety of Pursuit, even in any single Branch. The Situation of the Navy Surgeons, as has been before observed,[4] strongly points to the Use and Advantage of such an Institution, and considering the superior Opportunities they have for many particular

---

[1] Alluding to *Medical Essays and Observations Revised and Published by a Society in Edinburgh* (Edinburgh, 1733), vol. i, intended to be the first in an annual collection of medical essays.

[2] Benevolus's point is substantiated by a comment in the Preface to the collection: 'We cannot conclude, without returning Thanks to the Gentlemen who have furnished the Materials for this first Volume, and must presume that their Example and this convincing Proof of our being in good earnest to execute our Proposals, will soon encrease our Correspondence' (*Medical Essays* [Edinburgh, 1733], pp. xxiii–xxiv). The first volume included essays by the distinguished physicians Alexander Monro, Andrew Plummer, and William Cockburn.

[3] Not in Tilley, but cf. G315, 'Good though long stayed for is good'.

[4] In *CGJ* No. 38.

Disquisitions, it is somewhat a Surprise, that this naval Society was not more early formed. For to take it in its whole Extent, it is the first of the Kind, that this Kingdom, or any other has produced. It is especially adapted to the Genius of a maritime Power; to the Benefit, Welfare and Preservation, of that useful Body our Sailors; the Instruments of British Glory, the Nerves and Sinews of this Land.

The Diseases to which these are peculiarly incident, and the many Obstacles to a Cure, which by their Manner of living upon that Element they must necessarily encounter with require the greatest Skill in the Surgeon. Hence, it will appear, that this Undertaking has a manifest Tendency to advance the public Service. Upon Maxims therefore of sound Policy, or a national Concern, it is to be hoped, that Success will attend the Labours of the Society, which has already made some Progress, and is daily assiduous in pursuing the Means to beneficial and lasting Attainments.

Natural History being as it were the Path to Medicine, the Society's Claim to Enquiries, in that Branch of Knowledge, is too evident and justifiable to be disputed. Besides, their transplanting the Improvements of other Countries, and availing themselves of every useful Hint from Men of Science in foreign Climes, they likewise propose to furnish themselves with what natural and rare Materials the habitable Parts of the Globe produce. For to whom is mostly owing every Collection of Rarities, but to those, who for a while, "occupy their Business upon the great Deep?"[1] Every Repository of this Sort, is enriched by them; nor is it intended that any Recess, where Britons visit, shall escape their laudable Curiosity.

Every Member employed on board any of his Majesty's Ships in foreign Voyages, is desired to give the Committee a seasonable Notice of their Departure, that they may recommend to them such Memorandums and Enquiries, as they judge most interesting and necessary for the Society, the most conducive to the common Weal, and the acommodating Speculation to useful Practice.[2]

So far, for the Propriety and Consistence, in their including such a fundamental Part of Medicine as natural History. Nature under a certain Limitation is their Object, for which Physic is well known to be but a synonymous Term. As to the subaltern Classes as specified in their Plan, their Title to them is too palpable to need explaining.

The successful Labours of the Royal Society are above my Animadversions;[3] and it is no Reflection upon the Body itself, or on those great and

---

[1] Adapted from Psalm 107: 23, 'They that go down to the sea in ships, that do business in great waters'.

[2] This paragraph is a paraphrase of Article III of the Plan of the Society of Naval Surgeons.

[3] The tone reflects the solid standing of the Royal Society at mid-century. It was, however, still subject to attack; see John Hill's *A Review of the Works of the Royal Society* (1751), *A Dissertation on Royal Societies* (1750), and Fielding's satire in *CGJ* No. 70.

excellent Persons which compose it, that of all the Papers exhibited there, the Majority of its Members pay the least Attention to medical Subjects. They have, besides, such ample Fields to range in, such inexhausted Considerations, in the Stores of Learning, that no Wonder they should consider the immediate Cultivation of Medicine and its Relatives, as less adapted to general Study, and more suitable to the Pursuit of particular Bodies.

BENEVOLUS.

TUESDAY, MAY 26, 1752.   NUMB. 42.

——Me literulas stulti docuere parentes.

MARTIAL.[1]

> My Father was a Fool,
> When he sent me to School.

Mr. Censor,

It hath been a common Observation, *That great Scholars know nothing of the World.*[2] The Reason of this is not, as generally it is imagined, that the Greek and Latin Languages have a natural Tendency to vitiate the human Understanding; but in solemn Truth, Gentlemen who obtain an early Acquaintance with the Manners and Customs of the Antients, are too apt to form their Ideas of their own Times, on the Patterns of Ages which bear not the least Resemblance to them. Hence they have fallen into the greatest Errors and Absurdities; and hence, I suppose, was derived the Observation abovementioned.[3]

Numberless are the Instances which may be produced of these Errors of

---

[1] *Epigrams*, lxxiii. 7: 'Me, foolish parents taught paltry letters' (Loeb).

[2] Cf. Tilley, S 135, 'A mere scholar is a mere ass', for variations of this proverbial notion; also C 409, 'The greatest clerks are not the wisest men'.

[3] Fielding's irony here and in what follows is directed not, of course, at classical education but at the 'Notions of the World'; for his serious view of university education as 'much the best we have', see *CGJ* No. 56. With his ironic contrast in this essay between universities and worldly values, cf. Captain Bellamant to his father in *The Modern Husband* (1732): 'Suppose I had stayed at the university, and followed Greek and Latin as you advised me; what acquaintance had I found at court? what bows had I received at an assembly, or at the opera?' (II. ii); see also *The Temple Beau* (1730), I. iii, and *Amelia*, XI. ii. Fielding elsewhere makes amply clear that he rejects the conventional view that scholars are unfit for the world; see *Amelia*, VIII. v, where we are told that Booth's father, though intending a military career for his son, did not think 'that a competent Share of *Latin* and *Greek* would make his Son either a Pedant or a Coward'. Cf. especially Fielding's preface to his sister's *Familiar Letters between the Principal Characters in David Simple* (1747), where he argues against the notion that knowledge of human nature is to be gained more easily in the great world than in schools or colleges: 'The Truth of the Assertion, that Pedants in Colleges have seldom any Share of this Knowledge, doth not arise from any Defect in the College, but from a Defect in the Pedant, who would have spent many Years at *St. James's* to as little Purpose: for daily Experience may convince us, that it is possible for a Blockhead to see much of the World, and know little of it' (p. xv).

the Literati; so many indeed that I have often thought there is no less Difference between those Notions of the World which are drawn from Letters, and those which are drawn from Men, than there is between the Ideas of the human Complexion, which are conceived by one in perfect Health, and one in the Jaundice.

Let us suppose a Man, possessed of this Jaundice of Literature, conveyed into the Levees of the Great. What Notion will he be likely to entertain of the several Persons who compose that illustrious Assembly, from their Behaviour? How will he be puzzled when he is told that he hath before his Eyes a Number of Free-Men? How much more will he be amazed when he hears that all the Servility he there beholds, arises only from an eager Desire of being permitted to serve the Public.[1]

Again, convey the same Gentleman to a Hunting-Match, a Horse Race, or any other Meeting of Patriots.[2] Will he not immediately conclude from all the Roaring and Ranting, the Hallowing and Huzzaing, the Gaming and Drinking, which he will there observe, that he is actually present at the Orgia of Bacchus, or the Celebration of some such Festival? How then will he be astonished to find that he is in the Company of a Sett of honest Fellows, who are the Guardians of Liberty, and are actually getting drunk in the Service of their Country.

Introduce him next to a Drum or a Rout,[3] and if the Blaze of Beauty doth not blind him to any other Contemplation, how greatly superior will he think the British Ladies to all those of Greece and Rome——at their Needles? When he views all the exquisite Decorations of Art which set off the Persons of his fair Countrywomen, how will he despise all the Compliments paid heretofore to the Personages of the Greek and Roman Ladies of Quality, who claimed a Preference over each other from their superior Skill in handling their Needles? But what must be his Amazement, when he is assured that not one of these Ladies ever handled any such Instrument; that all the Ornaments of the best drest Woman there are owing to the Handywork of others, and that the whole Business of the Lives of all present, is only to toss about from the one to the other certain Pieces of painted Paper,[4] being a Pastime common to grown Persons and Children; with this Difference only, that the former play for the higher Wagers!

What Idea can we suppose such a Person could conceive of the Word

---

[1] See *CGJ* No. 2, above, p. 23 n. 3.

[2] i.e. the 'Country Gentlemen' of a political opposition, whose antics are here placed in no more favorable a light than the 'Court' figures of the preceding paragraph; on the term 'Patriot' see *CGJ* No. 28, above, p. oo n. o. In *JJ* No. 2 (12 Dec. 1747) Fielding associates the 'Orgia of Bacchus' with Jacobite political activity.

[3] See *CGJ* No. 17, above, p. 122 n. 2.

[4] Playing-cards.

Beau;[1] and if he could have no adequate Notion of the Word, much less would he be able to obtain any such Notion of *the Thing*! Should he behold a little dapper effeminate Spark, carried through the Sunshine in a soft Machine by two Labourers; his Body drest in all the Tinsel which serves to trick up a Harlot, and his Hair appearing to have been decked by the same Tire-woman[2] with hers. Would such a Sight as this recall to the Mind of our learned Friend, any Image of a Greek or Roman Soldier; or could he be easily persuaded, that the Insect before his Eyes was a military Commander; in Rank a Centurion or perhaps a Tribune?

In one Particular, and in one alone, it is possible he might form a true Judgment. The many Eulogiums on the Chastity of the antient Spartan and Roman Dames, and on the extraordinary Modesty of their young Females of Rank, must give him a perfect Idea of our present Ladies of Fashion.[3]

With this single Exception, I think I may aver, that a Scholar when he first comes to this Town from the University comes among a Set of People, as entirely unknown to him, and of whom he hath no more heard or read, than if he was to be at once translated into one the Planets; *the World* in the Town and that *in the Moon* being equally strange to him, and equally unintelligible.

How wise therefore is the Conduct of the present Age, in laying aside that foolish Custom of our Ancestors, who used to throw away many of the most precious Years of their Sons Lives by confining them to Schools and Universities; where what they learnt, was so far from being of any Use to them upon their *coming into the World*, as it is called, that it served only to puzzle and mislead them.[4] They were indeed obliged to unlearn all that had been taught them, before they could acquire that useful Knowledge mentioned in the Beginning of my Paper.

Whereas by the present Method of bringing Youth to Town, about the Age of fifteen or sixteen, and entering them immediately in those several Schools, where the Knowledge of the World is taught; such as the Play-houses, Gaming-houses and Bawdy-houses; a young Gentleman of any tolerable Docility, becomes at the Age of Eighteen, a perfect Master of all the Knowledge of the World at home; and it is then a proper Time for him to

---

[1] Cf. Fielding's definition of 'Beau' in his 'Modern Glossary', *CGJ* No. 4; see also *CGJ* Nos. 37, 56.

[2] A lady's maid; cf. the description of a beau fashionably dressed, *CGJ* No. 37.

[3] For similar irony on the chastity of women cf. *CGJ* No. 66; the virtue of Roman and Spartan women is again referred to in *CGJ* No. 67, where Fielding cites the punishments for adultery in past ages.

[4] What Fielding says here ironically was sometimes said in all seriousness. Cf. Peter Shaw, a physician, in his work *The Reflector* (1750): 'And it happens unluckily in the Situation [of seeking preferment], that what a Man learnt at School proves of little Service to him. . . . To succeed in Life, instead of *Latin* and *Greek*, a Man should furnish himself with Humility and Patience; and instead of courting the Muses, ingratiate himself with Ladies of Quality, or their Women' (p. 32; for similar passages, see pp. 56, 60–1).

set out on his Travels into foreign Parts, and to make himself acquainted with the World abroad.——This completes his Education; and he returns at One-and-Twenty, a most accomplished fine Gentleman; having visited all the principal Courts of Europe, and become versed in all their Fashions, at a Season of Life when our dull Forefathers knew nothing of those foreign People but from History, nor even of their Countries but from Geography.[1]

It was my Misfortune however to have a Father of the antique Way of thinking; by which Means, I lost the best Part of my Youth in turning over those Books, in which I have said there is little useful to be learnt. I remember a Passage out of Horace, who is the best of them, and who seems to be very particularly a Favourite of yours. His Words are these,

> *Vitæ summa brevis,*
> *Spem nos vetat inchoare longam.*[2]

Which may be thus rendered after your paraphrastical Manner. *The Shortness of Life affords no Time for a tedious Education.* How many indeed of my own Acquaintance, have I known to die of old Age at twenty-five! so that by the antient Method of educating our Sons at Schools and Universities, a great Part of them will be in Danger of going out of the World before they know any Thing of it.

> *Life* (says Mr. Pope) *can little more supply,*
> *Than just to look about us and to die.*[3]

Is it not therefore the Duty of a Father to give his Son an Opportunity of looking about him as soon as he can?

I am,

SIR,

Your most humble Servant,

TOM. TELLTRUTH.

A.

SATURDAY, MAY 30, 1752.   NUMB. 43.

> *Non quia, Mæcenas, Lydorum quicquid Etruscos*
> *Incoluit fines, nemo generosior est te;*
> *Nec quod avus tibi maternus fuit atque paternus,*
> *Olim qui magnis legionibus imperitarent;*

[1] Cf. Pope's *Dunciad* (1743), iv. 282–336. Criticism of the Grand Tour was commonplace, not only among satirists like Pope and Fielding but in tracts on education. See e.g. Locke, *Some Thoughts Concerning Education* (1693), sections 212–16, and *Free Thoughts upon University Education* (1751), pp. 16–21.

[2] *Odes*, I. iv. 15: 'Life's brief span forbids thy entering on far-reaching hopes' (Loeb).

[3] *Essay on Man*, i. 3–4.

Ut plerique solent, naso suspendis adunco
Ignolos, ut me libertino patre natum.
Cum referre negas, quali fit quisque parente
Natus, dum ingenuus——.

HORACE.[1]

MODERNIZED.

Tho' there is no Man of a better Family in Europe than your Lordship, no Man hath less in his Mouth that scornful Phrase, PEOPLE WHOM NO BODY KNOWS. *You apply it not even to me, whose Father was a Mechanic. On the contrary, I have heard you say; "It matters not what any Man's Parents were, provided that he behaves himself like a Gentleman."*

The following Letter had a Coronet[2] on its Seal.

TO

Sir Alexander Drawcansir, Knt.

Sir,

I read over your Paper on the Circle[3] with great Pleasure. You have there, with great Force of Eloquence, set forth the terrible Difficulties which we of the better Sort go through to keep *the Creatures*, as you very properly call them in your *Motter*, at a Distance.

But, dear Knight, why would you suffer that beastly Clerk to an *odious* Justice of Peace, to contaminate the dear Names of Drum and Rout, by putting the Word Mob close before them: For in your Account of High-Cunstables, and such Animals, in your Paper of the 2d of May, you tell us *of a Drum or Rout, where several hundred Mob assemble together.*[4]

You cannot imagine the Mischief you have done by this silly Paragraph. My Woman tells me that since the publishing it, some City-Creature[5] hath declared that she intends to keep Drums and Routs next Winter. Upon this News we had a Council at Lady Sadlife's in the Afternoon, where all the Ladies at once declared that it would be *odious* to use those Names any longer.

---

[1] *Satires*, I. vi. 1–8: 'Though of all the Lydians that are settled in Tuscan lands none is of nobler birth than you, and though grandsires of yours, on your mother's and father's side alike, commanded mighty legions in days of old, yet you, Maecenas, do not, like most of the world, curl up your nose at men of unknown birth, men like myself, a freedman's son. . . . you say it matters not who a man's parent is, if he be himself free-born' (Loeb).

[2] Signifying nobility.

[3] *CGJ* No. 37.

[4] See the 'Covent Garden' column of 1 May 1752 (printed below, Appendix I), in which Joshua Brogden, Fielding's clerk, speaks of a 'Mob drum or Rout' raided by the High Constable of Finsbury Division. On the terms 'drum' and 'rout', see *CGJ* No. 17, above, p. 122 n. 2.

[5] i.e. the wife or daughter of a 'citizen' or merchant of the City, such as the daughter of 'Paul Traffick', whose letter follows.

At the breaking up of the Assembly I was deputed to write to you, to desire you would invent us some new Terms for our Assemblies against the Winter. What think you of A RATTLE[1] for one; but this is submitted to you, by

SIR,

Your humble Servant,

ZARA GRANDEMONDE.[2]

The Lady cannot expect a hasty Answer in a Matter which she herself thinks of such Consequence. However, as I am resolved to observe the most perfect Impartiality on all Occasions, I shall here subjoin a Letter from a Gentleman, who sees my Paper of the 9th Instant in a Light very different from that in which it hath appeared to her Ladyship.

Mr. Censor,

I greatly honour you for that just Ridicule with which you have lately exposed the Follies of a Set of People, who affect a Desire of distinguishing themselves; not as Persons who are by Fortune, and sometimes by the Blindness of Fortune, placed above their Fellow Creatures and Fellow Countrymen, but as if they were really of a different Species, and by Nature constituted Beings of a higher Order than the rest of Humankind.

Such Distinctions, I apprehend, Mr. Censor, are totally inconsistent with the Religion professed in this Country, with the Liberty which we claim, and with that Spirit of Trade which all Men agree it is our Interest to encourage.

But farther, Sir, they are maintained in open Defiance of Truth, and even of common Sense. We are by Nature all equal. We bring with us the same Perfections and Imperfections (I speak generally) both of Body and Mind, into the World. And again, as we were equal in the Womb, so we are equal in the Grave.

Politicians, I own, have in different Nations set up different Distinctions. In some Virtue, in others Genius, in others military Atchievements have been the Marks which have raised one Man above another in the public Estimation. In some Countries perhaps these Marks have been mere chimerical; but among every trading People, as I take it, Money is that which stamps a Value on the Possessor, and places a Man at the Head of his Countrymen.

It was my Happiness (for so I think it) to be bred to Trade; and it hath been my Fortune to succeed so well in it, that I am worth what is called half a

---

[1] By analogy to 'Drum', but also with several other meanings applicable here: a dice-box; a constant chatter or uproar (*OED*).

[2] The name derives, perhaps, from the heroine of the tragedy *Zara* (1736), Aaron Hill's translation of Voltaire's *Zaire*.

Plumb;[1] indeed I believe if my Accounts were ballanced, I should find the Amount in Money and Stock, to be pretty near sixty thousand Pounds. All this, will one Day or other be the Property of an only Child, a Girl who in the Opinion of all my Acquaintance hath great personal Merit, and I have omitted no Care, nor spared any Expence in her Education.

This Girl, Mr. Censor, is now in the twentieth Year of her Age; and to speak an impartial Truth, I can discover but one Fault in her. In short, she is run mad with the Love of Quality. Within these two last Years, during which, I have given her, I am afraid, a little too much Liberty, she hath spent above half her Time at the other End of the Town. She goes often to Court, and is almost every Night of her Life (in the Winter Season) at some Drum or Rout, (as she calls them) with a Lady of Quality, who hath taken a great Liking to her; for which you will perhaps be able to account, when I tell you, my Girl hath lost about a thousand Pounds at Play, and her Ladyship is got above two thousand Pounds more into my Books.

This however, I do not much value: For I would please my Child at almost any Expence; but what I most regret is, the *apparent Loss of her Good-Breeding*,[2] since she hath kept this Quality Company. She was formerly the civilest of all young Women; but of late she hath learnt to toss up her Nose at all her Neighbours and Equals; nay indeed at her Betters, I mean, at the Wives and Daughters of Citizens, who are by some thousands, *better* Men than myself. It was but the other Day, that she absolutely refused to go to the Play-House with my Neighbour Curd the Cheesemonger's Daughters, tho' they had a Pit-Ticket to spare, which they offered her. I insisted strongly on her going, and what do you think was her Answer? "Indeed, Papa," said she, "I would not sit in the Pit on any Account; nor would I be seen with such People for the World!"[3]

In real Truth, Mr. Censor, I am sometimes afraid that she hath a Contempt for her own Father, tho' I cannot tax her with any disrespectful Behaviour to my Person, nor with any other Instance of Undutifulness, than in spending her Time in a Manner which she must know is disagreeable to my Inclinations, as I foresee no good Consequence can attend it.

The only Offer of Marriage which she hath hitherto had, was from a Man of Quality, (as they call him) but who could make no Settlement adequate to her Fortune. When I absolutely refused my Consent on any other Terms, (will you believe it, Sir;) this modest Gentleman had the Assurance to declare, that he might have expected some Concessions on the Account of Birth, from a Man who was never born.

[1] £50,000.

[2] See *CGJ* Nos. 55 and 56; see also General Introduction, above, pp. xlii–xliii.

[3] Cf. *CGJ* No. 27, in which Fielding analyzes ironically the social implications of various sections of the theater. The pit (the second most expensive area, after the boxes) is there said to be occupied by 'Shopkeepers Wives and Daughters'.

Be so good, Sir, as to tell me, what is the Meaning of this Word Birth, and of what Valuation it is; having never yet seen it brought to Account in any Journal or Leidger. Is not, think you, 30000l. rather too high a Price? Be pleased likewise to give me your Opinion, whether a Man whose Parents were honest and substantial Persons, may not only be said to be born, but to be well-born, even as well as any honourable Son of a —— in the World.

I am, Sir,

Your Humble Servant,

PAUL TRAFFICK.

Thames-street,[1]
May 20.

A.

TUESDAY, JUNE 2, 1752.   NUMB. 44.

——O bone, ne te
Frustrere, insanis et tu——.

HORACE.[2]

> My good Friend, do not deceive thyself;
> for with all thy Charity, thou also art
> a silly Fellow.

I have in a former Paper[3] endeavoured to shew, that a rich Man without Charity is a Rogue; and perhaps it would be no difficult Matter to prove, that he is also a Fool. If a Man, who doth not know his true Interest, may be thought to deserve that Appellation; in what Light shall we behold a Christian, who neglects the Cultivation of a Virtue which is in Scripture said *to wash away his Sins*,[4] and without which all his other good Deeds cannot render him acceptable in the Sight of his Creator and Redeemer.

Even in this World, it is surely much too narrow a view to confine a Man's Interest merely to that which loads his Coffers. To pursue that which is most capable of giving him Happiness, is indeed the Interest of every Man; and there are many who find great Pleasure in emptying their Purses with this View, to one who hath no other Satisfaction than in filling it. Now what can give greater Happiness to a good Mind, than the Reflexion on having relieved the Misery, or contributed to the well-being, of his Fellow

---

[1] 'A Place of a considerable Trade, and taken up by great Dealers, as well by Wholesale as Retale' (John Strype, [Stow's] *Survey of the Cities of London and Westminster . . . brought down . . . to the present Time* [1720], I. ii. 52). Cf. the comment made at a masquerade, *Amelia* (X. ii): 'the Gentleman smells strongly of *Thames-Street*, and, if I may venture to guess, of the honourable Calling of a *Taylor*'.

[2] *Satires*, II. iii. 31–2: 'My good sir, don't deceive yourself; you, too, are mad' (Loeb).

[3] *CGJ* No. 39 (16 May).

[4] The thought is that of I Peter 4: 8, 'for charity shall cover the multitude of sins', quoted by Fielding in the same context in *Champion*, 16 Feb. 1740, and the language is that of Acts 22: 16, 'arise, and be baptized, and wash away thy sins'.

Creature. It was a noble Sentiment of the worthy Mr. Thomas Firmin, "That to relieve the Poor, and to provide Work and Subsistence for them, gave to him the same Pleasure as magnificent Buildings, pleasant Walks, well cultivated Orchards and Gardens, the Jollity of Music and Wine, or the Charms of Love and Study gave to others."[1] This is recorded in the Life of a plain Citizen of London, and it as well deserves to be quoted, as any one Apophthegm that is to be found in all the Works of Plutarch.

A Christian therefore, or a good Man tho' no Christian, who is void of Charity, is ignorant of his own Interest, and may with great Propriety be called a silly Fellow. Nay, if we will believe all the great Writers whom I cited in my former Paper, to which I might add Plato and many more, a mere human Being who places all his Happiness in selfish Considerations, without any relative Virtues, any Regard to the Good of others, is in plain Truth a downright Fool.

I have been encouraged to treat the Want of Charity with the more Freedom, as I am certain of giving little Offence to any of my Readers by so doing. Charity is in fact the very Characteristic of this Nation at this Time.——I believe we may challenge the whole World to parallel the Examples which we have of late given of this sensible, this noble, this Christian Virtue.[2]

We cannot therefore surely be arraigned of Folly, from the Want of Charity; but is our Wisdom altogether as apparent in the Manner of exerting it? I am afraid the true Answer here would not be so much to our Advantage. Are our private Donations generally directed by our Judgment, to those who are the properest Objects? Do not Vanity, Whim, and Weakness, too often draw our Purse-Strings?[3] Do we not sometimes give because it is the Fashion, and sometimes because we cannot long resist Importunity? May not our Charity be often termed Extravagance or Folly; nay is it not often vicious, and apparently tending to the Encrease and Encouragement of idle and dissolute Persons?[4]

[1] Adapted from *The Life of Mr. Thomas Firmin, Late Citizen of London* (1698), p. 38; Firmin (1632–97), a London merchant and philanthropist, established a workhouse for the poor and thus may have been of special interest to Fielding.

[2] Fielding's seriousness here is indicated by his essay in the *Champion*, 16 Feb. 1739/40, where he argues at length that 'the amiable characteristic of the present age is charity'. See also *Champion*, 19 and 21 Feb. 1739/40, in the second of which he specifies further that the nation is to be congratulated particularly for its charity in founding hospitals; cf. Johnson on the same topic in *Idler*, No. 4 (6 May 1758).   [3] i.e. open our purses; for a similar usage see *CGJ* No. 58, below.

[4] Cf. the sermon written by Samuel Johnson and preached by Henry Hervey Aston in 1745: 'We are not to suffer our Liberality to be abused to the Indulgence of Idleness, or to the Encouragement of Vice, for this, like all other Virtues, is estimable for its Effects' (*A Sermon Preached at the Cathedral Church of St. Paul Before the Sons of the Clergy* [1745], pp. 24–5); cf. also Isaac Barrow in 'The Duty and Reward of Bounty to the Poor', a sermon cited below by Fielding: 'He *disperseth* them *to the poor*, not dissipateth them among vain or lewd persons in wanton or wicked profusions, in riotous excesses, in idle divertisements' (*Works* [1741], i. 304). For Fielding's list of the proper objects of charity, see *Champion*, 16 Feb. 1739/40.

It would be almost endless to attempt to be particular on this Head. I shall mention therefore only one Instance, namely the giving our Money to common Beggars.[1] This Kind of Bounty is a Crime against the Public. It is assisting in the Continuance and Promotion of a Nusance. Our wise Ancestors prohibited it by a Law,[2] which would probably have remained in Force and Use to this Day, had not the Legislature conceived, that after the severe Penalties which have been since inflicted on Beggars, none would have the Boldness to become such; and that after the sufficient legal Provision which hath been made for the Poor, no Persons would have so little Regard, either to common Sense or to the Public, as to relieve them.

But instead of staying to argue with such People, I shall hasten to the other Branch of Charity, which is of a public Nature; of which there are many Species in this Kingdom.

The Origin of this Kind of Charity, was no better than Priestcraft and Superstition. When Men began to perceive the near Approach of that great Enemy of human Nature, who was to deprive them of all their ill-gotten Possessions, and not only so, but might as they apprehended, deliver them into the Hands of an Almighty Justice, to punish them for all those Knavish Arts, by which these Possessions were acquired; the Priest stept in, took Advantage of the Terrors of their Consciences, and persuaded them, that by consigning over a great Part, (sometimes the whole) of their Acquisitions to the Use of the Church, a Pardon for all Kind of Villainy was sure to be obtained.[3]

In this Attempt, the Priest found but little Difficulty when he had to do with a Mind tainted with Superstition, and weakened with Disease; especially when he could back all his other Arguments with one Truth at least, namely,—Give us THAT WHICH YOU CAN BY NO POSSIBLE MEANS KEEP ANY LONGER YOURSELF.

Thus the *unwilling Will*, as Dr. Barrow pleasantly calls it,[4] was at last

---

[1] See *CGJ* No. 2, p. 22, above, and n. 4; see also *Champion*, 16 Feb. 1739/40, where Fielding again argues that beggars are unworthy objects of our charity, and cf. his *Enquiry into the Causes of the late Increase of Robbers* (1751), pp. 45–6. On Fielding's view as typical of his period, see Malvin R. Zirker, Jr., *Fielding's Social Pamphlets* (Berkeley and Los Angeles, 1966), pp. 96–100.

[2] By 27 Henry VIII, c. 25, providing a penalty for any person making a 'common dole' or giving to any except through the common boxes; this act was replaced by 39 Eliz., c. 4, which made no such provision. The most recent law affecting beggars was 17 George II, c. 5; see Fielding's *Enquiry* (1751), Sect. IV, for a survey of the laws involving provisions for the poor.

[3] Cf. Mandeville, *Essay on Charity and Charity Schools* (1723): 'Nothing is more destructive to Virtue or Religion it self, than to make Men believe that giving Money to the Poor, tho' they should not part with it till after Death, will make a full Atonement in the next World, for the Sins they have committed in this' (*A Fable of the Bees*, ed. F. B. Kaye [Oxford, 1924], i. 261). Cf. also Fielding's attack on 'mercenary Goodness' in *CGJ* No. 29.

[4] Quoted from the sermon that was particularly meaningful to Fielding, 'The Duty and Reward of Bounty to the Poor'; the entire passage is relevant to Fielding's point: '*He hath dispersed*, and *given*, while he lives, not reserving the disposal of all at once upon his death, or by his last will; that unwilling will, whereby men would seem to give somewhat, when they can keep nothing; drawing to themselves

signed. The Fruits of Fraud and Rapine were allotted to the Use of the Church, and the greatest of Rascals died very good Saints, and their Memories were consecrated to Honour and good Example.

How notably these Attempts succeeded, is well known to all who are versed either in our Law or our History. So common was it for Men to expiate their Crimes in this Manner; and to finish all their other Robberies, by robbing their Heirs; that had not the Legislature often and stoutly interfered in crushing these supersititious (or as they were called charitable) Uses, they seemed to have bid fair for swallowing up the whole Property of the Nation.[1]

In Process of Time however, the Lawyer came to the Assistance of the Priest; (for like the Devil he is always ready at Hand when called for) and formed a Distinction between the superstitious and charitable Use.[2] Henceforward, instead of robbing their Relations for the Use of the Church, a Method was devised of robbing them for the Use of the Poor. Hence Poor-Houses, Alms-Houses, Colleges and Hospitals began to present themselves to the View of all Travellers, being always situated in the most public Places, and bearing the Name and Title of the generous Founder in vast capital Letters; a kind of *KTHMA ES AIEI*,[3] a Monument of his Glory to all Generations.

Thus we see the Foundation of this Kind of Charity, and a very strong one

---

those commendations and thanks, which are only due to their mortality; when as were they immortal, they would never be liberal' (*Works*, 5th edn. [1741], i. 305). On Isaac Barrow, see *CGJ* No. 4, above, p. 34 n. 5; on the significance of this sermon to Fielding, see *CGJ* No. 29, above, p. 183 n. 3.

[1] Fielding means 'Uses' in the legal sense of trusts. By these devices medieval religious houses sought to evade the laws of mortmain, which had the effect of limiting their acquisition of new lands. The statutes to which Fielding refers would include the Statute of Mortmain (7 Edward I, c. 13) and various laws restricting uses, such as 15 Richard II, c. 5, and the important Statute of Uses (27 Henry VIII, c. 10). For discussion see F. W. Maitland, *The Constitutional History of England* (Cambridge, 1955), pp. 223–6, and W. S. Holdsworth, *A History of English Law* (1903–24), iv. 407–80.

The most recent legislative interference with charitable donations was the Mortmain Act of 1736 (9 George II, c. 36), which restricted lands given for charitable uses to those given by a deed executed a year before the death of the donor. Both Fielding's language and his thesis in these paragraphs are similar to those found in arguments supporting this bill, which was introduced by Sir Joseph Jekyll and opposed by the bishops; cf., for example, this comment by a writer in the *Old Whig*: 'one great Intention of this Act was to prevent the mistaken Charity of Men, who . . . are apt to hope to compound for the Faults of their past Life, by a Fine to be paid by their Heirs to some Use which they call a Religious one' (as quoted in *GM* 6 [1736], 204). On the controversy surrounding the Mortmain Act of 1736, see also *GM* 6 (1736), 336–7, 722–6; John, Lord Hervey, *Some Materials towards Memoirs of the Reign of King George II*, ed. Romney Sedgwick (1931), ii. 530–6; and anon., *Some Plain Reasons Humbly offer'd against the Bill . . . to Restrain the Disposition of Lands* (1736).

[2] For the background of Fielding's statement see W. K. Jordan, *Philanthropy in England 1480–1660* (New York, 1959), pp. 109–17. In describing the shift from religious to secular philanthropy Jordan cites an act of 1531–2 'outlawing trusts for superstitious purposes' (23 Henry VIII, c. 10); the Statute of Uses in 1536; and Elizabethan statutes codifying the law of charitable trusts (39 Eliz., c. 6; 43 Eliz., c. 4).

[3] 'A possession for all time', Thucydides' description of his *History* (I. xxii).

it is, being indeed no other than Fear and Vanity, the two strongest Passions which are to be found in human Nature.[1]

It may be thought perhaps, that I have omitted a third, which some may imagine to be the strongest, and greatest of all, and this is Benevolence, or the Love of doing Good; but that these charitable Legacies have no such Motive, appears to me from the following Considerations.

First, if a Man was possessed of real Benevolence, and had, (as he must then have) a Delight in doing Good, he would no more defer the Enjoyment of this Satisfaction to his Death-bed, than the Ambitious, the Luxurious, or the Vain, would wait till that Period, for the Gratification of their several Passions.

2dly, If the Legacy be, as it often is, the first charitable Donation of any Consequence, I can never allow it possible to arise from Benevolence: For he who hath no Compassion for the Distresses of his Neighbours, *whom he hath seen*,[2] how should he have any Pity for the Wants of Posterity which he will never see?

3dly, If the Legacy be, as is likewise very common, to the Injury of his Family, or to the Disappointment of his own Friends in Want, this is a certain Proof, that his Motive is not Benevolence: For he who loves not his own Friends and Relations, most certainly loves no other Person.[3]

Lastly, if a Man hath lived any Time in the World, he must have observed such horrid and notorious Abuses of all public Charities,[4] that he must be convinced (with a very few Exceptions) that he will do no Manner of Good by contributing to them. Some indeed, are so very wretchedly contrived in their Institution, that they seem not to have had the public Utility in their View; but to have been mere Jobs ab initio.[5] Such are all Hospitals whatever,

---

[1] Cf. Mandeville: 'Pride and Vanity have built more Hospitals than all the Virtues together' (*An Essay on Charity and Charity Schools* [1723], in *Fable of the Bees*, ed. Kaye, i. 261). In the pages following this remark Mandeville, like Fielding, analyzes harshly the motives of those who hope to atone for unworthy lives by leaving charitable legacies: 'the rich Miser who refuses to assist his nearest Relations while he is alive . . . and disposes of his Money for what we call Charitable Uses after his Death, may imagine of his Goodness what he pleases, but he robbs his Posterity' (p. 261); see also 'The Third Dialogue' in *Fable of the Bees, Part II* (1729), ed. F. B. Kaye, ii. 119–21. Fielding, in his analysis of this false kind of 'charity', is clearly experiencing a Mandevillian moment; but he differs sharply from Mandeville, of course, in his celebration of 'real Benevolence' and the 'Delight in doing Good'.

[2] Echoing I John 4: 20, 'He that loveth not his brother whom he hath seen, cannot love God whom he hath not seen'; Fielding also uses this text in *True Patriot*, No. 2 (12 Nov. 1745).

[3] Cf. Fielding's emphasis on this point in his 'Essay on the Knowledge of Characters of Men', *Miscellanies* (1743), ed. H. K. Miller, Wesleyan Edn. (Oxford, 1972), pp. 175–6.

[4] The principal example which would occur to Fielding's readers was the scandal in 1732 over the Charitable Corporation for the Relief of the Industrious Poor, founded to lend money to the poor; its eight directors, three of them Members of Parliament, were convicted of embezzlement. Cf. the definition of 'Charitable Corporation' offered by a character in Fielding's *The Lottery* (1732): 'That is, Madam, a Method invented, by some very wise Men, by which the Rich may be charitable to the Poor, and be Money in Pocket by it' (sc. ii, p. 14).

[5] 'Job' in the sense of 'a public service or trust turned to private gain' (*OED*); *ab initio*: from the very first.

where it is a Matter of Favour to get a Patient admitted, and where the Forms of Admission are so troublesome and tedious, that the properest Objects, (those I mean, who are most wretched and friendless) may as well aspire at a Place at Court, as at a Place in the Hospital.[1]

From what I have here advanced, I know I have rendered myself liable to be represented by Malice and Ignorance as an Enemy to all public Charity; I hope to obviate this Opinion effectually in a future Paper,[2] in which I shall endeavour to point out who are really the Objects of our Benevolence, as well as to propose some Expedients by which the Obstructions which attend some of our best calculated Charities of the public Kind may be removed. I cannot however, conclude this, without paying a Compliment to the present Age for two glorious Benefactions, I mean that to the Use of Foundling Infants, and that for the Accommodation of poor Women in their Lying-in.[3]   C.

SATURDAY, JUNE 6, 1752.   NUMB. 45.

Juxta se posita magis elucescunt.[4]

When they are placed near together, they
will the better illustrate each other.

[1] Fielding refers to St. Luke's Hospital for Lunatics and to his current concern over the placement of lunatics in hospitals; see the ridicule of the admissions requirements of St Luke's in *CGJ* No. 45; see also the 'Covent Garden' column of 1 June, originally published with this leader, below, Appendix I.

[2] Not published; the topic suggested is, however, the subject of the *Champion*, 16 and 19 Feb. 1739/40.

[3] The Foundling Hospital (i.e. the 'Hospital for the Maintenance and Education of exposed and deserted young Children', as it was officially called) received a royal charter in 1739, with Captain Thomas Coram (1668?–1751) instrumental in its establishment. Hogarth was one of its benefactors, and the Head of the Corporation was Fielding's patron the Duke of Bedford. See R. H. Nichols and F. A. Wray, *The History of the Foundling Hospital* (Oxford, 1935); for a typical panegyric of this widely praised enterprise, see Thomas Cooke, *An Ode on Benevolence* (1753). Fielding's second reference is to the Lying-In Hospital for Married Women in Brownlow Street, Longacre, serving the 'industrious Poor' and described in a contemporary account as one of the 'Variety of Charities which are the Distinction and Glory of this Age and Nation' (*An Account of the Rise and Progress of the Lying-In Hospital* [1751], p. 1). Fielding was a Perpetual Governor of this hospital (a listing which cost 30 guineas), as was his friend William Hunter, who served as a surgeon and man-midwife there. See Fielding's praise of this establishment in the 'Covent Garden' column of 10 Jan., originally appearing with *CGJ* No. 3 and printed below, Appendix I; in *CGJ* No. 8 (28 Jan.) Fielding also printed an advertisement (not reprinted here) defending the hospital against innuendoes made in a hostile pamphlet about its use of man-midwives.

Both these institutions, it should be noted, had procedures for admission much simpler than those at St Luke's Hospital for Lunatics, to which Fielding alludes in the preceding paragraph and which he satirizes in *CGJ* No. 45. At the Foundling Hospital in these years admission was virtually unrestricted, though limited in number by a lottery; see *An Account of the Hospital for . . . exposed and deserted young Children* (1749), pp. 56–9, and Nichols and Wray, ch. 9. At the Lying-In Hospital the rules of admission were more complex but none the less lenient compared to those at St Luke's; see *An Account of . . . the Lying-In Hospital* (1751), pp. 13–14.

[4] A maxim in logic, usually beginning *contraria* or *opposita*. Cf. Dryden, *Essay of Dramatic Poesy*

Mr. Censor,

When you so justly recommended the two public Charities for Foundlings and Lying-in Women,[1] I was surprized you omitted that for Lunatics, which is lately established under the Name of St. Luke's-Hospital.[2] This, I apprehend, could arise from no other Cause than your Ignorance that there was any such existing. I have therefore enclosed you the printed Account of it,[3] in order that you may render it as public as possible, with all due Encomiums on so excellent and extensive a Benefaction, and am

Yours, &c.

Instructions to such Persons who apply for the Admission of Patients into St. LUKE's Hospital for Lunaticks.

I. That no Person shall knowingly be received as a Patient into this Hospital, who is not in Point of Circumstances, a proper Object of this Charity; that is, Poor and Mad.

II. Or who hath been a Lunatic more than twelve Kalendar Months.

III. Or who hath been discharged uncured from any other Hospital for the Reception of Lunaticks.

IV. Or who is troubed with Epileptick or Convulsive Fits.

V. Or who is deemed an Ideot.

(1666): 'The old Rule of Logick might have convinc'd him that contraries when plac'd near, set off each other'; in *Parallel of Poetry and Painting* (1695) Dryden calls it an 'old maxim' and quotes it in Latin, beginning *contraria.* Cf. Aquinas, *Summa Theologica,* Part II (1st Part), art. 3, ob. 3; Bacon, 'The Jurisdiction of the Marches', *Works,* ed. James Spedding *et al.* (New York, 1869), xv. 121, 139.

 [1] See *CGJ* No. 44, above.

 [2] Fielding's criticism at the end of *CGJ* No. 44 of hospitals 'where it is a Matter of Favour to get a Patient admitted' is now focused specifically on St Luke's, which he ridicules by printing first the actual rules of admissions and then, in the second letter, his parody of those rules. For his increasing concern over how to handle deranged figures brought into his court, see the 'Covent Garden' columns for 11, 22, and 29 May and 1 June, originally appearing in *CGJ* Nos. 38, 41, 43, and 44, and printed below, Appendix I.

St Luke's Hospital for Lunatics was established in 1751 at Windmill Hill, Upper Moorfields, by Dr Thomas Crowne and a group of concerned merchants. Its primary physician in this period was the pioneering Dr William Battie (1701–76), author of *A Treatise on Madness* (1758). Ironically, given Fielding's complaint about its own admission policies, one of the reasons cited for opening St Luke's was 'That the Expence and Difficulty attending the Admission of a Patient into the Hospital of *Bethlem,* had discouraged many Applications for the Benefit of that Charity, particularly on the Behalf of the more necessitous Objects' (*Reasons for the Establishing and Further Encouragement of St. Luke's Hospital for Lunaticks* [n.d.; dated by *Eighteenth-century Short Title Catalogue* as 1751?], p. 4; ironically, also, included in its earliest list of Governors was Fielding's current journalistic enemy, Bonnell Thornton; and among its first benefactors was 'The Society at Robin-hood Temple Bar', satirized in *CGJ* No. 8 (for the list, see *Reasons* [1751?]). See also C. N. French, *The Story of St. Luke's Hospital* (1951).

 [3] Except for two minor omissions, the document which Fielding prints is identical with the 'Instructions' printed in *Reasons for Establishing St. Luke's Hospital* (1760), pp. 37–8 and presumably also included in earlier editions of this pamphlet, although missing from the copy of the only earlier edition (1751?) I have located. French (Appendix III) also prints, but does not date, the 'original' instructions, again identical to those Fielding gives.

VI.   Or who is infected with the Venereal Disease.

VII.   Nor any Woman with Child.

And every such Person, who through Mistake or Misinformation shall be received into this Hospital, shall be discharged immediately on a Discovery of any of the above Disqualifications.

Therefore if the Patient is not disqualified by any of the above Rules, upon applying to Mr. *Thomas Webster*[1] the Secretary, at his House in *Queen-street, Cheapside*, or at the Hospital, the Forms of two printed Certificates, together with a Petition may be had; the first of which Certificates (after it is filled up) must be signed by the Minister and Churchwardens, or Overseers of the Poor of the Parish, or Place, where such Patient resides; and the other by some Physician, Surgeon, or Apothecary, who had visited such Patient; after which the Person or Persons who saw them sign must go before one of his Majesty's Justices of the Peace, or some other Person authorised to take Affidavits, and make Oath (or in Case of Quakers an Affirmation) in the Manner as is printed at the Bottom of the said Certificates.

When the Certificates have been thus signed, and Oath (or Affirmation) made thereof as aforesaid, the next Step is to fill up the Petition, and annex the Certificates thereto, and then apply to a Governor to sign the same, which being done, both the Petition and Certificates must be left with the Secretary, and the Petitioner must not fail to attend at the Hospital the next Friday Morning at 10 o'Clock, when the same will be laid before the Committee, and if approved, an Order will be made for the Patient to be brought for Examination, in his Turn as soon as a Vacancy happens; four Days, at least before which there must be left in writing with the Secretary, the Names and Places of Abode of two substantial Housekeepers residing within the Bills of Mortality, who must be present precisely at 11 o'Clock in the Morning, when the Patient is to be admitted, to enter into a Bond of 100 l. to take the Patient away when discharged by the Committee.

Sir,

Notwithstanding your Endeavours to obviate the Censure of being an Enemy to public Charity, I shall conclude you so, unless you immediately publish the underwritten Plan, of an Hospital for the Reception of the Widows of poor Clergymen, in the projecting which I have spent much Time and Labour; and I am persuaded, if duly carried into Execcution, it will be of as general Use as many of our celebrated Hospitals are at present.

That the Persons for whose Use this Hospital is intended, are in the highest Degree the Objects of our Charity, is a Truth which needs no

---

[1] A merchant and attorney (d. 1784?).

Proof.[1] The only Reason why no Provision hath been hitherto made for them, is, I apprehend, that the Evil seems too great for any Remedy, and the Distressed too numerous to be relieved. This Objection I have endeavoured to remove, by such Restrictions as must prevent any Danger of over-burthening the Charity, or swelling the Expence of my Hospital beyond the Disbursements of a moderate Income. But let my Plan speak for itself.

It is proposed that a Building be erected capable of containing one thousand Persons; for the Support of which, a Fund is to be raised by voluntary Contributions. That the Rules or Instructions for *such* Persons, *who*[2] apply for the Admission of Widows, shall be these following.

First, that no Person shall knowingly be received as a Widow into this Hospital, who is not in Point of Circumstances a proper Object of this Charity, that is to say, a Widow.

2dly, Or who hath been a Widow more than Twelve Kalendar Months.

3dly, Or who is under the Age of Forty-nine, or above the Age of Fifty; or who hath been married less than ten, or more than eleven Years; or, who is not intitled to the *jus trium liberorum*,[3] i.e. who hath had three Children. Note, Miscarriages are not to be included.

4thly, Or who is troubled with any Kind of Distemper, particularly with such as must make her the highest Object of Compassion.

5thly, Or who is not *deemed* to be a Person of good Sense. This to be *deemed* by the Secretary.

6thly, Or who is lousy.

7thly, Or who is poor, or hath Children, or was left with Child by her late Husband.

And if any Widow shall be admitted by Mistake, contrary to all and every of these Rules, she shall upon the Discovery be immediately kicked out.

A Widow qualified within the above Restrictions, must apply herself to the Secretary of the Hospital, from whom she is to receive five Certificates to be filled up as follows.

1. Certificate, That she is a Woman. This to be signed by the Parson of the Parish.

2. Certificate, That she was married to a Clergyman. To be signed by

---

[1] Although the context is satiric, Fielding is serious about the need for such a charity or at least for 'some Provision . . . for the Families of the inferior Clergy' (*Tom Jones*, IV. xiv); see *JJ* Nos. 21 (23 Apr. 1748), 29 (18 June 1748), 30 (25 June), 31 (2 July), and 32 (9 July); see also the account of Mrs Bennet in *Amelia* (IV. ix). Cf. Ferdinando Warner, *A Scheme of a Fund for the better Maintenance of the Widows and Children of the Clergy* (1752), proposing a fund to be governed by an incorporated body of all the bishops, deans, and archdeacons of the Church.

[2] As with '*deemed*' in the fifth provision below, Fielding uses italics to emphasize the impersonality of these words, which appear also in the Instructions for St Luke's.

[3] 'A privilege granted to such persons in ancient Rome as had three children, by which they were exempted from all troublesome offices' (W. Jowitt, *Dictionary of English Law* [1959]).

twenty Persons who were at the Wedding, two of whom are to be Justices of the Peace, one quorum.[1]

3. Certificate, That her Husband is dead; to be signed by the Physician, Surgeon, Apothecary and Nurse, who attended him in his last Illness; the Undertaker, Parson, Clerk and Sexton, who are all to make Oath, that he is *bona fide* buried.

4. Certificate, That she remains a true and chaste Widow, to be sworn to by any one credible Person.

5. Certificate, That she and her late Husband never had any Quarrel during their Cohabitation. This likewise it will be sufficient to prove on the Oath of one Person of Credit: and this Person is only required to swear to the best of his Knowledge, provided he or she was intimately acquainted with the Parties during one Kalendar Month.

Besides which two Persons must give in their Names and Places of Abode to the Hospital. These are to enter into Bond with a large Penalty, to bury the Widow when dead; and to prevent any Possibility of a Conspiracy between the Obligees, one of these must dwell in Cornwall, and the other in Northumberland.

These Certificates being properly returned to the Secretary, are to lie before him one Month, then to be laid before the Committee, who are to take Copies thereof; after which they are within two Months to be reported to the general Court, who may order as they shall think proper.

This, Sir, is a Sketch of my Design, the great Utility and Efficacy of which is so apparent, that it will, I doubt not, meet with the Approbation of the British Censor.

I am, Sir, &c.

TUESDAY, JUNE 9, 1752.   NUMB. 46.

Nec pudor obstabit.

JUVENAL.[2]

Let not your Modesty hurt you.

TO THE
CENSOR of Great Britain.

Mr. *Censor,*

As you was pleased to publish my last Letter,[3] I have sent you the further

---

[1] i.e a justice of the peace specially named in the commission of the peace without whom the others cannot proceed. 'They are usually Persons of greater Quality or Estates than the common Commissioners.' (Giles Jacob, *A New Law-Dictionary*, 7th edn. [1756], s.v. 'Quorum'.)

[2] *Satires*, iii. 60: 'No shyness shall stand in my way' (Loeb).

[3] In *CGJ* No. 40; on the problematic authorship of these letters signed 'Misotharsus', see above, p. 230 n. 2.

Productions of my Friend on the same Subject. Without further Preface then, my Friend after having vindicated the Honour of the Moderns, as being, tho' not the Inventors of the Pert,[1] yet the undoubted Improvers and Enlargers thereof, and its Introductors into almost every Species of Writing, proceeds, like a true systematick Writer, to enquire what Geniuses are the fittest to receive, imbibe, and digest, the Doctrine of the Pert; and to shine most in the practical Application and Exercise thereof. In this Disquisition, which is pretty prolix, he displays an extensive Knowledge of the human Heart, as well as of the human Understanding; and at last concludes, that those are the most susceptible of the Efficacy of his Precepts, who have the best Opinion of themselves; and, on the other Hand, that those will profit least by his Instructions, who are most deeply tinctured with that aukward shame-faced Thing called Modesty.[2] What he adds is somewhat extra-ordinary. "If a young Writer," saith he, "entertains a mean Opinion of his own Abilities, and is at the same Time, what is commonly called a Man of Sense, I despair of him, and I pronounce him incorrigible, and utterly incapable of relishing and profiting by my Instructions and Advices. He will jog on like a Mule at his own Pace, regardless of extrinsic Direction. But if he hath a tolerable Share of Folly, I have some Hopes of him, let him be ever so modest. Tho' he has a poor Opinion of his own Parts at present, yet, ten to one, he will change his Mind in Time, and come to think himself a pretty mettled Fellow." And a little farther on, "that Man," continues he, "who after having hastily run through King Arthur,[3] fancies himself qualified to compose a better Epic Poem than the Æneid; or who because he was in the Battle of ——, (no Matter whether he stood or fled) undertakes to write a System of the military Art; or who, by dipping in a Tindal[4] and Bollingbroke,[5] feels himself animated by a strong Impulse to subvert the Religion of his Country; that Man I admire, so promising a Genius I revere, and hail with a

Macte, nova virtute, puer.[6]

That Writer, if he attends to, and diligently follows my Instructions, will in

---

[1] See *CGJ* No. 40, above, p. 231 n. 2.

[2] A constant theme in the *CGJ*; see especially Nos. 48 and 53, which ridicule the impudence and 'assurance' ironically advocated in this treatise on the 'pert'.

[3] *King Arthur* (1697), an heroic poem in twelve books by Sir Richard Blackmore (1653–1729), a constant butt of the wits. Blackmore's poetry furnished many of the absurd examples cited by Pope in *Peri Bathous* (1728), where he is called 'the father of the *Bathos*' (ch. vi).

[4] Matthew Tindal (1653?–1733), deist, whose best-known work was *Christianity as Old as the Creation* (1730).

[5] See *CGJ* No. 15, above, p. 104 n. 5.

[6] Virgil, *Aeneid*, ix. 641, Apollo speaking to the triumphant Iulus, 'A blessing, child, on thy young valour' (Loeb).

Time make a wonderful Figure; he will climb up to the Pinnacle of the true Pert."

Having shewn that a good Opinion of one's own Parts is an indispensible Requisite in such as aspire to the Height of the Tharsus,[1] and to be all-accomplished in the Art of Swaggering in Print, he earnestly recommends and inculcates an unwearied Zeal and restless Efforts, to entertain, cherish and increase that hopeful and profitable Disposition; towards which, he says, nothing conduces more than the diving into, dwelling on, and exaggerating the Faults and Defects of Writers, especially those that are reputed the most excellent of their Kind, whether Ancient or Modern. And that the Pupil may see and perceive these the more fully and distinctly, he advises him to keep their Beauties and Excellencies out of his View as much as possible. His reasoning on this Head is curious, and, for ought I know, original. "As the natural Eye," saith he, "when accommodated to view minute Objects, is rendered unfit to take in large Prospects; so the Understanding when strained to find out and canvass Faults, becomes disqualified for comprehending Excellencies.[2] And as those Artists, who daily pore upon Miniatures, become near-sighted, their Eyes being by Force of Habit rendered unable to descry Hills, Woods, or Palaces, at a Distance; so the true Critic, whose Business it is to spy out every little Flaw or Blemish in a great Work, of course becomes incapable of perceiving the Beauties of its Disposition, and its principal Parts, they lying far beyond the Reach of his Discernment. But this Contractedness of Comprehension is so far from being a Loss to our Disciple of the Pert, that it is of double Advantage to him. For while it enables him to see the Faults of Writers distinctly and fully, as through a magnifying Glass, it removes their Excellencies from his View, and gives him the solid Pleasure of exulting and triumphing in his own Talents, while he reflects upon the Faults of others, from which he imagines himself free; without being mortified by the Images of unattainable Perfections, of which he can have no Idea."

My Friend next passes to the Consideration of such Helps, as our young Adventurer may use with Success for his Improvement in this fundamental Article; to wit, the spying out and magnifying the Faults of Writers.[3] "For altho," says he, "nothing will do here without a suitable Genius, yet the Horatian Precept *Doctrina vim promovet insitam*,[4] is of eternal and unlimited

---

[1] The pert; see *CGJ* No. 40, above, p. 231 n. 2.

[2] Cf. Pope: 'The critic Eye, that microscope of Wit, / Sees hairs and pores, examines bit by bit' (*Dunciad*, iv. 233–4); cf. also the advice in *Peri Bathous* for the bathetic writer: 'his Eyes should be like unto the wrong end of a Perspective Glass, by which all the Objects of Nature are lessen'd' (ch. v).

[3] Scriblerian satire frequently objected to the critical emphasis on faults rather than beauties; cf. Swift's ironic definition of a critic as '*a Discoverer and Collecter of Writers Faults*' (*Tale of a Tub*, sect. III, 'A Digression concerning Criticks'); cf. also Pope, *Essay on Criticism*, 100–7, describing the gradual change of criticism into an art of fault-finding.

[4] Adapted from *Odes*, iv. 33: 'yet training increases inborn worth' (Loeb).

Truth." And therefore he recommends the reading of such Authors, as have been most diligent, and most perspicacious in detecting and exposing the Imperfections of celebrated Authors. Upon this Occasion he pathetically laments the Loss all true Critics have sustained by the Shipwreck of the Works of the immortal Zoilus.[1] "Of what amazing Penetration, as well as Freedom of Thought," says he, "must that Man have been, who in a learned and enlightened Age, and in the Neighbourhood of the wittiest People that ever flourished, could spy out what no Body else so much as suspected; to wit, Spots and Blemishes in that Son of Poetry the idolized Homer? How invincible was his Fortitude, who durst publish his Discoveries at a Time, when, by so doing, he ran the Risk of being pelted, or knocked down by every Body he met with in the Streets, from the Prince to the Porter or Applewoman? And do we hesitate to proclaim him the Father of Criticism, the Parent of the Pert? But," adds he a little farther on, "this Loss, great as it is, is not a little alleviated by the celebrated Abbé Terraçon's Dissertations on the Iliad,[2] which I can never sufficiently praise and recommend to my hopeful Pupil; this invaluable Work I would have him

Nocturna versare manu, versare diurna."[3]

He afterwards mentions many other Authors of the same Stamp, amongst which Dennis,[4] of acutely austere Memory, shines with a distinguished Lustre; but he laments the Scarcity of their Works, and ardently wishes they were re-published. But that, he says, is *optandum potius quam sperandum.*[5]

"But," continues he, "tho' the Pupil may draw unspeakable Advantage from the Dead, he may no less profit by the Living. The rising Generation of both Sexes furnishes a numerous Army of Critics, who swarm in all Places of

[1] Greek grammarian and cynic philosopher of the 4th cent. BC, infamous for his criticism of Homer and thus frequently cited as the 'type' of fault-finding critics. None of his works have survived. Cf. Pope, *Essay on Criticism*: 'Nay shou'd great Homer lift his awful Head, / Zoilus again would start up from the Dead' (464–5); cf. also Swift's genealogy of the true critic, which begins with '*Momus* and *Hybris*, who begat *Zoilus*' (*Tale of a Tub*, sect. III).

[2] Jean Terrasson (1670–1750), a figure in the French war of ancients and moderns, whose work on the *Iliad* was first published in 1715 and translated in 1722–5 as *A Critical Dissertation Upon Homer's Iliad* (trans. Francis Brerewood). His 'pertness' is illustrated by his claim in the subtitle to be the founder of '*A New System of the Art of Poetry* . . . upon the Principles of Reason' and by his avowed attempt 'to set the Faults of *Homer*, and the Delusion of all his Admirers, in a full and clear Light' (I. xviii). With La Motte, Terrasson took up the assault on Homer begun by Perrault; Pope responds to him frequently in his notes to the *Iliad*. See also *CGJ* No. 11, above, p. 83 and n. 1.

[3] Adapted from Horace, *Art of Poetry*, 269: 'handle [Greek models] by night, handle them by day' (Loeb).

[4] Another 'Scriblerian' touch, for John Dennis (1657–1734) was regarded by the circle of Swift and Pope as a bombastic and 'furious' critic. He was attacked by Pope in *Essay on Criticism*, *Peri Bathous*, and the *Dunciad*; by Swift in *Tale of a Tub*; and by Fielding in the Preface to his *Tragedy of Tragedies* (1731).

[5] As Jensen points out (ii. 233), this appears to be an adaptation of Cicero, *De republica*, II. xxx: *optandam magis quam sperandam*, 'to be desired rather than hoped for' (Loeb), describing Plato's ideal state.

Rendezvous; amongst whom he will always find a dead Majority[1] on his Side, the Dissentients being so very few that they scarce dare open their Mouths in promiscuous Companies; but are reduced either to ruminate alone in their Garrets upon their own antiquated Notions, or, when they can afford to make Holiday, to give them vent over a Mug of Beer with their Fellows. But let my hopeful Disciple herd with the modish Majority; let him, with erected Ears, greedily drink in; let him retain, meditate upon, and digest their free, easy, and airy Effusions; Effusions not smelling of the Lamp but perfumed with a natural, unlaboured Essence; quickened with a light volatile Spirit, and gratefully acidulated with the poignant Juice of Cavil."

Yours, &c.
MISOTHARSUS.

SATURDAY, JUNE 13, 1752.　　　　　NUMB. 47.

——heu plebes scelerata!

SILIUS ITALICUS.[2]

——O ye wicked Rascallions!

It may seem strange that none of our political Writers, in their learned Treatises on the English Constitution, should take Notice of any more than three Estates, namely, King, Lords, and Commons,[3] all entirely passing by in Silence that very large and powerful Body which form the fourth Estate in this Community, and have been long dignified and distinguished by the Name of THE MOB.[4]

---

[1]　i.e. 'absolute' or 'complete' majority, but with an obvious pun on 'dead'.

[2]　*Punica*, ix. 636: *heu patria, heu plebes scelerata et prava favoris!* 'Alas for our country! Alas for our people who in their wickedness bestow their favour amiss' (Loeb). Used also in an expanded form as motto to the *Champion* for 1 Mar. 1740 and to *The Opposition: A Vision* (1741).

[3]　Properly speaking, the Three Estates of the Realm are the Lords Spiritual, the Lords Temporal, and the Commons; see Blackstone, *Commentaries on the Laws of England* (Oxford, 1765), i. 151. Fielding's misconception, based on the balance of legislative authority rather than on representation in Parliament, was common in the century; for an attack on the notion that the king is one of Three Estates, see *True Briton*, 12 June 1751.

[4]　For the immediate impetus behind both this essay on the mob and that in *CGJ* No. 49, see Fielding's comment on a news item about recent riots in Norwich, originally appearing in the 'Modern History' column of *CGJ* No. 9 (1 Feb.) and printed below, Appendix II; it was in reaction to the disturbances in Norwich that he first formulated his conceit of the mob as the 'fourth Estate'. In *Tom Jones* Fielding makes several comments on the mob that are comparatively light-hearted, suggesting that the term includes persons 'without Virtue, or Sense, in all Stations' (I. ix) and describing in bemused terms the plunder of the rich by 'that large and venerable Body which in *English*, we call the Mob' (XII. i). In his later writings, however, when as a magistrate he was sometimes faced with the problem of handling riotous crowds, he viewed the topic as a serious social and political issue; see his account of the 'licentious, outrageous mob' in *A True State of the Case of Bosavern Penlez* (1749), and see especially his lengthy reflections on the case 'between the mob and their betters' in *Journal of a Voyage to Lisbon* (21 [16] July), where he traces the problem to a mistaken idea of 'liberty'. On Fielding's increasing distrust of the lower classes, see Miller, *Essays*, pp. 96–103. For background of attitudes

And this will seem still the more strange, when we consider that many of the great Writers abovementioned have most incontestably belonged to this very Body.

To say precisely at what Time this fourth State began first to figure in this Commonwealth, or when the Footsteps of that Power which it enjoys at this Day were first laid, must appear to be a Matter of the highest Difficulty, perhaps utterly impossible, from that deplorable Silence which I have just mentioned. Certain however it is, that at the Time of the Norman Conquest, and long afterwards, the Condition of this Estate was very low and mean, those who composed it being in general called Villains; a Word which did not then bear any very honourable Idea, tho' not so bad a one perhaps as it hath since acquired.[1]

The Part which this fourth Estate seem antiently to have claimed, was to watch over and controll the other three. This indeed they have seldom asserted in plain Words, which is possibly the principal Reason why our Historians have never explicitly assigned them their Share of Power in the Constitution, tho' this Estate have so often exercised it, and so clearly asserted their Right to it by Force of Arms; to wit, by Fists, Staves, Knives, Clubs, Scythes, and other such offensive Weapons.

The first Instance which I remember of this was in the Reign of Richard I, when they espoused the Cause of Religion; of which they have been always stout Defenders, and destroyed a great Number of Jews.[2]

In the same Reign we have another Example in William Fitz-Osborne, alias Longbeard, a stout Asserter of the Rights of the fourth Estate.[3] These Rights he defended in the City of London, at the Head of a large Party, and by Force of the Arms abovementioned; but was overpowered, and lost his

---

toward the mob in this period, see George Rudé, 'The London "Mob" of the Eighteenth Century', *Historical Journal*, 2 (1959), 1–18; id., *The Crowd in History* (New York, 1964), esp. pp. 33–63; Michael A. Seidel, 'The Restoration Mob: Drones and Dregs', *SEL* 12 (1972), 429–43; and Herbert M. Atherton, 'The "Mob" in Eighteenth-Century English Caricature', *ECS* 12 (1978), 47–58.

[1] Cf. *Enquiry into the Causes of the late Increase of Robbers* (1751): 'The Villains were indeed considered in Law as a Kind of Chattle belonging to their Masters: for though these had not the Power of Life and Death over them, . . . yet these Villains had not even the Capacity of purchasing Lands or Goods' (p. ix).

[2] Since Fielding concentrates in his examples on various uprisings in London, he probably refers here not to the famous attack on the Jews in York during Richard's reign but to the earlier massacre of London Jews in 1189 arising from an incident at the coronation festival. See *The Annales or Generall Chronicle of England, begun first by maister Iohn Stow, and . . . continued . . . by Edmund Howes* (1615), pp. 158–9; Stow was one of the many historical works in Fielding's library (Baker, item 289).

[3] i.e. William Fitzosbert (d. 1196), who in 1196 'rais'd such a Tumult about a Tax, which he pretended was unequally laid, that in St. *Paul*'s Church-Yard many were slain, and the whole City was in great Danger' (Laurence Echard, *History of England*, 3rd edn. [1720], i. 95; Echard's work was also in Fielding's library, Baker, item 307); Stow says Fitzosbert 'moved the common people to seeke libertie and freedome' (p. 162). In *Journey from this World to the Next* (1743) Fielding represents Julian in one of his incarnations as a follower of 'Fitz-Osborn', who 'had raised himself to great popularity with the rabble, by pretending to espouse their cause against the rich' (I. xxiii).

Life by means of a wooden Machine called the Gallows, which hath been very fatal to the chief Champions of this Estate; as it was in the Reign of Henry III. to one Constantine, who having at the Head of a London Mob pulled down the House of the High-Steward of Westminster, and committed some other little Disorders of the like Kind, maintained to the Chief Justiciary's Face, "that he had done Nothing punishable by Law," i.e. *contrary to the Rights of the fourth Estate.* He shared however the same Fate with Mr. Fitz-Osborne.[1]

We find in this Reign of Henry III, the Power of the fourth Estate grown to a very great Heighth indeed; for whilst a Treaty was on Foot between that King and his Barons, the Mob of London thought proper not only to insult the Queen with all Manner of foul Language, but likewise to throw Stones and Dirt at her.[2] Of which Assertion of their Privilege, we hear of no other Consequence than that the King was highly displeased; and indeed it seems to be allowed by most Writers, that the Mob in this Instance went a little too far.

In the Time of Edward II. there is another Fact upon Record, of a more bloody Kind; tho' perhaps not more indecent: For the Bishop of Exeter being a little too busy in endeavouring to preserve the City of London for the King his Master, the Mob were pleased to cut his Head off.[3]

I omit many lesser Instances to come to that glorious Assertion of the Privileges of the Mob under the great and mighty Wat Tyler, when they not only laid their Claim to a Share in the Government, but in Truth to exclude all the other Estates; for this Purpose, one John Staw, or Straw, or Ball, a great Orator, who was let out of Maidstone-Gaol by the Mob, in his Harangues told them, that as all Men were Sons of Adam, there ought to be no Distinction; and that it was their Duty to reduce all Men to perfect Equality. This they immediately set about, and to do it in the most effectual Manner, they cut off the Heads of all the Nobility, Gentry, Clergy, &c. who fell into their Hands.[4]

---

[1] Fielding refers to events in 1222, when one Constantine Fitz-Arnulf (or Fitz-Athulf or -Alulf) 'by means of a Wrestling-Match between the Inhabitants of *London* and *Westminster*, raised a popular Tumult and attempted to set up Prince *Lewis*'; in the confrontation with the chief justiciar, Hubert de Burgh, Constantine is supposed to have declared '*That they had done no less than they ought, and that they would stand by it*' (Echard, i. 111); cf. Stow, p. 179, and Robert Brady, *A Complete History of England* (1685), i. 530–1 (in Fielding's library, Baker, item 294). Constantine was no ordinary member of a mob but a wealthy citizen, formerly a sheriff; see Christopher Brooke and Gillian Ker, *London 800–1216* (1975), pp. 333, 365, 373.

[2] The incident occurred in 1263 as the queen, Eleanor of Provence, attempted unsuccessfully to move from the Tower to Windsor; the 'Stones and Dirt' are specifically mentioned by Stow (p. 193) and Echard (i. 124).

[3] Walter de Stapledon, Bishop of Exeter since 1308, was beheaded in 1326 by Londoners loyal to Queen Isabella; Echard adds, 'They also got the Tower into their Possession, placing and displacing the Garrison and Officers at their Pleasure . . . They also set at Liberty all Prisoners' (i. 140).

[4] In this and the following paragraphs Fielding describes events of the Peasants' Revolt (June 1381), led by Wat Tyler (d. 1381) and his Kentishmen. In his account Fielding conflates into

With these Designs they encamped in a large Body at Blackheath, whence they sent a Message to King Richard II. *to come and talk with them, in order to settle the Government*; and when this was not complied with, they marched to London, and the Gates being opened by their Friends, entered the City, burnt and plundered the Duke of Lancaster's Palace, that of the Archbishop and many other great Houses, and put to Death all of the other three Estates with whom they met, among whom, was the Archbishop of Canterbury, and the Lord Treasurer.

The unhappy End of this noble Enterprize is so well known that it need not be mentioned. The Leader being taken off by the Gallantry of the Lord Mayor,[1] the whole Army, like a Body when the Head is severed, fell instantly to the Ground; whence many were afterwards lifted to that fatal Machine, which is above taken Notice of.

I shall pass by the Exploits of Cade and Ket[2] and others. I think I have clearly demonstrated, that there is such a fourth Estate as the Mob, actually existing in our Constitution; which, tho', perhaps for very politic Reasons, they keep themselves generally like the Army of Mr. Bayes,[3] in Disguise, have often issued from their lurking Places, and very stoutly maintained their Power and their Privileges in this Community.

Nor hath this Estate, or their Claims been unknown to the other three; on the contrary, we find in our Statute Books, numberless Attempts to prevent their growing Power, and to restrain them at least within some Bounds; witness the many Laws made against Ribauds, Roberdsmen, Drawlatches, Wasters, Rogues, Vagrants, Vagabonds; by all which, and many other Names, this 4th Estate hath been from Time to Time dignified and distinguished.[4]

one figure two of the other rebel leaders, Jack Straw and John Ball, a seditious priest; it was Ball who preached to the mob assembled at Blackheath a sermon on the text, 'When Adam dolve and Eve span, / Who was then a Gentleman?' (Stow, pp. 285–94).

[1] Sir William Walworth (d. 1385), who at Smithfield on 15 June 1381 was instrumental in dispatching Tyler.

[2] John Cade (d. 1450), leader of a revolt in Kent against Henry VI in 1450, again involving a march on London; and Robert Kett (d. 1549), a well-to-do landowner who led a rebellion in East Anglia in 1549 protesting enclosures.

[3] In Buckingham's *The Rehearsal* (1671) Bayes explains that the army of Prince Volscius 'lies conceal'd for him in *Knights-bridge*' (III. v); cf. the herald in v. i, 'The Army's at the door, and in disguise'. Cited also in *JJ* No. 1 (5 Dec. 1747).

[4] For the statutes to which Fielding refers, see his *Enquiry into the Causes of the late Increase of Robbers* (1751), sect. VI, where he traces the laws against vagabonds from the time of Alfred to the most recent Vagrant Act (17 George II, c. 5). See also his sketch of statutes against riots and insurrections in *A True State of the Case of Bosavern Penlez* (1749). Few distinctions can be drawn among the various names Fielding cites for the 'fourth Estate'; in the *Champion* for 7 June 1740 he explains that according to Coke '*Sturdy Beggars*, *Ribauds* and *Roberdsmen* were all one and the same Person', that 'Roberdsmen' derives from the gang of Robin Hood, and that 'hence the Name became general to any Set of Thieves and Rascals'. Again, in the *Enquiry*, Fielding indicates that from Robin Hood 'a great Number of idle and dissolute Fellows, who were called *Drawlatches*, *Ribauds*, and *Roberdsmen*, took their Rise, and infested this Kingdom for above a Century, notwithstanding the many Endeavours of

Under all these Appellations they are frequently named in our Law Books; but I do not perfectly remember to have seen them mentioned under the Term of 4th Estate in all my Reading; nor do I recollect that any Legislative or judicial Power is expressly allowed to belong to them. And yet certain it is, that they have from Time immemorial been used to exercise a judicial Capacity in certain Instances wherein the ordinary Courts have been deficient for Want of Evidence; this being no Let or Hindrance to the Administration of Justice before the Gentlemen who compose this 4th Estate, who often proceed to Judgment without any Evidence at all. Nor must I omit the laudable Expedition which is used on such Occasions, their Proceedings being entirely free from all those Delays, which are so much complained of in other Courts. I have indeed known a Pickpocket arrested, tried, convicted, and ducked almost to Death, in less Time than would have been consumed in reading his Indictment at the Old-Baily.[1] These Delays they avoid chiefly by hearing only one Side of the Question, concluding, as Judge Gripus did of old, that the contrary Method serves only to introduce Incertainty and Confusion.[2]

I do not however pretend to affirm any Thing of the legal Original of this Jurisdiction. I know the Learned are greatly divided in their Opinions concerning this Matter, or rather perhaps in their Inclinations; some being unwilling to allow any Power at all to this Estate, and others as stoutly contending, that it would be for the public Good to deliver the Sword of Justice entirely into their Hands.[3]

the Legislature from time to time to suppress them' (p. 82). The terms appear throughout the early statutes against vagabonds.

[1] Cf. Fielding's somewhat more tolerant description of mob justice in Letter XLI of his sister's *Familiar Letters between the Principal Characters in David Simple* (1747); after describing the ducking of a pickpocket by the mob, Fielding's persona, a French visitor, observes, 'they are a Court, which generally endeavours to do Justice, tho' they sometimes err, by the Hastiness of their Decisions. Perhaps it is the only Court in the World, where there is no Partiality arising from Respect of Persons' (ii. 320). Cf. Fielding's ironic proposal in *CGJ* No. 68 that adulterers be punished by the mob.

[2] Fielding refers to the corrupt Judge Gripus in Dryden's *Amphitryon* (1690), who, charged with deciding which is the true Amphitryon, does not want to hear evidence which will confuse the issue: 'hold your tongue, I charge you; for the Case is manifest'. After Jupiter shows that his arm has the same scar as Amphitryon's, Gripus says, 'Did not I charge you not to speak? 'twas plain enough before: and now you have puzzled it again' (v. i). Cf. *Champion* for 15 Mar. 1740, where Fielding says readers of commentaries on Virgil and Horace 'would be in as perplexed a Condition as that of Judge *Gripus*, who very humorously complains that every new Evidence only tends to darken and embarass a Case which was plain enough before'.

[3] Perhaps a wry reflection of Fielding's experiences in the Bosavern Penlez affair and a reminder of his encounters with Opposition mobs during the Westminster election of 1749. Cf. his forthright rejection of mob justice in *A True State of the Case of Bosavern Penlez* (1749): 'But surely it will not be wished by any sober Man, that open illegal Force and Violence should be with Impunity used to remove this Nuisance [bawdy-houses]; and that the Mob should have an uncontrolled Jurisdiction in this Case. When by our excellent Constitution the greatest Subject, no not even the King himself, can, without a lawful Trial and Conviction divest the meanest Man of his property, . . . shall we suffer a licentious Rabble to be Accuser, Judge, Jury, and Executioner . . . ?' (pp. 51–2). On the Westminster election, see M. C. with R. R. Battestin, 'Fielding, Bedford, and the Westminster Election of 1749', *ECS* 11 (1978), 154–66.

So prevalent hath this latter Opinion grown to be of modern Days, that the fourth Estate hath been permitted to encroach in a most prodigious Manner. What these Encroachments have been, and the particular Causes which have contributed to them, shall be the Subject of my next Saturday's Paper.[1]   C.

TUESDAY, JUNE 16, 1752.   NUMB. 48.

Ω μεγίστη τῶν θεῶν
Νῦν οὖσ' ἀναίδεια.

MENANDER.[2]

O thou greatest of all the Deities,
Modern Impudence.

There is a certain Quality, which, tho' universal Consent hath not enrolled it among the Cardinal Virtues, is often found sufficient, of itself, not only to carry its Possessor through the World, but even to carry him to the Top of it. It is almost perhaps unnecessary to inform my Reader, that the Quality I mean, is Impudence;[3] so dear is this to one Female at least, that it effectually recommends a Man to Fortune without the Assistance of any other Qualification. She seems indeed to think, with the Poet, that,

——*He who hath but Impudence,*
To all Things hath a fair Pretence,[4]

and accordingly provides that those who want Modesty, shall want nothing else.

What are the particular Ingredients of which this Quality is composed, or what Temper of Mind is best fitted to produce it, is perhaps difficult to ascertain; so far I think Experience may convince us, that, like some Vegetables it will flourish best in the most barren Soil. To say Truth, I am

---

[1] *CGJ* No. 49.

[2] *The Carian Wailing-Woman*, ll. 1–2: 'O thou who now art chief amongst the gods, O Effrontery . . .' (Loeb).

[3] A much-discussed topic in the period, both by Fielding and others; cf. especially Fielding's essay in the *Champion*, 29 Jan. 1740, which discusses impudence as one of the qualities equipping a man for preferment and which is very similar to his argument here. See also *Grub-street Journal*, No. 62 (11 Mar. 1731) [by Joseph Trapp]; *Craftsman*, 21 Oct. 1749; 'The School of Impudence', in *The Student, or the Oxford Monthly Miscellany*, No. 4 (30 Apr. 1750), pp. 140–5; David Hume, 'Of Impudence and Modesty', *Essays Moral and Political* (Edinburgh, 1741); *Some Remarks on the Life and Writings of Dr. J—— H——* (1752), pp. 51–5, 57–8; and *CGJ* No. 53. Fielding himself was congratulated on his *lack* of impudence by the anonymous author of *Rules for Being a Wit* (1753), who contrasts his 'consummate Modesty' with John Hill's impudence (p. 5).

[4] Samuel Butler, *Hudibras*, Part II, 'An Heroical Epistle of Hudibras to Sidrophel', 109–10; Hudibras here accuses the astrologer Sidrophel of the kind of successful imposture Fielding discusses in this leader. Fielding changes 'has' to 'hath' in his quotation of these lines, which are also cited in his essay in the *Champion*, 29 Jan. 1740.

almost inclined to an Opinion, that it never arrives at any great Degree of Perfection unless in a Mind totally unincumbred with any Virtue, or with any great or good Quality whatever. It would indeed seem that Nature had agreed with Fortune, in setting a high Value on Impudence, and had accordingly decreed that those of her Children who had received this rich Gift at her Hands were amply provided for without any further Portion.

And surely it is not without Reason, that I call this the Gift of Nature; indeed Genius itself is not more so. We may here apply a Phrase which the French use on an Occasion not so proper to be mentioned, and affirm, *That it is not in the Power of every Man to be impudent who would be so.*[1] A Man born without any Genius may as reasonably hope to become such a Poet as Homer, or such a Critic as Longinus; as one born without Impudence can pretend without any Merit to aspire to these Characters.

Tho' Nature however must give the Seeds, Art may cultivate them.[2] To improve or to depress their Growth is greatly within the Power of Education. To lay down the proper Precept for this Purpose, would require a large Treatise, and such I may possibly publish hereafter. In the mean Time it shall suffice to mention only two Rules which may be partly collected from what I have above asserted, and which are of universal Use. This is with the utmost Care to suppress and eradicate every Seed or Principle of what is any wise praise-worthy out of the Mind; and secondly to preserve this in the purest State of Ignorance, than which nothing more contributes to the highest Perfection and Consummation of Impudence; the more a Man knows, the more inclined is he to be modest, it is indeed within the Province only of the highest human Knowledge to survey its own narrow Compass.

It may, I think, be predicated in Favour of Impudence, that it is the Quality, which of all others, we are capable of carrying to the greatest Height, so far indeed, that did not the strongest Force of Evidence convince us of the Truth of some Examples, we should be apt to doubt the Possibility of their Existence. What but the concurrent Testimony of Historians, and the indubitable Veracity of Records could impel us to believe, that there have been Men in the World of such astonishing Impudence, as in Opposition to the certain Knowledge of many Thousands to take upon themselves to personate Kings and Princes as well in their Life-time, as after their Death?[3] And yet our own, as well as foreign Annals afford us such Instances.

[1] Not identified, but the context suggests a punning reference to 'potency'. On the need for genius in attaining impudence and the difficulty of counterfeiting it, cf. Hume, 'Of Impudence and Modesty', in *Essays Moral and Political* (Edinburgh, 1741).

[2] Fielding satirically applies to 'Impudence' the traditional dichotomy in neo-classical aesthetics between Nature and Art; cf. Dryden's advice to Shadwell, 'Trust nature, do not labour to be dull' (*Mac Flecknoe*, 166). At the same time, however, the passage which follows is testimony to Fielding's belief in the power of education to affect for good or ill the 'seeds' implanted by Nature. Cf. *CGJ* No. 10 on the 'Seeds of Taste' which can be improved by art or education; and see Miller, *Essays*, pp. 218–20.

[3] Cf. a recent case reported in the London newspapers: 'There is at present resident at Nancy in

But the greatest Hero in Impudence whom perhaps the World ever produced, appeared in France at the End of the last Century. His Name was Peter Mege,[1] and he was a common Soldier in the Marines. This Fellow had the Assistance only of one who had been a Footman to a certain Man of Quality called Scipion le Brun de Castelane, Seigneur de Caille & de Rougon, a Nobleman who had fled from France to Switzerland, to avoid a religious Persecution. With this Confederate alone, Peter Mege had the amazing Impudence to personate the young Seigneur de Caille, who was at that Time dead;[2] and this in the Life-time of the Father, in Defiance of all his noble Relations then in Possession of his forfeited Estate, upon the Spot where the young Gentleman had lived to the Age of Twenty-one; and all this without the least Resemblance of Features, Shape, or Stature; without being acquainted with any Part of the History of him whom he was to represent, or being able to give the least Account of any of his Family; indeed without being able to write and read.

But how much more will the Reader be surprized to hear, that this most impudent of all Attempts succeeded so far as to obtain a Sentence in the Parliament of Provence in favour of the Soldier?[3] And this Success would have been final, had not the Canton of Berne interposed, and obtained an Appeal to the Parliament of Paris, where at last the Impostor was defeated.[4]

To account for all this, and to asswage his Reader's Astonishment, the very ingenious Author of the Trial, when he informs us, that this Impostor was confronted with Twenty Witnesses, who swore to the Identity of Peter Mege, and as many more who had been Fellow-Students with the young Nobleman, and who on their Oaths declared that this Peter was not the Person, goes on thus: "But what was most strange was the steady

---

Lorrain, a certain Adventurer, who far surpasses all that have appeared on the publick Stage, either in this, or in any other Age. He has the Assurance to affirm, without blushing, that he was a Man in the Reign of Augustus', a claim proved by his reciting fragments out of Livy, heretofore missing (GA, 16 Aug. 1751).

[1] Fielding's source for the story of Pierre Mêge, who made his first claims as an imposter in March 1699, was François Gayot de Pitaval, *Causes Célèbres et Intéressantes, avec les Jugemens qui les ont Decidées*, 22 vols. (The Hague, 1735–45), ii (1735), 1–246; this collection was in Fielding's library (Baker, item 78). The case is entitled 'Pierre Mêge, Soldat de Marine, reconnu par le Parlement de Provence pour être le Sieur de Caille Gentilhomme, & pour être Pierre Mêge par le Parlement de Paris'. Gayot de Pitaval (1673–1743), himself 'avocat au Parlement de Paris' and thus thoroughly biased in his account, speaks of Mêge as having 'l'impudence la plus signalée, qui ait jamais paru sur la face de la Terre' (ii. 245); for a popularized version of the affair which leaves the imposture a matter of doubt, see B. Barbery, *L'Ephémère Seigneur de Caille* (Paris, 1932).

[2] Isaac de Brun de Castelane, known as 'le sieur Rougon', who died 15 Feb. 1696 at the age of thirty-two.

[3] The decree was delivered at Aix on 14 July 1706.

[4] Officials in Berne, feeling their integrity impugned because they had certified Isaac's death, complained to the king on 10 Sept. 1706. The case was then considered by the Conseil Royal, who on 12 July 1708 broke the decree of the Parlement of Provence and transferred the issue to the Parlement of Paris. That court issued its final decree on 17 Mar. 1712, ruling against the imposter, who subsequently died in prison (Gayot de Pitaval, ii. 25–7, 44, 217).

Countenance of the Soldier, which never once betrayed him, nor gave the least Symptom of any Doubt of his Success. It is in vain to form a Project of usurping the Name of another, to lay your Plan ever so regularly and systematically, if you do not provide yourself with a Stock of Impudence to support every Attack to which you may be exposed. In such an Attempt the Forehead must be furnished as well without as within; more indeed will depend on the Outside: For 'tis the Steadiness of the Front, Hardiness or downright Audacity which impose on Mankind the most, and make Amends for all Defects in the Understanding. The Soldier had made many Blunders; but his invincible Assurance repaired all, and brought over even his Enemies to his Side."[1] And to say Truth, I know scarce any Thing to which such a Degree of Assurance is not equal.

This Attempt indeed, of personating WHO you are not, seems to be attended with too great Difficulties; and to succeed in it is perhaps beyond the Power of Impudence; we are not therefore to wonder, that all the Heroes in this Way have been unsuccessful. In fact, we ought to fix our whole Attention on the undaunted Impudence of engaging in such a Design, and not to suffer the Defeat to lessen our Admiration; but to say of such a Hero, with Ovid,

>——*Si non tenuit, magnis tamen excidit ausis.*[2]

But if in personating the WHO, Impudence is found unequal to the Task; in personating WHAT we are not, it is almost sure to come off triumphant. Here I believe the Undertaker seldom fails, but thro' his own Fault; that is, by not being impudent enough.

My Lord Bacon advises a modest Man to shelter his Vices under those Virtues to which they are the nearest allied.[3] The avaricious Man, he would have to affect Frugality; the extravagant, Liberality; and so of the rest. Now the Reverse of this should be the Rule of our impudent Man.——If you are a Blockhead my Friend, be sure to commence Writer; and if entirely illiterate, be sure to pretend to Learning. If you are a Coward, be a Bully, and always talk of Feats of Bravery; if again you are a Beggar, boast of your Riches. In short, whatever Vice or Defect you have, set up for its opposite Virtue or

---

[1] Fielding translates fairly closely from Gayot de Pitaval, *Causes Célèbres*, ii. 14.

[2] *Metamorphoses*, ii. 328: 'though he greatly failed, more greatly dared' (Loeb), part of the epitaph on the tomb of Phaëthon.

[3] *De augmentis scientiarum*, VIII. ii. Fielding is ironic when he speaks of Bacon advising 'a modest Man', since the context of the passage recommends the very kind of impudence Fielding is describing. Cf. *Champion*, 26 Jan. 1740, in which a 'correspondent' addresses Captain Vinegar as follows: 'My Lord Bacon, somewhat a greater philosopher I think than yourself, was so far from attempting to establish real virtue, . . . that he only endeavoured to recommend her shadow. He advised men only to wear the mask of those virtues which were nearest allied to their vices.' Bacon's advice is also cited in *Champion*, 20 Nov. 1739.

Endowment. And if you are possessed of every ill Quality, you may assert your Title to every good one.

The last Species of Impudence which I shall mention, is to assert openly and boldly *what you really are*, let this be ever so bad. Own your Vices, and be proud of them; and in Time perhaps you may laugh Virtue out of Countenance, and bring your Vices into Fashion.[1] This however is a little unsafe to attempt, unless you are very sure of yourself, and of the Degree of Impudence which you possess. A modest Woman may be a W—e; but to behave with Indecency in public, indeed to throw off all that would recommend a Woman to a vicious Man of Sense and Taste; to shew, as De Retz says of a court Lady, not the least Sense of Virtue in the Practice of every Vice;[2] this requires the highest Degree of Impudence; that Degree indeed which is inconsistent with every great or good Quality whatever.

C.

SATURDAY, JUNE 20, 1752.   NUMB. 49.

Odi profanum vulgus.

HORACE.[3]

I hate the Mob.

In a former Paper[4] I have endeavoured to trace the Rise and Progress of the Power of the fourth Estate in this Constitution. I shall now examine that Share of Power which they actually enjoy at this Day, and then proceed to consider the several Means by which they have attained it.

First, tho' this Estate have not AS YET claimed that Right which was insisted on by the People or Mob in old Rome, of giving a negative Voice in the enacting Laws,[5] they have clearly exercised this Power in controlling their Execution. Of this it is easy to give many Instances, particularly in the

---

[1] Cf. Bacon: 'But there is a confidence which surpasses this other in impudence; and this is, for a man to brazen out his own defects, by putting them forward and displaying them to view; as if he believed himself especially eminent in those things wherein he is deficient.' (*De augmentis scientiarum*, VIII. ii, trans. R. L. Ellis and J. Spedding, *Philosophical Works*, ed. J. M. Robertson [1905], p. 600.)

[2] *Mémoires du Cardinal de Retz* (Amsterdam, 1719), i. 221; on De Retz see *CGJ* No. 17, above, p. 119 n. 2.

[3] *Odes*, III. i. 1: 'I hate the uninitiate crowd' (Loeb); Fielding uses the same line, with a different translation, as the motto for *CGJ* No. 33.

[4] *CGJ* No. 47 (13 June); see above, p. 259 n. 4, for the background of Fielding's attitude toward the mob.

[5] A reference, presumably, to the *tribuni plebis*, or tribunes of the plebs, who asserted a right of veto against any act performed by the magistrates (*Oxford Classical Dictionary* [1970], s.v. 'tribuni plebis'); cf. Lyttelton, who can barely suppress his astonishment at the tribunes' exerting their authority 'with a violence more resembling the anarchy of a state of war, than the orderly acts of regular magistrates in a well-ordered commonwealth' ('Observations on Roman History', *Works of George Lord Lyttelton*, ed. George Edward Ayscough, 3rd edn. [1776], i. 49–51).

Case of the Gin-Act some Years ago;[1] and in those of several Turnpikes which have been erected against the Good-will and Pleasure of the Mob, and have by them been demolished.[2]

In opposing the Execution of such Laws, they do not always rely on Force; but have frequent Recourse to the most refined Policy: For sometimes without openly expressing their Disapprobation, they take the most effectual Means to prevent the carrying a Law into Execution; those are by discountenancing all those who endeavour to prosecute the Offences committed against it.

They well know, that the Courts of Justice cannot proceed without Informations; if they can stifle these, the Law of Course becomes dead and useless. The Informers therefore in such Cases, they declare to be infamous, and guilty of the Crime LAESÆ MOBILITATIS.[3] Of this whoever is *suspected* (which is with them a synonymous Term with *convicted*) is immediately punished by Buffeting, Kicking, Stoning, Ducking, Bemudding, &c. in short, by all those Means of putting, (sometimes quite, sometimes almost) to Death, which are called by that general Phrase of *Mobbing*.

It may perhaps be said that the Mob, do, *even at this Day*, connive at[4] the Execution of some Laws, which they can by no Means be supposed to approve.

Such are the Laws against Robbery, Burglary and Theft. This is, I confess, true; and I have often wondered that it is so. The Reason perhaps is, the great Love which the Mob have for a Holiday, and the great Pleasure

---

[1] Fielding refers to the severely restrictive Gin Act of 1736 (9 George II, c. 23), which was both protested by riots and circumvented by clandestine trade; on the riots see *GM* 6 (1736), 421, 550–1, and John, Lord Hervey, *Memoirs*, ed. Romney Sedgwick (1931), ii. 569–70. As one writer put it in 1751, 'when the populace had rode triumphant over the law, the reviving vice spread wider and wider' (*GM* 21 [1751], 321) with the results depicted most famously in Hogarth's *Gin-Lane* (1751). The Gin Act was repealed in favor of a new bill in 1743, and other acts of 1751 and 1753 attempted to control the problem. See also Fielding's *Enquiry* (1751), sect. II, where he speaks of 'how easily all partial Prohibitions are evaded' (p. 21).

[2] From the late 17th cent. onwards, separate acts of Parliament had created separate Turnpike Trusts to maintain and levy tolls on specific pieces of road, with the years 1751–2 seeing the beginning of a rapid expansion of the system. Riots against turnpikes had occurred in Bristol and Gloucestershire in 1727, 1731, and again in 1749, and in Herefordshire in 1734–5. The most recent such disturbance had come in May 1752, just a month before Fielding's essay, at Selby, West Riding of Yorkshire; see *LDA*, 24 May 1752, *London Gazette*, 26 May 1752. See also Sidney and Beatrice Webb, *English Local Government*, vol. v, *The Story of the King's Highway* (1920), ch. 7; William Albert, 'Popular Opposition to Turnpike Trusts in Early Eighteenth-Century England', *Journal of Transport History*, NS 5 (1979), 1–17; and Robert W. Malcolmson, '"A Set of Ungovernable People": the Kingswood Colliers in the Eighteenth Century', in *An Ungovernable People*, ed. John Brewer and John Styles (1980), pp. 85–127.

[3] Fielding puns on *laesa majestas* (injured majesty), from which the term for treason, *lèse-majesté*, is derived. On the treatment of informers by the mob, cf. *Amelia*, II. ix, and *Enquiry into the Causes of the late Increase of Robbers* (1751): 'The Person of the Informer is in Fact more odious than that of the Felon himself; and the Thief-catcher is in Danger of worse Treatment from the Populace than the Thief' (p. 102).

[4] i.e. shut their eyes to, take no notice of (*OED*, citing this usage in the epilogue of Fielding's *Modern Husband* [1732]).

they take in seeing Men hanged;[1] so great, that while they are enjoying it, they are all apt to forget, that this is hereafter in all Probability to be their own Fate.

In all these Matters however, the Power of this Estate is rather felt than seen. It seems indeed to be like that Power of the Crown in France, which Cardinal de Retz compares to those religious Mysteries that are performed in the *Sanctum Sanctorum*; and which, tho' it be often exercised, is never expressly claimed.[2]

In other Instances the fourth Estate is much more explicit in their Pretensions, and much more constant in asserting and maintaining them; of which I shall mention some of the principal.

First, they assert an exclusive Right to the River of Thames. It is true the other Estates do sometimes venture themselves upon the River; but this is only upon Sufferance; for which they pay whatever that Branch of the fourth Estate called Watermen are pleased to exact of them. Nor are the Mob contented with all these Exactions. They grumble whenever they meet any Persons in a Boat, whose Dress declares them to be of a different Order from themselves. Sometimes they carry their Resentment so far, as to endeavour to run against the Boat, and overset it; but if they are too good natured to attempt this, they never fail to attack the Passengers with all Kind of scurrilous, abusive and indecent Terms, which indeed they claim as their own, and call Mob Language.[3]

The second exclusive Right which they insist on, is to those Parts of the Streets, that are set apart for the Foot-passengers. In asserting this Privilege, they are extremely rigorous; insomuch, that none of the other Orders can walk through the Streets by Day without being insulted, nor by Night without being knocked down. And the better to secure these Footpaths to themselves, they take effectual Care to keep the said Paths always well blocked up with Chairs, Wheelbarrows, and every other Kind of Obstruction; in Order to break the Legs of all those who shall presume to encroach upon their Privileges by walking the Streets.[4]

---

[1] See *CGJ* No. 25 for Fielding's view of these 'holidays'.

[2] *Mémoires du Cardinal de Retz* (Amsterdam, 1719), i. 175, discussing 'le mystère de l'Etat'; on De Retz, see *CGJ* No. 17, above, p. 119 n. 2.

[3] Cf. Fielding's Letter XLI of Sarah Fielding's *Familiar Letters between the Principal Characters in David Simple* (1747), and see also the first entry (26 June) of *Journal of a Voyage to Lisbon* (1755), where Fielding speaks of running the gauntlet 'though rows of sailors and watermen, few of whom failed of paying their compliments to me by all manner of insults and jests on my misery', the result, he adds, 'of an uncontrolled licentiousness mistaken for liberty'. His comment here on watermen's whimsically variable charges is surprising, since their rates were fixed by statute (e.g. 23 George II, c. 26). On their proverbial abusiveness, see, among many examples, *Weekly Register* of 8 Dec. 1733; *A Trip through the Town* (1735); and Béat Louis de Muralt, *Letters describing the Character and Customs of the English and French Nations* (1726), p. 40.

[4] Cf. Gay's *Trivia; or, the Art of Walking the Streets of London* (1716), esp. ii. 25–64 which describes those trades (barbers, bakers, small-coal dealers, dustmen, butchers, etc.) who are especially to be avoided on the streets; cf. also *A Trip from St. James's to the Royal-Exchange* (1744), according to which

Here it was hoped their Pretensions would have stopped; but it is difficult to set any Bounds to Ambition; for, having sufficiently established this Right, they now begin to assert their Right to the whole Street, and to have lately made such a Disposition with their Waggons, Carts, and Drays, that no Coach can pass along without the utmost Difficulty and Danger. With this View we every Day see them driving Side by Side, and sometimes in the broader Streets three a breast; again, we see them leaving a Cart or Waggon in the Middle of the Street, and often set a-cross it, while the Driver repairs to a neighbouring Alehouse, from the Window of which he diverts himself while he is drinking, with the Mischief or Inconvenience which his Vehicle occasions.[1]

The same Pretensions which they make to the Possession of the Streets, they make likewise to the Possession of the Highways. I doubt not I shall be told they claim only an equal Right: For I know it is very usual when a Carter or Drayman is civilly desired to make a little Room, by moving out of the Middle of the Road either to the Right or Left, to hear the following Answer. *D—n your Eyes, who are you? Is not the Road, and be d—n'd to you, as free for me as for you?* Hence it will, I suppose, be inferred that they do not *absolutely exclude* the other Estates from the Use of the common Highways. But notwithstanding this generous Concession in Words, I do aver this Practice is different, and that a Gentleman may go a Voyage at Sea with little more Hazard than he can travel ten Miles from the Metropolis.

I shall mention only one Claim more, and that a very new and a very extraordinary one. It is the Right of excluding all Women of Fashion out of St. James's Park on a Sunday Evening. This they have lately asserted with great Vehemence, and have inflicted the Punishment of mobbing on several Ladies, who had transgressed without Design, not having been apprized of the good Pleasure of the Mob in this Point. And this I the rather publish to prevent any such Transgressions for the future, since it hath already appeared that no Degree of either Dignity or Beauty can secure the Offender.*[2]

---

* A Lady of great Quality, and admirable Beauty, was mobbed in the Park at this Time.

the passages leading to the Houses of Parliament 'are in such disorder, that a Man is toss'd about like a Gin Informer, before he can get to them' (p. 30).

[1] Cf. the encounter of two French visitors with a drayman, described by Fielding in Letter XLI of Sarah Fielding's *Familiar Letters* (1747); cf. also Fielding's comment on a news item in *True Patriot*, No. 15 (11 Feb. 1746), that the insolence and rudeness of waggoners 'call aloud for the Notice of the Legislature'. On the various efforts by Parliament and by justices to control the nuisances alluded to here, see E. G. Dowdell, *A Hundred Years of Quarter Sessions* (Cambridge, 1932), pp. 121–3.

[2] The reference, both in the note and in the text, is probably to the Gunning sisters, who, as Horace Walpole reports, found themselves unable to walk in the park because of the mobs (see *CGJ* No. 12, above, p. 91 n. 3); Murphy refers to the same incident in the *Craftsman, or Gray's Inn Journal* for 28 Oct. 1752 (original issue), and in a later number brings a 'William Brazen' before the Censor for molesting a lady of fashion in the park (*Gray's Inn Journal*, No. 44, [18 Aug. 1753]). See also the report

Many Things have contributed to raise this fourth Estate to that exorbitant Degree of Power which they at present enjoy, and which seems to threaten to shake the Balance of our Constitution. I shall name only three, as these appear to me to have had much the greatest Share in bringing it about.

The first is that Act of Parliament which was made at the latter End of Queen Elizabeth's Reign, and which I cannot help considering as a Kind of Compromise between the other three Estates and this.[1] By this Act it was stipulated, that the fourth Estate should annually receive out of the Possessions of the others, a certain large Proportion yearly, upon an implied Condition (for no such was exprest) that they should suffer the other Estates to enjoy the rest of their Property without Loss or Molestation.

This Law gave a new Turn to the Minds of the Mobility. They found themselves no longer obliged to depend on the Charity of their Neighbours, nor on their own Industry for a Maintenance. They now looked on themselves as joint Proprietors in the Land, and celebrated their Independency in Songs of Triumph; witness the old Ballad which was in all their Mouths,

> *Hang Sorrow, cast away Care;*
> *The Parish is bound to find us, &c.*[2]

A second Cause of their present Elevation has been the private Quarrels between particular Members of the other Estates, who on such Occasions have done all they could on both Sides to raise the Power of the Mob, in

---

of the mobbing of a 'celebrated Courtezan' and also of a foreign lady, *LDA*, 7 July 1752, reprinted by Fielding without comment in the 'Modern History' column of *CGJ* No. 54.

[1] Fielding refers to the Elizabethan Poor Law of 1601 (43 Eliz., c. 2), which placed the responsibility for the care of the poor directly on the parish. In his *Enquiry* (1751), pp. 32–8, he summarizes and evaluates the main provisions of this law, which called for the overseers of the poor to arrange for apprenticing the children of the poor, to raise by a parochial tax materials for employment of the poor, and to use the same tax for various forms of relief of the 'impotent' poor, such as erecting houses or cottages for their maintenance. See Fielding's footnote to *CGJ* No. 54, below; and see also Malvin R. Zirker, Jr., *Fielding's Social Pamphlets* (Berkeley and Los Angeles, 1966), pp. 11–12.

[2] Cf. *Spectator*, No. 232 (26 Nov. 1711), where in the course of an attack on giving charity to common beggars, Sir Andrew Freeport argues that each parish should maintain its own poor: 'We have a tradition from our Forefathers, that after the first of those Laws was made, they were insulted with that famous Song, *Hang Sorrow, cast away Care, / The Parish is bound to find us, &c.* And if we will be so good-natur'd as to maintain them without Work, they can do no less in Return than sing us *The Merry Beggars.*' 'Find' means 'support, maintain, provide for' (*OED*). In at least one version, the ballad is not quite the 'Song of Triumph' Fielding makes it out to be: 'Hang fear, cast away care, / The Parish is bound to find us, / Thou and I / And all must die, / And leave this world behind us; / The Bells shall ring, / The Clerk shall sing, / And the good old wife shall winde us, / And John shall lay / Our bones in clay / Where the Devil ne'er shall finde us' (*The New Academy of Complements . . . with an Exact Collection of the Newest and Choicest Songs a la Mode* [1671], pp. 271–2). Cf. a similar version, beginning 'A Fig for Care', in *Merry Drollery* (1691), p. 217. A drinking song with the same first line, printed in *Roxburghe Ballads*, ed. W. Chappell and J. W. Ebsworth, 9 vols. (1869–97), i. 509, is alluded to in Fielding's *Historical Register for the Year 1736* (1737), iii. 258: 'since the bottle is out, hang sorrow, cast away care, e'en take a dance'.

order to avail themselves of it, and to employ it against their Enemies.[1]

The third and the last which I shall mention, is the mistaken Idea which some particular Persons have always entertained of the Word Liberty; but this will open too copious a Subject, and shall be therefore treated in a future Paper.[2]

But before I dismiss this, I must observe that there are two Sorts of Persons of whom this fourth Estate do yet stand in some Awe, and whom consequently they have in great Abhorrence. These are a Justice of Peace, and a Soldier. To these two it is entirely owing that they have not long since rooted all the other Orders out of the Commonwealth.　　　C.

TUESDAY, JUNE 23, 1752.　　　NUMB. 50.

——*Versus inopes rerum, nugæque canoræ.*

HORACE.[3]

——*Verses of Matter void, and trifling Rhimes.*

TO

Sir *Alexander Drawcansir*, Knt.

Sir Alexander,

I am one of the constant Readers of your Paper, and am greatly offended, that you seldom or ever[4] entertain us with any Thing but Prose. 'Prithee Knight hast thou no Harmony in thy Soul?[5] For my part, I've always had such a strange Disposition to Rhiming, that I may say with a great Poet,

I lisp'd in Numbers, for the Numbers came.[6]

You'll tell me perhaps, that a Poet and a Rhimer are two different Things, and that the coming of the Numbers signifies Nothing, unless Genius, Fire, Fancy, &c. comes along with them. You will confess however, that we often see the silliest Things applauded only because they're tagg'd with Rhyme?

---

[1] See *CGJ* No. 58, where Fielding depicts the 'fourth Estate' at work on the approach to a new Westminster election, evidence enough that as he wrote this paragraph he had particularly in mind the exploitation of mob violence in the Westminster election of 1749 and the Opposition's political use of both the riots against bawdy-houses and the execution of Bosavern Penlez the same year; see *CGJ* No. 47, above, p. 263 n. 3.

[2] Not written; but see *CGJ* No. 2, above, p. 22 n. 1, and General Introduction, p. xl, for Fielding's other comments on the topic; see especially *Journal of a Voyage to Lisbon* (21 [16] July).

[3] *Art of Poetry*, 322: 'verses void of thought, and sonorous trifles' (Loeb).

[4] A common confusion of 'seldom if ever' and 'seldom or never' (*OED*).

[5] Cf. Fielding's own comment in the Preface to his *Miscellanies* (1743) that his poems 'are indeed Productions of the Heart rather than of the Head. If the Good-natured Reader thinks them tolerable, it will answer my warmest Hopes. This Branch of Writing is what I very little pretend to, and will appear to have been very little my Pursuit.'

[6] Pope, *Epistle to Dr. Arbuthnot*, 128.

And did not the finest Poem in our Language, lie for Years neglected, for no other Reason (that I know) but its wanting that Advantage?[1] Without further Apology, I present you a Song which I have lately made on my Mistress.[2]

Tho' Polly's and tho' Peggy's Charms,
Each Youthful Poet's Bosom warms;
None gives the Heart such fierce Alarms,
　　　　As Lovely Jenny Weston.

No Violet, Jessamin, or Rose,
Or spicy Gale that Afric blows,
Does half such fragrant Sweets disclose,
　　　　As waft round Jenny Weston.

Let other Swains to Courts repair,
And view each glitt'ring Beauty there,
'Tis Art alone makes them so fair,
　　　　But Nature Jenny Weston.

What Paint with her Complexion vies?
What Jewels sparkle like her Eyes?
What Hills of Snow so white, as rise
　　　　The Breasts of Jenny Weston?

Give others Titles, Honours, Pow'r,
The Riches of Potosi's Shore,
I ask not Bawbles; I implore
　　　　The Heart of Jenny Weston.

Possest of this, of this alone,
On India's Monarch I'd look down,
A Cot my Palace, and my Throne
　　　　The Lap of Jenny Weston.

---

[1] *Paradise Lost*; see *CGJ* No. 19, above, p. 129 n. 4.

[2] Cross (ii. 381–2) tentatively attributes this poem to Christopher Smart, and the case for Smart's authorship, based entirely on internal evidence, has been argued by Arthur Sherbo in 'The Case for Internal Evidence (1): Can Mother Midnight's Comical Pocket-Book be attributed to Christopher Smart?' *Bulletin of the New York Public Library*, 61 (1957), 378–9. Sherbo's evidence has been strongly disputed by Karina Williamson, 'Christopher Smart: Problems of Attribution Reconsidered', *The Library*, 28 (1973), 119. Fielding himself, in fact, cannot be absolutely ruled out as the author; see Miller, *Essays*, p. 30 n.

And now, Sir, if you will not allow me to be inspired with the Raptures of Poetry you will at least allow me the Inspiration of a Lover; and as such I doubt not your Favour to,

> *Your very humble Servant,*
> GEOFFRY JINGLE.

Sir,

Perhaps your Readers will not be displeased with the Sight of the following Poem,[1] when they are told it was written by that ancient and venerable Bard, *Dan Jeffry Chaucer.* How it came to my Hands is another Question: All I hope at present is, that the *fayre Maydens* will take fair Warning from this good Counsel; or in other Words, that they will first take some Pains to read, and some more to practise.—Without further Ceremony,

> *I am, &c.*

A

PLESAUNT BALADE,

Or, Advice to the

FAYRE MAYDENS:

Written by DAN JEFFRY CHAUCER.

Listhnith, Ladies, to youre oldè Frende:
If yee be fayre, be fayre to sum gode Ende.
For Gallants rath or late must loken out
For thilk same Yoke, so ese out of Dout,
*Yclepid Marriage: Yet sootly Weman be,
Malum per accidens vel malum per se,[2]
As lerned Clerkes saie; this Latin is,
Ladies, that yee al bene Mannis chefe Blis.

---

* *Called.*

---

[1] Attributed to Fielding by Jensen (ii. 237) and Cross (ii. 382) and to Smart by Arthur Sherbo, 'Fielding and Chaucer—and Smart', *Notes and Queries*, NS 5 (1958), 441–2, primarily because of Smart's knowledge of Chaucer. See Williamson, 'Christopher Smart', p. 120. The present editor, however, believes the most likely candidate for authorship is Fielding's friend James Harris, whose 'A Fragment of Chaucer' in Robert Dodsley's *Collection of Poems in Six Volumes by Several Hands* (vol. v [1758], 296) has several similarities to this one. For confirmation of Harris's authorship of the fragment used by Dodsley, see Ralph Straus, *Robert Dodsley* (London, 1910), p. 142. On Harris and his contributions to *CGJ*, see the 'Court of Enquiry' from *CGJ* No. 21, below, Appendix I. On Chaucer's reputation in this period, see Geoffrey Tillotson, ed., *The Rape of the Lock and Other Poems*, Twickenham Edn. of the Poems of Pope, ii (1942), pp. 3–8.

[2] A scholastic distinction between 'that which is an evil accidentally and that which is so through itself, an evil as such by its own nature' (R. J. Deferari, *A Lexicon of St. Thomas Aquinas* [Baltimore, 1948], s.v. 'malus'). The lines which follow echo Chauntecleer's deliberate mistranslation of a Latin line in his address to Pertelote, *Nun's Priest's Tale*, 343–5.

And as a Wife is Mannis helpe and Comfort,
His Paradise, his Solace, and Disport;
So pardie, is Man Woman's chefe Stay,
Harknith then, Dames, to my moral Lay:
Ne stand ye *shill I, shall I;*[1] 'tis childis Play:
Eke dangerous, sings the Saw, is all Delay.[2]
Now listnith to my Similitude,
Gode is the Moral, tho' the Rime be rude.
 Where Medway's Stremes meandring, flowen
  wyde,
There many a Sole, and many a †Made abyde:
(Tho' on the Banks, God wot, few *Mades* doe walk,
And fewer *Soles*, that think rite wel and talk.)
Now thilke same Mades, fresh broughten to the
 "Chepe,
Are rated high; but little can they kepe:
Downs fals the Price. *Ah! benedicite!*
Who bies my Mades? Ne one, ne tway, ne three;
So handled they bene, by my Father's Kin,
The *Mades* wont sell, they are not worth a Pin.

Covent-Garden, June 22.

The following Letter which was sent to the Justice by an unknown Hand, hath been transmitted to us; and tho' perhaps some Points are carried a little too far, upon the whole I think it a very sensible Performance, and worthy the Attention of the Public.[3]

Bond-Street,[4] 22 June, 1752.

---

† *Fish so named.* ‖ *Market.*

[1] i.e. shilly-shally.
[2] Cf. Tilley, D 195: 'Delay breeds danger (is dangerous)'.
[3] Although Cross (ii. 370), giving no reasons, attributes this letter to Fielding himself, it is unlikely to be his. In *CGJ* No. 57 Fielding responds to the points raised here, and though he could have produced this letter in order to set up his later response, the piece bears no marks of his style and is probably a genuine contribution. Despite its heading as a 'Covent Garden' column, the letter was highlighted in the original issue by being printed in the same typeface as the leaders and is therefore so placed in the Wesleyan Edn.
 The letter has as its specific background the reactions to recent legislation (25 George II, c. 36) affecting prostitutes, but it must also be seen as part of a whole body of writing in the century assessing and re-assessing society's treatment of prostitutes, ranging from calls for extirpation of all forms of prostitution to highly sympathetic pleas for greater understanding of their plight and plans for their institutional reformation. For Fielding's own view and for specific examples of this literature, see *CGJ* No. 57 and notes.
[4] The fashionable address is perhaps designed to lend authority to a letter with unorthodox views on a topic concerning the lower classes.

Sir,

I know not whether 'tis usual for any Body beside Lawyers to make Remarks upon Acts of Parliament, to explain their Meaning, and shew their Consequences; but as every Man of common Sense, Reason and Understanding, is at Liberty to examine and judge of Laws, as well as obliged to obey them, I shall make bold to submit to your Consideration (whom I esteem as a very worthy and useful Magistrate) an Observation or two, which I think may be made on the late Act, against loose Women and Houses of ill Fame:[1] Altho' the Life of Laws consists in a proper Execution of them, yet if this present Act against Lewdness be carried on with the same Rigour it seems to have been hitherto, and as some of the Justices give in Charge to their Understrappers, I apprehend many ill Consequences will arise from it, and that the Remedy will be infinitely more fatal than the Disease complained of.[2] It is said that a Constable has a Power of searching all Houses where he suspects Women of ill Character are lodged, to apprehend and bring such Women before Justices, who are to commit them to Prisons.[3] If the Constables do their Office diligently, and our Prisons (already well stored with Inhabitants) are to be crouded with Multitudes of these unhappy Wretches, may not a contagious Distemper be apprehended? But suppose that should not happen, what is to become of these People, when the Time of their Imprisonment expires? Must they not return to their former Courses for Bread, or must they not inevitably become Beggars, and so increase the prodigious Numbers that throng the Streets already? If they take to their

---

[1] 'An Act for the better preventing Thefts and Robberies, and for regulating Places of Publick Entertainment, and punishing Persons keeping disorderly Houses' (25 George II, c. 36) had gone into effect three weeks earlier, on 1 June 1752; it required prosecution by constables and justices of persons accused of keeping bawdy-houses whenever information is provided by two inhabitants of a parish paying scot and lot and willing to enter into a recognizance of £20 each to produce evidence against such persons, the informers to be rewarded £10 each upon a conviction. For criticism of the law's dependence on informers, see *LDA*, 15 June 1752.

[2] Although the new law was aimed at 'keepers', it was at first vigorously enforced against street-walkers as well; see the 'Covent Garden' column for 12 June (*CGJ* No. 47), printed below, Appendix I. Cf. *LDA*, 11 June: 'Since the shutting up of the Receptacles of Lewdness, and the Disappearance of the Ladies of Pleasure in the Streets, the Court End of the Town already begin to complain of the Dulness of their nocturnal Excursions, and bid adieu to Frolick and Whim on this Side of the Water. Upon this Account the Inhabitants of Lambeth are likely to be encreased with Male as well as Female Libertines; but why an Act of Parliament should appear to be of less Force in Surry than in Middlesex seems not easy to be determined.' Within a week of the law's taking effect it was reported that 50 houses around the Strand had been closed and their inhabitants 'turned Printsellers' (*DA*, 8 June 1752). For reactions to the rigorous enforcement of the law, see *LDA*, 15 June and 5 Aug. 1752 and a sixpenny pamphlet by 'M. Ludovicus' (i.e. John Campbell [1708–75]), *A Particular but Melancholy Account of the great Hardships, Difficulties, and Miseries, that those unhappy . . . Creatures, the Common Women of the Town, are plung'd into at this Juncture* (1752); another pamphlet, presumably alluding to this number of *CGJ* and called *A Speech made in the Censorial Court of Sir Alexander Drawcansir*, has apparently not survived but was also intended to ridicule the recent act affecting prostitutes (see *Monthly Review*, 7 [1752], 74).

[3] By the new law constables were empowered to enter 'disorderly houses' and seize all persons found therein; see Giles Jacob, *A New Law-Dictionary*, 7th edn. (1756), s.v. 'bawdy-houses'.

former Course of Life, as undoubtedly they will and must, (for who is there that will take into Service any of those Persons, tho' ever so willing to abandon their Debaucheries) the Constables and Watchmen will meet with incessant Business to apprehend, and the Justices to recommit them; till in due Time the Miseries of Imprisonments shall destroy them by lingering Diseases and Death. A Case this, most shocking and terrible to happen in a Country of Christians, or indeed of Men. Punishments are with Ease devised for those, whose very Being, is a continual Torment to them. But reputable and useful Occupations for the Idle and Dissolute, require some Care, Discernment and Consideration, to contrive such as 'tis hoped our Legislators are qualified with, and being so, may be disposed to order and enforce.[1] Another Inconvenience arising from this Law, is the insolent Behaviour that honest sober Persons frequently meet with, from some ignorant, but officious Fellows, who are employed in the Execution of it. I have been informed of several Instances of very worthy People being laid hold of and dragged to the Round-house[2] by some of these dirty Fellows, under a Pretence of their being disorderly Persons. Nay I have been present, when a Man's Wife of unsuspected Character and Credit has been brought before a Justice for Examination against whom not the least Charge was given, but that she was passing along the Streets at ten o'Clock at Night.[3] I cannot say how much I might be transported by such Treatment from a low pitiful Fellow, puffed up with a little ill delegated Authority; whatever I might do, I verily believe there are Husbands and Brothers, who would make a severe Example of such a Scoundrel on such Provocation. When a Woman of Character is thus insulted by one of these Blockheads, he pleads in his Justification that she was picking up Men. By this means the Fame and Honour of the most virtuous Woman, may be violated without a Possibility of

[1] The passage reflects the sympathetic strain in attitudes toward prostitutes, common throughout the century but especially evident at mid-century and later, which led to the founding of Magdalen House for penitent women in 1758. See, among other examples, a letter (by Joseph Simpson, a lawyer) to Johnson's *Rambler*, No. 107 (26 Mar. 1751); *Rambler*, Nos. 170, 171 (2 and 5 Nov. 1751) by Johnson himself; a letter signed 'Sunderlandensis' in *GM* 21 (1751), 163–5; and *The Vices of the Cities of London and Westminster* (1751); see also *CGJ* No. 57, below, p. 308 n. 2. Cf. also a notice in *DA*, 19 June 1752, describing a plan by a 'Set of Gentlemen' to lend support to young girls 'who have been deluded by different Stratagems to give up their Virtue' and become prostitutes and whose distresses may have been increased by the recent Act of Parliament.

[2] A place of detention for arrested persons (*OED*); a scandal had occurred ten years earlier (July 1742) when a number of women died by suffocation in the St Martin's Round-house, St Martin's Lane, after having been arrested by drunk constables on charges of being disorderly (see *Yale Walpole*, xvii. 503–5).

[3] A not uncommon problem, against which Giles Jacob warns, ''tis held not lawful for a Constable, &c. to take up any Woman, as a *Nightwalker*, on bare Suspicion only, of being of ill-Fame, unless she be guilty of a Breach of the Peace, or some unlawful Act' (*A New Law-Dictionary*, 7th edn. [1756], s.v. 'Nightwalkers'); cf. the predicament of Hilaret in the first two acts of Fielding's *Rape upon Rape* (1730) and the girl wrongly sent to Bridewell by Justice Thrasher in *Amelia*, I. ii; see also *The Midnight-Ramble; or, the Adventures of two Noble Females* (1754), pp. 20–2.

Reparation. The Justices would not do amiss if they enquired of their Beadles and Watchmen; what is the Sense and Meaning of the vulgar Expression picking up Men, because any Woman who is seen with a Man by Night, may in their Sense be said to have picked him up, and consequently is liable to be picked up herself, and forced to take up her Lodging in one of their Spunging-Houses.[1]

I have been told that in other Nations no less tender of Religion and Morality than our own, certain places are allotted and tolerated for the Entertainment of Women who are kept under Regulations, and are always at the Service of such Customers as are disposed to deal with them. At Venice, a Man may hire a Woman for a Night, a Week, a Month, or a Year; suppose he leaves her with Child, she incurs no Punishment as in England she would, nor is the Infant when born refused Admittance into the Hospital, on account of its not being begot by a Man of Quality. Some People are so foolish as to think these Licences irreligious and infamous; but wiser Men are of another Opinion; who having more closely considered the Frailties of Mankind, have by allowing of these seeming Irregularities, certainly prevented Practices of the most detestable Nature.[2] It may be said, and is said frequently by Women who have neither Money nor any thing else to recommend them but Airs and Paint, that Men who are fond of Women, may and ought to marry. That they may is certain, if they like it; but it is not so certain that they ought. Whoever looks thro' the married State will find many Discouragements from entering into it. It is utterly inconvenient and imprudent for some; nor can every Man support the Charge of a modern Wife, and at the same Time provide for a Family of Children. The woeful Consequences of inconsiderate Marriages are almost infinite, thence is produced that formidable Body of Poor, which can hardly be maintained by compulsive Laws and charitable Contributions.[3] In low Life, People often intermarry with no other View or Regard, than the sensual Gratification of a present Appetite: The Copulation of the Mob is no better than legal or ecclesiastical Fornication, and tho' a Priest may join two Wretches together, in what is called the holy Bands of Matrimony, yet in a very short Time when

---

[1] A house kept by a bailiff, usually regarded as a place of preliminary confinement for debtors (*OED*).

[2] Among these 'wiser Men' was Bernard Mandeville, whose *Modest Defence of Publick Stews* (1724), despite its irony, seriously advances some of the arguments made in this letter, including the view that public whoring is less detrimental to society than private whoring; Mandeville also cites the 'Authority' of Italy and Holland in support of his project (p. 74). Cf. *The Gentleman and Lady's Palladium* (1752), in which 'Honestus Idem' makes the same argument (p. 21), and *Memoirs of the Bedford Coffee House* (1763), p. 33.

[3] See Fielding's defense of marriage in answer to these comments, in *CGJ* No. 57, below, and his essay on the same theme in *Champion*, 21 June 1740. One argument sometimes advanced in favor of legalized prostitution was that it improved marriages because experienced men make better husbands; see Mandeville, *Modest Defence of Publick Stews*, pp. 29–39, and *Satan's Harvest Home* (1749), p. 42.

the consummation Pleasures are over, the Bridegroom either takes another Wife, or the Bride another Husband; and very often this is the Case of both. In high Life, Marriage is a mere Trade, a Bargain and Sale, where both Parties endeavour to cheat one another; the Effects of such unnatural Unions frequently are seen in Courts of Delegates,[1] or by private Articles of Separation. To these it must be owned there are some Exceptions of Persons who engage with a Prospect of mutual Felicity and Designs of raising a Progeny that may contribute to the Welfare of Society, and preserve their own: I decline any further Reflections on this Subject, since daily Experience affords Variety, and shall only observe that as the Suppression of some very notorious and dangerous Houses is absolutely requisite, so the utter Extirpation of Women of Pleasure or of the Town, term them how you please, is impracticable, and would it be effected, would produce Irregularities of ten Times more criminal and odious Tendency. Of what Service is an Hospital for Foundlings on this Supposition; are none but the Bastards of our Great-ones to have the Benefit of it?[2] But as these Days will hardly admit of speaking or writing Truth or Fact, I stop my Pen and subscribe myself Sir,

Your Well-wisher and humble Servant,

HUMPHRY MEANWELL.

SATURDAY, JUNE 27, 1752.   NUMB. 51.

Hæ tibi erunt artes.——   VIRGIL.[3]

These must be your golden Rules.

Of all our Manufactures, there is none at present in a more flourishing Condition, or which hath received more considerable Improvements of late Years, than the Manufacture of Paper. To such Perfection is this brought at present, that it almost promises to rival the great staple Commodity[4] of this Kingdom.

[1] The court of appeal in ecclesiastical causes, its commissioners appointed by the Crown. On marriage in high life, cf. Bellamant in Fielding's *The Modern Husband* (1732): 'It is a stock-jobbing age, every thing has its price; marriage is traffic throughout' (II. vi). See also H. J. Habakkuk, 'Marriage Settlements in the Eighteenth Century', *Transactions of the Royal Historical Society*, 4th ser., 32 (1950), 15–30.

[2] On the Foundling Hospital, see *CGJ* No. 44, above, p. 251 n. 3. The charge made here was uncommon, since the usual belief was that the Hospital, by catering to the lower classes, was encouraging prostitution; cf. 'M. Ludovicus', *A Particular but Melancholy Account*, which calls it 'that most excellent, well-endow'd, and well-designed Structure for the Encouragement of Whoring' (p. 22). 'Meanwell's' point, like that of 'Ludovicus', is perhaps that charity would be better employed on the mothers than on the children; cf. *Rambler*, No. 107 (26 Mar. 1751).

[3] *Aeneid*, vi. 852: 'these shall be thine arts' (Loeb).

[4] i.e. wool. Cf. *Amelia*, VIII. v, where Booth says, 'the Pen and Ink is likely to become the Staple Commodity of the Kingdom'. On the flourishing state of paper-making at this period, see E. Chambers, *Cyclopaedia*, 7th edn. (1751), s.v. 'Paper'; R. Campbell, *The London Tradesman* (1747), p. 126; and the *Universal Magazine*, 10 (1752), 26–7, 324 ff.

The two principal Branches of this Manufacture are carried on by Painting and Printing. To what a Degree of Excellence the Artists are arrived in the former, I need not mention. Our painted Paper is scarce distinguishable from the finest Silk; and there is scarce a modern House, which hath not one or more Rooms lined with this Furniture.[1]

But however valuable this Branch may be, it is by no Means equal to that which is carried on by Printing. Of such Consequence indeed to the Public may this Part of the Paper Manufacture be made, that I doubt not but that with proper Care, it would be capable of finding an ample Provision for the Poor.[2] To which Purpose it seems better adapted than any other, for a Reason which I shall present assign.

Of Printing likewise, there are two Kinds; that of the Rolling, and that of the Letter Press,—or perhaps I shall be better understood by most of my Readers, by the Terms Prints and Books.

The Former (though of infinitely the less Consequence) hath been of late much improved; and though it doth not consume a great Quantity of Paper, doth however employ a great Number of Hands. This was formerly an inconsiderable Business, and very few got their Bread by it; but some ingenious Persons have of late so greatly extended it, that there are at present almost as many Print-Shops, as there are Bakers in this Metropolis.[3]

This Improvement hath been owing to a deep Penetration into human Nature, by which it hath been discovered, that there are two Sights which the Generality of Mankind do hunger after, with little less Avidity, than after their daily Bread. The one is to behold certain Parts which are severally common to one half of the Species exhibited to View, in the most amiable and inviting Manner; the other is to see certain Faces, which belong to Individuals, exposed in a ridiculous and contemptible Light.[4] By feeding both which Appetites the Print-makers have very plentifully fed themselves.

I come now to the second Branch of Printing, namely to that which is performed at the Letter-press, and which consists of Books, Pamphlets, Papers, &c. The flourishing State of this Manufacture needs no Kind of

---

[1] Cf. Thomas Mortimer's *Universal Director* (1763): 'The art of Painting and Staining of Paper of various patterns and colours for hanging of rooms, is lately become a very considerable branch of commerce in this country, . . . as it is not only a cheap, but an elegant part of furniture, and saves the builders the expence of wainscotting; for which reason . . . most of the new houses lately erected are lined throughout with Paper' (p. 54).

[2] Here, and later in the essay, Fielding uses as a satiric device a topic which he and others considered the chief problem in providing for the poor, 'finding', or supplying, a suitable means of employment for those able to work; see *CGJ* No. 36, above, p. 215 n. 1.

[3] Cf. R. Campbell, *The London Tradesman* (1747): 'Our Print Shopkeepers are mere Tradesmen: They set up any thing that offers in their Shops; if it sells, their End is answered; if not, they know not where to lay the Blame, for they are no more Judges of the intrinsic Worth of the Commodity than they are of Astronomy' (p. 136).

[4] On sex and scandal as the chief subjects of modern prints, see the 'Court of Censorial Enquiry' in *CGJ* Nos. 11 and 12, and a letter from a print-seller in *CGJ* No. 13.

Proof. It is indeed certain, that more Paper is now consumed this Way in a Week, than was formerly the Consumption of a Year.

To this notable Encrease, nothing perhaps hath more contributed, than the new Invention of writing without the Qualifications of any Genius or Learning. The first Printers, possibly misled by an old Precept in one Horace,[1] seem to have imagined, that both those Ingredients were necessary in the Writer, and accordingly we find they employed themselves on such Samples only, as were produced by Men, in whom Genius and Learning concurred; but modern Times have discovered, that the Trade is very well to be carried on without either; and this by introducing several new Kind of Wares, the Manufacture of which, is extremely easy, as well as extremely lucrative. The Principal of these, are Blasphemy, Treason, Bawdry and Scandal.[2] For in the making up of all these, the Qualifications above-mentioned, together with that Modesty, which is inseparable from them, would be rather an Incumbrance than of any real use.

No sooner were these new fashioned Wares brought to Market, than the Paper Merchants, commonly called Booksellers, found so immense a Demand for them, that their Business was to find Hands sufficient *to supply the Wants of the Public.* In this however, they had no great Difficulty, as the Work was so extremely easy, that no Talents whatever (except that of being able to write) not even the Capacity of Spelling, were requisite.

The Methods however which have been used by the Paper-Merchants to make these new fashioned Wares universally known, are very ingenious and worthy our Notice.[3]

The first of these Methods was for the Merchant himself to mount in the most public Part of the Town into a wooden Machine called the Pillory, where he stood for the Space of an Hour proclaiming his Goods to all that past that Way. This was practised with much Success by the late Mr. Curl,[4] Mr. Mist[5] and others, who never failed of selling several large Bales of Goods in this Manner.

---

[1] *Art of Poetry*, 408–10: 'Often it is asked whether a praiseworthy poem be due to Nature or to Art. For my part, I do not see of what avail is either study, when not enriched by Nature's vein, or native wit, if untrained' (Loeb).　　　[2] On this theme see also *CGJ* Nos. 5, 6, 14, and 16.
[3] With the 'Methods' described (the pillory, the gallows, and the whipping post), cf. Swift's 'Physico-logical Scheme of Oratorial Receptacles or Machines' (the Pulpit, the Ladder, and the Stage-itinerant) in *Tale of a Tub*, sect. I.
[4] Edmund Curll (1675–1747), notorious bookseller and pirate of the writings of Swift and Pope. Constantly in trouble with the authorities for publishing obscene books, Curll stood in the pillory on 23 Feb. 1728 for a political offense, publishing the *Memoirs of John Ker of Kersland*. He was well-used by the mob, having had printed papers dispersed to the crowd claiming that he was being punished for vindicating the memory of Queen Anne; see Ralph Straus, *The Unspeakable Curll* (1927), pp. 98–121. Fielding ridicules him as 'Bookweight' and 'Curry' in *The Author's Farce* (1730); he hits at him again in an essay on 'book-puffing' in *Champion*, 1 Mar. 1739/40, and in an article on the concept of literary property in *Champion*, 12 Aug. 1740, where he says Curll has pirated 5 numbers of the *Champion* itself.
[5] Nathaniel Mist (d. 1737), proprietor of the Tory newspaper *The Weekly Journal; or Saturday's Post*

Notwithstanding however the Profits arising from this Method of Publication, it was not without Objections; for several wanton Persons among the Mob, were used on such Occasions to divert themselves by pelting the Merchant while he stood exposed on the PUBLISHING-STOOL, with rotten Eggs and other mischievous Implements, by which Means, he often came off much bedawbed, and sometimes not without bodily Hurt.

Some of the more cunning therefore among the Merchants, began to decline this Practice themselves, and employed their Understrappers, that is to say their Writers for such Purposes: For it was conceived a Piece of Blasphemy, Bawdry, &c. would be as well sold by exhibiting the Author, as by exhibiting the Bookseller.

Of this probably they received the first Hint from the Case of one Mr. Richard Savage; an Author whose Manufactures had long lain uncalled for in the Warehouse, till he happened very fortunately for his Bookseller to be found guilty of a capital Crime at the Old-Bailey. The Merchant instantly took the Hint, and the very next Day advertised *the Works of Mr. Savage, now under Sentence of Death for Murder.* This Device succeeded, and immediately (to use their Phrase) carried off the whole Impression.[1]

Encouraged by this Success, the Merchant not doubting the Execution of his Author, bad very high for his dying Speech, which was accordingly penn'd and delivered. Savage however, was, contrary to all Expectation pardoned, and would have returned the Money; but the Merchant insisted on his Bargain, and published the dying Speech which Mr. Savage *should have made* at Tyburn, of which it is probable as many were sold as there were People in Town who could read.[2]

The Gallows being thus found to be a great Friend to the Press, the

---

(1716–28). He stood in the pillory on 20 and 23 Feb. 1721, having been found guilty of scandalous reflections on the king. Like Curll, he was well-treated by the crowd. In 1728 Mist fled to France, and Mist's *Weekly Journal* became *Fog's Weekly Journal*.

[1] Richard Savage (?1697–1743), poet and friend of Pope and Samuel Johnson, was convicted, sentenced to death, and then pardoned for killing one James Sinclair in a tavern fight on 20 Nov. 1727; Fielding owned an account of his trial in *Select Trials at the Old Bailey*, 4 vols. (1742), iii. 77–89 (Baker, item 552); see also Johnson's *An Account of the Life of Mr. Richard Savage* (1744), ed. Clarence Tracy (Oxford, 1971), pp. 31–8. Johnson makes no mention of the effort of publishers to capitalize on Savage's misfortune, and Clarence Tracy (*The Artificial Bastard* [Toronto, 1953], p. 91 n.) believes Fielding may have been thinking only of Savage's *Miscellaneous Poems*, designed for publication in 1726 and withdrawn. Cf., however, an advertisement in the *Daily Journal* on 18 Dec. 1727 for 'Books written by the present unhappy Mr. Savage', listing three works printed by Samuel Chapman, a bookseller who had printed Eliza Haywood's *Works* and for whom Pope found a place in the 1729 *Dunciad* (ii. 159). Accurate or not, Fielding's anecdote may have come from his own bookseller and friend Andrew Millar, who published a poem by Savage in 1730 and to whom Savage gave a promissory note in June 1731 (Bodleian MS Montagu d. 1, f. 141; I am indebted to Prof. Thomas Lockwood for this reference). Savage was also perhaps the 'Richard Savage' who subscribed to Fielding's *Miscellanies* (1743).

[2] No copy or advertisement of a 'dying speech' by Savage has been located.

Merchants for the future made it their chief Care to provide themselves with such Writers, as were most likely to call in this Assistance; in other Words, who were in the fairest Way of being hanged; and tho' they have not always succeeded to their Wish, yet whoever is well read in the Productions of the last twenty Years, will be more inclined perhaps to blame the Law, than the Sagacity of the Booksellers.

The whipping Post hath been likewise of eminent Use to the same Purposes; and tho' perhaps this may raise less Curiosity than the Gallows, in one Instance at least, it hath visibly the Advantage: For an Author tho' he may deserve it often, can be hanged but once, but he may be whipped several Times, indeed six Times by one Sentence, of which we have lately seen an Instance in the Person of Stroud,[1] who is a strong Proof of the great Profits which the Paper-Merchants derive from the whipping one of their Manufacturers.

Mr. Stroud, in Imitation of several eminent Persons, thought proper to publish an Apology for his Life. The Public, however, were less kind to him, than they had been to other great Apologists,[2] and treated his Performance with Contempt. But no sooner was he tied to the Cart's Tail, than the Work began to sell in great Numbers; and this Sale revived with every monthly Whipping; so that if he had been whipped, as some imagined he was to have been, once a Month during Life, the Merchant possibly might have sold as many Bales of his Works as have been sold of those of Swift himself.[3]

I shall conclude with hoping, that as the Merchants seem at present to have their Eye chiefly on the Whipping-post for the Advancement of their Manufactures, it is to be hoped Courts of Justice will do all that in them lies, to encourage a Trade of such wonderful Benefit to the Kingdom,[4] and which seems more likely than any other to provide a Maintenance for our Poor; as

---

[1] William Stroud, swindler, was sentenced on 11 Jan. 1752 at Westminster Hall to be committed to Tothillfields Bridewell for 6 months and to be publicly whipped through the streets once a month for 6 months (see *LM* 21 [1752], 42). He had undergone his final whipping just three days before this essay, on 24 June, when, according to a news item reprinted by Fielding in his 'Modern History' column of this number of *CGJ*, 'the Cart proceeded very slowly, and the Executioner treated him very severely. After his Discipline was over, he fainted away in St. James's Round-house.' Stroud himself referred to his punishment as 'these severe Inflictions, which is a Precedent of the Kind, and such a Sentence as was never adjudg'd to the most abandon'd Wretches' (*Genuine Memoirs* [1752], p. 56).

[2] Fielding hits at Colley Cibber's *Apology* (1740), a favorite butt of his ridicule, and possibly also at the *Apology for the Life of Bampfylde-Moore Carew* (1749), as well as at the *Apology* of the courtesan Teresia Constantia Phillips, published in 1748–9. He ridicules the fashion of autobiographical 'apologies' in *Tom Jones*, II. i.

[3] In fact, Stroud's *Genuine Memoirs of the Life and Transactions of W. S. . . . . written by himself* (printed for J. Fuller) did not appear until 21 Feb. 1752, after he had already received two whippings (16 Jan. and 15 Feb.). Stroud's bookseller did attempt to capitalize on his predicament, however, by printing a notice in *GA* on the day of the second whipping (15 Feb.), claiming that a false *Life of William Stroud* had been printed by J. Trueman and promising that the genuine work would soon be forthcoming; the Trueman publication, called *The Tradesman's Warning-Piece*, was advertised in *CGJ* No. 12 (11 Feb.).

[4] For another development of this theme, see *CGJ* No. 59 (15 Aug.), below.

no Qualification is required to the Production of these Wares, besides that of being able to write, nor any Tools or Stock to set up a Manufacturer, besides a Pen and Ink and a small Quantity of Paper; so that an Author may indeed be equipped at a cheaper Rate than a Blacker of Shoes.　　　　　　A.

TUESDAY, JUNE 30, 1752.　　　　　　Numb. 52.

> Graiis Ingenium, Graiis dedit Ore rotundo
> Musa loqui——.　　　　　　　　　　　Horace.[1]

> Her Wit, and flowing Eloquence, the Muse
> Gave to the Greeks.——

As a Proposal is now publish'd for a Translation of the Works of Lucian into our Mother-Tongue,[2] it may not be improper to acquaint our English Readers with the real Value of the Work which is offered to their Acceptance.

This Author may be almost called the Father of true Humour: Mr. Dryden says, he knows not whom he imitated, unless it might be Aristophanes.[3] This Supposition can certainly be meant only of that Attic Elegance of Diction, in which there is perhaps some Resemblance between these two Authors; and this is a Point, in which I am afraid we are at this time but little able to decide who deserves the Preference; the learned Photius gives the Palm of excelling all others in Diction, to our Author. τὴν μέν τοι φράσιν ἐστὶν ἄριστος.[4]

But surely our ingenious Countryman could not conceive, that Lucian in the exquisite Pleasantry of his Humour, in the Neatness of his Wit, and in

---

[1] *Art of Poetry*, 323: 'To the Greeks the Muse gave native wit, to the Greeks she gave speech in well-rounded phrase' (Loeb).

[2] The proposal was Fielding's own, advertised in this number of *CGJ* and in *CGJ* No. 51. It projects a printing by subscription (2 guineas from each subscriber) of a new translation in two volumes 'with Notes Historical, Critical, and Explanatory' by Fielding and the Revd William Young; and it lists as the booksellers involved in the proposal Andrew Millar, Robert Dodsley, and Samuel Baker. The proposed translation came to nothing, presumably for lack of subscribers. In 1742 Fielding and Young had also planned to follow their translation of *Plutus* with translations of other plays by Aristophanes, together with 'a very large Dissertation on the Nature and End of Comedy'; this project also failed to materialize.
For examples of Fielding's many tributes elsewhere to Lucian, the 2nd-cent. Syrian satirist and rhetorician whom he here credits with a profound influence on his own style, see *Tom Jones* (XIII. i); *Amelia* (VIII. v, a passage which also puffs his projected translation); and *Journal of a Voyage to Lisbon* (19 [14] July). For analysis of Lucian's influence on Fielding, whose library contained nine different editions of Lucian, see Miller, *Essays*, pp. 365–86, and Christopher Robinson, *Lucian and his Influence in Europe* (Chapel Hill, NC, 1979), pp. 198–235.

[3] *The Works of Lucian, Translated from the Greek, by several Eminent Hands. With the Life of Lucian, a Discourse on his Writings, and a Character of some of the present Translators. Written by John Dryden*, 4 vols. (1711), i. 43; Fielding owned this edition of Dryden's Lucian (Baker, item 44).

[4] 'However, he is best with respect to diction'; Photius (c. 820–91), Byzantine scholar and patriarch of Constantinople, makes this remark in his *Bibliotheca*, ch. 128. μέντοι is written as one word in modern texts, but not in the edition Fielding owned (Rouen, 1653), cols. 309–10 (Baker, item 305).

the Poignancy of his Satire, did condescend to be the Imitator of a Writer, whose Humour is often extravagant, his Wit coarse, and his Satire unjust and immoral. Indeed, Mr. Dryden himself, in the short Character which he presently after gives of Lucian's Writings, shews he could not have imitated the Greek Comedian. "Any one," says he, "may see, that our Author's chief Design was to disnest Heaven of so many immoral and debauched Deities: His next, to expose the mock Philosophers; and his last, to give us Examples of a good Life in the Persons of the true."[1] Of the first of these we may find, I allow, many Strokes in Aristophanes, how inferior to the Spirit of Lucian, I submit to the learned Reader; but as to the second, I remember no Instance: For I hope the base and barbarous Abuse of Socrates[2] will not be allowed an Attempt to expose the mock Philosophers. The Truth is, that Species of Wretches, who were the Objects of Ridicule at Rome, and who gained a Livelihood by being so, being, as Suetonius tells us,[3] the favourite Buffoons of the Emperors themselves, were unknown in the Days of Aristophanes. And as to *giving an Example of a good Life in the Persons of the true Philosophers*, this likewise could no more be learnt from Aristophanes, than a System of Ethics can be drawn from our modern Comedies.[4]

And as I am thus unwilling to think that Lucian was the Imitator of any other, I shall not be much more ready to grant, that others have been the Imitators of him. The Person whom I esteem to be most worthy of this Honour is the immortal Swift. To say Truth, I can find no better Way of giving the English Reader an Idea of the Greek Author, than by telling him, that to translate Lucian well into English, is to give us another Swift in our own Language.[5] I will add, however invidious it may appear, that when I allow to this excellent English Writer the Praise of imitating the Greek, I allow him that Praise only which the best Imitator can possibly claim, of being Second to his Original. Our Author will perhaps for ever continue to deserve the Title of inimitable, (*i.e.* unequaled) which the learned Mr. Moyle hath given him.[6]

[1] *The Works of Lucian* (1711), i. 43–4.   [2] In *The Clouds*.

[3] As Jensen (ii. 240–1) suggests, Fielding apparently refers to Suetonius' 'On Rhetoricians', v, especially to an anecdote about Sextus Clodius, a Sicilian rhetorician who was employed 'for the sake of his jokes' by Mark Antony when the latter was consul.

[4] On Fielding's attitude toward Aristophanes, which had undergone a marked change since he translated *Plutus* (1742) and contrasted Aristophanes' comedies to the likes of Cibber and other modern wits, see *CGJ* No. 10 and p. 74 n. 4. He was to refer yet again to the abuse of Socrates in his *Fragment of a Comment on Lord Bolingbroke's Essays* (1755).

[5] On Fielding's constant praise of Swift in *CGJ*, as elsewhere in his works, see General Introduction, above, p. xliv and n. 1; on the comparison of Swift with Lucian, cf. Fielding's eulogy of Swift in *True Patriot*, No. 1 (5 Nov. 1745), where Swift is ranked above Lucian, Rabelais, and Cervantes; and *Amelia* (VIII. v), where not even Swift is said to equal Lucian. For the view that only Swift would have been capable of translating Lucian properly, see Thomas Francklin, *Translation; A Poem* (1753), p. 11.

[6] Walter Moyle (1672–1721), wit, scholar, and one of the translators of the Dryden edition of 1711; Moyle's word is actually 'matchless' rather than 'inimitable' or 'incomparable', as Fielding says

In Fact, besides the Superiority of Genius which seems to me to appear in Lucian, when he is compared with any other humorous Writer, no other seems to have had such excellent Materials to work upon. What Fund of Pleasantry hath any Age produced equal to that Theology and to that Philosophy which he hath exposed![1]

Notwithstanding all his Merit, (I should perhaps rather say, as a Proof of his Merit,) this inimitable Author hath had his Critics, that is, as the Moderns use the Word, his Censurers. "Of this Number," says Dryden, "is the wretched Author of the *Lucien en belle Humeur*, who being himself as insipid as a Dutch Poet, yet arraigns Lucian for his own Fault, *&c.* but the best on't is, the Jaundice is only in his own Eyes, which makes Lucian look yellow to him. All Mankind will exclaim against his preaching this Doctrine against him."[2] The learned indeed are unanimous in their Elogiums on him; such amongst others are Photius, Grævius,[3] Erasmus,[4] D'Ablancourt,[5] Dryden, Mayn,[6] and the learned Mr. Moyle whom I have mentioned above.

To the Honour of Lucian it should be likewise remembred, that his Virtues and Abilities recommended him to the Favour of that Glory of human Nature, Marcus Aurelius, by whom our Author was employed in a very considerable Post in the Government. That great Emperor did not, it seems, think, that a Man of Humour was below his Notice, or unfit for Business of the gravest Kind.[7]

---

in citing the same passage in *Amelia* (VIII. v). The phrase occurs in Moyle's 'Dissertation upon the Age of the *Philopatris*', *Works of Walter Moyle* (1726), i. 288–9; Moyle's *Works* were in Fielding's library (Baker, item 230).

[1] On Lucian's campaign against all schools of contemporary philosophy and religion, see F. G. Allinson, *Lucian: Satirist and Artist* (1926), chs. 5, 6. As Miller points out (*Essays*, p. 366 n.), some of Fielding's contemporaries, like Edward Young, were disturbed by Lucian's inclusion of the early Christians among those he mocked; see, for another example, Peter Shaw, *The Reflector* (1750), p. 16.

[2] *The Works of Lucian* (1711), i. 36–7; Fielding omits a short passage and slightly changes the final sentence. The author referred to is Jean-Chrysostome Bruslé de Montpleinchamp (1641–1724), Belgian biographer and miscellaneous writer, whose *Lucien en belle humeur* (Amsterdam, 1694) consists largely of dialogues between contemporary Belgian figures, though the first dialogue (where the passage Dryden complains of occurs) is between Lucian and Perrot d'Ablancourt.

[3] Johann Georg Graevius (1632–1703), German classical scholar, published an edition of Lucian in Amsterdam in 1687. On his edition and the others Fielding cites, see Hardin Craig, 'Dryden's Lucian', *Classical Philology*, 16 (1921), 141–63.

[4] Erasmus, whom Prof. Craig calls 'the greatest of all Lucianists' (p. 141), translated portions of Lucian's work into Latin in 1506 and imitated his manner in the *Colloquies* and the *Praise of Folly*.

[5] Nicolas Perrot d'Ablancourt (1606–64), whom Fielding quotes below, a celebrated French translator of the classics, published his version of Lucian in 1654.

[6] Jasper Mayne (1604–72) translated part of Lucian in 1638, although the work was not published until after the Restoration (Oxford, 1663).

[7] Cf. Dryden, who gives as evidence for Lucian's blameless life his having 'so honourable an Employment under *Marcus Aurelius*, an Emperour, as clear sighted, as he was truly vertuous' (*Works of Lucian*, i. 33); in his *Apology* Lucian defends his acceptance of a post in the administration of Egypt on the grounds that his salary came from the Emperor himself, not from a private person; see G. W. Bowersock, *Greek Sophists in the Roman Empire* (Oxford, 1969), pp. 114–15 n. Fielding's

Nor can I omit the Honour done him by some of the first Planters of Christianity, who embraced his Arguments and applied them with good Success against the Advocates for the Heathen Deities, who could not resist his Raillery. "For my Part," says Dryden, "I know not to whose Writings we owe more our Christianity, where the true God has succeeded a Multitude of false; whether to the grave Confutation of *Clemens Alexandrinus, Arnobius, Justin Martyr, St. Augustin, Lactantius,* &c. or to the facetious Wit of *Lucian*: A Wit which is thus described by Monsr. *D'Ablancourt.* 'Qui a par tout de la Mignardise & de l'Agreement avec une humeur gaye & enjouée, & cette *urbanité Attique* que nous appellerions en nôtre langue une railleriè fine & delicate,' "[1] &c.——In a Word, I conclude, that all who have a true Taste of Humour must read Lucian with the most exquisite Pleasure, and those who have not, will find no other Means so proper to acquire that Taste.

Such is the Author now proposed to be translated, I may truly say, to be first translated into our Language: For as to the two Attempts hitherto made,[2] tho' one of them hath Mr. Dryden's Name to the Preface (for indeed he translated but little himself) they can give the Reader no more Idea of the Spirit of Lucian, than the vilest Imitation by a Sign-post Painter can convey the Spirit of the excellent Hogarth.[3]

As to the Abilities of one of the Gentlemen who propose this Translation I shall be silent; I will only venture to say, that no Man seems so likely to

comment on the fitness of a 'Man of Humour' for 'Business of the gravest Kind' alludes both to the ridicule he suffered as a novelist/magistrate and also to a common complaint which he shared with the other writers involved in the Opposition to Walpole in the period 1722–42, that men of literary genius were considered by those in power to be unsuited for serious employment; see B. A. Goldgar, *Walpole and the Wits* (Lincoln, Nebr., 1976), ch. 1.

[1] *The Works of Lucian* (1711), i. 39, a passage which Dryden gives as the 'Words, or near them' of Jasper Mayne. Fielding quotes accurately down to the quotation from Perrot d'Ablancourt, which Dryden gives later (i. 41) in English, not in French; for that quotation Fielding apparently went to his copy of Perrot d'Ablancourt's edition of *Lucien* (Amsterdam, 1697; Baker, item 19). I have not seen the 1697 edition, but the quotation as he gives it appears in the edition of 1655 (I. sig. e 1ᵛ). The figures cited in the passage adapted by Dryden from Mayne are all early Christian apologists who attacked paganism: Clement of Alexandria (Titus Flavius Clemens), 3rd-cent. Father of the Church; Arnobius the Elder (d. *c.* 327), teacher of Lactantius; St Justin Martyr (d. *c.*165), a converted Platonist; and Lactantius Caelius (*c.*240–*c.*320), another writer who attacked pagan philosophy. Dryden had cited Tertullian, St Augustine, and St Chrysostom as making use of Lucian in their attacks on heathenism, but he called it 'an oblique Service, which *Lucian* never intended us' (*Works of Lucian*, i. 24); see Craig, 'Dryden's Lucian', p. 152.

[2] Besides the project of 1711 bearing Dryden's name, Fielding may be referring to a translation of part of Lucian's works by Jasper Mayne, cited above; or he may mean the fraudulent English version by Ferrand Spence of Perrot d'Ablancourt's translation, published in 1684 and viciously attacked by Dryden in his *Life of Lucian*. On the Dryden edition, cf. Booth in *Amelia* (VIII. v): 'I have seen a wretched one published by Mr. *Dryden*, but translated by others, who in many Places have misunderstood *Lucian's* Meaning, and have no where preserved the Spirit of the Original.' On the translators employed in this work, see Craig, 'Dryden's Lucian', pp. 154–63.

[3] Cf. Fielding's example of vanity in 'An Essay on Conversation', *Miscellanies* (1743): 'If . . . a Sign-Post Painter set himself above the inimitable *Hogarth*. . . .' On Fielding and Hogarth, see *CGJ* No. 6, above, p. 49 n. 1.

translate an Author well, as he who hath formed his Stile upon that very Author.[1] Nor shall I trespass upon the Modesty of a Gentleman greatly endow'd with that Virtue, by saying much of the other.[2] In this, I believe, I shall have the universal Concurrence of those learned Men of this Age to whom he is known, that no Man now alive is better versed in that Language in which the Wit of Lucian lies as yet concealed. I shall add, that I doubt not but the Public will find a Pleasure in shewing some Regard to two Gentlemen, who have hitherto in their several Capacities endeavoured to be serviceable to them, without deriving any great Emolument to themselves from their Labours.   C.

SATURDAY, JULY 4, 1752.   NUMB. 53.

Quid dignum tanto feret hic promissor hiatu?

HORACE.[3]

What will this Gascoon be able to perform after this PUFF?

TO THE
CENSOR of GREAT BRITAIN.

Sir,[4]

Your Predecessors in the Censorship[5] were used to celebrate the several extraordinary Personages who appeared in their Time; as I doubt not to find in yourself the same good Disposition, I here send you an Advertisement printed in the Daily Advertiser of Monday last;[6] the Author of which must, I think, be esteemed the most extraordinary Person whom any Age hath produced.

"Un François, Homme de Lettres, est arrivé de Paris a Londres, pour y enseigner le François, la Fable, la Poesie, la Blason, la Philosophie Françoise, le Latin, sans exiger aucune etude de son Disciple; l'etude etant un obstacle a sa Methode. S'il y a des Temperamens trop foibles pour les

---

[1] Fielding, of course, means himself. Cf. 'Orbilius' in the hostile *Examen of the History of Tom Jones* (1749): Lucian 'was as great a Scoffer, and as *true* an *Historian*, as Mr. F. himself' (chap. ii).

[2] William Young (1702?–57); from 1731 to 1740 curate of East Stour in Dorsetshire, Young was a long-time friend of Fielding's and the original of Parson Adams in *Joseph Andrews*. In addition to collaborating with Fielding on the translation of *Plutus* (1742), he edited the fourth edition of Ainsworth's *Dictionary of the Latin Tongue* (1752) and the third edition of Hederich's *Greek Lexicon* (1755); see Cross, i. 344–7; iii. 80–1.

[3] *Art of Poetry*, 138: 'What will this boaster produce in keeping with such mouthing?' (Loeb).

[4] This letter is clearly Fielding's; one scholar, however, offering no evidence, has claimed it for Murphy, despite the fact that Murphy included it in Fielding's *Works* of 1762 (John Pike Emery, *Arthur Murphy* [Philadelphia, 1946], p. 13).

[5] i.e. not only Addison and Steele but their classical predecessors; see General Introduction, above, p. xxxiv.

[6] *DA*, 29 June 1752 (No. 6701); Fielding has quoted the advertisement accurately, supplying only occasional accents because *DA* used none in printing material in French.

contraindre, des Caracteres trop vifs pour les fixer, des Personnes trop agees pour s'appliquer a l'etude, & qu'ils veuillent apprendre quelqu'une de ces Sciences sur une Methode si simple, plus courte, & plus solide que tout ce qui a precede; they are desired to enquire at Mr. Bezançon's Snuff-Shop in Little-Earl-Street, the Black Boy, by the Seven Dials."[1]

As it is possible that some of your Readers may not have yet conversed with this surprizing Master, I shall, for his and their Sakes, endeavour to render it in English.

Thus then it runs.

"A French Man, a Man of Learning, is arrived at London from Paris, in order to teach the French Language, Fables, Poetry, Heraldry, FRENCH PHILOSOPHY, and the Latin Tongue; *without exacting any Study from his Scholars*, ALL STUDY BEING AN OBSTACLE TO HIS METHOD. If there be any Constitutions too weak to bear Contradiction, any Characters too lively to be capable of Attention, any Persons too far advanced in Life to apply themselves to Study, and who are willing to learn any of the above Sciences, by a simple Method, and one shorter as well as more solid than any which hath been hitherto practised, they are desired to enquire," &c. *as above.*[2]

I must confess myself so ignorant, that till I read this wonderful Performance, I did not know there was a Philosophy which was peculiar to France, and that went under the Name of French Philosophy! Perhaps this is what is meant by the French Marquè in St. Evremont, when he says, *Premierement, J'aime la Guerre, après la Guerre Madame de* ———, *après Madame de* ——— *la Religion, après la Religion* LA PHILOSOPHIE.—*Voila ce que J'aime, Morbleu!*[3] "My first Passion is THE WAR, my second is MADAME de ———, my third is RELIGION, and my fourth Passion is PHILOSOPHY.—Now I have told you what my Passions are, d—n me!" In which Passage it seems pretty plain, that *la Philosophie* is no other than what the French likewise call *la Danse*; and then it will be plain that the Artist

[1] In the parish of St Giles-in-the-Fields, an open area from which seven streets (including Little Earl Street) radiated. It was a poverty-stricken, crime-ridden district, not particularly noted for occupancy by the French, who tended to live in the parish of St Anne, Soho.

[2] Advertisements offering instruction in French were commonplace; see e.g. notices in *LDA*, 29 Apr. and 12 May 1752 and a comment encouraging such instruction in the *Monthly Review*, 7 (1752), 317. In ridiculing this notice Fielding may, also, however, be hitting obliquely at Philip D'Halluin, founder of the upstart Public Register Office in competition with the Fieldings' own Register Office, who had begun in this calling himself and had composed a *Compendious English Grammar, Calculated for Foreigners* (1750). See the advertisements for the Public Register Office in *LDA*, 29 Apr. 1752 and *GA*, 24 Mar. 1752; see also General Introduction, above, p. xxv.

[3] Charles de Marguetel de Saint-Denis, Seigneur de Saint-Evremond (1610–1703), 'Conversation du Maréchal d'Hoquincourt avec le P. Canaye', *Oeuvres*, 5th edn. (Amsterdam, 1739), ii. 185. Fielding has misquoted the French original: 'J'ai aimé la Guerre devant toutes choses; Madame de Montbazon après la guerre; & tel que vous me voyez, la Philosophie après Madame de Montbazon.'

abovementioned is no other than a Dancing-Master, to whose *Method* of teaching I do readily agree *that Study is often a very deplorable Obstacle.*[1]

But this will by no Means solve all the Difficulties: For tho' Dancing will possibly make a Man a great Adept in *the French Philosophy*, how he will be able to dance into any English Science, or into the Latin Tongue, is somewhat hard to conceive. Perhaps, by French Philosophy, the Author means what is also called *l'industrie, ou l'art de voler bien les Poches,*[2] which I must beg to be excused from translating into our coarser Language; in barbarous French it may be called the Art of peeka de poka. But if this be his Meaning, I fancy he will be greatly deceived in his Views, since I believe it is impossible to find more able Masters than some of his Countrymen have already shewn themselves here in that Art. Nor do I believe, that Study or intense Application can be an Enemy to this Art, since I know several of the English who have plodded on all their Lives on this very Science, and have at last, by mere Dint of Study, become very great Proficients in it.

To say the Truth, I am inclined to think, that by la Philosophie Françoise, is meant no other than *la bonne assurance*; that Assurance, which the French alone call good, and which it is very probable, they alone may call Philosophy.[3]

And this I the rather conclude to be the Undertaker's Meaning, as it is certain, that to the making any considerable Progress in this French Philosophy, Study is of all Things the greatest Obstacle. I have indeed observed in a late Paper,[4] that no Man of Learning was ever a Proficient in this Art. I must further observe, that the Disciples which our Master seems to have principally chosen, such, I mean, as can bear no Contradiction, such as are incapable of any Attention, and such aged Persons who are willing, all at once, without any Labour, to leap, as it were, into Science, are all excellently adapted to receive the strongest and most immediate Impressions of this Philosophy.

Nor can I help observing, which is a further Confirmation of my Opinion,

[1] The reference to the 'Dancing-Master', with its suggestion of 'Frenchified' foppery, is typical of the considerable anti-French satire of the period in Fielding, Hogarth, and countless others; at this point feelings against all things French were intensified by the recently concluded War of the Austrian Succession. On the hostility to French immigrants in particular, see M. D. George, *London Life in the Eighteenth Century* (1925), pp. 133–4, 360–1.

[2] i.e. 'l'industrie' as in 'Chevalier d'Industrie', a crook or swindler, from which term the English equivalent 'Knight of Industry' was derived. Fielding's association of the French with pickpockets was not commonly made, the usual view being that '*France* and *Italy* supply this Town with *Cooks, Catcalls*, and *Valets de Chambres*' (*A Ramble through London* [1738], p. 1).

[3] Cf. Fielding's *Love in Several Masques* (1728): 'For, be assured, widows are a study you will never be any proficient in, till you are initiated into that modern science which the French call *le bon assurance*' (IV. ix); cf. also a discussion in *Jonathan Wild* of 'that assurance to which the French very properly annex the epithet of good' (II. viii). On the identity of meaning between 'Assurance' and 'Impudence', see *Some Remarks on the Life and Writings of Dr. J— H—* (1752), pp. 57–8.

[4] *CGJ* No. 48, on Impudence.

how nobly our Artist hath contrived to convince the World of his Fitness for the Task he hath undertaken. I defy the Ingenuity of Man to invent a better Method of conveying to the Public in so few Lines, an Idea of a Capacity for any Undertaking whatever, than this astonishing Frenchman hath made Use of to shew this Nation how well qualified he is to teach them the French Philosophy, or the Good Assurance. I will not venture to prophesy what Success may attend so new and so extraordinary a Proposal. This, however, I cannot avoid remarking, that it seems to indicate what Opinion of the Understandings of the good People of this Island at present prevails among the French Philosophers abroad. I am well convinced, it would be extremely difficult to persuade the greatest Adept in the Good Assurance which this Kingdom ever produced, to expect any Success from such a Proposal even among the Hottentots,[1] if he could make himself enough understood to publish his Scheme among them.

I am, Sir,

Your most humble Servant,
ANTIGALLICUS.[2]

Sir Alexander having lately given some Hints of an Intention to resign his Office of Censor of Great Britain, on Account of his great Age; which Hints of his have, it seems, got abroad into the Public, the *whole Town* Yesterday waited upon his Censorial Dignity; when Counsellor ENGLAND, an elder Brother of that Major ENGLAND who was formerly celebrated in a Paper called THE INSPECTOR, made a most pathetic Oration, as well in his own Name, as in that of the *said whole Town*, humbly beseeching his Dignity to continue still in his said Office.[3] Mr. *England* concluded his Speech in the following Words. "Give us Leave, therefore, Sir, to hope that you will be graciously pleased to persevere in bestowing upon us your inestimable Papers, and that you will not withdraw from the Town its only remaining Ray of Light. It is you, Sir, who have so nobly stood in the Breach, and have alone defended the Cause of Wit, against the Incursion of an Army of

---

[1] See *CGJ* No. 9, above, p. 67 n. 3.

[2] The pseudonym is generic, but cf. 'The Laudable Association of Anti-Gallicans' which flourished in these years to oppose all things French, even 'the Cambrick Ruffles of a refractory Brother' which were cut off 'from a true Spirit of Patriotism' (*DA*, 19 Nov. 1751); see also *GA*, 31 Mar., and 16, 24 Apr. 1752.

[3] Fielding parodies here the character Major England, whom John Hill had introduced as a personal champion into his 'Inspector' column in *LDA* on 3 Apr. 1752. Fielding also emphasizes the phrase *whole Town* to ridicule Hill's response to a critic who claimed the town had turned against him because of his quarrel at Ranelagh with Mountefort Brown: '*If this Gentleman speaks as he hears, I am afraid we are to divide the Public . . . into two Towns on this Occasion*' (*LDA*, 26 May 1752); in *LDA* for 10 June Hill develops the theme by describing the two towns as 'upper' (people of understanding) and 'lower' (a worthless and frivolous group who consider themselves the 'town'). On Fielding's relations with Hill and on the Hill–Brown affair, see General Introduction, above, pp. xxxvii–xxxix; *CGJ* No. 60; and the 'Covent Garden' column of 11 May 1752, below, Appendix I.

Vandals,[1] who still threaten this glorious Cause with Destruction, and who, had not you opposed them, had long since accomplished their fatal Purpose.

"Persevere, therefore, great Sir, in an Undertaking which must be attended with such immortal Honour to yourself, and in which you must see daily greater Reason to hope for a final Success. The Wise and Good have been always your Friends; but at present, many who have little Title to these Epithets, and who were formerly suspected of favouring the Enemy, seem fully convinced of their Errors, and begin to join in your Applause. Indeed it scarce deserves the Name of Prophecy, to declare, that before another Winter is over, there is not a Man in this Kingdom who will not be your Friend; or if there should, he will be but little a Friend to himself if he owns the contrary."

The Censor, after some short Deliberation, answered. "This affectionate Address of the whole Town is very agreeable to me. I shall endeavour to deserve that Opinion which they are pleased to entertain of me; and to oblige them, and at their particular Request and Entreaty, I will continue to carry on this Paper once in every Week for the future, that is to say, on every Saturday. Nor do I doubt but that the Loss of one Half of my Papers will be amply recompensed to my good Readers by the superior Excellence of the other."[2]

Then the whole Town had the Honour of a gracious Smile from his Dignity, which infused into every Countenance the most universal Satisfaction. A.

SATURDAY, JULY 11, 1752. NUMB. 54.

——*His Juventus orta parentibus.*
Infecit Æquor sanguine Punico.

HORACE.[3]

---

[1] See 'Journal of the Present Paper War' in *CGJ* Nos. 1, 2, 3, and 4.

[2] In his move to weekly publication Fielding puts as good a face on the matter as he can. A notice printed in the original number at the end of this column indicates that no advertisements will be accepted under the price of 3 shillings, 'it being the Intention of the Proprietors always to confine their Number to very few'; in fact, however, the last two numbers had carried no advertisements at all except those for the Universal Register Office and for Fielding's own works, nor does this current number. See General Introduction, above, p. li. Hill, provoked perhaps by the ridicule of him here, returned to the topic of Fielding after a long silence and gloated good-naturedly on the shift to weekly publication: 'The *Censor* staggers on his new erected Throne; and, Darius-like, has given up one half of his Kingdom to secure the other' (*LDA*, 7 July 1752).

[3] *Odes*, III. vi. 33–4: '[Not] such the sires of whom were sprung the youth that dyed the sea with Punic blood' (Loeb). Fielding omits *Non* at the beginning of the quotation so as to adapt Horace's line to his own purpose. The ode mourns the degeneration of Rome from a more heroic past; Fielding's strategy involves a similar contrast, enabling him to depict an idealized Elizabethan age, in which there were virtually no beggars, or adulterous court ladies, and in which Members of Parliament served out of a sense of public duty. On the Lucianic qualities of the dialogue, see Miller, *Essays*, p. 367; it was

Such were the Heroes of that glorious Reign
That humbled to the Dust the Pride of Spain.

Mr. Censor,

You have formerly entertained the Public, by representing to them the Opinions which Posterity will be supposed to conceive of the present Age;[1] you will possibly furnish no less Amusement to your Readers, by casting your Eyes backwards into our Annals, as the Manners of their Ancestors will, I apprehend, appear no less strange to the present Age, than the History of these our Times can be thought hereafter.

After this short Introduction, I shall present you with a curious Dialogue which seems to have been written towards the End of the Reign of Queen Elizabeth. I have taken the Liberty to modernize the Language without doing the least Violence to the Sentiments of the Original.

A Dialogue between Mr. English, *Madam* English, *Miss Biddy* English, *and* Mistress Plumtree *the Mistress of the House.*

Mrs. Plum. I hope your Ladyship is very well this Morning after the Fatigue of your Journey.

Mad. Eng. Indeed, Mistress Plumtree, I never was more fatigued in my Life. Four Days together upon a hard trotting Horse are enough to tire any one; besides my Pillion was horridly uneasy, and I rode behind the Footboy, who was hardly able to support my leaning against him; but here's Biddy not in the least the worse for her Journey.

Miss Biddy. Upon my Word, Mamma, I never was in better Spirits in my Life. My Ride hath given me an Appetite; I have eat above half a Pound of Beef Steaks this Morning for Breakfast.

Mrs. Eng. I could have gone through any thing at your Age, my Dear, tho' I was never many Miles from home before I was married. The young Ladies have more Liberty in these Days, than they had formerly. Indeed it was entirely owing to your Father's Goodness that you came to London now.

Mrs. Plum. O Madam, I am sure your Ladyship would not have left Miss in the Country. It would have been barbarous not to have let her see the Tower, and the Abby, and Bedlam, and two or three Plays.

Mrs. Eng. Fie, Mrs. Plumtree! with what are you filling the Child's Head? One Play she is to see and no more. The Terms are all settled. One Play, One new Gown, and One Ruff. But now I mention these things, Pray, Mrs. Plumtree, what is become of the Mantua-maker I employed last Parliament when I was here?

reprinted, with no acknowledgment of source, in the *Ladies Magazine*, iii. 326–7 (Aug. 22–Sept. 16, 1752).

[1] In *CGJ* Nos. 12 and 17.

Mrs. Plum. Alas, poor Woman, she is dead; but I can recommend your Ladyship to another, one of the best in all London; she makes Gowns for the Lady Mayoress herself.

Mrs. Eng. I shall be obliged to you, good Mrs. Plumtree, to send for her to Day, for I have three Visits to make in London, and I shall like to do it in my new Cloaths.——O, Sir John, are you come at last? Dinner hath stayed for you 'till I suppose it is spoiled. It is almost two o'Clock.

Mr. Eng. The House is but just up, my Dear. We sate very late to Day. I assure you I was invited very much to dine with one of our Knights of the Shire at his Lodgings; he had a Haunch of Venison, a fat Goose, and an Apple-Pye for Dinner,——and all this I left for your Company.

Mrs. Eng. Well, Sir John, I do not blame you; but Parliament Hours are very dreadful things.

Mr. Eng. We must suffer some Inconveniencies for the Good of our Country, and we are employed upon a Scheme now that is of the utmost Consequence to the Nation. We are going to make such a Provision for the Poor that there will never be another Beggar in the Kingdom.*[1]

Mrs. Plum. I am heartily glad of that; and I am sure it is high Time, for it was no longer ago than last Summer that I saw two poor Wretches, in one Day, actually begging in the open Street.

Mr. Eng. Well Dame, and how doth my good Friend Master Plumtree hold it? We shall have another Game at Lantry Loo.[2]

Mrs. Plum. Indeed Sir John, you are too hard for my Husband. You won above ten Shillings of him last Parliament.

Mr. Eng. Your Family is not hurt by it: for I believe you are as much in my Debt on the same Account; but I beg you will not encourage this Girl to play! for she is too much inclined to Idleness.

Miss Biddy. Nay, Mamma, I am sure I never desire to play but in the Christmas Holidays.

Mrs. Plum. O, Madam, Miss will have something else to think on. Here is a young 'Squire that lodges in our Neighbourhood. A fine hardy young Spark. There are but few they tell me, that can either run or wrestle with him, and Heir to a noble Estate he is.

(At these Words Miss Biddy blushed extremely.)

* By this Passage it is supposed this Dialogue happened in the 43d Year of Queen Elizabeth, when the famous Statute was made for providing for the Poor; and which is the Corner-Stone of all our excellent Poor Laws.

[1] To understand Fielding's irony here and in his note, see his *Enquiry into the Causes of the late Increase of Robbers* (1751), sect. IV, where he discusses the 'nasty and scandalous Condition' of the poor and the problems arising from the laws intended to provide for them. On the Elizabethan poor law (43 Eliz., c. 2) specifically, see *Enquiry*, pp. 32–8, and Malvin R. Zirker, Jr., *Fielding's Social Pamphlets* (Berkeley and Los Angeles, 1966), pp. 11–15. See also *CGJ* Nos. 11, 36, and 44.

[2] i.e. Lanterloo, an older form of the card-game Loo.

Mr. Eng. Well let him look to it. Biddy won't turn her Back to him. But my Dear, I have a Show for you. The Queen goes to the Parliament House tomorrow; and there will be all the fine Lords and Ladies of the Court. I have hired a Balcony and my little Biddy shall go too.

Mrs. Eng. You see Biddy, how good your Papa is; and now, I hope you will be satisfied, and not desire to go out any more, except to one Play and to Church, whilst you stay in London. I am sure he is so liberal, he will be forced to send up for the other Twenty Pound.

Mr. Eng. Never mind that, my Dear! your Prudence in the Country will soon make it up. But now I talk of Court Ladies, I have a Piece of News for you. Indeed I can hardly believe it myself, and yet I was told it by a very great Person.

Mrs. Eng. What can it be, my Dear, that you introduce with all this Preface?

Mrs. Plum. I hope there are no more Spanish Armadas coming.

Mr. Eng. No, no, nothing of that Kind.——In short, it is so strange a thing, I scarce know how to mention it.——But, can you think it? they say there is a Court Lady that hath made a Cuckold of her Husband——A Woman of very great Quality I assure you.[1]

Mrs. Eng. This is strange News indeed, and impossible to be true.

Mr. Eng. Hardly impossible, my Dear, such things have been in Nature.——

Mrs. Eng. And what is become of the Lady pray?

Mr. Eng.. Why she is at Court still.

Mrs. Eng. Then it is impossible to be true; for if I could believe there was one such Woman of Quality, I am well convinced there are no other that would own her.

Mr. Eng. I only tell you what I hear.——But come, Dame Plumtree, is not your Dinner ready?——Upon my Word, I have been half starved. My Constituents shall find out some other to serve them in the next Parliament. It is a hard Duty, Mrs. Plumtree, and a very expensive one too. I never come up myself under twenty Pound, and if my Wife comes with me, the Expence is almost double.

Mrs. Plum. Well, Sir——but you know all Men must serve their Country.

Mr. Eng. Yes, Madam, and if all would, the Burthen would be less severe; but I have discovered a most wicked Corruption in the Borough, I serve for.——There are three Gentlemen in the Neighbourhood who have as good Estates as I have, and yet because they entertain the Mayor and Aldermen with more Strong Drink than I do, they have never once attempted to chuse them. The Moment there is but a Discourse of an

---

[1] As Jensen suggests (ii. 245), Fielding may be referring to Lady Vane (see *CGJ* No. 2, above, p. 23 n. 3), but the reference is probably general.

Election, to Toping they go.——So that they are sure of always escaping, and I am likely to serve my Country as long as I live.[1]

Mrs. Plum. It is very hard, I must confess, 'Squire, but then you will consider you have all the Honour.——However, Sir, Dinner is upon the Table at present.

Mr. Eng. Lead on then, my Dame, and I will shew you what a Stomach I have got in the Service of my Country.   A.

SATURDAY, JULY 18, 1752.   NUMB. 55.

———*Juvat integros accedere Fontes*
Atque haurire——.

LUCRETIUS.[2]

———*It is pleasant to handle*
An untouched Subject.

It hath been observed, that Characters of Humour do abound more in this our Island, than in any other Country; and this hath been commonly supposed to arise from that pure and perfect State of Liberty which we enjoy in a degree greatly superior to every foreign Nation.[3]

This Opinion, I know, hath great Sanction, and yet I am inclined to suspect the Truth of it, unless we will extend the Meaning of the Word Liberty, farther than I think it hath been yet carried, and will include in it not only an Exemption from all Restraint of municipal Laws, but likewise from

---

[1] Cf. *CGJ* No. 35, where Fielding ironically argues that one advantage of abolishing money would be to abolish corruptions in elections, so that the struggle would be 'not who shall serve their Country . . . but who shall be excused from serving it'. The 'wicked Corruption' here is similarly ironic, since it involves escaping from service rather than bribing one's way into Parliament, the usual theme of satires on corrupt electioneering such as Fielding's *Don Quixote in England* (1734) and *Pasquin* (1736). On Fielding's consistently held ideal of public service for the common good, see *CGJ* No. 2, above, p. 25 and n. 1.

[2] *De rerum natura*, i. 927–8: 'I love to approach virgin springs and there to drink' (Loeb); Lucretius is exhorting his readers to listen as he explains obscure matters by the charm of his verse.

[3] The *locus classicus* for the view of humor as specifically English, arising from the degree of English liberty, is Sir William Temple's essay 'Of Poetry', in *Miscellanea*, 2nd part, 3rd edn. (1692), pp. 356–8; Fielding owned this volume (Baker, item 487), but by his day the idea had become a commonplace. In addition to Congreve, whom he cites below, see also Steele's *Guardian*, No. 144 (26 Aug. 1713) and Corbyn Morris, *An Essay toward Fixing the True Standards of Wit, Humour, Raillery, Satire, and Ridicule* (1744), both of which follow the view established by Temple. For a foreigner's understandable irritation at the English claim to sole ownership of humor, see Abbé Jean Le Blanc's *Lettres d'un François* (The Hague, 1745), i. 84–5 (Letter XI), and cf. Swift's skepticism about this part of Temple's argument in his essay on Gay, *Intelligencer*, No. 3 (1728).
In what follows, Fielding takes a very different line from the usually favorable view of 'humour' traditional by mid-century, reverting to an earlier, Jonsonian sense of the term and attaching to it a stigma it had largely lost since the Restoration, when it could signify a dangerous individualism. On the history of the word and its changing meanings, see Stuart Tave, *The Amiable Humorist* (Chicago, 1960), pp. 91–118, and Edward N. Hooker, 'Humour in the Age of Pope', *HLQ* 11 (1948), 361–85. See also Fielding's comments in *CGJ* Nos. 19 and 56.

all Restraint of those Rules of Behaviour which are expressed in the general Term of good Breeding.[1] Laws which, tho' not written, are perhaps better understood, and tho' established by no coercive Power, much better obeyed within the Circle where they are received, than any of those Laws which are recorded in Books, or enforced by public Authority.

A perfect Freedom from these Laws, if I am not greatly mistaken, is absolutely necessary to form the true Character of Humour; a Character which is therefore not to be met with among those People who conduct themselves by the Rules of good Breeding.

For indeed good Breeding is little more than the Art of rooting out all those Seeds of Humour which Nature had originally implanted in our Minds.

To make this evident it seems necessary only to explain the Terms, a Matter in which I do not see the great Difficulty which hath appeared to other Writers.

Some of these have spoken of the Word Humour, as if it contained in it some Mystery impossible to be revealed, and no one, as I know of, hath undertaken to shew us expressly what it is, tho' I scarce doubt but it was amply done by Aristotle in his Treatise on Comedy, which is unhappily lost.[2]

But what is more surprizing, is, that we find it pretty well explained in Authors who at the same Time tell us, they know not what it is. Mr. Congreve, in a Letter to Mr. Dennis, hath these Words. *We cannot certainly tell what Wit is, or what Humour is*, and within a few Lines afterwards he says, *There is great Difference between a Comedy wherein there are many things humorously, as they call it, which is pleasantly spoken; and one where there are several Characters of Humour, distinguished by the particular and different Humours appropriated to the several Persons represented, and which naturally arise from the different Constitutions, Complexions, and Dispositions of Men.* And again *I take Humour to be a singular and unavoidable Manner of saying or doing any thing peculiar and natural to one Man only; by which his Speech and Actions are distinguished from those of other Men. Our Humour hath Relation to us, and to what proceeds from us, as the Accidents have to a Substance; it is a Colour, Taste, and Smell diffused through all; tho' our Actions are ever so many, and different in Form, they are all Splinters of the same Wood, and have naturally one Complexion,* &c.[3]

---

[1] On Fielding's current concern with the misuse of the term 'Liberty', see *CGJ* No. 2, above, p. 22 n. 1, and General Introduction, above, p. xl; on 'Good Breeding', see *CGJ* No. 56, 'An Essay on Conversation' in *Miscellanies* (1743), and General Introduction, above, pp. xlii–xliii.

[2] A reference to the lost second book of the *Poetics*, which would presumably have included a section on comedy to balance that on tragedy, as suggested by *Poetics*, VI. i (1449 b. 21); see *Poetics*, ed. D. W. Lucas (Oxford, 1968), p. xiv.

[3] Fielding quotes, with considerable accuracy, from separate passages in Congreve's *Essay concerning Humour in Comedy* in *The Select Works of Mr. John Dennis* (1718), ii. 515, 521; this edition was in Fielding's library (Baker, item 532).

If my Reader hath any doubt whether this is a just Description of Humour, let him compare it with those Examples of humorous Characters which the greatest Masters have given us, and which have been universally acknowledged as such, and he will be perhaps convinced.

Ben Johnson, after complaining of the Abuse of the Word, proceeds thus,

> Why Humour (as 'tis Ens) we thus define it,
> To be a Quality of Air, or Water,
> And in itself holds these two Properties,
> Moisture and Fluxure; as for Demonstration,
> Pour Water on this Floor, 'twill wet and run;
> Likewise the Air forc'd thro' a Horn or Trumpet
> Flows instantly away, and leaves behind
> A kind of Dew; and hence we do conclude,
> That whatsoe'er hath Fluxure and Humidity,
> As wanting Power to contain itself,
> Is Humour. So in every human Body,
> The Choler, Melancholy, Phlegm and Blood,
> By Reason that they flow continually
> In some one Part, and are not continent,
> Receive the Name of *Humours*. "Now thus far
> It may, by Metaphor, apply itself
> Unto the general Disposition:
> As when some one peculiar Quality
> Doth so possess a Man, that it doth draw
> All his Effects, his Spirits, and his Powers,
> In their Confluxions all to run one Way,"
> *This may be truly said to be a Humour.*
> But that a Rook by wearing a py'd Feather,
> The Cable Hatband, or the three piled Ruff,
> A Yard of Shoe-tie, or the Switzer's Knot
> On his French Garters should affect a Humour!
> O! it is more than most ridiculous.[1]

This Passage is in the first Act of *Every Man out of his Humour*, and I question not but to some Readers, the Author will appear to have been *out of his Wits* when he wrote it; but others I am positive will discern much excellent Ore shining among the Rubbish. In Truth his Sentiment when let loose from that stiff Boddice in which it is laced, will amount to this, that as the Term Humour contains in it the Ideas of Moisture and Fluxure, it was

---

[1] From the Induction to *Every Man out of his Humour*, ll. 88–114; the quotation marks setting off six lines appear to be Fielding's own 'gnomic pointing' for emphasis, since they appear in no printed texts of the play, which was not acted in the 18th cent.

applied to certain moist and flux Habits of the Body, and afterwards metaphorically to peculiar Qualities of the Mind, which when they are extremely prevalent, do, like the predominant Humours of the Body, flow all to one Part, and as the latter are known to absorb and drain off all the corporeal Juices and Strength to themselves, so the former are no less certain of engaging the Affections, Spirits, and Powers of the Mind, and of enlisting them as it were, into their own Service, and under their own absolute Command.

Here then we have another pretty adequate Notion of Humour, which is indeed nothing more than a violent Bent or Disposition of the Mind to some particular Point. To enumerate indeed these several Dispositions would be, as Mr. Congreve observes, as endless as to sum up the several Opinions of Men; nay, as he well says, the *Quot homines tot sententiæ* may be more properly interpreted of their Humours, than their Opinions.[1]

Hitherto there is no Mention of the Ridiculous, the Idea of which, tho' not essential to Humour, is always included in our Notions of it.[2] The Ridiculous is annexed to it these two ways, either by the Manner or the Degree in which it is exerted.

By either of these the very best and worthiest Disposition of the Human Mind may become ridiculous. Excess, says Horace, even in the Pursuit of Virtue, will lead a wise and good Man into Folly and Vice.———[3] So will it subject him to Ridicule; for into this, says the judicious Abbé Bellegarde, a Man may tumble headlong with an excellent Understanding, and with the most laudable Qualities.[4] Piety, Patriotism, Loyalty, Parental Affection, &c. have all afforded Characters of Humour for the Stage.

By the Manner of exerting itself likewise a Humour becomes ridiculous. By this Means chiefly the Tragic Humour differs from the Comic; it is the same Ambition which raises our Horror in Macbeth, and our Laughter at the drunken Sailors in the Tempest; the same Avarice which causes the dreadful Incidents in the Fatal Curiosity of Lillo, and in the Miser of Moliere;[5] the same Jealousy which forms an Othello, or a Suspicious

---

[1] *Select Works of Dennis*, ii. 515. Congreve quotes the phrase *quot homines tot sententiae* ('so many men, so many minds') from Terrence, *Phormio*, 454.

[2] Cf. Fielding's Preface to *Joseph Andrews*, where he traces the Ridiculous to affectation arising from vanity or hypocrisy, but makes no mention of the conflict between humor and good-breeding. In that discussion, as here, Fielding cites Bellegarde and pays tribute to Jonson.

[3] *Epistles*, i. vi, 15–16: 'Let the wise man bear the name of madman, the just of unjust, should he pursue Virtue herself beyond due bounds' (Loeb).

[4] Jean Baptiste Morvan de Bellegarde (1648–1734), *Reflexions sur le ridicule, et sur les moyens de l'eviter*, 10th edn. (Amsterdam, 1712), p. 1, cited also in *CGJ* Nos. 56 and 60. Cf. *Champion* for 15 Mar. 1739/40.

[5] George Lillo's play was first performed by Fielding's company at the Haymarket on 27 May 1736, with a prologue by Fielding. On Fielding's friendship with Lillo (1693–1739) and his respect for *The Fatal Curiosity*, see the comments by Thomas Davies in his edition of *The Works of Mr. George Lillo*

Husband.[1] No Passion or Humour of the Mind is absolutely either Tragic or Comic in itself. Nero had the Art of making Vanity the Object of Horror; and Domitian, in one Instance, at least, made Cruelty ridiculous.[2]

As these Tragic Modes however never enter into our Notion of Humour, I will venture to make a small Addition to the Sentiments of the two great Masters I have mentioned, by which I apprehend my Description of Humour will pretty well coincide with the general Opinion. By Humour, then I suppose, is generally intended a violent Impulse of the Mind, determining it so some one peculiar Point, by which a Man becomes ridiculously distinguished from all other Men.

If there be any Truth in what I have now said, nothing can more clearly follow than the manifest Repugnancy between Humour and good Breeding. The latter being the Art of conducting yourself by certain common and general Rules, by which Means, if they were universally observed, the whole World would appear (as all Courtiers actually do) to be, in their external Behaviour at least, but one and the same Person.[3]

I have not room at present, if I were able, to enumerate the Rules of good Breeding: I shall only mention one, which is a Summary of them all. This is the most golden of all Rules, no less than that *of doing to all Men as you would they should do unto you.*[4]

In the Deviation from this Law, as I hope to evince in my next, all that we call Humour principally consists. I shall at the same Time, I think, be able to shew, that it is to this Deviation we owe the general Character mentioned in the Beginning of this Paper, as well as to assign the Reasons why we of this Nation have been capable of attracting to ourselves such Merit in Preference to others.   A.

(1775), i, pp. xv–xvi, and Fielding's eulogy of Lillo in the *Champion* for 26 Feb. 1739/40. Molière's *L'Avare* was adapted by Fielding as *The Miser* (1733).

[1] *The Suspicious Husband* (1747), a comedy on the theme of jealousy, was by Benjamin Hoadly (1706–57), a physician and the son of the theologian Benjamin Hoadly, Bishop of Winchester. Both the younger Benjamin and his brother John (1711–76), a clergyman and also a playwright, were subscribers to Fielding's *Miscellanies* (1743).

[2] For examples of Nero's vanity (especially over his skill in the arts) resulting in horror, see Suetonius, *Nero, passim*; cf. Fielding's use of Nero to illustrate the misapplication of the ridiculous, in the preface to *Joseph Andrews* and in *JJ* No. 17, 26 Mar. 1748. On Domitian's 'ingenious Employment of Fly-spitting', see *CGJ* No. 24.

[3] In contrast to this view, cf. Shaftesbury, for whom the 'rallying humour', liberty, and good-breeding are thoroughly compatible: 'All politeness is owing to liberty. We polish one another, and rub off our corners and rough sides by a sort of amicable collision. To restrain this is inevitably to bring a rust upon men's understandings. 'Tis a destroying of civility, good breeding, and even charity itself, under pretence of maintaining it.' (*An Essay on the Freedom of Wit and Humour* [1709], in *Characteristics*, ed. J. M. Robertson [1900], i. 46.)

[4] Matthew 7: 12; Luke 6: 31. Fielding makes the same identification of good-breeding with the Golden Rule in his 'Essay on Conversation', *Miscellanies* (1743). For examples of his ridicule of false notions of good-breeding, see *Love in Several Masques* (1728), III. vi., and *Champion*, 19 Aug. 1740. On the concept of good-breeding, see General Introduction, above, pp. xlii–xliii.

SATURDAY, JULY 25, 1752.   NUMB. 56.

Hoc Fonte derivata.   HORACE.[1]

These are the Sources.

At the Conclusion of my last Paper, I asserted that the Summary of Good Breeding was no other than that comprehensive and exalted Rule, which the greatest Authority hath told us is the Sum Total of all Religion and all Morality.[2]

Here, however, my Readers will be pleased to observe that the subject Matter of good Breeding being only what is called Behaviour, it is this only to which we are to apply it on the present Occasion. Perhaps therefore we shall be better understood if we vary the Word, and read it thus: *Behave unto all Men, as you would they should behave unto you.*

This will most certainly oblige us to treat all Mankind with the utmost Civility and Respect, there being nothing which we desire more than to be treated so by them. This will most effectually restrain the Indulgence of all those violent and inordinate Desires, which, as we have endeavoured to shew, are the true Seeds of Humour in the Human Mind: the Growth of which Good Breeding will be sure to obstruct; or will at least so over-top and shadow, that they shall not appear. The Ambitious, the Covetous, the Proud, the Vain, the Angry, the Debauchee, the Glutton, are all lost in the Character of the Well-Bred Man; or if Nature should now and then venture to peep forth, she withdraws in an Instant, and doth not shew enough of herself to become ridiculous.

Now Humour arises from the very opposite Behaviour, from throwing the Reins on the Neck of our favorite Passion, and giving it a full Scope and Indulgence.[3] The ingenious Abbé, whom I quoted in my former Paper, paints this admirably in the Characters of Ill-Breeding, which he mentions as the very first Scene of the Ridiculous. "Ill-Breeding (L'Impolitesse)" says he, "is not a single Defect, it is the Result of many. It is sometimes a gross Ignorance of Decorum, or a stupid Indolence, which prevents us from *giving to others what is due to them.* It is a peevish Malignity which inclines us to oppose the Inclinations of those with whom we converse. It is the

---

[1] *Odes*, III. vi. 19; the entire passage is relevant to Fielding's essay: 'Sprung from this source, disaster's stream has overflowed the folk and fatherland' (Loeb).

[2] The reference is to Jesus and the Golden Rule; see the discussion of good-breeding and humor in *CGJ* No. 55, above.

[3] Fielding's phrasing suggests the familiar theory of the 'ruling passion' to explain human behavior, a theory given particular prominence in Pope's *Epistle to Cobham* (1734) and Epistle II of the *Essay on Man* (1733–4). Cf. Booth's exposition of the doctrine in *Amelia* (I. iii; VIII. x); for neither Fielding nor Pope, however, did the theory lead to the fatalistic conclusions drawn by Booth. See also *Champion*, 1 July 1740. For the background of the idea, and for its connection with the psychology of the humors, see B. A. Goldgar, 'Pope's Theory of the Passions', *PQ* 41 (1962), 730–43.

Consequence of a foolish Vanity, which hath no Complaisance for any other Person: *The Effect of a proud and whimsical Humour, which soars above all the Rules of Civility*; or, lastly, it is produced by a melancholly Turn of Mind, which pampers itself *(qui trouve du Ragoût)* with a rude and disobliging Behaviour."[1]

Having thus shewn, I think very clearly, that Good Breeding is, and must be, the very Bane of the Ridiculous, that is to say, of all humorous Characters; it will perhaps be no difficult Task to discover why this Character hath been in a singular Manner attributed to this Nation.[2]

For this I shall assign two Reasons only, as these seem to me abundantly satisfactory, and adequate to the Purpose.

The first is that Method so general in this Kingdom of giving no Education to the Youth of both Sexes; I say general only, for it is not without some few Exceptions.[3]

Much the greater Part of our Lads of Fashion return from School at fifteen or sixteen, very little wiser, and not at all the better for having been sent thither. Part of these return to the Place from whence they came, their Fathers Country Seats; where Racing, Cock-fighting, Hunting, and other rural Sports, with Smoaking, Drinking, and Party become their Pursuit, and form the whole Business and Amusement of their future Lives. The other Part escape to Town in the Diversions, Fashions, Follies and Vices of which they are immediately initiated. In this Academy some finish their Studies, while others by their wiser Parents are sent abroad to add the Knowledge of the Diversions, Fashions, Follies, and Vices of all Europe, to that of those of their own Country.[4]

Hence then we are to derive two great general Characters of Humour, which are the Clown and the Coxcomb, and both of these will be almost infinitely diversified according to the different Passions and natural Dispositions of each Individual; and according to their different Walks in Life. Great will be the Difference; for Instance, whether the Country Gentleman be a Whig or a Tory, whether he prefers Women, Drink, or

---

[1] Abbé Bellegarde, *Reflexions sur le ridicule*, 10th edn. (Amsterdam, 1712), p. 4; see *CGJ* Nos. 55 and 60. Fielding translates accurately, with the italicized passages representing his own emphasis.

[2] By Temple, Congreve, Steele, and others; see *CGJ* No. 55, above, p. 297 n. 3. Fielding seeks here to offer some explanation other than 'English liberty' for the prevalence of humor in Britain.

[3] On the subject of education see also *CGJ* Nos. 34, 42, and 48, where Fielding treats it with some irony; *JJ* No. 22 (30 Apr. 1748), where it is given a political turn; and *Champion*, 10 June 1740, where he makes ironic recommendations for a new educational system. See also *CGJ* No. 66, on the power of habit in forming our characters. On his general attitude toward the value of education see Miller, *Essays*, pp. 218–20, and C. R. Kropf, 'Educational Theory and Human Nature in Fielding's Works', *PMLA* 89 (1974), 113–19. Contemporary critiques of the deficiencies of a modern education are too numerous to cite, but for two attacks typical of the genre, see the essay by Fielding's friend Thomas Cooke, *Pythagoras, an Ode. to which are Prefixed Observations on Taste and on Education* (1752), and an article signed 'Britannicus' in the *Craftsman*, 22 Aug. 1752.

[4] A conventional comment on the Grand Tour; cf. Pope, *Dunciad* (1743), iv. 293–326.

Dogs; so will it be whether the Town Spark be allotted to serve his Country as a Politician, a Courtier, a Soldier, a Sailor, or possibly a Churchman, (for by Draughts[1] from this Academy, all these Offices are supplied); or lastly whether his Ambition shall be contented with no other Appellation than merely that of a Beau.

Some of our Lads however, are destined to a further Progress in Learning; these are not only confined longer to the Labours of a School, but are sent thence to the University. Here if they please, they may read on, and if they please they may (as most of them do) let it alone, and betake themselves as their Fancy leads, to the Imitation of their elder Brothers either in Town or Country.

This is a Matter which I shall handle very tenderly, as I am clearly of an Opinion that an University Education is much the best we have; for here at least there is some Restraint laid on the Inclinations of our Youth.[2] The Sportsman, the Gamester, and the Sot, cannot give such a Loose to their Extravagance, as if they were at home and under no manner of Government; nor can our Spark who is disposed to the Town Pleasures, find either Gaming-houses or Play-houses, nor half the Taverns or Bawdy-houses which are ready to receive him in Covent-Garden.

So far however I hope I may say without Offence, that among all the Schools at the Universities, there is none where the Science of Good-Breeding is taught; no Lectures like the excellent Lessons on the Ridiculous, which I have quoted above, and which I do most earnestly recommend to all my young Readers.[3] Hence the learned Professions produce such excellent Characters of Humour; and the Rudeness of Physicians, Lawyers, and Parsons, however dignified or distinguished, affords such pleasant Stories to divert private Companies, and sometimes the Public.

I come now to the beautiful Part of the Creation, who, in the Sense I here use the Word, I am assured can hardly (for the most Part) be said to have any Education.[4]

---

[1] 'The withdrawing, detachment, or selection of certain persons . . . from a larger body for some special duty or purpose' (*OED*).

[2] But cf. the Man of the Hill's description of the life of 'Sir George Gresham' at Oxford, *Tom Jones*, VIII. xi. The universities were, of course, a common topic of criticism, from masterpieces like Pope's *Dunciad* (Book iv) to trashy pamphlets like *An Essay on Modern Education* [1751], pp. 23–9; cf. Fielding's ironic treatment of the 'uselessness' of a university education in *CGJ* No. 42, above.

[3] i.e. the lessons taught by Bellegarde.

[4] Cf. the plea for better education of women in *An Essay on Modern Education* [1751], pp. 41–7, which, as Fielding does here, considers first the plight of the country gentlewomen and then that of the young lady in town. For Fielding's other criticisms of the superficial education given to young women, see his poem 'To a Friend on the Choice of a Wife', in *Miscellanies* (1743); *Joseph Andrews*, IV. vii; *Tom Jones*, XIV. i; and *Champion*, 4 Sept. 1740, where he says women are 'but half taught to read and write'. Despite these views, however, Fielding seems to have been skeptical about the value of a literary education for a woman; see *Amelia*, VI. vii, where Mrs Bennet's learning is satirized, and the note on this passage by Martin Battestin, Wesleyan Edn. (Oxford, 1983), p. 255. For background on

As to the Counterpart of my Country Squire, the Country Gentlewoman, I apprehend, that except in the Article of the Dancing-Master, and perhaps in that of being barely able to read and write, there is very little Difference between the Education of many a Squire's Daughter, and that of his Dairy-Maid, who is most likely her principal Companion; nay the little Difference which there is, is, I am afraid, not in the Favour of the Former; who, by being constantly flattered with her Beauty and her Wealth, is made the vainest and most selfconceited Thing alive, at the same Time that such Care is taken to instil into her the Principles of Bashfulness and Timidity, that she becomes ashamed and afraid of she knows not what.

If by any Chance this poor Creature drops afterwards, as it were, into the World, how absurd must be her Behaviour! If a Man looks at her, she is confounded, and if he speaks to her, she is frightened out of her Wits. She acts, in short, as if she thought the whole Sex was engaged in a Conspiracy to possess themselves of her Person and Fortune.

This poor Girl, it is true, however she may appear to her own Sex, especially if she is handsome, is rather an Object of Compassion, than of just Ridicule; but what shall we say when Time or Marriage have carried off all this Bashfulness and Fear, and when Ignorance, Aukwardness, and Rusticity, are embellished with the same Degree, tho' perhaps not the same kind of Affectation, which are to be found in a Court. Here sure is a plentiful Source of all that various Humour which we find in the Character of a Country Gentlewoman.

All this, I apprehend, will be readily allowed; but to deny Good-Breeding to the Town-Lady, may be the more Dangerous Attempt. Here, besides the Professors of Reading, Writing, and Dancing, the French and Italian Masters, the Music Master, and of Modern Times, the Whist Master,[1] all concur in forming this Character. The Manners Master alone I am afraid is omitted. And what is the Consequence? not only Bashfulness and Fear are intirely subdued, but Modesty and Discretion are taken off at the same Time. So far from running away from, she runs after the Men; and instead of blushing when a modest Man looks at her, or speaks to her, she can bear, without any such Emotion to stare an impudent Fellow in the Face, and sometimes to utter what, if he be not very impudent indeed, may put him to the Blush.—Hence all those agreeable Ingredients which form the Humour of a Rampant Woman of—the Town.

the question, see Lawrence Stone, *The Family, Sex and Marriage in England, 1500–1800* (1977), pp. 356–8.

[1] Cf. *Tom Jones*, XIII. v, where Fielding refers to the leading 'Whist Master', Edmond Hoyle, whose *Short Treatise* on the popular game had appeared in 1742. In the *Ladies Magazine* No. 1 (16–30 Nov. 1751, iii. 7–9) a writer speaks of the 'universal Esteem' the game is held in 'among the Polite part of Mankind'; cf. Edward Moore's satire on the manners of whist players, in *The World*, No. 7 (15 Feb. 1753).

I cannot quit this Part of my Subject, in which I have been obliged to deal a little more freely than I am inclined with the loveliest Part of the Creation, without preserving my own Character of Good-Breeding, by saying that this last Excess, is by much the most rare; and that every Individual among my Female Readers, either is already, or may be, when she pleases, an Example of a contrary Behaviour.

The second general Reason why Humour so much abounds in this Nation, seems to me to arise from the great Number of People, who are daily raised by Trade to the Rank of Gentry, without having had any Education at all; or, to use no improper Phrase, Without having served an Apprenticeship to this Calling.[1] But I have dwelt so long on the other Branch, that I have no Room at present to animadvert on this; nor is it indeed necessary I should, since most Readers with the Hints I have already given them, will easily suggest to themselves, a great Number of humorous Characters with which the Public have been furnished this Way. I shall conclude by wishing, that this excellent Source of Humour may still continue to flow among us, since tho' it may make us a little laughed at, it will be sure to make us the Envy of all the Nations of Europe. A.

SATURDAY, AUGUST 1, 1752. NUMB. 57.

——Meretricem esse similem sentis condecet
Quemquem hominem attigerit profecto aut malum, aut damnum dari.

A Common Strumpet should be like a Briar,
None should bear off a whole Skin, who come nigh her.

PLAUTUS in TRUCULENTUS.[2]

By means of a Letter which was about a Month ago published in this Paper, and which seemed to condemn the too rigorous Prosecution of Women of Pleasure, as they are called, I find I have obtained a Character among those Ladies and their Abettors of which I am not very ambitious, as it would indeed very little become a Man of my Years.[3] In short, I collect from various

---

[1] Fielding uses a phrase appropriate to trade. For a description of a tradesman aping the manners of gentry, see *CGJ* No. 33, above.

[2] *Truculentus*, II. i. 225–6: 'A courtesan ought to be like a bramble bush, and make certain that any man she touches gets stuck or stung' (Loeb); modern texts have a slightly different word order in the opening phrase and read *profecto ei aut malum* in the final phrase.

[3] The letter referred to was signed 'Humphry Meanwell' and published in *CGJ* No. 50; see that issue, above, for notes on the attitude toward prostitution in the period and the reaction to new legislation against bawdy-houses. Although Fielding jokes about the 'Character' he has received as a result of *CGJ* No. 50, he had good reason to be concerned about his reputation in this regard. In his *Charge to the Grand Jury* (1749) he had called for suppression of prostitution while admitting that the evil could never be completely eradicated (p. 49); nevertheless, his role in the Penlez affair that same year produced the charge among Opposition journalists that he was a paid protector of disorderly houses (see M. C. with R. R. Battestin, 'Fielding, Bedford, and the Westminister Election of 1749', *ECS* 11 [1977–8], 165 n.). When in his *Enquiry into the Causes of the late Increase of Robbers* (1751) he

Hints sent me by my Correspondents; that the Rakes and Harlots of the Town begin to regard me as their Well-wisher, as what Falstaff calls *a Friend to us Youth*.[1]

A grave Gentleman, as he appears by his Stile, reproves me very sharply. He tells me, "That grey Hairs look odious on a green Head, that a Colt's Tooth is detestable in a Mouth, which hath no other!" with other Sarcasms of the like Kind which I shall not repeat. Again Tom Wilding assures me, that old Sawney is the reigning Toast of all the Ladies at Jenny D—s's,[2] and compliments me much on being an *honest Fellow*, and, as he phrases it, *one of us*. Lastly, a fair one who signs herself MARI MURRAIN,[3] tells me I am a *hearty Cock*, and declares, with about twenty Oaths, that she is ready to rub down my old Back at any Time without a Present.

In real Truth, the first of these treats me with much more Severity, and the other with more Favour, than I deserve at their Hands. I do not indeed think with the virtuous Fury in Prior, *that all Whores should be burnt alive*;[4] nor am I a Well-wisher to the Punishment of Bridewell, especially while Bridewell continues to be what it is, a School rather for the Improvement, than for the Correction of Debauchery. I know a Magistrate who never sends a Woman thither, while she retains even any external Mark of Decency; and I have heard him declare, that he never yet saw a Woman

---

failed to discuss prostitution as a cause of crime, he was again subjected to the accusation that he was being bribed by the keepers of bawdy-houses; see the very hostile letter signed 'An Old Rake' in *LM* 20 (Mar. 1751), 128–30, and 'Philo-Patria's' *Letter to Henry Fielding, Esq.* (1751), which complains that 'these infamous Women' are 'the very Fountain-head, whence Robbery originally springs' (p. 8). In *A Scheme for a New Public Advertiser* (1753) Fielding was again to be closely associated with bawds and whores; see *CGJ* No. 72, below, p. 381 n. 3.

Given this reputation, Fielding would naturally seek to dissociate himself from the letter in *CGJ* No. 50, which itself had resulted in at least one work in reaction, *A Speech made in the Censorial Court of Alex. Drawcansir, Monday 6th June, 1752, concerning a late Act of Parliament*, a sixpenny pamphlet advertised in *GA*, 27 June 1752. Apparently the same piece with a revised title was again advertised in *GA* on 1 July as *A Serious Address to the Publick, setting in a proper Light, the Disadvantages that may arise from the late Act of Parliament for suppressing of Common Houses, in a Speech made in the Censorial Court of Sir Alexander Drawcansir. By P— W—*. No such pamphlet or pamphlets have been located, but their titles suggest Fielding himself was being connected with the stance taken by 'Humphry Meanwell'.

[1] Perhaps a reference to *1 Henry IV*, II. ii. 85, 'they hate us youth'; but Fielding may be thinking of *2 Henry IV*, III. ii., in which Justice Shallow brags to Falstaff of the 'wildness of his youth' when he consorted with whores.

[2] Jenny Douglas (d. 1761), known as 'Mother Douglas', '*Empress* o'er all the bawds around', as she is titled in *Covent-Garden: A Satire* (1756), p. 9; see also *The Humours of Fleet-Street and the Strand* [1748], pp. 5–12, and *The Modern Courtezan* (1751), pp. 10, 20. Fielding mentions her also in *Amelia*, X. ii, and she appears in Hogarth's *Industry and Idleness* (1747), *March to Finchley* (1750), and *Enthusiasm Delineated* (1761).

[3] Fielding puns on 'Mary' so that the name means 'diseased husband'; 'Murrain' is also a prostitute's name in *A Scheme for a New Public Advertiser* (1753).

[4] Prior's 'Paulo Purganti and His Wife: An Honest but a Simple Pair' (1708), in which the wife 'thought the Nation ne'er would thrive, / 'Till all the Whores were burnt alive'; Fielding cites this poem also in *Tom Jones*, XV. x, and in *Amelia*, IV. ii and XII. ii.

totally abandoned and lost to all Sense of Shame, who had not already finished her Education in that College.[1]

On the other Hand, I must as plainly confess that I cannot agree with those who look on a common W—e, as any very great, or very amiable Character.[2] I cannot indeed bring myself to treat the Profession with much Honour, however lucrative it may sometimes be. From me the modest Girl under a Basket of Oysters attracts more Respect, than the Punk in her Coach and Six.

In serious Truth, what can possibly be meaner and baser, than a Livelihood gained by Prostitution, whether the Professor be tumbled on Down, or rolled in a Kennel. If the poor Slave who lets out the Labour of his Body for Hire, be ranked in the lowest Order of the Commonwealth, what shall we say of one who lets out the Body itself! This is in Reality, to descend below the Dignity of Human Nature, and to partake of the Office of a Beast. Why, says the witty Doctor South, speaking of an Epicure, "Shall we esteem him to be less a Beast who carries his Burden in his Belly, than him who carries it on his Back?"[3] The Alteration of a single Letter, will bring the

[1] Fielding refers, of course, to himself; see his comments on these houses of correction in *Joseph Andrews*, IV. iii, *Tom Jones*, I. ix, IV. xi, and especially *Enquiry into the Causes of the late Increase of Robbers* (1751), sect. IV, where he inveighs against Bridewells as 'Schools of Vice', where inmates are 'confirmed in the Practice of Iniquity' (p. 63). For examples of his reluctance to send offenders to Bridewell, see the 'Covent Garden' columns of 9 Mar. and 10 Jan. 1752, below, Appendix I. Cf. *Satan's Harvest Home* (1749), p. 3, for a similar view.

[2] Fielding's attitude toward prostitutes was more complex than he here indicates. On the one hand, his harshness in this essay seems in striking contrast to the sympathetic and humane pleas, common at mid-century, for greater understanding of the plight of individual prostitutes; cf., among many examples, the story of Miss Williams in Smollett's *Roderick Random* (1748), chs. xxii–xxiii), whom Roderick regards as 'unfortunate, not criminal', or the similar theme in Johnson's *Rambler* essays Nos. 107, 170, and 171 (26 Mar., 2 and 5 Nov. 1751), or an essay by Edward Moore in *The World*, No. 97 (7 Nov. 1754). Fielding seems untouched here by this sentimental strain of thought, which usually depicted whores as helpless victims of cruel seducers and conniving bawds, and which led to a spate of pamphlets in 1758, when Magdalen Hospital was founded; see *CGJ* No. 50, above, p. 278 n. 1. Interestingly enough, Fielding's half-brother and sister both later contributed to this more compassionate view; see John Fielding's *An Account of the Origin and Effects of a Police . . . To which is added A Plan for preserving those deserted Girls in this Town who become Prostitutes from Necessity* (1758) and Sarah Fielding's *The Histories of Some of the Penitents in the Magdalen-House, as Supposed to be related by Themselves* (1760).

On the other hand, Fielding exhibited great sympathy toward the 'young, thoughtless, helpless, poor Girls' brought into his court; see the 'Covent Garden' columns for 10 and 24 Jan. 1752, below, Appendix I. His kindly instinct appears to be reflected in his practice as a magistrate faced with individual offenders, but when required to think in larger social terms, as in this response to 'Meanwell', he expresses a condemnation of whores at some variance both from the sympathy of the court reports and from the light-hearted cynicism of his treatment of the theme in *Covent-Garden Tragedy* (1732), *Miss Lucy in Town* (1742), and his ironic epilogue to Charles Johnson's play *Caelia* (1732). For an ambivalence on this subject similar to Fielding's see the pamphlet by his friend Saunders Welch, *A Proposal to render effectual a Plan to remove the Nuisance of Common Prostitutes from the Streets of the Metropolis* (1758), a fairly hard-headed tract which paradoxically describes prostitutes as 'true objects of compassion, as well as detestation' (p. 16). Cf. also Sarah Fielding: 'Tho' the profession of a prostitute is the most despicable and hateful that imagination can form; yet the individuals are frequently worthy objects of compassion' (*Histories of Some of the Penitents*, p. v).

[3] Slightly altered from Robert South's 'Sermon Preach'd at Christ-Church in Oxford, October 29,

Quotation home to my Purpose. Nay Human Nature is by such Prostitution debased below the Animal Creation, where no such Baseness is known. The Females of every Species among them are solicited and courted by the Males; and their Consent is an Indulgence of their own Inclinations, and an Obedience to the Dictates of their Nature. To prostitute herself for Hire, to give up the Freedom of Choice, to sin against Nature and Inclination, to receive into her Embraces a Wretch whom she must loath and despise. To defile herself with Age, Ugliness, Impotency, Disease, with a long, &c. of Filth, too odious to be mentioned. To do, to suffer all this for the sake of Lucre, is the Property only (I blush when I say it) of the Fairest and Loveliest of all terrestrial Beings.

And as such Prostitutes are the lowest and meanest, so are they the basest, vilest, and wickedest of all Creatures. It is a trite Observation, that when a Woman quits her Modesty, she discards with it every other Virtue.[1] To extend this to every frail Individual of the Sex, is to carry it too far; but if it be confined to those who are become infamous by public Prostitution, no Maxim, I believe, hath a greater Foundation in Truth, or will be more strongly verified by Experience.

Hence I suppose the Epithet of *honest*, was used in Contradistinction to this Vice, (for otherwise some Violence would appear to be done to the English Sense of the Word).[2] In fact their Minds are totally corrupted, and are a Compound of every Species of Dishonesty.

But not to attempt to blacken a Blackamoor, which would be at least as impertinent a Labour, as to endeavour to wash him white, I shall hint only at one Instance of their Wickedness, and one from which very few of them are exempt.

This is a Crime little short of Murder, it bears a near Resemblance to Poisoning, which is the worst of all Murder. Nay, in its Consequence it partakes of the Nature of the very worst of Poisonings, even that of poisoning a Fountain. The Contagion extends not only to an innocent Wife, but like the divine Vengeance, to the Children of the third and fourth Generation.[3]

1693', in *Twelve Sermons upon Several Subjects and Occasions*, 5th edn. (1722), iii. 75–6; on South, see *CGJ* No. 12, above, p. 85 n. 3. The alteration Fielding suggests is presumably from 'in' to 'on'. He quotes the same passage in *Champion*, 15 Apr. 1740.

[1] Tilley, M 1033: 'She that loses her modesty and honesty has nothing else worth losing.'

[2] 'Honest' in the sense of 'chaste, virtuous, usually of a woman'; *OED* cites Steele in *Spectator*, No. 118 (1711) as its latest example.

[3] See Exodus 20: 5, Deuteronomy 5: 9. The dangers of venereal disease were an obvious and frequently cited aspect of the attacks on prostitution and adultery. Cf., for example, Edward Cobden, *A Persuasive to Chastity* (1749), pp. 8–9; *Entertainer*, No. 3 (17 Sept. 1754). For a poem making much of the likelihood of contracting disease from the whores of Covent Garden, see *The Modern Courtezan* [1751], the author of which, with very good reason, wishes for the talent of a 'neighbouring *Squire*, / Whom some for *Law*, some for *Romance* admire' (p. 20). In *Journey from this World to the Next* (I. iii), Fielding personifies venereal disease as the lady 'Maladie Alamode'; cf. Mr Wilson's description of harlots as 'painted Palaces inhabited by Disease and Death', *Joseph Andrews*, III. iii.

I shall not dwell on this odious Subject, nor shall I fall into a Common Place, by expatiating on all the ruinous and dreadful Consequences which are almost certain to attend a Commerce with these Women. Such are to the Men of Business in particular, (besides the Danger already mentioned) the Loss of Reputation and of Credit, Neglect of their Families and Occupations, and Consumption of both their Time and their Money; all which visibly tend to and frequently end in Bankruptcy and Ruin, and sometimes, by an Endeavour to avoid these Consequences, in all Kinds of Fraud, Violence, and Rapine.

Thus then I think the Trade of a Prostitute, can scarce be called either a reputable or an innocent Calling, with Respect to the Prostitute herself, and with Regard to the Public, it seems, in great Propriety of Speech, to deserve the Name of an Evil.

Nor can I entirely agree with such as think it among those which are called necessary Evils; and which are to be tolerated, nay even encouraged, on account of some Good which they produce, or at least of some Mischief, which is to be apprehended from their total Extirpation.[1]

As to any positive Good arising to a Society from the Encouragement of Prostitutes, this I own exceeds my Penetration. It must be very great indeed, if it can counter-ballance the Mischiefs which I have here enumerated.

But great Mischiefs are, it seems, to attend the Extirpation of this Vice. Young Gentlemen (and perhaps old Gentlemen) must have Whores, or woe be to your Wives and Daughters.[2] Bolts and Bars, Laws and Blunderbusses, together with the impregnable Virtue of the Ladies themselves, are, I believe, their Security at present, or several of our Gallants (as well old as young,) would have a better Taste, than to confine themselves to the Stews, or the Streets. A fine Woman adorned with all the Sweetness of Innocence, and Loveliness of Modesty, is a very different Object to a Letcher of any Understanding, from a stinking painted Harlot, whose Mind and Body are alike a Mass of Corruption. Every Art that can be practised, every Snare that can be laid for Beauty and Virtue, are practised and laid at this Day, and little more might be justly apprehended, if there was not a Punk to be found in the Liberty of Westminster.

---

[1] The argument that prostitution is a necessary evil was made by 'Meanwell' in *CGJ* No. 50; for other references see above, p. 279 n. 2.

[2] Cf. Mandeville, *Fable of the Bees* (1734), Remark H: 'If Courtezans and Strumpets were to be prosecuted with as much Rigour as some silly People would have it, what Locks or Bars would be sufficient to preserve the Honour of our Wives and Daughters?' See also *An Essay on Modern Gallantry* (1750), which cites 'the Wisdom of the Antients, in securing their Wives and Daughters from the Arts and Violence of lascivious Men', although the author will not 'contend for the Toleration of *public Stews*, any farther than is necessary for the Preservation of *Chastity* and *Virtue*' (p. 37). On such views among the ancients, see John Potter, *Archaeologiae Graecae*, 4th edn. (1722), ii. 305–7, a work cited by the author of *Modern Gallantry* and owned by Fielding (Baker, item 48). This common argument for legalized prostitution was also censured by Johnson; see Boswell's *Life*, ed. G. Birkbeck Hill (Oxford, 1934), iii. 18.

A second Inconvenience suggested is, that our young Men would marry, and this would often prove their Ruin. I answer, that it can scarce ever ruin them so effectually, as the associating with loose and abandoned Women.[1] If a Gentleman indeed, is undone, who cannot keep his Wife a Coach, or if a Chaise and one be necessary to the well-being of a Married Tradesman, it will be difficult for them to match themselves every Day with such Views. But if the Wife will accommodate herself to the Fortune of her Husband, and do her best in her Vocation, there would not be such fatal Difference between the Expences of a single and a married State; nor would it be so impossible for younger Brothers to indulge their Inclinations in a legal Way, as is at present (with some Justice perhaps) imagined.[2] To say Truth, that this is not the Case arises in some Measure from the extravagant Habits which our young Men contract from their Conversation with Lewd Wenches, and from the Manners which our young Women imbibe by imitating them.

But if elder Brothers, and those elder Brothers only who have great Fortunes, are to marry, what becomes of the Interest of the Public, which is so greatly concerned in this Matter, that the wisest of Legislators have thought proper to encourage Marriage with many Rewards, and by attributing to it the highest Honours and Privileges![3]

And what is to become of our poor Daughters: for these have their Passions and Appetites, as well as our Sons! Is their Chastity to be rewarded with the comfortable Appellation of old Maids? Are they to pine away their Lives in a useless, and to most of them I will say a disagreeable State,

---

[1] Again, Fielding answers a point made by 'Meanwell' in *CGJ* No. 50. In a variant of the argument against marriage, Mandeville had claimed that prostitution at least puts marriages on a more realistic basis by ridding young men of their romantic fancies; see *A Modest Defence of Publick Stews* (1724), pp. 29–39, and cf. *Satan's Harvest Home* (1749), p. 42. In what follows Fielding is at pains to defend the entire institution of marriage, which with many others he felt to be threatened by prostitution. Cf. *Champion*, 21 June 1740, in which he protests that 'Marriage seems to be in a fair Way of being shortly laid aside' in favor of 'Guardianship' or 'keeping'; see also a letter reprinted in *LM* 20 (1751), 22–3, arguing laboriously that matrimony has some advantages not possessed by 'keeping harlots', and a letter supposedly from three spinsters in *LDA*, 26 Sept. 1752, attributing the decline of marriage to the presence of prostitutes.

[2] The 'accommodation' Fielding refers to was a common topic of concern. See, for example, *LM* 20 (1751), 318–20, on the disasters that occur if partners in a marriage fail 'to confine themselves, according to their station in life, to such sort of pleasures only, which their circumstances will admit of'. On the difficulties of 'younger Brothers', see H. J. Habakkuk, 'Marriage Settlements in the Eighteenth Century', *Transactions of the Royal Historical Society*, 4th Ser., 32 (1950), pp. 15–30, esp. pp. 20–4.

[3] For a similar argument in defense of marriage, see *An Essay on Modern Gallantry* (1750), pp. 20–3, which defends the public utility of the institution and remarks on the fact 'that all wise Nations have given great Encouragement' to it, citing laws of the Spartans, Athenians, and Romans. Cf. Defoe's suggestion that giving greater encouragement to matrimony would 'have a better Effect than all the Whippings, *Bridewels* and *Work-Houses*, which are invented as Discouragements to Vice' (*Some Considerations upon Street-Walkers* [1726], p. 7). A bill for the encouragement of marriage among the poor was brought into the House of Commons in 1751 but died in committee; see *DA*, 8 Mar. 1751, *LDA*, 15 Apr. 1751.

without any Opportunity of exerting their good Qualities in the two principal Female Characters, that of Wife, and that of Mother?

Lastly whence are our Prostitutes themselves to be supplied? Most of these are the Daughters of Parents, whom they have made miserable by their Infamy. Some of them are of good Families, and many, to the great Scandal of the Nation, the Offspring of the Clergy.[1] Indeed there is Reason to think that the Daughters and Wives too, of what are called (I know not why) the better Sort, will soon be enrolled in the Number of our Courtesans (I will not now use too coarse a Name). These Courtesans have already, as I have been told, begun to lead the Fashions, and how considerable a Step that is towards the same Lead in the Manners of the Female World I need not here observe. If such Patterns should once be admitted in both these, that is to say, if our fine Ladies should appear in public in the Dress, and with the Behaviour of Courtesans, whether they will stop here or go a very little little Step further; in a Word, whether they will constitute a new Order of Females that are *neither Whores nor modest Women*, is a Point which I am not so willing as I think I am able to determine.   C.

The Letter from a BY-STANDER *is greatly approved; but the Ingenious Writer may suggest to himself the Reason why it cannot be inserted in such a Paper as this.*

SATURDAY, AUGUST 8, 1752.   NUMB. 58.

> *Donec erunt Ignes Arcusque Cupidinis Arma*
> *Discentur Numeri, culte Tibulle, tui.*
>
>   OVID.[2]

> *While Flames and Darts Love's Weapons shall remain,*
> *Polite Tibullus, shall we learn thy strain.*

To Sir ALEXANDER DRAWCANSIR.

Sir,[3]

Tho' your own Genius, I think, turns not much to Poetry, I do not suppose

---

[1] In *JJ* No. 32 (9 July 1748) Fielding refers to 'that vulgar (I hope false) Assertion, that the greatest Part of the *London* Prostitutes are the Daughters of Parsons'; cf. *Rape upon Rape* (1730), II. v., where Hilaret, pretending to be a whore, says she and her fifteen sisters in the same profession are all the daughters of a country parson. See also Abbé Le Blanc, *Letters on the English and French Nation* (1747), ii. 67. The first story in Sarah Fielding's *Histories of Some of the Penitents in the Magdalen-House* (1760) is told by the daughter of a poor clergyman (pp. 8–127).

[2] *Amores*, I. xv. 27–8: 'As long as flames and bow are the arms of Cupid, thy numbers shall be conned, O elegant Tibullus' (Loeb).

[3] Cross (ii. 383–4) had no doubt that this letter and its translation of Tibullus are by Fielding himself; though external evidence is lacking, the reference to Fielding's study of Tibullus at Eton may be a coy hint that he is the translator. The translation, at any rate, bears no resemblance to other English versions of this elegy in the period, including an early translation by Fielding's friend and

you are an Enemy to the Musical Inhabitants of Parnassus; if therefore I
have done tolerable Justice to an incomparable Elegy which you must
formerly have got by Heart in a certain Book called *Electa Minora*,[1] or more
commonly at Eton, *Elector Minor*, you may, if you please present it to the Test
of the Public.

I am SIR, &c.

TIBULLUS. Book 1st. Elegy 1st.
Translated.

Give others to their Wish the shining Ore,
And Tracts of well-till'd Land to swell their Store;
Vainly amass'd—their Wealth new Cares supplies,
To drive the wholesome Slumber from their Eyes.
Whether the dread Alarm imprint with Fear,
Or Trumpets Clangour speak the En'my near.
  Me, may my Fate to humbler Scenes consign,
And on my Hearth my little Fire still shine!
Be mine the honest Farmer's pleasing Care,
Let me his Labour and his Profit share!
To plant the Vine, and make the Apple grow,
And have my Vats with gen'rous Juice o'erflow!
To pay the Gods due Homage, when I see
Adorn'd with Flowers some Stone, or Stump of Tree!
With due Libations to his sacred Name,
Vertumnus, yearly his Reward shall claim:
Thy Temples, Ceres, grac'd with yellow Corn,
The grateful Poet shall with Care adorn;
Nor thou, Priapus, Guardian of my Ground,
Without thy full Reward shalt then be found;
Nor shall thy Scythe, which frights the Birds away,
Undeck'd, disgrace the Honours of that Day;
And ye, my houshold Gods, whose constant Care,
No less my small, than larger Fortunes share,
Receive alike an Off'ring from my Hand,
And let a Lamb now for a Heifer stand.
Whilst round the Sacrifice the Rustics come,
To celebrate with me, our Harvest Home.

former classmate at Eton, George Lyttelton (see *The Works of Lyttelton*, ed. G. E. Ayscough [1776], ii.
121–4). If Fielding is in fact the translator, he may have been moved to print his version by the recent
publication in *LDA* (6 July) of a translation of the same poem by his enemy John Hill, whose
knowledge of Latin verse he was soon to ridicule in *CGJ* No. 60.

  [1] *Electa Minora ex Ovidio, Tibullo, et Propertio, usui Scholae Etonensis* (1705); as a school text, this
work contained, in actuality, only a little over half of the elegy (ll. 1–38).

Once fond of Greatness, emulous of Fame,
Life's vain Pursuits my only End became;
Now wean'd from Grandeur, with a Little blest,
I find more solid Happiness in Rest;
Now pleas'd in Shades, the Dog-star's Heat to shun,
While cooling Waters with soft Murmurs run;
Now not asham'd the two-grain'd Fork to wield,
Or drive the tardy Oxen to the Field;
Or in my Arms bear home the Kid or Lamb,
Left on the Ground by its forgetful Dam.
Spare my small Flocks, ye Men, and Beasts of Prey,
And let the larger Herds, your Rapine stay!
For this, the due Lustrations yearly made,
In Streams of Milk to Pales shall be paid;
Be present ev'ry God, nor scorn to take,
The humble Off'ring which the Poor can make;
What tho' the Gift be small, and Vessels mean,
In little Things, a grateful Heart is seen;
And long e'er Gold or Silver rose to light,
Vessels of Earth were no unseemly Sight.
　　To me, no Joy my Father's Wealth affords,
I envy not the rich Man's ample Hoards.
Give me a little Field to plant, or sow,
A little Bed where I my Limbs may throw!
How pleas'd at Night, when Winds disturb my Rest,
To clasp my Delia to my panting Breast.
Or when the drenching Rains around us sweep,
Lull'd by the Noise prolong our balmy Sleep!
Be this my Fate, be Wealth his sordid Care,
Who can Life's varied Toils and Dangers bear.
Perish all Thoughts of Gold, or Gem, or Stone,
E'er Delia's Eyes in Tears my Absence moan!
Triumph ye mighty Chiefs o'er Sea and Land,
Thro' Nations yet unknown, assert Command—
The Toil becomes—the Spoils your Country grace—
Renown shall spread your Fame from Place to Place.
Whilst I, in silken Chains of Pleasure bound,
A constant Porter at thy Gate am found.
Praise I contemn—To be, dear Girl, with thee,

Is more than Praise, is Happiness to me!
Lost to my Friends, or Country, idle, dull,
With thee, the Measure of my Joy is full;
And when to Fate I must resign my Breath,
How blest to clasp thee in the Pangs of Death!
With trembling Hands shake o'er the last Embrace
And die contented, gazing on thy Face!
Then thou my Delia, when thou see'st the Bier,
Shalt mingle Kisses with the friendly Tear—
For thou wilt weep—thy tender Heart will feel—
Thy Bosom was not made of Stone or Steel.
Then shalt each Youth in Tears his Grief make known,
Each Maid lament thy Sorrows as her own;
Yet hear, ah hear thy Lover's dying Pray'r,
Tear not thy Cheeks, nor rend thy flowing Hair;
This last, this dying Comfort let me have,
For sure thy Grief would pierce beyond the Grave.
　Mean time, while Fate permits, our Joys improve,
Too soon, alas! Death puts an End to Love.
Too soon, old Age with slow unheeded Pace,
Will steal on Love, and rob it of its Grace.
Ill suits the fond Caress the hoary Head;
Ill suits the active Wish, when Power is dead;
Ill suits the falt'ring Voice, the tender Sigh,
Or am'rous Glance from the long faded Eye.
Now, Venus, is thy Hour; now lightsome Play
Should drive each foolish Sense of Shame away.
Now blush not Youths, opposing Doors to break,
Or on your jealous Rivals Vengeance wreak.
Now press with Ardour each resisting Fair,
Now ev'rything for Love and Pleasure dare.
Here I, your Chief, and Leader will command,
And in the midst of Danger fearless stand.
Let the ambitious Fool for Honour fight,
And in the Instruments of War delight.
Far from my Sight remov'd go grace the Field,
I ask no Arms but those which Lovers wield.
Enough for Use is all I wish or prize,
And Wealth and Poverty alike despise.

To the CENSOR.

Sir,[1]

Upon the Approach of a new Election for Westminster,[2] the fourth Estate[3] begin as usual to exert themselves. A Shower of Rain drove me last Night into an Alehouse where a large Number of this Estate was assembled, and where the Election was the Subject of Debate. A Cobler began an Harangue with declaring that he did not value any Man in England, whereof, he said, he thought himself as good as any He that wore Heels to his Shoes. My Memory will not serve to repeat his Speech, nor am I able to give the Substance of it, as I cannot affirm I perfectly understood his Meaning. It consisted of frequent Repetitions of the Words Liberty and true Englishman,[4] but to what Purpose they were introduced, I must confess myself at a Loss to determine; so far I observed, that they conveyed to his Hearers a great Idea of the Dignity and Independency of the Speaker. He concluded by saying——*Whereof I don't know why I shan't Vote for who I please, and if I please to Vote for* Stroud,[5] *who says I shan't?*

Upon this, a sly looking Fellow, and who, if I mistake not, was what they call a dry Joker, spoke as follows: "Why I must own, Neighbour Jobson,[6] if

---

[1] Although the usual initial signature is missing, this letter is unmistakably Fielding's own.

[2] The reason for this election was the death of Sir Peter Warren, one of the Members for Westminster, on 29 July 1752. But Fielding's readers would immediately associate the phrase 'Westminster Election' with one of the most hotly contested elections of the century, the Westminster election of 1749 between Granville Leveson-Gower, Viscount Trentham, and the anti-Court candidate Sir George Vandeput. Because of his dependence on the Duke of Bedford, Trentham's brother-in-law, Fielding himself had been heavily involved in the election of 1749 in support of Trentham, who was eventually successful. For an account of his activities as writer and magistrate in this campaign, see M. C. with R. R. Battestin, 'Fielding, Bedford, and the Westminster Election of 1749', *ECS* 11 (1977/78), 154–75.

As this letter makes plain, at the approach of a new election Fielding sensed some of the same forces coming into play that had marked the election of 1749, especially the Opposition's manipulation of the 'mob' and the reiteration of slogans about 'Liberty'. At this point no candidates were known to the public, and interest in the possibilities of various candidates was running high; *LDA* (6 Aug.) commented, 'the real Candidates cannot be long a Secret', adding that every housekeeper who rents a house of nine or ten pounds a year or above is entitled to a vote, 'though sometimes lower Tenants have answered the End'. In the event, there was no contest; Sir George Vandeput was again put in nomination but withdrew a few days before the election, and the Court candidate, Edward Cornwallis, was chosen without opposition on 16 Jan. 1753 (*LM* 21 [1752], 382; 22 [1753], 42–3).

[3] i.e. 'the mob', as defined in *CGJ* Nos. 47 and 49.

[4] On Fielding's current concern with the true meaning of the word 'Liberty', see General Introduction, above, p. xl, and *CGJ* No. 2, p. 22 n. 1. But in this context, such phrases are specifically political, for Fielding regarded them as stock expressions of the Opposition to the Pelham government (as they had been earlier to Walpole). In the Introductory Essay to a 1749 *Covent-Garden Journal*, written in support of Lord Trentham in the Westminster election of that year, Fielding parodies the cant of the anti-Court faction; see M. C. with R. R. Battestin, 'Fielding, Bedford, and the Westminster Election', pp. 173–4. As other examples, the Battestins point to Fielding's *Dialogue between a Gentleman of London . . . and an Honest Alderman* (1747) and Bondum the bailiff's speech in *Amelia* (VIII. ii).

[5] William Stroud, the swindler; see *CGJ* No. 51, above, p. 284.

[6] A 'jobson' is a country fellow, a lout (*OED*).

suffering in the Great Cause of Independent Liberty[1] be a Recommendation, I cannot see that any Man can have more of that Merit, nor could any Man bear his Sufferings with more Courage and Resolution."[2] "None of your Jokes, Mr. Sneerwell," cried a Taylor, "We must have some good Gentleman that hath a Purse,"——"Ay and Strings to his Purse," cried the Master of the House, "and who is not afraid of drawing them![3] I will Vote for no Man that won't open my House, and I am sure, every honest Englishman will say the same."[4] They then repeated the Names of several very honourable Gentlemen. Every one of whom I found had both Friends and Opposers. A Chairman objected to one, that he never saw him in a Chair in his Life.——A Taylor produced a long Bill against another, and a Tallow Chandler objected to a third, that his Servants burnt the Ends of Wax Candles in his Kitchen. Motives of the like Kind were assigned on the favourable side. One was an honourable Gentleman, and as good Pay as any Man in England.[5] ——Another did not pay quite so well, but was as generous as a Lord, and valued not his Money of a brass Farthing. Nor can I help observing that Liberty was in all their Mouths, and served like Lillaburlero,[6] as a kind of Burthen to close the End of every Speech.

Upon the whole I could not help being pleased with this Instance of English Freedom, in which we so exactly resemble the Antient Greeks and Romans; and I heartily wish, Mr. Censor, that we may never resemble those once great People in the Loss of this Blessing, and in the Manner of losing it: I mean by extending it to such an intolerable Degree of Licentiousness, and ungovernable Isolence, as to introduce that Anarchy which is sure to end in some Species of Tyranny or other.[7]

I am,

Sir,

Your hearty Well-Wisher,

A true Englishman.

---

[1] More Opposition rhetoric; in the 1749 election the Vandeput supporters had called themselves the 'Independent Electors'.

[2] Stroud's 'Sufferings' were the result of his being whipped through the streets once a month for 6 months; see *CGJ* No. 51.

[3] i.e. 'not afraid of opening his purse'; for the same usage, see *CGJ* No. 44, above, p. 247.

[4] i.e. pay for an open house; cf. George Alexander Stevens, *Distress upon Distress* (1752): 'A Set of Sharpers now attend the Squire, / And Leech-like live upon him: 'Tis To-day / He's come to Age, & open House he keeps / At *Beverage* the Vintner's' (i. iii).

[5] i.e. 'as sure to pay his debts' (*OED*).

[6] Part of the refrain of the famous song with that title, dating from about 1688 (*OED*).

[7] Cf. Fielding's comments on 'wild Notions of Liberty' in his *Enquiry into the Causes of the late Increase of Robbers* (1751), which conclude 'Anarchy is almost sure to end in some Kind of Tyranny' (p. xv).

SATURDAY, AUGUST 15, 1752.　　　NUMB. 59.

——*Illachrymabiles*
Urgentur, ignotique longa
Nocte, carent quia Vate Sacro.

HORACE.[1]

Without a a Tear they fall, without a Name,
Unless some sacred Bard records their Fame.

There is a certain Affection of the Mind, for which tho' it be common enough in the People of this Country, we have not, I think, any adequate Term in our Language. The Greeks, tho' they likewise want a Name for the Abstract, called a Man so affected *ΥΠΕΡΦΡΩΝ*,[2] a Word which I shall not attempt to translate otherwise than by a Paraphrase; I understand by it a Man so intoxicated with his own great Qualities, that he despises and overlooks all other Men. In this Sense the Participle passive of the Verb ὑπερφρονέω is used in Thucydides, ὑπὸ τῶν εὐπραγούντων ὑπερφρονούμενος.[3] The Sentiment is in the Mouth of Alcibiades, and it is a very fine one. *As no Man*, says he, *will even speak to us when we are unfortunate, so must they bear in their Turn* to be despised by us when we are intoxicated with our Successes.

This disdainful Temper, notwithstanding its haughty Aspect, proceeds, if I am not much mistaken, from no higher Principle than rank Timidity. We endeavour to elevate ourselves and to depress others, lest they should be brought into some Competition with ourselves. We are not sufficiently assured of our own Footing in the Ascent to Greatness, and are afraid of suffering any to come too near us, lest they should pull us down, and advance into our Place.[4]

Of this pitiful Temper of Mind, there are no Persons so susceptible as the Brethren of the Quill. Not only such Authors as have been a little singular in their Opinions concerning their own Merit, and in whom it seems more excusable to bear a jealous Eye towards others; but even those who have far out-stripped their fellow Coursers in the Race of Glory, stretch their scornful Eyes behind them, to express their Disdain of the poor Wretches who are limping and crawling on at however great a Distance.

---

[1] *Odes*, IV. ix. 26–8: 'overwhelmed in unending night, unwept, unknown, because they lack a sacred bard' (Loeb); Fielding uses the motto ironically, since Horace's ode is on the power of verse to immortalize the worthy, not the unworthy.

[2] Haughty or arrogant.

[3] *History*, VI. xvi. 4: 'despised by those who prosper' (Loeb). Alcibiades is urging the Athenians to mount an expedition to Sicily against the advice of Nicias, who has made invidious reference to him; his motives are those of political ambition and self-interest, says Thucydides, who comments, 'it was precisely this sort of thing that most of all later destroyed the Athenian state' (VI. xv).

[4] On the 'disdainful Temper', see also *CGJ* No. 61 and Fielding's 'Essay on Conversation', *Miscellanies* (1743).

Many are the Methods by which this Passion is exerted. I shall mention only one, as it is much the most common, and perhaps the most invidious. This is a contemptuous Silence. A Treatment not much unlike to that with which the Buccaneers formerly used to treat their conquered Enemies, when they sunk, or as they phrased it, hid them in the Sea.

How many Names of great Writers may we suppose to have been Sunk by this base Disposition! Homer, as I remember, hath not perpetuated the Memory of a single Writer, unless that of Thersites, who was, I make no Doubt, from the Character given of him in the Iliad, an Author of no small Estimation.[1] And yet there were probably as many of the Function in those Days, as there are in this; nay Homer himself in his Odyssey, mentions the great Honours which Poets then received in the Courts of all Princes,[2] whence we may very reasonably conclude that they swarmed in those Courts, and yet the Names of three only of his Cotemporaries have triumphed over the Injuries of Time, and the Malice of their Brethren so as to reach our Age.[3]

The learned Vossius, who seems to have employed no little Pains in the Matter, hath not been able to preserve to us many more than two hundred down to the Death of Cleopatra,[4] and yet we are assured, that the famous Alexandrian Library contained no less than six hundred Thousand Volumes, of which, as the Humour of those Ages ran, we may conceive a sixth Part at least to have consisted of Poetry.[5]

---

[1] See *Iliad*, ii. 211–42. Thersites was not, of course, literally an author, but as a ranting and abusive character he is used by Fielding as the 'type' of a writer who envies his betters; cf. Pope's comment that Homer has here 'shewn great Judgment in the Particulars he has chosen to compose the Picture of a pernicious Creature of Wit; the chief of which are a Desire of promoting Laughter at any rate, and a Contempt of his Superiors' (Pope's note to his trans. of *Iliad*, ii. 255).

[2] See *Odyssey*, xvii. 381–7. But the reference to poets receiving honors in princely courts is to be found not in Homer but in Pope's translation (xvii. 466–9): 'But chief to Poets such respect belongs, / By rival nations courted for their songs; / These States invite, and mighty Kings admire, / Wide as the sun displays his vital fire.' Fielding might also have in mind *Odyssey*, viii. 477–81, where bards are said to be honored 'among all men that are upon earth'.

[3] The variety of traditions about Homer among the ancients themselves makes it difficult to know with any certainty what source Fielding is following here; see e.g. Thomas Parnell's discussion of such problems in *An Essay on the Life, Writings, and Learning of Homer*, prefixed to the first volume of Pope's translation of the *Iliad* (1715), Twickenham Edn., vii. 26–80. Parnell, puzzling over the sort of poets Homer saw in his own time, comments, 'The imperfect Risings of the Art lay then among the *Extempore*-Singers of Stories at Banquets, who were half Singers, half Musicians. Nor was the Name of *Poet* then in being, or once us'd throughout Homer's Works' (p. 66). However, Fielding is perhaps following Vossius, whom he cites in the next sentence and who suggests as Homer's possible contemporaries Hesiod, Arctinus of Miletus, and Creophylus of Samos (*De veterum poetarum temporibus* [Amsterdam, 1654], pp. 9–11).

[4] Gerhard Johannes Vossius (1577–1649), German classical scholar, surveys some 230 Greek poets from the earliest times to the death of Cleopatra in the first eight chapters of his *De veterum poetarum temporibus libri duo* (Amsterdam, 1654), pp. 1–54; this work was in Fielding's library (Baker, item 94).

[5] The number of books was variously estimated, but Fielding seems to be following Aulus Gellius, who gives the figure as 'nearly seven hundred thousand volumes' (*Attic Nights*, VII. xvii. 3).

Among the Latins how many great Names may we suppose to have been hid by the affected Taciturnity of Virgil, who appears to have mentioned only those Writers of Quality to whom he made his Court! Of his Friend Horace he had not the Gratitude to take any Notice; much less to repay those Praises which this latter Poet had so liberally bestowed on him.[1]

Horace again tho' so full of Compliments to Virgil, of poor Ovid is altogether as cruelly and invidiously silent.

Ovid, who was, I am confident, one of the best natured of Human kind, was of all Men most profuse in the Praises of his Cotemporaries; and yet even he hath been guilty of Sinking. Numberless were the Poets in his Time, whose Names are no where to be found in his Works; nay he hath played the Buccaneer with two, one of whom is celebrated by Horace, and both of them by Virgil. The learned Reader well knows I mean the Illustrious Names of Bavius and Mævius; whose Merits were so prevalent with Virgil, that tho' they were both his bitter Revilers, he could not refrain from transmitting them to Posterity.[2] I wish he had dealt as generously by all his Censurers, and I make no Doubt but we should have been furnished with some hundreds of Names, *quæ nunc premit Nox.*[3]

Among our own Writers, too many have been guilty of this Vice. Had Dryden communicated all those who drew their Pens against him, he would have preserved as many Names from Oblivion as a Land Tax Act;[4] but he was, I am afraid, so intoxicated with his own Merit, that he overlooked and despised all the great Satyrists who constantly abused, I had almost said libelled, his Works, unless they were some other way eminent, besides by their Writings, such as Shadwell, who was Poet Laureat, and Buckingham, who was a Duke.[5]

Of all the chief Favorites and Prime Ministers of the Muses, the late ingenious Mr. Pope was most free from this scornful Silence. He employed a whole Work for the Purpose of recording such Writers as no one without his Pains, except he had lived at the same Time and in the same Street,

---

[1] For Horace's compliments to Virgil, see *Satires*, I. v. 40, I. vi. 55, I. x. 45; *Art of Poetry*, 55; *Odes*, I. iii. 6, I. xxiv. 10, IV. xii. 13; *Epistles*, II. i. 247.

[2] Virgil 'celebrates' these two in *Eclogues*, iii. 90, a famous line which Fielding uses as the motto to *CGJ* No. 31 (Apr. 18). Horace wrote his *Epode* x against Maevius, but, as Fielding says, Ovid makes no mention of the pair.

[3] 'Which night now covers'; Fielding is perhaps remembering Horace, *Odes*, I. iv. 16: *iam te premet nox fabulaeque Manes*, 'Soon shall the night of Death enshroud thee, and the phantom shades' (Loeb).

[4] Each of these acts lists for each county the names of the Commissioners who will 'put this Act in Execution' and thereby preserves 'from Oblivion' relatively obscure figures.

[5] Thomas Shadwell (1642?–92), playwright and Poet Laureate after 1689, was attacked by Dryden in *Mac Flecknoe* (1682) and *The Second Part of Absalom and Achitophel* (1682). George Villiers, 2nd Duke of Buckingham (1628–87), was caricatured as 'Zimri' in *Absalom and Achitophel* (1681), after Buckingham had ridiculed Dryden in his play *The Rehearsal* (1671). In his *Discourse concerning the Original and Progress of Satire* (1693) Dryden claimed that he had usually been silent in the face of attacks, although, he protested, 'More Libels have been written against me, than almost any Man now living'. On Dryden's enemies, see also *CGJ* No. 23, above.

would ever have heard of. He may indeed be said to have raked many out of the Kennels to Immortality, which, tho' in somewhat a stinking Condition, is to an ambitious Mind preferable to utter Obscurity and Oblivion;[1] many, I presume, having, with the Wretch who burnt the Temple of Ephesus,[2] such a Love for Fame, that they are willing even to creep into her common Shore.

In humble Imitation of this Great Man, in the only Instance of which I am capable of imitating him, I intend shortly to attempt a Work of the same kind, in Prose I mean, and to endeavour to do Justice to a great Number of my Cotemporaries, whose Names, for far the greater Part, are much less known than they deserve to be. And that I may be the better enabled to execute this generous Purpose, I have employed several proper Persons to find out these Authors. To this End I have ordered my Bookseller to send me in the Names of all those Apprentices and Journeymen of Booksellers and Printers who at present entertain and instruct the Town with their Productions. I have besides a very able and industrious Person who hath promised me a complete List of all the Hands now confined in the several Bridewells in and about this City, which carry on the Trade of Writing, in any of the Branches of Religion, Morality, and Government; in all which every Day produces us some curious Essay, Treatise, Remarks, &c. from those Quarters.[3]

I shall conclude this Paper with some very fine Lines from the third Book of the Dunciad, which gave indeed the first Hint to my charitable Design: For what a melancholy Consideration is it, that all *these Armies* there spoken of should perish in the Jaws of utter Darkness, and that the Names of such Worthies should be as short-lived as their Works!—The Verses are Part of the Speech of Settle to his Son Cibber.

> And see, my Son! the Hour is on its Way,
> That lifts our Goddess to Imperial Sway.
> This fav'rite Isle long sever'd from her
> Reign,
> Dove-like she gathers to her Wings again.

[1] Cf. Pope's anticipation of this criticism in the 'Letter to the Publisher' (signed 'William Cleland') which he prefixed to the *Variorum Dunciad* (1729): 'The first objection I have heard made to the Poem is, that the persons are too obscure for Satyre. The persons themselves, rather than allow the objection, would forgive the Satyre. . . .' (Twickenham Edn., v. 14). Cf. Swift's advice to Pope (26 Nov. 1725): 'Take care the bad poets do not outwit you, as they have served the good ones in every Age, whom they have provoked to transmit their Names to posterity' (*Correspondence of Alexander Pope*, ed. George Sherburn [Oxford, 1956], ii. 343; for Swift's comment on the obscurity of the Dunces, see ii. 504). Cf. *Champion*, 27 Nov. 1739.

[2] Herostratus, who supposedly set fire to the temple of Diana to make himself forever memorable. According to Aulus Gellius (*Attic Nights*, II. vi. 18) it was decreed that no one should ever mention his name. See also Valerius Maximus, *Factorum et dictorum memorabilium*, viii. 14, ext. 5. Cited also in *Champion*, 27 Nov. 1739.

[3] Cf. Fielding's essay connecting the book trade with whipping posts and the gallows, *CGJ* No. 51 (27 June).

Now look thro' Fate! behold the Scene she
draws!
What Aids, what Armies to assert her
Cause!
See all her Progeny, illustrious Sight!
Behold, and count them as they rise to
Light.
As Berecynthia, while her Offspring vye
In Homage to the Mother of the Sky,
Surveys around her, in the blest Abode,
An hundred Sons, and ev'ry Son a God:
Not with less Glory mighty Dulness crown'd,
Shall take thro' Grubstreet her triumphant
Round;
And her Parnassus glancing o'er at once,
Behold an hundred Sons, and each a
Dunce.[1]

A.

SATURDAY, AUGUST 22, 1752. NUMB. 60.

'Υπὲρ σεαυτοῦ μὴ φράσης ἐγκώμια'[2]

Be not the Trumpeter of your own Praise.

A French Author, a great Favorite of mine, and whom I have often quoted in
my Lucubrations, observes "that it is very common for Men to talk of
themselves, of their Children and their Family, and always in the Terms of
Commendation. But," says he, "if those who accustom themselves to such
Narratives could conceive how troublesome and tiresome they are to the rest
of the World, they would possibly learn to contain themselves a little better,
and to shew more Complaisance to the Patience of their Hearers. It is
moreover Matter of great Astonishment to me, that Men who are perpetually
praising themselves, scarce ever mention the Name of another Person but in
order to abuse it. Perhaps they intend to avail themselves of the Contrast,
and to recommend their own Conduct to general Approbation, by the
Censure of their Neighbours."[3]

---

[1] *Dunciad* (1729), iii. 115–30. The lines are part of the prophetic vision given in the Underworld to Colley Cibber, newly anointed as king of dullness, by the ghost of Elkanah Settle (1648–1724), dramatist and poet to the City of London.

[2] The line is one of the 'Sententiae' attributed to Menander in late antiquity; see *Menandri Sententiae*, ed. Siegfried Jaekel (Teubner, 1964), p. 78, l. 778.

[3] Abbé de Bellegarde, *Reflexions sur le ridicule et sur les moyens de l'eviter*, 10th edn. (Amsterdam, 1712), pp. 26–7; Fielding quotes from this work in *CGJ* Nos. 55 and 56 and here translates closely.

The Motive to the former of these Vices is clearly Vanity; which, as the ingenious Dr. Young says,

> Makes Dear Self on well-bred Tongues prevail,
> And I the little Hero of each Tale.[1]

The Motive to the latter is Malice; and to say a plain Truth, I firmly believe there is no Bosom where Vanity is to be found in any great Degree, which is not at the same Time pretty considerably tainted with Malice. Praise is a Mistress, in the Pursuit of which every vain Man must have many Rivals, and what Temper of Mind Men preserve to a Rival, need not to be here repeated.

To both these Impulses of Mind, there is no Man, I am afraid so liable as the Writer. Fame is sometimes his only Pursuit; but this is always blended with his other Views, even in the most mercenary, and for this simple Reason that it leads directly to Pudding. He must at least respect Fame, as the Cit in the Play doth his Reputation, because *the Loss of it* may tend *to Loss of Money.*[2] But in Fact his Views are commonly more noble; Vanity not Avarice is the Passion he would feed, and there is scarce an Inhabitant of Parnassus, even among the Poor of that Parish, who will not be more pleased with one who commends his Works, than with one who gives him a Dinner; which being the Case, it follows of Course that they must be all Rivals for the aforesaid Mistress, and may consequently be all suspected of bearing Malice to each other.

Again there is no Writer who can so easily indulge both these Inclinations, as the Writer of Miscellaneous Essays. It required the Genius of Cicero or Bolingbroke, to introduce their own Praises into every political Oration or Pamphlet;[3] or the Wit of Lucian, or South, to drag the Philosophers and Dissenters, into almost every Subject.[4] But such Essayist having a full Liberty to write not only what, but on what he pleases, may fill up very Page with his own Commendations, and with the Abuse of all other Writers.

When I meditate on these Matters, I can scarce refrain from taking some Praise to myself; I am even vain enough to think the Public have some little

[1] Edward Young, *Love of Fame, the Universal Passion: Satire I* in *The Poetical Works of . . . Edward Young* (1741), i. 174; Fielding owned this edition (Baker, item 529) and was a great admirer of Young (1683–1765), whose verse he often spoke of along with Pope's.

[2] Tipkin in Steele's *The Tender Husband* (1705), v. ii: 'Loss of reputation may tend to loss of money'; Fielding cites the same line, again without identifying the source, in the *Champion*, 4 Mar. 1739/40. The editor is indebted to Prof. W. B. Coley for this reference.

[3] Cf. Addison on this trait of Cicero: 'It is observed of *Tully*, . . . that his Works run very much in the First Person' (*Spectator*, No. 562, 2 July 1714); on Bolingbroke, see *CGJ* No. 15, above, p. 104 n. 5.

[4] On Lucian and the 'Philosophers', see Fielding's remarks in *CGJ* No. 52; for Robert South, see *CGJ* No. 18, above, p. 124 n. 4. One example of the tendency Fielding has in mind may be cited: South, in a sermon on the virtuous education of youth, works in a reference to Charles I having been murdered by 'a Company of *Coblers, Taylors, Draymen,* . . . and *Broken Tradesmen*; though since, I confess, dignify'd with the Title of *the Sober part of the Nation*' (*Sermons* [1717], v. 21).

Obligation to me, for that Silence which I have hitherto so inviolably maintained with Regard to my own Perfections;[1] and perhaps the more candid among my Readers, would allow some Applause to this Forbearance, if they knew what a Sacrifice I make of my own Inclinations, by thus consulting their Ease and Pleasure; for surely nothing can equal the Satisfaction which a Man feels in writing Encomiums on himself, unless it be the Disgust which every other Person is as sure to conceive at reading them.

In this Mood of thinking likewise I am apt to challenge to myself some Degree of Merit, towards my cotemporary Writers, especially those who write in my own Way. As these Gentlemen are I doubt not well assured of that immoderate Envy which I must bear to their great Genius and Learning, they will certainly acknowledge that to confine all this to myself, to smother these scorching Flames within my own Breast, without suffering even a Spark to escape, seems a little to deserve their Commendation.

But to deal ingenuously on this Occasion, I must acknowledge there are some prudential as well as generous Motives to this Silence. Two Considerations may perhaps be suspected of having some little Weight, in dissuading a Man even for his own Sake, from exhibiting his own Praise. First, that he will be sure of being very little read, and in the next Place of being much less believed. The Fear of this latter Fate, may likewise have some Share in prevailing on a Man to stifle his Envy notwithstanding all the Pleasure which is to be found in giving it Vent. However sweet it was to those great Men, whose Names are recorded in the Preface to the Dunciad, and in the Dunciad itself, to abuse the Characters of Pope, and Swift, and to assert, as they did, that the one wanted Humour, and the other was no Poet;[2] I much doubt whether they would not have bought their Pleasure too dear, at the Price of Public Scorn, even tho' the former had treated them with the same silent Contempt, with which they were treated by the latter. For this Reason I shall carefully avoid any Satire against the Popes and Swifts of the present Age. Tho' Envy of these great Men should boil in my own Bosom, I will never suffer it to boil over so as to run abroad into the Public.

To suppress two such powerful Passions as Vanity and Envy, is by no means an easy Task. It requires indeed little less Resolution than what animated the Spartan Youth, who concealed a Fox under his Garment, and

---

[1] For another instance of Fielding's fondness for treating 'Silence' in an ironic vein, see *CGJ* No. 59; see also Fielding's essay on political silence, appearing in *Common Sense* (13 May 1738), the manuscript of which has been discovered, described, and reprinted by M. C. with R. R. Battestin, 'A Fielding Discovery, with Some Remarks on the Canon', *SB* 33 (1980), 131–43.

[2] Fielding refers to the 'Testimonies of Authors Concerning our Poet and his Works' prefixed to the *Dunciad Variorum* (1729) and subsequent editions; those whose attacks on Pope are cited include John Dennis, John Oldmixon, Lewis Theobald, Leonard Welsted, as well as lesser 'dunces'. As an appendix Pope also included 'A List of Books, Papers, and Verses, in which our Author was abused . . . with the true Names of the Authors'. Pope's notes on the text of the poem are also larded with citations of writers who have abused him and Swift. See also *CGJ* No. 59.

rather than he would produce him openly, suffered the Vermin to gnaw his very Bowels.[1] To say Truth, I am afraid I should not have been able to persevere so long, had I not contrived a certain cunning Method of discharging myself in private; and which as it is a most curious Secret, I shall now communicate for the Use of others, who, if they pursue the same Method, will, I doubt not, meet with the same Success.

I will give it by Way of Receipt; and can truly say, it hath every Quality, with which Remedies are usually recommended; being extremely cheap, easy, safe and practicable.

A Receipt to prevent the ill Effects of a raging Vanity in an Author.[2]

[1] Plutarch, *Life of Lycurgus*, xviii; Fielding also alludes to this story in *Tom Jones*, v. vi.

[2] The 'Receipt' which follows is primarily an attack on John Hill, whom Fielding had scarcely alluded to since the 'paper war' of the early numbers of *CGJ*; see Nos. 1–4 and General Introduction, pp. xxxvii–xxxix. The details of the satire refer to an absurd incident which had occurred over two months earlier. On 6 May 1752 Hill was assaulted at Ranelagh by a young man named Mountefort Brown, who thought Hill had slandered him in his column in *LDA*, 30 Apr. In his 'Inspector' column in the following weeks Hill gave his readers almost daily bulletins on Brown's supposed flight to avoid prosecution—he had indeed left town—and on his own state of health following the assault: on 9 May he speaks of losing 'the Stream of Life'; on 11 May he reports that his doctors fear an 'Empyema' will develop on his side and have refused him visitors; on the following day he lists the surgeons attending him and prints a leader bravely accepting death; and on 14 May he reports improvement—his doctors consider sending him into the country 'under a proper Regimen of Asses Milk'. Fielding was drawn into this bizarre affair on 9 May, when Brown appeared before him and was admitted to bail; see the account in the 'Covent Garden' column of 11 May, printed below, Appendix I, in which Fielding makes a point of defending Brown against some of Hill's insults in *LDA*. Eventually, Brown appeared at the sessions at Hick's Hall and was discharged for lack of a prosecution, and though Hill pretended he was considering an action against him in the Court of King's Bench, the episode was at an end (see *LDA*, 30 May).

Hill had cut a ridiculous figure through all this; his hypochondriac claims of mortal injury, his varying accounts of the attack itself, his efforts to prove that Brown had no right to the title 'Esquire', and his dark hints that more was involved in the affair than met the eye all made him the butt of a parade of satiric pamphlets and prints. See, for example, *A Narrative of the Affair between Mr. Brown, and the Inspector* (1752); *The Inspector's Rhapsody or Soliloquy on the Loss of his Wigg* (1752); *Libitina Sine Conflictu; or, A true Narrative of the untimely Death of Doctor Atall* (1752), attributed to Arthur Murphy by another pamphlet, *Rules for Being a Wit* (1753), p. 15; and two satiric prints, 'A Night scene at Ranelagh on Wednesday 6th of May 1752' and 'Le Malade Imaginaire, or the Consultation', both of which quote extracts from Fielding's 'Covent Garden' column of 11 May (see *Catalogue of Prints and Drawings in the British Museum. Division I. Political and Personal Satires*, Nos. 3183 and 3184). The flamboyant 'Inspector', for once, had lost the favor of the town.

Fielding himself, however, did not contribute to these attacks on Hill in May and June, although his role in support of Brown was often alluded to (see e.g. *A Narrative of the Affair*, pp. 23–4). His return to satirizing Hill now, in late August, was no doubt prompted by a new and even more astounding demonstration of Hill's effrontery, the publication of a piece called *The Impertinent* on 13 Aug., which attacked Fielding, Smart, and John Hill; as Johnson pointed out in his notice of the piece in *GM* for Aug., *The Impertinent* was by Hill himself, even though Hill had pretended to attack it and to defend Fielding and Smart in his 'Inspector' column of 25 Aug. This episode, as Cross points out (ii. 421–2), was outrageous enough to cause Fielding to break his silence on Hill and enter the fray once more. At the same time, of course, Hill was an obvious example to employ in any essay on the vanity and self-praise of writers; *Some Remarks on the Life and Writings of Dr. J—— H——, Inspector-General of Great Britain* (1752) calls Vanity the 'ruling Principle, or Spring of Action' of his life (pp. 22–7). The 'receipt' formula Fielding uses for his satire was also conventional; cf. John Kennedy's *Whipping Rods for Trifling, Scurrhill, Scriblers* (1752), p. 32, for 'A Receipt for the Writing of Inspectors' making the same point as Fielding's.

When the Fit is at the highest, take of Pen, Ink, and Paper. Q.S.[1] Make a Panegyrick on yourself; Stuff it well with all the cardinal Virtues; season to your Taste with Wit, Humour, and Learning. You may likewise add, as you see Occasion, Birth, Politeness, and Such like.

In the choice of your Ingredients, be sure to have a particular Regard to your Sore Part.[2] If your Ears be Sore with any fresh pulling, or your Br——ch with any fresh Kicking, infuse a double Portion of Courage. If you have lately betrayed your Ignorance so grosly as to make Ovid guilty of two false Quantities in one Line, dash plentifully with Learning.[3]

If you are publicly known to be an infamous Liar, Season very high with Honour; if you are notoriously sprung from the *Dunghill*, take of Ancestors from the English History at the least half a dozen.[4] *Et sic de cæteris.*[5]

When you have writ your Panegyrick, you may read it as often as you please; but take Care that no body hears you, and then be sure to——burn your Panegyrick.

This last Operation, I own, will cause some Pain, but when it is considered that if you do not burn it yourself, other People will; nay perhaps will treat it yet worse, and bring it to a much more dishonourable and stinking End, a wise Man will soon force himself to the Resolution of putting his Panegyrick beyond the Reach of Malice.

As to the Cure of Envy, I need not give the Receipt for it at length. It is sufficient to direct the Choice of the very contrary Ingredients; that is to say, instead of all the good, make use of all the bad Qualities both of the Head and Heart.

And here likewise you are to examine your own Sore Part; if any Man hath ridiculed you with Wit and Humour, Take of Blockhead, Dunce, and Fool; of each three Penfulls. If another hath kicked and cuffed you lustily, be sure to becoward him well, and if the Assault was in Public, before the Eyes of many Gentlemen, the Word Coward can never be too often repeated.[6]

---

[1] *quantum sufficit*, as much as suffices.

[2] Referring to Hill's concern with the 'Empyema' on his left side, as well as to his shifting account of the manner of his injury; cf. *Libitina Sine Conflictu*: 'he was, with great Reason, lugged by the Nose, which it is insisted was the only Assault made on the Doctor' (p. 8).

[3] Hill's bad Latin, especially in the mottos for his 'Inspector' column, was frequently ridiculed; see *Some Remarks on the Life and Writings of Dr. J—— H——, Inspector-General of Great Britain* (1752), pp. 45, 62; William Kenrick's *Pasquinade* (1753), p. 23; and Arthur Murphy in the *Gray's Inn Journal*, No. 3 (4 Nov. 1752). Fielding may be referring specifically to Hill's motto from Ovid for his column in *LDA* for 13 May, at the height of the controversy with Brown: *Et herbarum subjecta est potentia nobis*, in which the word *est* is an interpolation by Hill which creates the prosodic problem Fielding indicates. The full line from Ovid (*Metamorphoses*, i. 522) is *dicor, et herbarum subiecta potentia nobis*.

[4] For similar hints that Hill had sought to elevate himself by false claims of honors or degrees, see *Some Remarks*, p. 13, and Kennedy's *Whipping Rods*, p. 32; cf. *CGJ* No. 72, below. Fielding also uses the 'Dunghill' image in *CGJ* No. 3, above.

[5] 'And thus concerning the others.'

[6] Hill had called Brown a coward in his 'Inspector' column in *LDA* for 9 May and had repeated the charge as recently as *LDA*, 19 Aug.; his original paper which provoked the incident had also laid on

But with Regard to this last, great Caution must be had; first, that the Person so to be becowarded, be first under a Prosecution at Law for the Assault, and secondly, that he be then out of the Kingdom.[1] These Precautions are however useless, if you apply your Satire, as you are above advised to apply your Panegyrick, I mean to the Flames; otherwise they will be abundantly necessary, to prevent your Ears from being pulled, 'till they resemble those of the Ass, lately exposed at the Bedford Coffee-House.[2]

I shall conclude this Paper with two Quotations; the first is from the Mouth of Socrates. *Never speak of yourself: for he who commends himself is vain; and he who abuses himself is absurd.*[3] The other is from the witty Dr. South. He advises *an abusive Writer to be, of all others, most circumspect as to his own Actions, seeing he is so sure of meeting with no Quarter.*[4] A Man must, indeed, be most furiously mad, who sets up for a Satirist, when it is scarce possible for him to discharge a single Vice at any other, that will not recoil on himself. In a Word, with my Friend Horace, *melius non tangere clamo.*[5] A Hint, which those of my cotemporary Writers, who understand Latin, will for the future, I hope, observe.   A.

Brown 'an Imputation of Cowardice' (*A Narrative of the Affair* [1752], p. 5). Cf. the satiric rehearsal of Hill's 'Dying Words' in *Libitina Sine Conflictu* (1752): 'I'll brazen it out—a d——d two-handed Fellow—call him a *Coward* in my next Paper—Caracature of me by *Hogarth*—Nuts to *Fielding* . . .' (p. 13). For some of the 'Gentlemen' who were present at Ranelagh during the assault and who appeared in Fielding's court on Brown's behalf, see the 'Covent Garden' column of 11 May, printed below, Appendix I.

[1] Brown had gone about 50 miles from London on private business; see Fielding's defense of him on this point in the 'Covent Garden' column of 11 May, Appendix I, below; according to *A Narrative of the Affair* (p. 22), Hill, in a deposition sworn before Justice Lediard, also accused 'one Mr. *Fay*, a Gentleman who now is, and was long before the Affair happened, in *Ireland*'.

[2] Referring to the Lion Hill had placed in the Bedford Coffee-House (see *CGJ* No. 2, above, p. 26) and also, of course, to Hill himself, who to the delight of his enemies had been prescribed 'Asses Milk' for his 'Empyema'. Cf. *Some Remarks* (1752): 'every Ass of your Acquaintance has had an Opportunity of braying his Sentiments through that damned Lion' (p. 9).

[3] Not located in the mouth of Socrates, but proverbial. Plutarch reports that Cato in one of his speeches says, 'self-praise and self-depreciation are alike absurd' ('Comparison of Aristedes with Marcus Cato', *Life of Marcus Cato*, v. 2), and a similar saying is in the collection of moral apothegms of unknown authorship called the *Distichs of Cato*, ii. 16. Self-praise was a common topic among the classical rhetoricians; see Plutarch's essay 'On Praising Oneself Inoffensively', *Moralia*, 539–47.

[4] As Jensen suggests (ii. 256), Fielding is probably paraphrasing roughly a passage in the Preface to South's *Animadversions upon Dr. Sherlock's Book* (1693): '*And if this be his Way and Temper,* never to give Quarter, *I am sure he has no cause to expect any, whatsoever he may find*' (p. iii). The thought is a constant theme in this work of South's; see also e.g. p. 330 and all of ch. xi. On South's controversy with Sherlock, see *CGJ* No. 18, above, p. 124 n. 4.

[5] *Satires*, II. i. 45: ' "Better not touch me!" I shout' (Loeb).

SATURDAY, AUGUST 29, 1752. NUMB. 61.

Τὸν ἐλάττω μὴ ἀποσκυβαλίσῃς

CLEOBULUS.[1]

Do not despise your Inferiors.

There is not in Human Nature a more odious Disposition, than a Proneness to Contempt.[2] Nor is there any which more certainly denotes a bad Mind. For in a good, and a benign Temper, there can be no Room for this Sensation. That which constitutes an Object of Contempt to the Malevolent, becomes the Object of other Passions to a worthy and good-natur'd Man: For in such a Person, Wickedness and Vice, must raise Hatred and Abhorrence; and Weakness and Folly will be sure to excite Compassion; so that he will find no Object of his Contempt, in all the Actions of Men.

And however detestable this Quality, which is a Mixture of Pride and Ill-Nature, may appear when considered in the serious School of Heraclitus, it will present no less absurd and ridiculous an Idea to the laughing Sect of Democritus,[3] especially as we may observe, that the meanest and basest of all human Beings are generally the most forward to despise others. So that the most contemptible are generally the most contemptuous.

I have often wished that some of those curious Persons who have employed their Time in enquiring into the Nature and Actions of several Insects, such as Bees and Ants, had taken some Pains to examine whether they are not apt to express any contemptuous Behaviour one towards another; the plain Symptoms of which might possibly be discovered by the Help of Microscopes.[4] It is scarce conceivable that the Queen Bee, amongst the hundred Gallants which she keeps for her own Recreation, should not

---

[1] One of the 'Seven Sages of Greece' who flourished 620–550 BC; the proverb Fielding quotes is found in various collections of their sayings, e.g. *Dicta septem sapientum* (Paris, 1558), p. 4.

[2] A frequent theme with Fielding; see e.g. 'An Essay on Conversation' in *Miscellanies* (1743), (ed. H. K. Miller, Wesleyan Edn. [Oxford, 1972], pp. 134–9), where Fielding also analyzes contempt as a compound of pride and ill-nature, adding that 'Murder is not a much more cruel Injury' than contempt of others, 'the truest Symptom of a base and a bad Heart'. See also *Champion*, 13 Mar. 1740, and *CGJ* Nos. 59 and 65.

[3] Referring to the traditional antithesis between Democritus, the 'laughing philosopher', and Heraclitus, the 'Weeping Fool-ass-ofer, that for fear of looking Old, never Laugh'd in his Life' (Thomas Flatman, *Heraclitus Ridens* [coll. edn., 1713], i. 19). Cf. the prologue to Fielding's *The Author's Farce* (1730): 'Bred in Democritus his laughing schools, / Our author flies sad Heraclitus' rules', and the poem 'Weep, Heraclitus' prefixed to Burton's *Anatomy of Melancholy*, 6th edn. (1651/2).

[4] Fielding has in mind such moralizing works of natural history as *An Account of English Ants* (1747) by his cousin, William Gould, a work which he discusses in *CGJ* No. 70, or John Thorley's *Melissalogia, or Female Monarchy; being an Enquiry into the Nature, Order, and Government of the Bees* (1744), which describes the justice, honesty, temperance, sobriety, chastity, etc., of bees. Cf. Mandeville's demonstration that 'Envy is visible in Brute Beasts' in Remark N of *Fable of the Bees*, and see *CGJ* No. 65, where Fielding, as he does here, speculates on envy and contempt among lice.

have some especial Favorites, and it is full as likely, that these Favorites will so carry themselves towards their Brethren, as to display sufficient Marks of their Contempt to the Eye of an accurate Discoverer in the Manners of the Reptile World. For my own Part, I have remarked many Instances of Contempt amongst Animals, which I have farther observed to increase in Proportion to the Decrease of such Species, in the Rank and Order of the Animal Creation. Mr. Ellis[1] informs me that he never could discover any the least Indication of Contempt in the Lions under his Care; the Horse, I am sorry to say it, gives us some, the Ass many more, the Turky-cock more still, and the Toad is supposed to burst itself frequently with the Violence of this Passion.[2] To pursue it gradually downwards would be too tedious. It may be reasonably supposed to arrive at a prodigious Height before it descends to the Louse. With what a Degree of Contempt may we conceive that a substantial Freeholder of this Kind, who is well established in the Head of a Beggar Wench, considers a poor vagabond Louse, who hath strayed into the Head of a Woman of Quality; where it is in hourly Danger of being arrested by the merciless Hands of her Woman!

This may perhaps seem to some a very ridiculous Image, and as ridiculous as I apprehend to a Being of a superior Order, will appear a contemptuous Man; one puffed up with some trifling, perhaps fancied Superiority, and looking round him with Disdain, on those who are perhaps so nearly his Equals, that to such a Being as I have just mentioned, the Difference may be as inconsiderable and imperceptible between the Despiser and the Despised, as the Difference between two of the meanest Insects may seem to us.[3]

And as a very good Mind, as I have before observed, will give no Entertainment to any such Affection; so neither will a sensible Mind, I am persuaded, find much Opportunity to exert it. If Men would make but a moderate Use of that Self Examination, which Philosophers and Divines have recommended to them, it would tend greatly to the Cure of this Disposition. Their Contempt would then perhaps, as their Charity is said to

---

[1] John Ellis or Ellys (1701–57), portrait painter and lifelong friend of Hogarth, had been given by Walpole the sinecure of master keeper of the lions in the Tower, as reward for his services in buying paintings for the collection at Houghton; see John B. Shipley, 'Ralph, Ellys, Hogarth, and Fielding: The Cabal Against Jacopo Amigoni', *ECS* 1 (1968), 313–31. Fielding was almost certainly the author of 'An Epistle to Mr. Ellys the Painter', a poem appearing in *The Comedian, or Philosophical Enquirer*, No. 5 (Aug. 1732), pp. 36–8, edited by Fielding's good friend Thomas Cooke. See Shipley, p. 322, and Thomas Lockwood, 'Fielding's *Champion* in the Planning Stage', *PQ* 59 (1980), 238–41.

[2] Fielding may be thinking of the Aesopian fable of the envious toad who burst trying to be as large an an ox (Babrius, Fable 28; in Phaedrus, Fable 24, the story is of a frog, not a toad).

[3] Cf. Addison in *Guardian*, No. 153 (5 Sept. 1713): 'If there be any thing which makes human Nature appear *ridiculous* to Beings of superior Faculties, it must be Pride'; Addison goes on to ridicule vanity by observing a molehill inhabited by rational pismires. This essay had recently been reprinted, without attribution, in Robert Dodsley's *The Preceptor* (1748), i. 7–8. See also *Spectator*, No. 621 (17 Nov. 1714).

do, begin at Home. To say Truth, a Man hath this better Chance of despising himself, than he hath of despising others, as he is likely to know himself best.

But I am sliding into a more serious Vein than I intended. In the Residue of this Paper, therefore I will confine myself to one particular Consideration only, one which will give as ridiculous an Idea of Contempt, and afford as strong Dissuasives against it, as any other which at present suggests itself.

The Consideration I mean, is, that Contempt is, generally at least, mutual, and that there is scarce any one Man who despises another without being at the same Time despised by him, of which I shall endeavour to produce some few Instances.

As the Right Hon. the Lord Squanderfield, at the Head of a vast Retinue, passes by Mr. Moses Buckram, Citizen and Taylor, in his Chaise and one.[1] "See there!" says my Lord, with an Air of the highest Contempt, "That Rascal Buckram, with his fat Wife, I suppose he is going to his Country House, for such Fellows must have their Country House, as well as their Vehicle. These are the Rascals that complain of Want of Trade." Buckram on the other Side is no sooner recovered from the Fear of being run over, before he could get out of the Way; than turning to his Wife, he cries, "Very fine, Faith! an honest Citizen is to be run over by such Fellows as these, who drive about their Coaches and Six, with other People's Money. See my Dear, what an Equipage he hath, and yet he cannot find Money to pay an honest Tradesman. He is above 150l. deep in my Books; How I despise such Lords."

Lady Fanny Rantun, from the side Box, casting her Eyes on an honest Pawnbroker's Wife below her, bids Lady Betty her Companion take Notice of that Creature in the Pit; "did you ever see, Lady Betty," says she, "such a strange Wretch? how the aukward Monster is dressed!" The good Woman at the same Time surveying Lady Fanny, and offended perhaps, at a scornful Smile, which she sees in her Countenance,—whispers her Friend.— "Observe Lady Fanny Rantun. As great Airs as that fine Lady gives herself, my Husband hath all her Jewels under Lock and Key, what a contemptible Thing is poor Quality!"[2]

Is there on Earth a greater Object of Contempt than a poor Scholar to a splendid Beau; unless perhaps the splendid Beau to the poor Scholar![3] The

---

[1] Fielding uses here the conventional contrast between the tradesman or 'cit' and the aristocrat; cf. the letters from 'Zara Grandemonde' and 'Paul Traffick' in *CGJ* No. 43. 'Buckram' suggests a 'stiff and starched manner' (*OED*), and 'Squanderfield' is the name of the husband in Hogarth's *Marriage à la Mode* (1745). For another instance of reciprocal pride proceeding down the social scale, cf. Mandeville, *Fable of the Bees*, Remark M.

[2] Again the contrast is between social classes, with 'Rantun' suggesting noisiness and rant (cf. 'Drum' and 'Rout'). On the placement of various classes in the theater, see the essay on 'Betters' in *CGJ* No. 27 and 'Traffick's' letter in No. 43.

[3] Cf. *CGJ* No. 42.

Philosopher and the World; the Man of Business and the Man of Pleasure; the Beauty and the Wit; the Hypocrite and the Profligate; the Covetous and the Squanderer, are all alike Instances of this reciprocal Contempt.

Take the same Observations into the lowest Life, and we shall find the same Proneness to despise each other. The common Soldier, who hires himself out to be shot at for five pence a Day; who is the only Slave in a free Country, and is liable to be sent to any Part of the World without his Consent, and whilst at Home subject to the severest Punishments, for Offences which are not to be found in our Law Books;[1] yet this noble Personage looks with a contemptuous Air on all his Brethren of that Order in the Commonwealth, whether of Mechanics or Husbandmen, from whence he was himself taken. On the other Hand, however adorned with his Brick-dust coloured Cloth, and bedaubed with worsted Lace of a Penny a Yard, the very Gentleman Soldier is as much despised in his Turn, by the whistling Carter, who comforts himself, that he is a free Englishman, and will live with no Master any longer than he likes him; nay, and tho' he never was worth twenty Shillings in his Life, is ready to answer a Captain if he offends him.—*D—n you, Sir, who are you? is it not WE that pays you?*

This contemptuous Disposition is in Reality the sure Attendant on a mean and bad Mind in every Station; on the contrary, a great and good man will be free from it whether he be placed at the Top or Bottom of Life. I was therefore not a little pleased with a Rebuke given by a Blackshoe Boy to another, who had expressed his Contempt of one of the Modern Town-Smarts. "Why should you despise him, Jack," said the honest Lad, "we are all what the Lord pleased to make us."

I will conclude this Paper with a Story which a Gentleman of Honour averred to me to be Truth. His Coach being stopt in Piccadilly by two or three Carts, which, according to Custom, were placed directly across the Way;[2] he observed a very dirty Fellow, who appeared to belong to a Mud Cart, give another Fellow several lashes with his Whip, and at the same Time heard him repeat more than once—*D—n you, I will teach you Manners to your Betters.* My Friend could not easily from these Words divine what might possibly be the Station of the unhappy Sufferer, till at length, to the great Satisfaction of his Curiosity, he discovered that he was the Driver of a Dust Cart drawn by Asses.

---

[1] These were common observations about soldiers; cf. *LM* 6 (1737), 477, giving a parliamentary 'speech': 'They are not free Subjects, they are Soldiers, not governed by the Laws of their Country but by a Law made for them only.' The same passage points out that 'an *English* Soldier is much more a Slave than any Soldier in *France* can be'; see also *LM* 15 (1746), 442; and 20 (1751), 587.

[2] See *CGJ* No. 49, above, p. 271.

SATURDAY, SEPTEMBER 16,[1] 1752.   NUMB. 62.

Insanire parat certe ratione modoque.[2]

To Sir ALEXANDER DRAWCANSIR, Knt.
Censor of Great Britain.

Bedlam, Apr. 9, 1752.

Sir,[3]

I have been confined in this Place four Years; my Friends, that is, my Relations, but, as I call them, my *Enemies*, think me Mad, but to shew you I am not, I'll send you a Specimen of my Present State of Mind.——About a Week ago, a grave Gentleman came to the Grate of my Cell and threw me in a Pamphlet, written it seems by a Gent. of Cambridge.[4] I read it over, and approve the Drama much, but I must send you some Thoughts that occur'd to me from Reading the Prefix'd Five Letters.——the Author it seems lives at Pembroke-Hall, in Cambridge, where Sophocles, Euripides, and Æschylus, have, I don't doubt, been his darling Studies, not forgetting the abominable Rules of Aristotle, who indisputably wrote very properly concerning Dramatic Poetry at his Time of Day, but what a Figure wou'd a Modern Tragedy make with his three Unities![5]——if Shakespeare had observed them——he wou'd have flown like a *Paper-Kite*, not *soar'd like an*

---

[1] By the Calendar Act of 1751, the day following 2 Sept. 1752 was 'called, reckoned, and accounted' 14 Sept. 1752, with the intermediate eleven days simply omitted; despite the dates on the essays, then, only a week had elapsed since *CGJ* No. 61.

[2] 'He is surely preparing to go mad by rule and method'; adapted from Horace, *Satires*, II. iii. 271 (*insanire paret certa ratione modoque*), with the subjunctive changed to indicative.

[3] This letter and portions of the second are marked through in Hope Folio 11 (see General Introduction, above, p. xxx). The use of 'has' causes Jensen (ii 259) to doubt Fielding's authorship, though Cross (ii. 375–6) accepts it. Arthur Sherbo argues on the basis of internal evidence that the first letter is by Arthur Murphy and reprints the entire essay in his *New Essays by Arthur Murphy* (East Lansing, 1963), pp. 174–5; the claim for Murphy's authorship had been made earlier by John P. Emery, *Arthur Murphy* (Philadelphia, 1946), p. 13. See p. 334 n. 5, below, on the authorship of the second letter in this leader. No reason has been suggested for the early date of Apr. 9 on the letter by 'Tragicomicus'.

[4] The reference is to *Elfrida, A Dramatic Poem. Written on the Model of The Antient Greek Tragedy* (Mar. 1752), by William Mason (1724–97). Mason prefixed to his play five 'Letters concerning the following Drama', dated from Pembroke Hall, Cambridge, in which he defended his use of a classical form. Along with praising the use of a chorus and calling for strict observance of the unities of time and place, he saw fit to argue that veneration of Shakespeare is the groundwork of false criticism of the drama. Shakespeare, he says, was naturally great, but 'if we had a Tragedy of his form'd on the Greek model, we should find in it more frequent, if not nobler, instances of the high Poetical capacity, than in any single composition he has left us' (p. ix). Both Mason's play and his critical views were eulogized in *Remarks on Mr. Mason's Elfrida* (May, 1752) and severely criticized, perhaps by Samuel Johnson, in *GM* 22 (May, 1752), 224–6. For a poem in its praise see *GM* 22 (1752), 136.

[5] Cf. Johnson's later assault on the unities of time and place (not actually suggested by Aristotle's *Poetics* but among Renaissance accretions to neo-classical theory) in his *Preface to Shakespeare* (1765). The author of *Remarks* praises Mason for observing them without his genius being 'strait'ned or cramp'd' (p. 56).

Eagle[1]——Again, Sir, as to his *Chorus* he is so fond of, why that did very well amongst the Greek Writers; but methinks this *Mr. Chorus* would be a very impertinent Fellow if he was to put in his Observations on any of Shakespeare's interesting Scenes;[2] as for Example, what do you think of this same *Chorus*, if he was to be upon the Stage when, in the Play of Othello, Iago is imprinting those exquisite Tints of Jealousy upon Othello's Mind in the third Act;[3] or suppose when Desdemona drops the fatal Handkerchief, the *Chorus* was to call after her to bid her take it up again, or tell the Audience what was to happen in Case she did not.——Or suppose, Sir, this same *Chorus* was to stand by, and tell us Brutus and Cassius were going to differ, but that they would make it up again——would not this prevent the noble Anxiety this famous Scene[4] in Julius Cæsar raises in the Minds of a sensible Audience? Another Use this ingenious Gentleman finds out for the *Chorus*, and that is, to explain the Characters and Sentiments of the several Personages in the Drama, to the Audience.[5] Now, Sir, there is a Nation in the World which has found out a way of doing this very effectually without *interrupting the Action*—and that is, the *Chinese*; these People always make the Characters of the Drama come upon the Stage before the Play begins, and tell who they are, as thus Sir.

Enter Dramatis Personæ.

1. I am Taw Maw-shaw, King of Tonchin, Brother to Hunfish, am to be dethroned by my Brother, and killed with the Sabre of the renowned Schimshaw.

2. I am Hunfish, Brother to Taw-Maw-shaw, I am to dethrone him, and usurp his Crown.

3. I am Schimshaw Master of the great Sabre which is to kill the King Taw-Maw-shaw.[6]

---

[1] A conventional image; cf. the prologue to James Miller's *The Universal Passion* (1737), admitting his inability to 'soar like Shakespeare's Eagle Wing', and a song by Garrick about Shakespeare in *Harlequin's Invasion* (1759) containing the line, 'He could soar with the eagle, and sing with the wren' (*Poetical Works* [1785], ii. 393). Sherbo (p. 210 n.) cites a similar expression by Murphy in *Gray's Inn Journal*, No. 41.

[2] Mason, in Letter III (p. vii), had proclaimed, 'I have, I know not how . . . contracted a kind of veneration for the old Chorus; and am willing to think it essential to the Tragic Drama'. Among other things, he argues that admitting a chorus will restore the unities of time and place 'to equal rights' with unity of action and will restrain modern playwrights from revelling in secret intrigues and business instead of 'Simplicity, Nature, and Pathos' (p. viii). Cf. Johnson's (?) response in *GM* 22 (1752), 224: 'A chorus is purely artificial, and wholly foreign to every natural event; it is only an expedient which was used to assist the representation before a better was discovered.' *Elfrida* has a chorus of British Virgins.

[3] III. iii.   [4] IV. ii, iii.

[5] What Mason actually says is that the audience may be instructed by the Chorus 'how to be affected properly, with the characters and actions which are represented' (p. xii), i.e. how to make the morally correct interpretation.

[6] The view of Chinese drama given here may be found in the influential *General History of China* by Jean Baptiste du Halde, translated and printed in four volumes in London (1736). After explaining that the Chinese know nothing of the unities, Du Halde remarks, 'In the printed Books they seldom set

Thus, Sir, do these wise People let you into the Characters of the Drama; which is to be sure a much wiser way, than by a *Chorus*, who interrupt the Actors to cram in their stupid Remarks.——Indeed, when Dramatic Poetry first appeared, the whole was represented *by one Person*,[1] and there it was necessary the *Chorus* should come in, to give the poor Solo Speaker a little Breath, but as I have half a dozen Plays by me which I intend to bring upon the Stage, I beg you will insist upon it that this learned Cantab[2] says no more about his *Chorus*, for it would be very hard upon me if I had not the same Indulgence which has been shewn *to all my Cotemporaries*; which is to let the Audience find out the Meaning of my Characters if they can, of themselves; if not, let them depart as wise as they came.——

I am,

Sir, Yours in clean Straw,

TRAGICOMICUS.

N.B. I have no Objection to the Choruses of the immortal Handel.[3]

If you observe, Sir, this learned Gentleman finds fault with Shakespeare's *Chorus* in Harry the Vth, and says it would do better in other Metre.[4]——If I had him here, I believe I should do him a Mischief.

Mr. Censor.[5]

I was the other Day in Company with a young Lady, with whose Alliance I

---

down the Name of the Person who speaks, because . . . he always tells the Spectators who he is himself, and begins with telling his Name, and the Part he is to act in the Play' (iii. 196). The sample play which follows opens with a character saying, 'I am *Tou Ngan Cou*, Prime Minister of War in the Kingdom of *Tsin*' (iii. 197) and relating the motives and circumstances of his role—but not, as in the Tragicomicus letter, revealing the future action.

[1] See Aristotle's *Poetics*, iv. 12, 13.

[2] Cantabrigian, member of the University of Cambridge.

[3] On Handel, see *CGJ* No. 26, p. 168 above, n. 2.

[4] Mason, arguing that Shakespeare would be improved by classical dress, had said, 'I think you have a proof of this in those parts of his historical plays, which are call'd Chorus's, and written in the common Dialogue metre. And your imagination will easily conceive, how fine an ode the description of the night, preceding the battle of Agincourt, would have made in his hands, and what additional grace it would receive from that form of composition' (p. ix).

[5] Cross (ii. 376) again accepts this letter as Fielding's own, but Jensen (ii. 260), pointing to 'has' and 'does', rejects it. Sherbo (*New Essays*, p. 175) believes Murphy wrote this letter and the comment following it, but admits there is no internal evidence to support his view except Murphy's use of the pseudonym 'Philomath' elsewhere. John P. Emery (*Arthur Murphy*, p. 13) again ascribes the letter and comment to Murphy, offering no argument except a note which says, 'The writer of this monograph has not published his proof of Murphy's authorship of parts of the *Covent-Garden Journal*' (p. 175 n.). For doubt about Emery's conjectures, see Howard H. Dunbar, *The Dramatic Career of Arthur Murphy* (New York, 1946), p. 4. The present editor believes that the comment following the letter is certainly by Fielding, and probably the letter as well. See Martin Battestin, 'Fielding's Contributions to the *Universal Spectator* (1736–7)', *SP* 83 (1986), 94, which points out that this letter 'bears every mark of Fielding's own style' and that 'Philomath' was a common pseudonym, used (probably) by Fielding himself in a contribution to the *Craftsman* in 1737.

hope some Time to be honoured: We accidentally fell into a Discourse concerning Religion; during which I defended my Argument pretty warmly, and, according to my usual Openness, declared myself a Freethinker; at which she was much concerned, as she had conceived a most horrible Idea of that Sect of People. You must know, Mr. Censor, that by a Freethinker I mean a Man who in the Old Testament, as well as in all other Writings, makes use of his Reason as a Guide, and will believe nothing contradictory to that or common Sense, and who does not put faith in Matters he does not comprehend.

Now the Reason of my troubling you with this is, that as a Unity of Sentiment is quite necessary for Happiness in the Matrimonial State, you will in your next Paper lay down, how far a Man is to be conducted by Reason in the Scriptures (which I think God has given him as the grand Criterion by which he is to judge of every Thing) and whether God requires us to believe any Thing which we cannot understand, which my female Disputant imagines absolutely necessary to Salvation.

I always thought *that* Man the happiest, who made choice of a sensible Woman to spend his Life with; but I begin now to see, that unless a Woman is as deep-read as a Man (which I believe seldom or never happens) or so fond of him and good natured, as to give the Preference to his Judgment in matters of such a Nature, there will be Foundation for endless Feuds and Cavils, which of course will intirely imbitter and render that State disagreeable.[1] I assure you, I have known the like in my own Family. If therefore you will in your next Paper, settle how far a Woman may interest herself and meddle with her Husband's Principles, it will be a certain Means of preventing a great deal of Unhappiness, and be ever acknowledged, by

Your constant Reader, and Admirer,

PHILOMATH.

My Correspondent must excuse me from presuming to decide in such great Points as the Qualifications, Limits, Merit, &c. of Faith; but as to his last Question, *how far a Woman may interest herself and meddle with her Husband's Principles*, I shall give him the Opinion of a very ingenious Casuist, which tho' delivered on no very similar Occasion, may serve to give a sufficient Hint of my own Opinion in the present Case.

There happening once a Dispute between a certain Author and a certain Actress, concerning the retaining or striking out some Lines in the Author's Play, and which were to be repeated by the Actress; the Author, as usual,

[1] The statement is in accord with Fielding's own view of the basis of a happy marriage; see his poem 'To a Friend on the Choice of a Wife', *Miscellanies* (1743), and the discussion by Miller, *Essays*, pp. 103–13. On the question of learned women, see the satire on Mrs Bennet in *Amelia*, VI. vii and x. i, and Martin Battestin's note, Wesleyan Edn. (Oxford, 1983), p. 255.

alledged that they were the very best Lines in his whole Play, indeed the best he had ever writ; that they were particularly approved by all his Friends, and that he was sure they would actually be called for on the Stage, if omitted. In Answer to all this the Actress only persisted, that she did not understand them, and consequently could convey no Idea of them to the Audience. The Decision of this Dispute was at length referr'd to Mr. Quin;[1] who, having perused the Lines, with great Gravity and Silence at last returned the Actress her Part, and gave Judgment in favour of the Author, That the Lines should be spoke if he desired it; for sure, Madam, added the Judge, every Gentleman hath a right to be Damned in his own Way.[2]

SATURDAY, SEPTEMBER 23, 1752.   NUMB. 63.

Mr. Censor,[3]

Had not I long resolved to be intimate with no Man, I do not know any Gentleman's Acquaintance I should covet sooner than your Worship's. However, as I have not debarred myself the Privilege of writing to those from whom I run no risque of an Answer, I intend to trouble you now and then with a Letter. Perhaps you may think me a troublesome Correspondent, as I am a very odd Fellow. And in order that you may have some Idea of my Oddities, I shall give you a short Account of myself, the darling Subject of every Author's Pen, but your own.[4] In the first Place, I must inform you that I am of no Business, have neither Relations, Friends or Acquaintance. I spend exactly a Hundred a Year, which is all my Income. Neither Ambition or Avarice, disturb my Rest. I went to School till I was Eighteen, at which Time my Father proposed to buy me a Cornetcy of Dragoons, but he died before my Commission was bought, and left my Mother too poor to lay down so much Money without distressing herself. My Eagerness to have a Cockade made me suffer much at this disappointment. Indolence succeeded Disappointment, and I kept my Chamber for a whole Year. When I was five and twenty I lost my Mother, and renewed my Desires of going into the Army, and contracted a warm Friendship with a Schoolfellow who was to assist me in this Affair, but he, by the Contrivance of my wicked Footman,

---

[1] On James Quin, see *CGJ* No. 26, above, p. 167 n. 1. This anecdote is typical of Quin, whose jokes, according to the *Life* published in 1766, 'may be called the standing jests of the town' (pp. 1–2).

[2] Cf. a story told in *Quin's Jests* (1766): Theophilus Cibber, seeking Quin's opinion on a play he had written, was finally advised 'not to bring it on in his life-time. "Why so, said he with no small astonishment?" "Because, resumed Quin, when you are *dead, you* and your *play* may be *damned* together"' (pp. 76–7).

[3] This letter is probably not Fielding's. It is struck through in the Bodleian Library (Hope Folio 11); see General Introduction, p. xxx. Cross (ii. 377–8), offering no evidence, suggests Sarah Fielding as the 'E. R.' who contributed this letter and another in the following number; for the more likely possibility that both are by John Fielding, see the notes on No. 64, below.

[4] Cf. Fielding's development of this theme in *CGJ* No. 60, above.

made a shift to cheat me out of Seven hundred Pounds. This put an end to my Opinion of Friendship, and gave me a Disgust to Servants. The next two Years I led in perfect Idleness, and lived every Day in danger of an Apoplex, and should have slept away the rest of my Life, had not I been rouzed by a sprightly Cousin of mine from this lethargic State. With her I fell desperately in Love, and began once more to think of going into the World. I drest gaily, followed her close, got her Consent; the Writings were drawn, and the Day fixed for our Marriage. But O, Mr. Censor, how shall I tell it? That very Day a cursed Fever snatched the lovely, innocent Maid from Life and me. Now Fortune had done her worst. What I did for a whole Year after this Accident I can't tell. Her Tomb was the only Place I visited, and Books my only Amusement. In a Word, my Life was as inanimate as that of an Oyster. However, being naturally active, I grew tired of myself, and resolved to spend the rest of my Days in the Gratification of my Curiosity. I bought me an Annuity for my Life, hired an old Woman for my Servant, (for I was determined to let no Man come near me again) furnished myself with Cloaths of different Sorts, with a View of visiting every public Place in or near Town, and to know as much of every Man's Business as I could, thinking by this Means to acquire a perfect Knowledge of human Nature. In order to begin at the Top, I made my first Appearance at Court, which I frequented some Time without any sort of Satisfaction. Whispering, Bowing, and Cringing, seemed to be the whole Business of this Assembly. My next Visit was to the City, where I soon found myself despised as an idle Fellow; and one Day got a Pull by the Nose by a Jew, for listening to a Conversation between him and a Broker. For fear this Accident should have made me remarkable at that end of the Town, I resolved to spend some Time in the Coffee-Houses in Westminster: But this Scheme proved as unsuccessful as the former; for I could learn nothing in these Places, every Man seeming void of every other Intention but that of killing Time; nor had I hitherto met with any Adventure worth Notice, but returned Home every Night dissatisfied. At length I resolved to dress meanly, and mix with that Order of Men which are to be found at Alehouses and Cellars. Adventures now began to flow in upon me, and I soon discovered that all the Wit and Humour in this Kingdom, was to be found in Alehouses. Here human Nature appeared in her native Simplicity, and it is from these Fountains that I owe the little Knowledge I have of Mankind. I have many Adventures to communicate to you, which I dare say will make you laugh. But I met with so extraordinary a one the other Day, that I cannot omit giving it the first Place, tho' I am persuaded it will make your Heart ake. About Seven one Evening I stept into a very low Alehouse near the Hay Market, filled with a strange Mixture of Mortals; for there were Soldiers, Footmen, Chairmen, Porters, Hackney Coachmen, Carmen, Taylors, Shoemakers, and Oyster Women.

But in one Corner of the Room in a small Box all alone, I saw a young Gentleman leaning in a melancholy Posture on his Hand. His Dress bespoke him a Clergyman, but every Feature in his Face seemed to be burdened with Affliction. And, as it is my constant Custom to enter into Conversation with every Person I find that has any Thing singular about them, I placed myself close by him, and concluding that his Distress was Love, I broke Silence on that Subject; but soon found that his Misery flowed from a different Cause. Nor had we spent much Time together before he consented to give me his History, if I would retire with him into a back Room; which he did in a Manner so becoming a Gentleman, a Man of Sense and a Christian, that I am sure I shall injure his Relation by the Repetition of his Story. "Sir," says he, "I am the very unfortunate Son of an extravagant Father, who about five Years ago left my Mother, myself and Sister in great Distress.

"My poor Mother," (at this Word I observed a Tear stole down his Cheek) "was always desirous of my being brought up to the Church. She therefore persuaded some of her Friends to assist me at the University; which they were so kind to do. I staid long enough at College to take my Bachelor's Degree, but being then too young to go into Orders, and losing the Friend that then supported me, I was obliged to quit the University, and for a Livelihood engaged as Usher in a little School. As soon as I was of Age to take Deacon's Orders, I procured a Testimonial from College, got a Curacy by way of Title, and was favoured with a private Ordination, a Circumstance that gave great Joy to my poor Mother and Sister.[1] I was no sooner settled in my Curacy, but my merciless Creditors from Oxford, where I owed about forty Pounds, drove me this Day from the Rector's House, into that Box where you first found me. My dear Mother, who lodges at a small Distance from this Place, is an intire Stranger to what has happened, and how to communicate it to her, is at present my great Difficulty." The tender Affection, the filial Love this young Man expressed for his Mother, engaged me so strongly in his Behalf, that I offered to go home with him, and promised him all the Assistance in my Power. He accepted my Offer, and in about ten Minutes we were conveyed into a two-pair-of-stairs Room,[2] where we found his Mother and Sister. The former a comely, chearful, neat old Gentlewoman, the latter a modest, sprightly, innocent young Creature. The

---

[1] A deacon had to be 23 years old, and before being ordained needed to present 'Letters Testimonial of his good Life and Conversation' from his Oxford or Cambridge college; a candidate for ordination also had to present a 'Title' demonstrating that he had obtained or been promised some 'certain Place where he might use his Function' (Edmund Gibson, *Codex juris ecclesiastici Anglicani*, 2nd edn. [1761], i. 140–7). On the common ways of circumventing these rules, see Norman Sykes, *Church and State in England in the XVIII Century* (1934), 97–8, 112–14, 200–1. For a complaint against the use of 'friendship and power' in overcoming obstacles on the way to ordination, see *LM* 20 (1751), 405–7. The Universal Register Office dealt as broker in the sale and exchange of curacies as well as military offices like the 'Cornetcy' mentioned earlier. See also *Amelia*, VII. iv.

[2] On the second floor.

Joy that flash'd from each of their Countenances, at the Sight of my Companion, was inexpressible; but the Mother soon saw the Son's Chearfulness was affected, and with Eagerness said, "Child, what is the Matter?" when he told her what I have above related; which she heard in a Manner becoming the greatest of Characters. His Sister indeed dissolved into Tears; upon which the Mother addressed herself to her Children, in a Speech so fraught with Arguments drawn from the very Essence of Christianity, with so much Steadiness, and at the same Time with such Tenderness, that they soon recovered themselves to a State of Chearfulness, which nothing but Innocence and good Sense could produce, where there was so much real Distress. I remember Seneca somewhere says, That a noble Mind, bearing up under Distresses with Chearfulness, is an Object the Gods themselves behold with Pleasure.[1] The old Lady indulged me with the History of her Family, which I shall not trouble you with at present, tho' it is well worth your hearing. It is a trite, but a true Observation, that one Half of the World do not know how the other Half live.[2] For it is really amazing to think in what Manner they have lived, having no real Dependance. The Daughter, tho' bred to no Trade, has learnt several; but that of a Mantua-maker she has succeeded in best, and tho' she might do extreamly well by going out into the World, she has resolved to give up every Advantage, and to continue with her Mother so long as she lives. In their little Room they have two Beds, which are inexpressibly neat, tho' evidently old, as is most of their Furniture.

Upon the whole, if the benevolent Mind feels a real Pleasure, in relieving a worthy Object, this little Family, I really think, is as true a One of Generosity as ever I have seen in all my Travels. But there is one Circumstance which I must not omit to inform you of, as I know it will give you Pleasure; namely, the Son has now got a Curacy, so that if by any Means you could raise about forty Pounds, you would relieve this little Family from the only material Affliction they now labour under. I have inclosed a Direction of their Mother's Lodging, unknown to her, which you may communicate to any Gentleman or Lady whose Goodness may induce them to exert their Generosity on this Occasion, and I do assure you, whoever is the Author of their Relief, will be the Object of my Envy, for had it been in my Power to have done that for them, which I think they deserve, you would not have heard any thing of it: And whoever visits this two-pair-of-stairs Room, will be thoroughly convinced that they, nor any Person related to

---

[1] Seneca, *On Providence*, ii. 7–8: 'For my part I do not wonder if sometimes the gods are moved by the desire to behold great men wrestle with some calamity' (Loeb).

[2] See Tilley, H 46.

them, have any Hand in this Solicitation,[1] and that they really are what I have represented them to be.

I am Sir,

Your obliged humble Servant,

E. R.

P.S. I beg these Directions may be given to nobody, whose View is Curiosity only.

SATURDAY, SEPTEMBER 30, 1752.　　　NUMB. 64.

Quid Romæ faciam? mentiri nescio.

JUVENAL.[2]

——*What shall I do at Rome, who can't lie?*

Mr. Censor,[3]

It is the Observation of somebody, that the greatest Evils in Society are those which are out of the reach of the Law.[4] This is in nothing so true as in that free and inconsiderate Manner in which Persons are apt to speak of the Absent. It is but very lately that I travelled with an old Lady in a Stage Coach from the West, who entertained me a whole Day by giving me the Characters of my Father, Mother, Brothers, Sisters, and of many Dorsetshire Gentlemen of my Acquaintance, not one of whom, I was convinced, before we parted, she had ever seen, from the very unfair Picture she gave of them. The Women she spoke of, were all Ugly, Proud, or Ill-tempered, and the Men, either Brutes or silly Fellows. When I came to Town, I stepped into a Coffee-House to refresh myself before I went Home, where I met with an exact Contrast to my Stage Coach Acquaintance; for here I found a Gentleman entertaining a whole Box with the finest Characters in the World; many of which were given of Men, most of whom, to my certain Knowledge, are the vilest Fellows in the present Age. I was so surprized at these two extraordinary Occurrences, that I could not help considering in my own Mind, what could be the Motives of such uncommon Behaviour; the

---

[1] There is no evidence elsewhere in the *CGJ* that such a collection was begun.

[2] *Satires*, iii. 41.

[3] This letter is struck out in the Bodleian copy (Hope Folio 11) and is probably not Fielding's (see General Introduction, p. xxx). Cross (ii. 377–8) saw Sarah Fielding's hand in both this letter and the one in *CGJ* No. 63, but Jensen's suggestion (ii. 261) that 'E. R.' is John Fielding seems much more likely, especially when one compares this letter with one signed by John in *LDA*, 21 Nov. 1751; see below, p. 341, n. 2; p. 342, nn. 1 and 2.

[4] Proverbial; the conception of laws as cobwebs catching only small flies is attributed to Anacharsis in Plutarch's *Life of Solon*. Cf. Pope, *Essay on Man*, iii. 191–4, and the lines added by Johnson to Goldsmith's *The Traveller* (1764): 'How small of all that human hearts endure, / That part which law or kings can cause or cure.'

former abusing every Body without the least shadow of Excuse, the latter, as indiscriminately praising. In this Search, the following Characters presented themselves to my View; the Inconsiderate, the Vain, and the Malevolent. The former is really a harmless Animal, who speaks of Persons by Hearsay, takes Characters upon Trust, intends no Ill to any one, tho' they are often the Occasion of much Mischief. The vain Man speaks well of all indiscriminately, intending good to no one, but hopes that this kind of Candour will procure him the Character of a good-natured well-bred Man. But when he talks of his Grace, My Lord, or Sir John, it is only to shew you that he keeps the best Company. The last and most injurious Monster, is the malevolent Man, who, conscious of his own Unworthyness, cuts, pares, hacks, hews, and mangles every Character, 'till he has reduced it below his own Standard.[1] There are doubtless several other Reasons why Men speak unjustly, well or ill of others. These I shall leave for your Discovery and Discussion. I remember a comical old Gentleman of my Acquaintance, who always went the last out of every Company; for which he gave the following Reason, namely, that he was resolved never to give them an Opportunity to abuse him, which he said they would be sure to do, if he left any body behind him. And indeed I scarce ever have seen a Person leave Company but his Character has been immediately entered upon by those who remained. Perhaps the Inconveniencies arising from these sorts of Misrepresentations between Equals, are not of so much Consequence as they appear to be. But I am very sure, and that from Experience, that the Characters given by Superiors of their Inferiors, are dreadful to the last degree: what I mean is the unjust Characters given of Servants; an Order of People, who are moved out of one Station into another, and are admitted into Places of Trust according to their Recommendations.[2] For my own Part, from the Deceits I have lately met with, I began to think that Truth had taken her Departure from this Earth, with her Sister Justice. My Wife having Occasion for a Nursery Maid, had one recommended to her in the strongest Manner imaginable, as a sober, honest, careful, Creature, who got drunk the very first Night she came into my Service, and had like to have burnt my Child, and set fire to my House. Inraged at this Treatment I posted to her Recommender, who had no better Excuse to make, but that she was unwilling to take the Creature's Bread away, and gave her a Character out of

[1] Cf. Fielding's essay on slander, *CGJ* No. 14.

[2] Although unreliable character references were generally recognized as a major problem in the employment of servants in the period (see Dorothy Marshall, 'The Domestic Servants of the Eighteenth Century', *Economica*, 9 [1929], 29–30), this particular account sounds very much like a special plea on behalf of the Universal Register Office, which depended heavily on accurate 'characters'. See the *Plan* (1752), pp. 15–16; the advertisement at the end of Fielding's *Enquiry* (1751), p. 128; and especially the letter by John Fielding printed in *LDA*, 21 Nov. 1751, which explains the responsibilities of the public to help the Register Office in this regard and which is very close to the points expressed here. See the two notes following.

pure good Nature. On telling this Story to a Friend, he assured me that he lately hired a Man Servant, of whom he had the vilest Character in the World, and was in reality the best Servant he ever had in his House, but that there was apparently so much Spleen, and undeserved Resentment mix'd in the Account he had of him, that he was determined to try him at all Events. Now really, Mr. Censor, is not this shocking? And what can be the Motive of such unwarrantable Proceedings? It is very plain that false good Nature will recommend the Undeserving, and improper Resentment traduce the Worthy.[1] But by the Stories I have heard from my Friends since my own Accident, one would imagine that half the Masters and Mistresses of this Kingdom, by the Characters they give their Servants, live in fear of, and are dependent upon them. I declare for the future, that whoever acts in my Family in the Capacity of a Servant, shall, when he or she leaves it, have that Character from me which their Behaviour entitles them to, be it good, bad or indifferent, and I wish from my Soul you would set forth the Consequences of the contrary in such a light, as may deter every Gentleman and Lady from saying more or less of any Servant than they deserve; as this will prevent the greatest Irregularities in decent Families,[2] hinder the Idle and Worthless from eating the Bread of the Faithful and Industrious, and be an Encouragement to the Worthy to deserve well.

I am Sir,

Your obliged humble Servant,

E. R.

Mr. Censor,[3]

I have been long over Head and Ears in Love with the adorable Cleora. I have drest at her, made her Presents, wrote Sonnets on her, made a Cross Sticks on her Name; in a Word, I have performed all the Duties of a sincere Lover, but without Success; for I have a Rival, and such a one too, as I can never conquer; he is too contemptible an Animal to draw upon, and yet he has got fast hold of her Heart. How you will laugh when I tell you that my Rival is a Monkey, a Creature which I have a natural Antipathy to, my Mother having received a Fright from one when she was with Child of me!

[1] Cf. John Fielding on character references for servants: 'I have often observed, and with Concern too, that, on the one hand, Resentment has been as industrious to aggravate Foibles into Faults, as, on the other, foolish Good-nature has been sollicitous to conceal dangerous Vices, and to palliate very criminal Misconducts with the specious Names of Weakness, Youth, Ignorance, &c.' (*LDA*, 21 Nov. 1751).

[2] Cf. John Fielding: 'For my own part, I think . . . that those that knowingly are the Occasion of the Admission of a Liar, Drunkard, immodest or disorderly Servant, into a decent and regular Family, are, in a great Measure, answerable for the Consequences of their Conduct' (*LDA*, 21 Nov. 1751).

[3] The authorship of this letter is again in doubt; J. P. Emery attributes it to Arthur Murphy, but offers no evidence, either internal or external (*Arthur Murphy* [Philadelphia, 1946], p. 13).

Dear Sir, what is to be done? for I cannot sit in a Room where a Monkey is, and my dear Cleora and this Beast are inseparable.

I can neither live with the one, nor without the other. In vain have I attempted to laugh her out of this ridiculous Passion. She calls him her Darling, her sweet Soul, her little Beau, her Sweetheart, fondles him, caresses him, suffers the little Rascal to sleep on her Bosom, smothers him with Kisses, nay, admits him to her Bed; and I expect every Day that she will keep a Footman to wait on him, and all she can say to justify herself is, that Monkeys are now in Fashion, that every Lady of Taste keeps one, and that she is determined not to part with her dear Pug to the best Man alive.[1] What makes this the more shocking is, that the lovely Cleora has every Charm that a wise Man could wish in a Lady, or a good Man deserve of a Wife. Pray Mr. Censor write a Satire upon Monkeys, extirpate these little Rascals from this Kingdom, and at the same Time say a Word or two against lap-Dogs and Kittens. For my Cleora's Pug must have a fresh Kitten every Month by way of Playfellow. What a Degeneracy is this! and how must our Sex have behaved to be thus transplanted by such Vermin!

I am Sir,

Your obliged humble Servant,

X. W.

P.S. Within this two Months, I have been almost frightened to Death, for I can scarce go into any House of Fashion, but I find a Monkey.

SATURDAY, OCTOBER 7, 1752. NUMB. 65.

——rabiosa Silentia rodunt.

PERSIUS.[2]

Mr. Censor,[3]

As you are as well acquainted with the Movements of human Nature, as was the late learned Dr. Whiston[4] with those of the Stars, you seem to be as

---

[1] A common topic of satire; cf., for one example, *Spectator*, No. 343 (3 Apr. 1712), where Addison ridicules 'One of those Ladies who throw away all their Fondness on Parrots, Monkeys and Lap-dogs' and where the monkey is also named 'Pugg'.

[2] *Satires*, iii. 81: 'champing and muttering to themselves like mad dogs' (Loeb) is the translation of the entire line, *murmura cum secum et rabiosa silentia rodunt.*

[3] The authorship of this letter is uncertain; the first half is struck through in the Bodleian Library copy (Hope Folio 11; see General Introduction, p. xxx). The use of 'has' also argues against Fielding's authorship, but the letter's themes, allusions, and verbal parallels to his known works argue in favor of it. Cf., for example, his essay on 'Silence' in *Common Sense*, 13 May 1738, the manuscript of which has been reproduced by M. C. and R. R. Battestin in 'A Fielding Discovery, with Some Remarks on the Canon', *SB* 33 (1980), 131–43. J. P. Emery, with no evidence to offer, attributes the letter to Murphy (*Arthur Murphy* [Philadelphia, 1946], p. 13).

[4] William Whiston (1667–1752), heterodox and eccentric divine, mathematician, and astronomer, who had died on 22 Aug.; the news columns of *CGJ* No. 61 reprint a long eulogy of Whiston,

proper a Person to be consulted with on any extraordinary Phænomenon in the former, as he was on any such Phænomenon in the latter. Without farther Preface, therefore, I am by Profession an Apothecary, a Business I have followed in Partnership with a Gentleman, who, for his Knowledge in Diseases, Dignity of Aspect, and Size of Wig, deserves to be a Physician. No Man more acceptable to his Patients, more valuable to his Friends, more agreeable to his Acquaintance, more generous to his Enemies, or more compassionate to the Poor. In a Word, I scarce know a worthier Character; for in him are happily united a good Head and an excellent Heart. Yet he has an Oddity about him, which I can no more account for, than I can find out the Longitude;[1] but the finest Diamonds have sometimes a Flaw. We live together in the same House, and in general, as happy as two Men can do; and I believe there are few Friendships more perfect than ours: but my Partner sometimes takes it into his Head to lay an Embargo upon his Tongue, and scorns to speak for a whole Week together. The frequent Loss of so much agreeable, nay, such instructing Conversation as his, I do most bitterly lament. At these Times, if he has any Business with me, he writes it down, if I ask him a Question, he answers me by Signs. For this last Fortnight his Tongue, which, like Milton's, drops Manna,[2] has performed Quarantine, and I am afraid he will never speak again. I sometimes think he is bewitch'd, and at other times I fear he has lost the Use of Speech. But these Fits of Silence have generally been owing to some trifling Dispute. Our last I remember, was because I would not have my Wig made by his Barber; and as Silence is a Mark of Contempt, he is angry with any of his Servants that treat me with Civility. A few Days ago he discharged his Man Servant for giving me a clean Plate when he called for some Small Beer, and that very Evening beat a favourite Dog for jumping with Fondness on my Knee. We breakfast, dine, and sup together like Mutes at a Funeral, and we appear to our Servants like Ghosts, which, they say, cannot speak 'till they are spoke to.[3] Now, pray Mr. Censor, from what dark, dirty Hole of human Nature, does this Kennel[4] flow? Sometimes it smells like Pride, sometimes like Contempt, sometimes it looks like a Distemper, and sometimes it has neither Smell nor Taste. I am sure he is too good a Man to act from an unworthy

abstracted from *LDA*. Among his works were *A New Theory of the Earth* (1696) and *The Astronomical Principles of Religion* (1717). See also *CGJ* No. 12, above, p. 88 n. 2; and *CGJ* No. 70.

[1] Alluding slyly to Whiston's continuing efforts to devise a method for determining the longitude, a project first announced in 1713 and the subject of one of his tracts as late as 1738. Whiston and the longitude project were ridiculed by Swift and other Scriblerians; see B. A. Goldgar, *The Curse of Party* (Lincoln, Nebr., 1961), pp. 8–10.

[2] It was, of course, not Milton's but Belial's tongue which 'Dropd Manna, and could make the worse appear / The better reason' (*Paradise Lost*, ii. 113–14).

[3] Cf. *Hamlet*, I. i. 45; the superstition is also alluded to in *Tom Jones*, XI. ii and in the *True Patriot*, No. 9 (31 Dec. 1745).

[4] A drain or gutter.

Motive, and I know he loves me. Perhaps it may be constitutional; if so, I pity him from my Heart. I remember in the Preface to a modern Romance,[1] an excellent Account of Ridicule and its Objects, of which Affectation is justly made the Ground-work; and as to Affectation he has none. I cannot therefore laugh at him, tho' I can scarce avoid it. If he has any Pride it is of the nobler sort; and as to Envy, he has no more than he should have. As I am naturally of an open Disposition and forgiving Temper, I could not help giving myself up one Evening to Melancholy on Account of his Behaviour; and being half angry with him, I was inclined to believe that this not-speaking Passion was the Child of Pride: But as this led me into Reflections to his Disadvantage, and to my own Uneasiness, I endeavoured to amuse myself another way; for it is dangerous to think lightly of ones Friends. I therefore betook myself to the usual Entertainment of my idle Hours, namely, the Observation of Insects;[2] and Lice happened, that Evening, to be the Subject of my Enquiry; but of this I soon grew tired, and went to Bed, where Sleep presently relieved me from my unpleasant state of Mind, and produced a Dream as ridiculous as is possible. I think it is observed by Cicero, that Dreams are the imperfect Traces of our waking Thoughts;[3] which from what follows appears to be a Truth; for I found myself with my Microscope in my Hand, in which were two Lice placed for Inspection, the one so very old that he was silvered o'er with Age, the other appeared to be young. But how was I surprised when these two Insects entered into the following Dialogue! For the old one placing himself in an erect Posture, broke silence first, and said to his Companion, "Pray Piddy, what is become of your inseparable Companion Tiddo?" "Alas," says Piddy, "our Friendship, like that of superior Beings, is dissolved, and that for as trifling a Reason as often makes Breaches in theirs. Tiddo and I lived together for many Years in one Scab, undisturbed by Combs, unmolested by Nails, and unfrequented by Neighbours. Our Conversation was sweet to each other, and we shared equally both good and bad Fortune. But Tiddo at last grew impatient of Contradiction, and after any little Dispute that happened, he would keep Silence for a whole Day together. If I offered to interrupt him, he would enter into a long Discourse about the Dignity of Louse Nature, and tell me I should learn to distinguish between Lice and Lice; for tho' their Form was the same, yet there were different Orders among them, and due Preference should always be paid where there was a Superiority either in Understanding, Birth, Size, or Colour. For, said he, a Louse born in the Head of a Beggar,

[1] Fielding's Preface to *Joseph Andrews* (1742).

[2] A response perhaps to *CGJ* No. 61, where Fielding calls for an observer of insects to describe their 'contemptuous Behaviour one towards another'. See also *CGJ* No. 70.

[3] *De divinatione*, II. lxii, citing Aristotle; see also *De republica*, VI. i ('the dream of Scipio'), and cf. the discussion of Atkinson's dream in *Amelia*, IX. vi, and the note by Martin Battestin on the passage, Wesleyan Edn. (Oxford, 1983), p. 379.

or bred up in a Workhouse, is a mean Animal when compared to a Gentleman Louse. In a Word, he worked himself up into such a Passion, that he left the Scab, nor have I seen him since." Upon which the old one replied, that it was common to mistake accidental Differences for real ones, arising from their own Merit. "Ay," says Piddy, "that is the Case of my Friend, for he has got a blue Spot on his right Shoulder, on which he values himself much; and he has accustomed himself so long to look at it, that he is grown quite wry-neck'd; but I think," says he, "that handsome is as handsome does." This Speech of Piddy's put me so much in mind of a ridiculous old Knight of my Acquaintance, that grew stiff-necked at keeping his Eye constantly on the Star on his Breast, that I broke into a Laugh which waked me. Many Reflections followed this Dream, with which I shall not trouble you. But to go on with this not-speaking Subject, pray Mr. Censor, does not this sort of Silence arise sometimes from a Sullenness of Disposition? And is not this what we call riding Grub,[1] Master's Back is up, Miss is in her Airs; or the old Gentleman is in the Dumps, &c. &c? But this one finds either among the Very Polite, who, if you ask for any Person of their Acquaintance they have lately quarrelled with, their Answer is, *I really don't know, for we have not spoke for some time*; or else in a Country Village, between a Plowman and his Mistress, who never go the same side of the Way with one another, nor speak to each other for a long Time, if perchance they have had a Miff. I was once in Company with a Farmer's Son and his Sweetheart, when quarrelsome Tempers was the Subject of Conversation; when the young Farmer, in order to raise himself in the Esteem of his Girl, declared he never quarrelled with any one in his Life. "For," says he, "if Vather, Mother, or any of our Volks contradicts me, I never speak to 'um for half a Year." This open Declaration of so sweet a Disposition, joined to the Addresses of a less sulky Lover, broke off the Match. This Sort of Conduct among the Illiterate, I can laugh at, but when I see it in genteel Families, I own it grieves me. For is it not shocking to see a Father and Son, Husband and Wife, Brothers, and Sisters, or two Friends, passing and repassing in the same House, setting together like Mutes in the same Room, as if they were all Lodgers and unacquainted. But I am convinced my Friend's Case differs from all these. I therefore desire you would probe it to the Bottom, and tell me the Cause of such singular Behaviour in so sensible a Man, *et eris mihi magnus Apollo.*[2]   W. W.[3]

---

[1] Being sulky or bad-tempered (*OED*, overlooking its use this early).

[2] Virgil, *Eclogue*, iii. 104: 'And you shall be my great Apollo' (Loeb); in Virgil the line is similarly used in the posing of a riddle. Fielding uses the line as the motto to *CGJ* No. 9.

[3] Possibly meant to suggest William Whiston.

SATURDAY, OCTOBER 14, 1752.   NUMB. 66.

Fac tibi consuescat; nil Consuetudine Majus.

OVID.[1]

Do as you should, and in Time you may do as you would.

The English Words of my Text are rather a Translation of a Passage of Cicero, than of the above Line of Ovid. *Optimum Genus Vitæ eligito,* says the Orator, *Consuetudo nam faciet jucundissimum.*[2]

Habit hath been often called a second Nature, the former may indeed be said to govern and direct the latter.[3] I am much deceived, (and so was Mr. Lock too) if from our earliest Habits we do not in a great Measure derive those Dispositions, which are commonly called our Nature, and which afterwards constitute our Characters.[4] Nor is this Force of Habit or Custom exemplified only in Individuals; Nations are governed by the same Impulse.

Hence the Truth of that fine Observation in Livy, *Sunt tam Civitatum quam singulorum Hominum mores: gentesque aliæ Iracundæ, aliæ audaces: quædam timidæ, &c.*[5] Nations as well as Individuals have their peculiar Manners: Some are fierce and bold, some timorous, &c.

If this Diversity arose from the Difference of Climates, it would be constant and perpetual; and this we see is not the Case.[6] The same Sun which formerly warmed the Spartans and the Romans, now shines on the modern Greeks and Italians. The antient Gaul and French Petit-Maitre breathed the same Air; so did those poor Wretches, so lamentably described by Gildas, who sent over for Hengist and Horsa,[7] with those Heroes who in

---

[1] *Art of Love,* ii. 345: 'See that she grows used to you; than use and wont naught is mightier' (Loeb). The accepted text reads *adsuetudine* rather than *consuetudine.*

[2] A familiar maxim which Plutarch attributes not to Cicero but to Pythagoras, *Moralia,* 602C: 'Choose the best life and familiarity will make it pleasant' (Loeb); Addison quotes the same line as a saying of Pythagoras, *Spectator,* No. 477 (2 Aug. 1712).

[3] See e.g. Aristotle, *Nicomachean Ethics,* vii. 10; Cicero, *De finibus,* V. xxv. 74; and Addison, *Spectator,* No. 477 (2 Aug. 1712).

[4] See Locke's *Essay concerning Human Understanding* (1690), II. xxxiii. 6, and *Some Thoughts concerning Education,* 5th edn. (1705), sects. 10 and 66. On Fielding's conflicting views about human educability and determinism, see Miller, *Essays,* pp. 218–20; cf. also *CGJ* No. 55.

[5] Quoted with slight changes from *History,* XLV. xxiii. 14: 'The character of states is like that of individual men; some nations are hot-tempered, some bold, some diffident. . . .' (Loeb).

[6] Fielding takes issue here with the prevailing view that national stereotypes are determined by climate; for the background, see J. W. Johnson, ' "Of differing Ages and Climes" ', *Journal of the History of Ideas,* 21 (1960), 465–80. Sir William Temple, for example, had found the source of the English propensity to 'Humour' in 'the unequalness of our Clymat' (*Of Poetry,* 1692; cf. Fielding's views on humor in *CGJ* No. 55). In earlier works, however, Fielding sometimes took for granted the effect of climate on character; see e.g. *Champion,* 15 Dec. 1739, and the opening passage of 'An Essay on the Knowledge of the Characters of Men', *Miscellanies* (1743).

[7] Gildas (*c.*516–70), British monk whose lament on the ruin of Britain, *De excidio et conquestu Britanniae,* includes a description of the decision by a 'proud tyrant' (Vortigern) to invite the Saxons to

the Days of Edward III, crossed the Seas, and made bold to borrow the Person of his Majesty of France, and to bring him over with them to this Kingdom.[1]

It is not therefore the Difference of Climate, but of the Customs and Institutions of Men, which produces the different Characters of Nations. This indeed is expressly averred by Cicero, in his Oration against Rullus. *Non ingenerantur hominum mores tam a Stirpe Generis et Seminis quam ex iis rebus quæ a Vitæ Consuetudine suppeditantur.*[2] The Manners of Men are not born with them; or derived from their Ancestors. Their true Source is no other than Custom, or the general Habit of their Lives.

Now so great is the Force of this Habit, that we find it superior even to those Affections which seem to have the fairest Claim to be thought the primary Instincts of our Nature. Such is first the Love of Life; from an eager Desire of which, says Aristotle in his Politics,[3] Men are contented to struggle with many great Evils, as if there was a certain Delightfulness and natural Sweetness in the Thing itself: So Homer in his Odyssey.

$$Πάντες \; μὲν \; στυγεροὶ \; θάνατοι \; δειλοῖσι \; βροτοῖσιν·^4$$

Nay the brave Achilles, in the Iliad, confesses that all the Riches of the World are not to be put in any Competition with Life.

$$οὐ \; γὰρ \; ἐμοὶ \; ψυχῆς \; ἀντάξιον \; κτλ.^5$$

And yet as Monsieur la Motte observes, this very Achilles despises Death when opposed to Glory, and runs upon his certain Fate with his Eyes open.[6] Such was the Force of Habit; which, if we believe his Ghost in the Odyssey, impelled the Heroe to make a silly Choice.[7]

Under the same Impulse of Habit we see this King of Terrors despised by whole Nations, and not only by the Men, but by the Women. The Story of the Indian Wives who ambitiously contended for the Honour of being burnt with their dead Husbands, is well known.[8] The Æthiopians, says Diodorus

---

defend Britain; the 'ferocious Saxons', led by Hengest and Horsa, thus entered like wolves invited to the fold. See the edition and translation by Michael Winterbottom (1978), sect. 23.

[1] Referring to the exploits of Edward the Black Prince at the battle of Poitiers (19 Sept. 1356), when King John of France was captured and taken to England. See Joshua Barnes, *The History of . . . Edward III* (Cambridge, 1688), pp. 495–525, a work which Fielding owned (Baker, item 649).

[2] Slightly adapted from *De lege agraria (contra Rullum)*, II. xxiv. 95; Fielding's translation follows.

[3] III. vi. 5.

[4] *Odyssey*, xii. 341: 'All forms of death are hateful to wretched mortals' (Loeb).

[5] *Iliad*, ix. 401; Fielding quotes only the opening of the line; the line-and-a-half segment reads, 'For in my eyes not of like worth with life is even all that wealth that men say Ilios possessed' (Loeb).

[6] See Antoine Houdar de la Motte, *Discours sur Homère* (1714), in *Œuvres* (Paris, 1754), p. 37; on La Motte and his quarrel with Madame Dacier over Homer, see *CGJ* No. 11, above, p. 83 n. 1.

[7] See *Odyssey*, xi. 488–91.

[8] The story was common in the 18th cent., especially as describing a Bengalese custom; see Alexander Hamilton, *A New Account of the East Indies* (Edinburgh, 1727), ii. 8–9, and an extract of a letter of 1743 printed in *Richardsoniana* (1776), pp. 69–74. Fielding probably has in mind a recent

Siculus, never execute any Malefactors; their Custom is to send an Officer of Justice, bearing with him an Image of Death; upon the Sight of which the Condemned retires to his own House, and voluntarily destroys himself. There was an Instance, of one only who refused to obey this Hint, upon which his Mother strangled him with her own Hands that he might not, says my Author, appear scandalous in the Eyes of his Neighbours.[1]

So very forcible was this Custom or Habit amongst these People, as the same Author tells us; that when the College of their Priests pleased to consign any of their Kings to Death, they had only to signify to him their Orders, which were instantly obeyed. In this Obedience their Kings persisted for many Ages, till at last one of them less complaisant than the rest, besieged the Priests in their Temple, took it and put them all to the Sword.[2]

The Contempt of Death, when the Good of their Country demanded their Lives, so universal both among the Spartans and Romans, could have no other possible Source than this natural Habit.

And next to that Instinct which Nature seems to have implanted in Men for the Preservation of their own Lives, is that by which they are prompted to continue their Species, and to give Life to others. This too is within the Power of Habit to controll, of which we have a notable Instance in the Roman History. Among the old Romans it was thought infamous in a Widow to marry; and those, saith Valerius Maximus, who were content with one Husband, received public Honours in Reward of their Chastity.[3] Hence nothing was more rare than second Marriages among the Roman Ladies of any Rank; and one of the Fathers in his Epistle to Furia, a Lady of the Camillan Family, compliments her that there had been no Example of a second Marriage in the Ladies of that House for a great many Generations.[4] Now these Instances of Continence were among the same People, and in the same City, where in other Ages a W——e and a Woman of Quality were synonymous Terms.

From these Considerations, I have often comforted myself, while I have been reading the Histories of the most profligate Times, that the very Persons who have acted the most infamous Parts at such a season, derived

account in *LDA*, 4 July 1752, reprinted in the news columns of *CGJ* No. 54, which tells of a Bengalese girl who 'stepped upon the Pile, and quietly laid herself down by the Corpse of her Husband'. See also *GM* 22 (1752), 335.

[1] Diodorus Siculus, *Bibliotheca*, III. v. 3.

[2] Ibid., III. vi. 1–4.

[3] Valerius Maximus, *Factorum et dictorum memorabilium libri*, II. i. 3; this same question is the subject of a learned discussion in *Amelia* (VI. vii) between Booth and Mrs Bennet, in the course of which the same passage from Valerius Maximus and the same epistle by St Jerome are cited.

[4] St Jerome, *Epistle* LIV (*Ad Furiam de viduitate servanda*), written in 394 to Furia, a noble lady who had rejected the idea of remarriage after the death of her husband. For the compliment to the family, see sect. i.

their Iniquity rather from the general Corruption which then prevailed, than from any extraordinary Disparity in their own Nature; and that a Livilla, a Messalina, an Agrippina or a Poppæa,[1] might in better Times have made chaste and virtuous Matrons. In short, I am willing to read those Lines of the Poet with a small Variation,

> That if weak Women go astray,
> *The Age* is more in Fault than they.[2]

But if a good natured Man may thus afford some Excuse for the ill Behaviour of Individuals in a Season of general Depravity; it must be observed that, from the very same Consideration, the Crimes of those who sin even against the Fashion, will contract the greater Degree of Abhorrence. The Man indeed who bears up his Vices against the Torrent of the Times, and who is wicked in Defiance of numberless good Examples before his Eyes, deserves to be stared at as a kind of Prodigy or Monster in the Society.

I shall single out therefore a Vice or two, against which the present Age have declared the most universal Abhorrence, and in which consequently if some few Persons among us should venture to indulge themselves, they must appear in the most scandalous Light to the rest of their Countrymen.[3]

The first of these is Gaming, a Vice so universally condemned by the Lords and Commons, that these ten or twelve last Years have, I think, produced no less than four several Laws for its Punishment and Extirpation.[4] These are indeed virtually to be considered as the Censures of the whole Nation; but they must be considered as positively and expressly the Sentiments of all the greatest Men in it. How singular and contemptible the Character of a Gamester would appear in such an Age as this, needs very little Argument or Illustration.

---

[1] Livilla (13 BC–AD 31), mistress of Sejanus and poisoner of her husband; Valeria Messalina (d. AD 48), the notoriously profligate third wife of Claudius; and Julia Agrippina or Agrippina Minor (AD 15–59), mother of Nero and later wife of her uncle Claudius, whom she poisoned; these were all included by Fielding in a long list of depraved 'heroines' in *Amelia*, I. vi. Poppaea Sabina (d. AD 65) was the mistress and later the wife of Nero.

[2] Matthew Prior, 'Hans Carvel': 'She made it plain, that Human Passion / Was order'd by Predestination; / That if weak Women went astray, / Their Stars were more in Fault than They' (ll. 9–12), in *Poems on Several Occasions*, 6th edn. (1741), p. 85.

[3] Cf. *CGJ* No. 2 (7 Jan. 1752) for similar irony about the virtues of the age.

[4] Recent laws to restrain gambling included 12 Geo. II, c. 28 (1739); 13 Geo. II, c. 19 (1740); 18 Geo. II, c. 34 (1745); and 25 Geo. II, c. 36 (1752), the last of which, though not specifically an anti-gaming law, encouraged prosecution against keepers of both gaming and bawdy-houses. It was presumably to the 1752 law that Lady Jane Coke referred in August of that year as 'the Act of Parliament that has put a stop to publick gaming' (*Letters*, ed. Mrs Ambrose Rathborne [1899], p. 110). For Fielding's other condemnations of gaming, see *A Charge Delivered to the Grand Jury* (1749), pp. 54–5; *Enquiry into the late Increase of Robbers* (1751), sect. III; *CGJ* No. 17 (29 Feb. 1752); and many passages in *Amelia*, e.g. X. v, vi. Neither in his legal writing nor in his practice as a magistrate was Fielding able to address directly the problem of gambling among the wealthy upper classes, a fact which explains his insistent irony in passages such as this.

The next Vice against which the Popular Torrent may be said to run very high at present, is a criminal Conversation between the Sexes.[1] Against this, not only our Courts of Legislature and Justice have expressed the utmost Severity, but so far have the People in general carried their Zeal, that they have endeavoured to expel Lewdness out of her own Temples, as the morose Part of Mankind formerly called them.[2] The Theatres themselves are reduced to the strictest Rules of Modesty. Neither Pit nor Gallery will bear an indecent Idea, if they smell it out; and an obscene Jest would throw them into such a violent Fit of Groaning, that a Foreigner might suspect they were all bewitched.[3] At such a Season what a Figure must a profligate Woman in high Life make amongst her chaste Sisterhood! A Figure indeed so odious, that I shall not rest my Contemplation upon it.

Many more such Examples might be drawn from this virtuous Age; but to conclude as I began, with the Language of a Sermon,[4] I shall reserve the rest for some future Opportunity. C.

SATURDAY, OCTOBER 21, 1752. NUMB. 67.

Fæcunda culpæ sæcula nuptias,
Primum inquinavere, et genus, et domos.
Hoc Fonte derivata clades
In patriam, populumque fluxit.

HORACE.[5]

Pollution in our wicked Times,
(Fruitful of every kind of Crimes)
First rises in the Marriage Bed,
There is its muddy Fountain Head.

[1] For continuation of this theme see *CGJ* Nos. 67 and 68.

[2] On Fielding's use of the word 'morose' for an 'over-sanctified' spirit, see *CGJ* No. 29, above, p. 186 n. 4. By 'Temples' of lewdness Fielding may be referring to bawdy-houses and to the misplaced zeal of those rioting against them, as in the Bosavern Penlez affair of 1749; or, given the passage which follows, he may mean the theaters, as viewed by both the Puritans and by Jeremy Collier or similar anti-theatrical writers (see e.g. Collier's *Short View of the . . . English Stage* [1698], p. 141). Cf. Fielding's comment on the attitude toward the stage during the Cromwell period in his essay in the *Daily Journal* (25 Mar. 1737): 'But notwithstanding what a Puritanical Spirit, mixed with Dulness and Spleen, may suggest, the Theatre has always been supported in our politest Times. . . . Indeed I will ask the Enemies to this Amusement, Whether they will undertake to withdraw the Minds of Men from the Love of all Pleasure whatever?' (as printed by Thomas Lockwood, 'A New Essay by Fielding', *MP* 78 [1980], 52).

[3] Fielding himself had suffered from the same hypocritical reaction of audiences he treats so ironically here; see his comments on the reception of his play *The Wedding Day* (1743) in the Preface to *Miscellanies* (1743), ed. H. K. Miller, Wesleyan Edn. (Oxford 1972), i. 7–8.

[4] Alluding to the phrase 'my Text' in the opening paragraph.

[5] *Odes*, III. vi. 17–20: 'Teeming with sin, our times have sullied first the marriage-bed, our offspring, and our homes; sprung from this source, disaster's stream has overflowed the folk and fatherland' (Loeb). A phrase from this passage is the motto to *CGJ* No. 56.

Thence in more Torrents than the Nile,
It overflows and wastes our Isle.

"It is very remarkable," says M. Dacier, "that Horace should attribute all the Miseries of Rome, and all the civil Wars of the Romans to no other Cause than to their Adulteries."[1] And this seems to me the more remarkable when we consider the Character of the Poet who hath given us this Opinion. We have not here the Sentiments of a recluse Pedant, who might be suspected of Ignorance, of a cynic Philosopher, who might be accused of Malice, or of a Christian Divine, whom some would insinuate to be swayed by Interest; but we have before us the Words of a Man of the World, who lived in the politest, and most splendid of Courts, and in the Intimacy of the greatest Men of that Court; of one who united in himself the several Characters of the Gentleman, the Politician, the Moralist, the Scholar, the Poet, the Wit, and the Man of Sense.

Nor is there in these Lines the least Appearance of Jest or Irony; on the contrary they are introduced in one of his gravest Odes, and which was written on the most solemn Occasion; an Ode addressed to his Countrymen, lamenting the wretched Condition into which they were fallen, tracing their political Diseases up to their Source, and pointing out the Methods of their Cure. In this Ode he mentions the Pollutions of the Marriage Bed as the Cause of all the Corruptions of Rome.

And that this was his serious Opinion, appears further from his repeating it in other Places. In the 24th Ode of the same Book, he seems to prefer the Manners of the Getes and Scythians to those of his own Country, principally on account of the superior Virtue of their Women, *who neither attempt to govern their Husbands, nor listen to an adulterous Beau.*[2] Again in the 5th Ode of the 4th Book, he pays a Compliment to Augustus Cæsar, for the Institution of the Lex Julia, by which capital Punishment was inflicted on Adulterers; and speaks of this Law as likely to produce the greatest Advantages to the Public.[3]

Under the Authority therefore of so fine a Gentleman as Horace, I may

---

[1] Fielding translates accurately from André Dacier, *Remarques Critiques sur Les Œuvres D'Horace, avec une Nouvelle Traduction*, iii (1683), 168; Fielding owned this ten-volume edition of Dacier's Horace (Baker, item 559).

[2] *Odes*, III. xxiv; Fielding is translating lines 19–20.

[3] In *Odes*, IV. v. 21–4, Horace alludes to, but does not mention specifically, the *Lex Julia de Adulteris Coercendis*, which in 18 BC made adultery a criminal offense punishable by exile and loss of property. The Lex Julia did not, however, as Fielding implies, make death an automatic penalty but simply permitted the father and husband of a woman caught in the act of adultery to kill the adulterer (and the father to kill the daughter) under certain very restricted circumstances; see the discussion in *The Cambridge Ancient History*, ed. S. A. Cook *et al.* (Cambridge, 1934), x. 443–7. The death penalty is erroneously ascribed to the *Lex Julia* in the *Institutes* of Justinian; see J. B. Bury, *History of the Later Roman Empire* (1923), ii. 411 n.

venture, without apprehending the Imputation of Pedantry or Moroseness[1] to encounter the present general Opinion, and to question whether Adultery be really that Matter of Jest and Fun which it is conceived to be, and whether it might not be decent and proper to contrive some small Punishment for this Vice in a civilized (much more in a Christian) Country.[2]

I will begin then with examining as far as my Reading and Memory will enable me, what Punishment hath been inflicted on this Crime by the Laws of other Countries. And hence I think will appear, that most Legislators agreed with Horace in their Opinions of the civil Consequences of this Crime.

In that First and most perfect Table of Law, which God himself was pleased to divulge to the Jews; Adultery is among the ten Articles expressly forbidden;[3] and in this Table it follows immediately after the Crime of Murder, to which it was equalled in its Punishment: for in Leviticus we read, *The Man that committeth Adultery, even he that committeth Adultery shall surely be put to Death.*[4] Well therefore might the wise Author of the Proverb say, *Whoso committeth Adultery lacketh Understanding.*[5]

The Egyptians were somewhat less severe in their Animadversion on this Crime. They distinguished likewise between the Punishment of the Men and the Women. The former of whom was to receive a thousand Lashes, and the latter to have her Nose cut off: for they thought it reasonable, says Diodorus, to deprive lascivious Women of those Charms which they used to the Purpose of unlawful Lust.[6]

Among the old Arabians this Crime was punished with Death: for their Philosophers, as we read in Alexander ab Alexandro, thought it worse than Perjury.[7] What Sense the antient Greeks had of this Crime may appear from

---

[1] On Fielding's use of this term, see *CGJ* No. 29, above, p. 186 n. 4.

[2] Cf. Fielding's complaint in the 'Covent Garden' column of 4 May (printed below, Appendix I) that he was unable to issue a warrant against the paramour of a poor man's wife, 'Adultery being no Crime by the Laws of England'. For his other condemnations of adultery and his concern that it was not punishable by law, see the strictures delivered by Dr Harrison in *Amelia*, IX. v and X. ii, in the latter of which he points out that many non-Christian nations have punished it 'with the most exemplary Pains and Penalties'. Cf. also *Champion*, 11 Oct. 1740, which similarly points to the fact that the death penalty is exacted for adultery in many other countries.

Although the vehemence of Fielding's attack on adultery was perhaps unusual in his period, he was not alone in condemning it. Edward Cobden pointed to the prevalence of the vice in fashionable circles in a sermon preached before the king (*A Persuasive to Chastity* [1749]), a sermon promptly ridiculed and censured (see *The Foundling Hospital for Wit*, No. 6 [1749], pp. 2–3). And Fielding's tactic here of reciting the punishments inflicted on adulterers by the 'wise Nations' of the past was also common. See e.g. an essay called 'The Sentiments of many of the Ancients concerning Adultery' in *GM* 20 (1750), 457–9; the article entitled 'Adultery' in Ephraim Chambers's *Cyclopaedia*, 7th edn. (1751); and *An Essay on Modern Gallantry* (1750), pp. 23–5, which seeks to demonstrate that this crime has always been regarded as 'prejudicial to the public Peace and Welfare of Mankind' (p. 26).

[3] i.e. the Ten Commandments, Exodus 20.

[4] Leviticus 20: 10.   [5] Proverbs 6: 32.

[6] Diodorus Siculus, *Bibliotheca historica*, I. lxxviii. 4.

[7] i.e. Alessandro Alessandri, Italian jurist and scholar (1461–1523), whose *Dies geniales* (1522) was

Homer: for whether the Rape of Helen was the Cause of the Trojan War, or was only feigned to be so by Homer, as I am apt to imagine, in either Case the great Abhorrence of this Crime in these Ages, will be equally manifest; since we cannot suppose that Homer would have brought together all the Princes of Greece to avenge by a common War, an Injury which had not in his Time been thought of the highest Nature.[1]

As for that Passage in the third Iliad, λάϊνον ἕσθο χιτῶνα κτλ upon which M. Dacier remarks that Hector threatens Paris with being stoned to Death, which was the Punishment for Adulterers in the East, I omit it as the Words will by no Means bear that Interpretation; for Hector is there representing not the Punishment which he deserved of the Greeks for his Crime, but of the Trojans for its Consequences.[2]

By the Laws of the Locrians which were established by the famous Zaleucus, the Punishment of Adultery was the Loss of Eyes. Valerius Maximus after having passed very high Encomiums on these Laws, relates that the Son of Zaleucus[3] himself having been condemned for this Crime, the Father could not be prevailed upon by all the Entreaties of the Citizens to remit the Execution any farther than by redeeming one of his Son's Eyes, by pulling out one of his own.[4]

The Athenians gave to any Man who caught another in the Act of Adultery, full Liberty to punish him as he pleased, either by Castration, Mutilation, or by Death itself. This Law whether instituted first by Draco as Plutarch seems to think, or by Hyettus, according to Pausanias, received afterwards the Sanction of the mild Solon.[5]

---

modelled on the *Attic Nights* of Aulus Gellius. The passage Fielding cites is located in the edition he owned (Baker, item 371), *Genialium dierum libri sex* (Leiden, 1673), i. 863.

[1] In this reflection, and in much of what follows, Fielding appears to be indebted to John Potter's *Archaeologiae Graecae: or, The Antiquities of Greece* (Oxford, 1697–9), ii. 322–34; this work, which Fielding owned (Baker, item 48), surveys the punishments for adultery among the Greeks and is cited as the source of a similar section in *An Essay on Modern Gallantry* (1750). Potter discusses the 'long and bloody War occasion'd by *Paris*'s Rape of *Helen*' in ii (1699), 324. His work is cited frequently in Fielding's notes to *Plutus* (1742).

[2] It is Madam (not Monsieur) Dacier who makes the interpretation to which Fielding objects, in *L'Iliade d'Homere, Traduite en Français, avec des remarques* (Paris, 1711), i. 387. On Anne Dacier, see above, p. 83 n. 1. The line in question (*Iliad*, iii. 57) literally means 'thou hadst put on a coat of stone'; it is also cited by Potter (ii. 324) as evidence of the Greek punishment for adultery. Cf. Pope's note on the line: '*Giphanius* would have it to mean stoned to death on account of his Adultery: But this does not appear to have been the Punishment of that Crime among the *Phrygians*. It seems rather to signify, destroy'd by the Fury of the People for the War he had brought upon them' (Twickenham Edn., VII. i. 193).

[3] Lawgiver of the Italian Locrians (*c.* 650 BC), noted for his severity. See Plutarch, *Moralia*, 543A and Diodorus Siculus, XII. xx, the latter of whom describes his legislation as non-punitive.

[4] *Factorum et dictorum memorabilium*, VI. v, ext. 3.

[5] See Plutarch, *Solon*, xvii. o and xxiii. 1; Pausanias, *Description of Greece*, IX (*Boeotia*), xxxvi. 6–8. Fielding seems to have inferred Plutarch's opinion about Draco from a passage in which Draco's widespread use of the death penalty is described. Pausanias, after recounting the exile of Hyettus of Argo for killing a man caught with his wife, remarks, 'This Hyettus was the first man known to have

There were many kind of corporal Punishments for this Crime at Athens, one of which was the Παρατιλμὸς, which is alluded to both by Aristophanes and Juvenal.[1] I must explain it no farther here than by saying that it was a Mixture both of Pain and Shame.

Two Punishments of the Women, I cannot omit. The one was by prohibiting them to dress themselves in any Manner of Finery, the other was by forbidding their Husbands to have any future Converse with them under the Penalty of Infamy and Loss of Freedom.[2] The former of these may possibly by some be thought the more grievous Penance.

The Spartan Lawgiver, it is true, inflicted no Penalty on this Crime, of which he thought with a very singular Levity. How greatly therefore to the Honour of the first Spartan Ladies is this Passage in Plutarch's Life of Lycurgus. "They were so far (says he) from making any ill use of that natural and political Liberty which was allowed them by their Law, or of indulging themselves in the Freedom taken by Women in later Ages, *that it was entirely incredible to them that any Woman could be guilty of Adultery.*" Nor can I pass by the Story of Geradas, the antient Spartan, which Plutarch immediately subjoins. "He was asked by a Stranger how they punished Adulterers; to which he answered, 'We have no Adulterers.' 'But suppose there should be such?' says the Stranger. 'His Fine,' answered Geradas, 'would be a Bull that could stand at Taygetus and drink out of the Eurotas.' 'Where is such a Bull to be found?' answered the Stranger. 'Where,' replied Geradas smiling, 'is an Adulterer to be found in Lacedemon?' "[3]

In the earlier Days of Rome, the Punishment of Adultery was only by Fine, and of this I remember only one Instance in Livy.[4] Indeed from what Valerius Maximus tells us, that till the five hundred and twentieth Year of Rome there was not a single Divorce, we shall not lose much Time in searching into the Laws against Adultery; nor can it seem strange that there

exacted punishment from an adulterer. Later on, when Dracon was legislator for the Athenians, it was enacted that the punishment of an adulterer should be one of the acts condoned by the State' (Loeb). Cf. Potter, *Archaeologiae Graecae*, ii (1699), 327.

[1] The Greek word, meaning 'plucking out hair', refers to a punishment which John Potter describes as follows: 'having *pluck'd* off the Hair from their Privities, they threw hot Ashes upon the Place, and thrust up a *Radish*, Mullet, or some such thing into their Fundament' (*Archaeologiae Graecae*, ii [1699], 328–9). Potter, who says only the poor were subjected to this punishment, cites Aristophanes, *The Clouds*, 1083, and Juvenal, *Satires*, x. 317, alluding to 'the punishment of the mullet' (Loeb). See also Aristophanes, *Plutus*, 168; Fielding's note to that line in his and William Young's translation of *Plutus* (1742) explains modestly, 'The Greek here alludes to a particular Punishment for this Crime, which we could not literally translate into *English*' (p. 14).

[2] Cf. Potter, ii (1699), 329, citing Demosthenes' Oration *In Neaeram*, 85–7.

[3] Fielding translates accurately from Plutarch, *Lycurgus*, xv. 9–10; cf. Plutarch's *Moralia*, 228C, where the story is again told, with the name of the ancient Spartan given as 'Geradatas'. The anecdote is used also in the article on 'Adultery' in *The Student's Companion* (1748), p. 5.

[4] *History*, x. xxxi. 9: 'In this year Quintus Fabius Gurges, the consul's son, assessed a fine of money against a number of married women who were convicted before the people of adultery, and with this money erected the temple of Venus which is near the Circus' (Loeb).

was so little of either, in a Nation where, as the same Author informs us, the Honour of their Matrons was so sacred, that the Outworks of their Chastity were inviolable, insomuch that the Officers of Justice were not permitted to lay their Hands on a married Lady.[1]

Banishment, or Deportation into an Island, was another Punishment of this Crime among the old Romans. This Suetonius, in the Life of Augustus, calls the heavier Punishment.[2] By that Emperor not only Death was inflicted upon Adulterers, by the Julian Law, but the Offence was raised into Treason. A Severity which Tacitus censures, and Juvenal himself, when he says Domitian revived it, calls it *a bitter Law*.[3]

This Law, in the Decline of the Roman Commonwealth, was most probably grown obsolete: for we find the Punishment of Death again revived in Case of Adultery among the Constitutions of Constantine.[4]

In the Novels of Justinian there is a Distinction in favour of the Wife, who is only to be Whipt and lose her Dower, whereas Adultery remains capital in the Husband. With which Distinction the Empress Theodora is said to have favoured her own Sex, as the weaker Vessel.[5]

Among the Pisidians, as we find it in Stobæus,[6] the Adulterer and Adulteress were both conducted round the City, riding on an Ass; which Procession continued during several Days.

"The Punishment of Adultery among the antient Germans was immediate, and executed by the Husband himself. The Wife was stript stark Naked, and

---

[1] *Factorum et dictorum memorabilium*, II. i. 3, 4–5. The passage does not actually involve 'Officers of Justice' but indicates only that no one calling a married woman to court was permitted to touch her body, so that the wife's garment (*stola*) would be left unviolated by the touch of another's hand. Fielding cites the same passage in *Amelia*, VI. vii. Some manuscripts of Valerius Maximus give a date for the first divorce considerably earlier than the five hundred and twentieth year; the case was that of Spurius Carvilius, who separated from his wife because of her inability to bear children. Cf. Aulus Gellius, *Attic Nights*, IV. iii. 1–2, and Dionysius of Halicarnassus, *Roman Antiquities*, ii. 25.

[2] See Suetonius, *Augustus*, v, where the phrase *gravior poena* is apparently used not in contrast to the death penalty, as Fielding implies, but to indicate the harsher of two forms of banishment; see the note by J. H. Westcott and E. M. Rankin, eds., *De vita Caesarum libri I–II* (New York, 1918), p. 197. On the Julian Law, see above, p. 352 n. 3.

[3] Tacitus, *Annals*, iii. 24, where Augustus, by designating adultery by the names of sacrilege and treason, is said to have 'overstepped both the mild penalties of an earlier day and those of his own laws' (Loeb); Juvenal, *Satires*, ii. 29–33, in which Domitian is called an adulterer who 'revived the stern laws that were to be a terror to all men' (Loeb).

[4] *Codex Theodosianus*, IX. xl. 1; XI. xxxvi. 4.

[5] Fielding refers to the *novellae constitutiones* which Justinian compiled from 534 until his death in 565 and which supplemented his *Institutes* and *Digest*. For the 'Distinction' Fielding has in mind, see *Novellae* No. 134, ch. x, which also provides that a woman adulterer must be sent to a nunnery from which she may be recalled by her husband after two years but where if not recalled she must remain for life. Procopius, *Secret History*, (xvii. 24) describes Theodora's habit of protecting women accused of adultery and devising punishments for the husbands who accused them; on the notion that she influenced Justinian to lessen the severity of the law on adultery, see Ephraim Chambers, *Cyclopaedia* (7th edn., 1751), s.v. 'adultery'.

[6] Author of an anthology of extracts from poets and prose writers, probably compiled in the 5th cent. AD; Fielding refers to his 'De legibus et consuetudinibus', Sermo xlii. 30, in *Stobaei sententiae ex thesaurus Graecorum delectae* (1609), p. 292, a volume which he owned (Baker, item 625).

her Hair cut off: then in the Presence of her Neighbours, she was turned out of Doors, and whipt by her Husband through the whole Town. This Crime however," says Tacitus, "was extremely rare with these People;" for which he very well accounts by telling us, that "the Morals of their Women were corrupted by no Allurements of public Shows, nor their Desires provoked by any luxurious Entertainments.—And again the Woman who had lost her Reputation, was sure to receive no Pardon; nor could the united Charms of Youth, Beauty and Fortune ever procure her a second Husband; for there," says he, "*Nemo Vitia ridet. No one can turn off his Vices with a Joke.*"[1]

Modern Travellers tell us of very severe Punishments inflicted on this Crime in various Nations. Death according to M. Nieuhoffe is its Punishment in the Kingdom of Patane, especially among the Nobility.[2]

In Cochin China Adulterers are to be killed by Elephants, and the Method of Execution, which is very curious, may be seen in Borris's Voyages, which is in the second Volume of Churchill's Collections.[3]

In some Parts of Guinea, according to Mr. Barbott, Adultery is punished by the Loss of an Ear, in others by Castration, in others by so severe a Fine, that it ruins the whole Family; and in others by Death.[4]

I shall mention but one Instance more from these Nations. In Fida, this Crime is punished in the following Manner: The Adulterer is placed in an open Field as a Mark for several of their Great Men to dart at by Way of Diversion, with their Javelins. "After he hath been thus tormented, he undergoes a second Punishment in the Presence of the Adultress. Both the Criminals are then bound and put into a deep Pit, when boiling Water is by small Quantities dropt on their Heads, till a large Pot is half empty; after which the Remainder is poured upon them, and then the Pit is closed up and they are both buried with what of Life remains in them."[5]

I should now proceed to our own Punishments of this Crime, but as I have already exceeded the Length of my Paper, it is very lucky for me that we have none.[6]   C.

---

[1] Fielding translates with some rearrangement of sentences from Tacitus, *Germania*, 19; the text of the last phrase in the Tacitus passage actually reads, *nemo enim illic ridet*. Cf. the use of this passage by 'Eugenio', who was also a correspondent to *CGJ* No. 28, in an essay on 'Chastity and the Matrimonial State', *LM* 21 (1752), 550–1.

[2] 'Mr. John Nieuhoff's Remarkable Voyages and Travels to the East-Indies', in Awnsham and John Churchill's *A Collection of Voyages and Travels*, 6 vols. (1732), ii. 183. Fielding carefully fails to note one point made by Nieuhoff: 'Notwithstanding this severe punishment, adultery is very frequent among them, by reason of the extraordinary lasciviousness of the women. . . .'

[3] Christopher Borri, 'An Account of Cochin-China', in Awnsham and John Churchill's compilation, *A Collection of Voyages and Travels*, ii. 737.

[4] John Barbot, 'A Description of the Coasts of North and South-Guinea', in Churchill's *Collection of Voyages*, v. 300, 372.

[5] Fielding is paraphrasing, rather than quoting, from John Barbot's 'Description of the Coasts of North and South-Guinea', in Churchill's *Collection of Voyages*, V. 337.

[6] For Fielding's continuation of this discussion, see *CGJ* No. 68.

SATURDAY, OCTOBER 28, 1752.   NUMB. 68.

At placet Urfidio Lex Julia.——

JUVENAL.[1]

The Julian Law (against Adultery) pleases Urfidius.

Beside the Quotation from Tacitus in my last[2] concerning the Manners of those antient Northern Nations from which our Saxon Ancestors derived their Original, I find in Master Speed's Chronicle the following Passage.[3]

"Greater Punishments than these (namely those mentioned by Tacitus, to be inflicted on Adulterers by the Germans) the Pagan Saxons executed upon such Offenders as by the Epistle of Boniface an Englishman, Archbishop of Mogunce, which he wrote unto Ethelbald King of the Mercians in reproving his Adulterous Life is manifest; for (saith he) in the antient Country of the Saxons where there was no knowledge of God, if a Maid in her Father's House, or one having a Husband became a Whore, she should be strangled with her Hands close to her Mouth, and her Corrupter should be hanged upon the Pit wherein she was buried; if she was not so used, then her Garment being cut away down from the Girdle Steed, the chaste Matrons did scourge and whip her, and did prick her with Knives, and she was sent from Town to Town, where other fresh and new Scourgers did meet and torment her unto Death.

"These severe Laws a long Time remaining in the Days of Christianity, declare with what Rigour without regard of Person, they both examined and punished this Offence, &c." And this Punishment he says continued till about the Year 750, when it was abolished by Pope Stephen the second.

Among the Laws of Canute the Dane, made about the Year 1017 or 18, this was one, that a married Woman convicted of Adultery should be infamous, lose her whole Fortune, and should have her Nose and Ears cut off. By which, among other good Laws, says Mr. Echard, *Sin and Looseness were much restrained, and the Nation piously and justly governed.*[4]

---

[1] *Satires*, vi. 38; Fielding errs, perhaps out of playfulness, in his parenthetical insertion in the translation of the line, for the Julian Law referred to by Juvenal is the *Lex Julia de maritandis ordinibus* (18 BC) to encourage marriages and parenthood, not the Lex Julia to punish adultery discussed by Fielding in *CGJ* No. 67. Fielding had earlier conflated the two laws in his burlesque of Juvenal's satire in *Miscellanies* (1743), ed. H. K. Miller, Wesleyan Edn. (Oxford, 1972), i. 88–9, where his Latin gloss on the line points out that men are impelled to marriage by a law to punish adultery.

[2] From *Germania*, 19, in *CGJ* No. 67, above.

[3] Fielding quotes accurately from John Speed's *The History of Great Britaine Under the Conquests of the Romans, Saxons, Danes and Normans*, 3rd edn. (1650), p. 289; this edition of the work of Speed (1522?–1629) was in Fielding's library (Baker, item 313).

[4] Quoted from Laurence Echard, *The History of England. From the First Entrance of Julius Caesar and the Romans, to the Conclusion of the Reign of King James the Second*, 3rd edn. (1720), p. 45; Fielding has substituted 'piously' for the word 'peaceably' in his source. This work, which Fielding owned (Baker, item 307), is included in a list of partisan histories in *Joseph Andrews* (III. i), where it is set in opposition to the Whiggish work of Rapin. Echard's Tory bias is also hinted at in *A Charge to the Grand Jury*

Later than this, I do not remember any Constitution by which Corporal Punishment is inflicted on this Crime. Indeed, Henry I. as we read in Rapin, intending to reform the numerous Abuses which his Brother had permitted among his Courtiers, published a very severe Edict against all Offenders in General, but more particularly against Adulterers.[1] But what the Punishment was under this Edict, I do not remember to have seen.

By what means our Laws were induced to consider this atrocious *Vice* as no Crime, I shall not attempt to determine. Such however is the Fact: for as to the Action for criminal Conversation, tho' some have severely smarted by it, yet the Lawyers well know the Difference between criminal and civil Proceeding, between that Process which is instituted for Punishment and Example; and that which hath merely the Redress of an Injury and Damages only in its View.[2]

No longer ago than the Reign of King William, a Bill, as I have been told, was brought into the House of Commons to make Adultery Capital, when one of the Members standing up and saying, "That he had no Objection to the Severity of the Punishment, but hoped the Crime might be put on the Footing of Treason as to the Manner of Conviction, in which Case, a late Act of Parliament required two Witnesses to the same Overt Act." Some

---

(1749), and Fielding incorporates him in the figure of 'Geoffrey Bechard' as part of his parody of John Oldmixon in *CGJ* No. 17. For Fielding's slighting reference to another work by Echard, *The Roman History*, see *Tom Jones*, VI. ii, and *A Journey from this World to the Next* (1743), I. ix.

[1] Summarized (and partially quoted) from *The History of England. Written in French by Mr. Rapin de Thoyras. Trans. N. Tindal*, 2nd edn. (1732), i. 190, the edition of Rapin which Fielding owned (Baker, item 308). For his other references to this well-known work of 'Whig history', translated and completed by Nicholas Tindal, see *Joseph Andrews* (III. i), *Tom Jones* (VI. ii), and *A Charge Delivered to the Grand Jury* (1749).

[2] By the 'Action for Criminal Conversation' Fielding means a 'Common law action . . . at the suit of a husband to recover damages against an adulterer' (W. A. Jowitt, *Dictionary of English Law* [1959], s.v. 'Criminal conversation'). Cf. Fielding's 'Part of Juvenal's Sixth Satire Modernized', in *Miscellanies* (1743), Wesleyan Edn., p. 89: ' "We'll all (he cries) be Cuckolds, *Nem. Con.* / While the rich Action lies of *Crim. Con.*" '; and Jonathan Wild's threat to bring Fireblood into Westminster Hall, 'the modern method of repairing these breaches and of resenting this affront' (IV. x). In his *Charge to the Grand Jury* (1749), Fielding cites Coke's *Third Part of the Institutes* (206) to the effect that adultery was in ancient times punished by fines and imprisonment, but, Fielding adds, 'later Times have given up this Matter in general to ecclesiastical Jurisdiction' (pp. 44–5). In 1650 Parliament made adultery a felony punishable by death, but at the Restoration, as Blackstone points out, 'it was not thought proper to renew a law of such unfashionable rigour. And these offences have been ever since left to the feeble coercion of the spiritual court' (*Commentaries*, 5th edn. [Oxford, 1773], iv. 64–5).

For others who shared Fielding's indignation at this state of affairs, see *CGJ* No. 67, above, p. 353 n. 2. CF. also Sollom Emlyn's similar views in his Preface to the 2nd edn. of *A Complete Collection of State Trials*, 6 vols. (1730); Emlyn (1697–1754), professing himself puzzled at the lenity shown to this 'enormous Crime', complains that the 'Severity of our Law in inflicting capital Punishments upon the lighter Crimes of Pilfering and Thieving seems the more extraordinary, when one considers the great Indulgence shewn to one of the first Magnitude, and which is productive of much more mischievous Consequences, I mean *Adultery*, which it is holden does not by our Law admit of any Prosecution in a criminal way' (I. ix–x). And, like Fielding, he buttresses his argument with a parade of citations to show that 'the Laws of other Nations had a different Sense of it, and treated it in a Severer manner'.

Conceits presently prevailed, upon which the House began to be merry and the Bill was laughed out of it.[1]

I shall not much wonder if what I have advanced or shall advance on this Subject, should be likewise the Object of Laughter to my Reader. I can indeed very truly appropriate the Words of Dr. South on a like Attempt to oppose the general Opinion. "Such ever was," says he, "and is, and will be, the Temper of the generality of Mankind, that, while I send Men for Pleasure to Religion, I cannot but expect, that they will look upon me, as only having a Mind *to be pleasant with them myself.* Men are not to be worded into new Tempers or Constitutions; and he that thinks that any other can persuade, but he that made the World, will find that he does not well understand it."[2]

I am therefore prepared to hear from those who do not know me, that all this is only *the Copy of my Countenance*;[3] and from those who do, that a Lecture against Adultery, very well becomes a Man of threescore and ten.

In Defiance, however, of all such Sarcasms, I shall persist in declaring my Opinion, that to have no Law at all against Adultery, is a small Defect at least in a Christian Society. Nay, I will venture farther, and will propose some Provisions on this Head; from the Moderation of which, I doubt not but I shall appear to an impartial Eye in the Light of a cool and wise Politician, rather than that of an inflamed and rash Zealot.

First, I think, it might be at least negatively declared, that Adultery is not honourable, or indeed not *bonum in se*;[4] by which means Ambition and Love

[1] The 'late Act' requiring two witnesses to treason is 7 William III, c. 3, 'An Act for regulating of Trials in Cases of Treason and Misprison of Treason' (1698). The bill which would have made adultery a capital offense and which Fielding says was laughed out of the House was probably the one 'for the more effectual discouraging and suppressing Profaneness and all manner of Vice and Immorality', brought in on 23 Dec. 1698 and considered by the House as a Committee of the Whole several times; the *Journal of the House of Commons* makes no further reference to it after 9 Feb. 1698/9. Though its provisions are not known, evidence that this is the bill Fielding has in mind is provided by a pamphlet of 1699, *Reasons for the Passing of the Bill for the more Effectual suppressing Vice and Immorality*, a pamphlet directed primarily against adultery. Although the 'Vice and Immorality' bill was not passed, another bill, introduced in the House of Lords, to suppress profaneness and blasphemy did become law (9 & 10 William III, c. 32) but did not concern itself with adultery. Despite Fielding's anecdote, the atmosphere in the last years of the century, when societies for the reformation of manners were beginning to flourish, was propitious for such legislation; see e.g. *The Humble Address of the House of Commons to the King* (Edinburgh, 1698) and *A Help to a National Reformation* (1700). As unseasonably early as 1675 one pamphlet had called for a law to punish adultery with death and, as Fielding was to do three-quarters of a century later, had cited the ways in which past cultures had punished a crime which (the writer says) the present age calls by the 'soft and gentle *French* Names of *Gallantry* and *Divertisement*' (*A Letter to a Member of Parliament* [1675], p. 6).

[2] Fielding quotes with trivial changes from Robert South's *Epistle Dedicatory* to Edward Earl of Clarendon of the first volume of South's *Twelve Sermons Preached upon Several Occasions*, 5th edn. (1722), i. sig. [A3]. On South, see *CGJ* No. 12, above, p. 85 n. 3.

[3] i.e. 'a mere outward show or sign of what one would do or be; hence, pretence' (*OED*, citing *Jonathan Wild*, III. xiv); cf. Wild's maxim in IV. xv: 'That the heart was the proper seat of hatred, and the countenance of affection and friendship'.

[4] A good in itself.

of Glory, would cease any longer to be Motives to this Vice, as there is great Reason to think they have sometimes been.

Secondly, tho' this may be a Matter merely indifferent to the moral Character of a young Gentleman, especially in those of the Army, or those of Wit and Pleasure about Town,[1] it is far otherwise with Men of a graver Character. A Magistrate or a Clergyman who lies with his Neighbour's Wife, may be justly I think esteemed as infamous as he who picks his Neighbour's Pocket, and therefore might with no Impropriety suffer that same Punishment which the Mob inflict on the latter Crime, viz. ducking in a Horsepond.[2] All chaste and sober Matrons to be under the same Predicament; and this indiscriminately, whether they belong to the Parish of St. James's or to that of St. Giles's.[3] For which Purpose a Proviso may, I conceive, be added.——"That it may be lawful for the said Mob to proceed to Execution, without any Regard to the Finery of the Offender, and her to duck, all Silks, Velvets, and Brocades in any wise notwithstanding."

Thirdly, That after such Ducking, the Offender, if a Man, shall henceforth forfeit all Claim to that Respect which was originally designed (however it may have been corrupted) as a Tribute to Wisdom, Virtue or Sobriety; nor shall it be lawful afterwards for any Man (unless an Author in a Dedication) to call such ducked Person, Honourable, Worshipful, or Reverend, save only in such Cases where the Monosyllable *Right* is prefixed to any of these Titles. And tho' a Lady may after ducking appear in Public, and visit and be visited as before, yet shall it not be lawful for her ever to mention the Word *Honour*, either by Way of Panegyric on herself, or Censure on any of her Acquaintance.

Fourthly, That as in the Case of the Benefit of Clergy, so no Officer shall claim *the Benefit of the Army*[4] more than once. Provided, however, that all Landladies at Inns where the said Officers are Quartered, shall be totally excepted out of this Law, unless in Cases where the Husband can prove that he hath strictly forbidden his Wife to converse with the said Officers, and hath taken all Means in his Power to prevent the same.

Fifthly, Provided likewise that no Husband shall be entitled to any Prosecution of his Wife for Adultery, who lives in a state of Separation from

---

[1] On the propensity of Army officers to 'Gallantry'—a reiterated theme in *Amelia* (1751)—see also *CGJ* No. 20, above, p. 137; on gentlemen of wit and pleasure, cf. *An Essay on Modern Gallantry. Address'd to Men of Honour, Men of Pleasure, and Men of Sense* (1750), *passim*.

[2] On adulterous magistrates, cf. Justice Squeezum in Fielding's *Rape upon Rape* (1730), who compiles material toward a history of all the women he has seduced (IV. vi); the play concludes with the lines, 'No reverence that church or state attends / Whose laws the priest or magistrate offends'. For Fielding's description of a mob ducking a pickpocket, see his Letter XLI contributed to Sarah Fielding's *Familiar Letters between the Principal Characters in David Simple* (1747); the sentence, he says, 'is immediately executed with such Rigour, that he hardly escapes with his Life' (II. 319).

[3] See *CGJ* No. 17, above, p. 122 n. 3.

[4] See n. 1, above; on 'Benefit of Clergy', see *CGJ* No. 14, above, p. 103 n. 1.

her, either at Bed or Board; or who connives at her keeping *Drums, Routs*,[1] or any such kind of disorderly House; or who suffers his Wife to play for large Sums of Money, or to converse with either Men or Women of dissolute and abandoned Characters, or to haunt suspected Houses; or lastly, who lives himself in an open and avowed State of Adultery with other Women. In all such Cases nevertheless, the Mob on due Proof may *ex Officio* proceed to Judgment and Execution.

And here I apprehend (viz. in the Matter of Proof,) will lie all the Difficulty. On this Head to demonstrate my extreme Lenity, I shall insist that the Conviction be by the unanimous Consent of *the whole World*; by which I cannot be supposed to mean every Individual in Europe, Asia, &c. but that Body of People which are in common Speech so called, and which consists of an indefinite Number, sometimes of five or six.[2] But I shall suffer no less than twelve, that is to say the Number of an English Jury to make a Quorum, or the whole World on this Occasion. I shall likewise allow to the Defendant all Challenges of the Jurors, either for Prudery or Rivalship; or because any or all of the said World have been themselves ducked.

But as in the old Law of England (as some perhaps know) a Thief taken with the Manner, *i.e.* surprized in the Fact with the Goods upon him, (*meinor, manœuvre*) was executed without farther Trial;[3] so here all Matrons who are guilty of indecent and profligate Behaviour with Men in Public, shall be deemed to be taken with the Manner, and may together with the said Men, be immediately Ducked without farther Ceremony.

Perhaps it will be objected that I am giving a Jurisdiction to improper Persons; but such Objection deserves little Answer in an Age when it seems to be generally agreed, that the Sword of Justice can never be in better Hands than those of the Mob; which Opinion is, I suppose, founded on this Argument, that as this is a very heavy Sword, the Hands of the Mob being the strongest, are the best able to wield it.[4]

C.

---

[1] See *CGJ* No. 17, above, p. 122.

[2] Cf. *CGJ* No. 4, where Fielding in his 'Modern Glossary' defines 'World' as 'your own Acquaintance'.

[3] Giles Jacob's version of the 'old Law' is a little less extreme: 'And anciently if one guilty of Felony or Larceny had been freshly pursued, and *taken with the Manner*, and the Goods so found upon him had been brought into Court with him, he might be tried immediately, without any Appeal or Indictment' (*A New Law–Dictionary*, 7th edn. [1756], s.v. 'Manner'). Fielding uses the term playfully in *Joseph Andrews*, I. xvii. On the etymology, see *OED*, s.v. 'mainour'.

[4] Cf. the French visitor in Fielding's Letter XLI, contributed to his sister's *Familiar Letters* (1747): 'The Mobs . . . are a Court, which generally endeavours to do Justice, tho' they sometimes err, by the Hastiness of their Decisions. Perhaps it is the only Court in the World, where there is no Partiality arising from Respect of Persons.' But to understand the extent of Fielding's irony in this concluding paragraph, see his essays on the Mob, *CGJ* Nos. 47 and 49, above.

SATURDAY, NOVEMBER 4, 1752.   NUMB. 69.

Nimirum insanus paucis videatur eo ˈquod,
Maxima pars hominum morbo jactatur eodem.

HORACE.[1]

Few Men may Madness this or Folly name,
For most Men are infected with the same.

There are a kind of silly Fellows, whom I do not remember to have seen fully animadverted upon by any Author, antient or modern. Many have indeed given us several shrewd Hints concerning them, have attacked them as it were obliquely and in the dark; but none have ever fairly declared War against them, and have dared to oppose them in open Field; the true Reason of which seems to be, that the World in general will be almost sure to be of their Side, and to maintain their Cause.

Not to keep my Reader in too long a Suspence, the silly Fellows I here mean, are those to whom the common Voice gives the Appellation of *Wise Men*. A People whom, however they may be fortified and secured, it is absolutely necessary to encounter and utterly to abolish, before it will be possible to introduce any true Notions of Goodness, Virtue, or indeed of common Sense, among Mankind; for to all these the said Wise Men are professed Enemies, and all such Notions they will be sure to laugh, or rather to shake out of the World, by that dangerous shaking of their Heads, with which they are usually so certain of triumphing over their Adversaries.[2]

It is scarce, I think, necessary to premise, that by Wise Men here I do not understand Persons endowed with that Wisdom of which Solomon was possessed, which he tells us is more eligible than Gold; to which he advises us to open our Ears and to incline our Hearts.[3] Which David tells us, cometh out of the Mouth of the Righteous, and which Solomon says, is despised by Fools.[4]

Neither do I mean that Wisdom here which was the Deity of the antient Philosophers, which Seneca says, is superior to all the Efforts of Fortune, and which, according to Horace, makes a Man a King of Kings, and places him in Rank next to Jupiter himself.[5]

---

[1] *Satires*, II. iii. 120–1: 'Few, doubtless, would think him mad, because the mass of men toss about in the same kind of fever' (Loeb). Used also as the motto to the *True Patriot*, No. 23 (8 Apr. 1746).

[2] Cf. *Champion*, 26 Jan. 1739/40, where Fielding, posing as a cynical correspondent and ironically citing Bacon's advice to assume virtues nearest our vices, makes this comment: 'This is indeed arguing like a wise man, like a man who understands the world, and the way of living in it. This is such philosophical diet as a man may grow fat by feeding on. No chimerical system, which hath starved all its professors . . .' On his distinctions between true and false wisdom in *Tom Jones*, see Martin Battestin, *The Providence of Wit* (Oxford, 1974), pp. 164–92.

[3] Proverbs 16: 16 and 2: 2.   [4] Psalms 37: 30; Proverbs 1: 7.

[5] Seneca, *De constantia sapientis* (*Dialogues*, II), v. 4; viii. 3, and *passim*; Horace, *Epistles*, I. i. 106–7. Fielding had appealed to the Stoic conception of the wise man in his 'Of the Remedy of Affliction for

By Wisdom here I mean that Wisdom of this World, which St. Paul expressly tells us *is Folly*; that Wisdom *of the Wise*, which, as we read both in Isaiah and in the Corinthians, is threatened with Destruction:[1] Lastly, I here intend that Wisdom in the Abundance of which, as the Preacher tells us, there is *much of Grief*;[2] which, if true, would be alone sufficient to evince the extreme Folly of those who covet and pursue such Wisdom.

But tho' the Scriptures in the Places above cited, and in many others do very severely treat this Character of worldly or mock Wisdom, they have not, I think, very fully described it, unless perhaps Solomon hath done this ironically under the Name of Folly.[3] An Opinion to which I am much inclined; and indeed what is said in the 10th Chapter of Ecclesiastes of the great Exaltation of a Fool, must be understood of a Fool in Repute, and such is the Wise Man here pointed at.[4]

In the same Manner, the best Writers among the Heathens have obscurely and ironically characterized this Wisdom. *What is a covetous Man?* says Horace, *he is both a Fool and a Madman.*[5] Now Avarice is the very highest Perfection and as it were Quintessence of this Kind of Wisdom. Again says the same Horace, *Chuse any Man you please out of the Crowd; he is either oppressed with Avarice, or miserable Ambition.*[6] Here you have the two great Characteristics of this Wisdom, Avarice and Ambition, in one Verse, which, the Poet tells us, were the Pursuit of all the wise Men in Rome, as indeed they have been in all other Countries.[7]

And with this Opinion the Judgment of the World hath so absolutely coincided, that I am extremely doubtful whether by a *Wise Man* is generally meant any other than a Man who is pursuing the direct Road to Power or Wealth, however dirty or thorny it may be. A wise Man, in short, in the common Estimation, is he who becomes great or rich; nor are all the Labours he undergoes, or all the Frauds and Villanies which he commits ever taken into the Account, or in the least considered as any Objections to his Wisdom.

But however wise a Man may be who outwits and over-reaches others, he

---

the Loss of our Friends', *Miscellanies* (1743); in this essay, however, he argues from within the specifically Christian context of the promise of immortality. On his attitude toward the Stoics, see Miller, *Essays*, pp. 254–63.

[1] Isaiah 29: 14; I Corinthians 3: 19.   [2] Ecclesiastes 1: 18.

[3] As e.g. in Proverbs 15: 2: 'The tongue of the wise useth knowledge aright: but the mouth of fools poureth out foolishness.'

[4] Ecclesiastes 10: 6.   [5] *Satires*, II. iii. 158–9.

[6] *Satires*, I. iv. 25–6. Cf. Aristotle, *Politics*, II. vi. 19.

[7] Cf. Fielding's description of these two frequently coupled vices in his 'Essay on Nothing', *Miscellanies* (1743): 'our two greatest and noblest Pursuits, one or other of which engages almost every Individual of the busy Part of Mankind'; both pursuits, however, end in nothing. Avarice and Ambition are the passions which dominate the mind of Blifil (*Tom Jones*, VI. iv). Cf. also Fielding's Letter XLIV in Sarah Fielding's *Familiar Letters* (1747), as well as the allegorical 'Vision' which follows that letter and concludes the second volume.

seems not much to deserve that Name who outwits and over-reaches himself; and this, I am afraid, is always the Case with the most absolute Slaves of either of these Passions, that is to say, with the wisest of Men.

It is certain that a Man may (tho' perhaps with greater Difficulty) impose on himself as well as on others; for it hath been asserted, and I doubt not truly, that an habitual Liar will come in Time to believe his own Lies.[1] In the same Manner may a Man make a Fool of himself, and this is perhaps the highest Degree of worldly Cunning. Thus very artful Children do sometimes outwit those who have the Care of them, and by such Means do fall into all kinds of Mischief; on which Occasions, I think none will dispute but that the little Wretches have likewise been too hard for themselves.

Divines, pursuing I suppose the Opinions above cited from Solomon and St. Paul, have taken great Pains to prove that the Man who sacrifices his Hopes in another World to any Acquisitions in this, however wise he may call himself or may be called by others, is in Reality a very silly Fellow.[2] These have endeavoured to shew us, that a Rascal gibbeted up as it were on the Mount of Ambition, or a Wretch wallowing in the Mire of Avarice, is in Truth a Fool, and will be convinced of his Folly when it is too late.

But if there be any Persons who, in Opposition to all the Arguments which have been urged to support this Doctrine, still guide their Opinion by the old Proverb of a Bird in the Hand,[3] &c. and conclude that those are wisest who make sure of the present World, yet all must, I think, confess that he is a Fool who gives up both; who without any Prospect or Hopes of a future Reward, takes care to be at present as miserable as he possibly can.

Now that this is the Case with the Slaves of Ambition and Avarice, is so very manifest, that it seems an Affront to the human Understanding to endeavour to prove it. Take a Picture in Miniature of the former from the ingenious Dr. South. "The ambitious Person (says he) must rise early and sit up late, and must pursue his Design with a constant indefatigable Attendance; he must be infinitely patient and servile, and obnoxious to all those Persons whom he expects to rise by; he must endure and digest all Sorts of Affronts; adore the Foot that kicks him, and kiss the Hand that

---

[1] Proverbial; see Tilley, L 221, citing Bacon, *History of the Reign of Henry VII* (1622), p. 446, and Prior's *Alma* (1718), iii. 9.

[2] Cf., for example, Robert South's sermon on 1 Corinthians 3: 19, 'For the Wisdom of this World is Foolishness with God', demonstrating that 'such as act by the . . . Rules of Worldly Wisdom, are eminently foolish', *Twelve Sermons Preached upon Several Occasions*, 5th edn. (1722), i. 334–73; John Tillotson, Sermon CXXXIII, 'The Wisdom of Religion Justified', *Works* (1752), ii. 193 ff.; Isaac Barrow, Sermon I on 'The Pleasantness of Religion', contrasting true wisdom with the seeking of power and dominion, *Works*, 5th edn. (1741), i. 1–8; and, for an example closer to the time of Fielding's essay, Edward Pickard, *Solomon's Preference of Wisdom Considered* (1752). Fielding's formula for definition, 'by Wise Men I do not understand . . . Neither do I mean . . .' is common in sermons of this sort; cf. Pickard, 'By *Wisdom* I do not mean *bare Knowledge* . . . Much less by *Wisdom* do I mean . . . By *Wisdom* therefore I mean . . .' (16–17).

[3] Tilley, B 363.

strikes him."[1] Of the latter, you have as lively a Description in the excellent Dr. Barrow. "Other vicious Inclinations combat Reason, and often baffle it; but seldom so vanquish it, as that a Man doth approve or applaud himself in his Miscarriage: but the covetous Humour seizeth on our Reason itself, and seateth itself therein; inducing it to favour and countenance what is done amiss. The voluptuous Man is swayed by the Violence of his Appetite, but the Covetous is seduced by the Dictates of his Judgment: he therefore scrapes and hoards and lets go nothing, because he esteems Wealth the best thing in the World, and then judges himself *most Wise* when he is most base. Labour not to be Rich, *cease from thine own Wisdom*, saith Solomon; intimating the Judgment such Persons are wont to make of their Riches; whence of all Dispositions opposite to Piety, this is the most pernicious."[2]

With Examples of the Misery, the Folly, and indeed the Absurdity of these Pursuits, History so abounds, that as there is perhaps no more profitable, so there seems to be no more apposite *Use of that Study*,[3] than to learn a just Contempt of Ambition and Avarice. History may make a half-witted Fellow a Politician, and may point out to him the Means of acquiring Power or Wealth; but it bids fair to raise the Man of solid Sense into a true Philosopher, and to teach him the Contempt of both.

Cræsus, King of Lydia, having received a Favour from Alcmæon the Athenian, gave him as much Gold as he could carry. Alcmæon not contented with loading his Pockets, which were for the Purpose made immensely large, and filling a vast Pair of Boots with Gold, tied several Ingots of Gold to his Hair, and crammed his Mouth with the same Metal. In this Condition when Cræsus saw him coming out of the Treasury, Herodotus tells us, he burst into a most immoderate Fit of Laughter, at the extreme Avarice of the Man.[4]

In solemn Truth, there is nothing more ridiculous than the Labours of either Avarice or Ambition; and for this Reason especially that those who undergo them, undergo them to no Purpose. No Fable was ever so finely conceived as that of Tantalus, to represent the State of a Miser; who, as *Bion*

---

[1] Quoted with minor changes from 'The Practice of Religion enforced by Reason: in a Sermon . . . upon Prov. x. 9', in South's *Twelve Sermons Preached upon Several Occasions*, 5th edn. (1722), ii. 27–8. On Robert South, see *CGJ* No. 12, above, p. 85 n. 3.

[2] Isaac Barrow, Sermon XXXI, 'The Duty and Reward of Bounty to the Poor', in *Works*, 5th edn. (1741), i. 317. On Barrow, see *CGJ* No. 4, above, p. 35 n. 5; on the significance of this sermon to Fielding, see *CGJ* No. 29, above, p. 183 n. 3.

[3] A sly gibe at Bolingbroke, whose *Letters on the Study and Use of History* had been published in two volumes by Millar in March of 1752; on Bolingbroke, who had died in Dec. 1751, and on Fielding's objections to his free-thinking, see *CGJ* No. 15, above, p. 104 n. 5. Fielding's allusion to the *Letters* in the context of an essay on true wisdom and Christian immortality is especially pointed, for this work was widely censured as containing 'little more than some objections to Revelation' (*GM* 22 [Mar. 1752]). See e.g. *Some Remarks on the Letters of the Late Lord Bolingbroke* (1752); Robert Clayton, *A Vindication of the Histories of the Old and New Testament* (Dublin, 1752); James Hervey, *Remarks on Lord Bolingbroke's Letters* (1752); and similar pamphlets by Peter Whalley and John Leland in 1753.

[4] Herodotus, *History*, vi. 125. The usual spelling is 'Croesus'.

finely said, "Surveys the Heaps of another Man, as if they were his own, and his own as if they were another Man's, being indeed not in Possession of his Wealth, but possessed by it."[1]

And what is the Case of the ambitious Man when he hath gained the Power he aimed at? Can he call it his own, or ensure himself the Enjoyment of it? Notwithstanding all the Slavery and unwearied Diligence with which he must court the Supporters of his Power, how liable are they every Hour to slide from him! what a Bargain did that Wretch make who purchased the Roman Empire, and was butchered at the End of two Months, by those military Auctioneers that sold it him?[2] And yet we read of one in the History of Spain, who would have been contented with a shorter Term in his Royal Estate. "In the Dissentions among the Moors, in the Kingdom of Cordova, when about a dozen successive Kings had been put to the Sword, a Youth of a Royal Family," says Mariana, "assisted by a Company of wild young Fellows, entered the Palace, and desired the Soldiers to proclaim him King. They represented to him the Disloyalty of the Citizens, and advised him to take Warning by so many who had already perished. He wisely answered. *Call me but King to Day, and kill me to morrow.* Such," says my Author, "is the inordinate Desire of reigning";[3] *and such,* I add, *is the inordinate Folly of Ambition.*

And yet these two are the great Business which the World espouses; to the Pursuit of which it assigns the Appellation of Wisdom; and to which, if we will attain that Honour, we must sacrifice all the real Enjoyments of Life.

But in plain Truth, if it was as certain that there is no other World, as I take it to be certain that there is, he would be the wisest Man who made the most of the Conforts of this, while the Wretch who spends his Days in Cares and Misery that he may die greater or richer than other Men, is the silliest Fellow in the Universe.   C.

---

[1] Bion of Borysthenes, sophist of 3rd cent. BC; Fielding's source is perhaps Diogenes Laertius, *Lives of Eminent Philosophers* (iv. 51): 'Referring to a wealthy miser he said, "He has not acquired a fortune; the fortune has acquired him" ' (Loeb); cf. *The Apophthegms of the Ancients* (1753) on Bion: 'He once told a sordid rich miser, "You don't possess your wealth, but 'tis your wealth possesses you" ' (ii. 239).

[2] Servius Sulpicius Galba (*c.*3 BC–AD 69), who was made emperor after huge sums were promised in his name to the Praetorian Guards. The money was never paid, and he was killed by them in Jan. 69; see Plutarch, *Galba*, ii, and Suetonius, *Galba*, xvi and xx.

[3] Juan de Mariana, *The General History of Spain*, trans. Capt. John Stevens (1699), p. 133; Fielding has mixed paraphrase with quotation from the original, apparently to make the situation Mariana describes clearer out of context. This translation of Mariana (1536–1623) was in his library (Baker, item 469); Fielding cites him also in *Joseph Andrews* (III. i), Preface to the *Miscellanies* (1743), and *Journey from this World to the Next* (1743), where (I. xvii) he criticizes the historian for telling a 'silly story' as a 'solemn truth'.

SATURDAY, NOVEMBER 11, 1752.　NUMB. 70.

Cælum ipsum petimus Stultitia.

HORACE.[1]

Our Folly would look into Heaven.

I have lately read over a very entertaining little Book, called an Account of English Ants.[2] A Performance which appears by its Date to have been five Years in the World, in which, if the Author had been better known, his Work would have had the same Fate, and have been ranked, as it deserves, among the most curious Productions of this Age. But as the Name of the Reverend Mr. Gould, tho' a Gentleman, a Scholar, and a Master of Arts, is not yet famous in the Republic of Letters, this excellent Work hath hitherto, I apprehend, been suffered to sleep among the Rubbish of the Times.[3]

From the many extraordinary Discoveries which the ingenious Writer hath made in the Ways of this surprising Insect, he proceeds to draw some moral Lessons for the Use of Mankind. "Their incredible Affection towards their Young," says he, "might teach us to value Posterity and promote its Happiness. The Obedience they pay their respective Queens, might read us a Lecture of true Loyalty and Subjection. Their incessant Labours may serve to enliven the industrious, and shame the lazy Part of Mankind. The unanimous Care exerted by each Colony for the common Emolument, might let us know the Consequence of public Good, and tempt us to endeavour the Prosperity of our Countrymen. From their Œconomy we may learn Prudence, from their Sagacity Wisdom, &c."[4]

Many great Authors have spoken largely of the Understanding of these little Insects. Horace expressly recommends their Example to the Imitation of Mankind,[5] and Solomon himself sends us to the Ant, as to the School of Wisdom.[6]

While I was meditating on the astonishing Instances of Sagacity, Prudence, and Art, which are exemplified in the Œconomy of Ants, and

---

[1] *Odes*, I. iii. 38: 'Heaven itself we seek in our folly' (Loeb); quoted also in *Joseph Andrews* (II. xii) and (second half of line) as motto of *True Patriot*, No. 17 (25 Feb. 1746).

[2] William Gould, *An Account of English Ants* (1747).

[3] Fielding appears to be sincere in these flattering comments; Gould, who received his MA from Exeter College in 1739, is listed in Foster's *Alumni Oxoniensis* as the son of Davidge Gould, Sharpham Park, Somerset, and was thus Fielding's first cousin. His book, moreover, had been published by Andrew Millar, whose publications are frequently puffed in *CGJ* (see General Introduction, above, p. xxx). Gould's book was not entirely unnoticed; an abstract by Henry Miles was read before the Royal Society on 15 Jan. 1747, and reprinted in *LM* (16 [1747], 522, 557–60).

[4] P. 108. Gould's moral reflections were omitted in the abstract by Miles, but are typical of the humanistic application of the observation of nature which Fielding calls for in *CGJ* No. 61; see above, p. 328.

[5] *Satires*, I. i. 33–8.

[6] Proverbs 6: 6–8; cf. Pope, *Essay on Man*, iii. 169–98.

which are displayed by the ingenious Author of the abovementioned little Book, it occurred to my Imagination, that these little Insects may possibly resemble the human Species in many Particulars, of which it may be beyond the Reach of the most curious Enquirer, to discern the least Trace or Footstep. They may possess many of our Sciences which we can never discover, as we do their Skill in Architecture, from the Effect; and that for a very simple, tho' a very convincing Reason, because those Sciences among the Ants, as indeed among us, do end in nothing, and produce no Effect at all.

Such for Instance among us are the higher Branches of Natural Philosophy; that Philosophy, I mean, which is always prying into the Secrets of Nature, and lying in wait as it were to peep into her dressing Room to view her naked, and before she is drest in any kind of Form.[1] A bold Attempt, and for which the Philosophers have been often deprived of that little Share of Sense which they before possessed. Indeed, I am apt to think, that if a superior Being was to examine into the Ways of Man, with the same Curiosity with which my Author hath searched into those of Ants, he would not be able to make any thing of this Philosopher, nor to discover what he was about when he was employed in his Lucubrations.[2]

In the Course of my Meditation, however, a Thought suggested itself to me, that it was very reasonable to think there might be some such Insects as these Natural Philosophers among the Ants, and when the Thought was once started, it afforded such Entertainment to my Fancy, that I could not avoid pursuing it, till it threw me into a kind of Reverie, in which I fell asleep, and was amused with the following Dream.

I dreamt I was lying down near a large Ant-hill, where I perceived a Number of those little Insects assembled together; and as I had in my Reverie already gifted them with the Use of Speech, I dreamt that one of them informed me, that they were a set of Philosophers assembled to

---

[1] For the image, cf. Samuel Butler, *Hudibras*, i. 560–2: 'He had First Matter seen undressed: / He took her naked, all alone, / Before one rag of form was on'; cf. also George Herbert, *Vanity (I)*, st. iii. On Fielding's consistently satirical attitude toward the Royal Society and the 'virtuosi', see Miller, *Essays*, 326–31. Cf., among many examples, *CGJ* No. 24, above; 'Some Papers Proper to be Read before the Royal Society', in *Miscellanies* (1743); *True Patriot*, No. 22 (1 Apr. 1746); and Letter XL in Sarah Fielding's *Familiar Letters between the Principal Characters in David Simple* (1747). Fielding's game in the present essay, however, is not simply the Royal Society or the 'Diligence in Trifles' of the virtuosi but, as the motto from Horace indicates, the proud pretensions of natural philosophy itself, which like Pope and Swift he satirizes in the long tradition of humanist attacks on science. For one example of a similar view within the scientific community itself, see Colin Maclaurin's *An Account of Sir Isaac Newton's Philosophical Discoveries* (1748); in this work, which Fielding owned, Maclaurin assaults system-builders like Descartes and Spinoza who 'have attempted to form a scheme of philosophy that far surpasses the human faculties' (p. 90).

[2] Cf. Addison's use of ants as a device for ridiculing human pride in *Guardian*, No. 153 (20 Sept. 1713).

enquire into the Cause of a violent and sudden Deluge which had happened some time before and had swept off almost a whole Colony.[1]

There is in Dreams, a strange Jumble and Mixture of Phantoms and Realities. Now what brought this Subject of their Enquiries into my Mind was, an Accident to which I was last Summer an Eye-witness, when I saw a very large Cow discharge a vast Shower on an Ant-hill, which as I afterwards observed, had destroyed a great Number of the Inhabitants.

But to return to my Dream: On a sudden one of the Insects, that was elevated above the rest on a small Bit of Earth, about thrice as large as a moderate Pin's Head, seemed to address himself to the rest in the following Speech, which I wrote down the Moment I awaked.

"It behoves every Ant that desires to excel other Insects, to avoid with the utmost Diligence the wasting his Life in Silence, like those Insects which Nature seems to have formed for no other Purpose, than to eat or to be eaten. Now all our Energy is placed either in the Body or in the Mind; that is formed to command, and this to obey;[2] that we partake in common with the meanest Fly, this we enjoy in Partnership with the Gods. To me therefore, it

---

[1] Reference to the 'Deluge' provides the key to Fielding's twofold strategy in what follows: he satirically allegorizes 'scientific' attempts to interpret the biblical account of the Deluge, a problem which in the late 17th cent. had been the prime focus of efforts to reconcile science and scripture; and he incorporates into this general satire a parody of a specific paper on the Deluge read before the Royal Society in 1694 by the astronomer Edmund Halley. See Bertrand A. Goldgar, 'Fielding, the Flood Makers, and Natural Philosophy: *Covent-Garden Journal* No. 70', *MP* 80 (1982), 136–44.

For an excellent brief account of the Deluge controversy, see Ephraim Chambers, *Cyclopaedia*, 7th edn. (1751–2), s.v. 'deluge'. For modern commentary see Ernest Tuveson, 'Swift and the World-Makers', *Journal of the History of Ideas*, 11 (1950), 54–74; Marjorie Hope Nicolson, *Mountain Gloom and Mountain Glory* (Ithaca, NY, 1959), chs. 5 and 6; and Joseph Levine, *Dr. Woodward's Shield* (Berkeley, 1977), pp. 25–40. Essentially the debate over the natural causes of the Flood involved differing theories about the origin of the water, since it was assumed the oceans did not contain a sufficient quantity to match the details of the Mosaic account. Among the major controversialists were Thomas Burnet (*Telluris Theoria Sacra*, 1681, 1689), John Ray (*Three Physico-theological Discourses*, 1692), John Woodward (*An Essay toward a Natural History of the Earth*, 1695), and William Whiston (*A New Theory of the Earth*, 1696). Although the first three found the source of the waters in 'the subterranean Abyss', and differed mainly about the mechanism for bringing the water to the surface, Whiston attributed the Flood to the earth's passing through the tail and atmosphere of a comet, a theory which may have taken its hint from Halley's papers read in 1695 but not printed until 1724.

Given Fielding's indictment here of the pride and presumption of the modern scientist, his choice of the Deluge controversy as a focus for his theme was almost an obvious one. Even some of the scientific contemporaries of the theorists had warned that the effort to square relevation with science could easily subvert religion itself; cf. the mathematician John Keill, who, in the course of demolishing Burnet and Whiston on scientific grounds, asserts, 'These contrivers of Deluges, have furnished the Atheist with an Argument, which . . . is not so easily answer'd as their Theories are made' (*An Examination of Dr. Burnet's Theory of the Earth* [Oxford, 1698], pp. 19–20). And Swift, Arbuthnot, and the other Scriblerian satirists, in various works known to Fielding, had also included the 'flood-makers' in the course of their attacks on the excesses of the new science; e.g. in the *Memoirs of Martinus Scriblerus*, the pedant-hero is said to know 'all the new *theories* of the *Deluge*' (ed. Charles Kerby-Miller [New Haven, 1950], p. 166 and n., pp. 329–31; for similar Scriblerian satires on the controversy, see Tuveson, pp. 66–74; and Nicolson, pp. 247–9).

[2] Fielding appears inadvertently to have reversed the positions of 'that' and 'this' in this sentence.

seems wiser to seek Glory from our Wit, than from our Strength; and since our Life is but short, to lengthen out our Memory as far as we can.

"Now by what can we hope to effect this so certainly, as by that Investigation of Nature, that Search into the first Causes of things, which as it is the noblest and most useful of all Studies, so is it most fitly accommodated to the Dignity of an Ant, the noblest Insect which this World ever saw. A Study of such infinite Benefit to *Ant-kind*, that without it, that most useful Art of curing Distempers which we call Physic, could never have been improved as it hath been to such a Degree of Certainty and Perfection.[1]

"Other Branches there be of this Philosophy, which may reasonably be presumed to have their Utility, tho' this is sometimes not so very apparent. In these learned Ants have most notably bestirred themselves in all Ages to their immortal Honour; and from which, the World have been enriched with that vast Treasure of Opinions; it being remarkable that scarce any two Ants, or any two Ages, have concurred in the same.

"Among those honorary or diverticulating Articles of Enquiry, on which so many learned Ants have spent their whole Lives, none, I think, hath exercised the Talents of the ingenious, more than an Enquiry into the Causes of that mighty Deluge which happened in the Reign of Queen Pissmiris the 10th, by which this whole Ant-hill which we now inhabit was laid under Water; and scarce a single Ant escaped save only the Queen with fifty-nine of her Lovers, who were then retired with her Majesty for her Recreation to the inmost Recesses of the Hill, and were happily preserved.[2]

"To repeat to you all that hath been advanced on this Subject, would be endless. None, I apprehend, have yet hit on the true Cause. As for that mighty Ant, Dr. Hook,[3] who would account for this Deluge by a *Compression of the Earth into a prolate Spheroid*, so as thereby to squeeze out the Waters of the Abyss, this would only drown the two extreme Zones of the Hill, whereas the middle Zone would thus be squeezed up instead of down, and so could

---

[1] But cf. the final paragraph of *CGJ* No. 41, where it is argued that the Royal Society pays little attention to medical subjects. Fielding, of course, found little 'Certainty and Perfection' in medical practice; see e.g. *Tom Jones*, II. ix; *Journey from this World to the Next* (1743), I. ii–iv; and *Amelia*, v. ii (1st edn. only, 1751).

[2] By the escape of the Queen and her lovers, Fielding represents the preservation of Noah and the Ark, an event the 'comet theory' had trouble explaining; see below, p. 372 n. 2, and cf. William Whiston, *A Vindication of the New Theory of the Earth* (1698), p. 37.

[3] Robert Hooke (1635–1703), eminent physicist and at one time Secretary of the Royal Society; for his theory (and the quoted statement) see 'A Discourse of Earthquakes', in Hooke's *Posthumous Works*, ed. Richard Waller (1705), pp. 351 ff. Although Fielding merely takes the reference to Hooke from Halley (see the note following), Hooke in some ways represented the type of presumptuous natural philosopher Fielding is ridiculing; cf. Waller's description of him as possessing 'more than common, if not wonderful Sagacity, in diving into the most hidden Secrets of Nature', and Hooke himself claimed that studying natural philosophy will enable a man to advance his state 'above the common Condition of Men, and make him able to excel them as much, almost, as they do Brutes or Ideots' (*Posthumous Works*, pp. xxviii, 3).

never be immerged.[1] And as for the egregious Ant who would have it to be occasioned by the Choc of a Comet, which instantly changing the Poles and diurnal Rotations of the Globe, would occasion a Puddle of Water to recede from those Parts, towards which the Poles did approach, and to encrease upon and overflow those Parts wherefrom the Poles were departed; it is sufficient to observe, that the learned Ant himself did afterwards confess, he had forgot to consider the great Agitation such a Choc must necessarily occasion in the Puddle; and tho' he would not give up his Hypothesis (which no Ant ever did or will) he yet confesses it would be extreme difficult to conceive how her Majesty and her Court could be preserved alive in such a Convulsion.[2]

"Before I undertake to consider the Cause of this Deluge, I shall premise that it is agreed on all Hands, that the Air had been greatly obscured for a long Space of Time, and that violent Bellowings had been heard in it.[3] The Cloud too which then overspread the Hill, hung so extremely low, that it is computed if five hundred Ants were heaped on each other, the uppermost Ant would have reached up to it. Another Circumstance agreed is, that the Waters no sooner began to fall, than they rushed down in a continued Cataract, and with inconceivable Violence.

"I account therefore for this Deluge, in the following Manner.

"A learned Ant hath long since proved, by some curious Hydrostatic

---

[1] This passage begins Fielding's parody of Edmund Halley's 'Some Considerations about the Cause of the Universal Deluge, laid before the Royal Society, on the 12th of Dec. 1694', printed for the first time in *Philosophical Transactions*, 33, No. 383 (1724), pp. 118–25, and included later in a volume Fielding owned, *Philosophical Transactions . . . Abridged*, 6 (1734), pt. 2, 1–5 (Baker, item 585); Halley had originally rejected publication of his two papers on the Deluge because of concern over his non-scriptural approach to the problem. The first passage Fielding parodies is as follows: 'Dr. *Hook's* Solution of this Problem, as he has not fully discovered himself, I cannot undertake to judge of; but his Compression of a Shell of Earth into a *prolate Spheroide*, thereby pressing out the Waters of an Abyss under the Earth, may very well account for drowning two extream opposite Zones of the Globe; but the middle Zone, being by much the greater Part of the Earth's Surface, must by this means be raised higher from the Center, and consequently arise more out of the Water than before' (pp. 120–1).

[2] This passage is again a close parody of Halley: 'In Num. 190 of these Transactions, I have proposed the casual *Choc* of a *Comet*, or other transient Body, as an Expedient to change instantly the Poles and Diurnal Rotation of the Globe; at that Time only aiming to shew how the *Axis* of the *Earth* being chang'd, would occasion the Sea to recede from those Parts towards which the Poles did approach, and to encrease upon and overflow those Parts wherefrom the Poles were departed; but at that Time I did not consider the great Agitation such a *Choc* must necessarily occasion in the Sea, . . . raising up Mountains where none were before, mixing the Elements into such a Heap as the Poets describe the old *Chaos*. . . . In this Case it will be much more difficult to shew how *Noah* and the *Animals* should be preserved, than that all Things in which was the Breath of Life, should hereby be destroyed' (*Philosophical Transactions*, 33, No. 383 [1724], 121–2). Halley himself is thus the 'egregious Ant' who refused to give up his hypothesis; although in the second of the two papers read before the Royal Society (19 Dec. 1694) he admits that his theory does not quite fit the case of the Deluge, he simply leaves the matter at that.

[3] One of the points of contention between Keill and Whiston was how a comet could produce the Darkness which the Primitive Chaos had, according to scripture; see Keill, p. 184.

Experiments,[1] that Water, tho' it hath not all the energetic Powers of an animated Insect, hath yet the Power of Motion. Indeed, such Experiments were scarce necessary, since we see it come and go every Day, which certainly nothing can do but what can move. And what is more common than to see it come into our Cells to-day, and remove itself to-morrow.

"Secondly, tho' Water may be divided into Drops, otherwise it could not have been calculated for the Use of us Ants, yet these Drops whenever they have an Opportunity will run to one another, so that they have been strongly concluded to be male and female.[2] They likewise have an adhesive Quality, by which they are able to unite themselves so strongly in one Body, that to separate them immediately into Drops again, would require an immense Number of Ants.

"Thirdly, Water when it ascends upwards, doth always ascend in Drops, and those almost too small for our Sight; but when it descends or falls down, it falls in a Body of two, three, four or more Drops together, as we often see in the falling of Clouds, which are only so many united Bodies of Drops of Water; most commonly male and female; as a learned Ant observes, who very ingeniously derives hence the Propagation of all kinds of those delicious Fruits which Nature hath so abundantly produced for the Use of Ant-kind.[3]

"Upon the whole then, an infinite Number of Drops of Water having perpendicularly ascended, (occasioned probably by a long Frost, which had dried up the Moisture of the Air) and these Drops having been cemented and coagulated together by that glutinous Quality of the Frost, did remain aloft in the Air about the Altitude of 500 Ants, and cause that Opacity above remembered, till their Compages[4] being released by the Wind, they all poured down on the Hill with such Violence, that the whole was immediately covered, and all the Ants near the Surface destroyed. And this appears to me to have been the true Cause of the Deluge."

Here a violent Applause from the whole Assembly, put an End to my

[1] Such experiments were frequently reported on by members of the Royal Society and figure occasionally in the Deluge controversy. In what follows Fielding burlesques the language and manner of numerous explanations in the *Philosophical Transactions* of the properties of water and the nature of rainfall; for specific examples and possible sources, see Goldgar, 'Fielding, the Flood Makers, and Natural Philosophy', p. 143. The philosopher-ant labors through four paragraphs of contemporary scientific jargon, merely to conclude that the cause of the Deluge was rain.

[2] Apparently Fielding's own terminology for an accepted principle: '*The Particles of Water attract one another.* This, I think, is now universally acknowledged, and therefore needs no Demonstration'(James Jurin, in *Philosophical Transactions . . . Abridged*, 4 [1721], 431). Fielding may also be glancing at Hooke's description of body and motion as 'the *Male* and *Female* of Nature, from the Co-operations of which the most of Natural Productions are effected' (*Posthumous Works*, p. 172).

[3] Possibly a reference to John Woodward; see *An Essay toward a Natural History of the Earth* (1695), pp. 128–9, and cf. Chambers's *Cyclopaedia* (1751): 'But Dr. Woodward endeavours to shew the whole a mistake: *water* containing extraneous corpuscles, some of these, he shews, are the proper matter of nutrition' (s.v. 'water').

[4] i.e. solid or firm structure (*OED*), a term used by Whiston, among others (*A New Theory of the Earth*, p. 372).

Sleep. I will here likewise put an End to this Paper, after having observed, that there are some Subjects on which a Wit and a Blockhead, a Man and an Ant, will exert themselves with the like Success. The Author of a Treatise on Politics, of another on Rhetoric, and of a third on Ethics, the merit of all which I think hath not yet been equalled, hath left us a Treatise on the Soul in three Books;[1] which will require some Degree of Genius to equal; since it will be no easy Task to pour forth so great a Profusion of incomprehensible Nonsense in the same Number of Pages.

A.

SATURDAY, NOVEMBER 18, 1752. NUMB. 71.

Nec quenquam jam ferre potest Cæsarve priorem,
Pompeiusve parem.

LUCAN.[2]

Rich can no longer bear to see the House of Garrick fuller than his own;
Nor Garrick that of Rich so full.

The War which is so lately broke out between the two powerful States of Drury-Lane and Covent-Garden,[3] seems to have much surprized the World

---

[1] Aristotle's *De anima*; cf. Fielding's *JJ* No. 12 (20 Feb. 1748): 'Are not all the Opinions of the Ancients concerning the Soul, which are preserved in the first Book of *Aristotle* on that Subject, . . . stark staring Nonsense?' On Fielding's generally admiring view of Aristotle, see *CGJ* No. 4, above, p. 37 n. 4.

[2] *Pharsalia*, v. 125–6: 'Caesar could no longer endure a superior, nor Pompey an equal' (Loeb). Quoted also in *Amelia*, v. iii.

[3] On Fielding's partiality to Garrick and Drury Lane in the rivalry between the two theaters, see the notes to *CGJ* No. 3, p. 31, above, where the major figures mentioned here are also identified. The current 'War' began in early November, when Rich, manager of Covent Garden, imported Anthony Maddox, a 'wire dancer' and acrobat, from Sadlers Wells and simultaneously introduced a set of 'strange animals' into his pantomime *The Fair* (2 Nov.). Both Maddox and the menagerie were immediately successful. On 6 Nov. Garrick countered by ridiculing Rich's entertainment in burlesque scenes added to a Drury Lane pantomime, *Harlequin Ranger*; Richard Cross, prompter at Drury Lane, recorded in his diary the nature and effect of this burlesque: 'A new Scene was introduc'd of Beasts in Mr Rich's Entertainment as an Ostrich a Lyon, Dog, Monkey, 2 small Ostrichs & A Figure like Maddox upon ye Wire . . . Hiss'd a good Deal' (*London Stage*, Pt. 4, i. 329). Despite the evident disapproval of the town, this mock-pantomime was repeated five times over the next week. On 10 Nov. came the crucial episode in the current battle; on that night a party 'determined to damn' Garrick's mock entertainment went to Drury Lane, and amidst the boos and hisses one 'person of some distinction', Richard Fitzpatrick of Hanover Square, threw an apple at Henry Woodward, who was playing Harlequin. According to Woodward's affidavit, he responded merely with an ironic '*Sir, I thank you*'; according to Fitzpatrick's statement, Woodward issued an impudent challenge, '*I have noticed you in particular, and I shall meet with you again*' (*GA*, 16 Nov. 1752, *LDA*, 17 Nov. 1752; for an account of the whole affair highly favorable to Garrick and Woodward, see *GM* 22 [1752], 535). Fitzpatrick's cause was immediately championed by John Hill, who in his 'Inspector' column in *LDA* (14 Nov.) commented, 'The Town is with *Rich*, but Mr. *Woodward* is with Garrick'; a few days later Hill assaulted Woodward as 'one of the Meanest of Mankind' (*LDA*, 17 Nov.) After tumult and some fighting at Drury Lane on 13 Nov., Garrick withdrew the new scene, but the affair was far from over; on 18 Nov. affidavits from Cross and from Mrs Elizabeth Simson, an eyewitness, appeared in *GA*, along with Woodward's denial of any intended insolence. Yet it required the Lord Chamberlain to convince Fitzpatrick to drop his complaint (see Cross's comment, *London Stage*, Pt. 4, i. 332). Hill

in general, tho' some of our Theatrical Politicians pretend to have foreseen this Event of some time, even as long ago as when Mrs. Cibber went to France (or as they say was sent thither) the Beginning of last Summer.[1]

I do indeed remember, when that Matter was the Subject of public Discourse, to have heard a young Gentleman of the Law, who for many Years hath applied his Thoughts solely to theatrical Affairs, expressing himself in the following Manner: "A wise Step of Rich! Then we shall have the best Dancers at that House. This is an Imitation of French Politics; they have often succeeded in very deep Schemes by sending over their fine Women hither." And when one of the Company said he believed she was only gone thither on a Journey of Pleasure, the other, shaking his Head with great Appearance of Penetration, answered, "Ay, ay, Journey of Pleasure! very considerable Transactions have been carried on under the Cover of a Journey of Pleasure. Rich is a wise Man, and I always thought it."

Some Weeks afterwards I again met my Friend, who asked me if I did not perceive a Storm rising in the North, where it seems Mr. Garrick then was? but, without waiting for an Answer, he whispered in my Ear——"I do assure you the Treaty is already opened at Sadler's Wells. It is a Subsidy-Treaty, and Drury-Lane stipulates for a hundred Pound a Month. It is a wise Measure and will greatly distress the other House." This Treaty, however, was never signed, and the Plenipos of Rich afterwards found Means to draw off the Powers of Sadler's Wells, and signed a Subsidy-Treaty with them.[2]

---

continued to attack Woodward and Garrick in *LDA*, and the usual spate of pamphlets and essays appeared. See e.g. *A Letter from Henry Woodward . . . to Dr. John Hill* (1752), sometimes attributed to Garrick and Fielding but denied by Garrick (*Letters*, i. 190); 'Sampson Edwards', *A Letter to Mr. Woodward on his Triumph over the Inspector* (1752); 'Simon Partridge', *A Letter to Henry Woodward* (1753); *The Adventurer*, No. 3 (14 Nov. 1752); Thornton's *Spring-Garden Journal*, No. 2 (23 Nov. 1752); and Murphy's *Gray's Inn Journal*, Nos. 4 and 5 (11, 18 Nov. 1752).

Fielding was drawn into the episode in several ways. The affidavits of Woodward, Cross, and Simson were all sworn before him, and his friendship with Garrick and sympathy for Garrick's efforts to banish folly from the stage are evident throughout the *CGJ*. Moreover, Hill's role in the controversy obviously irked Fielding, whose own quarrel with the 'Inspector' earlier in the year made them natural antagonists in the current theatrical dispute; see *GM* 22 (1752), 535 for comment on the revival of the Fielding–Hill enmity, and cf. the report in one pamphlet that Hill 'rail'd at Squire F—LD–NG, D—n him, says he, *he has knock'd me up, tho' I don't allow it in print*' ('Simon Partridge', *A Letter to Henry Woodward* [1753], p. 12). On Fielding's relations with Hill, see General Introduction, above, pp. xxxvii–xxxix. This leader of *CGJ* was reprinted without title or acknowledgment in *Universal Magazine*, 11 (1752), 233–5.

[1] On Susannah Arne Cibber, see *CGJ* No. 3, above, p. 32 n. 3. Cf. Garrick, writing to Somerset Draper on 17 Aug. 1751: 'have you not heard whether Cibber is engaged or not?—Is she gone to France for some time—or what is the mystery of her leaving us at this time?—*Quere*—does she not want to get rid of *Barry*, and takes this method of doing it delicately?' (*Letters*, ed. D. M. Little and G. M. Kahrl [1963], i. 172). Garrick himself had left France in some haste the same year, apparently under suspicion of trying to entice French dancers to England, a political offense (see *Letters*, 171 n.); Fielding's speaker in the following paragraph hints that Rich has sent Mrs Cibber to France for the same purpose.

[2] The 'Subsidy' or subsidiary treaty was for the services of Maddox, the wire dancer. Cf. Hill's comment in the course of his attack on Drury Lane's burlesque of Maddox: 'Was he not apply'd to

When this Affair became public, I must confess, tho' I have not the Penetration of my Theatri-Political Friend, I began myself to think a Rupture was almost unavoidable; and this Opinion seemed to be more and more favoured by the several Advices which we daily received of the great Diligence which both Parties used in order to strengthen themselves, and to over-reach the other in Negotiation.

In this threatning Posture of Affairs a Body of Forces belonging to Drury-Lane, consisting chiefly of Irregulars, marched suddenly out of their Quarters in the Beginning of September: for as to Garrick himself, he did not take the Field till some Time afterwards, probably not 'till he heard that the Army of Covent-Garden was likewise in Motion.[1]

It is true indeed that Rich, on the first Advices of the Enemy's Appearance, did cause a Body of Troops to assemble; but these were so ill disciplined, that very little could be expected from them, especially as they were without a General of any Name or Character; so that Covent-Garden was now given for lost; for no one imagined that the Army of Rich could ever be brought to any Action; or even to look the Forces of Garrick in the Face. It was therefore expected that he would be soon in Possession of the Town without Opposition.*[2]

Garrick, however, to the Surprize of every one, chose to lie still in his Camp, sending forth only three Times a Week small Parties of his Irregulars to forage, and very seldom appeared himself in the Field. What was the Cause of this Inactivity is difficult to say, my political Friend above assures me the true Reason was, that the Town, as Garrick well knew, was at that Time deserted by most of its greatest and richest Inhabitants, and that he lay still in Expectation of their Return, when the said Town would be the better worth taking.

While Matters were in this Situation, and Covent-Garden seemed more

---

* The Town (which perhaps all my Readers do not know) is a fair, large, and opulent City, situated between the two contending Parties, and extremely commodious to them both. Upon this Town they have both for Time immemorial laid what Taxes they please, and have by many Treaties, agreed to share it between them; but these Treaties, like those between other Potentates, have bound no longer than either Party hath thought himself strong enough to seize the whole; which both have often attempted, but have hitherto miscarried in their Attempt.

---

from this very Stage on which he is now ridicul'd? Was he not even engag'd there? He was.' (*LDA*, 9 Nov. 1752.) While at Sadlers Wells Maddox was advertised as able to 'play on the Violin, sound the Trumpet, and beat the Drum, and balance a Coach-Wheel on the Wire' (*DA*, 29 Apr. 1752).

[1] Garrick appeared only once in Sept., the major roles that month being taken by lesser players, and only eight times during Oct.

[2] For Fielding's other comments on the 'Town', see *CGJ* No. 7, above, p. 56 n. 1. In *The Address of the Town to Common Sense* (1752), the Town claims to have 'observed a strict Neutrality in the present theatrical Dispute', adding, 'I was no Ways concerned in the Opposition at the Old House . . . and I further declare, that those Persons who pretended to be my Acquaintance, are absolutely as much Strangers to me as they are to you' (p. 5).

and more to decline Daily, so that it was thought impossible that Rich should keep the Field much longer; we were on a sudden alarmed with the News that Mrs. Cibber, otherwise called Cibberini, Queen of the Amazons, had openly embraced the Side of Rich, and that General Barry[1] was likewise taken into the same Service. Sadler's Wells was also reported to have fulfilled her Engagements, and that Maddox the Chief of the Wire-dancers was in full March to Covent-Garden.[2]

Garrick now roused from his Lethargy, (which perhaps was only of the Political Kind). He did every Thing which a wise General could do, at such a Juncture. He first reinforced the Forces under Macbeth,[3] which before consisted of only five Pair of fighting Men, with three Pair more of Candle-snuffers and Scene Men; so that between the Trees of Birnam-Wood, they made a most formidable Appearance. He was almost every Day in the Field, where he exerted himself with unwearied Diligence. He now likewise caused the Lieutenant Generals Mossop and Dexter,[4] who were before placed in the Front to fall into the Rear, and himself supported only with General Woodward led the Van, giving to three Amazons the Conduct of his main Body.

Rich, no sooner received the Strength abovementioned, than he immediately put himself in Motion. General Barry he placed in the Van, with Lieutenant General Macklin[5] to support him. Queen Cibberini at the Head of the Main Body, he opposed to all the Amazons of the Enemy; and to the Chief Maddox supported by the chief of the People called Dancing-Masters, he entrusted the Rear.

And now while both Armies were in this Disposition, and at no great Distance from one another, News was brought to Garrick that one of his detached Parties had surprized and taken a pretty considerable Body of Forces, who were escorting a large Number of dreadful Animals to the Enemy, which it was imagined would have had as terrible an Effect as the Elephants had which Pyrrhus first brought against the Romans.[6] Garrick

---

[1] On Spranger Barry see *CGJ* No. 3, above, p. 32 n. 3. Fielding is alluding to the fact that Barry and Mrs Cibber did not appear in the 1752–3 season until 21 Oct., in *Romeo and Juliet*. This was quickly followed by their performances in *Othello* (24 Oct.), *The Orphan* (27 Oct.), and *Macbeth* (30 Oct.).

[2] See n. 3, above. Maddox's appearance in Rich's pantomime *The Fair* on 2 Nov. prompted this hopeful comment from Richard Cross of Drury Lane: 'Mr. Maddox ye Ballance Master perform'd in it. Great Expectations not answer'd' (*London Stage*, Pt. 4, i. 329).

[3] *Macbeth* had been played by Mossop on 16 Oct., but on 30 Oct. Garrick appeared in the role, competing with Barry's performance as Macbeth the same night at Covent Garden.

[4] On Mossop, see *CGJ* No. 9, above, p. 71 n. 3. John Dexter (1726–64) was, like Mossop, a young Irish actor recruited by Garrick. He joined Drury Lane in Oct. 1751, making a great success in *Oroonoko*.

[5] Fielding's friend Charles Macklin (1697–1797), who joined Rich's company in 1750. See General Introduction, pp. xlvii–xlviii; *CGJ* No. 8, p. 60 n. 4; and *Tom Jones*, ed. Martin Battestin, Wesleyan Edn. (Oxford, 1974), i. 329 n.

[6] See Plutarch, *Pyrrhus*, xvii.

immediately dispatched Orders to General Woodward, to endeavour to turn the Force of these very Animals against Rich himself, which was immediately executed, and at first with Success: for having wheeled round, they fell so violently on the Rear, that they had like to have cut off Maddox with his whole Party; upon which a large Body of the Town that had before sided with Rich began to desert to Garrick; but Cibberini so stoutly exerted herself, that she soon restored the Face of Things, relieved Maddox, and brought back the Town in great Numbers to the Side of Rich.

Soon after this, a Body of People called *Ninnies*, who were Inhabitants of the Town, fell suddenly upon Garrick's Head-Quarters.[1] These People very much resemble the Croats and Pandours;[2] they being little better than Savages. They are armed with a dangerous Weapon called a Catcall, and attack with a most terrible Noise compounded of hissing, howling, yawning, groaning, shouting, &c. They caused at first some Confusion; but were soon put to the Rout by the Garrickeans. They all ran away except the Trumpeter, who having an *Empyema* in his Side, as well as several dreadful Bruises on his Breech, was taken.[3]

When he was brought before Garrick to be examined, he said the *Ninnies*, to whom he had the Honour to be Trumpeter, had resented the Use made of the Monsters by Garrick. *That it was unfair, that it was cruel, that it was inhuman* to employ a Man's own Subjects against him.[4] That Rich was lawful Sovereign over all the Monsters in the Universe, with much more of the same Kind; all which Garrick seemed to think unworthy of an Answer; but when the Trumpeter challenged him as his Acquaintance, the Chief with great Disdain turned his Back, and ordered the Fellow to be dismissed with full Power of trumpeting again on what Side he pleased.[5]

---

[1] Alluding to the protests during the performances of *Harlequin Ranger*, with its scene ridiculing the pantomime at Covent Garden. Hill was much offended by Fielding's language here: 'Let it not appear strange, that while one Writer is paying this Deference to the Publick, another is holding it in the most extreme Contempt. This respectable Body with me, are with the *Drawcansir* of the Age, to borrow for the Occasion his own high Wit and elegant English, *Ninnies*. I don't know what Dictionary may explain the Term; but with all the Reproach and Contumely that he carries, he has not less Cause, whatever may be the Share of Reason for the Use of it, than that I have for my Respect.' (*LDA*, 21 Nov. 1752.)

[2] Soldiers organized by Baron Trenck in 1741 to clear his Croatian estates of robbers; hence synonymous with 'brutal Croatian soldiers' (*OED*). Cf. *Tom Jones*, VI. ii.

[3] John Hill; the '*Empyema*' refers to the injury Hill claimed to have suffered when attacked by Mountefort Brown at Ranelagh (see *CGJ* No. 60, above, p. 325 n. 2). On the term 'Trumpeter' for Hill, cf. the motto to *CGJ* No. 60, 'Be not the Trumpeter of your own Praise'; the word is again applied to Hill in Woodward's *Letter . . . to Dr. John Hill* (1752), p. 21.

[4] In the first of the 'Inspector' columns complaining of Drury Lane's burlesque of the wire dancer and the animals, Hill had written, 'There is Severity in it: What is much more there is Justice; for the Subject is worthy Ridicule; but there is not Humanity.' The conduct of Drury Lane 'is unjustifiable, and it is cruel' (*LDA*, 9 Nov. 1752).

[5] Hill claimed Garrick as his acquaintance in *LDA*, 14 Nov. 1752: 'It has been imagined, that some private Pique between the Author of this paper and the Manager of Drury-Lane Theatre, has occasioned his Attack upon this Scene: It is much otherwise. . . . I think him the best Player I have seen; and added to all this, I have a personal Acquaintance with him; an Acquaintance, which . . . I the more respect, as one of the greatest Men in the Kingdom was pleased to occasion it.'

I cannot, however, dismiss him without observing that tho' he is the meanest and basest that ever took a Trumpet in his Hand,[1] he had the Impudence to declare in the Camp, that he was the principal Leader of the Town, by which Means he took in several Sutlers, and others for certain small Sums of Money as well as Drink, &c.

Such is at present the Situation of both these Armies, upon whose Motions the Eyes of Europe are fixed with such Attention. It is however believed by the most discerning, that instead of coming to a general Action, they will content themselves with levying Contributions on the Town as usual, in which, he who succeeds the least, will most probably make a very comfortable Campaign.   A.

SATURDAY, NOVEMBER 25, 1752.   NUMB. 72.

Cestus, artemque repono.

VIRGIL.[2]

Proceedings at a Court of Censorial Enquiry.

John Hill, Doc. Soc. Burg. &c.[3] alias Hill the Apothecary,[4] alias Jack the Herb-gatherer, alias Player-Jack,[5] alias Hilly-Pilly, alias Silly-Hilly, alias Jack the Trumpeter, alias Jack the Spectre of Great Britain,[6] &c. &c. &c. was indicted for that he, not having the Fear of Wit before his Eyes, but being moved and seduced by certain Diabolical Spirits of Vanity, Folly and Malice, on the First of April, &c. at the Parish of Billingsgate, in the Kennel there, one large Mouthful of Dirt did lick up, and that said Mouthful of Dirt, from his said Mouth then and there, in and upon his most serene Honour

---

[1] Cf. *CGJ* No. 3, where Hill is described as 'among the meanest of those who ever drew a Pen'; Fielding is also responding in kind to Hill's description of Woodward as 'one of the Meanest of Mankind' (*LDA*, 17 Nov. 1752).

[2] *Aeneid*, v. 484: 'I lay down the gauntlet and my art!' (Loeb).

[3] On Hill and his relations with Fielding, see General Introduction, above, pp. xxxvii–xxxix; for the immediate controversy, see *CGJ* No. 71. In the honorific abbreviations Fielding parodies Hill's habit of listing himself as 'Acad. Reg. Scient. Burd. &c Soc.' to indicate membership in the Royal Academy of Science of Bordeaux; cf. the similar ridicule in a mock-will satirizing Hill: '*Item*, My Review of the *Philosophical Transactions* I desire may be presented to the Society of *Bordeaux*, as a Testimony of that Gratitude I bear them for incorporating me with their Number; an Honour I could not obtain in my own Country' (*Libitina Sine Conflictu; or, A true Narrative of the untimely Death of Doctor Atall* [1752], p. 15). Skepticism about Hill's alleged titles and degrees was common in works ridiculing him; see Henry Woodward, *A Letter . . . to Dr. John Hill* (1752), p. 17; *Some Remarks on the Life and Writings of Dr. J— H—* (1752), p. 13; and *Spring-Garden Journal*, No. 4 (7 Dec. 1752), p. 84.

[4] Hill began his career as an apothecary; Woodward's *Letter* (1752) has as its motto 'I do remember an Apothecary' and is at some pains to contrast that stage in Hill's life with his present pretensions to be a gentleman (see p. 7). Cf. Fielding's reference to 'Hilly-Pilly', below.

[5] Alluding to Hill's theatrical career, which was not a notable success; cf. Woodward: 'We have been Rivals, Mr. *Inspector*, and my success has exerted in you all the Rage of a disappointed *Jealousy*' (*A Letter*, p. 4; for similar ridicule of his attempts as an actor, see *Some Remarks*, pp. 14–15).

[6] 'Spectre', of course, is a pun on 'Inspector'; for Hill as 'Trumpeter', see *CGJ* No. 71.

Alexander, by universal Consent, the known and undoubted Censor of this Kingdom, did throw and put, against all Common-sense, and Decency, &c.[1]

The Prisoner pleaded to the Jurisdiction of the Court, that he was below its Notice, and his Plea was allowed.[2]

I shall here lay down a Paper, which I have neither Inclination or Leisure to carry on any longer.

Many of my graver Friends, have chid me for not dropping it long ago; indeed for undertaking it at all. They have been pleased to think it was below my Character, and some have been kind enough to tell me, that I might employ my Pen much more to the Honour of myself, and to the Good of the Public.[3]

How partial such Representations have been, I may perhaps be hereafter so unfortunate as to prove; however, I hope I shall be admitted yet to take the Advice of my Friends, and to avail myself of an old Proverb, which says, *It is never too late to grow wise.*[4]

Without a Word more therefore of Apology for myself, or of Reflection on any other, I here lay down my Pen, with this Desire only to the Public, that they will not henceforth father on me the Dulness and Scurrility of my worthy Cotemporaries; since I solemnly declare that unless in revising my former Works, I have at present no Intention to hold any further Correspondence with the gayer Muses.

The World, I know, pay but little Regard to a Writer's Promises of this Kind; I hope, however, if they will now and then lay a little Dulness at my Door, they will at least require very good Evidence before they convict me of Abuse: Since I never yet was, nor ever shall be the Author of any, unless to Persons who are, or ought to be infamous; and it is really hard to hear that scandalous Writings have been charged on me for that very Reason which

[1] Fielding in this passage parodies the form of an indictment for murder: 'The Jurors . . . present, that *A. B.* late of M. in the said County, yeoman, not having God before his Eyes, but being moved and seduced by the Instigation of the Devil, on the Day of, &c . . . with Force and Arms made an Assault in and upon one C. D. then and there being in the Peace of God . . . against the Peace of our said Sovereign Lord the King, his Crown and Dignity' (Giles Jacob, *A New Law–Dictinary*, 7th edn. [1756], s.v. 'murder'). Fielding thus, once again, hints at the parallel between slander and murder, one of his favorite themes; see *CGJ* No. 14, above. The date of 1 Apr., presumably, is meant to connect Hill's behavior with All Fools' Day; cf. the date of the letter from Bedlam in *CGJ* No. 35, above. For an imitation of Fielding's mock-indictment of Hill, see Murphy's *Gray's Inn Journal*, No. 4 (11 Nov. 1752), which brings in 'the *Inspector*, alias Dr. *Bobadil, Acad. Reg. Scien. Burd. &c. Socius*' on the charge that he 'not having a due Regard to Decency, hath presumed to rail with all the Vehemence of a Billingsgate Orator' against Christopher Smart.

[2] Cf. the exoneration of 'B— T—' in *CGJ* No. 15, above.

[3] i.e. in social tracts and pamphlets.

[4] Cf. Tilley, L 153, 'Never too late to learn'.

ought to have proved the contrary, namely because they have been scandalous.[1]

But I must submit to bear that Character which my worthy Cotemporaries have been pleased to give me; and indeed if those who know me only by their Writings, have not a bad Opinion of my Morals, they must be strangely incredulous, or extremely candid.

I am running on further than I intended, so pleasant it is to talk of one's self; I will however controll this Pleasure, and conclude like Horace.

Verbum non amplius addam.[2]

As I have now taken Leave of the Public, I shall recommend to their Acquaintance, a Paper which I have some Reasons to think will deserve their Encouragement better than any which hath been yet published.[3]

LONDON, NOV. 25, 1752.

To the PUBLIC

The PROPRIETORS OF
The GENERAL ADVERTISER,

Enabled by their Success, and in Gratitude for the many Favours received from the Public, during the Space of Eighteen Years past, have determined to enlarge the Plan of their Paper; and, for that Purpose have settled a real Correspondence at *Paris*, and at the *Hague*, in order to receive a better and more authentic Account of Foreign Affairs, than hath hitherto been transmitted: And have also taken every Method in their Power, to procure the most early Intelligence of all material Transactions in *Great Britain* and *Ireland* (fit to be made public).—From the first Establishment of this Paper, they not only acquit themselves, but they hope the Public also will acquit them, of having ever indulged the Liberty of aspersing the Characters of particular Persons; and they will always endeavour to conduct it in the same decent and impartial Manner.

As they are thus attempting still more to deserve a general Encouragement;

---

[1] A sore point with Fielding; see *CGJ* No. 4, above, p. 39 n. 2. Cf. his sister Sarah's comment when ascribing five letters to her brother in *Familiar Letters between the Principal Characters in David Simple* (1747): '*I should have thought this Hint unnecessary, had not much Nonsense and Scurrility been unjustly imputed to him by the* Good-Judgment *or* Good-Nature *of the Age*' (ii. 294).

[2] *Satires*, I. i. 121: 'Not a word more will I add' (Loeb); the same line concludes the leader in *True Patriot*, No. 10 (7 Jan. 1746) and is quoted in *Amelia*, x. i.

[3] Fielding puffs the *Public Advertiser* because he owned shares in it and because it was to carry on for him some of the functions of the *CGJ*: public notices about criminal activity, advertisements for the recovery of stolen goods, and advertisements for the Universal Register Office. His connection with the paper was ridiculed in *A Scheme for a New Public Advertiser* (n.d.), 'Printed for Justice *Fail-Paper*, in Arrow-Street'; on this pamphlet and Fielding's involvement with the new paper, see General Introduction, above, p. lii.

and have, in hopes of it, somewhat altered, and much extended the Plan of their Paper, it will from the End of this Month, (on Account of the subsequent Agreement,) be continued and carried on under the Title of *The Public Advertiser*; and will contain, as usual, the Play-Bills of both Theatres, which are in no other Paper, and all other Advertisements with which the Public may be pleased to favour it.

And as great Confusion and Inconvenience hath arisen, both to the Public and to the Pawnbrokers, from publishing Advertisements of Goods lost and stolen, in different Papers; the principal Pawnbrokers within the Bills of Mortality have entered into the following Agreement.

We the under-written, being the principal Pawnbrokers within the Bills of Mortality, do agree to take in a certain Daily Paper, called the PUBLIC ADVERTISER; *and if any stolen Goods shall be advertised in that Paper, we will, to our utmost, endeavour to secure the Property for the Owner, and to bring the Offender to Justice.*[1]

Mr. Justice FIELDING likewise gives notice, That all Advertisements and Articles which concern the Public, and which come from his Clerk's Office, shall for the future be inserted in this Paper ONLY. And that *Magistrate* hath consented, that his Clerk shall from time to time receive from any Person, and transmit to this Paper, all Advertisements of Things lost or stolen, or which particularly concern the Good of the Public.—And all such Advertisements shall be inserted with the utmost Care and Dispatch, immediately after those of the Public Offices; and in so conspicuous and regular a manner, that they may be discerned with a single Cast of the Eye.

N.B. No Care or Expence will be omitted, that may contribute to support the Credit, and increase the present considerable Sale of this Paper; which will continue to be delivered at the Houses of such as desire it as usual.

ADVERTISEMENTS for the *Public Advertiser*, are taken in by the Printer,

---

[1] There follows a list of 59 pawnbrokers, omitted in the present text. This agreement represents an effort toward self-regulation on the part of pawnbrokers, notorious as receivers of stolen goods. By a recent act of Parliament (25 George II, c. 36) 'the Advertising a Reward with no Questions asked, for the Return of Things which have been lost or stolen' was condemned as an encouragement of thefts and made subject to a fine, but the practices of corrupt pawnbrokers were still a problem. An effort to regulate pawnbrokers by statute had failed in 1745 (see *GM* 15 [1745], 457–8, 697–701), and a similar bill early in 1752 had been rejected by the House of Lords (see *LM* 20 [1752], 317–18). One of the provisions of the 1752 bill called for stolen goods to be advertised 'in a publick paper to be specified for that purpose', so that pawnbrokers could no longer plead ignorance that goods were stolen; although the bill failed to pass, the *Public Advertiser* clearly sought to take over the role of the specified paper, with pawnbrokers voluntarily agreeing to watch its columns for descriptions of stolen property. Fielding, obviously, was much concerned with the problem; see his *Enquiry* (1751), sect. V and *Amelia*, XI. vii, XII. iii. See also John Fielding, *An Account of the Origin and Effects of Police* (1758), where the need is still stressed for 'some one Public News Paper to be fixed on' by pawnbrokers as a place where the public might advertise lost or stolen goods (p. 57).

W. Eglesham, the Corner of *Ivy-Lane*, *Pater-noster-Row*; at Mr. *George Woodfall's*, at the *King's–Arms*, near *Craig's–Court*, *Charing–Cross*; Mr. *Shuckburgh*, at the *Sun* between the two *Temple Gates*, in *Fleet Street*; and Mr. *Brackstone*, at the *Globe* in *Cornhill*.

ADVERTISEMENTS are also taken in at the *Universal Register Office*, opposite *Cecil-street*, in the *Strand*, and in *Bishopsgate Street*; and by Mr. *Brogden*, at Justice *Fielding's*, in *Bow Street, Covent Garden*.

APPENDIX I

1. Two Columns of Doubtful Authorship from the 'Court of Censorial Enquiry'

The following two columns, the first appearing originally in *CGJ* No. 21 (14 Mar. 1752) and the second in *CGJ* No. 23 (21 Mar.), are probably not by Fielding. As with other secondary columns of doubtful authorship, they have accordingly been placed in an appendix; the texts of these columns have, however, been collated and given the same bibliographical analysis as the leading essays of the *Journal*, with emendations listed in Appendix V.

Proceedings at the Court of Censorial Enquiry, *&c.*

A Book called Hermes[1] *was read, and most highly approved by the Censor, and the following Recommendation of it ordered to be published.*

If the Reader has any Curiosity to know why this *Treatise* is intituled HERMES, it might not be improper to inform him that *Aristotle* gave a Name, derived from *Hermes*, to a Book concerning the Combination of simple Terms, or Words, into Propositions: And that *Demetrius* likewise gave the same Appellation to what he wrote concerning the Method of rhetorically combining Words, according to all the several Species or Characters of Stile.[2] From the same Idea of *Hermes*, being the God of Eloquence, the Genius of Elocution, our Author perhaps gave this Name to his Book, which treats of those Principles which are essential to Speech or Language; and which if they were taken away, or denied us, there could be no longer either Logic, or Rhetoric, or even common Discourse, but the Life of Man would be like the Life of Beasts.

Having said so much concerning the Title, I come now to consider the Book itself,

---

[1] *Hermes: or a Philosophical Inquiry concerning Language and Universal Grammar* (1751), by 'J. H.', i.e. James Harris (1709–80) of Salisbury. Harris and Fielding were close friends; in 1745 they had both pledged security for a debt contracted by a mutual friend, Arthur Collier. Despite its reputation for obscurity, *Hermes* was frequently republished in the second half of the century, and Fielding, whose concern with language is everywhere apparent, may have had a genuine interest in the work beyond the claims of friendship. See Glenn Hatfield, *Henry Fielding and the Language of Irony* (Chicago, 1968), p. 31; on Fielding's relations with Harris, see Austin Dobson, ' "Hermes" Harris', *Later Essays, 1917–1920* (1921), pp. 48–57, and Clive T. Probyn, 'James Harris to Parson Adams in Germany: Some Light on Fielding's Salisbury Set', *PQ* 64 (1985), 130–7. Harris's dialogue 'Concerning Happiness' was read in manuscript by Fielding and is alluded to in his 'Essay on Conversation', *Miscellanies* (1743).

Fielding does not appear to have written this abstract. Cross argues (ii. 379), with more wit than evidence, 'Nobody but Harris knew what the book meant, and consequently nobody but Harris could have been the author of the review'. But stylistic similarities and the explanation of the title *Hermes* (not present in the work itself) do suggest that Harris himself contributed this piece; see *CGJ* No. 30 for another of his contributions.

[2] The treatise by Aristotle is entitled Περὶ Ἑρμηνείας, conventionally translated as *On Interpretation*; the work doubtfully ascribed to Demetrius of Phalerum (*c.*350 BC) has the same title in Greek but is conventionally translated as *On Style*.

which opens with the Dignity of the Subject; and our Author having premised that Speech is not only the peculiar Distinction of Man, but that 'tis likewise the joint Energy of our best Faculties, *viz.* of our Reason and our social Affections; he then considers Speech as divided into its constituent Parts, or as resolved into its *Matter* and *Form*: And this different analyzing or Resolution constitutes *Universal Grammar*.

Hence with great Perspicuity and Order he treats concerning the analyzing of Speech into its smallest Parts; and reduces their seeming indefinite Natures to certain definite Classes; and lays down this Proposition, that every Sentence will be either a Sentence of Assertion or a Sentence of Volition. Sentences are the longest Extension of Speech, with which Grammar has to do; having therefore defined what a Sentence is, he shews that the Knowledge of the Species of Words must needs contribute to the Knowledge of Speech; and with great Precision and Accuracy, from the ancient Philosophers and Grammarians, gives each of these Species a separate Consideration; and very elegantly introduces many Illustrations of his Doctrine from some of the politest Authors of Antiquity, or of later Years.

Having finished those principal Parts of Speech, the Substantive, and the attributive, which are significant when alone, he proceeds to those auxiliary Parts which are only significant when associated. And these make the Subject of the second Book. *What Remains of our Work* (says the Author) *is a Matter of less Difficulty, it being the same here, as in some historical Picture, when the principal Figures are well formed, 'tis an easy Labour to design the rest.*[1]

He recapitulates the whole of his two Books, by observing that all Words are either significant by themselves, or only significant when associated:——Those significant by themselves denote either *Substances* or *Attributes*, and are called for that Reason *Substantives* and *Attributives*: The *Substances* are either *Nouns* or *Pronouns*: The *Attributives* are either primary or secondary: The primary *Atrributives* are either *Verbs*, *Participles*, or *Adjectives*; the secondary *Adverbs*.—Again, the Parts of Speech, only significant when associated are either *Definitives* or *Connectives*; the *Definitives* are either *articular* or *pronominal*; the *Connectives* are either *Prepositions* or *Conjunctions*.

And thus our Author has resolved Language, as a whole, into its constituent Parts, which was the Thing proposed in the Course of his Inquiry.

In the third Book, after taking Notice in general of the Act of the Mind in mental Separations, he considers the elementary Principles of Language in particular, with a View to its *Matter* and *Form*: Its *Matter* is recognized when 'tis considered as a Voice; its *Form*, as 'tis significant of our several Ideas; so that upon the whole *Language* may be defined, *A System of articulate Voices, the Symbols of our Ideas, but of those principally which are general or universal.*[2]

The two last Chapters are a Kind of Corrollaries, and very requisite to obviate some Objections that modern Philosophers might be induced to make against the *Aristotelian* Doctrine, newly revived and explained by our Author. The fourth Chapter is highly metaphysical and treats of general Ideas. The last Chapter has the following Contents, *Subordination of Intelligence—Difference of Ideas in particular Men and in whole Nations—different Genius of different Languages—Character of the English, Oriental, Latin and Greek Languages—Superlative Excellence of the last—Conclusion.*

[1] *Hermes* (1751), p. 213.   [2] Ibid., p. 349.

Nothwithstanding the Subject Matter of this Treatise is of such a Nature, and indeed written after so methodic and orderly a Manner as hardly to admit, what now a-days is called Embellishments; yet if the Reader will examine the easy Flow of the Periods and Sentences, and with what Precision the whole is written——even this alone will appear no small Beauty. Let me add likewise, which is mentioned in the Preface, that the Author does not merely confine himself to what the Title of the Book promises, but expatiates freely into whatever is collateral; aiming on every Occasion to rise in his Enquiries, and to pass from small Matters to the greatest. Of such Nature we may reckon his most elegant and acute Reply [from p. 293, to p. 303.] to such Objectors as ask the *Cui bono?* of such Inquiries. To this may be added what he writes concerning *Time, Truth, Being, Mind, God,* &c.—His Philosophical Inquiry [from p. 308, to p. 313.] into *Matter* and *Form.*—His metaphyiscal Chapter [p. 350.] concerning *general* or *universal Ideas*: In which if there are any oblique Glances at modern Philosophers, those Philosophers, perhaps, are to be blamed for first departing from *Plato* and *Aristotle*.

There are likewise interspersed several Criticisms of the *lesser Kind*, and more adapted to what is generally called by that Name! such for Instance is that Observation [p. 269.] of Philosophers either new-coining of Words, or of transfering Words by Metaphor from common to special Meanings.—And that [p. 58, 59, 60.] where is shewn how elegantly *Milton* uses *His* instead of *Its.*—And [p. 133, 134, 135.] where 'tis instanced from *Virgil*, how frequently he joins in the same Sentence, the compleat and perfect present with the extended and passing present.—Add likewise the Etymologies [p. 368.] of Επιστήμη, *Scientia*, understanding—Again, [p. 259, 260.] his Reflections on the *Attic* Writers abounding in Particles of all Kinds, and our modern Way of writing without, hardly, any Connectives at all.—Nor let me forget the concluding Chapter of his Book mentioned just above.

In a Word our Author is so much *Aristotle* both as to the *Matter* and *Form* of his Treatise, that he perpetually keeps him in his Eye, and thus after the old *Stagerites* Manner concludes his Book.

And so much at present as to general Ideas, how we acquire them, whence they are derived, what is their Nature, and what their Connection with Language, and universal Grammar.[1]

Proceedings at the Court of Censorial Enquiry, *&c.*

At a Court of Censorial Enquiry, the following was read and ordered to be printed, with the Censor's Approbation.[2]

---

[1] Quoted directly, this is the final paragraph of *Hermes*, p. 426.

[2] Fielding most probably did not write the extended puff which follows (the writer uses 'has' rather than 'hath', for example), but there are two reasons why he would have wanted to include it in *CGJ*: the work described was published by Andrew Millar, and was dedicated to Fielding's friend and patron, George Lyttelton. The book is *The History of the Portuguese during the Reign of Emmanuel* by Jerome Osorio (i.e. Osorio da Fonseca), newly translated from Latin by James Gibbs (1682–1754), the well-known architect who designed St Martin-in-the-Fields and the Radcliffe Library at Oxford. The Latin text by Osorio (1506–80), Portuguese churchman and historian, had appeared in 1571. Gibbs's translation, which Fielding owned (Baker, item 241), was advertised as 'this Day published' in *CGJ* No. 12 (11 Feb. 1752) with the claim that the work was esteemed by Dryden and Pope as '*a most elegant, useful, and noble History*'.

The Translation of a Work in high and just Esteem into our own Language, is an Acquisition of a very peculiar Kind; for tho' it be taken from, it is not at the Expence of our Neighbours. We are enriched, but they are not impoverished; and perhaps it may be said with Truth, that in this Case only, those who take without Ceremony, are so far from being held guilty of Rudeness, that they are thought to confer a Kind of Obligation. The History of Don Emanuel of Portugal, so well known to the learned World, in the elegant Latin of the most learned Prelate that Kingdom produced, has been lately rendered into English, and perhaps it may be no unuseful, at least I am sure it is a well intended Task, to recommend this illustrious Stranger, by saying something of the Author, and of the Means by which he acquired so extensive a Reputation, of the Nature of that Character he established in the Republic of Letters, and more especially of the Worth of this Book, which having long ago appeared in most of the other Languages of Europe, is now at length come abroad, and merits a kind Reception in our own.

Jerom Osorio was the Son of Juan Osorio de Fonseca, and of Francisca Gil de Govea, both of noble Families in the Kingdom of Portugal, where he was born, in the capital City of Lisbon, in the Year 1506. He was distinguished even in his Infancy by his Affection for Learning, to which he applied himself with such Diligence and Success, that at the Age of thirteen he was sent to the University of Salamanca, where, having acquired a perfect Knowledge in the Latin and Greek Tongues, he applied himself for some Time to the Study of the Laws. When he was about nineteen he was sent to Paris, that he might make himself Master of the Philosophy of Aristotle, the only one then in Esteem. Some Years after he went to Bologna in Italy, where, to the Science he had already acquired, he joined the assiduous Study of the Holy Scriptures, and of the Hebrew. Upon his Return to Portugal he grew into great Favour with King John the Third, whose Brother Cardinal Henry, Archbishop of Evora, honoured him with his Friendship, and made him Archdeacon. He did not, however, arrive at the Episcopal Dignity by his Favour, but by that of the Queen Dowager Catherine, who governed the Kingdom during the Minority of the famous but unfortunate Don Sebastian.[1]

That Princess bestowed upon him the Bishoprick of Silves, in the Province or Kingdom of Algarve. A Place seated near the Sea-Coast, and, tho' far from being either well built or populous, is certainly one of the pleasantest little Cities in Europe. It stands in the midst of a fruitful Plain, laid out on every Side into Gardens or Groves of Fruit-Trees, and, from the Similitude of its Situation, has obtained the Title of Parayso or Paradise. There he passed his Days in a Kind of learned Retirement, 'till the King Don Sebastian formed the Project of invading Africa, when, foreseeing the fatal Consequences that would attend it, our Prelate, under various Pretences, found means to make a Tour to Rome, where he was extremely well received by Pope Gregory the thirteenth. But he had scarce continued there a Year before he was recalled by the King his Master, and within a short Space after his Return to Silves, he had the afflicting News of that Monarch's Defeat and Death. It was then those Troubles began, which he had so much apprehended. He laboured,

---

[1] Sebastian, King of Portugal from 1557–78, led a crusade against the Moors and was killed in a disastrous battle at Alcazar in 1578; he is the subject of Dryden's play *Don Sebastian* (1689).

however, to preserve the Tranquillity of his Diocese, but with little Effect. The People conceived a Prejudice against him on the Score of his being attached to the Spanish Interest, and he took the ill Treatment he received on this Account so heavily, that it threw him into a lingering Disease, of which he died August the 20th, 1580, at the Age of seventy four. Ten Years after his Demise the Episcopal Chair was removed from Silves to Faro, as it had formerly been from Ossonoba to Silves.

He was a Man of a sweet Temper and a generous Disposition, thoroughly versed in the whole Extent of polite Learning, and the constant Patron and Friend of Men of Letters. He had commonly several of these in his Episcopal Palace, who were the Companions of his leisure Hours and at Table. While they were at Dinner one of his Pages read commonly some Passage or other out of the Works of St. Bernard, and after the Meal was ended they disputed amicably upon any weighty Point that Passage contained. Our Prelate was a great Writer, and upon a vast Variety of Subjects, such as Commentaries on the Holy Scriptures, Treatises on Civil and Christian Nobility, of the Duty and Office of a King, and many others; which, tho' very nice Subjects, he held with so much Judgment, and with so good Temper, that he not only avoided giving any Offence, but secured to himself a sincere and general Applause.

The distinguishing Excellency of his Writing was an easy flowing Eloquence, and so happy an Imitation of the great Roman Orator, that he left most of those who affected the same Manner, and they were not a few, at a very great Distance. The only reproach he sustained in his Life-time, has served not a little to exalt his Memory. He wrote in five Books a Treatise *de Gloriæ*, in which his Sentiments were so elevated, his Remarks so natural and yet so judicious, and above all his Stile so easy and so truly classical, that it was given out and believed he had found among the Dust and Cobwebs of some Italian Library, that Treatise of Cicero upon the same Topic,[1] the Loss of which has been so much regretted, and digested it into or published it as his own. This Notion, which was altogether groundless, and the pure Effects of Envy, serves to shew how masterly a Writer he was in the Latin Tongue; for certainly a stronger Proof cannot be desired, than the Assertion that he had blended the Thoughts and Words of Tully with his own, in such a Manner as put it out of the Power of the Critics to determine where he was an Author and where a Plagiary.

His Memoirs of the Life of Emanuel King of Portugal,[2] were first published in Folio at Lisbon, in 1571, and have been very often reprinted since. They are in all Respects highly valuable, and are at least as perfect in their Kind, as any, that have fallen from the Pen of a Modern. This History has every Thing that can recommend it in Point of Dignity, Instruction, or Entertainment. Don Emanuel, is allowed both by Portuguese Writers, and Strangers, to have been the greatest Monarch, ever sat on that Throne, and was very near being the most potent Monarch in Europe, in Right of his first Queen, the Infanta Isabella, who was acknowledged to be the sole Heiress of Castile and Arragon, and the Son he had by her, would have been first sole

---

[1] *De gloria*, one of Cicero's lost works, written at about the same time (45–44 BC) as *De senectute* and *De amicitia*.

[2] Manuel I, king of Portugal in the period 1495–1521, called 'The Fortunate'; he was responsible for the consolidation of Portuguese influence in the East and the expansion of Portuguese interests into India and Brazil.

Monarch of Spain, if he had not died in his Cradle. It was owing to the Wisdom and Fortitude of Emanuel, that the East-Indies were discovered by Vasquez de Gama: In short, the Glories of his Reign, were so numerous and great, and his Reputation rose to such a Pitch, that our Henry the Eighth, who was nearly allied to him, or rather to his Queen, in Blood, sent him the Order of the Garter, which Circumstance considered, we may justly wonder, that this vauable Performance, so much esteemed, and so justly commended, by many of our best Writers, should not have been translated till now.

Amongst other Advantages, it has been remarked, that this History is admirably well disposed, so that the Division of it into twelve Books, breaks it naturally into proper Periods, which at the same Time, shew the Writers Skill, and very much assists the Reader's Memory. There is a wonderful Propriety in the Stile, never rising too high, or sinking too low, perfectly natural and clear, without any of those perplexing Parentheses, which often disfigure Works of this Nature. But above all, it is remarkable for its Sincerity; the Author, tho' he represents Emanuel, as a great King, acknowledged that he had Faults, and shews us, what they were. He is just to his Virtues, without dissembling his Foibles. In a Word, it is an admirable Model, for any who shall undertake to give us a full and free Account of a single Reign. It has hitherto been considered in this Light, by the greatest Critics in all Countries, and will probably maintain its Character, at least till that great Work shall appear which has been so long expected from the illustrious Patron of this Translation.[1]

2. The 'Covent Garden' columns

Most numbers of the *CGJ* carried a column dated from 'Covent Garden', set in smaller type than the leading essays and reporting on cases brought before Fielding in his capacity as a magistrate for Westminster and Middlesex. As explained in the General Introduction (p. xxxi), many of these were written by Fielding's law clerk, Joshua Brogden, especially those simply reporting on the disposition of cases; others, however, appear to have been written by Fielding himself, especially those which editorialize in strong terms about the social or legal issues raised by the cases. Because of the uncertainty of authorship, selected columns have been placed in this appendix.

The text which follows includes all the columns which make editorial comments or which include such features as narrative sketches or humorous dialogue. It excludes, however, seventeen columns which merely give a bare record of cases presented and actions taken (namely, the columns of 6, 16, 20, 23 Mar.; 31 July; 7, 21 Aug.; 15, 22, 29 Sept.; 6, 20, 27 Oct.; and 3, 10, 17, 24 Nov.). The column of June 22 is printed with its original number (*CGJ* No. 50, above, p. 276) because in the copy-text it is printed in the same type as the leading essays and thus accorded a more significant status. The texts of these columns from 'Covent Garden' have been collated and given the same bibliographical analysis as the leading essays of the *Journal*, with emendations to both substantives and accidentals listed in Appendix V. Annotation of

---

[1] George Lyttelton (1709–73), Fielding's friend and patron; the 'great Work' is his *History of the Life of Henry the Second* (3 vols., 1767–71), on which he spent much of the last part of his life.

this material, however, is less detailed and extensive than that given to the leading essays.

THE COVENT-GARDEN JOURNAL, No. 1, 4 Jan. 1752

Covent-Garden, *Jan.* 3.

Wednesday last William Baylis, about 18 Years of Age, was brought before Justice Fielding, and charged with Burglary, for having broke open the House of Mr. Francis Taylor in Tottenham Court Road.—About half an Hour past Four in the Morning, Mr. Taylor was alarmed by a Danish Dog which he kept in the House, and which had then laid hold of the Thief; who, nevertheless, made a Shift to get loose from the Dog, and was afterwards found concealed in the back Cellar, when Mr. Taylor found several of his Goods upon him. The Prisoner confessed the fact, desired to be admitted an Evidence for the Crown, and charged several Persons; but unluckily for him, the first Man he named proved his Innocence by many unquestionable Witnesses; upon which the Justice immediately committed Baylis to Newgate, and bound over several persons to prosecute him. He is, tho' so young a Man, a most hardened Offender, and was but just discharged from Bridewell when he committed the above Fact. And before he left the Justice's House he confessed that the Man he had charged was innocent.

In the above Examination, Mary Brown, Servant of the House deposed literally as followeth. "The Bitch came up Stairs as I was coming down Stairs, and she put her Nose to the Ground; and for that I says, Ruose, what is the Matter with you, and the Bitch looked up in me, and seemed as if to say somebody is below, and I said Ruose what is the Matter with you; and then I said just so to the Bitch, If you will go into the Tap Room, I will go with you, and the Bitch went down Stairs before me, and we both went into the Tap Room together, and there I saw the Chap behind the Door, and said what in the Name of God do you do here; and then he fell upon me, and aimed to strike me in the Head, for he hit me in the Shoulders, and then I run up and called my Master."

The same Day Elizabeth Flowers was before the said Justice, bailed out of New Prison, to which she had been committed for keeping a Bawdy House in the Parish of St. Giles.

The same Day Jeremiah Andrews was committed by the said Justice, for Stealing Money out of the Till of Daniel Jones, of Bologne Court in the Strand.

THE COVENT-GARDEN JOURNAL, No. 2, 7 Jan. 1752

Covent-Garden, *Jan.* 6.

There never was a more perfect Calm in the political World than at present.[1] You hear it, indeed, repeated twenty Times a Day, in all Companies, *that there is no News.* How wonderful therefore, must be the Ingenuity of our modern Historians, vulgarly called News Writers, who furnish us daily with the same Quantity of Intelligence! As I

---

[1] See *CGJ* No. 16, p. 114 n. 2.

am sensible of my Want of this original Genius, I have endeavoured, like that laborious Race of Men, the Commentators on the Classics, to raise my Reputation by pointing out the Merits of others, and, as it were, to mount into the Temple of Fame on their Shoulders. But I find, by sorrowful Experience, that however nobly these Historians may soar themselves, they are not able to bear another; and I seem to myself much more likely to sink into the Abyss of the Profound, than to reach the aforesaid Temple by such Means.[1]

But besides the utter Impossibility which I find of giving any Satisfaction to my Reader by these Comments, there is a pernicious Consequence which attends reading over these several diurnal Histories, and which, I am convinced, my Readers themselves must have often experienced; this is a certain Languor, or Stupor, or, to express myself in more plain English, a total Dulness, that seizes me whenever I have travelled through two or three of these Authors. If indeed, I can preserve myself from Sleep so long (which is a difficult Matter,) I am always thrown, by such Reading, into a State so perfectly lethargic, that I am scarce able to utter a Word of common Sense for several Hours afterwards. Should I, in short, continue these Studies a little longer, I must, I fear, be obliged to lay down my Paper, or, at least, oblige my Readers to lay it down.

For the future, therefore, I shall date from Covent-Garden, all such historical Matters, as are in the least worthy any Person's Notice, either of the political, the moral, or the entertaining Nature. And the better to enable me to do this, I do very humbly address myself to all Ministers of State, and do entreat them to send me in an Account of all their secret Transactions, and Negotiations; and likewise, I beg Leave to desire all Gentlemen who are, or intend to be, in Opposition, to transmit me all their private Schemes, and Plans of Operation; and do promise, that I will handle both the one, and the other, with the utmost Discretion, and will display them to the best Advantage.

To the learned World I shall likewise be obliged for their constant Communications, as I shall to all Gentlemen and Ladies, who will be so kind, to send me from time to time, an exact Narrative of whatever passes at Assemblies, Routs, Riots, and Drums; and I doubt not, but that I shall soon convince them, by my publishing no more than is proper, that I am a very prudent Person, and proper to be entrusted with Secrets.

I have already secured the Play-houses, and other Places of Resort in this Parish of Covent Garden, as I have Mr. Justice Fielding's Clerk,[2] who hath promised me the most material Examinations before his Master.

As I hope, therefore, by this Means to be enabled to give the Public a much better Journal of Occurrences than hath been ever yet printed, I shall henceforth turn over the other modern Historians to a Man of so wakeful a Capacity,[3] that he defies the Juice of Poppy itself to set him asleep. This Gentleman hath Orders to extract the best

---

[1] 'Temple of Fame' and 'Abyss of the Profound' are both allusions to works by Pope, the *Temple of Fame* (1715) and *Peri Bathous* (1728).

[2] Joshua Brogden; see General Introduction, p. xxxi, on Brogden's role in producing this column.

[3] Perhaps Fielding's friend and collaborator, Revd William Young; see *CGJ* No. 52, p. 289 n. 2.

Intelligence he can find, and to endeavour as seldom as possible at a Joke, which is, I find a very offensive Thing to tender Years.

Mr. Fielding's Clerk hath just transmitted the following.

On Saturday last, Mr. Welch,[1] High Constable of Holbourn, brought before that Magistrate a Person who calls himself Bernard Agnew; who, after a very long Examination, was committed to Prison, on Suspicion of having forged a Note of 25 *l.* from the late Captain Agnew, to the said Bernard, with Intent to defraud the Captain's Widow, and Executrix. This Note was tendered by an Attorney, to Mrs. Agnew, who perceiving that the Hand-Writing did not in the least, resemble her late Husband's, and not at all knowing this Bernard, or believing that the Captain had ever had any Transactions with him, suspected it to be a Forgery; and this Suspicion being, upon some Enquiry into the Matter, farther confirmed, she applied first to an Attorney, and then, by his Advice, to the Justice, for a Warrant. But as there was yet no legal Evidence, either of the Forgery, or Publication, a Scheme was laid to appoint this Bernard Agnew, who had informed the Lady's Attorney that he had two Witnesses to the Transaction, to meet together with the Witnesses at a Tavern, in order to give Mrs. Agnew the Satisfaction of the Note's being attested by those Witnesses. This Plot succeeded.—Bernard Agnew produced, and published, the Note, and two Witnesses attested it. Upon this Mr. Welch, who was concealed in the Company, discovered himself, and brought all three to the Justice, who took the Pains to examine them separately, during seven Hours, by which Means they involved themselves in so many Contradictions, and the Iniquity of the whole Affair so plainly appeared, that the Justice thought proper to commit them all.

THE COVENT-GARDEN JOURNAL, No. 3, 11 Jan. 1752

COVENT-GARDEN, *Jan.* 10.

Several Bills for the more effectual discouraging and detecting Robbers, for suppressing the Places of their Reception and Entertainment; and for making it extremely difficult, if not impossible for them to dispose of their Booties in Watches, &c. with Safety and Advantage, will be very shortly brought into Parliament.[2]

This Week Jane Hinton, Judith Carlton, Elizabeth Brown, and Anne Williams, were committed to Prison by Henry Fielding, Esq; for several Larcenies.

On Tuesday Night, Mr. Carne, the High Constable of Westminster, with a Warrant from Justice Fielding stormed a most notorious Bawdy-House at the Back-side of St. Clements, and brought the Master of the House, with his Chattles, that is to say, four young Women, before the said Justice. One of these Girls, who seemed younger and less abandoned than the rest; was fixed on as a proper Person to give Evidence against the others but could not be prevailed upon that Evening; upon

---

[1] On Fielding's good friend Saunders Welch, later a magistrate and partner in the Universal Register Office, see General Introduction, p. xvii.

[2] Resolutions on prevention and punishment of robbery were read in the House of Commons on this date; the 'Bill for better preventing of Thefts and Robberies' (25 Geo. II, c. 36) received the royal assent on 26 Mar. For the history of this legislation and an assessment of Fielding's role in it, see Hugh Amory, 'Henry Fielding and the Criminal Legislation of 1751–2', *PQ* 50 (1971), 175–92.

which she was confined separately from the rest; and the next Morning being assured of never becoming again subject to her late severe Task-Master, she revealed all the Secrets of her late Prison-House, Acts of Prostitution, not more proper to be made public, than they are capable, as the Law now stands, of being punished. The Master of the House was committed to Goal for want of Sureties; whence he will have a Right, in a few Days, to come out. Three of the Women were sent to Bridewell, whence they will return, if possible, worse than they went thither, and the young Girl was recommended by the Justice to the Parish of St. Clements to be passed to her Settlement in Devonshire. She was very pretty, under 17 Years of Age, and had been 3 Years by her own Confession upon the Town. The following few Words would redress this Grievance. "Be it enacted, that for the future, no *Certiorari* shall be brought on the Part of the Defendant to remove any Indictment taken before the Justices, &c. for the Offence of keeping an idle, disorderly House, into his Majesty's Court of King's Bench; nor shall any Persons charged on Oath with this Offence (at least any against whom such an Indictment is found) be liable to be let to Bail or Mainprize."[1]

These few Words, or some others to this Effect, would, in a great Measure, put an End to a very exorbitant, and yet growing Evil, the daily Cause of the Misery and Ruin of great Numbers of young, thoughtless, helpless, poor Girls, who are as often betrayed, and even forced into Guilt, as they are bribed and allured into it.[2]

On Wednesday last, George Buddle, a Hackney-Coachman, was committed to Prison by the said Justice, for stealing a Pair of Pistols, the Property of Capt. Clavering. The Pistols were, together with several other Parcels of Goods, delivered by the Captain's Valet de Chambre to the Coachman, to drive to Sir Thomas Clavering's, where the Coachman delivered the other Goods, but went off with the Pistols. He, at first, denied the having them, but afterwards confessed it; and said he kept them in Expectation of seeing a Reward advertised; but the Justice thinking the Trust determined by the Delivery of the other Goods at the House, and that the carrying off the Pistols from thence was a new and felonious Taking, bound over the proper Persons to prosecute the Coachman for Felony at the ensuing Sessions.

The same Day a very remarkable Affair happened before the same Justice. One John Smith, a young Fellow, was charged with a Rape of an old Woman of Seventy. Smith alledged that she was his lawful Wife. The Woman replied, that she knew not of any Marriage with him, and if there was any, that it was done without her Consent, or even Knowledge, when she was by some Liquor, the Strength of which was unknown to her, intoxicated and deprived of her Senses. In Conseqeunce of which Marriage, she said Smith the next Day broke open her House, came to Bed to her,

---

[1] 'Mainprize' is 'Taking of a Person into Friendly Custody, who otherwise might be committed to Prison, upon Security given that he shall be forth-coming at a Time and Place assigned' (Giles Jacob, *A New Law-Dictionary*, 7th edn. [1756]). Fielding's concern in this paragraph is that keepers of bawdy-houses are escaping punishment by obtaining a writ of *certiorari* to remove the case from a lower court to a higher on the complaint that they have received 'hard Usage' or are 'not like to have an indifferent Trial' in the lower court (Jacob); see the 'Covent Garden' column for 24 Jan., below, and Fielding's note in *Amelia*, I. iv. The bill which Parliament enacted in March did in fact forbid the practice in cases involving keepers of brothels; see Amory, p. 189.

[2] On Fielding's attitude toward prostitutes, see *CGJ* No. 57, p. 308 n. 2.

and asserted the Right of a Husband, and against her Consent, with the Assistance of two Women, ravished her; after which he carried off all she was worth, to the Value of several Hundred Pounds. This was done several Months ago, and tho' she hath long had a Warrant against her pretended Husband and the Women, she never could meet with any of them till Yesterday.

Smith then in a very oratorical Manner, delivered himself literally as follows.

"May it please your Worship; this fair Lady being old, had no great Occasion to carry her Interest to the Grave. On the 14th of January last, in the Year 1751, I was married to this fair Lady, with Expectation of Fortune, and not for Beauty, as you see;—And this Dr. Keith's Annals[1] will tell you. We lived together off and on until this Time; but I had Business to go into the Country: She then brought several Blood hounds to hoot me out of the House, and because I can't live in my own House, she brings Warrants. I am the Husband of that Wife, and she brings Assins[2] against me. Mr. Keith's Substitute is ready to make Oath of the Licence upon a Five Shilling Stamp: Upon my Honour, I did as much as I could do as a Husband, did I not, Madam?—Here is Mr. Smith, the Constable, who saw us live in the Respect of Man and Wife.—Mr. Justice Fielding, as you are the Godfather of Goodness, I will live with this Woman as a Wife. She was recommended to me, a ten Thousand Pounder; but I found not one Thousand Pound with her; however, I will take the Blank, and be quiet. She is an exorbitant Usurer, and will lend your Worship eighteen Shillings, upon a Note for twenty.—But, pray let your kind Gospel be my Friend, and if I live, or die, I will remember never to marry her any more."

All this, and much more, the Justice had the Patience to hear, upon a private Information, that he was suspected of another capital Offence, and that the Witnesses against him were coming. At last arrived Dr. Hill,[3] and his Man; the latter of whom charged the Prisoner with robbing his Master on the 26th of December last, on the Highway; and swore not only to his Face, but to his Voice. The Prisoner desired to send for a Witness to prove an *alibi*. This was one Jane Tate, who appeared; but, by a fatal error, on a separate Examination, though they agreed in every other Circumstance, they disagreed as to the Day, which they had forgot previously to settle between themselves.

Another unfortunate Circumstance was, that this Jane Tate was one of the Women charged in the Accusation of the Rape; so that, in the Conclusion, Mr. Smith, and his Witness, shared the same Fate, and were committed to several Prisons.

This Smith is a genteel young Fellow, and appeared in a handsome laced Wastecoat, with a fashionable Wig, and good Linnen; but behaved himself, during the whole Time of his Examination, which lasted near four Hours, in a most ridiculous and absurd Manner. ,

Thursday Morning, eleven married Women, all big with Child, appeared before the said Justice, at one and the same Time, to receive their Certificates for the Lying-

---

[1] Alexander Keith (d. 1758), who had conducted clandestine marriages in a chapel in Mayfair, was now in Fleet prison; his business, however, was continued by his associates.

[2] Presumably *assigns*, agents or deputies.

[3] On the role of this episode in Fielding's relationship with John Hill, see General Introduction, p. xxxvii.

in Hospital in Brownlow Street. A Sight highly pleasing to a good Mind, and a Charity which doth great Honour to those who first planned it, and to those who contribute to it.[1]

COVENT-GARDEN, *Jan.* 11.

It is currently reported that a famous Surgeon, who absolutely cured one Mrs. Amelia Booth, of a violent Hurt in her Nose, insomuch, that she had scarce a Scar left on it, intends to bring Actions against several ill-meaning and slanderous People, who have reported that the said Lady had no Nose, merely because the Author of her History, in a Hurry, forgot to inform his Readers of that Particular, and which, if those Readers had had any Nose themselves, except that which is mentioned in the Motto of this Paper, they would have smelt out.[2]

The *Right Honourable* the Lady Viscountess V–ne[3] hath lately eloped again from the noble Lord her Husband. *This being Elopement the Thirteenth.*

THE COVENT-GARDEN JOURNAL, No. 4, 14 Jan. 1752

COVENT-GARDEN, *Jan.* 13.

Of several Letters we have received, for which we kindly thank our Correspondents, we hope the Reader will not impute to Vanity, that we have published the two following.

To the Author of the Covent-Garden Journal.

Sir,

Walking lately to Islington, I saw the following Lines written under a Sign of the Moon with a Parcel of Curs barking under it.

> Ye little silly Dogs, why bark ye so;
> When I'm so high, and ye so very low?

This, Sir, I believe every Reader of Taste in the Kingdom, will agree to be the Case between yourself, and *——,[4] and his Brethren.

I am, &c.

A. B.

---

* *Here was inserted a Name, with which we scorn to stain our Paper.*

[1] Fielding himself was one of the Perpetual Governors of this hospital for married women. See *CGJ* No. 44, p. 251 n. 3.

[2] This is Fielding's facetious response to his notorious lapse in *Amelia* concerning his heroine's nose, which was 'beat all to Pieces' (II. i) in an accident. Critics ridiculed the presentation of a noseless beauty; see *CGJ* Nos. 7 and 8, pp. 58, 65. For an effort to identify the surgeon, see J. Paul de Castro, 'A forgotten Salisbury Surgeon', *TLS*, 13 Jan. 1927, p. 28, and *Amelia*, ed. Martin Battestin, Wesleyan Edn. (Oxford, 1983), p. 68 n. For the motto to *CGJ* No. 3, see above, p. 26.

[3] On Lady Vane, see *CGJ* No. 2, p. 25 n. 1.

[4] Presumably John Hill. Cf. an epigram by 'C. D. F. R. S.' defending Fielding from Hill's attacks, *GA*, 18 Jan. 1752.

To the Censor of Great-Britain.

When once a Genius soars above
The Vulgar, as if born t' improve
   Mankind, and writes with Flame;
Whole Crowds of nibbling Critics rise,
All Grub-Street takes th' Alarm, and tries
   To damp his growing Fame.

So, in the hottest Summer Days,
When Sol with irresistless Blaze
   Shines out in all his Pow'r,
What Swarms of Insects cloud the Sky,
Buzz, flutter for a while, then die,
   And plague the World no more![1]

Saturday last Anne Kircham was committed to Prison by Justice Fielding, for Theft.

The same Day, after a full Hearing of the Evidence on both Sides, one David Cooper a Labourer, was convicted before the said Justice upon the Statute of the 17th of his present Majesty, of embezzling several Firkins of Beer, the Property of Mr. William Shepherd a Brewer, and was committed to Bridewell, to hard Labour for a Month. This Fellow, while in Mr. Shepherd's Service, had carried on a private Trade, and had delivered Beer in the Name of another Brewer, for which he himself received the Money.

Yesterday Job Franklyn, and James Bignal, two of the Gang who have so long infested the Public at Blackmary-Hole, were, after a long Examination, convicted before the aforesaid Justice of being Rogues and Vagabonds, and committed, as such, to Clerkenwell Bridewell.

Two others of the Gang, who came to give Evidence on Behalf of their Friends, were likewise charged in the Presence of the Justice, and shared the same Fate.

They will be all brought up again this Day exactly at five in the Evening, when it is hoped all Persons who have been plundered by this Gang will appear against them.

The same Day John Bennitt, a Soldier of the Guards, was committed by the same Justice to Newgate, for stealing a Gold Watch Case set with Diamonds out of the Show-Glass of Mr. Stephen Trequet. This Fact was committed by Bennet as he was conducting from the Savoy to the Parade to be whipt.

The same Day William Neale was charged before the same Justice with stealing Iron-Rails, the Property of Sir Francis Head, and was committed for further Examination.

THE COVENT-GARDEN JOURNAL, No. 5, 18 Jan. 1752

Covent-Garden, *Jan.* 16.

His Majesty was pleased to return the following Answer to the Address of

---

[1] Cf. Pope: 'So morning Insects that in muck begun, / Shine, buzz, and fly-blow in the setting-sun' (Epistle II: *To a Lady*, 27–8).

Condolance of the Right Hon. the House of Peers, presented to him on Thursday last, on the Death of the late Queen of Denmark,[1] viz. "That he thanked the House of Lords for the kind Concern they had expressed for the great Loss which he had sustained, and had the justest Sense of this fresh Mark of their Zeal and Duty to him, and of their Affection for his Family."

The Behaviour of this great Prince on several late melancholy Occasions hath been so truly heroic, and contained in it such a Mixture of Tenderness and Fortitude of Mind, that we may apply what Tacitus says of Agricola, on a like Loss. *Neque ut plerique fortium Virorum ambitiose, neque per Lamenta rursus ac Mærorem muliebriter tulit.*[2] He bore not the Loss of his Son with the Ostentation which some great Men have shewn on such Occasions; nor with Lamentations, and effeminate Sorrow.

Covent-Garden, *Jan.* 17.

Thursday last, Paul Buchanan, Samuel Sheffield, and Isaac Daniel, were committed to Prison by Justice Fielding, for simple Felonies.

The same Day a very extraordinary Person was sent, by the Colonel of St. James's Guard, before the said Justice. He had been apprehended in the Mall, dispersing Papers of a most scandalous Nature, charging a Lady of the very highest Rank with being married to the Young Pretender, and with having an Intent to poison his most Sacred Majesty and the Duke.[3]

He owned all this before the Justice, and charged the Jacobites with having poisoned 36 Noblemen, the Prince of Wales, the Lord Mayor Pennant, the horned Cattle, &c.

But tho' it appeared from such Discourse, as well as from the Account given by the Man where he had lodged several Months, that he was undoubtedly mad, there was not the least Appearance of Madness, either in his Countenance or Behaviour, and he talked very sensibly on every other Subject; but persisted in the above Account; and on Friday Morning sent the Justice a long Narrative to much the same Purpose, declaring, he can make great Discoveries, but will do it only to the King or the Duke.

This unhappy Man, sometime since, endeavoured to destroy himself by fasting, and actually lived on Water only, during 26 Days.

The same Day Mary Daily prayed the Peace against Thomas Mears, and swore as follows.

"He came bodily through my Room, and I might have been murthered, and nobody the wiser; and then a Woman came in bodily through the Room: I'll tell you her Name by and by, but I am justly in a Hurry. I had a bit of Fire at the Bottom of the Grate, but it would not light a Candle. He called me an old defrauding B——, and then he threatned to knock me down; and I hope your Worship will let me have good Bail or Goal for my Life: For I will take a thousand bodily corporal Oaths, that my Life is in Danger from that Snake there, for a Snake he is."

[1] Louisa, daughter of George II and wife of Frederick V, King of Denmark.

[2] *Agricola*, 29; Fielding translates the line in the next sentence. Other deaths in the royal family in recent months included those of Frederick, Prince of Wales (Mar. 1751) and William IV, prince of Orange, son-in-law of George II (Oct. 1751).

[3] William Augustus (1726–65), Duke of Cumberland, youngest son of George II.

The Defendant spoke thus. "Ant please your Worship, the Policy of the Thing is this. My Wife formerly took a Warrant against this Woman, and she could not draw Cogniz,[1] and now she wants my Substance, and I came to ask her why my Grates should be used, and be wearing and tearing; for you must know that I went away a Week before Michaelmas, because whereof my Rent was to be due at Michaelmas, for you must know that she is my Landlady, and I went away only because I could not pay her then, and she threatned to fetch a Marshalsea Write:[2] For to be sure there is no Sense in a Man's going to Prison when he cannot pay, and so she has gotten my Grates, and all my Things, whereof to be sure your Worship must know there is no Justice in that."

THE COVENT-GARDEN JOURNAL, No. 6, 21 Jan. 1752

Covent-Garden, *Jan.* 20.

On Saturday last Elizabeth Ainsworth was committed to Prison by Justice Fielding, for stealing a Hat, the Property of Gaspar Valle, of the Haymarket. This Theft was detected in the following Manner: Mr. Valle has lately lost several Hats out of his Shop, upon which he made Use of the following Stratagem; he fastened a Bell to the Crown of a new Hat, on the Inside, and then having tied a String of about two Yards long to the Hat, and nailed the other End of the String to a Chest, he placed it on the Counter, and then concealed himself in the Shop. This Trap had not been long set before his Prey was caught. The Bell was soon heard to ring, and Mr. Valle leaping from his hiding Place, saw the above Elizabeth Ainsworth drop the Hat from her Hand; upon which he immediately seized her, and carried her before the Justice.

On Sunday Morning last, Mr. Holwell set out in a Coach for Gravesend, to go on board one of the Ships bound to the East-Indies, he being one of the Council appointed for the Service of that Company. When he came to New Cross Turnpike, he missed his Trunk, in which were contained many Letters from private Persons to their Friends in India, and all the Papers containing the Orders of the Directors, and other Matters relating to the Company; so that the Loss seemed very great and irretrievable. This Trunk had been, by some Villain, cut from behind the Coach on the Road, and the poor Gentleman, in the utmost Despair, dispatched a Messenger back to Governor Davis of Norfolk-Street, who immediately applied to Justice Fielding for his Advice. In this Dilemma, as Advertisements would be too late, the Ship being to sail the next Morning, the Justice advised to have the Trunk cried in all the neighbouring Villages; and, at the same Time sent for an old and experienced Thief-taker, as the Person best acquainted with the Haunts of Rogues, and their Methods of stealing. This Man presently set out with two Servants of the governor to Peckham, where the Trunk had been last seen; and then conceiving, as he says, that as the Theft was committed at Noon-Day, the Rogues would not attempt immediately to carry off their Booty, as the Trunk was very large, but would endeavour to conceal it in some Place till the Evening, he bethought himself of

---

[1] i.e. cognizance, judicial notice or the hearing of the cause.
[2] A writ from the Court of Marshalsea.

searching all the Ditches in the adjacent Fields, in one of which the lost Goods were soon found in *statu quo*.[1]

He and his Companions then carried the Trunk to an Inn at Peckham, where they were all three charged with having stolen it, and delivered into the Custody of a Constable, and what was worse, the Trunk was seized by a Custom-House Officer. The Thief-taker, however, at last obtained his Liberty, by Means of a Sheriff's Officer of Surry, to whom he was known, and returned back to Justice Fielding, where he met Mr. Holwell, who was likewise returned to Town. The Justice then wrote a Letter to Mr. Copeland, one of the Magistrates of Surry, informing him of the whole Matter. With this Letter, Mr. Holwell set out at Seven at Night in a Post-chaise, and, when he arrived at Peckham, the two suspected Men were set at Liberty, and the Trunk was re-delivered to him; but he was obliged to break it open for the Satisfaction of the Custom-House Officer, (for a Servant who was gone by Water had the Key.) Mr. Holwell then proceeded directly to Gravesend, having thus wonderfully and to his highest Satisfaction, recovered the Possession of Papers of such Consequence, that, had they been lost, the East India Company's Ship must have delayed her Voyage.

THE COVENT-GARDEN JOURNAL, No. 7, 25 Jan. 1752

COVENT-GARDEN, *Jan.* 24.

On Tuesday last William Neal was committed to Prison by Justice Fielding, for stealing several iron Rails, the Property of Sir Francis Head: as was Christopher Emners, for picking the Pocket of Mr. Rolte of a silk Handkerchief; and John Marsh on an Indictment of wilful and corrupt Perjury. The same Day one Thomas Halwyn, charged Catharine his Wife, and Benjamin and Samuel, two young Lads, her Sons by a former Husband, with beating him.

Thomas Halwyn swore as follows: May it please your Worship, this Woman my Wife, is a very sober, discreet, and intemperate Woman as can live, for Matter o that: as for sober, I mean that she is a very sober Woman; that is, now and then when she does not take a Cup or so; for indeed when she does she is the veriest *Balragger*[2] upon the Face of the Earth; and whenever that is, which to be sure is oftener than it shou'd be, she flies upon me like any Dragooness: indeed I shou'd be Man enough for her, for that Matter, but then here's her two Sons that take her Part; and so Yesterday, as I was saying, they all fell upon me, and beat my poor Head to a Mummy, or a Jelly, as a Man may say. To be sure they wou'd have murthered me, if I had not run away from them, which I did for dear Life; and so I charged a Constable with them, and I hope your Worship will send them all to Goal, that I may have a quiet House for hereafter.

After the Orator had finished, it appeared from the Testimony of several of their Neighbours, of Substance and Credit, that the Wife was a very honest, industrious Woman, and that her Husband constantly deprived her of the Fruit of her own Labour; that he had long used her with the utmost Cruelty, and had beat, and

---

[1] i.e. in the condition in which they were.

[2] A scold; not listed in *OED*, but cf. the phrase 'scolding or ballaragging' in the *Drury-Lane Journal*, No. 7 (27 Feb. 1752). See *OED*, s.v. 'bullyrag'.

threatened to kill her; upon which the Justice discharged the Mother and her Son, and sent the Complainant himself, for want of Sureties, to Goal in their Room.

On Wednesday John Russel and David Conner, were committed; the former for stealing several Carpenter's Tools, and the latter for picking the Pocket of Colonel Sandford of a Handkerchief.

The same Day Twenty Guineas, remitted by Governor Davis to the Justice, to be by him distributed to the Finders of Mr. Holwell's Trunk,[1] were divided by the Justice in the following Manner: *viz.* Nine Guineas to Mr. Bath the Thief-catcher, Five Guineas each to the Two Boys, who, in searching by his Directions, found the Trunk; and Half a Guinea each to two Men who assisted in the Search, and taking Care of the Trunk when found.

Thursday Mr. Labrosse, who keeps the Coffee-House of the four Nations, was brought before the same Justice, and charged by a Girl who had lived with him as a Servant, with having ravished her and given her a bad Distemper.

The Charge was positive, but being laid[2] to be done so long ago as September last, and not complained of to a Magistrate before, a Circumstance which is always held to be very suspicious in this Offence, the Justice took great Pains in shifting out the Truth; and after an Examination which lasted many Hours, and in which there appeared many Contradictions, Improbabilities, and even Impossibilities, in the Evidence of the Accuser, it came clearly out, that this very Girl who had sworn herself to be a Virgin at the Time of the Rape, had been before notoriously guilty of Incontinency; and the Man-Servant of Mr. Labrosse, declared himself that he had unfortunately and ignorantly given the Girl that Distemper of which she complained.

The Matter appearing in this Light, the Justice ventured to admit Mr. Labrosse to Bail, to the great Satisfaction of all who were present during the Examination; and by which means Mr. Labrosse, who is a Person of very good Character, was saved from long Imprisonment, which must have been his Ruin, however sure he was of being acquitted at his Trial.

The same Evening, Mr. Welch, the High Constable, brought several lewd Women before the same Justice; when one Philip Church, at whose House three of them were apprehended, appeared, and offered to bail the Women; but as one of them became a Witness against Mr. Church for keeping a Bawdy-House, the Justice chose to commit him likewise. He behaved very insolently, and being asked how he knew a certain Tavern to be a Bawdy-House, as he had asserted it was, he answered; *Because I am there every Night myself with a Whore, and I thank G— I can afford it.*

Among the Women taken at this House, was one Mary Parkington, a very beautiful Girl of sixteen Years of Age, who, in her Examination said, That she was the Daughter of one Parkington a Hatter, in the Parish of St. Catharine's; that her Father dying, her Mother married again; that she lived with her said Mother till within these three Weeks; that about three Weeks ago she was seduced by a young Sea-Officer, who left her within a Day or two; that being afraid and ashamed to go Home to her Mother, and having no Money, she was decoyed by a Woman to this Bawdy-House, where she was furnished with Clothes; for which she gave a Note for Five Pounds;

---

[1] See the column for 20 Jan., above.

[2] i.e. 'presented in legal form as having been done' (*OED*).

that she was there prostituted to several Men for Hire; and all the Money, except a few Shillings, she was obliged to pay over to the Mistress of the House; that since she was in the aforesaid House, her Mother, as she heard, had used great Pains to enquire after her; and that she would have returned to her, if she could, but was kept a Prisoner there, against her Will and Consent, and the Doors always locked, to keep her and other Women within the said House; and sayeth that she was threatened by Church, if she offered to make her Escape, that he would arrest her on that Note of Five Pound, which she had given for Clothes, apparently not worth Ten Shillings.

As the Law now stands, it will require above a Year, and cost upwards of 50 l. to bring any of these Fellows to Justice; whereas, was the Power of removing such Indictments, by *Certiorari*, taken away, and the Offence made unbailable, and to be tried as Felonies are, the Prosecution would be so cheap and easy, that the Keepers of these Houses would be at least afraid of committing such dreadful Outrages, and of driving Youth, Beauty, and Modesty (for this Girl was possessed of all three) headlong to the Ruin both of Body and Soul; and not permitting them to quit the Ways of Vice, tho' ever so desirous.[1]

In the Conclusion, the Justice committed Mr. Church and his Man, and four of the Women, and recommended the Care of Mary Brown, and another Girl of the same Age, and under much the same Circumstances, to a sober and discreet Constable, 'till the next Morning.

Yesterday being Friday, Mr. Carne, High Constable of the Liberty of Westminster, brought before Henry Fielding, and George Errington, Esqs; a great Number of idle, loose, and disorderly Persons, whom he had apprehended the Night before. And John Garway, William Miers, William Merryfield, John Smith, John Sawler, and John Revill, all impeached by an Accomplice, were committed for further Examination, 'till Tuesday next, when they may be all seen; and all whose Pockets have been lately picked, will, it is hoped, attend in Bow-Street at that Time.

The same Day, Esther Pouch, and Anne Fisher, were committed by the same Justices for receiving stolen Goods, knowing them to be stolen.

Anne Fisher confest the buying several Things of the Thief who swore against her, *but to prove she did not know, or suspect, they were stolen*, said "she had often given the Lad Advice to leave off Thieving, and had told him, that it would certainly bring him to the Gallows in the End."

The same Day, one Hall, of the City of Coventry, and a Soldier of the Guards, were committed by Mr. Fielding, for uttering counterfeit Money, knowing it to be counterfeited.

To the PUBLIC.

All Persons who shall for the Future, suffer by Robbers, Burglars, &c. are desired immediately to bring, or send, the best Description they can of such Robbers, &c. with the Time, and Place, and Circumstances of the Fact, to Henry Fielding, Esq; at his House in Bow-Street.[2]

---

[1] See the column for 10 Jan., above, p. 393 n. 2.
[2] This notice appeared with some frequency in *CGJ*.

THE COVENT-GARDEN JOURNAL, No. 8, 28 Jan. 1752

COVENT-GARDEN, *Jan.* 26.

Yesterday several Persons who had been committed by the Right Honourable the Lord Mayor, on Suspicion of having been concerned in, or privy to, the Murder of George Carey the Higgler, in Essex, were, by his Lordship's Order, and at the Desire of several Gentlemen of Fortune, in the County of Essex, brought before Henry Fielding, Esq; who spent near eight Hours in examining them all separately; by which Means such Discoveries were made, as it is believed, will soon bring the Persons guilty of that barbarous Act to the Fate they deserve.

The same Justice was on Friday and Saturday last, engaged above Twenty Hours in taking Depositions concerning this Fact, when a Person who had been suspected of being privy, at least, to the Murder, made his Innocence appear so evident, that he was very honourably discharged.

This Morning William Smith and John Jessett, Two of the Constables of Shoreditch, brought before the said Justice, the following idle, lewd, and disorderly Persons, *viz*. James Drake, Simon Jones, Mark Preistman, Eleanor Stuffs, George Gibbon, Edward Kendall, Susanna Brown, Elizabeth Delaheus, Elizabeth Panthen, and Elizabeth Lancaster. Simon Jones appeared to be a very dangerous Fellow, and was committed for assaulting the Contable. Drake and Priestman were bound to their good Behaviour, and the rest were committed to hard Labour.

This Morning Hannah Hains was charged before the same Justice, by Antony La Fortune, with having brought to him three Brilliant Diamonds, which he suspected were stolen, and accordingly stopt them. These Diamonds, Mr. Lacan[1] swears, he believes to be the same that he sold some time ago to the Hon. Col. George Townshend, for the Use of his Lady the Right Hon. the Lady Ferrers; and were picked out of the Colonel's Pocket; but as the Colonel did not appear to prove the Property , she was committed for further Examination.

The same Morning Mr. Welch the High Constable of Holborn, brought before the same Justice, the following idle and lewd Persons, whom the said High Constable had apprehended the Night before, viz. Thomas Holmes, Anne Brooks, *William Haines*,[2] Mary Garnidge, Thomas Darnell, Benjamin Jacobs, Anne Chandler, Edward Ward, Catharine Ward, William Freeman, Elizabeth Rose, Joshua Evans, Catharine Warren, George Gough, Mary Bensted, Samuel Etch, and Thomas Laxton. Several of those were committed to Bridewell as idle and disorderly Persons, and others bound over to their good Behaviour.

The same Day Joseph Gerardini, an Italian, was brought before the same Justice, for the Murder of Christopher Albani. It appeared that the said Joseph had stabbed the said Christopher, and cut his Throat from Ear to Ear, so as almost to cut his Head off; the Prisoner confest the Murder, but said he did it in his own Defence, that the Deceased came to his Room, and demanded Money of him, upon which a Quarrel arose, and the Consequence was a Struggle, and the Death of Christopher,

---

[1] See *CGJ* No. 19, above, p. 129 n. 3.
[2] Unidentified; it is unclear why this particular name should be italicized.

as aforesaid. This Joseph had a slight Wound in his Hand, but was all over covered with Blood of the other.

THE COVENT-GARDEN JOURNAL, No. 9, 1 Feb. 1752

COVENT-GARDEN, *Jan.* 31.

This Week Mary Worth, Anne Goodey, Ralph Williams, George Barker, and Anna Maria Cranford, were committed to Prison by Justice Fielding for several Felonies; as were upwards of Twenty to Bridewell, as idle and disorderly Persons.

On Thursday the Woman who was apprehended on Suspicion of having stolen several Diamonds, the Property of the Hon. George Townshend, Esq; was re-examined before the said Justice, when the Colonel not being able to swear that the Ring was stolen from him, nor the Jeweller to the Identity of the Diamonds, the Woman was discharged, and the Diamonds delivered back to her.

The same Day Hook and White were again examined before the said Justice, relating to the Murder of George Carey,[1] when it appearing that they were perfectly innocent of the Fact, they were both discharged. In their Examinations they appeared to be both guilty of Deer-stealing; but as their confessing this was necessary to their Defence, and as they had been induced to their Confession by a Promise of Indemnity as to any Crimes of the inferior kind, the Justice absolutely refused to detain them on that Account.

By means of the Confession of these Men, and by the Examination of some others, the Persons of the Murderers, tho' not yet apprehended, are well known, and will be described in his Majesty's Proclamation.

This Evening being Friday, the two High Constables are to search the Streets and suspected Places; and the several Persons apprehended will be examined in Bow-Street, To-morrow being Saturday at twelve, when and where all those who have been lately robbed are desired to attend and see them.

THE COVENT-GARDEN JOURNAL, No. 10, 4 Feb. 1752

COVENT-GARDEN, *Feb.* 3.

Saturday last the two High Constables brought above 30 idle, dissolute, and suspicious Persons before Mr. Justice Fielding; when, after a long Examination, seven were discharged, five bound to their good Behaviour, and the rest were committed. Among the last were five notorious Pickpockets, who have long infested the Passage to Drury-Lane Play house. Several Members of Parliament were present at the above Examination, who all declared themselves sensible of the Necessity of a Law to detain all such suspicious Vagabonds, till they can be advertised, and seen by Persons lately robb'd.[2]

[1] See the column for 26 Jan., above; see also *GM* 22 (1752), 41, and the 'Modern History' column for 18 Jan., below, Appendix II.

[2] Cf. Fielding's *Enquiry into the Causes of the late Increase of Robbers* (1751), sect. vi, where he recommends detention of 3 days in such cases. Detention of 6 days was provided for by the new Act in Mar. (25 Geo. II, c. 36, sect. xii).

The same Evening a little Urchin of about 12 Years old, was brought before the said Justice, and charged with Theft. The Parents of the Child (both of whom had an extreme good Character) appeared; and the Mother fell into Agonies scarce to be conceived. In Compassion to her, and to the tender Years of the Child, the Justice, instead of sending him to Prison, which would have probably ended in the Death of the Mother, and in the Destruction of the Son, recommended to his Father to give him an immediate private Correction with a Birchen Rod. This was executed with proper Severity, in the Presence of the Constable; and the Parents, overwhelmed with Joy, returned home with their Child.

THE COVENT-GARDEN JOURNAL, No. 11, 8 Feb. 1752

COVENT-GARDEN, *Feb.* 7.

Tuesday Night last, one Richard Beckett was brought before H. Fielding, Esq; and charged by James Brown, with having robbed him in the Street of 18 d. on the 31st of December last.

Brown. I am positive that this is the Man who robbed me.

Q. How do you know him?

B. By his Nose.

Q. Had he the same Clothes on as now?

B. I can't tell.

Q. Had he the same Wig on?

B. I can't tell that neither, but I swear to his Nose.

(*Now this happened to be no wise remarkable, but his Clothes and Wig were extremely so.*)

Q. Was it Light or Dark when the Robbery was committed?

B. So Dark I could not see my Hand.

Q. How then could you see the Prisoner, so as to distinguish him?

B. I swear to his Nose. I swear positively to him. He is the Man, and he had this very Nose on when he robbed me.

The Justice being unwilling to commit a Man on such extraordinary Evidence, and as it was very late at Night, adjourned the further Examination 'till the next Day; when the several Particulars appeared in Favour of Beckett, Brown still persisted in his Charge, 'till it was reduced to writing and he was required to sign it. This he was incapable of doing immediately by the violent trembling of his Hand, which being observed, he threw the Pen down, declared he was convinced of his Mistake, and very heartily asked the Prisoner's Pardon.

The same Day John Lewis was committed to New-Prison, for stealing half a Guinea, the Property of Thomas Francis of King's-Street Bloomsbury.

Francis had out of Friendship to the Prisoner admitted him to a Share in his Bed, and had the very Day before lent him a Shilling. Lewis confessed the Fact, pleaded Necessity, and appeared truly penitent and ashamed of his Ingratitude.

The Gentlemen of the *Gambling Society*, to enable them to appear with as little Charge as possible, among many of their Acquaintance at the *Masquerade*, made use of the following Stratagem to obtain proper Habits for that *virtuous* Entertainment. One of the Fraternity went to Mrs. Walker's a Milliner and Habit maker, and ordered her to send three Dominos' to Pon's Coffee-House directly, which Order she exceeded by sending five by a Porter, that her Customers might have proper Choice. The Porter upon coming up to the Door of the Coffee-House, was accosted by another of the Fraternity with a Napkin upon his Arm, who asked the Porter if he had the Dominos for the Gentlemen? The Fellow answered yes.—Upon which the Sharper told him he must run back and get another Domine for a Lad of sixteen, and he would carry those to the Gentlemen; the Porter obeyed the supposed Waiters Order, and while he hasted back for the Domino for little Master, Mr. Sharper moved off with the other five.

This Morning the Body of a poor Wretch who perished last Night in the Street, with Cold, Hunger and Disease; was brought to the Round-House at St. Giles's.

THE COVENT-GARDEN JOURNAL, No. 12, 11 Feb. 1752

Covent-Garden, *Feb.* 10, 1752.

The following is the Account which Samuel Redman,[2] who was confined for publishing certain scandalous Papers, gives of himself in his own Words; "Samuel Redman, a Clergyman's Son, educated with Design to make him a Clergyman, and can produce a Diploma from the University of Glasgow, has continued in the Naval Service of England during the late War, and afterwards remained upwards of a Year in Rome and about a Year more in other Parts of Italy, and came to London about two Years ago, where he spent what Money he had, and paid every Body honestly as long as it lasted; but that failing, and being an utter Stranger in London and destitute of Friends, and not willing either to beg, steal, or use any unlawful Means to procure Money, took to fasting in the Month of April last, and continued twenty-six Days with no other Sustenance, than about one Pint of Water daily, and also suffered many other Hardships."

This unhappy Man, whose Brain seems to have been disordered by his Distress, was firmly persuaded, that the Horned-Cattle have been poisoned by some Emissaries from Rome; with some nonsensical Conceits not proper to be mentioned. In every other Particular, he talks well and sensible; and is very sober, decent and civilized. He was brought before Mr. Fielding and another Justice, on Friday, and was discharged from his Confinement. He appears much better than when he was committed, and if it was possible to relieve his Distress, might probably avoid a Relapse. He is a good Accomptant, writes an excellent Hand, and is willing to undertake any Business. If this poor young Man who is at present destitute of Money, Friends and Employment, shall appear an Object of Compassion, any Charity which shall be sent for him to Mr. Fielding, will be delivered to him.

[1] 'Dominos' were loose cloaks with masks, commonly worn at masquerades. The 'Gambling Society' may be a generic term rather than a specific organization; cf. Smollett's reference to a group of gamesters as 'the association', 'the confederacy', 'the fraternity', and 'the order' in *Peregrine Pickle*, II. lxix.

[2] The madman described in the 'Covent Garden' column for 17 Jan., above.

Saturday Morning a Victualler in this Town was complained of before Justice Fielding, for refusing Quarters to a Soldier. He said in his Defence, that another Soldier, and not this, had been billeted by the Constable. The Case appeared to be, that the Serjeant had exchanged one Soldier for another, because the Man who had been billeted was afraid to lie in his Room, a Person having lately flung himself out at the Window of that Room and broke his Neck. And this Fear appeared to be so strong and incurable in the poor Man, that the Justice ordered the Exchange to be made accordingly.

The same Day a Man who keeps a Cook's Shop, was committed for cruelly and inhumanly beating his Wife.

The same Day, Ann Goodwin was committed to Newgate for stealing out of the Lodgings of John Cope, Esq; in Somerset-House, one silver handled Knife, two Pair of Shoes, three Shirts, and several other Things.

THE COVENT-GARDEN JOURNAL, No. 13, 15 Feb. 1752

COVENT-GARDEN, *Feb.* 14.

On Tuesday last Mary Harbins was committed to the Gatehouse, for stealing a Promissory Note of Five Pounds the Property of Thomas Jones.

On Wednesday last Mary Welsh was committed to the same Place, for stealing one Guinea from the Nurse belonging to Covent-Garden Workhouse. And,

On Thursday John Barkerville, a Hackney-Coachman, was committed to Bridewell to hard Labour for fourteen Days, being guilty of a certain Misdemeanor in his Employment; to wit, in embezzling his Master's Money and for suffering another Person to drive his Master's Coach and Horses, whilst the said Barkerville was regaling himself at an Alehouse, contrary to the Statute of the 20th of the present King.

Whereas a tall young Fellow in a green short Wastecoat and a whitish Coat with Brass Buttons, a Silk Handkerchief about his Neck, with a short grey Wig and a flapped Hat, was apprehended at Finchley on Wednesday last, and brought on Thursday Morning before Justice Fielding; by whom he was committed for further Examination on Tuesday next, at twelve in the Forenoon; all Persons who have been lately robbed on Finchley Common, or any where on that Road, are desired to be present at the aforesaid Time, at the House of the said Justice in Bow-street, in order to see the Prisoner.

A Spur was found concealed in the Lining of his Coat.

Sent to Mr. Fielding, for the Use of Samuel Redman.

£.	s.	d.		£.	s.	d.
0	2	6		1	1	0
2	2	0		1	1	0
0	10	0		0	10	6
0	5	0				
5	5	0		11	2	6
0	5	0				

I do hereby acknowledge to have received from the Hands of Henry Fielding, Esq; the several Sums of Money above-mentioned, amounting to eleven Pounds, two Shillings and Sixpence; for which said Sum of Money, I return my hearty and sincere Thanks to my kind Benefactors: As Witness my Hand this 14th Day of February, 1752.

SAMUEL REDMAN.[1]

Yesterday Morning his Grace Duke Hamilton was married to the younger Miss Gunning. A Lady really of great Beauty and Merit.[2]

THE COVENT-GARDEN JOURNAL, No. 14, 18 Feb. 1752

COVENT-GARDEN, *Feb.* 17.

On Friday last Bridget Lynch was committed to the Gatehouse, for stealing a great Quantity of Linen from one Ann Adams a Washerwoman, near Grosvenor Square.

The same Day, David Murphy was committed to Clerkenwell Bridewell, for stealing one Pewter Pot, the Property of Thomas Newsom.

The same Day James Hammond was committed to the same Place for returning from Transportation.

On Saturday last, George Upton was committed to Clerkenwell Bridewell, for stealing several Pewter Pots the Property of Thomas Lucas.

This Day Richard Sneesby was committed to Newgate for stealing one Coat, a great Quantity of Iron, and other Things, the Property of Samuel Miller of Kentish Town.

As was Mary Williams, the Mother in Law of Richard Baxter, for being an Accessary after the Fact to the said Richard Baxter, in the Murder of George Carey the Higler of Epping.[3]

This Mary Williams was taken up and brought before Mr. Fielding on Saturday last; when she was charged with being privy to the Murder; as Richard Baxter, against whom there is very strong Evidence, for having actually committed the Fact, lodged at her House, and was supposed to have made his Escape by her Means; but there appearing then no Kind of Evidence against her, she was discharged. She was at that Time asked by the Justice, Whether she had ever seen any Clogs in the Possession of Baxter? (for Carey at the Time of the Murder was robbed of several Pair) and she answered positively in the Negative.

This Question about the Clogs being afterwards mentioned in Kensington by one who was present at the Examination of Williams, Elizabeth, the Wife of Edward Hide, who is a Turnspit in the King's Kitchen having heard it, declared that Mary Williams had given her 4 Pair of Clogs to sell about a Fortnight since, and that she had sold 3 Pair for her, and had delivered the 4th back again. This was afterwards deposed before the Justice by Elizabeth Hide; upon which he caused the said

---

[1] See the column for 10 Feb., above.
[2] See *CGJ* No. 12, above, p. 91 n. 3, for the Gunning sisters.
[3] See the column for 26 Jan., above.

Williams to be again taken up, who then confessed the Fact, and said she had received the Clogs from Baxter.

It unluckily happens, that one Pair of these Clogs was sold to a Gentlewoman who lay in privately at Kensington, in the House where this Elizabeth Hide lodges, and a second to that Gentlewoman's Maid. These therefore are not very likely to be produced; and the third Pair was sold to a Woman who is since gone far into the Country. However, Hide swears to the Number marked on them, and that corresponds with the Mark advertised to have been on those which were taken from the Higler.

It is very remarkable that Richard Baxter hath already twice very narrowly escaped from Justice; once at Belfond, where he was apprehended by four Country Fellows, whom he prevailed upon to let him go, as not being the Person; and a second Time from Kensington, where five Fellows beset the House where he was above Stairs, and not one of them had the Courage to go up to him. Such Care however, is now used, that it is most probable he will be very soon taken. By the Evidence now before Mr. Fielding, it appears that Rolfe, whose Voice was sworn to by Green, is an innocent Man.

Since Saturday Morning several Sums of Money have been sent to Mr. Fielding for the Use of Mr. Redman, all which were returned by the Servants.[1] Mr. Redman lodges at Mr Powel's a Breeches-Maker in Round-Court, in the Strand; to which Place he may be sent for by any who are charitably inclined towards him.

THE COVENT-GARDEN JOURNAL, No. 15, 22 Feb. 1752

COVENT-GARDEN, *Feb.* 21.

Tuesday last Mary Rompster was committed to Prison by H. Fielding, Esq; for Theft.

The same Day Alexander Anderson, a Hackney-Coachman, was committed to Bridewell, on the Statute of the 20th of the King, for a Month to hard Labour and to be whipped, for a Misdemeanour in his Employment, by embezling his Master's Money, and for suffering another Person to drive his Master's Coach without his Consent. This is the second Person lately punished for this Offence.

Wednesday a stolen Ass was recovered by a search Warrant, and produced before the Justice; when Joseph Wood, a very old Man and the Master of the Ass swore as follows.

Sir, this is my Ass, I should know him among all the Asses in the World, and he would know me, wouldst not thou, poor Duke? Sir, we have lived together these many Years, ay that we have, as a Man and Wife, as a Man may say; for Sir, I love my Ass as my Wife; the best twenty Horses in the World, no nor a King's Ransom to boot, should not buy my poor Ass. Poor Duke! Thou hast had many an *empty Meal* since I saw thee, and so has thy Master too for Want of thee. For Sir, I do not love him without Reason. Poor Thing he has got me many a good Meal's Meat, and many a good one he will get me I hope. Poor Duke! We shall never part more, I hope, whilst I live.

[1] See the column for 10 Feb., above.

Then followed a Scene of Tenderness between the Man and the Ass, in which it was difficult to say, whether the Beast or its Master gave Tokens of the higher Affection.

The same Day a young Woman was committed to New-Prison, on Suspicion of High Treason, in diminishing the Coin. She is to be re-examined To-morrow.

On Thursday one Thomas Ashley of Isleworth, was committed to Newgate, on an Indictment for wilful and corrupt Perjury, in the famous Cause between Goddard, and a certain Jew.

Yesterday Morning one John Salisbury, a Soldier in Colonel Buckland's Regiment of Foot, was committed to the Gatehouse, for robbing John Thompson, one of the Collectors at the Turnpike on Smallberry-Green.

Thompson swore that this Salisbury came to the Turnpike on Horseback, at one in the Morning. That he hung his Horse at the Gate and came into the House, saying he was very cold, and desired to warm himself at the Fire. That on a sudden he leapt up, laid hold of Thompson, and attempted to murder him, and actually did make a great Wound in his Throat, by which he lost a large Quantity of Blood; but he had the good Luck (tho' apparently the weaker Man) to wrest the Knife from the Villain's Hand, who then attempted to choak him, which Thompson likewise prevented, and getting the Villain's Thumb in his Mouth, bit it very heartily. Salisbury then robbed him of some Shillings and a Watch, and hearing some Persons coming by, ran away and left his Horse behind him. A Man who then past by on Horseback, refused to stop and give poor Thompson Assistance; however he described the Robber to the Person who returned to Town from guarding the Mail, who having given an Alarm on the Road, the Robber was pursued, and in the Morning at six, taken at Hide-Park Corner. Thompson swears positively to him, as well as to a Piece of Money found in his Pocket; and the Bite appeared very visibly on his Thumb; and when he was taken the Watch was found within a few Yards, he having most certainly thrown it from him. He is a young Fellow remarkably handsome and genteel, seemed under no Concern, and very confidently denied the Fact.

THE COVENT-GARDEN JOURNAL, No. 16, 25 Feb. 1752

COVENT-GARDEN, *Feb.* 24, 1752.

On Saturday Morning Mary Mariston was again brought up before H. Fielding, Esq; when there not being sufficient Evidence to prosecute her for coining, she was bound over to answer to an Indictment for uttering false Coin, knowing it to be false.

The same Day a poor Woman, Mother of three small Children, was charged before the said Justice, with a paultry Larceny[1] of a Cap value 3 d. but the Evidence not being positive, she was discharged.

By the Law of England, as it now stands, if a Larceny be absolutely committed, however slight the Suspicion be against the accused, the Justice of Peace is obliged in

---

[1] i.e. petit larceny, stealing goods valued at a shilling or under, punished by whipping, as distinguished from grand larceny, stealing goods valued at more than a shilling, a capital crime; see Fielding's *Enquiry into the late Increase of Robbers* (1751), sect. V.

strictness to commit the Party; especially if he have not Sureties for his Appearance to answer the Charge.

Nor will the trifling Value of the Thing stolen, nor any Circumstance of Mitigation justify his discharging the Prisoner. Nay Mr. Dalton says, that where the Felony is proved to have been done, should the Party accused appear to a Demonstration innocent, the Justice cannot discharge him, but must commit or bail.[1] And however absurd this Opinion may appear, my Lord Hale hath thought fit to embrace and transcribe it in his History of the Pleas of the Crown.[2]

Thus for a Theft of two-pence or three-pence value, a poor Wretch may lie confined and starving in Gaol near two Months in this Town, and in the Country above half a Year, before he is brought to his Trial. The Consequences of which are,

First, that he is even thus punished infinitely beyond the Degree of his Guilt.

Secondly, that he is absolutely undone; his Business lost, and his Reputation gone for ever.

Thirdly, that his Morals are totally contaminated and corrupted, by the Conversation with notorious Thieves, from whom he is taught all the Arts and Mysteries of Iniquity. So that however slightly his Mind is tainted with Vice at his going into the Prison, he is sure to come out abandoned. He hath now learnt Cunning, Boldness and all the Ingredients of a Rogue. His Character and his Business are both gone. In a Word he hath lost all Restraints, and acquired every Incitement to Villany and every Qualification for it.

4thly, If he be a Master of a Family, his Family however innocent must share in his Ruin.——And if the petty Thief be the Mother of a young Child, the poor Innocent is almost certain of being destroyed: For the Gaoler will not nor can be obliged to receive it; and the Humanity of Parish Officers on such Occasions is well known. Thus a Woman is undone, and a little Infant too often destroyed for a trifling Theft, dictated perhaps by absolute Necessity.

Nor is the Case of the Prosecutor without its Hardships: For he is obliged to an Attendance (perhaps of several Days) on a Court of Justice; to Expence and Loss of Time, in order to prosecute a little Offender, whom he at the same Time compassionates in his Heart.

To do this, however, he must enter into a Recognizance before the Justice; and therefore to avoid it, nothing is more common, than to suffer these Thefts indiscriminately to go unpunished.

Now the whole might be remedied by giving the Justice of Peace a Power, where the Value of the Thing stolen amounts to no more than   [3] where no Circumstance of Robbery, or any other Matter appear to aggravate the Theft, and when the Party shall appear to the Justice to be no old nor hardened Offender, either to order the Criminal to be whipt by the Constable, &c. or commit him or her to hard Labour for

---

[1] Michael Dalton, *The Country Justice* (1635), ch. 111, explains, 'For it is not fit that a man once arrested and charged with felony (or suspition thereof) should be delivered upon any mans discretion, without further triall' (p. 296).

[2] Sir Matthew Hale, *History of the Pleas of the Crown* (1736), 11, ch. xiv, p. 121, and ch. xi, p. 93.

[3] The number is left unspecified.

any Time, not exceeding   In which Case the Prisoners will be kept apart from the Felons, and not sent to Newgate as now they are.

By this slight Alteration of the Law; I am convinced the Lives of many Hundreds of his Majesty's Subjects will be saved; and the first Theft will often prove the last, which at present I am afraid is very rarely the Case.[1]

THE COVENT-GARDEN JOURNAL, No. 17, 29 Feb. 1752

COVENT-GARDEN, *Feb.* 24, 1752.

As the Character of Lord Lempster[2] hath been most cruelly injured in an infamous Paragraph, inserted in one of the Daily Papers[3] of this Week, we have thought proper to print the following, which tho' perhaps not so in Law, will at least in Honour, be a full Justification of his Lordship, as it will appear from it, that the unhappy Gentleman who fell in the Contest, was entirely in the wrong, from the Beginning to the End of the fatal Affair.

Capt. Collingwood and Lord Lempster dining together at the Bedford-Head, Covent-Garden; after Dinner, Lord Lempster told Mr. Collingwood, that Capt. Grey was on Duty at the Tilt-yard, Mr. Collingwood replied, it was some Time since he had seen Capt. Grey, and if it was agreeable to his Lordship, they would go and spend the Evening with Capt. Grey, which they did; and when they came to the Tilt-yard, Capt. Grey received them with great Civility, and said it was very charitable in them, to come and spend the Evening with him; they sat in the Coffee-Room till they chose to go to Supper, and after Supper Lord Lempster and Capt. Collingwood, not chusing to drink, and Capt. Grey being on Duty, and having no Inclination, Lord Lempster and Capt. Collingwood amused themselves at Piquet, at Half-a-Crown a Game; during the Play, a Conversation arose about ten Guineas Lord Lempster denied to lend to Capt. Grey, at the last Masquerade but one; Capt. Collingwood is not certain who began it, and for some Time the Conversation did not appear material; but on stating the Manner of refusing it, they disagreed, and the first Word of an Affront that passed, was the Lie, given by Capt. Grey to Lord Lempster; on which Lord Lempster retorted very severe Language, which was returned by Capt. Grey; and Capt. Grey presently started up, and drew his Sword, which Lord Lempster perceiving went to his, which lay a little Way from him: Capt. Collingwood started up immediately and took hold of Capt. Grey, who to do him Justice, did not offer to advance, 'till Lord Lempster had his Sword drawn. He stood at the further End of the Room, and tho' no-body could oppose him, never came near Capt. Grey. Mr. Collingwood insisted on their not fighting; on which they both put up their Swords. Capt. Collingwood being a Friend to both, desired them to forgive one

---

[1] Cf. Fielding's caution against an excess of compassion in cases involving 'notorious' robbers, *Enquiry* (1751), sect. VII.

[2] George Fermor, Baron Lempster (1722–85), later Earl of Pomfret. Horace Walpole commented on the episode related here: 'Poor Lord Lempster has just killed an officer in a duel about a play debt, and I fear was in the wrong. There is no end of his misfortunes and wrongheadedness!' (*Yale Walpole*, xx. 303–4).

[3] Unidentified.

another, and declared on his Honour, what had passed should never be known, and of Course no Slur upon their Reputation could ever ensue: They sat down after this near two Hours, and seemed very good Friends, not one Syllable passing in regard to the unhappy Dispute; and if Mr. Collingwood had not been thoroughly convinced they were Friends, he would have put them under an Arrest: Lord Lempster being an Officer, as well as Capt. Grey; tho' he well knew, the great Risk that must have attended Capt. Grey's Commission on his drawing his Sword in a private Dispute, when on Guard: Lord Lempster and Capt. Collingwood went Part of the Way together in their Way Home, to their Respective Lodgings, and Lord Lempster seem'd in chearfuller Spirits than usual, which Capt. Collingwood imputed to their Reconciliation; and did not at first believe Lord Lempster when he came the next Day and told him what a Misfortune Capt. Grey had forced on him, and declares, he so much believed they parted good Friends, that he told Lord Lempster, he was sure he joked, but my Lord's Countenance too soon spoke the unhappy Truth.

The Maid-servant where Lord Lempster lodged, has an Account, how that Capt. Grey asked if Lord Lempster lodged there, and sent up his Name and that he must see him; the Maid having said she believed he was not at home: Lord Lempster's Servant, and two Tradesmen of good Repute confirm the Maid's Evidence, as to the knocking at the Door, and enquiring for Lord Lempster. Nothing but Civility passed on both Sides at my Lord's Lodgings; and my Lord's Servant and one of the Tradesmen who help'd to put my Lord's Clothes on, whilst his Lordship's Servant was gone to fetch some Chocolate for them, (which Lord Lempster drank one Dish of, but Capt. Grey refused with Civility) thought they were going on a Party of Pleasure; for Capt. Grey proposed a Coach, my Lord saying it was a fine Day, they had better walk: There is no Evidence of any Thing more, 'till the unhappy Affair began, which was seen by Mr. William Powell, a Master of Music; who declared on Oath, that when he saw the two Gentlemen walking in the Field, he thought they came to take the Benefit of the fine Day; but turning about he saw them both engaged, and Lord Lempster giving Ground; but soon saw Capt. Grey stumble on one Knee, on which Lord Lempster retired from him, nor ever offered to make one Pass more; but Capt. Grey a little recovering, he made several Thrusts at Lord Lempster, which his Lordship parried, and continued retreating; 'till the Captain fell dead. The Surgeon and all the Gentlemen present as well as the Jury; declare there was but one Wound, and that very fair, but unhappily too deep.

The Public may be assured, that this is a full Account of the whole Transaction; to which we shall only add, that the noble Lord is universally acknowledged by all his Acquaintance to be the furthest of all Men from a quarrelsome Disposition.

The Coroner's Inquest after a full Enquiry into the Matter, and an Examination of many Witnesses, found a Verdict of Manslaughter.[1]

On Tuesday last, John Bryan and Margaret Leonard were committed to New-Prison, by Henry Fielding, Esq; the said John Bryan for stealing a great Quantity of

---

[1] Lord Lempster was found guilty of manslaughter at the Old Bailey in April; see *GM* 20 (1752), 190.

Lead off the Foundling Hospital, and the said Margaret Leonard, for receiving the same knowing it to be stolen.

On Wednesday last Catherine Messenger was committed to the same Place by the same Gentleman, for stealing one Pair of Sheets, two Handkerchiefs, two China-cups, one Glass-salt, and several other Things the Property of William Lloyd.

The same Day William Merredith was committed to the Gatehouse, by the same Gentleman, for privately picking the Pocket of Mrs. Judith Simmons, as she was going into Covent-Garden Playhouse, of half a Guinea in Gold, one Crown-piece, one Silver Groat, one Pocket-piece, one Silver Two-pence, and one Farthing with two Heads; and upon searching the said William Meredith in the Presence of the Justice, there were found upon him, several of the aforesaid Things; and particularly the Farthing with two Heads, which the said Judith Simmons swore to be her Property.

As was Samuel Smith, otherwise Black Sam, a notorious Pickpocket, to Tothill-Fields Bridewell, for being taken up at the same Time in Picking Pockets at the Playhouse.

THE COVENT-GARDEN JOURNAL, No. 18, 3 Mar. 1752

COVENT-GARDEN, *March* 2, 1752.

Saturday last a Watchman of this Parish was bound over to the Sessions by H. Fielding, Esq; for assaulting a young Gentlewoman in the Street a little after nine o'clock, and offering to drag her to the Round-house.

The Watchman in his Defence alledged that the Prosecutrix assaulted his Lanthorn, by brushing it with her Petticoat, as she past hastily by him; but finding that would not do, he attempted to throw some Slurs on her Character, which appeared to have no just Foundation.

The same Day a Frenchman who hath lately been robbed on the Highway, came to ask the Justice his Opinion, whether he might not kill a Thief who offered to rob him? and being told he might, answered——*Auh! bien! Je tirerai donc sans doute. Parblieu! Je tirerai.* If all our English Gentlemen would take the same noble Resolution, the Roads would soon be free from Robbers.

The same Day a poor Girl who had come from Wapping to see the new Entertainment[1] which is so much and so justly admired, at Covent-Garden Theatre, had her Pocket cut off in the Crowd before the Doors were open. Tho' she knew not the Pickpocket she came immediately to lay her Complaint before the Justice, and with many Tears lamented not the Loss of her Money, but of her Entertainment. At last having obtained a sufficient Passport to the Gallery, she departed with great Satisfaction, and contented with the Loss of fourteen Shillings, tho' she declared she had not so much more in the World.

The same Day a Foreigner swore the Peace against a Bricklayer in the following Words. *Sar, dis Man he come a my House, he came in my Room. He call a my Wife de Beesh, de grand a Beesh. Sar, my Wife be one Woman, she be no Beesh. Upon dis, I take a de Poker, I make one Blow; begar, I am of advice if I had but a de Pate of de Fripon, he never*

[1] *Harlequin Sorcerer;* see *CGJ* No. 17, p. 123 n. 4.

call my Wife de Beesh again.—But he did run away, and my Wife she catch up de Candlestick, she run after him, she trow de Candlestick at de Fripon, and break a my Candlestick.—Here it is in my Pocket all broke a spoil a.—It cost me five Shilling.

The Justice who hitherto saw no great Occasion for Fear on the Side of the Complainant, asked him, how he could possibly swear he was afraid of this Person, who seemed to have much the greater Reason for Fear of the two.—To which he answered, *Begar, Sar, I am afraid he will come again, and if he do call my Wife de Beesh, begar I will kill him, begar, I will knock a his Brains out; for I am ver passionate Man and so is my Wife too.*

The Prisoner was discharged, but the Justice recommended to him to abstain for the future from the passionate Gentleman's House, which he faithfully promised to do. It appeared that the Bricklayer and the Foreigner, who was a Taylor, had formerly been Rivals for the same Lady, who had preferred foreign Politeness to English Simplicity.

The same Day Martha Marshall was committed to New-Prison, by Henry Fielding, Esq; for picking the Pocket of William Pallin of a Silver Watch.

And Yesterday John Smith was committed to the same Place by the same Gentleman, for picking the Pocket of William Squires of a Linen Handkerchief.

This the the tenth Pickpocket committed by the Justice within this Fortnight.

THE COVENT-GARDEN JOURNAL, No. 20, 10 Mar. 1752

COVENT-GARDEN, *March* 9, 1752.

Saturday last one Sarah Matthews, a Woman of near fourscore, brought a Woman of about Twenty-five before Mr. Fielding, and charged her with several violent Bruises. The young Woman said in her Defence, that the old one had taken away her Husband, to whom she had been married many Years, and to whom the old one, as was proved by a Certificate, was married in May last. It appeared at last by indisputable Evidence, as well as by the Declaration of the Husband, who was present, that the former Marriage was a Falsehood, and that the old Lady was the lawful Wife. She was not indeed very charming in her Person, but she was however possessed *of every Qualification to make the married State, &c.*[1] namely of twenty Guineas, with which she had purchased a brisk young Fellow; and had prevailed with him to quit his former Mistress; who having no Bail was sent to Prison, and the old Lady marched off with her Husband under her Arm; but not before she had received several lusty Blows from her Rival in the Presence of the Justice: For so enraged was this young Amazon, that had not the Constable and other Persons interposed, the happy Wife would most probably have fallen a Victim to the Resentment of the unfortunate Mistress. As for the Husband, he observed a perfect Neutrality; seemed well satisfied to be so honourably contended for, and ready with perfect Resignation to have taken up the Conqueror.

The same Day, Joseph Hall was committed to Clerkenwell-Bridewell, for being concerned with divers others, not yet taken, in stealing a great Quantity of Lead the Property of Counsellor Theed.

[1] See General Introduction, p. xxxii.

As was one William Hall to New-Prison for further Examination; he being charged before the Justice, by an Accomplice, with divers Felonies and Burglaries.

The same Day, four Persons, viz. three Men and a Woman, were bound over to the next Sessions at Hicks's–Hall, for keeping Bawdy-Houses; as were several Persons of ill Fame, to their good Behaviour; among whom was a young Woman remarkably handsome, genteel, well dressed, and behaved herself with great Decency before the Justice. Notwithstanding which Appearance, it was sworn that she had been extremely drunk in the Streets the preceeding Night, and had picked up the Constable. She expressed however so much Penitence, that the Justice shewed her all the Compassion in his Power; and as it was the first Time of her coming before him; instead of committing her to Bridewell; bound her over as above. *What doth that Wretch deserve, that was the Destroyer of an innocent lovely young Creature, who seems once to have so well merited Happiness herself? and to have been so capable of bestowing it on an honest Man?*[1]

I was much pleased with the foregoing Observation of Mr. Brogden;[2] who, tho' he hath drawn so many thousand Commitments, is a Man of great Humanity. The Reader will perceive how well this Sentiment agrees with those exprest by my Friend Axylus, in the Letter printed above.[3]

This Morning John Davis was committed to the Gatehouse by Henry Fielding, Esq; for defrauding Joseph Gray of a Quantity of Money, by a certain false Token.

The same Day Thomas Presser was committed to the same Place, by the same Gentleman, for stealing two silver Spoons, the Property of Mathew Smith.

The same Day Matthew Doharty was committed to the same Place by the same Gentleman for stealing a great Quantity of Burgundy, Champagne, and other Liquors, the Property of Richard Plimpton.

The same Day James Hall was committed to Newgate by the same Gentleman for picking the Pockets of William Payne and David Forrester, of two Linen Handkerchiefs.

This Felony was committed at Mr. Wesley's Tabernacle.

THE COVENT-GARDEN JOURNAL, No. 21, 14 Mar. 1752

COVENT-GARDEN, *March* 13, 1752.

Our worthy Correspondent Mr. Brogden being gone to the Essex Assizes, we have no Communications from Covent-Garden to insert this Time.

[1] For Fielding's view of such women, see *CGJ* No. 57, p. 308 n. 2; and see the column for 11 Jan., above.

[2] On Joshua Brogden's role in the preparation of these columns, see General Introduction, p. xxxi; see also the columns for 7 Jan. and 13 Mar.

[3] i.e. in *CGJ* No. 20.

THE COVENT-GARDEN JOURNAL, No. 25, 28 Mar. 1752

COVENT-GARDEN, *March* 27.

At the Execution at Tyburn, which was on Monday last, the Croud was more numerous than hath been usually seen on such an Occasion.[1] The Criminals themselves behaved with the wonted Affectation of Mock-Heroism; and instead of endeavouring to give any Marks of true Contrition and Repentance, seemed to vie with each other in displaying a Contempt of their shameful Death, and a total Indifference as to what might befal them after it. The Fool-hardiness of these miserable Wretches received perhaps no little Support from their Friends and Successors in Shame, who are destined to be the Heroes of a future Holiday. These Fellows seemed to have exerted their utmost Skill, by all Manner of Sports and Pastime, to keep up the Spirits of the present Sufferers. For this Purpose great Numbers of Cats and Dogs were sacrificed, and converted into missile Weapons, with which together with Dirt, Brickbats, and such like Ammunition, a sham Fight was maintained, the whole Way from Newgate to Tyburn: I could, I think, paint this Scene in a more ludicrous Light if I chose it; but I do not. It is not my Intention to raise my good Reader's Mirth, but his Indignation, and by that Means to prevail with those in whose Power it is, to prevent for the future the exhibiting of these horrid Farces, which do really reflect so great a Scandal to the Nation, and so much Disgrace to Humanity. If any one can invent a better Scheme than was advanced last Winter* for the Remedy of this Evil, I wish he would give it the Public: or if that Scheme wants only a greater Authority, I wish some greater Man *would alter a few Words in it, and make it his own.*[2] The real Fact at present is, that instead of making the Gallows an Object of Terror, our Executions contribute to make it an Object of Contempt in the Eye of a Malefactor; and we sacrifice the Lives of Men, not for *the Reformation, but for the Diversion of the Populace.*

I cannot help adding, as an Instance of the greater Efficacy of such Executions as are recommended in the Book I have hinted at, what I myself observed on Saturday last, when a Report prevailed, that three of the Felons were executed in Newgate. The Horror which this Report spread among the lower People is astonishing. Of this I myself saw many Instances, and many more have been well attested to me.

The Public may be assured, that the following very remarkable Incident is strictly true. By the Conviction of Miss Blandy and Miss Jeffries, two Copyholds escheat to

* See Fielding *on the Encrease of Robberies,* &c.

[1] The executions on 23 Mar. were of 'sixteen Malefactors', several of whom had attempted escape from Newgate; see *GA* for 23, 24 Mar. The first two paragraphs of this column are intended to support the argument Fielding made less directly in the accompanying leader for *CGJ* No. 25; both the leader and this commentary (perhaps by Brogden) comment on the failure of the recent 'Murder Act' (25 Geo. II, c. 37) to provide for private executions, which Fielding had argued for in his *Enquiry into the Causes of the late Increase of Robbers* (1751), sect. XI.

[2] For Fielding's 'Scheme', see *CGJ* No. 25 and notes. On the need for a 'greater Authority', cf. Fielding's comment in his Dedication of the *Enquiry* to Hardwicke: 'I hope I have no immodest Opinion of my own Abilities; but, in truth, I have much less Confidence in my Authority. Indeed the highest Authority is necessary to any Degree of Success in an Attempt of this Kind.'

one and the same Lord.[1] Thus the same Person enjoys the same Benefit, by the Conviction of two very remarkable Women, living at distant Parts of the Kingdom, unknown to each other, and both convicted at the same Lent Assizes, of the same Crime of Parricide.

A Gentleman who was present at the Trial of Miss Blandy, and who had his Eyes on her when the Hon. Mr. Bathurst, in a most eloquent and masterly Speech, opened the Charge against her, informs us, that the unfortunate Woman who had seemed unmoved at all the rest, could not bear a Hint which seemed to reflect on the Power of her Charms.[2] It was insinuated that Miss Blandy's supposed Fortune of 10000 l.— might possibly be the chief Allurement to her Lover. She who could without Emotion hear herself accused of Want of Humanity, could not bear the least Hint of Want of Beauty; but the Fire kindled in her Eyes, and she discharged a Look at the Speaker, full of such Indignation and Contempt, that is inconceivable to any except those who beheld it.

No Felon of any Kind, hath been brought before Mr. Fielding since Monday last. We cannot however flatter ourselves much, that this is owing to Reformation, since we hear almost Daily of Robberies and Murders. Two Robberies particularly have been committed this Week, in the Middle of Covent-Garden Square. The Servant of Capt. Cunningham, whose Skull was broke in that barbarous Manner, so as to have several large Pieces taken from it, is within Hopes of Recovery. He is under the Cure of Mr. Tomkins the Surgeon.

On Wednesday last, a Tragi-comical Cause was heard before the said Justice, between one Elizabeth Bewley and her Niece. The Aunt, who is about Sixty-year's of Age, brought her Niece of about Twenty-five before the Justice for beating her; which indeed she had done in no perfunctorious Manner, having given the old Gentlewoman two Black-Eyes, and beat out one of her Teeth. The Niece confessed the Fact, and indeed gloried in it, alledging as a full Justification, that her Aunt held a criminal Converse with her Husband, which she declared she would not tamely submit to while she had a Drop of Blood left in her Body. And now the Husband himself came forward, when lo! the very Picture of Shadow, the Woman's Taylor appeared.[3] He seemed hardly to deny his Wife's Accusation, upon which he was

---

[1] Elizabeth Jeffreys (?1717–52) was convicted at Chelmsford Assizes on 14 Mar. of being an accessory with John Swan in the murder of her uncle, Joseph Jeffreys, at Walthamstow on 3 July 1751. She was executed on 28 Mar., the date on which this column appeared. On Blandy, see *CGJ* No. 11, p. 84 n. 2.

The phrase 'copyholds escheat' means that lands being held in tenure 'at the will of the lord according to the custom of the manor' lapse to the lord of the manor on the death of the owner intestate without heirs (*OED*). In this instance Gillingham Cooper, a banker in the Strand, received, as lord of the manor at Henley, two fields belonging to Blandy and a malthouse belonging to Jeffreys (*DNB*, s.n. 'Blandy').

[2] The reference is to Henry Bathurst, later 2nd Earl Bathurst and Lord Chancellor (1714–94), Counsel for the Crown. His speech was both printed and praised in *The Genuine Speech of the Hon. Mr. ———— at the Late Trial of Miss Blandy* (1752). According to the notes in this pamphlet, when Bathurst said Cranstoun 'fell in love—not with her, but with her Fortune', Miss *Blandy* who stood seemingly unaffected thro' all the other Parts of this Oration, . . . yet cou'd not bear this trifling Reflection on her Charms, but cast a Look of the utmost Indignation and Contempt upon the Speaker' (pp. 7–8).

[3] A conflation of two of Falstaff's recruits in *2 Henry IV*, III. ii, Simon Shadow and Francis Feeble, the 'woman's tailor'.

asked how he could be guilty of the Sin of Adultery and Incest, (which are by the by no Crimes in our Law)[1] without any Temptation: For the Wife, besides being Young was Pretty, whereas the Aunt had not, at least since her Beating, any Remains of Comeliness, when poor Shadow thought proper to deny the more Criminal Part; but confessed the running away from his Wife: In Excuse for which, he declared that she had beat him every Day for a Fortnight together, which Batteries did indeed remain of Record, very legible on his Face. The Justice recommended an Accommodation between all the Parties; but while the Treaty was carrying on in an outward Room, something happening to provoke the Wife, she fell violently on the supposed Lovers, and laid both her Husband and her Aunt sprawling at her Feet. For this Fact she was ordered to be committed, when a *very substantial* Housekeeper, with another Person became her Bail. The Justice however in the End admonished the Husband concerning the horrid Sins charged upon him; but poor Shadow protested his Innocence, and with great Earnestness, and possibly with great Truth, declared, *That he would rather have one Pot of good Beer than all the Women in Europe.*

Mr. Arthur, of White's Chocolate-House, hath been lately robbed of ten Long-lawn Frocks, 3 Children's Napkins, marked A. one Child's Shift, five White Aprons, two coloured Handkerchiefs. It is hoped that any Pawn-broker, to whom such Goods are offered, will acquaint Mr. Brogden, Clerk to Mr. Justice Fielding.

THE COVENT-GARDEN JOURNAL, No. 26, 31 Mar. 1752

COVENT-GARDEN, *March* 30.

On Saturday last an Application was made to Mr. Justice Fielding, on the following very extraordinary Case.

Monsieur *Mathieu Bertin, Marquis de Frateaux*, Son of Monsieur *Bertin*, Master of the Requests, and Counsellor of the Parliament of Bourdeaux, was on some Family-Quarrel conveyed from France into Spain, by some of his Relations. There he was afterwards arrested by Virtue of a Lettre de Cachet, and imprisoned. From this Imprisonment he found Means to escape by the Assistance and Interest of the Count *Marcillac*, who is his Cousin, (for the Marquis is a Person of Distinction and related to many great Families.) About three Years ago, he came over from Spain into England, where he has resided in a private Manner ever since, and lodged with one Mrs. *Giles*, in the Parish of Marybone; at whose House he was on Friday last, late at Night, arrested by one *Alexander Blasdale*, a Marshal's-Court Officer, who had with him as a Follower, an Italian; a Person it seems before known to the Marquis: For the Moment that Fellow appeared, the Marquis started up and cried, I AM A DEAD MAN, and refused to go with the Officer. Mrs. Giles then sent for the Rev. Mr. Nicholas Robart, who is Minister of the French Chapel at Marybone; to whom on his Arrival, *Blasdale* shewed his Writ against the Marquis, who then, upon the Persuasion of the Minister, obeyed the Arrest, and went to the Bailiff's House; whither one *Monsieur Dobies* accompanied him, intending to stay with him till the next Morning; when Mr. Robart was to procure and bring him Bail. But the Marquis and his Friend had not

[1] See *CGJ* Nos. 67 and 68.

been together above Half an Hour in the upper Room in the Bailiff's-House, before the Italian Follower came up Stairs, and acquainted Mr. *Dobies*, that there was one below who wanted to speak with him. Upon this Message, Mr. *Dobies* went down Stairs, where he found no other Person than the Bailiff, by whom he was roughly told, that he must not lie that Night with the Marquis. Mr. *Dobies* desired to stay in any other Room, but that likewise was refused him; and he was in a Manner thrust out of Doors. What became of the unhappy Prisoner after that Time, is not yet known, for Mr. *Dobies* returning in the Morning, with some other Friends of the Marquis's, to the Bailiff's House, was informed by a Servant Maid and a Boy, who were the only Persons then in the House, that the Marquis was gone thence in Company with several Gentlemen, and that the Bailiff himself was gone out of Town. Mr. *Dobies* says, that he saw at the Bailiff's House, a large Hamper and Trunk packed up as for a Journey, and a Pair of Horse-Pistols lying thereon.

A Warrant hath been granted against the Bailiff, on a Supposition of Murder; but he hath not been seen or heard of since. Application hath been likewise made to the Lord Chief-Justice, for a Habeas-Corpus; as well as to the Secretary of State, to prevent the carrying this unfortunate Gentleman against his Consent out of the Kingdom; but all we fear will be to no Effect. We cannot help observing on this Occasion, that the Laws to prevent or punish such an audacious Attempt as this, of *Kidnapping* the Persons of his Majesty's Subjects, for any other Purpose, except those of Murder or Robbery, are much less effective and severe, than one would expect them to be in a Nation so proud and jealous of its Liberties; for as the Law now stands, a Villain may with less Danger, steal away your Child from your House, than he can privately take a Shilling, or forcibly take a single Farthing from your Person.[1]

The same Day, an Affair of a very different Kind was heard before the said Justice. One David Smith, a Welchman, and a Sailor, complained against Margaret Price, for having privately stolen Twenty-Shillings from his Pocket, and deposed as follows. "I came into the House of one Mrs. Owen. She is a Welchwoman; but not a Bit the less an honest Woman for that I'm sure, I wish I had never dealt with any other; not but Margaret Price, is a Welchwoman too; but there be Rogues of all Countries, and I am not ashamed of my Country for that. But there, Sir, as I was saying, I found this Woman; and I presently picked up an Acquaintance with her, *whereby* I intended, to make her my Wife; *whereby* I gave her eight Guineas; *whereby* I had but twenty Shillings in my Pocket left; and then as I was sitting and smoaking my Pipe, she took the twenty Shillings."

He was then asked, if she took them privately, and without his Consent? "To be sure, Sir," answered he, "it was privately; tho' I cannot say it was quite without my Consent neither: For as I told you, Sir, I intended to make her my Wife, *whereby*, I

---

[1] According to Giles Jacob, kidnapping was simply an offense at common law, punishable by fine or pillory (*A New Law-Dictionary*, 7th edn. [1756]). This case attracted considerable attention; see *The Unfortunate Officer; or, the History of Monsieur Bertin, Marquis de Fratteaux* (n.d.), a translation of a French pamphlet of 1753, which commented, 'An Act of this Nature made very strong Impressions in *England* on the Minds of People. . . . Men of Humanity were concerned that their Country afforded such a Wretch as *Blazdell*' (pp. 187–8). On 2 May *GA* advertised another pamphlet on the affair, *An Address to Those in Power*; see also a long letter of protest in *DA* (9 Apr.). Fielding's account was reprinted in part in *GM* 22 (1752), 191, as part of its 'Historical Chronicle'.

thought she was fitter to keep the Money than I; but, to be sure, I did not give her the twenty Shillings *graciously*, as I did the eight Guineas, for those I did give her *graciously*, that is the Truth on it, but as to the twenty Shillings"—He then turned to the Prisoner and cried, *Woot ha' me, Peg, or no, d—n me, if woot not, I'll swear thy Life.*

All Appearance of Felony being now vanished, the Justice recommended to the Woman either to return the Man his Money, or to take him into the Bargain, as it appeared she had promised. After some little Hesitation, she consented to the latter; they then went directly to the Fleet, where they were married, the Constable performing the Office of Father for the Bride and giving her away.

This Afternoon, John Stevens, an Ostler at the White Hart in St. John's-Street, was committed to Prison by the same Justice, for robbing and ravishing one Elizabeth, the Wife of William Humphreys of Highgate, on Saturday Night last, near Islington. The Woman appeared before the Justice to be a very decent and sober Person, and swore both the Facts very positively against the Prisoner. The Husband who was bound over to prosecute, tho' but a poor Man, expressed the highest Concern on the Insult offered to his Wife, and had been indefatigable in hunting out and apprehending the accused Person.

THE COVENT-GARDEN JOURNAL, No. 27, 4 Apr. 1752

COVENT-GARDEN, *April* 3, 1752.

On Monday Night last, at the Desire of the Lord Chamberlain, Mr. Justice Fielding, and another Justice, attended by several Constables, and assisted by a Party of the Guards attacked the Play-House in May-Fair. The Guards were appointed to march through the Park to Buckingham-Gate, where they were met by the Civil-Power, and the following Disposition was made. Mr. Welch with the Constables and a Corporal and six Men led the Van. These were supported by a Serjeant and twelve Men; and these again by the two Justices, with the Officer at the Head of the remaining Part of his Command. Mr. Welch with his Party immediately entered the Playhouse, rushed upon the Stage, and seized the Players; whilst the rest of the Guards drew up before the House to prevent any Disturbance from the Audience, which was very numerous, and, except a few Persons, all of the Mobile Order, seemed well enough inclined to have resisted, had it appeared in any Manner practicable. The Play was the Tragedy of Phædra and Hypolitus, (or as some of the Spectators called it Pheder and Polipus.)[1] Theseus and Ismena found Means to escape; the rest were all taken and conducted into Bow-street, when they were examined before Justice Fielding.

They appeared to be a Set of Apprentices, who acted only for their Diversion (the Money being taken for the Benefit of others.) The Justice therefore discharged them all, but not without many severe Rebukes, and Exhortations to abstain for the future from Diversions so very improper for Persons of their Condition, and which could

---

[1] i.e. *Phaedra and Hippolitus*, by Edmund Smith (1672–1710), which had been revived at Drury Lane in Nov. 1751. See *CGJ* No. 19.

not fail of bringing on them Habits of Idleness that must necessarily end in their Ruin.[1]

On Tuesday the military Power was again called in to the Assistance of the Civil. A Constable having a Warrant on Suspicion of Felony against a Girl who dwelt in a House in the Strand, went thither and enquired for her; upon which several Persons of both Sexes fell upon the Constable and very severely beat him. He then obtained a Party of the Guards, seized a great Number of the Offenders, and carried them before Mr. Justice Fielding; by whom some were bound over and others committed. One of the Women imposed on the Humanity of the Justice, by pretending to be taken in Labour; for no sooner was she got into Covent-Garden in a Chair, than she called to the Chairmen to set her down; and when the Chair was opened, she jumpt forth, took to her Heels and ran away; at which the Mob gave a great Shout; nor did the Chairmen think proper to pursue her for their Fare.

Yesterday a Gentleman was brought before the same Justice for assaulting a young Lad of 13 Years of Age, and ducking him in a Horsepond. The Gentleman confessed the Fact and gave Bail to answer it at the Sessions. He then charged the Lad in his Turn with having picked his Pocket of his Handkerchief, and which on his missing, he found concealed in the Boy's Bosom. This was sworn by two Witnesses; upon which the orignal Complainant was committed to Prison, and the Gentleman again bound over to prosecute; which he declared he would now do with the utmost Rigour, tho' he had first intended to content himself with the Punishment of the Horse-Pond.

Yesterday William Carney who lately broke out of New-Prison, was retaken and conveyed before Mr. Fielding, who committed him to Newgate.

The same Day William Harvey was committed to the same Place, by the same Gentleman, for feloniously conveying to one William Carney, then a Prisoner, committed to New-Prison for Felony; a certain Disguise, with Intent to aid and assist the said William Carney to facilitate his Escape without the Privity or Consent of the Keeper, contrary to the Statute of the 16th of his present Majesty.[2]

THE COVENT-GARDEN JOURNAL, No. 28, 7 Apr. 1752

COVENT-GARDEN, *April* 6.

On Friday Night last, two Men and a Woman apprehended in Hampshire, on Suspicion of the Murder of Carey the Higler of Epping,[3] were brought before Mr. Fielding.

They were viewed by a Man who was intimately acquainted with the Men who are

[1] *The London Stage* (Pt. 4, i. 303), which prints an erroneous account of this incident taken from *GA* and ignores Fielding's role in the episode, identifies the playhouse as New Wells, Shepherds Market, Mayfair. For other examples of Fielding's leniency toward apprentices who wished to be players, see the 'Covent Garden' columns of 13 'Apr. and 14 Aug. *LEP* (4 Apr.), seeking to make political capital out of Fielding's action, points up in its account all of Fielding's phrases which might suggest the exercise of arbitrary power.

[2] 16 Geo. II, c. 31, which specifies that assisting a prisoner to escape is a felony if the prisoner is guilty of any felony but petty larceny.

[3] See the columns for 26, 30 Jan. and 17 Feb., above.

accused of the Murder, and were both discharged not proving to be the Persons. One of them greatly resembled the Hard-ware Man; but the other had little Resemblance to Baxter.

Above a Dozen different Vagabonds have been taken up in several Parts of the Kingdom for this Murder; the supposed Perpetrators of which have been pursued by the Magistrate with great Expence, and unwearied Diligence, tho' hitherto without Success.

William Darby, the Brother to Robin Darby, convicted at the late Assizes at Kingston of robbing the Western Mail in July last, was some Time since bound to the next Sessions at the Old-Baily, there to answer a Charge against him as an Accessary after the Fact, to his said Brother. Last Night his Bail, who were bound in very large Sums for his Appearance, surrendered the said William, before the same Justice, who committed him to Prison.

This Morning one Rebecca Hart, a poor Woman belonging to the Parish of St. James's, was committed to Prison for stealing several Quantities of Coals, the Property of Mr. Nathan Robley. It was sworn against her that she had declared, "It was no Sin in the Poor to rob the Rich; and that if it was, J—— C—— had died to procure the Pardon of all such Sinners." The Prisoner all the Time she was before the Justice, appeared with uplifted Eyes, and behaved herself as if she had been engaged in her Devotions, appealing to Heaven for her Innocence, and invoking the most sacred Names as Witnesses of her not having committed a Fact, of which there appeared unquestionable Evidence.

THE COVENT-GARDEN JOURNAL, No. 29, 11 Apr. 1752

Covent-Garden, *April* 10.

On Tuesday last one Robert Archer was committed to Newgate by Henry Fielding, Esq; for feloniously marrying one Mary Blake, Spinster, his first Wife being then alive.

On Wednesday Philip Roberts, and John Rosse, were committed to Newgate by the same Gentleman, for stealing a great Quantity of Lead the Property of William Jarvis.

As was Christopher Emero, to the same Place, for picking the Pocket of Mr. Daniel Hugh Gordon of a Silk Handkerchief.

On Thursday one Mary Yardley was charged, before the said Justice, with having stolen a Blanket; but as the Evidence was not very positive, and the Prisoner appeared to be rotting alive with a foul Distemper given her by her Husband, the Justice, instead of sending the poor Wretch to Gaol, recommended her to an Hospital.

THE COVENT-GARDEN JOURNAL, No. 30, 14 Apr. 1752

Covent-Garden, *April* 13.

This Day Mr. Fielding began to distribute Gratis, his little Book,[1] just published,

[1] *Examples of the Interposition of Providence in the Detection and Punishment of Murder*, published by

which contains a great Number of Instances of the Interposition of Providence, in the Detection and Punishment of Murder. An Example, which, it is hoped, will be followed by all who wish well to their Country, or who have indeed any Sentiments of Humanity.—No Family ought to be without this Book, and it is most particularly calculated for the Use of those Schools, in which Children are taught to read: For there is nothing of which Children are more greedy, than Stories of the Tragical Kind; nor can their tender Minds receive more wholesome Food, than that which unites the Idea of Horror with the worst of Crimes, at an Age when all their Impressions become in great Measure, a Part of their Nature: *For those Ideas which they then join together*, as Mr. Locke judiciously observes, *they are never after capable of separating.*[1]

Yesterday Barnard Seers, and George Grayham, were committed to New Prison by Henry Fielding, Esq; being charged with breaking the House of James Blackwell, a Grocer, in John-street, Golden-Square, and taking from thence a great Quantity of Linen, Wearing-Apparel, Money, and other Things, the Property of Joseph Sewell.

The following is an extraordinary Instance of the Discharge of the Duty of the Office of Constable. About ten Days ago, four young Gentlemen went into a House dedicated to Venus; when, about two o'Clock in the Morning, came in a Man with a long Staff, at first to the great Terror of the Ladies, but the Kind Officer soon relieved their Fears, by producing a Fidler, who having played a Tune or two, a Watchman went round the Company, and collected Six-pence apiece, after the Receipt of which, the Constable, or pretended Constable, took a formal Leave, and left the Company to pursue their Inclinations.

This Night an Information was given to Henry Fielding, Esq; that a set of Barbers Apprentices, Journeymen Staymakers, Maid-Servants, &c. had taken a large Room at the Black-Horse, in the Strand, to act the Tragedy of the Orphan;[2] the Price of Admittance one Shilling. About eight o'Clock the said Justice, issued his Warrant directed to Mr. Welch, High Constable, who apprehended the said Actors, and brought them before the said Justice, who out of Compassion to their Youth, only bound them over to their good Behaviour. They were all conducted through the Streets in their Tragedy Dresses to the no small Diversion of the Populace.[3]

Millar on 13 Apr., a work both encouraged by and dedicated to Isaac Maddox, Bishop of Worcester. Advertisements for the book in *CGJ* for 11 and 14 Apr. assert its occasion to be the many murders committed within the past year, its purpose to induce 'Horror at this most heinous Sin', and its intended audience the youth of both sexes 'whose natural Love of Stories will lead them to read with Attention, what cannot fail of infusing into their tender Minds an early Dread and Abhorrence of staining their Hands with the Blood of their Fellow-Creatures'. The title-page credits Fielding with the introduction and conclusion to the collection of case histories.

[1] Not an actual quotation but a conflation of the points made in *An Essay Concerning Human Understanding*, II. xxxiii, 8–10; Locke, however, is warning against 'the undue connexion of ideas in the minds of young people'.

[2] Otway's *The Orphan; or the Unhappy Marriage*, performed recently at both Drury Lane (17 Mar.) and Covent Garden (1 Apr.). The Black-Horse was a tavern next to Andrew Millar's shop (Hugh Phillips, *Mid-Georgian London* [1964], p. 170).

[3] See also the columns for 3 Apr. and 14 Aug.

Appendix I

THE COVENT-GARDEN JOURNAL, No. 31, 18 Apr. 1752

COVENT-GARDEN, *April* 17.

This week one Curtis was brought before the Justice, and charged by his Wife with threatning to murder her, and carrying a Knife to Bed with him for that Purpose. He was greatly rebuked for this Behaviour, which he confessed, and for which he declared himself truly penitent. The Wife at last, by the Persuasions of the Justice, forgave the past, and they went away reconciled, taking with them the little Book against Murder,[1] which the Man promised to read over before he slept.

On Tuesday last John Smith, alias Brown, alias Thompson, a notorious Rogue, was committed to New-Prison for returning from Transportation.

The same Day William Turner was committed to the Gate-house, for privately stealing out of the Shop of Mr. Edward Lyres, a Linnen-Draper in York-street, Covent-Garden, a Quantity of Lawn and Muslin. The Goods were found on the Prisoner, and he confessed the Fact to those who apprehended him. When before the Justice, this unhappy Man appeared under the utmost Confusion and Horror, and scarce returned any Answer to the Questions which were asked him. Soon after he arrived in the Prison, he cut his Throat in so desperate a Manner that it is imagined he cannot recover.

On Wednesday Cicely Mullier was committed to the same Place, for stealing several Pieces of Houshold Furniture.

The same Day a Woman was charged with a trifling petty Larceny; when several of her Neighbours appearing to her Character, and offering to be bound for her, as the Theft was small and the Evidence circumstantial, the Justice admitted her to Bail.

On Thursday one Mary Baitin, a Girl of 13 Years of Age, was charged by another Girl about the same Age with stealing a Gown, the Property of the Accuser's Mother. The Girl who was the Witness told a very circumstantial Story to the Constable and others, and persisted a long Time in the Truth of her Charge; but before the Justice, who was then abroad, came home, having been closely examined by several of the Neighbours who disbelieved the Fact, on Account of the very good Character of Mary Batin, the Accuser declared that she was entirely innocent, and that an old Woman had committed the Felony, and had prevailed upon her not only to conceal the real Thief, but to lay the Crime on an innocent Person.

This Evening an Action brought by Dr. Thompson,[2] against an Apothecary for scandalous Words, was tried in the King's Bench before the Chief Justice of England, when, after a Hearing of near four Hours, the Jury gave a Verdict for the Doctor, with considerable Damages.

In this Cause his Grace the Duke of Roxborough, the Earl of Middlesex,

---

[1] Fielding's *Examples of the Interposition of Providence*; see the column for 13 Apr., above.

[2] Thomas Thompson, MD (d. 1763), the controversial physician praised by Fielding in the first edition of *Amelia* (v. ii). Thompson's *Enquiry into the Origin, Nature, and Cure of the Small-Pox* had just been published by Millar. Since the case reported here does not involve Fielding, its inclusion in the 'Covent Garden' column was prompted simply by his admiration for the physician. Thompson had attended Fielding during an illness in December 1749; see *Amelia*, ed. Martin Battestin, Wesleyan Edn. (Oxford, 1983), pp. xxix–xxx.

Mr. Doddington, Sir Francis Dashwood, Mr. Leveson Gower, Sir Francis Eyles, and other Gentlemen of Fashion, appeared in Support of the Doctor's Character, and upon their Oaths attested the very great Opinion they had of him, both as a Man and a Physician; and the great Success he had had in their Families, and among their Acquaintance. One Gentleman in particular declared on his Oath, that out of near fifty Persons for whom he had known the Doctor to prescribe, not one had failed while under his Hands.

THE COVENT-GARDEN JOURNAL, No. 32, 21 Apr. 1752

COVENT-GARDEN, *April* 20.

On Saturday last one of the Knights of Industry[1] was brought before the Justice, and charged with having conspired with several of the Companions of that honourable Order, to cheat a poor Farmer of his Money and Goods; when the Case appeared to be as follows.

One Minett, who rented an Estate in the marshy Lands in the Isle of Ely, was lately drowned out, as is sometimes the Case in that Country. Upon this he repaired to Gravesend, and there was taken in by a Farmer to work at Husbandry. Here a Knight of Industry, who had been formerly acquainted with him, found the poor Man, and decoy'd him to a Public-House, where they were joined by two others of the same Order. Minett was first made drunk, and then seduced to play, the Consequence of which was presently the loss of his Watch and ten Pound. The same Misfortune befel likewise his own Friend and one of the Strangers. For this 30 l. the three Losers joined in a Note to the successful Person. Minett came soon after to Town and went to a House in Shoreditch, where he had not been long before he and his Friend were arrested, and carried to the Habitation of one who may be called the Mirror[2] of this Kind of Chivalry. The Master of the House immediately offered to bail Minett's Friend; upon which the Officer, or pretended Officer, swore he would directly carry Minett himself to Prison, unless he found Bail or paid the Debt. Terrified at this Menace, and being incapable of complying with the Bailiff's Demand, Minett applied to the Master of the House, who was at last persuaded to become Bail for him also, upon Condition that he would make a Bill of Sale of his Goods, which were near of the Value of 30 l. This was soon complied with; and then the Bail recollecting himself that he should not have sufficient Security in his Hands, insisted likewise that Minett should give him a Note for 30 l. by way of collateral Surety. The Dread of a Prison forced the poor Man into this Concession also, and the Note was accordingly drawn and signed; when the unmerciful Rogues bethought themselves that Minett was yet possessed of a Mare. This he was likewise obliged to surrender, and then the Knights very generously suffered him to carry off his Skin, having stript him of his Watch, his Houshold-Goods, his Mare, and two Notes of Hand: For tho' he saw the joint Note in the Possession of his false Friend, who was arrested or rather pretended to be arrested with him, that Gentleman refused to deliver it to him.

[1] Swindlers (*OED*).
[2] i.e. the model of excellence, the exemplar.

For this Fact, the false Friend, whose Name was Robert Hall was committed to Prison, to which he was conveyed by a strong Party of the Guards.

The Villanies and Cruelties daily committed on the Subjects by Bailiffs,[1] under Colour of Law, are ONE Object of the Consideration of the Legislature; and it is pity some Reform was not made among them by those whose immediate Officers they are: If the Goals of this Metropolis were well inspected, it is my Opinion a Scene would be discovered of the most shocking Kind; and it would appear that our Liberties, no more than our Laws, are within the Reach of the Unhappy and Necessitous.

This Day Judith Pierce was committed to Clerkenwell Bridewell, for stealing a Guinea from one Alice King, whose Husband is now confined in Prison, the Fees of which this Guinea (which was all she had) was intended to pay, and for the Loss of which the poor Wretch appeared almost in a State of Distraction. The barbarous Woman saw the Money received, and knew the Purpose for which it was designed; notwithstanding which, there is great Presumption that she took the Opportunity of being her Friend's Bedfellow, to perpetrate the above Fact.

THE COVENT-GARDEN JOURNAL, No. 33, 25 Apr. 1752

COVENT-GARDEN, *April* 24.

On Tuesday last there was the greatest Drum or Rout at Sir Thomas Robinson's[2] in Privy-Garden, that was ever yet known. There were more People of Quality and Distinction present on this Occasion, than were supposed to be in Town. Notwithstanding the immense Assembly of Company, every thing was conducted with the greatest Order and Decorum, with the greatest Elegance and Magnificence. The House from Top to Bottom was most splendidly illuminated with waxen Tapers, and the Entertainment was of the politest Kind. The whole displayed the exquisite Taste of the Master of the House, and gave the highest Satisfaction to all. So great was the Crowd at the Door and on the Stairs, that several could not get farther than the first Stairs, and many more could not mount into the upper Apartments.

A Robbery of a very unusual, and almost ridiculous Kind, was lately committed in the Parish of St. Giles's. A young Girl, with a fine Head of Hair, was seized by a Robber and conducted into a blind Alley, where the Rogue with a Pair of Scissars cut off her Hair, and then giving her a Kiss dismissed her.

No great Criminals have been this Week brought before the Justice. Several accused of paultry Crimes, supported by circumstantial Evidence only, have been discharged; and Judith Campbell, and Elizabeth Marshall, for several Thefts, were committed to Prison.

This Week one Stephen Coleman, a Drayman was convicted of riding upon his Dray in the Streets, and paid the Penalty.

This Evening the following strange Case came before the Justice. One Rachael

---

[1] With this complaint about bailiffs, cf. *Amelia*, VIII. x. and XII. v.

[2] Sir Thomas Robinson (?1700–77), formerly governor of Barbados and well known for his fashionable entertainments and his extravagance; Fielding gently jokes at his expense in *Joseph Andrews* (III. vi.), where he is called a 'long *English* Baronet of infinite Wit, Humour, and Gravity'.

Davis was charged with having given some poisonous Ingredients to Thomas Greensmith, a Boy of eighteen Years of Age, by means of which the Boy had become raving mad. One Alice Allen swore that she herself having given the Lad some Jallop at Christmas last, in a Jest; Rachael Davis said, if she gave him any thing, she would give something better than that, and that she had afterwards brought something under the Name of Love Powder. Rachel confest she had made Use of the Expression, but denied having given any Thing to the Boy; she likewise confessed the buying the Love-Powder, but said she had bought it for a young Woman of her Acquaintance. The Apothecary's Journeyman was then sent for and deposed, that Rachael Davis had come to his Master's Shop to enquire for Love-Powder, when by the Orders of his Mistress, he gave her some Powder of Liquorice. It appeared on all Hands, that there was neither any particular Affection or Hatred between the Boy and the Accused, nor any Reason that she should give him such Powders either to do him Harm, or with a View of creating any Affection in him towards herself. It appeared likewise that the Powders brought of the Apothecary were entirely innocent; upon which the Justice was about to discharge the Woman; when the Journeyman delcared, that on the Day after that in which he had delivered her the Love Powder, she returned and asked him for a Halfpennyworth of Ratsbane. Upon this Circumstance, the Justice committed her for further Examination; and immediately sent for a proper Person to examine into the Condition of the Lad, whom the Journeyman aforesaid (being his only Doctor) reported to be dying.

This odd Story seems to have taken its rise from the Case of Miss Blandy.[1] As more of the Kind may be expected, it is hoped all Apothecaries will be cautious to whom they deliver any Drugs which are capable of doing Mischief.

THE COVENT-GARDEN JOURNAL, No. 34, 28 Apr. 1752

COVENT-GARDEN, *April 27.*

Saturday last, Rachael Davis was re-examined by the Justice.[2] She persisted in declaring that she had fetched the Love-Powder, as she called it, for the Use of another Girl, at whose Desire likewise, she had enquired for the Ratsbane, but had got none. She absolutely denied having given the Boy any Kind of thing whatever, nor was there any Evidence that she did. The Boy remains in a very strange Way, but an eminent Surgeon who visited him at the Desire of the Justice, declared that he had not the least Apprehension his Complaints which lay in his Head could be occasioned by any Thing poisonous given him by the Girl, as his Stomach or Bowels were not in the least affected, nor had he any violent Sickness or other Symptoms, which attend those who have taken Poison. Several Persons likewise came to the Character of the Girl, who gave her a very good one, particularly her Mistress; she appeared herself likewise, with all the Marks of Innocence and Simplicity; upon the whole therefore, and as it was acknowledged by all, even by the Boy's Sister, that there was neither Love nor Hatred between the Parties, the Prisoner was discharged.

It is a little surprising, that the Singularity of this Boy's Case as it appears upon the

---

[1] See *CGJ* Nos. 11 and 20.   [2] See the column for 24 Apr.

Report of the Surgeon, should not awaken the Curiosity at least of some of the Faculty, to enquire after him. He is reduced not only to the Loss of his rational, but most of his animal Faculties; and this, as I apprehend without any violent Fever, or any immediate Danger of Death.

Saturday Evening Mary Macculloh and Jane Macculloh were brought before the Justice, for beating Elizabeth Macculloh. After much Altercation on all Sides, the Justice thinking it a Family Quarrel, advised an Accomodation; when it appeared, that the Relationship between the Parties was such as is not known or acknowledged in our Law, they being indeed all the Wives of one and the same Husband. Matters now seemed irreconcileable by any, unless perhaps by Solomon himself; however, as the last Wife was the Complainant, and the Beating not very severe, indeed much less than might have been suspected, or seemed in this Case to have been deserved; the Magistrate refused to interpose. He then recommended to the first Wife to endeavour to bring her Husband to Justice, but that was plainly impossible, there being no Evidence in England of the first Marriage; and the Estate of the Husband, and the Fortunes of the three Wives amounting only to oo oo oo.

This Morning one Thomas Guilliam was committed to Prison for stealing near 300 lb. Weight of Lead from the House of Mr. Edward Turner. As this was affixed to the Freehold, the severing it, and immediately taking it away was no Felony, 'till made so by a late Act of Parliament.[1]

The same Morning a young Fellow, genteel, handsome and well drest, was brought before the Justice; being apprehended the Night before in the Embraces of a very ugly old Woman who stunk alive. The Woman was committed to Bridewell, and the young Fellow bound over to his good Behaviour. Indeed he seemed to have had Punishment enough before, and by some Symptoms appearing on his Paramour, may have yet a greater Punishment to come.

This Day five Malefactors were executed at Tyburn. No Heroes within the Memory of Man ever met their Fate with more Boldness and Intrepidity, and consequently with more felonious Glory. As Leake was conveying to the Place of Execution, he spied the Officer who apprehended him, and with all the Force he was then Master of discharged an Orange at his Head. At the very Place of Execution, the same worthy Personage called out to his Friends who were then assembled to protect his Body from the Surgeons, and after some Dispute with them, said twice or thrice, "I will have it my own Way." The Cart then moving, he called out to the Executioner, and said in a jesting Manner, "Pray Sir, don't hang us before our Time." In short, by his whole Behaviour, he endeavoured to shew the utmost Contempt of, or rather a total Unconcern of his Fate. And this Behaviour was imitated by three others of his Companions, to the great Encouragement of all future Heroes of the same Kind.[2]

---

[1] 4 Geo. II, c. 32, 'An Act for the more effectual punishing stealing of lead or iron bars fixed to houses', effective 24 June 1731.

[2] For Fielding's view of public executions, see also *CGJ* No. 25 and the 'Covent Garden' column for 27 Mar.

THE COVENT-GARDEN JOURNAL, No. 35, 2 May 1752

COVENT-GARDEN, *May* 1.

This Morning, between the Hours of One and Two, a Fire broke out at the House of Mr. Pierce, a Baker in Hynde-Street Bloomsbury, by Means unknown to the unhappy Sufferers, which in less than an Hour destroyed it; but by timely Aid was prevented from doing further Mischief, altho' the Street is narrow; and by reason of a large Quantity of dry Wood brought in the preceding Day to heat the Oven, the Flames burst forth with dreadful Impetuosity. Mr. Sells, formerly a Poulterer in Bloomsbury-market, who by many Years Application had acquired a Fortune, with which he retired from Business, and lodged in the First Floor, unhappily perished in the Flames. Mr. Pierce, his Wife, and an Infant, happily escaped; he with only a Fustian Frock, his Wife and Child without any other Covering than their Linnen, which was all that they saved. This unfortunate young Couple, who might truly be said to be happy, both in their Industry and mutual Affection for each other, and who had the pleasing Prospect of a comfortable Subsistance from their united Endeavours, are now totally stripped of every Conveniency of Life, by this sudden and unavoidable Calamity. To describe the Distress of this unhappy young Family is impossible; it drew Tears from many who were Spectators of this dreadful Scene, and will be felt by every good Mind to whose Knowledge it shall come.

The above Narrative is in the Words of Mr. Welch,[1] the worthy High-Constable of Holbourn Division; we are desired to add, that a Subscription for the Benefit of this unhappy Family, so truly the Objects of Charity, is now opened at Justice Fielding's in Bow-street, where Contributions will be received, and an Account thereof published in this Paper.

On Tuesday last Elizabeth Mills was brought before the Justice, and committed to the Gatehouse, being charged by Mr. Richard Kirby, with stealing a Gold-Ring, and a Quantity of Linen from his Wife.

As was Mary Jones, for stealing Wearing-Apparel from John Spencer.

Wednesday Mary Turner was committed to the same Place; being charged with stealing three Muslin Aprons the Property of a young Lady of Fashion.

In this Case, the Pawnbroker where they were pledged, very learnedly argued with the Justice, that the Aprons could not be stolen, because they were delivered; but there happening to be a Distinction in Law where the Property of the Goods delivered is altered, as was the Circumstance here, which had escaped the Pawnbroker's Reading, it was thought proper to refer the Matter to the Determination of the Judges.[2]

On Thursday a great Number of Persons, who were apprehended the Night before by Mr. Hurford, the High Constable of Finsbury Division, were examined by Mr. Fielding, and Mr. Dyot, another Justice of the Peace for the County of Middlesex. They were taken at a Mob DRUM or ROUT,[3] where several Hundreds

---

[1] Saunders Welch, close friend of the Fieldings, later a partner in the Universal Register Office.
[2] Cf. Giles Jacob: 'But Persons have the Possession of Goods by Delivery, may in some Instances be guilty of Felony, by taking away Part thereof' (*A New Law-Dictionary*, 7th edn. [1756], s.v. 'larceny').   [3] See the reaction to this phrase by 'Zara Grandemonde' in *CGJ* No. 43, above.

assemble Nightly, to the great Disturbance of the Neighbourhood, and Danger of the King's Peace, as well as to the debauching and Ruin of Apprentices, and the Youth of both Sexes.

The Prisoners all produced some credible Person to their Character, and appeared to be guilty of nothing more than Idleness, for which after a severe Reprimand, they were all discharged.

This Week a Housekeeper of Reputation was charged by one who had been his Maid-Servant, with a Rape (or rather several Rapes); and after a very long Examination, such Circumstances appeared, that he was admitted to Bail, two very substantial Persons becoming his Sureties.

In the Rigour of the Law, no Bail can be taken against an Oath of this Kind; but the higher Courts have indulged a Latitude to Magistrates—*Dabitur Licentia sumpta prudenter:*[1] For was it otherwise, no Man living could say this Night, that he was certain he should not lie in Newgate To-morrow.

This Week a Man was bound over to the Sessions for beating a Woman. In Revenge of this, he gave an Information against the Woman for pretending to tell Fortunes contrary to the Vagrant-Act; upon which, she was apprehended and brought to the House of the Justice while he was at Dinner. Before he was ready to examine her, she found means to make her Escape in so extraordinary a Manner, that she hath greatly convinced the Mob of the Truth of her Art, tho' perhaps she had only learnt the Method of *crossing the Hand*, a Ceremony always used in Fortune-telling.

THE COVENT-GARDEN JOURNAL, No. 36, 5 May 1752

COVENT-GARDEN, *May* 4.

N. B. *The Loss of this poor Family*[2] *who are entirely destitute even of Clothes, is computed at near two hundred Pounds.*

Last Week a certain Colonel of the Army bought a large Number of the Book called *Examples of the Interposition of Providence in the Detection and Punishment of Murder,*[3] in Order to distribute them amongst the private Soldiers of his Regiment. An Example well worthy of Imitation!

On Saturday last one Patrick Moore, was brought before the Justice, for violently beating his Wife, who deposed in the following Words.—"An't please your Worship, I have been married to this Man, if he be a Man, for it is more than I know, but I have been married to him these six Months; and ten good Pounds besides several other good Things of mine he has had, whereby I should not mind that, if he was to have made me a good Husband in Return; but instead of that, he and his Whore,—O Patrick, you know very well that you has no Need of a Whore, nor of a Wife neither; but that is neither here nor there, for that to be sure is none of your Worship's Business; but an't please your Worship he has tore me all to Pieces, he has tore me,

---

[1] Horace, *Art of Poetry*, 51: 'licence will be granted if used with modesty' (Loeb); the reading should be *pudenter.*

[2] The opening paragraph of this column, omitted here, repeats the story of the fire at the home of Pierce, the baker; see column for 1 May, above.

[3] Fielding's work; see column for 13 Apr., above.

that I have bled a Pint of Blood out at my Ears, and I have it all in my Cap here to shew. Indeed he has murdered me several Times within this Month, and I can bring good Witnesses of it; for the Neighbours all cry Shame, and if he be not sent to Prison, I shall be murdered again before To-morrow Morning: For to be sure such as he are not deserving of an honest Woman."

The Defendant traversed[1] the Murder; but admitted the beating his Wife the Evening before; for which he alledged by Way of Excuse, that he had caught her in Bed with a Foot Soldier. This was attested likewise by one of the Neighbour's a Man of Credit, who gave the Husband a good Character, as a peaceable and quiet Fellow. This Person likewise added, that he had been very industrious and laborious, till he had been injured by a Fall from a Ladder, by which he had strained his Back, so that he was yet scarce able to stand upright. An Accident which had unfortunately happened to him within a Day or two of his Marriage.

The Justice then recommended a Pacification between the Parties, to which the Wife after a severe Reprimand, pretended to agree, but that very Evening left her Husband in Company with her Paramour. The poor Man returned to the Justice for a Warrant against this Fellow, but could obtain none, ADULTERY BEING NO CRIME BY THE LAWS OF ENGLAND.[2]

The same Day Margaret Griffin was committed to the Gatehouse for Theft.

This Morning Esther Johnson was charged with stealing a Cap, a Muslin Apron, and a Sack by a Lady who said she was the said Esther's Mistress; but it appearing plainly, that both Mistress and Maid had an equal Property in the Goods, and wore them alternately she was dismissed. It appeared likewise, that the Lady and the Servant were Maid and Mistress by Turns.

The same Day one Sturges was charged by Mary Sheppard with a Rape; but the Accuser soon quitted that Accusation, and charged him with an Assault and Attempt to ravish. For this Offence the Justice gave the Man Time to find Bail; but whilst he waited for his Sureties, and perhaps began to despair of getting any, he offered his Hand to the Woman, who immediately accepted it; and instead of returning before the Justice, they went directly before the Parson.

The following is an Instance of Honesty which would have done Honour to any Age or Country. Mr. Pierce, for whom the Collection above mentioned is designed, in searching into the Rubbish of his late House, found several Pieces of Gold and Silver Coin, a Watch, and some half-melted Plate; all which he hath delivered into the Hands of Mr. Welch, saying that he had himself no Claim to them, but that they had, he supposed, belonged to the unhappy Gentleman who perished in the Flames; for whose Representative they are all preserved by the said Mr. Welch.

Whoever can without Emotion read such an Instance of Honesty, so nobly superiour to the Temptation of the highest Distress, must have a Heart Proof against every Impression of Humanity, and which nothing but Fire itself is capable of melting.

---

[1] i.e. formally contradicted, denied (legalism).
[2] A theme which forms the basis for Fielding's essays in *CGJ* Nos. 67 and 68.

THE COVENT-GARDEN JOURNAL, No. 37, 9 May 1752

COVENT-GARDEN, *May* 8.

The Subscription for Mr. Pierce, the Baker, still continues open at Justice Fielding's.[1]

This Week Mr. Welch brought several idle and dissolute Persons before the Justice. Among them were three little Girls; the eldest of whom, about fourteen Years of Age, was quite rotten with the foul Disease; the other two, who were under thirteen, had been both upon the Town, as it is called, above a Twelvemonth.

A Boy of about twenty Years of Age, who had been taken in Bed with a Girl of Seventeen, were of the Number. The Girl was pretty, and had not lost all Marks of Innocence, nay there was Reason to think, that she had been debauched by this very Fellow. After a Reprimand from the Justice, and some Threats, the Lad declared he was willing to make her all the Reparation in his Power, and to marry her immediately; to this she gave a ready Assent, and they were soon after made Man and Wife accordingly.

This Week have been committed by the Justice, the following Persons, viz.

1. Elizabeth Row, for privately stealing twenty-six Shillings from William Scott.
2. Richard Burton, for stealing several Dishes out of the King's Kitchin.
3. Samuel Harrison a Carman, on Account of the Death of Thomas Rogers, who was killed by the Cart, which the said Harrison was driving on Shoreditch Road; but as the Coroner's Inquest found it Chance-Medley,[2] he was bailed the same Day.

Tuesday last three Informations on the Game-Act were heard before the Justice, when after a long Hearing, the Defendants were all discharged. One not being within the Time limited. A second on the Evidence, and the third on a Point of Law which the Justice conceived to be in Favour of the Defendant.

THE COVENT-GARDEN JOURNAL, No. 38, 12 May 1752

COVENT-GARDEN, *May* 11.

On Saturday last Mountefort Brown, Esq;[3] surrendered himself before the Justice, to answer the Complaint of Dr. Hill, for a supposed Assault at Ranelagh, on Wednesday last; when upon the Affidavit of an eminent Physician, that Dr. Hill was not in any Danger of his Life, Mr. Brown was admitted to Bail, two Housekeepers of great Credit and Substance becoming his Sureties.

Whereas several scandalous Paragraphs have been published in a common News-

---

[1] See the column for 1 May.

[2] 'The casual Killing of a Man, not without the Killer's Fault, though without any evil Intention' (Giles Jacob, *A New Law-Dictionary*, 7th edn. [1756]).

[3] For the background and details of this case, see *CGJ* No. 60, above, p. 325 and n. 2. On the same day as this column appeared, Hill published a letter supposedly from a person of fashion, who commented, 'I hear they have flown for protection to Mr. F———g' (*LDA*, 12 May 1752). Part of Fielding's intention in this column is to justify Brown's claim to be a gentleman, impugned by Hill in columns in *LDA* throughout the month. Brown's use of the title 'Esquire' particularly irritated Hill; in a footnote in *LDA* for 30 May he wrote that 'Brown, when asked by Mr. Fielding in the Prosecutor's House, whether he signed himself *Esquire*' answered 'No'.

Paper, intending to vilify and misrepresent the Character of Mr. Brown; we think it an Act of Justice to declare, that nothing against the Honour of Mr. Brown appeared before the Justice; and so far was he from running away with an Intent to avoid Prosecution, that, having gone about 50 Miles from London on his private Business, he returned back on receiving an Express from his Friends with an Account of what was published against him, in order to surrender himself as aforesaid. We think ourselves farther obliged to inform the Public, that Lord Boyle, Colonel Churchill, Mr. Hamilton, Mr. Stewart, and many others of Fashion who were present at Ranelagh at the Time, appeared before the Justice on Mr. Brown's Behalf; which the Public will not, I believe, suppose they would have done on the Part of one who was not a Gentleman, and who had not behaved as such.

Saturday last Redman, the unhappy Person disordered in his Senses, formerly mentioned in this Paper was again brought before the Justice.[1] He appeared to be furiously mad, had several strange Papers in his Hat, and a very dangerous Weapon called a Tuck,[2] which darted a sharp Spike of a Foot long from the End of a Stick, in his Hand. The Justice committed him to New-Prison, and it is recommended to the Governors of the several Madhouses in Town, to procure him a Reception in one of them.

N. B. They are desired to apply to the Justice for that Purpose.

The Subscription for Mr. Pierce the Baker, will remain open till Friday Noon, when it will be closed, and an Account of the Contributions published in this Paper on Saturday.

On Saturday last James Hall and Jeremiah Barker, were committed to Newgate by the Justice, the said James Hall, for breaking the dwelling House of Thomas Bowden, a Cloathier, in the Night-time, and taking from thence eleven Pieces of Scarlet Cloth; and the said Jeremiah Barker, for receiving the same, knowing it to be stolen.

This Day Cath. Wickham was committed to the same Place, being charged by Mary Anderson, with stealing a great Quantity of Linen, and other Things.

As was William Sundell to New-Prison, for stealing an Iron Grate, the Property of a Person unknown, for further Examination.

THE COVENT-GARDEN JOURNAL, No. 39, 16 May 1752

COVENT-GARDEN, *May* 15.

The following is an Account of the Sums received by the Justice, for the Use of Mr. Pierce the Baker.[3]

---

[1] See the column for 10 Feb., above.

[2] A slender, pointed, thrusting sword (*OED*).

[3] See the column for 1 May, above. In the following list of those who contributed directly to Fielding may be found a number of people whose connections with him are well known: George Lyttelton, his patron and friend; Thomas Birch, the scholar and man of letters with whom Fielding was friendly; and Henry Gould, Fielding's first cousin. Others were well known public figures: Sir Thomas Robinson (see the 'Covent Garden' column for 24 Apr.); Alexander Hume Campbell (1708–60), brother of the Earl of Marchmont, MP, and friend of Pitt and Chesterfield; and George Errington (d. 1769), like Fielding a justice of the peace for Middlesex and later a Sheriff of London (1759–60).

Appendix I

	£.	s.	d.
Lord A	4	4	0
T. W. from St. James's Coffee-House	2	2	0
Anon. by the Rev. Mr. Birch	2	2	0
H. H.	2	2	0
Mrs. M. P.	2	2	0
Hon. Alex. Hume Campbel, Esq;	2	2	0
A. B.	1	16	0
K.Z.	1	16	0
George Errington, Esq;	1	1	0
H. H.	1	1	0
W.	1	1	0
Mr. Cooper	1	1	0
Sir Thomas Robinson, Bart.	1	1	0
Mr. Ravenell	1	1	0
Sir George Lyttleton, Bart.	1	1	0
Lady Lyttleton	1	1	0
Z. Y.	1	1	0
Mr. John Morris	1	1	0
Henry Fielding, Esq;	1	1	6
N. A.	0	10	6
Mr. Baker	0	10	6
Collected by Do. at the Genoese Arms	0	19	6
S. D.	0	10	6
Mr. Hunter	0	10	6
Collected by him	1	11	6
H. G.	0	11	6
Mr. Parnell	0	10	6
Mrs. P—e	0	10	6
Henry Gould, Esq;	0	10	6
D. Gash, Esq;	0	5	0
A. C.	0	5	0
T. C.	0	5	0
Mr. Craven	0	5	0
Collected in less Sums	4	2	6

The underwritten Sums were collected by Mr. Welch.

Lord Leicester	2	2	0

D. Gash (or Gach) (d. 1765) was a druggist in the Strand not far from the Universal Register Office, John Morris was perhaps the haberdasher of that name in Bond Street, and 'Mr. Hunter' was probably William Hunter, the prominent surgeon and friend of Fielding (see *CGJ* No. 38, above). The others are unidentified.

The second list, of those who contributed through Saunders Welch, includes Thomas Coke, Earl of Leicester (1697–1759); Joseph Andrews, a lawyer and Fellow of the Royal Society; and William Wyndham, again a lawyer and FRS, perhaps the '—— Wyndham, Esq.' who subscribed to Fielding's *Miscellanies* (1743). The rest are unidentified, although 'Mr.' should perhaps be 'Rev.' William Warburton, for whom see above, p. 192 n. 3.

	£.	s.	d.
Joseph Andrews, Esq;	2	2	0
Messrs. Gifford and Jarman	2	2	0
J. F. from Doyley's Coffee-House	2	2	0
William Wyndham, Esq;	1	1	0
——Sweete, Esq;	1	1	0
Mr. Francis Goodge	1	7	0
Mr. William Goodge	0	10	6
Mr. Higginson	0	10	6
Mr. William Edwards	0	10	6
——Mann. Esq;	0	10	6
Mr. William Warburton	0	10	6
A. B.	0	10	6
Mr. Morris	0	5	0
Mr. Scrafton	0	2	6
Mr. Foyster	0	2	6
Anonymous	0	1	0
	£. 57	6	6

I do acknowledge to have this Day received of Henry Fielding, Esq; the Sum of Fifty-seven Pounds, Six Shillings and Six-pence; for which I most humbly and gratefully return my hearty Thanks to my worthy Benefactors.

May 15,
1752.

William Pierce.

If any Person shall be yet willing to contribute to the Relief of this honest Man, their Contributions will be received at the Justice's, as before.

On Wednesday last a Woman applied to the Justice for a Warrant against a Staymaker in the Strand, and represented that he had enticed the said Woman to go over the Water on Sunday last, to his Brother's at Lambeth, which she agreed to; that as soon as they got into the House, the said Man took her up Stairs, and there put her into a Room, and locked the Door and kept her there all Night, and the next Day and Night; and during that Time that he assaulted and ravished her against her Will and Consent, and repeated such Ravishment several Times. A Warrant was accordingly granted, and the Prisoner arrested and brought to the Justice's House; but before the Justice was ready to examine the Matter, the Prisoner said to the Woman, "My Dear, you know very well we were married on Monday Morning at the Fleet." Upon which she burst out into Tears, and confessed it to be true; alledging as an Excuse for what she had done, that she had been over persuaded to it. The good Man presently forgave the Offence, and they departed very lovingly together.

The same Day John Purser was committed to New-Prison by the Justice, for defrauding Mr. William Young, a Silversmith, of two Silver Watches. He persisted in denying that he was the Person, tho' positively sworn to by three unexceptionable Witnesses.

Yesterday George Oglevey was committed to the Gatehouse, being charged by an Accomplice with Burglary, in breaking and entering the House of James Miller, near Battle Bridge, in the Parish of Pancras, and feloniously taking from thence a great Quantity of Houshold-Furniture.

THE COVENT-GARDEN JOURNAL, No. 40, 19 May 1752

COVENT-GARDEN, *May* 18.

The Subscription for the Benefit of Mr. Pierce[1] the Baker, will continue open 'till Friday next at Noon, when it will be closed, and a final Account of the whole Sum collected will be published in this Paper on Saturday.

On Saturday last three Barbers were tried before the Justice, on the Statute of Charles II, for exercising their Trade on the Lord's Day,[2] one of whom was convicted and paid the Penalty.

The same Day two Women accused of two several small Thefts, were discharged on the Insufficiency of the Evidence; as was a third on the Insufficiency of the Fact, the Goods stole being, at a high Valuation, worth three Farthings.

This Morning several Women were brought before the Justice, and accused as idle and disorderly; but no Fact being proved against them, they were all discharged. *Note.* The Law hath been formerly held to be otherwise, by some learned Justices of Peace.

This Day one Elizabeth Scott, swore the Peace against her Husband; and gave the following Reasons, which were transcribed verbatim. "Sir, he has *mortified* me all over, and I goes in Danger of my Life, Night and Day. I have bore him nine Children, whereof I am with Child now of the tenth, and whereof, I am sure, I would not make my *Afferdavy* to any thing that was false for the whole World; but I can safely take my *Afferdavy*, that he has mortified me from Head to Foot, and so he has my Child too. Whereof I could shew your Worship, if your Worship was a Woman; but to be sure our Sexes Modesty can't go as far, that is, whereby before Men, to be sure your Worship however understands me very well; and I hopes you will do me Justice, and send him to Gaol;" which however, as every Word of the foregoing, appeared to be false, was not done, but they were both dismissed; and the Accuser severely reprimanded. One of the Neighbours, a very credible Person, swore, that he believed, *there was not a better Husband nor a worse Wife in the King's Dominions.*

The Reply of Benevolus to Crito in the Gazetteer of Saturday last, will be published in our next, as we shall be very glad of contributing to the Establishment of so useful a Design as this, of erecting the Sea-Surgeons into a Society, promises to be;[3] and it is with Pleasure we observe the prodigious Improvements which this most

[1] See the columns for 1 and 15 May.

[2] 29 Charles II, c. 7. The prescribed penalty was five shillings for people in most classes of occupations.

[3] For the Society of Naval Surgeons, see *CGJ* No. 38. The criticism of the society in the *London Gazetteer* of 16 May by 'Crito' is answered in *CGJ* No. 41; this number of the *Gazetteer* has not been located.

noble Art of Surgery, the elder Sister to that of Physic, hath lately received in this Country, and the much greater which it is in a fair Way of receiving; we wish we could say as much of the younger Sister.

THE COVENT-GARDEN JOURNAL, No. 41, 23 May 1752

COVENT-GARDEN, *May* 22.

Yesterday one Samuel Sutherwood, a noted Gambler, was committed to Clerkenwell Bridewell by the Justice, for cheating and defrauding one Henry Bentley, a raw country Lad, of six Pounds thirteen Shillings, by a Game called Pricking at the Garter.[1]

The same Day John Allen was committed to New-Prison, for defrauding Samuel Farey of a Guinea by false Tokens.

This Week a Servant of a noble Lord was committed to Prison, for a most notorious Insult on his Lordship.

As was a Carter, for wilfully and maliciously breaking the Chariot of another noble Peer.

Note, There are now confined in Prison two mad Persons, and it is most earnestly desired that some Governors of Madhouses will apply to the Justice, otherwise they must be shortly let loose among the People. Quære, To what Use are all the Madhouses about Town? Are not the large Contributions for the Support of such Houses, mere Impositions on the Public?[2]

The following is an Account of the whole Collection by Mr. Fielding, for the Use of Mr. Pierce the Baker.[3]

	£.	s.	d.
Lady Maynard	1	1	0
M. B.	0	5	0
L. B.	0	5	0
T. T.	0	2	6
A. B. C.	0	10	6
Peter Delme, Esq;	2	2	0
F. P.	0	10	6
Mrs. G.	0	5	0
P. D.	0	2	6
J. F. Esq;	10	10	0
Mr. James Collett	2	2	0
£.	17	16	0
Received before———	57	6	6
Total	75	2	6

[1] A swindling game; see *OED*, s.v. 'fast-and-loose'.
[2] See *CGJ* No. 45, where Fielding satirizes one such institution.

[*For note 3 see next page.*]

I acknowledge to have received from the Hands of Henry Fielding, Esq; the above Sum, for which I return my most sincere and grateful Thanks to all my worthy Benefactors; and I shall constantly pray, that that great and glorious Being, who can alone reward true Goodness, may reward their Bounty to me and my Family.

William Pierce.

THE COVENT-GARDEN JOURNAL, No. 42, 26 May 1752

COVENT-GARDEN, *May* 25.

Saturday last one Henry Child was committed to Prison for stealing several Pewter Plates, the Property of Mr. Hammond.

The same Day a search Warrant was granted to search for a Trunk in which were several Things of Value, and which had been advertised with ten Guineas Reward. To obtain this an Oath was made of a Suspicion of Felony, and of the Place where the Trunk was supposed to be deposited. When the Officer went to search, he was told the Trunk had been left there, but was taken away; upon which the Party went away, highly vexed at his Loss; but this, however, was not so grievous as he imagined it; for at his Return home he found his Trunk, which a Person in his Absence had left for him, and had received the ten Guineas.

The same Day a Man was bound over to keep the Peace, for cruelly beating his Wife, and two Women for beating their Husbands.

This Morning one Thomas Wilford was committed to Newgate for the Murder of Sarah his Wife, by giving her several Stabs, and cutting her Throat is such a Manner as almost to sever her Head from her Body.

The Prisoner confessed the Fact, and said that he had married this Woman on Wednesday last, that he had a very violent Love for her, and that Jealousy was the Motive to this rash Action. He said his Wife had left him last Night at Seven, and staid out 'till past Eleven; that he was vexed at her long Stay, and questoned her about it at her Return; to which she gave him very short and unsatisfactory Answers. This threw him into a Rage, which being further kindled by provoking Words, he snatched up a Knife and committed the above Fact.

He was extremely bloody, and particularly on one Knee, with which he had knelt on his Wife while he cut her Throat.

When he had perpetrated this horrid Fact, he ran hastily down from the second Floor, where he lodged, to the first, and offered to make his Escape out at the Window; but a Woman who lodged in the Room opposite to him, who had heard his Wife groan, crying out Murder, he stopt suddenly and returned, saying he had killed the Woman whom he loved best of all the World, and was contented to suffer for it. After this he made no more Offer at escaping, which he might easily have effected;

---

[3] See the columns for 1 and 15 May. In the list of additional contributors, Lady Charlotte Maynard (d. 1762) was the wife of Sir William Maynard, Bt., of Essex; and Peter Delmé (1710–70), MP for Southampton, was one of the governors of the Foundling Hospital and a frequent subscriber to literary works, including Sarah Fielding's *Familiar Letters* (1747). One hopes that the charitable James Collett, otherwise unidentified, is not the one who advertised a few months later that his wife had eloped (*DA*, 13 Nov. 1752).

but staid quietly with the Man of the House 'till the Constable came, who took him into Custody.

He appeared greatly affected, and full of Contrition before the Justice, professing that he desired to die for his Offence. He was exhorted to spend his whole Time, 'till his Trial, in true Repentance and Prayer, to abstain from all strong Liquors, and to confine himself to Bread and Water, which he promised to do. He then begged the Justice to give him the little Book on the heinous Sin of Murder,[1] lately published, which when he received, he shed a Shower of Tears, and wished he had read it before.

He is a young Fellow just turned of 17 Years of Age, born only with one Arm, of a comely and modest Countenance, and his Behaviour, with the extreme Horrors with which he appeared to be possest, drew some Pity from the Croud who were present, notwithstanding he confessed, that he was near a Quarter of an Hour in the Commission of the Murder; during which Time, it was remarkable, that no Person heard more than two or three of the Woman's dying Groans.

This Day one Dupie, a Foreigner, was committed to Prison for stealing sixty Guineas from his Master George Pitt, Esq;

THE COVENT-GARDEN JOURNAL, No. 43, 30 May 1752

COVENT-GARDEN, *May* 29.

This Week one James Lory, a Lad of about sixteen Years of Age, was committed to Prison, on Suspicion of stealing a Quantity of Brass belonging to Coaches; which an honest Broker, to whom they were offered to sale, stopt, together with the Lad. He gave several Accounts of himself, and of the Goods, none of which proved to be true. By this Kind of Theft, an Injury to the Amount of several Pounds, is done to a Gentleman's Coach, while the Purchase to the Thief is scarce as many Pence.

Three Men who were taken up by the Watch, with a Bundle of Linen found on them, were likewise committed for farther Examination at the End of five Days, and the Goods advertised in Pursuance of an Act of Parliament past last Sessions;[2] the Excellency of which Law hath appeared in this Instance, the Owner having already appeared, and will by these Means recover his Goods.

No less than five People have been this Week convicted on the Act against prophane Swearing;[3] some of whom paid the Penalty, and others were committed to Bridewell. Besides religious Motives to the putting this Act in vigorous Execution, it would answer many civil Purposes, and would check the licencious Insolence of the Vulgar, better than any other Law in Being.

Wednesday last an unhappy Gentleman, who is disordered in his Senses, and hath comitted many Acts of Violence, and threatened greater, was sent before the Justice

---

[1] Fielding's *Examples of the Interposition of Providence*, published on 13 Apr.; see the 'Covent Garden' column for that date, above.

[2] 25 Geo. II, c. 36, which provided for advertisements describing suspicious persons and the things found on them.

[3] 19 Geo. II, c. 21 (1746); offenders were subject to conviction by a justice of the peace on the oath of a constable or other officer.

by Order of the Government, and by him committed to New-Prison.[1] A Gaol which will shortly deserve the Name of a Madhouse, there being no less than three dangerous mad People now confined there by the Justice, for want for a more proper Place of Confinement; and from whence (unless some of the Governors of Madhouses should acquire a little Humanity) they must shortly be turned loose on the Public.

O Proceres! Censore Opus est an Haruspice nobis.[2]

This Day Jane Stagg was committed to New-Prison, on an Indictment of Felony at Guild-hall.

THE COVENT-GARDEN JOURNAL, No. 44, 2 June 1752

COVENT-GARDEN, *June* 1.

Saturday last, Anne Flowers was committed to Prison by the Justice, on the Accusation of Thomas Marshal of having privately stolen a Watch from his Person.

As was William Haynes for further Examination, on Suspicion of stealing a Quantity of Iron, the Property of a Person unknown. He was taken up by the Watch, at Two in the Morning with a Bag of Iron in his Possession, and could not or would not give any Account how he came by it.

The same Day Margaret Meredith brought one Sarah Cole before the Justice, and charged her with an Assault in the following Words. "An't please your Worship, I was standing in Covent-Garden Market, when this Woman came up to me, and there was Mary Falkner and Bess Groves, standing by.—Upon which I moved off to a Block just by, and I had got a Bit of Paper in my Hand, whereby to set down my Jobs; for an't please your Worship, we always sets down our Jobs; and so she came up to me, and said, she had a great Mind to drive her Fist into my Jaw, and I said, do if you will, and then I said, I had never laid with a Man in Newgate under Condemnation, nor I was never washed out of Newgate, and so without any Offence to your Worship, I says again.—And upon this she came up to me again, and swore she would wash her Hands in my Heart's Blood, and dance a Hornpipe over my Breast-Bone; and then she would have let drive her Fist in my Face, if Bess Groves had not prevented her, and then she swore I should not be alive two Days to an End, not tho' I had as many Lives as a Cat, and all the World knows she has a-got nine."

Mo . . . ce,[3] notwithstanding which the Justice thought he might safely venture the Life of the Subject without Sureties, and therefore dismissed the Accused on her Honour not to meddle any more with the Prosecutor's Basket, which was it seems the Cause of the Quarrel.

---

[1] New-Prison at Clerkenwell, described as 'a prison of ease to Newgate for the county of Middlesex' (John Noorthouck, *A New History of London* [1773], p. 752). For Fielding's further expression of concern on the disposal of lunatics, see *CGJ* No. 45.

[2] Juvenal, *Satires*, ii. 121: 'Oh ye nobles of Rome, is it a soothsayer that we need, or a Censor?' (Loeb.)

[3] The line is missing in all extant copies, the result of 'frisket-bite'.

This Day John Bradford was committed to the Gatehouse, for stealing two large Silver Spoons, the Property of Mr. Packington Tomkyns, at the Shakespeare's Head.

As was Anne Lloyd, otherwise Howard, for stealing a Pair of Sheets and other Things, the Property of John Hart.

N. B. There are now several Dangerous mad People confined by the Justice, who must shortly be let loose; of which timely Notice will be given in this Paper, *that his Majesty's sober Subjects may shut themselves up in their Houses.*[1]

THE COVENT-GARDEN JOURNAL, No. 45, 6 June 1752

COVENT-GARDEN, *June* 5.

This Week upwards of thirty Persons have been committed by the Justice to several Prisons for various Offences; seven of whom are accused of capital Crimes, viz. Robbery upon the Highway, Rape, Smuggling and Forgery.

The Devizes Caravan having been three Times robbed by the same Person at the same Place, the Master applied to one William Norton, and asked him if he would venture to ride in the Caravan, and to attempt the taking the Highwayman. Norton presently undertook it; and was attacked at the usual Place. He affected a Fright, and begged the Robber to give him Time to take his Money out of his Pocket; but whilst he held forth some Silver in his left Hand, he presented a Pistol in his Right, and snapt it; upon which the Robber fell down, and then got up and ran away. Norton immediately jumped from the Caravan, pursued, and took him. When brought before the Justice, he impeached three of his Companions (all the Drivers of Post-Chaises) who have been since apprehended and committed for farther Examination on Tuesday next.

The Accusation of the Rape of an Infant was re-heard this Day, when the Person accused was after a very long Examination committed, and several bound over to prosecute at the next Sessions at the Old-Bailey.

This Week a young Woman was charged before the Justice with stealing a Silver Spoon; but the Proof being very defective she was dismissed. Upon this she threatened her Master, who had been her Accuser, with an Action; which so incensed him that he advertised the Spoon. A Pawnbroker then produced it, and swore positively against the Girl, upon which she was committed to Prison.

The Man accused of Forgery was apprehended in Kent, and sent before the Justice by the Justices of that County. There were several Accusations against him, on one of which the Prosecutor was bound over in the Penalty of 500 l. to appear against the Prisoner.

A Woman was committed for uttering a false Guinea, knowing it to be false and counterfeit. She behaved herself very outrageously before the Justice, and seemed to affect the Part of a Madwoman.

---

[1] Another expression of Fielding's increasing irritation at the admission policies of asylums for lunatics; see *CGJ* No. 45.

THE COVENT-GARDEN JOURNAL, No. 46, 9 June 1752

COVENT-GARDEN, *June* 8.

This Morning three Women were bound over to the Sessions, by the Justice, for assaulting a fourth, and threatening to burn her for being a WITCH. One of the Accused declared to the Justice, that the Accuser had bewitched two of her Children. There was, it seems, a Quarrel between this Woman and the Prosecutrix, and the latter had denounced Vengeance against the former, and told her her Children should not live a Month. Both of these were since dead of the Small-Pox; but the Witch was a little mistaken in Time, seven Weeks having elapsed before the Death of the second Child.

This Day Mary Hilton was committed to Prison, on Suspicion of stealing several China Plates, and a silver Spoon, the Property of Mr. Goodburn.

As was the Widow of the late Mr. Field who was hanged, for assaulting and beating the Widow of the late Mr. Thrift, the Hangman.

THE COVENT-GARDEN JOURNAL, No. 47, 13 June 1752

COVENT-GARDEN, *June* 12.

On Tuesday last the three Persons taken up on Suspicion of robbing on the Highway, were brought before the Justices to be re-examined; when, after all the Pains which the Justices had taken, and the Expence which they had been at in advertising, not one Prosecutor thought proper to appear. In a Nation where there is such Zeal for the Public in every Man's Bosom, it is wonderful there are no more Robbers.

Since Tuesday only one Person hath been committed for Felony, namely Sarah Rock, for privately stealing several Pair of Stockings, out of the Shop of William Finch, a Hosier in Covent-Garden. She is an old Woman, and an old Offender, having been eleven Times whipt at the Cart's Tail.

On Wednesday one Thomas Heyerd was committed to New-Prison, for cheating Mr. Holmes of Limehouse of 500 Tiles and upwards, by Means of a false Token. He confessed the Fact, appeared very penitent, and pleaded Poverty.

The late Act of Parliament, by which a Reward of 10 l. is allowed to any two Inhabitants of Parishes paying Scot and Lot, for the Prosecution of the Keepers of Bawdyhouses, and which became in Force on the 1st of June, hath struck a most extraordinary Panic into the lower Order of that Profession, many of whom have left their Houses; nay the Streets are reported to be cleared of Ladies in an Evening. It is probable, however, they will all return to their Stations by the Beginning of the Winter.[1]

---

[1] On the reaction to this new law (25 Geo. II, c. 36), see *CGJ* Nos. 50 and 57 and notes.

THE COVENT-GARDEN JOURNAL, No. 48, 16 June 1752

COVENT-GARDEN, *June* 15.

On Saturday last Henry Incleton was committed to the Gatehouse, being accused by John Utridge of Hammersmith, of stealing one Sheet, one Quilt, and one Pair of Curtains, out of his ready furnished Lodgings.

The same Day Robert Callder was committed to the same Place being charged by William Perry, a Waterman, with stealing forty Shillings out of the Boat of the said William Perry, near Queen-Hithe.

As was Mary Blinkcoe to the same Place, being charged with stealing one Sheet, one Brass Candlestick, one Pewter Dish, and one Pewter Plate, out of her ready furnished Lodgings, the Property of Patrick Nowland.

This Day David Murray was committed to the same Place, being accused by Nathan Holmes, a Porter at the Saracen's Head, on Snow Hill, of stealing a Box containing several valuable Things, the Property of Mr. Edward Stratford.

This Day three Persons were charged with Burglary before the Justice, by an Accomplice, and were committed for Examination.

A Virago was brought before the Justice for beating another Woman; and being ordered to Prison, she fell immediately on the Prosecutrix, and gave her several Blows in the Face, with the Force and Dexterity of a true Boxer.

This Day several idle and disorderly Persons were brought before the Justice, from the several Roundhouses; some of whom were committed, some bound over, and some discharged.

THE COVENT-GARDEN JOURNAL, No. 49, 20 June 1752

COVENT-GARDEN, *June* 19.

Tuesday last Maria Newman, was brought before the Justice, and charged on Oath by Henry Jenkins, a Welshman, with having picked his Pocket of ten Guineas in Gold, four Shillings and Six-pence, and a Gold-Ring. The Prosecutor had picked up the Prisoner in the Streets, and carried her to a House near Temple Bar; where they went to Bed together, and in the Morning he missed both his Bedfellow and his Money. The Woman confessed taking the Silver and the Ring, but denied seeing the Gold. She was committed to Prison.

The same Day one John Page a Soldier, who had lately listed himself into the Army, and one John Meadows, were accused of Burglary before the said Justice, on the Oaths of Mr. Caister and Jane Llewin, in breaking open the House of the said Mr. Caister, in the Night-time, and stealing from thence several large Pieces of China and other Goods. An Accomplice was likewise a Witness against the Accused.

The same Day one Mackenzie, who had formerly lived a Servant with Counsellor Gascoigne,[1] was committed to Prison for violently assaulting his Master, and striking him on the Head, with Intent, as he declared, to murder him. This was in Revenge

[1] Presumably Bamber Gascoyne (1725–91), the barrister and later MP who was son of Sir Crisp Gascoyne, just elected Lord Mayor of London.

for a Blow given him by his Master two Years before, when this Mackenzie was in his Service; for which he had sued his Master, and received a Sum of Money.

Notwithstanding which, he lay in wait for the Counsellor behind a Pillar in the Temple, and assaulted him in the Manner aforesaid.

Wednesday, Benjamin Breach was committed to Prison for Burglary, in breaking and entering the House of Michael Gibbons, in Gray's-Inn-Lane, and stealing six great Coats.

Thursday several Wretches who had been apprehended the Night before by Mr. Welch, were brought before Mr. Fielding and Mr. Errington;[1] when one who was in a dreadful Condition, being all over covered with the Itch, was recommended to the Care of the Overseers; another who appeared guilty of no other Crime but Poverty, had Money given her to enable her to follow her Trade in the Market; one Man was bound to his good Behaviour, one discharged, and the rest committed to Bridewell.

The same Day in the Afternoon, Mr. Welch routed a Mob Gaming-house in Holborn, where he apprehended thirty idle Persons, all of them Apprentices, Journeymen and Gentlemens Servants, and all in the high Road to Ruin. Some were only admonished and discharged, some bound in their own Recognizances according to the Statute of Henry VIII. some with Sureties by the Statute of the present King,[2] and some of the most notorious were committed to Prison. The Master of the House was bound with very great Bail to the Sessions, where he will be prosecuted pursuant to the new Act of Parliament,[3] upon which, this is the first Information which hath been laid before the Justice.

THE COVENT-GARDEN JOURNAL, No. 51, 27 June 1752

Covent-Garden, *June* 26.

Persons charged with the following capital Offences, have been committed by the Justice to be tried at the present Sessions at the Old-Baily, viz. Murder, Rape, Robbery on the Highway, Burglary, Smuggling, Forgery, privately stealing in Houses, and privately stealing from the Person. And this Week upwards of forty Persons have been committed by the Justice to the several Prisons in the County of Middlesex, and in the Liberty of Westminster.

This Week the following remarkable Charge was laid before the Justice. Sunday last a young Woman went to a House while the Husband was at Church, and the Wife left alone in the House. The Stranger immediately fell upon the Wife, and gave her three violent Cuts on the Head with a Cleaver, and then left her for dead. She was aprehended and carried before a Justice. Whither the Husband after his Return from Church came, having first viewed his Wife weltring in her Blood. He was there Sworn a Witness as to the Situation in which he had found his Wife; and the Woman upon his and other Evidence, was committed to Prison, whither he went with her in the same Coach. When there, he was asked if he knew this Woman who was then in

---

[1] For George Errington, see the column for 15 May, above.
[2] Referring to 23 Henry VIII, c. 6 and 2 Geo. II, c. 28.
[3] 25 Geo. II, c. 36, encouraging prosecution 'against persons keeping bawdy houses, gaming houses or other disorderly houses', effective 1 June 1752.

Man's Cloaths, which he denied. The next Day this very Person was charged on Oath by another Woman, with having enticed the Prisoner to commit the Fact; with having himself drest her in a suit of his own Clothes for that Purpose; and with having taken a Woman with him to Church who lodged in the House, in order to leave his Wife alone. It appeared that he had had a Child by the Prisoner, had lived with her in a State of criminal Conversation two Years. And when this Woman was told in the Prison, that both she and her Lover would be hanged, she cried out in an Agony, *Hang me, hang me,—but Spare him*. It is said the Husband had promised to marry his Mistress as a Reward for making him a Widower; tho' he seems afterwards to have repented this Promise, and to have been well contented with the Prospect of being rid of both. This however is not likely to happen; for the Wife, tho' desperately wounded, is in a fair Way of Recovery.[1]

This Day five notorious Vagabond Wenches, who had long disturbed the Neighbourhood of Chelsea, lying in the Streets, and committing all manner of Disorders and Indecencies, were on the Complaint of a great Number of Housekeepers, sent to Bridewell, to hard Labour. When they had received their Sentence, they all fell a laughing, cursing, and swearing and talking of B—dy; and behaved in a Manner which shocked the Decency of all the Mob who saw them.

THE COVENT-GARDEN JOURNAL, No. 53, 4 July 1752

Covent-Garden, *July* 3.

This Week the following Cause was heard before the Justice. One Frances Crane was accused by Jane Porter with violently assaulting and beating her. Frances made the following Defence to the Accusation. "This Woman, an't please your Worship, lives with my Husband, that is I don't mean that she lives altogether with him, but she lies with him that she does to be sure, and that is more than I can say, who am his lawful Wife for manys the good Day—and so, Sir, I says to her, *Mary, what do you mean by lying with my Husband*? Whereof, to be sure, no Woman upon Earth can bear to have that done in my own poor House and upon my own poor Bed; wherefore she had the brazen Face to tell me she had a better Right to him than I had, and she called me Wh—re, which I thought very hard, an't please your Worship, having as I have my Certificate in my Hand to shew and two fine Children by him, which that vile Creature there, there she stands, I defies her to shew any such Thing, tho' she have had two Husbands before she have had mine—And so, Sir, I do own, that upon her calling me Wh—re, I did lend her a Bit of my Resentment, that I must confess, whereof, to be sure, no Woman alive would have done any other."

Jane in her Reply, produced a counter Evidence to the Certificate, that is to say

[1] See the later reference to his case in the *Public Advertiser* for 25 Jan. 1753; after a paragraph indicating that both parties went without punishment, a comment of protest follows, written either by Brogden or Fielding himself: 'By the ancient Laws of this Kingdom . . . a manifest Attempt to murder was equally capital with Murder itself. Quere, For what Reason, and by what Authority, hath this so sensible and excellent an Institution been altered . . . ? At this Day the most flagitious Attempt to murder, heightened with Barbarity and every atrocious Circumstance whatever (unless with a Design to rob, which perhaps in reality rather lessens the Wickedness of the Intention) can only be punished as a Misdemeanour.'

another Certificate dated at the same Place, to wit, at the Fleet. The same Man's Name was in both, and tho' that of Jane was dated two Years after the other, as she appeared innocent of the Bigamy, the Justice recommended an Accommodation between the Wives, and that they should both join in Prosecuting the Husband; against whom a Warrant was granted accordingly.

On Wednesday last Sarah Osborne was committed to New-Prison, for stealing a quantity of Linen and other Things, out of the dwelling House of Edward Roberts, a Brewer in Denmark Street, St. Giles's.

On Thursday last Charles Vain was committed to Clerkenwell-Bridewell, for stealing a quantity of Lead the Property of John Fitzer, a Farmer at Hodsden.

And Yesterday Martha Carter, was committed to New-Prison, for stealing one Pair of Sheets, one Tea Kettle; and several other Things the Property of Margaret Grange.

As was Ann Finch to Clerkenwell Bridewell, for stealing one Sheet, one Apron, and one Handkerchief, the Property of Elizabeth Basset.

No Matters of any Consequence have been before the Justice this Week. A Man was taken up on Suspicion of being concerned in the Murder of Carey the Higler;[1] but appeared perfectly innocent on his Examination.

THE COVENT-GARDEN JOURNAL, No. 54, 11 July 1752

COVENT-GARDEN, *July* 10.

This Week a most extraordinary Lad of about ten Years of Age, was brought before the Justice and charged with having Stolen two Silver Spoons from his Master Mr. Langley, an Apothecary, in Chancery Lane. He confessed the Fact, and likewise declared that he had entered into a Conspiracy with six Ruffians, who were to enter his Master's House while he was absent at a Funeral, to murder the Journeyman and Maid Servant, and to rob the House, and that he himself was to have a fourth Share of the Booty. All this he confessed without the least Concern or Emotion; in which hardened Condition he continued, notwithstanding all the Endeavours of the Justice to shew him the great Atrociousness of his Guilt.

This Week likewise, two other notorious Offenders appeared before the Justice, namely the Woman who some Time ago gave a married Woman, two very barbarous and dangerous Wounds on the Head, with a Cleaver; and the Husband who is accused of having induced her to commit this horrid Fact.[2] The Woman confessed the giving the Blows, and accused the Man of having advised and incited her to it, and this likewise was sworn positively by another Woman, who through a Window, saw him dress this Female Assassin in his own Cloaths for that Purpose; and heard the Appointment made. When the Justice ordered the Husband to be removed from his present Prison to Newgate, the Wife who was so far recovered of her Wounds as to be able to attend, fell on her Knees, and begged that he might be dealt more gently with; and declared if he was sent to Newgate it would occasion her Death. She

[1] See the 'Covent Garden' column for 26 Jan., above.
[2] See the column for 26 June, above.

likewise expressed a Readiness to forgive them both, but especially her Husband.

This Week Mary Cole was committed to Clerkenwell Bridewell, being charged with stealing a quantity of Household Goods, the Property of George Hicleton. As was Abigail Frances to the same Place, on suspicion of stealing a silver Watch, the Property of a Person unknown. And William Randall, otherwise Shock Randall, was committed to Tothillfields Bridewell, being charged by William Bedwin, with robbing him on the King's Highway, on Smallberry Green, near Hounslow, of some Money and other Things.

Yesterday Morning one Cole was committed to New Prison, on Suspicion of having stole a large Quantity of Jewels, with a gold repeating Watch, and other things, the Property of a little Girl lately come from the West-Indies. They were chiefly the Trinkets of her late Mother, and were left in a Cedar Box by the Carelessness of a Servant at an Inn in Blandford, whence they were stolen. Some of the Jewels to the Value of about sixty Pounds are recovered, having been sold to a Jeweller in this Town by the above Cole.

THE COVENT-GARDEN JOURNAL, No. 55, 18 July 1752

COVENT-GARDEN, *July* 18.

On Monday last eleven Wretches were executed at Tyburn, and the very next Night one of the most impudent Street-Robberies was committed near St. James's Square; an Instance of the little Force which such Examples have on the Minds of the Populace.[1]

In real Truth, the Executions of Criminals, as at present conducted, serve, I apprehend, to a Purpose diametrically opposite to that for which they were designed; and tend rather to inspire the Vulgar with a Contempt of the Gallows than with the Fear of it.

The Day of Execution is a Holyday to the greatest Part of the Mob about Town. On every such Occasion they are sure to assemble in great Numbers and as sure to behave themselves with all kinds of Disorder. All the Avenues to Tyburn appear like those to a Wake or Festival, where Idleness, Wantonness, Drunkenness, and every other Species of Debauchery are gratified.

And as the Looks and Behaviour of the Spectators so well bespeak them to be assembled to see some Shew or Farce, those who are to exhibit the Spectacle seem brought thither only as the Performers of such ridiculous Drama. Some indeed, as in the Case of all Players, perform their Parts beyond others, have much more Mirth in their Countenances, and of Jest in their Mouths, and do consequently entertain the good Company better than their Companions; but even among those who fall shortest of such Merit, there are very few who do not preserve the Appearance of Indifference at least, and tho' all cannot force a Laugh, there is scarce one who doth not refrain from Tears, and from every other Mark of Fear or Contrition.

Can such a Scene as this impress the Fear of Death on the Minds of the Vulgar?

[1] With these remarks and those that follow, Fielding returns to the subject of *CGJ* No. 25 (28 Mar.) and of his *Enquiry into the Causes of the late Increase of Robbers*, sect. XI; see *CGJ* No. 25, above, and notes, and the 'Covent Garden' column of 27 Mar., above.

Can the Politician invent any other more powerful Method of teaching them to dispise it? Is it not to exemplify all the laboured Receipts of the Philosophers, and to prove the Truth of those Doctrines, which are summed up in the Lines of Lucretius?

> *Multo igitur Mortem minus ad nos esse putandum,*
> *Si minus esse potest, quam quod nihil esse videmus.*[1]

And if the Fear of Death cannot be inculcated this Way, neither can the Fear of Shame. Here likewise the Example operates directly contrary to what is intended: for however contemptible these Wretches may appear to a wise and good Man, it is manifest that they are seen in a very different Light by their Companions, by all those who are capable of learning either a good or bad Lesson from their Fate.[2] However atrocious his Crimes were, the Thief who suffers with Resolution and Boldness (as is now commonly the Case) looks on himself as a Hero, and is regarded and spoken of as such by others.

Where then is the Remedy? I answer the Remedy hath been prescribed already, and may be found at the End of the Treatise on the Encrease of Robberies published last Year; Namely private Executions before the Face of the Court.

To the Arguments there used, I have never heard more than one Objection, which is, that the Execution of Criminals would be a very disagreeable Sight to the Magistrates. So I believe it is in Holland, where the Magistrates all attend on these Occasions;[3] so to a good-natured Judge, in England is the Office of condemning a Man to be hanged, to a tender-hearted Man perhaps scarce less disagreeable than to see his Sentence executed.

But I shall reply no farther to an Objection, which when opposed to the good of the Public, is absolutely ridiculous.[4] I will only add that if no Method can be found of making our capital Punishments more terrible and more exemplary, I wish some other Punishments were invented; and that we may no longer proceed to string up hundreds of our Fellow-Creatures every Year, a Matter as shocking to all Men of Humanity, as it is entertaining to a dissolute Rabble, who (I repeat it again) instead of being terrified, are hardened and encouraged by the Sight.

THE COVENT-GARDEN JOURNAL, No. 59, 15 Aug. 1752

COVENT-GARDEN, *August* 14.

This Week only three Persons have been committed for Felonies, and those of no very considerable Kind. On Tuesday last Information was laid before the Justice by a

---

[1] *De rerum natura*, iii. 926–7: 'Death therefore must be thought of much less moment to us, if there can be anything less than what we see to be nothing' (Loeb). Fielding's *nihil* should be *nil*, and *putandum putandumst.*

[2] Cf. *Enquiry*, sect. XI, where Fielding argues that 'To unite the Ideas of Death and Shame is not so easy as may be imagined' and adduces evidence from drama and from Montaigne to support his proposal that private executions follow immediately after conviction.

[3] A point made also in the *Enquiry*, where executions in Holland are called 'incredibly solemn'.

[4] Fielding's scheme for executions was criticized, though not on this ground, in *Observations on Mr. Fielding's Enquiry* (1751) by 'Ben Sedgly', attributed to Richard Rolt in William Kenrick's *Pasquinade* (1753).

Tradesman in Westminster, That one of his Apprentices had robbed him, in order to equip himself for acting a Play, and that the said Play was to be acted that Evening by several Apprentices, and other idle Persons, at the Old Tennis Court in James's Street. Upon this the Justice dispatched Mr. Welch in the Evening with a Party of Soldiers to apprehend the Persons concerned in the Representation of the Play, which was the Tragedy of Venice Preserved.[1] Jaffier, Pierre, Belvidera, and most of the other principal Characters were taken, and some of them, particularly Belvidera, were brought in their Theatrical Attire before the Justice. The Men all appeared to be young Apprentices, and the Woman a young Millener; wherefore the Justice was unwilling to proceed against them as Rogues and Vagabonds, as they are made by the last Vagrant Act;[2] in which case they must have been committed to Bridewell, which might have proved their Ruin: He treated them therefore as guilty of an unlawful Assembly, and a common Nusance; for which they were either bound to their good Behaviour, or committed for Want of Sureties, and soon after discharged. It was sworn before the Justice that Sunday had been the usual Day of rehearsing their Parts.[3]

THE COVENT-GARDEN JOURNAL, No. 66, 14 Oct. 1752

COVENT-GARDEN, *Oct.* 13.

This Week a Tradesman in the Strand applied for a Warrant to search the Garret of a Man whom he had several Years imployed as a Porter at nine Shillings per Week, on a Suspicion that this Porter had embezled some of his Goods. On searching the aforesaid Lodgings, the Constable found several Bags of Money hid in different Parts of the Room, to the Amount, as afterwards appeared, of near 500l. Upon his Examination before the Justice, the Man could produce no other visible Means of acquiring this large Sum, than the aforesaid Sallary which he had enjoyed near twenty Years, during all which Time he said (and his Neighbours seemed to confirm it) that he had lived only on what he had begged, and had saved his whole Wages. However there being very strong Suspicion against him, the Justice thought proper to commit him. When he came first to the Prison he pleaded Poverty and lay all Night on the Boards to save a Shilling for his Bed. His Garret resembled a poor Broker's Shop, it had in it above twenty Pair of old Shoes, as many old Wiggs and other Goods of the like Kind. He is an old Man.

On Monday last Elizabeth Wood was committed to New-Prison, being charged by James Wilson of Kentish Town with picking his Pocket of a Six and thirty Shilling Piece of Gold.

On Tuesday last John Langston was committed to the Gatehouse, being charged with stealing two Coats, the Property of John Calverley.

The same Day Elizabeth Ash was committed to New-Prison, being charged with stealing two Shirts and one Muslin Neck-cloth the Property of Sarah Bedford.

[1] Otway's *Venice Preserved* had been regularly performed at Covent Garden in the season of 1751–2 and was revived by Garrick at Drury Lane in Oct.

[2] 17 Geo. II, c. 5; by 25 Geo. II, c. 36 unlicensed places of public entertainment were also considered disorderly houses.

[3] For other examples of Fielding's leniency in such cases, see the columns for 3, 13 Apr. above.

On Wednesday last Margaret King was committed to the Gatehouse, being charged with stealing one Pair of Stays, one Pettycoat, one Holland Shift, one Silk Handkerchief, two linnen Caps, and other Things, the Property of Mary Coles.

The same Day Zachariah Duncomb was committed to Clerkenwell Bridewell, being charged by Richard Orme with picking his Pocket of a Handkerchief.

The same Day Matthew Davies was committed to the same Place, for picking the Pocket of Isack Moresley of a Handkerchief.

As was William Smith for stealing one Gold Ring the Property of John Cordwell.

APPENDIX II

The 'Modern History' Columns

EACH number of *CGJ* carried a column called 'Modern History', consisting of news items reprinted from other newspapers. In the first twenty numbers (except for *CGJ* Nos. 8 and 17), Fielding and his assistants followed many of the reprinted items with brief, italicized commentary. His purpose in this exercise was to continue his satirical assessment of contemporary journalism with the same device he had used in his earlier papers, although some of the comments here are serious reflections on the social implications of the items reprinted. The authorship of the individual comments cannot be determined with certainty, but—despite the array of initials and pseudonyms with which they are frequently signed—Fielding's hand is clearly present in many of them (e.g. all those signed 'C.'), and all were printed under his supervision.

The text which follows includes all the commentary, with no effort made to determine authorship. Moreover, this material has not been given the same bibliographical analysis as was accorded the more important texts of the essays or of the 'Covent Garden' columns; obvious printer's errors have been silently corrected. Where necessary· and possible, the items reprinted from other papers have been shortened, with omissions indicated by ellipsis. Commentary original with *CGJ* follows the reprinted item and is placed in italic fount, as it is in the copy-text, with the conventional exceptions for emphasis. Where the identification would otherwise be unclear, the initials of the newspaper in question have been substituted for the abbreviation 'Id.' used in the copy-text. Items from other papers which are not followed by editorial comment from the *CGJ* are, of course, not reprinted here. Annotation of this material has been kept at a minimal level.

The copy-text uses the following abbreviations for the names of contemporary newspapers:

D. A.	*The Daily Advertiser*
D. G.	*The Daily Gazetteer*[1]
G. A.	*The General Advertiser*
G. E.	*The General Evening Post*
L. D. A.	*The London Daily Advertiser*
L. E.	*The London Evening Post*
L. G.	*The London Gazetteer*
St. J. E.	*The St. James's Evening Post*
W. E.	*The Whitehall Evening Post*

---

[1] Since December 1748 this paper had been called *The London Gazetteer*, but Fielding and others continued on occasion to refer to it by its old name. The initials 'D. G.' and 'L. G.' thus refer to the same paper.

Appendix II

THE COVENT-GARDEN JOURNAL, No. 1, 4 Jan. 1752

MODERN HISTORY.

CUM NOTIS VARIORUM.

—Sunt quædam mediocria; Sunt mala plura.[1]

WEDNESDAY, *Jan.* 1.

It is reported, that several Projects of great Importance will be infallibly brought upon the Carpet soon after the Holidays, when some that have been already carried into Execution, but with very indifferent Success, will be also *retouch'd*, and that some Pieces of good News will be likewise made publick about the same Time.   G. A.——
What these Projects are which have been lately carried into Execution with such indifferent Success, I no more know than I do the good News here prophecied of; but both, it is probable, will end in RETOUCHING.

Some private Letters from Italy assure us, that the Sword is half unsheathed again in Corsica, where it is asserted, that one Chief has challenged the other, and that this Challenge has been accepted; but Advices from Genoa treat all this as Fiction, but acknowledged at the same time, that Difficulties have arisen which hinder, and are like to hinder, the Pacification from taking Place this Year, or perhaps the next.   Id.——*If the Challenge, which hath been accepted, should not take Place sooner than the Pacification, the Advices* FROM GENOA *seem to treat the Matter more justly than those* FROM ITALY.

Last Week was performed, with great Applause, the Tragedy of Cato, by the Boys of the Free Grammar School in Nottingham, and for their Encouragement, a Collection was made at the Theatre, amounting to the Sum of 90 l. 6 s. 6 d. L. D. A.——*I do not see what Encouragement this can give to Boys to prosecute their Studies; I would propose therefore to read the Passage thus,* for their Encouragement *to become Actors,* a Collection was made, &c.

We are assured there will be no Ode performed in the Great Council Chamber at St. James's this Day, as has been usual on New-year's Day.   Id.——*If this Fact be true, the Town will have this Year escaped both the annual Odes; and the true Lovers of the Muses may hope, that the Laureate will, for the future, make a* Sine Cure *of his Office.*

A Comedy, written in French by a Lady, called Cenie, and translated by the Rev. Mr. Francis . . . will soon be acted. This Comedy, which is of the genteel Species, without any Intermixture of low Characters, met with great Success at Paris; and by its Fate on our Stage will be seen, whether the English Taste can be pleased with that Kind of Comedy, which, as it has no Drollery, can never excite Laughter. D. G.——*That Kind of Comedy which has no Drollery, is in Truth no Comedy at all. And so is the Case at present; for this Comedy (as I have heard) happens to be a Tragedy.*

THURSDAY.

Yesterday Mr. Halford, who serv'd Mr. David Trinder, an eminent Cooper and

---

[1] 'There are some indifferent things, there are more things bad' (Loeb); adapted from Martial, *Epigrams,* I. xvi. I.

Hoopbender at Shadwell, was married to Miss Elizabeth Trinder, eldest Daughter of the late Mr. Thomas Trinder; an agreeable young Lady with a handsome Fortune. D. A.——*If instead of* young Lady *we read* young Woman, *the young Lady will appear to have made* a more agreeable Choice.

On Tuesday Night two Persons going to Newington were attack'd between Shoreditch and Kingsland, by three Fellows well arm'd, who robb'd them of their Money, and demanded their Watches; but upon their telling them they had none, wished them a good Walk home. S. J. E.——*By the Civility of these Fellows, there certainly was no* Hackney Coachman *among them.*

It appears upon Enquiry, that several Persons have bred Silk-Worms with great Success in this Country; so that there is no Doubt, with proper Encouragement, we might be enabled to raise as much Silk here as would, at least, supply our Manufactures. This and the Herring Fishery would effectually employ, and comfortably support, all the indigent Persons in this Nation that are inclined to be industrious, and both might be carried to Perfection at much less Expence than is annually levied for the Relief of the Poor of London only.——*This political Scheme is mentioned by various Authors; and so far, as least, it would be certainly effectual; that the Manufacture would be capable of providing Nets for the Fishery, and the Fishery might reciprocally maintain the Manufacture with red Herrings.*

They write from Copenhagen, that, on Occasion of the Death of the Queen of Denmark, his Danish Majesty has issued an Edict, forbidding, for a whole Year, all Plays, Balls, Operas, Concerto's, &c.—Heaven preserve us from such Mourning, which would send at least half of our gay, polite Gentry to the Grave! G. E.——*And half of our gay, polite Tradesmen to the Dogs.*

We hear that a Party of Soldiers in Sussex last Week made a Seizure of a great Quantity of Tea and Brandy, and also secured some of the Persons *running* the same. Id.——*These Persons, it seems, could not* out-run *the Soldiers.*

This Week several Waggon-Loads of Wine were brought to Town from Rochester, having been landed at that Port, to have the additional Duty of Forty Shillings per Pipe; the Winking at which proves to be a great Disadvantage to the fair Traders: And 'tis hoped . . . the Commissioners will order the Duty of Out-Ports to be made the same as in London. Id.——*If an Order were made for the Advantage of the* fair Traders *in Wine; Quere, Who would be literally within it?*

Last Sunday died, at his House in Cowley-Street, Westminster, Mr. Solomon Despayres, an eminent Jew Merchant, of considerable Fortune, which he acquired with a good Character. G. A.——*Some Historians leave out the latter Part of this Paragraph, as thinking it, I suppose, immaterial.*

Yesterday died at his House in Tothill Street, Westminster, Mr. Bargrave, an eminent Attorney at Law, possessed of a good Fortune, acquired with a fair Character. G. E.——*A Loss greatly to be regretted.*

It is said that several worthy *Magistrates* have, upon mature Deliberation, resolv'd amongst themselves to exert their *Authorities*, and to punish as the *Law* directs such as shall be brought before them for being *drunk*, and to take away the *Licences* of such Public Houses as shall continue to permit *tippling* at unreasonable Hours; or who suffer any Kind of *Gaming* in their *Houses*, by which they may render *eminent Service* to their *Country* without injuring DIANA, or giving *Offence* to the *Craftsmen*. L. E.——*Some Manuscripts for* DIANA, *read* BACCHUS, *and for* CRAFTSMEN, QUAFFSMEN, *and this seems to be the truer Reading: for by executing the present Laws against Drunkenness, very little Injury would be done to the Votaries of this Deity*. See Fielding on the Encrease of Robbers, et al.

FRIDAY

Last Tuesday Afternoon a Gentleman was attacked upon Hounslow Heath by two Highwaymen exceedingly well mounted, who robbed him of five Guineas in Gold, and five Shillings and Sixpence in Silver; after which they returned him Twopence, which they told him was to pay for the two Turnpikes, and wished him well home. L. D. A.——*By the Care which these Gentlemen took not to rob the Turnpikes, it appears that one Rogue seldom cares to rob another.*

Wednesday Morning James Pease, Esq; set out for his Seat near Doncaster in Yorkshire, in order to celebrate his Nuptials with a young Lady in that Neighbourhood, endowed with all the necessary Accomplishments to make the married State happy, and a Fortune of 12000 l. Id.——*This is the first Time that these amiable and valuable Qualities have been bestowed on a Lady unknown; but no Man can be too careful to conceal so inestimable a Jewel.*

Yesterday, about 11 o'Clock, a Servant of the most Hon. the Marquis of Rockingham, in Grosvenor-Square, discharging a Fuzee and Pistol out of the Garret Window, (the Muzzles of each being directed upwards, as the Man says) one of the Balls went quite a-cross the Square, and shot the Hall Window of Lord Robert Manners. The Ball luckily struck the Rail, and did no more Mischief than breaking three Panes of Glass. There were at least a Dozen People in the Hall, and some very near the Window; the Ball rebounded quite a-cross the Area, and went into the Channel. Id.——*If the Servant of the Marquis is after speaking Truth, upon my Shoul, Honey, the Ball must have gone out at the Touch-hole.* Patrick Oshane.

Also was married by the Rev. Mr. Jones, Mr. Ventris, an eminent Soapboiler in Holborn, to Miss Morgan, of Clarges-street; a young Gentlewoman of great Beauty and Merit, with a Fortune of 2000 l. G. A.——*It is observable that Gentlemen content themselves with moderate Qualifications in their Wives; while all the Ladies of great Beauty and Merit, engaging Sweetness of Temper, and every Qualification requisite to make the Marriage State happy, fall to the Share of eminent Builders, Soap-boilers, Shoemakers, Butchers, &c.*

On Saturday last were committed to Maidstone Goal, by Andrew Long, Esq; Mayor of the City of Rochester, Matthew Keyes, Michael Hartley, and John Allwitt, charged on the Oaths of Edward Gilham and Anne his Wife, with feloniously assembling themselves with several others, at the Dwelling-house of the said Edward Gilham, . . . and with assaulting the said Edward Gilham, and Anne his Wife, and breaking the Windows of his Dwelling-house. G. A.——*If there be no more Felony in the Mayor's Commitment than is recorded by this Historian, these Fellows will soon recover their Liberty.*

On Tuesday last a Gentleman was robb'd by three Fellows near West-ham in Essex, who took from him his Watch, Money, and Hat. There was another Gentleman within 50 Yards of him, but he had his Sword in one Hand, and a Link in the other, neither of which Weapons they chose to contend with, and so he got clear off. Id.——*The latter Gentleman should certainly have lent one of his Weapons to the former.*

THE COVENT-GARDEN JOURNAL, No. 2, 7 Jan. 1752

MODERN HISTORY.

CUM NOTIS VARIORUM.

—Sunt quædam mediocria; Sunt mala plura.

SATURDAY, *Jan.* 5.

A Few Days ago a Quarrel happened in a very eminent Coffee-House in the Strand: A Taylor and a Cabinet Maker were chattering over a Dish of Coffee, when the Taylor took an Opportunity to reprove the Cabinet-Maker for prophane Swearing, which Usage the Cabinet-Maker resented with some severe Sarcasms on his Antagonist's Profession, and that he was sorry he ever should stand in Need of the Advice of a Taylor. This enraged the Taylor so much, that, *in Honour of his Profession,* he struck him a Blow; the Cabinet-Maker made no Return, but challenged him at Sword and Pistol, with which the Taylor was willing likewise to comply; but his Antagonist, upon second Thoughts, refused that also, and declared he would take the Law for this Usage; upon which the Taylor swore that he should not take the Law for nothing, and repeated his Blows with double Keenness; and after giving him a hearty Drubbing, desired him calmly to walk Home, and hold a Consultation with his Attorney. D. G.——*Nothing can be more glorious than the Light in which this Taylor here appears; who was at once the Champion of his Religion and of his Profession. It is Pity, however, that so Great a Man should give a Countenance to the present abominable Custom of Duelling, which, it seems, had the Cabinet-Maker been of a non-legal Disposition, he was inclined to have done.*

On Thursday Night the Wife of Richard Broughton went to see her Husband, who is now chain'd down in the Cells in Newgate, for robbing Capt. Gould of a Gold Watch and several Guineas, a few Weeks since, when, after staying some Time, she took her Leave of him, and went out and robb'd one Mr. John Busher of his Silver Watch, for which she was Yesterday committed to Newgate; when it is to be hoped they will both go out together next Time, and receive a proper Punishment due to their Crimes. Id.——*It is indeed Pity to part so fond a Couple, who seem to possess that Congruity of Inclinations, so necessary to make the married State happy.*

Last Thursday was married, Mr. Richard Barber, of Buckletsbury, to Miss Cooke of Ludgate Hill, an agreeable young Lady, *with all Accomplishments to render the*

Marriage State truly happy. L. D. A.——Q. *What are the Accomplishments necessary to render this State truly happy?*

Yesterday Morning a Chairman and a Groom went to fight in Hyde Park: The first Blow was given by the Groom, and the second was given by the Chairman, which killed the Groom on the Spot; the Chairman was taken into Custody.——*This is a better Way of duelling than with Sword and Pistol; and, as it appears, equally effectual to all good Purposes.*

Yesterday three loose and disorderly Women, were committed to Bridewell to hard Labour, by Benjamin Cox, Esq; not being able to give a good Account of themselves. Id.——*How is it possible that loose and disorderly Women should give a good Account of themselves?*

Dublin, Dec. 28. We have the Pleasure of informing the Public, that the Hospital for Lunaticks and Ideots, founded by the late Dr. Swift, is so forward, by the Care of the Governors, as to be intirely prepared for the Reception of Female Patients, there being 27 Cells in the Eastern Range of the Building made ready for the Accommodation of Women. Id.——*And we have the Pleasure of informing the Governors that we have full as many female Patients intirely prepared for the said Hospital.*

It is a Point of great Consequence in the *Education* of *Youth*, to instil virtuous and useful *Habits* as soon as possible; the good Effects of which will appear . . . from the following Observation, in the *Journal* of a *Foreign Merchant*: 'The Children at *Nurembergh*,' said he, 'are imploy'd in *making Toys*, at the very same Age that the Children in *London* spend their Time in *breaking* them.' The Consequence is very just, and very rational: The first Price of the Toys is the *Premium* which the *Nuremberghers* receive for promoting *Industry* so *early*, and which might remain *here*, if the Children of such as have *no Money* to *buy* Toys, were employed in *making* them for *those* that *have*. L. E.——*Persons who have Money in this Kingdom, have very little Regard for the Children of those who have none.*

Last Saturday Mr. Robert Gillingham, an eminent *Malt Distiller* in Barbican, was married to Miss Wells, *a Cornfactor* in the Borough; an agreeable *young Lady*, with a Fortune of 3000 l. L. D. A.

And at the same time was married Mr. Wells, Junior, to Miss Gillingham, Sister of Mr Robert Gillingham; *a young Lady* of fine Accomplishments with a Fortune of 2000 l. Id.——*Nothing can be more natural than this double Alliance between Meat and Malt.*

Last Saturday the Jury sat on the Body of the Man kill'd in Hyde Park in a Boxing-Match, and brought in their Verdict, Accidental Death. D. A.——*This is, I suppose, according to the usual Phrase* accidentally on Purpose.

On Friday Night two of the Malefactors under Sentence of Death in Newgate attempted to make their Escape, by sawing their Irons off, but were prevented by the Keepers, and more strongly secured by being chain'd down. Id.——*Fellows who have had a Right to be delivered out of Newgate so long ago, are not to be blamed for attempting to escape.*

Last Friday a young Woman in Piccadilly stabb'd her Uncle in the Back with a Case-Knife. A Surgeon was directly sent for, and, 'tis hop'd, the Wound will not prove mortal. Id.——*Parricide is become very common among the Fair Sex.*[1]

THE COVENT-GARDEN JOURNAL, No. 3, 11 Jan. 1752

MODERN HISTORY
ABRIDG'D.

CANTERBURY, Jan. 8. We hear last Saturday Evening about Six o'Clock, Mr. Michael Lade, on his Return to his House at Boughton from this City, was attacked by a Footpad at some Distance beyond Harbledown Turnpike, who suddenly took hold of the Bridle of his Horse, when Mr. Lade saying he would not be robbed, was soon knocked off; but, making a stout Resistance, he saved his Money, tho' the Villain took an Opportunity to mount his Horse, and rode off towards London.

It is said that one of the Dragoons quartered here is very much suspected, he having been missing ever since the Affair happened. W. E.——*If this Suspicion should prove true, the Thief was Horseman, Footman, and Dragoon.*

THE COVENT-GARDEN JOURNAL, No. 4, 14 Jan. 1752

MODERN HISTORY
ABRIDG'D.

SATURDAY, *Jan.* 11.

We hear that several Parishes, in and about the City of London; as also a great many Towns, in different Parts of this Kingdom, have sent Proposals and Petitions to the Gentlemen who have the Conduct of the Undertaking of the Herring-Fishery; desiring *that their numerous and burthensome Poor* may be employed in making Nets and Cordage, for the British Busses. G. A.——*Perhaps we should read a Part of their numerous,* &c. POLITICUS.

On Monday Night last, *a most sorry Fellow,* a Hackney Coachman, overturn'd Mr. Kent, a Common council-man and his Wife, wilfully in his Coach upon Clerkenwell Green, but providentially they received no great Damage, only spoiling their Cloaths; but a Prosecution is carrying on against the Fellow, to *make an Example* of him. Id.——*The Prosecution will possibly make him* a more sorry *Fellow than he is; but he is already* an Example *to all his Brother Coachmen.* PUNICUS.

We hear that the several Holes in the Pavement in Part of Cheapside, by which many Coaches have of late narrowly escaped being overturned, are to remain so for a considerable Time longer; for when it becomes much worse in general than it is, and some notable Mischief is done by it, 'twill be time enough new-pave the whole in a handsome and elegant Manner, as it is one of the finest Streets in Europe. Id.—— *Here the Coachmen seem to have a Right to call for an* Example *in their Turn; as this*

---

[1] Alluding to the case of Mary Blandy; see *CGJ* Nos. 11 and 20.

Passage seems to *imply that there are* some very sorry Fellows *who do not live by* driving; *unless it be* by driving a Trade. Pu.

Yesterday at Noon a Man about Fifty meanly dressed, was beat down at the End of Charles Court in the Strand, by a Porter that had on his Back Three Iron-Bars; by which Accident he was killed on the Spot. The Porter was coming up the Court just as the Poor Man passed the End of it; and the Irons unluckily met his Temple. He was immediately carried to St. Martin's Roundhouse to be own'd. Id.——*Some little Enquiry ought likewise to have been made after the Porter: For the worthy Body who are called by that Name, by their Insolence and Carelessness, make one Species of those numerous Nusances that infest the public Streets.* POL.

Last Thursday as a Gardener was lading his Cart with Dung in Whitecross-Street, he luckily found concealed in Papers a Quantity of Halfpence, to the Amount of Ten Pounds, in five Shilling Parcels, and tied with Packthread; *but how they came there, is at present a Secret.* L. G.——*Where should a Quantity of Halfpence be so properly deposited? for if Gold to a Wise Man is but Dirt, sure Brass cannot be better than Dung; and the wise Man who found these Halfpence seems to think so; or it would have been as profound a Secret how they went from the Dunghill, as how they came there.* GELOSOPHUS.

Yesterday Morning, about Seven o'Clock, Mr. Lebass, *an eminent* and wealthy Malster of Mansfield, was married at St. George's Bloomsbury, to Miss Louisa Manshall, of the same Place; *an agreeable Lady*, with a Fortune of 5000 l. Id.—— *For* LADY, *must be read* GENTLEWOMAN; *for Mr. Censor suffers no Ladies to marry Malsters, though ever so eminent and wealthy.* C. C.

Yesterday Morning two private Centinels of the First Regiment of Foot Guards were severely whipt on the Parade in St. James's Park. As they were bringing from the Savoy to the Parade, guarded by a File of Musqueteers, one of them broke the Shew-Glass of a Silversmith in the Strand, and took out a Gold Watch, which was found on him in St. James's Park, and delivered to the Owner. S. J. E.——*The Historian is silent to what became of the Offender: For whipping could not be the Punishment for this Offence.* POL.

Yesterday Mr. Henderson, Author of the Edinburgh History of the Rebellion, was admitted Keeper of Westminster Hall; a Place of great Trust and considerable Profits. Id.——*It seems more easy to account for* the great Profits, *than for* the great Trust. INCERTI.

We hear that, in a *certain* Country, there are still some *wrongheaded* People, who remain firmly persuaded that while *Taxes* are *high*, and *Interest low*, *Sine Cures* in Government, that is, *Offices* not executed, or not executed by *those* who hold them, are *Grievances* in the *same Proportion* with the *Profits* arising from them.

—There seems to be just Reason to *apprehend*, from that Eagerness with which a certain Nation lays hold of every Opportunity of setting in *new Islands*, and breaking up *fresh* Ground for *Sugars* in the *West Indies*, that they carry on some *collusive Trade* to *Europe*, as well as that which is *apparent*; tho' the latter is so very *considerable*. So that, in Time, those that have been their *Rivals*, may come to be their *Dependents*.

—Certain Advices from *Germany*, which have been likewise printed in our *own* Language, seem to intimate, that it is not enough for a *Nation*, that shall be at present *nameless*, to remain *steady* herself to the *Common Cause*; but that it is expected she should furnish a certain *Weight* of *Metal* to *fix* all such as are *wavering*, either thro' *Interest* or *Inclination*. L. E.——*Several Critics have puzzled in vain on these three obscure Paragraphs; but as from the many Italic Characters we are sure they contain both Wit and Politics, it is no wonder they are unintelligible.*

THE COVENT-GARDEN JOURNAL, No. 5, 18 Jan. 1752

MODERN HISTORY.

CUM NOTIS VARIORUM.

A Grant has also pass'd the Great Seal for a new invented Oil that gives almost present Ease in Fits of the Gravel and Stone. G. A.——*This is a very good Article of News, if the latter Part of it be true.* INCERTI.

We hear from Dublin, that they talk much of a Scheme which has been proposed to the Lord Lieutenant for erecting in that Country an Academy for teaching military Exercises, and modern Languages . . . ; it were to be wished that they could have taken the *Hint* of such a Thing from us, who want it at least as much, and can afford it better; but perhaps we shall not be ashamed to *follow an Example which we ought to have shewn.* Id.——*If this Politician intends to convey* any Hint *to the Government,* he ought to have shewn *a little more what he means.* I.

They write from Newcastle, that George Bowes, Esq; Member for the County of Durham, has given 200 l. to be distributed in several Parishes in Newcastle, amongst the Poor that are sick. Id.——*This is an Example which no Man, I am sure, need be ashamed to follow.* I.

Tuesday Evening some Rogues found means to get into the Kitchen Window of a House belonging to Mrs. Stevens in Crane Court, Fleet-Street, and stole from thence Kitchen-Furniture, to the Amount of Five Pounds, notwithstanding a Watchman is placed at the Bottom of the Court. Id.——*This is a hard Reflection upon a Watchman, who was, perhaps, asleep, or warming himself at a Night-House; in either of which Cases he could not possibly have prevented the Robbery.* G.

Yesterday the large spread Brilliant Diamond, was sold at Chadwell's Coffee House, to Mr. How, a Banker in Lombard-Street, for 312 Pounds. D. A.——*This was either no very large Brilliant, or no very large Price.* G.

This Day a general Court-Martial will sit on the Grenadier, who, a few Days ago, would not submit to be punished on the Parade, but requested to be tried by a general Court-Martial. This Fellow was once himself a Corporal, but by some Act of Misdemeanour was reduced to a common Station. His Crime was for striking his Corporal, when he came to call him, and some others who were asleep in the Guard-Room, to go out upon Duty: He imagined the Corporal used him roughly, and, as it was by his Means that he himself was reduced from that Station, he beat him heartily, for which 150 Lashes were decreed him, and *now that he has exposed himself to a second Trial, it is thought his Lashes will be doubled.* D. G.——*If so he will pay very heavy Costs for his Appeal. But, whatever be the Fate of this poor Fellow, his Spirit seems too great for the common Station he is reduced to, or even to the uncommon Station he was reduced from.* C.

On Tuesday last two Serjeants were examined before the Worshipful Justice Fraser, charged by a Woman who keeps a disorderly House in Spring Gardens, for not paying the Reckoning she charged them, which they imagined was exorbitant. In the Course of the Riot the Serjeants broke a Punch-Bowl, which his Worship ordered them to pay for, and, as her Reckoning seemed an Imposition, the Serjeants were dismissed, and she ordered to Bridewell. Id.——*There must be some Mistake* in the Report of this Case *before the Worshipful Justice. Persons who keep a disorderly House may, on a proper Information, be bound over to the Sessions, and committed for Want of Sureties; but by no Law of England can a Housekeeper be sent to Bridewell* because her Reckoning seemed an Imposition. C.

We hear that the learned English Dog, so much talked of, and mentioned in the Papers, that, in an inimitable Manner, performs vast Variety of surprising Actions, far beyond what the late Chien savant, or any other Creature of that Kind, was ever capable of, *is now learning the Greek Alphabet*, and will shortly be exhibited to the Speculation of the Curious somewhere about Charing-Cross. D. A.——*This is not at all surprizing: for the Greek Language hath been long since gone to the Dogs.* C.

Yesterday Stroud, who has defrauded several Tradesmen to a very great Value, received the first Part of his Sentence, by being severely whipt by the common Hangman, in Gerrard-street. Mr Carne, the High Constable of Westminster, rode in the Cart to see the Executioner do his Duty, and two Constables walked at the Horses Heads, to prevent the Driver going too fast. L. D. A.——*Whatever the Driver did, it is hoped the Hangman whipt on.*[1]. Pu.

THE COVENT-GARDEN JOURNAL, No. 6, 21 Jan. 1752

MODERN HISTORY.

Cum notis variorum.

Saturday, *Jan.* 18.

Yesterday in the Dusk of the Evening, a Gentleman going along Walbrook, was knock'd down by a Tile that fell from the Top of one of the old Houses facing the Mansion-House.—It is very extraordinary that such a shocking Piece of Ruins should be suffered to remain Year after Year in a principal Part of this populous City, every one that passes by being in danger of losing his Life, and when this Truth is proved by the Loss of a few of his Majesty's Subjects, the Proprietor doubtless to retaliate for so Trifling an Affair, will consent to their being pulled down. G.A.——

[1] See *CGJ* No. 51.

If a Nusance of this Kind, which is abatable by Law, be suffered to continue, the Proprietor is not the only Person in Fault. C.

On Wednesday last, between Ten and Eleven at Night, betwixt the thirteen and fourteen Miles Stone, about two Miles and a half from Epping, . . . George Carey, Higgler, with his Son and two other Men, returning from Leadenhall Market, in a Cart, were stopp'd by two Footpads; one of which got into the Cart, and, with his Pistol at the Head of Carey, demanded his Money: Carey gave him eleven Shillings; he insisted he had not given him all; the poor Man desired him to have Patience; but, while he was searching for the rest, the Villain shot him through the Head, and immediately flung his Body out of the Cart. He then asked his Comrade for another Pistol, which he snapp'd twice at another Man in the Cart, calling him by his Name, Jack Green; and asked him if he did not know him, and bid him look in his Face; which he did, and protested he did not know him. He then took down Jack Green's Breeches, and was going to cut off his private Parts; but, changing his Mind, cut him about the Face with a long Knife, and give him two or three Thrusts with it in his Side. He then cut the Son of the Deceas'd over the Head, and threaten'd him with his Father's Fate if, ever he travell'd that Road again. Then they emptied the Cart of all the Baskets; which, when they had rifled, they helped to throw again into the Cart, as also the dead Body. . . . L. E.——*The Barbarity of these Villains is grown to such an enormous Height, that the immediate Suppression of them is become a Matter of the utmost Consequence. This we can, with Pleasure, assure the Public, is at present the chief Attention of Parliament; but, even as the Law now stands, if every honest Man would think it as much his Concern, and his Duty, as it really is, to detect such Villains as these, they would not long escape the Punishment they deserve.* C.

A young Tradesman in a small Market-Town in the Fens of Lincolnshire, desirous of getting a large Fortune with all Expedition, resolved on Smuggling, as the most convenient Method; accordingly he agreed with a Smuggler for a Hundred Weight of Tea, at eleven Guineas, and to pay him upon the Delivery of the Goods, which was punctually performed; but, upon opening the Bag, to his great Disappointment, found all his Tea, (except a very small Quantity) *metamorphosed into Black Oats.*—A just Reward of such fraudulent Practices. W. E.——*As the Smuggler had plainly made an Ass of this Tradesman, I suppose he thought Oats were more agreeable to his Palate than Tea.* M.

On Thursday next the Royal Society will chuse one of their Members into the Council; and on Saturday elect a Secretary; both vacant by the Death of Dr. Mortimer. G. A.——*It is generally believed that the Rev. Mr. Birch, a Gentleman of great Merit in the learned World, will be chosen.*[1] C.

Yesterday was married at St. Giles Church, Mr. Whittle the younger, *an eminent Carver* and Gilder, to Miss Phipps of Old-street, Niece to the late Mr. Gabriel Johnston of New Inn, a young Lady possessed of many amiable Qualities, and a Fortune of 3000 l.——*This young Lady hath* carved eminently well *for herself.* PUNICUS.

---

[1] Thomas Birch (1705–66), historian and friend of Fielding.

We are assured, that at the Rev. Mr. Keith's Chapel in May Fair, 2340 Couples have been (happily, it is hoped) united in the *lasting Noose*, within the Space of two Years. Id.——*Other Copies read* last Noose; *which is not agreeable to Truth, some of them having, to our Knowledge, been tied in another Noose since, more according to Law. It is Pity, however, that the Epithet of* lasting *is not taken* away *from this* Chapel *by the Legislature, it being the Occasion of infinite Mischief to the Society.*[1]   C.

On Friday last a pretty singular Instance happened to a Gentleman in Westminster, as he was standing at the Door of his own House; a Person plainly dress'd, with a Box in his Hand, came up to him, and told him that he came from the City, and was desired to deliver it to him. . . . Upon opening the Box, there was found a Letter, written in a great Variety of Hands, to prevent a Discovery, and two Playhouse Bills, in which something seemed to be wrapp'd: On opening the Bundle, eight Guineas were carefully concealed, and in the Letter was wrote, "Sir, the Inclosed is your's honestly your's, ask no Questions, and you shall never know from whom this come." D. G.——*This is a new Kind of Sharper, but his Gang is probably not very numerous.*

THE COVENT-GARDEN JOURNAL, No. 7, 25 Jan. 1752

MODERN HISTORY.

CUM NOTIS VARIORUM.

WEDNESDAY, *Jan.* 22.

Saturday last died, aged 84 Years, *an eminent and wealthy Hardwareman* at Mile End. His Fortune, which is very considerable, he has bequeathed to his two Nephews, with this remarkable Clause in his Will, that they never presume to smoke any Tobacco, on the Forfeiture of losing the Interest of 4000 l. and to devolve to their Sisters. D. G.——*The name of this anonymous eminent Person, (if he had any) will possibly, by means of this Clause, be well known in Westminster-Hall.* M.

Last Week died, at Seafield, near Whitehaven, in the County of Cumberland, Mr. Henry Townson and Bridget his Wife, aged 100 Years each; who after *living in conjugal Affection nigh* 70 Years, and enjoying a perfect State of Health till almost the last, expired within a few Minutes of each other. D. A.——*Both these seem to have enjoyed every Qualification necessary to make the married State happy.* M.

Yesterday there was the highest Tide that has been known for some time; the Houses, Kitchens, and Cellars about Scotland-yard, Whitehall, &c. were all filled with Water; *as was also Westminster-Hall*, and all the Houses about New Palace-Yard and Vine-street, and the Horse-ferry, Westminster. G. A.——*This Rising of the Tide the first Day of Term, portends possibly some good Omen to the Law, which hath lately been at* a very low Ebb. M.

---

[1] Although the Revd Alexander Keith (d. 1758) was currently a prisoner in the Fleet, marriages continued to be performed in his chapel in Mayfair without banns or license. The practice was ended by the Marriage Act of 1753 (26 Geo. II, c. 33).

THE COVENT-GARDEN JOURNAL, No. 9, 30 Jan. 1752

MODERN HISTORY.

Cum notis variorum.

Thursday, *Jan.* 30.

They tell us from Cudderstone in Yorkshire, that on the 25th ult. one Mark Newby eat at one Meal, and in less than half an Hour's Time, twenty Pounds of Pudding, eleven of Mutton, four Gallons of Broth, three of churn'd Milk, and an entire Giblet Pye.   G. E.——*This Fellow may be said to have had a good Swallow; and the Historian seems to think his Readers have no bad one.*   C.

Last Saturday Morning . . . Stage-Coaches were robbed by a single Highwayman. . . . He had on a drab colour'd Frize Horseman's Coat, his Hat a little flapt, a brown Natural Wig, and affected much the Air of a *Drover:* He behaved with great Civility as a Highwayman, for being desired (as he seem'd timorous, and his Hand shook) to withdraw his Pistol, he immediately returned it into his Bridle Hand, desiring the Passengers would not be affrighted, his Intent being only to get a little Money to supply a present Necessity. On his riding off, he dropt 4 s. 6 d. to treat the Passengers in one of the Coaches with a Breakfast.   Id.——*Tho' I have not disturbed the Text, from the Description of this Man's Behaviour, I suspect that instead of* Drover, *we should read* Courtier.   C.

Extract of a Letter from Norwich, Jan. 27.

"Last Week this City was full of Uproar and Riot, with the Mobbers, they began this Day again with Drums and Clappers, beating the People, &c. and tho' Mr. Wheatly had three Constables to guard him, they beat him and the Constables in a barbarous manner, and so covered them with Dirt and Mud, that they could hardly be known." . . .   S. J. E.——*The Writers on our Constitution, when they mention only three Estates, are guilty of a great Omission in leaving out the fourth Estate,* the Mob; *which seem at present in a fair Way to get the better of all the rest.*   C.[1]

On Tuesday last a Gentleman, who lives next Door to the Turk's Head Bagnio, Spring-Gardens, had two Suits of Laced Cloaths stolen from him by his Barber, a Fellow who has shav'd him for seven Years; he stript the Lace off them, and went to Mr. Kilby, an eminent Salesman, and sold it; who upon seeing them advertised, returned it immediately to the Gentleman, and great Search is making for the Thief.   D. G.——*If the eminent Salesman had been as circumspect when he bought the Lace, as he was honest when he returned it,* this cunning Shaver *would not have been now to search after.*   M.

Yesterday was committed to Newgate, by William Withers, Esq; Anne Walson, . . . upon a violent and strong Suspicion of the said Anne Walson's violently assaulting Anne Ellard, a Child, about fourteen Years of Age, and forcibly strangling the said Anne Ellard with a Woolen Garter, that she died on the Spot.   Id.——*More shocking*

---

[1] Cf. *CGJ* Nos. 47 and 49.

Murders have been committed within this last Year, than for many Years before. To what can this he so justly imputed, as to the manifest Decline of Religion among the lower People. A Matter which, even in a civil Sense, demands the Attention of the Government.

THE COVENT-GARDEN JOURNAL, No. 10, 1 Feb. 1752

MODERN HISTORY.

CUM NOTIS VARIORUM.

SATURDAY, *Feb.* 1.

A Gentlewoman, and her Daughters . . . were attacked by two Highwaymen, one of whom stopt the Coach, and the other came to the Door, to demand their Money; upon which the Gentlewoman, presenting a Pistol, *told him she was prepared for him*, and ordered the Coachman to drive on, which he did accordingly, and the Highwaymen put Spurs to their Horses *and rode off* full Speed towards London, without their Booty. G. E.——*The Part of a Man was acted on this Occasion, but not by the Highwaymen, who rode away from the Lady, when she said she was prepared for him.*

Thursday being the Anniversary of the Martyrdom of King Charles, according to annual Custom, forty poor Taylors walked in Procession to Black-Friars Church, agreeable to the Will of Mr. Cato, a Master Taylor, and heard a Sermon preached by the Rev. Mr. Grainger, Rector of that Parish: 'Tis worth observing that the Donor's Will is always read by the Minister in the Church, who has 1 l. 15 s. for preaching a Sermon suitable to the Occasion, and the poor Men each 20 s. St. J. E.——*It is hard that the Minister should be no better paid for preaching his Sermon, when the Taylors are so well paid for hearing it.* M.

We hear from Esher in Surry, *that a young Gentleman of an academical Education*, on Saturday last, met with two Gypsey Women, who undertook to tell him his Fortune, but said they could not do it without the Help of Gold, and that they must make use of four Guineas, which they would seal up in a Handkerchief, and give him again, but that he was not to open it till next Day; (when by the Help of their Art) he would be directed to an hundred Pounds and a Gold Watch, concealed in a certain Place; accordingly he gave them four Guineas, which the Fortunetellers pretended to seal up in the Handkerchief, and then took their Leave. On the Expiration of the Time, he opened the Charm, and found that the four Guineas were metamorphosed into four Halfpence, which fully satisfied his Expectations as to the Money and Watch he was promised to be directed to. Id.——*If this silly Story be true, the young Gentleman must have had his Academical Education in the* University of Goatam. M.

There happened lately a very odd Affair, at a Village in Surry; a Rag-man driving an Ass, which was some Distance before him, there stood a Bason of *Julep* at an Apothecary's Door, which the Ass drank up; he had scarce finished when the Apothecary seized and detained him till his Driver came up, to whom he complained, his Ass had drank a Bason of Julep which cost him a Crown, and insisted on his paying for it, which the Rag-man refusing, he took him before a Justice, whom he informed of the Affair, and desired his Worship would oblige the Rag-man to give him Satisfaction. The Justice, after searching his Statute Book, paus'd some time, and at last told them it was an Affair he could not well decide himself, and referred them to a boozing Cobler in the Neighbourhood, who, he said, understood those Matters as well as any Man in England. Both Parties agreed to stand by Crispin's Decision, and he was accordingly sent for; the Justice immediately inform'd him upon what Account, and the Cobler, seem'd pleas'd with his Office, but desired, if he was to act as a Justice, he might sit in his Worship's Chair. The Justice complied, and the Cobler being seated, the whole Matter was laid before him; Pray, Sir, said the cobling Magistrate, did the Ass drink the Julep at one Draught? which was answered in the Affirmative. Very well, replied the worshipful Crispin, Did the Ass sit down? he was answered No. Why then said he I can decide this Affair immediately. It is a Custom among Topers, that any Man may drink once standing for Nothing; therefore you, Rag-man, go about your Business. The Case being given against the Apothecary, so enraged him that he cursed the new Justice, who made him pay for his Oath, and advised him to put the next Julep he made out of the Ass's Way. Id.——*A famous Punster on reading this facetious Paragraph declared that this Julep was* JULAPIUM ASSMATICUM. T.

On Wednesday died advanced in Years, at his Lodgings at Hampton, Mr. Wade, formerly an eminent Apothecary in the Strand, but having acquired a handsome Fortune, had retired from Business. G. A. And,

On Wednesday died Mr. Harding, an eminent Apothecary, *in Partnership* with Mr. Monk in Crutched-fryars. Id.——*It may, perhaps, be thought extraordinary that an Apothecary and an Half should die on the same Day.* M.

On Friday Night last, some Rogues found Means to take the Leaden Spouts off the Top of a Gentleman's House in Albermarle-Street, but as they were letting them down by Ropes into the Street, they missed their Hold, and the Spouts fell into the Area, which made a great Noise, and alarmed the Family, and the Watchmen coming, they saw two Fellows upon the House Top, whom they went in search of but to no Purpose, *for they got clear off.* Id. ——*Q. Where the Watchmen went to search?* M.

Some Measures are concerted, and will soon be proposed to Parliament, for preventing all Beggars from being seen in the Streets, by which it is thought a great Number of Robberies will be prevented, as Thieves often follow People disguised like Beggars, and when they are in a convenient Place, throw off the Mask, and more easily commit a Robbery. D. G.——*Whoever finds a Way to put an End to Beggars, will incidentally, I believe, put an End to Thieves.*

The following Epigram was made by a Gentleman of Distinction on his third Marriage.

> Terna mihi ducta est variis Ætatibus Uxor,
> Hæc Juveni, illa Viro, tertia nupta Seni est
> Prima est propter *Opus*, teneris mihi nupta sub Annis
> Altera propter *Opes*, tertia propter *Opem*. L. D. A.

Three Times I took for better and for worse,
A Bed-Fellow, a Fortune, and a Nurse:
How blest the State, which such good Things produce!
How dear that Sex which serves such various Use! C.

THE COVENT-GARDEN JOURNAL, No. 11, 8 Feb. 1752

MODERN HISTORY.

Cum notis variorum.

Thursday, *Feb.* 6.

On Tuesday a Precept was issued by the Lord Mayor, strictly enjoining all the Constables, Beadles, and other Officers of this City and Liberties thereof, to apprehend all idle and disorderly Persons, who shall be found assembling together about illegal Sports and Pastimes, particularly with Wheelbarrows or other Things for playing with Dice; or who shall be found on Shrove Tuesday, or any other Day, throwing at Cocks, &c. And it is hoped that every sober and humane Person, under whose Observation Irregularities of this Kind may fall, will . . . have the Spirit to exert themselves, and give Notice to the Constables, &c. that they may execute the abovesaid Order, which none of them can refuse without incurring severe Penalties.   L. D. A.——*A certain Magistrate of the County of Middlesex, riding in his Coach through Broad-Street on Thursday Morning, while a large Mob was there assembled throwing at Cocks, stopt his Coach, and sent his Servant for a Constable; but just before the Officer's Arrival, some Person to whom the Justice was known, gave the Alarm, and within two Minutes, neither Mob nor Cocks were to be seen.* C.

On Tuesday Morning, between One and Two o'Clock, three House-breakers attempted to get in at the two Pair of Stairs Window backwards, of the House of Mr. Savage, the Red-Lion, at Stoke-Newington, but were over-heard by the Maid-Servant, who alarmed her Master, and a Soldier who was quartered there, on which they *made off, leaving behind them a Ladder and a Pair of Shoes.*   L. G.——*These Fellows will scarce make off at least without their Shoes, or without a Ladder.*   M.

On Tuesday last the Waiting Maid of a Lady in Burlington-Street, went into a Linnen-Draper's Shop and cheapned some Goods, and found an Opportunity of stealing some Lawn, &c. but the People of the Shop perceiving it, followed her Home, and found their Goods upon her, upon which she was immediately *discharged her Service.*   Id.——*It is hoped this Waiting Maid was not so soon discharged as she appears to have been in this Paragraph.*   C.

Friday.

Last Saturday a Serjeant in a Marching Regiment came to London to receive a Legacy of 50 l. . . . Early on Monday Morning the Soldier set out on his Way Home, but on Barnes-Common was overtaken by three Fellows dressed like Sailors, who walked with him about half a Mile, when they all pulled out Pistols and demanded his Money, but he making some Resistance with his Sword, they cut and beat him in a most terrible Manner, robbed him of all his Money, and left him for dead, making off towards Putney. D. A.——*It is so extremely easy to take these Fellows, that if they escape, it is hoped this brave unhappy Serjeant will be redressed by the Hundred.*

We hear the Comedy called *The Comical Lovers* will be revived for the Benefit of Mrs. Clive on Monday the 9th of March; to which will be added *Miss in her Teens*, the Part of Fribble by Mr. Garrick, being the only Time of his performing it this Season. G. A.——*Mrs. Clive in her Walk on the Stage is the greatest Actress the World ever saw; and if as many really understood true Humour as pretend to understand it, she would have nothing to wish, but that the House was six Times as large as it is.* C.

THE COVENT-GARDEN JOURNAL, No. 12, 11 Feb. 1752

MODERN HISTORY.

CUM NOTIS VARIORUM.

SATURDAY.

An Order is issued out to the High Constable of Westminster to apprehend all Persons, who shall be found gaming in the Court of Requests, and Places adjacent, during the Sitting of Parliament. D. A.——*This Order, we apprehend, doth not extend through the whole Liberty of Westminster.* C.

Tuesday died Mrs. Matthews, Wife of Mr. Matthews, *an eminent Glover*, opposite Bow Church in Cheapside. St. J. E.

The same Day died Mr. Price, *an eminent Timber Merchant* at Black-Friars. Id.

Thursday died in the Cells of Newgate, William Baylis, who was capitally convicted the last Sessions for a Burglary. Id.——*He was an eminent Rogue.* M.

Yesterday died at his Lodgings in Red Lion Street, aged 76, Mr. Peter Doubiac, an eminent Jeweller; a Man famous for his extensive Knowledge in old Coins. G. E.——*But more famous for his extensive Life.*

MONDAY.

On Thursday last *an uncommon Piece of Villany* was transacted in the Fields between Stepney-Causeway and Shadwell: As two Gentlemen were passing along, a Fellow comes running up to them without Hat or Wig, declaring he had been robbed, and entreated their Assistance to take the Rogues, which they agreed to; but they had not gone far before two other Villains jumped from behind a Hedge, who, with the former that pretended to be robbed, set upon the Gentlemen and robbed them of their Money and Watches, and then made off. L. D. A.——*This is a very common Piece of Villany.*

THE COVENT-GARDEN JOURNAL, No. 13, 15 Feb. 1752

MODERN HISTORY.

CUM NOTIS VARIORUM.

Yesterday Mr. Thompson and Mr. Spiers, two Farmers of Ealing, ran each a Cart

Load of Hay, drawn by two Horses, from Ealing to the White-Horse in Rupert-street, near the Haymarket, for a Wager of 3 Guineas, which was won by the former.   G. A.——*If this extraordinary Race had been run down St. James's Street, very considerable Betts might possibly have been laid upon it. But since this sportive Humour is descended among the Farmers, some Races between Dung-Pots are shortly expected of which it is hoped, timely Notice will be given.*   C.

Last Week was married at Hatfield in Yorkshire, Mr. William Calvert, an eminent *wholesale Cheesemonger* in Thames-street, to Miss Okes, of Stockton.   D. A. . . .

Last Week Mr. Thomas James, an *eminent Gardiner* at Lambeth, was married to Mrs. Ann James, an agreeable Widow Lady, with a Fortune of 600 l. per Ann.   L. D. A.

We hear that there is a Treaty of Marriage on Foot between Mr. George Brown, an eminent Double Japanner, and Mrs. Thumper, Relict of Mr. Edward Thumper, late an eminent Drummer in the Third Regiment of Guards. An agreeable Widow Lady of great Merit, Beauty and Fortune; and every, &c.

THE COVENT-GARDEN JOURNAL, No. 14, 18 Feb. 1752

MODERN HISTORY.

Cum notis variorum.

Saturday.

On Thursday Morning a Bye-Coach from Bath, in which were *three Ladies of Pleasure*, was attacked near Hamersmith, by two Highwaymen, who robbed them of eighteen Shillings and a Metal Watch.   G. E.——*They will possibly return the Ladies their own with Interest.*   C.

Last Night, between Six and Seven o'Clock, four young Gentlemen were attacked and robbed by two Footpads with Pistols, in the Field between Marybone and Cavendish-square, of about six Guineas. They were both young Lads, and pretty well dressed, and one of them had on a Bag-Wig. The young Gentlemen were much frighted, and went to a Publick-House, from whence some Company pursued them, but to no Purpose, for they were got clear off.   G. A.——*It is not very clear from this Historian, whether the four young Gentlemen, or the two young Gentlemen, were the frighted Persons.*

We are credibly informed that Mr. Powell, the surprizing Fire-Eater, that has had the Honour of exhibiting his surprizing Performance before most of the Nobility and Gentry of London and Westminster, . . . is to exhibit the same . . . this Evening at Six o'Clock, at Mr. Compton's, at the Bull-Head, Bread-street, Cheapside.   Id.

Yesterday Afternoon, about Four o'Clock, a Fire broke out in the Sugar-House of Mr. Lechmere, in Three-Tun Court, in Thames-street, which by timely Assistance of several Engines, and a great Plenty of Water, was prevented from spreading to any other House.   G. A.——*Quare, Whether the abovementioned Mr. Powell might not be of Service on such Occasion.*

On Saturday last Stroud was whipped the second Time, from the Admiralty-Office to the Mews Gate. As soon as he got out of the Coach in which he was brought from the Goal, he threw some Money amongst the Mob, who thereupon pressed so close on the Executioner, that he had not Power to strike ten Times during the whole Length of the Way. He is to be whipt again the 16th of March, from the Corner of the Haymarket, through Pall-mall, to the Turning into St. James's-square. Id.——
Another Historian says the Crowd was so great that it was difficult to pass the Streets. To say Truth, these monthly Whippings are a Novelty to the People of England. C.[1]

THE COVENT-GARDEN JOURNAL, No. 15, 22 Feb. 1752

MODERN HISTORY.

CUM NOTIS VARIORUM.

THURSDAY.

We hear from Covent-Garden that a certain Justice has so well learnt the Art of getting a Penny, that he sold the first Number of an excellent Journal, wrote by his good Friend Sir Alexander Drawcanster, at the small Price of Half a Crown; *cum Notis var.*—A remarkable Piece of Modesty this, as of the great Esteem he has for his own Lucubrations. D. G.——*If this Story, which is a notorious Lie, was true, it would be a Proof that there is another Person who hath these Lucubrations in some Esteem besides the Author. As there have been in this Paper many false and dirty Reflections published against this certain Justice, we will only tell one remarkable Piece of Modesty and other good Qualities in the supposed Author.[2] He was some Time since for a Breach of the Peace, brought before this certain Justice whom he had libelled for many Years together. The Justice so much disdained mixing any private Resentment with his public Character, that instead of sending this Fellow to Prison, which as it was very late at Night, he might immediately have done, he let him stay in his House whilst he sent for his Friends, nay even suffered him to sit down in his Presence, and at last by his Persuasion assisted those Friends in compromising the Matter, and obtained Forgiveness for him of the Prosecutor.*

On Wednesday Night died Mr. Mawtass, *Brush Maker*, on Fishstreet-hill. L. D. A.
The same Night died, aged seventy-eight, at his Lodgings at Islington, Mr. Waller, *Hartshorn-Rasper* in the old-Change. Id.——*We hear after lying in State, they will be both interr'd in the Vaults of their Ancestors.*

[1] See *CGJ* No. 51.

[2] Although Fielding uses the initials 'D. G.', the paper to which he refers is presumably the *London Gazetteer*, the successor to the *Daily Gazetteer*; see the introductory notes to this appendix. The editor has been unable to locate a copy of the *London Gazetteer* for 20 Feb. 1751/2, apparently the issue containing the item reprinted here. The 'supposed Author' to whom Fielding refers is probably William Horsley, who wrote under the name of the 'Fool' and whom Fielding had earlier identified as the author of the *Daily Gazetteer* (see *JJ* No. 10, 6 Feb. 1748). Horsley, a writer on economics, was at this date still writing for the *Gazetteer*. He announced his resignation from the paper in a letter, signed with his own name, to *LDA* of 7 July 1752, adding 'What his Wisdom, Sir Alexander, will say on this Occasion, is not, I apprehend, as yet seeded in the Womb of Futurity; but if I have any Skill in Prophecy, he will write a Farce about it, and give the Yclepment of *The Fool turn'd Courtier.*' The 'Covent Garden' columns make no mention of Horsley's appearance in Fielding's court. For ridicule of Fielding's response here, see Thornton's *Drury-Lane Journal*, No. 7 (27 Feb. 1752).

THE COVENT-GARDEN JOURNAL, No. 16, 25 Feb. 1752

MODERN HISTORY.

CUM NOTIS VARIORUM.

SATURDAY.

We hear that *the Quarrel* between the Proprietors of a Pamphlet, lately published, intitled Andro, a new Game at Cards, is amicably adjusted, and that this Day is published the Second Edition of the said Pamphlet, and is to be had of M. Cooper at the Globe in Pater-noster Row, and E. Rowlands, at Pope's Head in Exeter Exchange, and all the Book and Pamphlet Shops in Town and Country.   L. D. A.— —*This Quarrel seems to have ended in a Puff.*   M.

Whereas it hath been falsely asserted in several News Papers, only to impose on the Publick, that I perished by Shipwreck in my Passage to France: This is therefore to convince my Friends of the Untruth, and to assure them, that I intend to return to London, in Pursuance of my Promise, as soon as my Birds shall have acquired sufficient Skill to amuse the Ingenious, when I shall also exhibit my Chien Savant, or learned French Dog . . . P. le Moine.   Id.——*We hear that at the Return of Mons. le Moine, these two learned Dogs are to argue a Question at the Robinhood, for the Entertainment of all Critics in Dog-Learning. The Question will be on the Nature of the human Soul; and one of the Actors at Covent-Garden Theatre is to be the Moderator.*[1]

THE COVENT-GARDEN JOURNAL, No. 18, 3 Mar. 1752

MODERN HISTORY

ABRIDGED.

SATURDAY.

The Crowd was so great on Thursday at the new Entertainment of Harlequin Sorcerer, that a Lady lost one of her Shoes going into the House and sat with a Gentleman's Glove on her Foot; and the Gentleman lost his Hat and Wig, and sat during the Performance with a Handkerchief over his Head.   G. E.——*This Gentleman and Lady, if not Hand and Glove, were at least Foot and Glove.*

A Man and his Wife are committed to Malden Goal, for threatening to kill their Neighbours for upbraiding them with Cruelty. It seems, the Woman used frequently to stick Pins in a Child (to which she was Mother-in-law) and stir up the Fire with its Feet, so that its Toes rotted off; on which the Parish took it from her on the Neighbour's Complaint, and put it in the Workhouse, where it is since dead: But we don't hear that there are any Proceedings against her yet on this Score.   Id.—— *More Murders and horrid Barbarities have been committed within this last Twelvemonth, than during many preceding Years. This, as we have before observed, is principally to be attributed to the Declension of Religion among the common People.*   C.

[1] Cf. *CGJ* No. 17, above, p. 123. On the Robin Hood Society see *CGJ* Nos. 8 and 9; the actor referred to is Charles Macklin, who regularly attended the sessions at the Robin Hood.

The Death of the Rev. Mr. Page, Rector of Beccles in Suffolk, and Justice of the Quorum for the County, being mentioned in this Paper of the 20th Instant, this is inserted to contradict that mistaken Paragraph, that Gentleman being in perfect Health, and above twenty Years younger than therein mentioned, to the no small Disappointment and Mortification of the malicious Authors of that Piece of fictitious Intelligence. L. D. A.——*As malicious as this Paragraph is, we are assured it comes from one who doth not so much desire the Rector's Death as his* LIVING. M.

The Paragraph in one of last Saturday's Papers, of the Marriage of Mr. Overton, Printseller, without Newgate, with a young Lady in that Neighbourhood, is not true. D. A.

The Paragraph in one of the Daily Papers on Saturday, and in one of the Evenings of the same Day, mentioning the Marriage of Mr. Henry Overton, Printseller, without Newgate, to Miss Dawson, was premature. L. G.——*The Public may be assured that as soon as this Match becomes either true or mature, they shall have timely Notice.* M.

THE COVENT-GARDEN JOURNAL, No. 19, 3 Mar. 1752

MODERN HISTORY

ABRIDGED.

THURSDAY.

MARGATE, March 2. The young Woman mentioned in my last, lost her Life in the following Manner: Two Men follow'd her out of Deal about Seven o'Clock at Night, and seeing her go into the Halfway-House between Deal and Sandwich, they went in likewise, and soon after she went from thence they came up to her and began to use her very ill; but she would not consent to their base Designs, one of them pulled out a Knife and cut off her Gown, ript the fore Part of her Stays up, and stript her to her Shift, then used her in a cruel Manner, and left her for dead. . . . W. E.——*If something be not done to prevent it, Cruelty will become the Characteristic of this Nation.* C.

EDMUNDUS CASTLE, S.T.B. hujus Ecclesiæ Rector,
C.C.C. apud Cantabrigienses Custos, Decanus Herefordienses,
Obiit Jun. 6, 1750. Ætat. 52.
Quisquis es,
Qui nuperam Virtutem fastidiose premis,
Morum antiquorum & prisci Temporis Laudator;
Scias
Neque Literis instructiorem,
Neque Moribus simpliciorem,
Vetustatem exhibuisse.
Fidem, Justitiam, Pietatem,
Si quis unquam, vere excoluit;
Summa Charitate SUOS complexus est:
SUOS autem duxit HUMANUM GENUS. Id.

The Epitaph in English.

Whoever thou art
That lookest with Disdain on
The Virtue of modern Times,
While thou commendest the
Manners of the Antients
Know
That a Man more adorned with Learning
And with Simplicity of Manners,
Antiquity never produced.
Sincerity, Justice, Piety,
If ever they belonged to Man,
Belonged to Him.
He exerted the utmost Charity
To HIS OWN,
But HIS OWN WERE ALL MANKIND.   M.

Yesterday in the Evening the Earl of Coventry was married to Miss Maria Gunning,[1] Eldest Daughter to John Gunning, Esq; Barrister at Law, Sister to the Dutchess of Hamilton and Brandon, and Grand-daughter to the late Lord Viscount Mayo, of the Kingdom of Ireland.   D. A.——*A Lady possessed of that exquisite Beauty, and of those Accomplishments which will add Grace and Dignity to the highest Station.*

THE COVENT-GARDEN JOURNAL, No. 20, 10 Mar. 1752

MODERN HISTORY

ABRIDGED.

SATURDAY.

Dublin, Feb. 29. Lately died in the Barony of Iveraagh, and County of Kerry, Daniel Bull M'Carthy, Esq, of a very antient Family, in the 112th Year of his Age.... He was always a very healthy Man; no Cold did ever affect him; he could not bear the Warmth of a Shirt at Night, but put it under his Pillow, for these seventy Years past. When in Company he drank plentifully of Rum and Brandy, which he called the Naked Truth; and if, in Compliance with other Gentlemen, he drank Claret or Punch, he always drank an equal Glass of Rum or Brandy to qualify those Liquors: This he called a Wedge. No Man remembers to have seen him spit. His Custom was to walk eight or ten Miles in a Winter's Morning, over Mountains, with Greyhounds and Finders, and seldom failed to bring home a Brace of Hares. He was an honest Gentleman, and inherited the social Virtues of the antient Milesians.   D.A.——*This is a very extraordinary Character; but we recommend only the last Part to the Imitation of those, who are desirous of living so long.*   M.

On Thursday Evening Mr. Dalton presented to the Royal Society the second Part

---

[1] See *CGJ* No. 12, above, p. 91 n. 3.

of his Views and Antiquities of Greece and Egypt, which met with a general Approbation. G. A.——*These Views, which were all taken on the Spot by this ingenious Gentleman, are delineated with the utmost Care and Exactness. They are the Representations of the most curious and valuable Remains of Antiquity, and will not only afford the highest Entertainment to those who are well versed in classical Learning; but must be greatly pleasing, and even instructive, to such as want that Advantage; since they convey to us the noblest Ideas of those great People, among whom the Arts and Sciences did in their very Infancy arrive to such a Degree of Perfection.*[1] C.

We hear from Limerick, that a few Nights ago a very extraordinary Robbery was committed in that Town. A Lady had invited about twenty Female Friends to spend the Evening, all of whom accordingly came, and left their Capuchins, Shades, &c. in the Window of the Room; but, notwithstanding the Company were present all the while, when they were going home they found that some Thief had slipped in and carried all off, not leaving a single Shade for the Ladies. Id.——*This Method of dividing the Shade from the Substance, is a new Discovery in Philosophy, and hath greatly puzzled the Learned; but an Irish Gentleman observes, tho' the Company were all present, they were possibly in another Room.* M.

On Friday in the Afternoon, between Three and Four o'Clock, the Bath Stage-Coach was robbed by a single Highwayman about two Miles this Side of Maidenhead, who took from the Passengers between four and five Pounds, *behaved very genteely*, and made off. L. G.——*It is but lately that robbing on the Highway has been called* behaving genteely. C.

We are assured from undoubted Authority, that the Justices of the City and Liberty of Westminster in their Petition to Parliament, have prayed Liberty to assess only Two-pence in the Pound, and not Ten-pence as mentioned Yesterday. Id.——*A Sum, which if any of the Inhabitants refuse towards building a Sessions-House, it may be said they would not give Two-pence for Justice.* M.

Thursday was preached at St. Andrew's, Holborn, before the Governors of the Small-pox Hospital, a most excellent Sermon, by the Right Rev. the Lord Bishop of Worcester; at which were present his Grace the Archbishop of Canterbury, the Duke of Marlborough, the Earl of Northumberland, Lord Viscount Gage, Lord Parker, Sir William Beauchamp Proctor, Sir William Calvert, and several other Governors, and about 3000 Ladies. . . . W. E.——*This worthy Prelate is a true* Labourer in the Vineyard. *To his great Care and Diligence, the late Act against Spirituous Liquors was chiefly owing. A Law, which, if it hath not abolished, hath very considerably lessened the pernicious Practice of Gin-drinking.*[2] C.

Last Wednesday Night the Wife of an eminent Attorney in Clement's-Inn was

---

[1] Referring to Richard Dalton's *Museum Graecum et Egyptiacum* (1752).

[2] Isaac Maddox (1697–1759), Bishop of Worcester, had preached in 1750 a famous sermon against gin-drinking, *The Expediency of Preventive Wisdom*. Fielding dedicated to Maddox his *Examples of the Interposition of Providence in the Detection and Punishment of Murder*, which appeared a few weeks after this comment.

interred in St. Clement's Church-Yard. She desired before her Death . . . to be buried in a Lawn Hood and Cap, with white Ribbands, and the Curls which she had used to wear, in a Holland Shift tied also with white Ribbands, in white Stockings, and to have at the Bottom of her Coffin a Mattress; to be then wrapped up in a Winding-Sheet, and to be covered with a white Calicoe Covering; all which Circumstances were punctually observed. . . . S. J. E.——

So Ovid says of Lucretia.

> *—Ne non procumbat honeste,*
> *Respicit; hæc etiam Cura Cadentis erat.*[1]

> *—Dress was her latest care;*
> *And her last fault'ring Breath cry'd—curl my Hair.*

M.

Last Saturday one Harris, Servant to Mr. Clarke, of Bury-Street, St. James's, having set his Basket down with fourteen Quartern-Loaves in it, besides Flour; at the Earl of Clarendon's House in Berkeley-Square, it was carried away, while he went down into the Kitchen, by a Fellow dressed like a Baker. Several other Bakers have lately been served in the same Manner in that Part of the Town. D. A.——*These Robberies are plainly committed by Wretches who are in Want of Bread.* M.

---

[1] *Fasti*, ii. 833.

APPENDIX III

List of Emendations

A Plan of the Universal Register-Office

[NOTE: The only emendations, either accidental or substantive, to the text of the *Plan* are as listed below; for the sigla employed, see the head-note to the Historical Collation of the *Plan*, Appendix VI.]

8.18 particular] II–III; particalar I
10.6 *om.*] W; *FINIS.* I

APPENDIX IV

List of Substantive Emendations

Covent-Garden Journal

NOTE: As the Textual Introduction indicates, for most of the material in the *Covent-Garden Journal* only the original numbers published in 1752 have any authority. There are, however, two exceptions to this general rule. The first arises from the fact that an incomplete run of the *Journal* at the Bodleian Library (Hope Folio 11) contains a few changes and additions to the text in Fielding's own hand, as well as a few minor corrections in an unknown hand and occasional deletions of undetermined source. The second exception to the authority of the first edition involves the 26 leaders from the *Journal* included in the posthumous *Works* of 1762. As explained in the Textual Introduction, these essays seem to have been reprinted from the same marked copy as those surviving in the Bodleian, and their substantive variants must thus be presumed to have some authority. For these 26 leaders only, the text included in the *Works* constitutes a second edition. In the textual apparatus to the present edition these various texts will be designated as follows: I (the first edition, i.e. the original numbers of 1752); II (the second edition, both octavo and quarto); II^a (the second edition, quarto); II^b (the second edition, octavo); and Bodl. MS (Hope Folio 11).

Except for the silent emendations specified in the Textual Introduction, the list which follows records all substantive changes to the first-edition copy-text, together with their immediate source. Substantive emendations are drawn from II when the editor believes that they represent changes or additions made in Fielding's hand in the marked copy used by the printer. A few 'semi-substantive' variants listed here, mostly corrections of misprints, have also been drawn from II as the earliest printed source of the correction, although there is no reason to believe that Fielding himself had a hand in the changes. When emendations are drawn from II, the editor has silently changed the accidentals of II so as to conform to the 'accidental texture' of I (see Textual Introduction, p. lxi).

Each emendation listed below also includes readings of the editions earlier than the immediate source. 'W' indicates that the emendation is the responsibility of the present editor and that the reading is not to be found in I or II. The swung dash ~ stands for the word provided in the lemma to the left of the bracket and is used when the emendation involves a matter of punctuation; the inferior caret ∧ indicates the absence of punctuation as the point of variance. An asterisk before the page-line reference indicates the presence of a Textual Note (Appendix IX).

30.29 forbidden] II; forbid I
49.26 Minds of] W; Minds Children I
53.16 Gentleman] W; Gentlemen I
66.15 *mihi*] II; *milii* I

66.32 δ εν] W; δ ἐ I–II

68.3 Assemblies] II; Assembles I

75.27 Writings] II; Writing I

97.21 to] W; *om.* I

97.27 Gentleman] W; Gentlemen I

99.25 Ethics] W; Eluis I

121.3 Men] II; Man I

124.7 *Auroram*] W; *Aurorem* I

150.6 promulging] II; enacting I

150.7 seems] II; seem I

155.29–30 him: for it would have been very unsafe for the *Town* of Rome to damn his Performances.] II; him. I

158.13–14 Barrow, which gives a very serious, but very just Turn to this Subject.] II; Barrow. I

188.5 guess.] W; ~ ? I

190.17 learnt] W; learn I

192.1 *Miss.*] W; *Mr.* I

192.4 *Mr.*] W; *Miss.* I

203.10 begun] II; began I

204.24 Give] II; with give I

204.36 *of*] II; *in* I

205.2 as] II; a I

215.21 Creatures] W; Creature I

218.12 φάσεων] II; φασίων I

223.22 its] W; it I

*227.11 us to enjoy?] W; us? To enjoy. I

*228.14 shewn] Bodl. MS; thrown I

242.4 become] II; *om.* I

246.26 a view] II; *om.* I

247.7 to] II; *om.* I

248.28 YOURSELF] II; *om.* I

249.9 have] II; *om.* I

252.2 When] W; Then I

255.6 buried] Bodl. MS; dead I

266.23 very] II; *om.* I

268.10–12 Taste; to shew . . . this] II; Taste, I

*268.11 De Retz] W; De Roty II

270.17 Persons] II; Person I

270.21–2 Terms, which . . . Language.] II; Language. I

271.7 we see them] II; *om.* I

271.32 A Lady . . . Time] II; *om.* I

283.27 to] II; of I

284.13 whipping] II; whip- / one I

285.4 be] II; he I

288.9 une] W; un I

294.26 *Mrs.*] II; *Mr.* I
296.38 Aldermen] II; Alderman I
*303.21 Fashions] W; Fashion I–II
310.30 alike] W; a like I
312.10 begun] W; began I
*319.8 single] W; simple I–II
*327.13 sets] W; sits I–II
328.7 a] II; *om.* I
342.28 too] W; to I
345.3 of] W; *om.* I
345.23 Dialogue!] W; ~ ? I
353.13 follows] W; follow I
361.27 Provided] W; Provide I
362.23 Men] W; Man I
366.11 wont] W; want I

APPENDIX V

NOTE: For the sigla and system of notation used in this list, see the head-note to Appendix IV (List of Substantive Emendations). As explained in the Textual Introduction, the minor corrections and revisions in Fielding's hand in the incomplete Bodleian Library copy of the *Journal* are substantive in nature; there is thus no reason to believe that accidental variants in the 26 leaders from this run reprinted in the *Works* of 1762 are the result of Fieldings own intervention. When in the list below the editor indicates the acceptance of an accidental variant from II, he does so not because he believes such variants have any particular authority but because they represent the earliest printed source of an emendation he believes to be necessary.

I. LIST OF ACCIDENTALS EMENDATIONS: *COVENT-GARDEN JOURNAL*

13.7 Anglicé] W; Anglice I
17.10 ∧are] W; '~ I
17.24 A.] W; ~∧ I
19.7 A.] W; ~∧ I
24.13 A.] W; ~∧ I
26.18 A.] W; ~∧ I
30.35 A.] W; ~∧ I; *om.* II
32.12 he,∧] W; ~,' I
33.13 A.] W; ~∧ I
37.7 World.] II; ~, I
38.21 A.] W; ~∧ I; *om.* II
40.2 Grub-street] W; ~∧ ~ I
44.11 living] W; li ng I
44.25 A.] W; ~∧ I
46.25 A.] W; ~∧ I
51.10 Year!] W; ~ ? I
51.21 A.] W; ~∧ I
57.18 *Readers.*] W; ~∧ I
59.3 Reason] W; Reas n I
63.22 *Laugh.)*] W; ~.∧ I; ~.] II
63.24 I thinks] II; Ithinks I
63.34 Chandler;] II; ~, I
64.18 Materials?] II; ~. I
65.11 A.] W; ~∧ I; *om.* II
66.15 *Apollo.*] II; ~, I
68.6 *Robinhoodians*] II; *R obinhoodians* I
71.11 A.] W; ~∧ I; *om.* II
74.23 secondary] II; seeondary I

79.12 Anglicé] W; Anglicè I
82.8 Abbé] W; Abbè I
83.11 Distress,] W; ~. I
86.21 opprobrious] W; opprobious I
95.27 and] W; aad I
105.23 Interruption] W; Intteruption I
110.26 Learning,] W; ~. I
113.12 Ancestors] W; Ancesto s I
113.18 amiable] W; aimable I
114.3 Source.] W; ~ ? I
132.26 Conqueror] W; Conquetor I
133.26 flows] W; flow I
140.1 *amiable*] II; *aimable* I
154.4 Young,] II; ~∧ I
154.18 *childish*] II; *hildish* I
155.26 Artifex] II; Artifix I
157.5 Memoirs] II; Memoi s I
158.7 *Triflers*] II; *Trifl rs* I
158.17 trifling] II; triffling I
158.25 Imitation.] II; ~, I
179.35 tiresome] W; tiresom I
182.4 amiable] W; amable I
182.17 amiable] W; aimiable I
184.29 proceed] W; poceed I
201.2 with——.] W; ~.—— I
203.21 said,] II; ~∧ I
203.21 By] II; by I
206.28 extremely] II; extreemly I
212.3 of] II; o I
212.10 Secondly,] II; ~∧ I
218.24 them.] II; ~∧ I
219.15 Covent-Garden] II; ~ ∧ ~ I
227.20 (after] W; ∧~ I
233.3 old-fashioned] W; old-fashion I
247.30 Persons?] II; ~. I
250.7 First,] II; ~∧ I
253.10 Overseers] W; Overseres I
255.4 Illness;] W; ~ ? I
257.28 unattainable] W; unatainable I
259.17 political] II; polical I
266.8 Caille] II[b]; Caile I–II[a]
271.20 Words,] II; ~∧ I
271.21 Gentleman] II; Genleman I
273.21 *came.*] W; ~, I
278.25 Blockheads] W; Blo kheads I

282.21 Spelling,] II; ~; I
283.12 probably] II; probablly I
289.1 translate] W; transllate I
291.17 *assurance*] II; *asseurance* I
291.22 Study] II; Sudy I
294.37 here?] II; ~. I
295.6 last?] II; ~. I
295.22 it?] II; ~. I
295.34 *extremely*.] II; ~∧ I
296.28 ready?] II; ~∧ I
299.20 Now] II; now I
299.37 this,] II; ~∧ I
302.26 Abbé] W; Abbè I–II
303.30 Life.] II; ~∧ I
305.35 agreeable] II; agreable I
307.6 other!] W; ~ ? I
312.2 Mother?] W; ~. I
314.22 Hoards.] W; ~∧ I
315.8 thou∧] W; ~, I
317.6 them!] W; ~ ? I
317.13 assigned] W; assign d I
317.18 Lillaburlero,] W; ~. I
320.18 *quae . . . Nox*] II; roman I
326.1 Pen, Ink,] II; ~∧ ~∧ I
326.12 *Et . . . caeteris*] II; roman I
329.12 arrive] II; arive I
330.18 cries,] II; ~. I
330.27 dressed!] W; ~ ? I–II
331.11 Husbandmen] II; Hussbandmen I
332.15 Aeschylus] W; Aeschilus I
335.25 presuming] W; persuming I
336.24 Cornetcy] W; Cornecy I
337.15 Servant,] W; ~ ; I
339.36 pair-of] W; ~ ∧ ~ I
342.23 E.] W; ~∧ I
343.5 Sweetheart] W; Sweatheart I
346.18 is,] W; ~. I
346.27 Declaration] W; Declaratiion I
350.2 Disparity] W; Desparity I
353.7 enable∧] W; ~, I
353.14 read,] W; ~. I
354.7 Iliad,] W; ~. I
355.22 found?] W; ~, I
355.22 Stranger.] W; ~ ? I
357.9 he,] W; ~∧ I

360.11 will] W; well I
366.11 intimating] W; in ima ing I
367.19 *inordinate*] W; *inordiate* I
368.16 its] W; i s I
373.15 three,] W; ~∧ I
376.15 Covent-Garden] W; ~ ∧ ~ I
377.7 Covent-Garden] W; ~ ∧ ~ I

2. LIST OF EMENDATIONS: 'COURT OF ENQUIRY' COLUMNS OF DOUBTFUL AUTHORSHIP

385.17 significant∧] W; ~, I
385.17 alone,] W; ~∧. I
385.40 revived] W; reuived I
386.23 understanding —] W; ~∧ I
388.2 against] W; against against I

3. LIST OF EMENDATIONS: 'COVENT GARDEN' COLUMNS

SUBSTANTIVE EMENDATIONS

398.7 then] W; than I
412.15 has] W; was I
427.10 to] W; *om.* I
427.22 its] W; it I
442.11 to] W; *om.* I
445.9 he] W; she I
448.3 Lines] W; Lives I
448.11 Crimes] W; Crime I
449.1 Tradesman] W; Tradesmen I

ACCIDENTALS EMENDATIONS

390.4 COVENT-GARDEN] W; ~ ∧ ~ I
390.35 COVENT-GARDEN] W; ~ ∧ ~ I
390.25 COVENT-GARDEN] W; ~ ∧ ~ I
393.19 Girls] W; Gils I
395.15 COVENT-GARDEN] W; ~ ∧ ~ I
396.39 COVENT-GARDEN] W; ~ ∧ ~ I
397.34 Room;] W; ~ ∧ I
398.12 COVENT-GARDEN] W; ~ ∧ ~ I
399.19 COVENT-GARDEN] W; ~ ∧ ~ I
402.2 COVENT-GARDEN] W; ~ ∧ ~ I
403.4 COVENT-GARDEN] W; ~ ∧ → I
403.16 Deer] W; Deeer I
403.28 COVENT-GARDEN] W; ~ ∧ ~ I
404.11 COVENT-GARDEN] W; ~ ∧ ~ I

405.10 little] W; lltle I
405.15 Covent-Garden] W; ~ ∧ ~ I
408.3 unluckily] W; unlackily I
409.31 Covent-Garden] W; ~ ∧ ~ I
411.7 Covent-Garden] W; ~ ∧ ~ I
412.11 when] W; hen I
412.39 Manslaughter] W; Manslaghter I
413.20 Esq;] W; ~ : I
413.29 *tirerai.*] W; ~∧ I
414.3 Candlestick] W; Cnndlestick I
414.10 recommended] W; reccomended I
416.33 the] W; the the I
418.3 the] W; the the I
418.15 *Europe*] W; Europe I
425.31 likewise] W; likwise I
426.29 unusual] W; unusal I
426.37 Coleman] W; Colemmn I
427.8 Woman] W; Waman I
431.6 Defendant] W; Defendat I
431.9 Character,] W; ~. I
431.36 had] W; hhad I
431.37 Gentleman] W; Gen leman I
439.8 received] W; recieved I
441.26 Old-Bailey]; Old-Bail I
442.11 Prison] W; Prioson I
443.10 Candlestick] W; Candlestic I
444.31 following] W; foll wing I
444.31 Charge] W; Ch rge I
445.2 Fact;] W; ~ : I
450.1 Gatehouse,] W; ~. I

APPENDIX VI

Historical Collation

A Plan of the Universal Register-Office

NOTE: This list records all substantive variants from the edited text within the first three editions. The list is complete only for the introductory material down to the beginning of the list of articles (p. 6), since it is only this portion of the tract which may be reasonably attributed to Henry Fielding; as explained in the Textual Introduction, the list of services performed was greatly expanded in the editions of 1752 and 1753, which also included notices signed by John Fielding. None of these additions, apparently the work of John Fielding, have any authority for an edition of Henry Fielding's *Works*, and no useful purpose can be served by including them here. The lemma, or reading to the left of the bracket, is that of the present edited text; the absence of the sigla for any edition indicates that its reading is that of the edited text. In this collation the following sigla are employed: I: first edition, 1751; II: second edition, 1752; III: third edition, 1753.

3.11 several] sev ral III
3.11 different] *om.* II–III
5.27 hath] has II–III
6.1 Advertisements] Registers II–III
6.6 On] Upon II–III
6.6 is now erected] was erected on *February* 19, 1749, II–III
6.7 and] *om.* II–III
6.7 *Cecil-street*; the] ∼, and has been since carried on by a Society of Gentlemen of Honour and Abilities. The II–III
6.7 which is] which Office is II–III
6.8–10 Seller, the Master and the Scholar, the Master and the Apprentice, and the Master and Servant] ∼ Tutor and the Pupil, the Master, the Scholar and Usher, the Rector and Curate, the Man of Taste and the ingenious Artificer, the Virtuoso with Curiosities, the Traveller and a Companion, the Tradesman and Partner, the Master and Apprentice, or Bookkeeper, the Master and the Servant, *&c.* II–III
6.17 him. Several] ∼, and several II–III
6.25 that] this II–III

APPENDIX VII

Historical Collation

Covent-Garden Journal

NOTE: This list includes all substantive variants from the edited text within the first two editions, with the second edition consisting only of the 26 leading essays from the *Journal* which were chosen for inclusion in the *Works* of 1762 (both quarto and octavo). The list thus records the history within these editions of all substantive alterations to the copy-text included in the List of Substantive Emendations, as well as the history of all rejected substantive variants from both issues of the second edition. The lemma, or reading to the left of the bracket, is that of the present edited text; the absence of the sigla for an edition or issue indicates that its reading is the same as that of the edited text to the left of the bracket. For the sigla used in this list, see the head-note to the List of Substantive Emendations, Appendix IV. For the history of variant readings in the manuscript revisions of the Bodleian copy of the *Journal*, see Appendix VIII. An asterisk before the page-line reference indicates a Textual Note (Appendix IX).

27.3 19] nineteen II
27.4 last] least II^a
29.26 18] eighteen II
30.1 5000*l.*] five thousand pound II
30.11 criticise] criticse II^a
30.29 forbidden] forbid I
33.24 8] viii II
*61.8 1 51] 1751 II
61.13 ist it] ist it is II^b
61.15 beter] better II
61.18 that will] that it will II^a
62.29 Smallness] smallest II^a
63.24 I thinks] Ithinks I
63.35 Mr. Budge] Mr. Buge II
64.19 we] he II
65.3 3000] three thousand II
66.15 *mihi*] *milii* I
66.32 δ'ἐν] δ'ἐ I δὲ II
68.3 Assemblies] Assembles I
69.1 the] *om.* II
72.12 Horace] *om.* II
75.27 Writings] Writing I
120.18 36th] thirty sixth II

*120.25–6 Fems] ems II
121.3 Men] Man I
142.1 thousand Pound] thousand pounds II
150.6 promulging] enacting I
150.7 seems] seem I
152.1–2 neither . . . or] neither . . . nor II
152.26 only] not only II[a]
155.29–30 him: . . . Performances.] him. I
156.4 that] the II
156.10 4000] four thousand II
158.13–14 Barrow, . . . Subject.] Barrow. I
158.18–19; 202.16; 267.7 'tis] it is II
158.18 a] *om.* II
202.1 April 25] April 23 II
203.10 begun] began I
203.15 were] was II
*204.18 *Vitals*] vituals II
204.22 *Gent.*] gentleman II
204.24 Give] with give I
204.36 *of*] *in* I
205.2 as] a I
205.38 or] nor II
205.38 or any] nor any II
208.2 50 l.] fifty pounds II
208.18 farther] further II
210.16 Apr.] April II
211.23 extirpating] extirtating II[a]
211.33 this] these II
218.12 φάσεων] II; φασίων I
219.7 this] the II
*219.32 *armed*] arms II
241.7 or] and II
242.4 become] *om.* I
246.26 a view] *om.* I
247.5 gave] give II[a]
247.7 to] *om.* I
248.28 YOURSELF] *om.* I
*249.1 allotted] trusted II
249.2 of] *om.* II
249.9 have] *om.* I
249.19 AIEI] AEI II
250.12 2dly] Secondly II
250.17 3dly] Thirdly II
251.12 Foundling] the Foundling II
259.17 political] polical I

260.26 lost his] losthis 11ᵃ

262.25; 263.3; 263.8 4th] fourth II

264.25 think] thing II

266.22 very] *om.* I

268.10–12 to shew . . . this] *om.* I

*268.11 De Retz] *om.* I De Roty II

270.17 Persons] Person I

270.21–2 Terms, which . . . Language.] Language. I

271.7 we see them] *om.* I

271.32 A lady . . . time] *om.* I

271.18 *as for you*] as you II

283.27 to] of I

284.13 whipping] whip- | one I

285.4 be] he I

290.22 in] de IIᵃ

290.28 Passage] passion IIᵃ

291.9 peeka] peka II

291.16 la] *à la* II

294.26 *Mrs.*] *Mr.* I

295.35 43d] forty-third II

296.38 Aldermen] Alderman I

303.6 think very] think I very IIᵃ

*303.21 Fashions] Fashion I–II

304.14 Inclinations] inclination IIᵃ

305.6 is,] *om.* II

318.4 *Vate*] *vato* II

319.3 with] *om.* II

*319.8 single] simple I–II

319.14 Cotemporaries] cnotemporaries IIᵃ contemporaries IIᵇ

320.9; 321.9 Cotemporaries] contemporaries II

320.14 Maevius] Maebius II

321.13 those] these IIᵃ

324.9; 327.16 cotemporary] contemporary II

*327.13 sets] sits I–II

328.7 a] *om.* I

330.12 Hon.] Honourable II

330.19 than] then II

330.23 1500l.] fifteen hundred pounds II

APPENDIX VIII

Corrections and Revisions in the Bodleian Library Copy of the *Covent-Garden Journal*

NOTE: The copy of the *Journal* in the Bodleian Library (Hope Folio 11) contains manuscript corrections and revisions, some of which are definitely in Fielding's hand and a few of which are probably not. On the provenance of this copy and its relation to the *Works* of 1762, see Hugh Amory, 'Fielding's Copy of the *Covent-Garden Journal*', *Bodleian Library Record*, 11 (1983), 126–8; see also Amory's discussion of these corrections in 'What Murphy Knew: His Interpolations in Fielding's *Works* (1762), and Fielding's Revision of *Amelia*', *PBSA* 77 (1983), 140–1. The alterations in manuscript have been examined not only by Dr Amory, who first identified the hand as Fielding's, but also by Professor Martin Battestin and the present editor; all agree on the certainty or uncertainty of Fielding's hand in each case of manuscript addition, correction, or revision. As well as the changes recorded below, Hope Folio 11 also includes a few marginal notations, apparently in a third hand, next to advertisements in Nos. 30, 39, 41, and 43, and deletions of entire essays or letters to the editor in Nos. 28, 38, 40, 41, 62, 63, 64, and 65; on the possible significance of these deletions to the question of Fielding's authorship, see the notes to the numbers in question. The hand of Arthur Murphy, whose copy this supposedly was, appears nowhere in Hope Folio 11.

The list which follows records all manuscript corrections, revisions, and additions to the text, regardless of handwriting, and all marginal notes that are definitely in Fielding's hand. Deletions of entire contributions are not included. The reading to the left of the bracket is that of the present edited text; the presence of an asterisk indicates a textual note. For the convenience of the reader, material accepted as definitely in Fielding's hand is marked [F].

128.8 indeed] *deleted*   Bodl. MS
128.12 then] there   Bodl. MS
*173.6 ʌBetters] our Betters   Bodl. MS
*228.14 shewn] thrown I
233.26 Add these 2 Letters to yᵉ next Paper.   Bodl. MS [F]
233.31 Baker] *marked for note at bottom of page*: An unhappy poor Man who would have been ruined by Fire had not a very large Collection been set on Foot for him in this Paper.   Bodl. MS [F]
235.20 accomplished.] ~ ; by any but my self; who seem [?] alone to . . . rd [*indistinct*] its [?] Utility.   Bodl. MS [F]
255.6 [F] buried] dead I

APPENDIX IX

Textual Notes

61.8 1 51] The alteration in II of the date to '1751' is an obvious error, since Fielding in *CGJ* No. 9 jokes about the date '1 51'.

120.25–6 Fems] The reading in II ('ems') is rendered dubious by the retention in II of 'fems' in the third occurrence of the word in this same passage.

173.6 Betters] The word 'our' has been inserted before 'Betters' in the Bodleian copy, but the hand is probably not Fielding's and the addition results in the awkward phrase 'these same our Betters'.

204.18 *Vitals*] Since 'stap my Vitals' is the phrase being quoted from Vanbrugh's *The Relapse*, the reading 'vituals' in II is rejected in W.

219.32 *armed*] The alteration in II to 'arms' destroys Fielding's effort to pun in his footnote on the phrase in his text, '*armed* Vehicles'.

227.11 us to enjoy?] The alteration to the accidentals of I changes the meaning, but the emendation in W is in accord with the passage in Locke which Fielding quotes and is demanded by the context.

228.14 shewn] Although the hand making the change in the Bodleian copy is probably not Fielding's, the correction of the reading in I ('having thrown some Difficulties') has been accepted in W as necessary in the context.

249.1 allotted] The word is effaced in all copies of I examined except that at Cambridge University Library. The reading in II ('trusted') thus appears to be someone's guess at the word originally intended for the blank.

268.11 De Retz] Since the passage cited is from Cardinal de Retz, the name in II ('De Roty') is an error. Moreover, as Dr Hugh Amory points out, the compositor's misreading testifies to Fielding's hand in the added passage; see Amory's 'What Murphy Knew: His Interpolations in Fielding's *Works* (1762), and Fielding's Revision of *Amelia*', *PBSA* 77 (1983), 141. The error is further evidence that the 26 essays from *CGJ* in II were set from a marked copy containing occasional corrections, revisions, and additions by Fielding of the type surviving in the Bodleian run of the *Journal*.

303.21 Fashions] Although uncorrected in II, the singular form in I appears to be an error; cf. the same phrase exactly in the very next sentence, 'Diversions, Fashions, Follies and Vices'.

319.8 single] The context demands the rejection of 'simple', the reading in I–II; Fielding's point in the paragraph is the *number* of writers whose names have disappeared over time, and the two words could easily be confused by a compositor.

327.13 sets] *OED* provides no authority for the 'sits' of I–II, but cites 'to set up for' as the phrase meaning 'to put oneself forward as'.

APPENDIX X

Word-Division

NOTE: No hyphenation of a possible compound at the end of a line in the Wesleyan Edition is present in the copy-text except for the following readings, which are hyphenated within the line in the copy-text. Hyphenated compounds in which both elements are capitalized are excluded.

A PLAN OF THE UNIVERSAL REGISTER-OFFICE

7. 39–8.1 Patent-places
8.22–3 Cook-maids
8. 36–7 Penny-post

THE COVENT-GARDEN JOURNAL

90. 3–4 twenty-third
106. 26–7 Green-room
126. 19–20 Perry-shop
130. 1–2 well-known
156. 2–3 Fly-spitting
207. 25–208.1 two-thirds
215 8–9, 21–2 No-body
220. 18–19 Black-bird
251. 13–14 Lying-in
257. 4–5 all-accomplished
377. 10–11 Candle-snuffers

THE 'COVENT-GARDEN' COLUMNS

392. 33–4 Back-side
394. 40–395. 1 Lying-in
403. 9–10 re-examined
411. 18–19 Tilt-yard
413. 4–5 China-cups
418. 16–17 Long-lawn

NOTE: The following compounds, or possible compounds, are hyphenated at the end of the line in the copy-text. The form in which they have been given in the Wesleyan Edition, listed below, reflects the usual practice of the copy-text as far as it may be ascertained from other appearances. Hyphenated compounds in which both elements are capitalized are excluded.

A PLAN OF THE UNIVERSAL REGISTER-OFFICE

5.24 Warehouse

THE COVENT-GARDEN JOURNAL

48.24 Trunk-makers
54.19 Fox-hunter
96.22 so-forth
147.18 Chamber-door
147.30 Chamber-door
173.1 Oyster-woman
185.25 Taskmasters
204.6 Exciseman
206.11 undertaken
208.11 Heart-achs
210.22 Countrymen
215.17 No-body
216.4 No-bodies
217.9 Every-body's
220.19 Tomorrow
241.31 Gaming-houses
244.18 Humankind
246.6 well-born
254.4–5 over-burthening
255.5 Undertaker
271.13 Highways
271.15 Drayman
281.27 Print-makers
282.13–14 abovementioned
282.17; 284.6 Booksellers
291.1 abovementioned
294.36 Mantua-maker
296.3 Tomorrow
302.18 over-top
307.16 Well-wisher
331.11 Commonwealth
343.5 Sweetheart
345.9–10 not-speaking
361.28 Landladies
364.31 outwits
370.6 Ant-hill
372.5 wherefrom
373.19 Ant-kind
382.9 Pawnbrokers

THE 'COVENT GARDEN' COLUMNS

394.17 Godfather
411.16 Tilt-yard
413.9 Pocket-piece
423.14 John-street
430.21 Fortune-telling
441.38 Madwoman

3. SPECIAL CASES

NOTE: The following compounds or possible compounds are hyphenated at the end of the line in the copy-text and in the Wesleyan Edition.

COVENT-GARDEN JOURNAL

254. 4–5 over-burthening
282. 13–14 above-mentioned
345. 9–10 not-speaking

APPENDIX XI

Press Variants and Bibliographical Descriptions

A PLAN OF THE UNIVERSAL REGISTER-OFFICE

(1) THE FIRST EDITION

Title-page: A | PLAN | OF THE | Universal Register-Office, | OPPOSITE | CECIL-STREET in the STRAND. | [*ornament*] | LONDON: | Printed in the Year MDCCLI.

Collation: 8°: π² (−π2) A⁸χ (=π2); $4 signed (−A1); 10 leaves, pp. *i–ii, 1–2, 4–16, 17–18.*

Press Figures: (sig.-page-fig.): A5-9-3.

Contents: π1: half-title 'A | PLAN | OF THE | Universal Register-Office, | OPPOSITE | CECIL-STREET in the STRAND.' π1ᵛ: blank; A1: title (verso blank); A2: [*ornament*] followed by half-title 'A |PLAN | OF THE| Universal Register-Office.' followed by text ending on A8ᵛ with *FINIS* [*ornament*]; χ1 and χ1ᵛ blank.

Copies collated: British Library (T. 325 [2]); King's College, Cambridge (Keynes coll. E. 4. 18); Yale (Ndn54. G6. 751 f). No press variants were observed.

(2) THE SECOND EDITION

Title-page: A | PLAN | OF THE | Universal Register-Office, | OPPOSITE | CECIL-STREET in the STRAND, | AND OF | That in BISHOPSGATE-STREET, the Corner | of CORNHILL. Both by the same PROPRIETORS. | [*ornament*] LONDON: | Printed in the Year MDCCLII. | [Price Three-pence]

Collation: 8°: A⁸ B²; $4 signed (−A1, A2, B2); 10 leaves, pp. *1–5, 6–19, 20.*

Press Figures: (sig.-page-fig.): A7ᵛ-14-4.

Contents: A1: title; A1ᵛ: blank; A2: [*type-ornament*] 'To the READER.' signed John Fielding (verso blank); A3: half-title 'A | PLAN | OF THE | Universal Register-Office.' and text ending on B2ʳ with printer's ornament (inverted); B2ᵛ blank.

Copies observed: British Library (12230 f 26 [7]); University of London (Goldsmith's Library); Bodleian Library (Gough London 35).

(3) THE THIRD EDITION

Title-page: A | PLAN | OF THE | Universal Register-Office, |OPPOSITE Cecil-Street in the Strand, |AND OF | The UNIVERSAL REGISTER OFFICE, in | Bishopsgate-Street, near Cornhill, | Both by the same PROPRIETORS. | [*ornament*] | LONDON: | Printed in the Year MDCCLIII. | [Price Three-pence.]

Collation: 8°: A⁸ B²; $4 signed (−A1, A2, B2); 10 leaves, pp. *1–5, 6–19, 20.*

Press Figures: (sig.-page-fig.): A5ʳ-9-3.

Contents: A1: title; A1ᵛ: notice beginning 'Universal *Register-Office*', signed John Fielding; A2: [*type-ornament*] 'To the READER.' signed John Fielding (verso blank); A3 [*ornament*] half-title, as in 2nd edn., and text ending on B2ʳ with printer's ornament; B2ᵛ blank.

Copies observed: Yale (Beinecke Library, NZ 753fi).

[NOTE: These three editions are the only ones appearing in Fielding's lifetime which the present editor has located. Another edition (8° in 4s, 12 leaves) appeared in 1755, its title-page calling it the 'Eighth Edition'; this edition has no authority for an edition of Fielding's *Works*, its revisions and additions merely reflecting the increased business of the Register-Office. The only printings of the *Plan* indicated by entries in the Strahan ledger from its beginning in 1752 through 1760 are as follows: Dec. 1752: 2,000 Plans, 1 sheet and 1/4; Sept. 1753: 2,000 Plans, 3 halfsheets; Feb. 1755: 2,000 Plans, 3 halfsheets (BL Add. MS 48803A).]

THE COVENT-GARDEN JOURNAL

(1) THE FIRST EDITION

Title-page: The Covent-Garden Journal. | [*rule*] | By Sir ALEXANDER DRAW-CANSIR, Knt. Censor of GREAT BRITAIN. | [*rule*] | SATURDAY, JANUARY 4[–NOVEMBER 25.] 1752. NUMB. I[–72] | [*rule*] | To be continued every TUESDAY and SATURDAY. | [*rule*]

Colophon of No. 1: LONDON: Printed, and Sold by Mrs. DODD, at the *Peacock*, *Temple-Bar*, and at the UNIVERSAL REGISTER | OFFICE, opposite *Cecil-street*, in the *Strand*; where ADVERTISEMENTS and LETTERS to the AUTHOR are taken in.

Copies collated: University of London Library ([S. L.] I [Fielding-1752] fo.), missing Nos. 44, 46, 48, 50; British Library (L¹) Burney 447), missing No. 61, lacking one leaf Nos. 71–2; British Library (L²) (Burney 447*), missing Nos. 15, 49, 61–3, 69, 71–2, and lacking one leaf Nos. 34, 55, 70; Cambridge University Library (CCA. 14. I), complete; London Library (Safe-Folio), lacking one leaf Nos. 47, 48, 51–60, 62–5, 67–9, 72; Bodleian Library, Oxford (Hope Folio 11), missing Nos. 1–4, 8–10, 17, 21, 23, 24, 33–5, 37, 42, 44, 47–9, 51, 53–6, 59–61, 71, 72.

Copies observed: University of Texas, Humanities Research Center (Wrenn Library, WWk F460 7520), complete; University of Illinois Library (x052 COV), missing Nos. 16, 49, 61; private copy of Viscountess Eccles, missing Nos. 13, 71, two copies of No. 70. The Texas and Illinois copies were examined on microfilm.

Press Variants:
86.19 Thing] Things *uncorrected all copies except Bodleian*
87.10 where] whre *uncorrected all copies except Bodleian*
246.13 *et tu*] ettu *uncorrected all copies except Cambridge, London Library*
249.1 allotted] *blank printed in all copies except Cambridge*

[NOTE: The run at the University of Texas contains two well-known contemporary prints satirizing John Hill, 'Le Malade Imaginaire, or the Consultation' and 'A Night Scene at Ranelagh on Wednesday 6th of May 1752', both dated 29 May but bound in with *CGJ* No. 38, 12 May. As reported to the editor, the prints appear to be inserted into rather than being integral with the text of *CGJ*.]

(2) THE SECOND EDITION (1762) in *Works*, First Issue 4°, vol. iv.

[The second edition contains the leading essays only of the following numbers of the *Covent-Garden Journal*: Nos. 3, 4, 8–10, 17, 21, 23, 24, 33–5, 37, 42, 44, 47–9, 51, 53–6, 59–61.]

General title-page: THE | WORKS | OF | HENRY FIELDING, Esq; | WITH | The LIFE of the AUTHOR. | In FOUR VOLUMES. | VOLUME the FOURTH | [*double rule*] | LONDON: | Printed for A. MILLAR, opposite Catherine-Street, in the Strand. | M.DCC.LXII.

Half-title: THE | Covent-Garden Journal. | By Sir ALEXANDER DRAWCANSIR, Knt. | Censor of GREAT-BRITAIN.

Collation (*Covent-Garden Journal* only): 4°: Aaa 3, 4 Bbb–Iii⁴ Kkk 1, $2 signed, 35 leaves, pp. [365–367], 368–433 (misnumbering 393 as 395, 396 as 398, 397 as 399, 400 as 402).

Contents (*Covent-Garden Journal* only): Aaa3 half-title, verso blank; Aaa4 text, with HT '[*double rule*] THE | Covent-Garden Journal. | By Sir ALEXANDER DRAWCANSIR, Knt. | Censor of GREAT-BRITAIN', ending on Kkk 1 with ornament, verso blank.

Press Figures: 368–5; 375–5; 381–5; 386–5; 394–5; 408–5; 425–5.

Copies bibliographically collated: BL (92. g. 10); NjP (3728. 1762).

(3) THE SECOND EDITION (1762) in *Works*, Second Issue 8°, vol. viii.

General title-page: THE | WORKS | OF | HENRY FIELDING, Esq; | WITH | The LIFE of the AUTHOR. | In EIGHT VOLUMES. | VOL. VIII. | The SECOND EDITION. | [*orn.*] | [*double rule*] LONDON: | Printed for A. MILLAR, in the Strand. | M. DCC. LXII.

Half-title: As in 4° First Issue.

Collation (*Covent-Garden Journal* only): 8°: N6, 7, 8 O–X⁸ Y1, 2, $4 signed, 69 leaves, pp. [187–189] 190–353, misnumbering 208 as 08, 215 as 214, 249 as 2, not numbering 248.

Contents: N6 half-title, verso blank; N7 text with HT '[*double rule*] | THE Covent-Garden Journal. | By Sir ALEXANDER DRAWCANSIR, Knt. | Censor of GREAT-BRITAIN: | [*single rule*]', ending with ornament on Y2, verso blank.

Press Figures: [2]08–5, 212–1, 237–5, [248]–5, 264–1, 287–4, 303–4, 320–4.

Copies bibliographically collated: BL (1493. r. 46); NjP (3738 .1762 .11).

INDEX OF NAMES, PLACES, AND SELECTED TOPICS

IN INTRODUCTIONS, TEXTS, APPENDICES, AND NOTES

(Fielding's own notes are designated by an asterisk in front of the number. Indexing of Appendix I. 2 covers only major figures and editorial issues, excluding names and places listed in accounts of routine court cases. Indexing of Appendix II covers only the *CGJ* comments, not the extracts reprinted from newspapers. Single-letter signatures are also excluded from the index.)